Tradition and Survival

A BIBLIOGRAPHICAL SURVEY OF EARLY SHĪ'ITE LITERATURE

VOLUME ONE

Tradition and Survival

A BIBLIOGRAPHICAL SURVEY OF
EARLY SHĪʿITE LITERATURE

VOLUME ONE

HOSSEIN MODARRESSI

ONEWORLD
ACADEMIC

TRADITION AND SURVIVAL: A BIBLIOGRAPHICAL SURVEY OF EARLY SHĪʿITE LITERATURE

Oneworld Publications
10 Bloomsbury Street
London WC1B 3SR
England

A CIP record for this title is available from the British Library

ISBN 978-1-85168-331-4

Cover design by Saxon Graphics, Derby, UK
Typeset by LaserScript Ltd, Mitcham, UK

Contents

Preface xiii

I 'Alī and His Personal Associates 1

1. 'Alī b. Abī Ṭālib 2
2. Fāṭima al-Zahrā' 17
3. Abū Rāfi' 22
4. 'Ubayd Allāh b. Abī Rāfi' 25
5. Rabī'a b. Sumay' 33
6. 'Alī Zayn al-'Ābidīn 33
7. Muḥammad al-Bāqir 37

II Kūfan Shī'ism in the Umayyad Period 39

1. Maytham al-Tammār 42
2. Ḥārith al-A'war 45
3. Aṣbagh b. Nubāta 59
4. Kumayl b. Ziyād 74
5. Zayd b. Wahb 80
6. Sulaym b. Qays al-Hilālī 82
7. Jābir al-Ju'fī 86
8. Ibn Abī Ya'fūr 103
9. Sālim b. Abī Ḥafṣa 105
10. Abān b. Taghlib 107

11. Abū ʻUbayda al-Ḥadhdhā’ 116
12. Sa‘d al-Iskāf 118
13. Abū ’l-Jārūd 121

III The Period of Persecution (136–198) 127

1. Abān b. ‘Uthmān al-Aḥmar 129
2. ‘Abbād b. Ṣuhayb al-Kalbī 131
3. ‘Abd al-‘Azīz b. ‘Abd Allāh al-‘Abdī 133
4. ‘Abd al-Ghaffār b. Ḥabīb al-Jāzī 134
5. ‘Abd al-Ghaffār b. al-Qāsim al-Anṣārī 135
6. ‘Abd al-Karīm b. ‘Amr al-Khath‘amī 137
7. ‘Abd Allāh b. Ayyūb al-Zuhrī 138
8. ‘Abd Allāh b. Bukayr al-Shaybānī 140
9. ‘Abd Allāh b. Ghālib al-Asadī 141
10. ‘Abd Allāh b. al-Ḥakam al-Armanī 142
11. ‘Abd Allāh b. Ibrāhīm al-Ja‘farī 143
12. ‘Abd Allāh b. Maymūn al-Qaddāḥ 145
13. ‘Abd Allāh b. Muskān 150
14. ‘Abd Allāh b. al-Qāsim al-Ḥārithī 155
15. ‘Abd Allāh b. Sinān 157
16. ‘Abd Allāh b. Ṭalḥa al-Nahdī 161
17. ‘Abd Allāh b. Waḍḍāḥ 162
18. ‘Abd Allāh b. Yaḥyā al-Kāhilī 162
19. ‘Abd Allāh b. al-Zubayr al-Rassān 163
20. ‘Abd al-Malik b. Ḥakīm al-Khath‘amī 165
21. ‘Abd al-Malik b. ‘Utba al-Nakha‘ī 165
22. ‘Abd al-Mu’min b. al-Qāsim al-Anṣārī 167
23. ‘Abd al-Raḥmān b. al-Ḥajjāj 168
24. ‘Abd al-Raḥmān b. Kathīr al-Hāshimī 171
25. ‘Abd al-Raḥmān b. Muḥammad al-‘Arzamī 174
26. ‘Abd al-Ṣamad b. Bashīr al-‘Urāmī 176
27. Aḥmad b. ‘Āidh al-Aḥmasī 177
28. Aḥmad b. Rizq al-Ghumshānī 178
29. ‘Alā’ b. al-Fuḍayl al-Nahdī 179
30. ‘Alā’ b. Razīn al-Qallā’ 180
31. ‘Alī b. ‘Abd al-‘Azīz 181
32. ‘Alī b. Abī Ḥamza al-Baṭā’inī 183
33. ‘Alī b. ‘Aṭiyya al-Ḥannāṭ 187

34. 'Alī b. Ḥassān al-Hāshimī 188
35. 'Alī b. Ri'āb al-Ṭaḥḥān 189
36. 'Alī b. Shajara al-Nabbāl 191
37. 'Alī b. 'Uqba al-Asadī 193
38. 'Alī b. Yaqṭīn 194
39. 'Ammār b. Marwān al-Thawbānī 198
40. 'Ammār b. Mūsā al-Sābāṭī 199
41. 'Amr b. Jumay' al-Ḥulwānī 200
42. 'Amr b. Khālid al-Wāsiṭī 202
43. 'Amr b. Shimr/Shamir al-Ju'fī 204
44. 'Amr b. Thābit Abī 'l-Miqdām 205
45. Anas b. 'Iyāḍ al-Laythī 207
46. 'Anbasa b. Bijād al-'Ābid 208
47. Asbāṭ b. Sālim Bayyā' al-Zuṭṭī 209
48. 'Āṣim b. Ḥumayd al-Ḥannāṭ 210
49. 'Āṣim b. Sulaymān al-Kūzī 211
50. Ayyūb b. al-Ḥurr al-Ju'fī 212
51. Burayd b. Mu'āwiya al-'Ijlī 213
52. Dāwūd b. Farqad 214
53. Dāwūd b. al-Ḥuṣayn 214
54. Dāwūd b. Sirḥān 215
55. Ḍaḥḥāk Abū Mālik al-Ḥaḍramī 216
56. Dharīḥ b. Muḥammad al-Muḥāribī 217
57. Durust b. Abī Manṣūr al-Wāsiṭī 218
58. Faḍl b. 'Abd al-Malik al-Baqbāq 220
59. Faḍl b. Abī Qurra al-Armanī 221
60. Faḍl b. Yūnus al-Kātib 222
61. Fuḍayl b. 'Iyāḍ 223
62. Fuḍayl b. 'Uthmān al-A'war 224
63. Fuḍayl b. Yasār al-Nahdī 225
64. Ghālib b. 'Uthmān al-Minqarī 226
65. Ghiyāth b. Ibrāhīm 227
66. Ḥafṣ b. al-Bakhtarī 230
67. Ḥafṣ b. Ghiyāth al-Qāḍī 231
68. Ḥafṣ b. Sālim Abū Wallād al-Ḥannāṭ 235
69. Ḥafṣ b. Sūqa al-'Amrī 235
70. Ḥakam b. Miskīn al-A'mā 236
71. Ḥammād b. Abī Ṭalḥa 238
72. Ḥammād b. 'Uthmān al-Nāb 239

73. Ḥamza b. Ḥumrān al-Shaybānī 239
74. Ḥanān b. Sadīr al-Ṣayrafī 240
75. Ḥārith b. al-Mughīra al-Naṣrī 242
76. Ḥārith b. Muḥammad al-Aḥwal 243
77. Ḥarīz b. 'Abd Allāh al-Sijistānī 244
78. Hārūn b. Ḥamza al-Ghanawī 247
79. Hārūn b. al-Jahm 248
80. Hārūn b. Khārija 249
81. Ḥasan b. 'Alī b. Abī Ḥamza 250
82. Ḥasan b. al-Ḥusayn al-'Uranī 254
83. Ḥasan b. Rāshid 255
84. Ḥasan b. Ṣāliḥ b. Ḥayy 256
85. Ḥassān al-Jammāl 257
86. Ḥātim b. Ismā'īl al-Madanī 258
87. Hishām b. al-Ḥakam 259
88. Hishām b. al-Muthannā 268
89. Hishām b. Sālim al-Jawālīqī 269
90. Ḥudhayfa b. Manṣūr 272
91. Ḥujr b. Zā'ida al-Ḥaḍramī 272
92. Ḥumayd b. al-Muthannā al-'Ijlī 273
93. Ḥumayd b. Shu'ayb al-Sabī'ī 274
94. Ḥusayn b. Abī 'l-'Alā' 274
95. Ḥusayn b. Abī Ghundar 275
96. Ḥuṣayn b. Mukhāriq al-Salūlī 275
97. Ḥusayn b. al-Mukhtār al-Qalānisī 277
98. Ḥusayn b. 'Uthmān al-Aḥmasī 277
99. Ḥusayn b. 'Uthmān b. Sharīk al-'Āmirī 279
100. Ḥusayn b. Zayd b. 'Alī Dhū al-Dam'a 280
101. Ibrāhīm b. Abī 'l-Sammāl 283
102. Ibrāhīm b. 'Īsā Abū Ayyūb al-Kharrāz 285
103. Ibrāhīm b. Mihzam b. Abī Burda 286
104. Ibrāhīm b. Muḥammad b. Abī Yaḥyā 286
105. Ibrāhīm b. Nu'aym Abū 'l-Ṣabbāḥ al-Kinānī 289
106. Ibrāhīm b. Rajā' al-Shaybānī Ibn Harāsa 290
107. Ibrāhīm b. 'Umar al-Yamānī 291
108. 'Īṣ b. al-Qāsim al-Bajalī 293
109. 'Īsā b. 'Abd Allāh al-'Umarī 294
110. 'Īsā b. Dāwūd al-Najjār 298
111. Isḥāq b. 'Ammār al-Ṣayrafī 299

112. Isḥāq b. Bishr al-Kāhilī 300
113. Isḥāq b. Jaʿfar al-Ṣādiq 301
114. Isḥāq b. Jarīr al-Bajalī 302
115. Ismāʿīl b. ʿAbd al-Khāliq al-Asadī 303
116. Ismāʿīl b. Abī Ziyād al-Sakūnī 304
117. Ismāʿīl b. Jābir al-Khathʿamī 305
118. Jaʿfar b. Muḥammad al-Ḥaḍramī 306
119. Jamīl b. Darrāj al-Nakhaʿī 307
120. Jamīl b. Ṣāliḥ al-Asadī 308
121. Jarrāḥ al-Madāʾinī 309
122. Kathīr b. Ṭāriq al-Qanbarī 309
123. Khālid b. Awfā Abū ʾl-Rabīʿ al-Shāmī 310
124. Khālid b. Jarīr al-Bajalī 311
125. Khālid b. Mādd al-Qalānisī 311
126. Khālid b. Saʿīd al-Qammāṭ 312
127. Khālid b. Ṭahmān al-Salūlī 313
128. Khallād al-Sindī al-Bazzāz 313
129. Khaybarī b. ʿAlī al-Ṭaḥḥān 314
130. Kulayb b. Muʿāwiya al-Ṣaydāwī 315
131. Layth b. al-Bakhtarī al-Murādī 315
132. Lūṭ b. Yaḥyā al-Azdī Abū Mikhnaf 316
133. Mālik b. ʿAṭiyya al-Aḥmasī 316
134. Maʿmar b. Yaḥyā b. Sām 317
135. Manṣūr b. Ḥāzim al-Bajalī 317
136. Manṣūr b. Yūnus Buzurj 318
137. Marwān b. Muslim 319
138. Masʿada b. Ṣadaqa 319
139. Masʿada b. al-Yasaʿ al-Bāhilī 322
140. Masʿada b. Ziyād al-Rabaʿī 323
141. Mismaʿ b. ʿAbd al-Malik Kurdīn 325
142. Muʿallā b. Khunays 326
143. Muʿāwiya b. ʿAmmār al-Duhnī 327
144. Muʿāwiya b. Wahb al-Bajalī 332
145. Mufaḍḍal b. Ṣāliḥ al-Asadī Abū Jamīla 333
146. Mufaḍḍal b. ʿUmar al-Juʿfī 333
147. Muḥammad b. ʿAlī b. Abī Shuʿba al-Ḥalabī 337
148. Muḥammad b. ʿAlī b. al-Nuʿmān Ṣāḥib al-Ṭāq 338
149. Muḥammad b. ʿAmr al-Zubayrī 340
150. Muḥammad b. Furāt 340

151. Muḥammad b. Ḥakīm al-Khath'amī 341
152. Muḥammad b. Ḥumrān al-Nahdī 342
153. Muḥammad b. Maymūn al-Za'farānī 343
154. Muḥammad b. Muslim al-Thaqafī 344
155. Muḥammad b. Qays al-Bajalī 345
156. Muḥammad b. Tamīm al-Nahshalī 347
157. Muḥammad b. Thābit b. Dīnār al-Thumālī 348
158. Muḥammad b. 'Ubayd Allāh b. Abī Rāfi' 348
159. Muḥammad b. 'Udhāfir al- Madā'inī 350
160. Muḥammad b. Yaḥyā al-Khath'amī 351
161. Munakhkhal b. Jamīl al-Raqqī 351
162. Murāzim b. Ḥakīm al-Madā'inī 353
163. Mūsā b. Bakr al-Wāsiṭī 354
164. Mūsā b. Ibrāhīm al-Marwazī 354
165. Mūsā b. Ukayl al-Numayrī 355
166. Mūsā b. 'Umayr Abū Hārūn al-Makfūf 355
167. Mushma'ill b. Sa'd al-Nāshirī 356
168. Muthannā b. al-Walīd al-Ḥannāṭ 357
169. Muṭṭalib b. Ziyād b. Abī Zuhayr 357
170. Qāsim b. Burayd b. Mu'āwiya al-'Ijlī 358
171. Qāsim b. Sulaymān al-Baghdādī 359
172. Qāsim b. 'Urwa 359
173. Rabī' b. Muḥammad al-Muslī al-Aṣamm 360
174. Rifā'a b. Mūsā al-Nakhkhās 360
175. Rib'ī b. 'Abd Allāh al-Hudhalī 361
176. Rawḥ b. 'Abd al-Raḥīm 362
177. Ruzayq b. Zubayr al-Khulqānī 362
178. Ṣabbāḥ b. Ṣabīḥ al-Fazārī 363
179. Ṣabbāḥ b. Yaḥyā al-Muzanī 364
180. Sa'd b. Abī Khalaf al-Zāmm 365
181. Ṣafwān b. Mihrān al-Jammāl 365
182. Sa'īd b. 'Abd Allāh al-A'raj 365
183. Sa'īd b. Ghazwān al-Asadī 366
184. Sa'īd b. Yasār al-Ḍuba'ī 366
185. Ṣāliḥ b. 'Uqba 367
186. Ṣāliḥ b. Sa'īd al-Qammāṭ 367
187. Sālim b. Mukram Abū Khadīja al-Jammāl 368
188. Sallām b. 'Abd Allāh al-Hāshimī 368
189. Sallām b. Abī 'Amra 369

190. Samā‘a b. Mihrān al-Ḥaḍramī 369
191. Sarī b. ‘Abd Allāh al-Sulamī 370
192. Sayf b. Amīra al-Nakha‘ī 371
193. Shu‘ayb al-‘Aqarqūfī 371
194. Sufyān b. ‘Uyayna 372
195. Sulaym al-Farrā’ 373
196. Sulaymān al-Daylamī 373
197. Sulaymān b. Khālid al-Aqṭa‘ 374
198. Suwayd b. Muslim al-Qallā’ 375
199. Ṭalḥa b. Zayd al-Shāmī 375
200. Abū Ṭālib al-Sha‘rānī 376
201. Thābit b. Dīnār Abū Ḥamza al-Thumālī 377
202. Thābit b. Shurayḥ al-Anbārī 379
203. Tha‘laba b. Maymūn al-Naḥwī 380
204. ‘Ubayd Allāh b. ‘Alī al-Ḥalabī 380
205. ‘Ubayd Allāh b. al-Walīd al-Waṣṣāfī 382
206. ‘Ubayd b. Zurāra b. A‘yan 383
207. Udaym b. al-Ḥurr 384
208. ‘Umar b. Abān al-Kalbī 385
209. ‘Umar b. ‘Abd Allāh b. Ya‘lā al-Thaqafī 385
210. ‘Umar b. Udhayna 387
211. ‘Umar b. Yazīd al-Thaqafī 388
212. ‘Uqba b. Khālid al-Asadī 388
213. Wahb b. ‘Abd Rabbih 389
214. Wahb b. Wahb Abū ’l-Bakhtarī 389
215. Walīd b. Ṣubayḥ al-Asadī 391
216. Wuhayb b. Ḥafṣ al-Mantūf 391
217. Wuhayb b. Khālid al-Karābīsī 393
218. Yaḥyā b. al-‘Alā’ al-Rāzī 393
219. Yaḥyā b. ‘Imrān al-Ḥalabī 394
220. Yaḥyā b. al-Qāsim Abū Baṣīr al-Asadī 395
221. Yaḥyā b. Sa‘īd al-Qaṭṭān 396
222. Ya‘qūb b. Sālim al-Aḥmar 397
223. Ya‘qūb al-Sarrāj 397
224. Ya‘qūb b. Shu‘ayb al-Maythamī 398
225. Yāsin al-Ḍarīr 398
226. Yazīd Abū Khālid al-Qammāṭ 399
227. Yūnus b. Ya‘qūb al-Duhnī 399
228. Zakariyyā b. Muḥammad al-Mu’min 400

Preface

This study attempts to locate and identify the written heritage of the Imāmite Shī'ite branch of Islam in the first three centuries of its history. The beginning of the research goes back many years to a festschrift paper I wrote on the surviving remnants of a book ascribed to 'Alī in early Islamic sources. The article remained unpublished since the festschrift itself, for which the piece was originally intended, was never published. The research, however, encouraged me to embark on a more comprehensive venture encompassing other works of early Imāmite Shī'ism as a supplement to the relevant chapter of Fuat Sezgin's *Geschichte des arabischen Schrifttums* 1: 524–52. The present study has, however, a shorter time frame as it only covers the first three centuries of Shī'ite history, divided, as presented in the two volumes of the present work, into five periods covering from the time of 'Alī to the end of the Minor Occultation (329 AH/941 AD). A final chapter will attempt a general evaluation of the entire corpus.

The beginning of specifically Shī'ite literature can be traced to the late Umayyad period with a number of anti-Umayyad sectarian pamphlets and a book. Already by then, some transmitters of *ḥadīth*, Shī'ites included, had started to keep written records of narratives they had heard from their teachers.[1] More formal books on topics such as Qur'ānic sciences and law soon followed. The first systematic Shī'ite

1. See Kashshī: 225.

work on law[2] is said[3] to have been the book that ʿUbayd Allāh b. ʿAlī al-Ḥalabī, a transmitter from Imām Jaʿfar al-Ṣādiq, wrote in the first half of the second century. By the middle of that century, works on law by a non-Shīʿite majority reportedly[4] abounded.

The records that early transmitters of *ḥadīth* kept of what they received through oral transmission, conventionally known as *juz'*, *nuskha*, *aṣl*, *ṣaḥīfa*, or *kitāb*,[5] served as the main sources for the larger collections of *ḥadīth* that were soon to appear. In the Shīʿite tradition, those early records are mostly referred to as *kitāb*s or *aṣl*s. This latter term had a clear meaning in general Islamic,[6] as well as in more specific Shīʿite,[7] literature on the sciences of *ḥadīth*. It conveyed the sense of a personal notebook of material received through oral transmission,[8] perhaps originally simply a jotter, although later it was also applied to an organized and structured work, compiled out of the material received through oral transmission.[9] Some four hundred of those notebooks were believed to have been left by transmitters from the Imāms.[10] They would have been among some one thousand Shīʿite works that were available at the end of the third century.[11]

2. This book was in the form of a collection of reports transmitted from the Imāms but apparently organized in chapters according to subject matter. See Najāshī: 231; *Fihrist*: 106–7 (see also Murtaḍā, *Rassiyya al-ūlā*: 331).
3. Barqī: 73.
4. Kashshī: 384.
5. For possible minor distinctions between the original usages of some of these terms, see the many examples of the *nuskha*s, *juz's* and *aṣl*s already published (see also Aʿẓamī, *Dirāsāt*: 343–5, 477).
6. The examples of the use of the term in this sense in the Sunnī tradition are too numerous to enumerate; I mention only a few that I happened to note in passing: ʿUthmān al-Dārimī, *Jahmiyya*: 1; Ibn Abī Ḥātim 5: 147; Ibn ʿAdī: 2303; Abū Nuʿaym, *Akhbār Iṣbahān* 1: 129, 2: 152; Khaṭīb, *Talkhīṣ*: 471, 516; idem, *Ta'rīkh* 3: 96–8, 5: 467, 6: 379; Ḥaskānī: passim; Abū Ṭāhir al-Silafī, *Muʿjam al-safar*: 299, 423; Rāfiʿī, *Tadwīn* 2: 302; Ṣarīfīnī: 16, 38, 317, 401, 424 (cf. ibid.: 35, 83, 107; Ṣūlī: 217; Samʿānī 10: 57 [also *Mabānī*: 91], 386, 540; Ibn Funduq: 183 for an alternative usage); *Mīzān* 1: 127; Ibn Ḥajar, *Tahdhīb* 5: 176, 8: 154, 11: 180; Suyūṭī, *La'ālī* 1: 263.
7. See, for instance, Nuʿmānī: 18; *Kamāl*: 19; *Fihrist*: 174–5 (see also *Faqīh* 2: 117; *ʿUyūn* 1: 256; Khazzāz: 309; Ṭūsī, *Amālī*: 413; *Manāqib* 1: 299). For the use of the term in the Zaydī tradition, see, for instance, ʿAbd Allāh b. Ḥamza, *Shāfī* 1: 58, 2: 116.
8. See, for instance, Mufīd, *ʿAdadiyya*: 24.
9. See Murtaḍā, *Rassiyya al-ūlā*: 331; *Fihrist*: 63.
10. Ṭabrisī, *Iʿlām*: 410, 439. See further Etan Kohlberg, "*Al-uṣūl al-arbaʿumiʾa*." According to *Manāqib* 2: 197, one hundred of those notebooks were left by the students of Imām Jaʿfar al-Ṣādiq alone. Early indices actually ascribe more than one hundred notebooks to the students of Jaʿfar al-Ṣādiq. Muḥaqqiq, *Muʿtabar* 1: 26 even assumes that all four hundred were left by them.
11. *Fihrist*: 64.

It has already been established that later collections of *ḥadīth* obtained most of their material through earlier written records, and that *isnāds* predominantly represented authors' chains of transmission to those earlier records rather than oral transmission of individual quotations. These points have been convincingly argued by Muḥammad Muṣṭafā al-A'ẓamī in his works[12] with ample documentation from Sunnī sources.[13] Much parallel evidence can be supplied from Shī'ite works.[14] However, in my attempts to ascertain whether a later work quotes directly from an earlier source, I have tried to rely on more concrete evidence. Quotation through the same chain of transmission, or at least the ultimate transmitter, that early bibliographies identify as the transmitter of a work from the author[15] may most probably have originated from the work in question. The same seems true where a large number of reports are quoted from an early author through the same *isnād*,[16] and where an author is always quoted simultaneously through several identical *isnāds*.[17] The common link in this latter case would most likely represent a written record. I only include works from which a fair number of quotations have survived, adequate enough for the work to be deemed partially extant.[18]

---

12. See his *Dirāsāt*: 587–94 (see also 382–5) and *Ḥadīth*: 74–9.
13. Consider this one example: Bukhārī 4: 112–13 quotes a report from 'Amr who quoted Muḥammad b. Ja'far using the common, standard formula *ḥaddathanā*, conventionally understood to signify oral transmission. There is a word missing in the report. Bukhārī quotes 'Amr explaining that the word was missing in the book of Muḥammad b. Ja'far.
14. Here are a few random examples: Abū Ghālib: 129–33 (see also 153–4); *Ma'ānī*: 149–50; *'Uyūn* 2: 20–22; *Faqīh* 3: 72; Ṭūsī, *Amālī* (Najaf, 1964) 2: 207. See also *Kāfī* 1: 52, 53. Authors sometimes noted if a report did not appear in the notebook of the ultimate authority for an oral transmission, a sign normally taken to indicate that the ascription was not reliable (e.g. Mufīd, *'Adadiyya*: 24; Ṭūsī, *Tahdhīb* 4: 169 [whence Ibn al-Barrāj, *Sharḥ*: 175]).
15. In many instances, however, those indices mention only one chain of transmission for a work out of several. See Najāshī: 3, 116, 127, 231.
16. That is even more so where all of those quotations appear together as is the case with many quotations in, for instance, 'Abd Allāh b. Ja'far al-Ḥimyarī's *Qurb al-isnād* and Ṭūsī's *Amālī*.
17. Such is the case with, for instance, Ibn Bābawayh's *Faqīh* where individual quotations normally appear under the name of the ultimate transmitter of the material from an Imām with no *isnād* attached, but then in an appendix, the author gives a full account of his chains of transmission to all of the aforementioned authorities and their works. Many times, he notes that for all quotations from a specific transmitter he simultaneously has two or more different *isnāds* to that person.
18. I have thus excluded authors who are quoted in later works but not, or only in a few cases, through those specified as the transmitters of their works in early bio/bibliographical sources. An appendix at the end of volume 2 will provide names and lists of quotations for these authors.

Various other points also deserve attention at the outset:

Most of the material for this book was compiled before the advent of modern electronic resources for the study of *ḥadīth*, in fact even before the publication of modern concordances of Shīʿite *ḥadīth*. The data base currently being prepared at Qum for the *isnād*s of Shīʿite collections of *ḥadīth* has not been accessible to me. Clearly, the availability of these modern tools of research will enhance both the speed and the accuracy of future scholarship in this field.

When I began to collect the material, I strove to gather all available information about early Shīʿite *mutakallimūn* and their views on various theological issues. But the appearance of Josef van Ess's *Theologie und Gesellschaft im 2. und 3. Jahrhundert Hidschra* has persuaded me to review and exclude material which would now appear as redundant or repetitive. Numerous recent publications attempt to reconstruct works long lost to us by tracing quotations from them in later works, or to collect quotations from early authorities of Shīʿite tradition in special volumes. I have benefited immensely from this resurgence of interest as it has enabled me to discard similar findings of my own as superfluous and trim my work accordingly. In addition, the recent publication of indices of the main works of Shīʿite *ḥadīth* makes it no longer necessary to add the long list of surviving citations from every early Shīʿite notebook of *ḥadīth* which I had originally compiled for inclusion. This also helped to reduce the size of the present work considerably. However, in the instances where the indices proved inadequate in the context, references from my original lists have been inserted.

References to early works do not always signify an acknowledgement of their authenticity. There are serious suspicions, for instance, of interpolation in the case of a large part of the material of the current "greater" version of Ṣaffār's *Baṣāʾir al-darajāt*, as will be discussed in the appropriate place in the present work. In line with a well-established tradition in narrating the events of the major battles of the Arabs (*ayyām al-ʿArab*), some of the accounts on early civil wars among the Muslims used in sources such as Naṣr b. Muzāḥim's *Waqʿat Ṣiffīn* are clearly historical novels. Much of the contents of a book called *Dalāʾil al-imāma* and works by authors such as Shādhān b. Jibrīl al-Qummī, Ḥusayn b. ʿAbd al-Wahhāb, Quṭb al-Dīn al-Rāwandī, and Ḥasan b. Sulaymān al-Ḥillī come from unorthodox, esoteric sources. Authors of these works may have believed in the authenticity of the material they quoted but not necessarily on the basis of traditional methods of authentification.

However, this does not mean the exclusion of works as such from this study, drawing as it does on a whole array of probabilities and conjectures.

There are works that are commonly ascribed to wrong authors. An early index of the names of some Shīʿite transmitters of *ḥadīth* known as *Rijāl al-Barqī* is ascribed to the scholar Aḥmad b. Muḥammad b. Khālid al-Barqī (d. 274–280). The text, however, contains citations from someone who was a student of this scholar and should thus belong to a later period.[19] Najāshī: 392 mentions a work by Ibn Bābawayh al-Qummī (d. 381) as *Kitāb al-maʿrifa bi-rijāl al-Barqī*, apparently an index of the transmitters that Barqī quoted in his comprehensive collection of transmissions, *Kitāb al-maḥāsin*. This may be the same as the work in question (discrepancies between the information supplied in this index and that provided in Ibn Bābawayh's *Mashyakha* can naturally represent the author's state of knowledge in the different time frames in which the two lists were prepared). The *Kitāb al-īḍāḥ* of Ibn Rustam al-Ṭabarī has been published, erroneously attributed on the sole basis of some recent manuscripts to Faḍl b. Shādhān al-Naysābūrī. The *Tafsīr* commonly ascribed to ʿAlī b. Ibrāhīm al-Qummī is not by that scholar. The status of these and other similar works will also be discussed in the present work. For the sake of clarity in identification, common ascriptions of titles to authors will be respected in the bibliographic references, even where the attribution is obviously wrong.

Quotations from earlier works are usually repeated in numerous later collections. Here, only the earliest work is mentioned, unless there is sufficient ground to believe that a later work quoted directly, or through a different route, from a now lost original. This is usually the case when a quotation appears in a later work with a different *isnād* or with substantial variations in the text. The same rule is followed for the biographical works where only the original or redactions of earlier but extinct sources are mentioned. An example of the latter category is provided by Ṭūsī's *Kitāb al-fihrist*, obviously a redaction of an earlier Shīʿite bibliography[20] that has not survived but was available to Najāshī who noted, and tried to correct, its errors in numerous cases.

---

19. Unless the citations in question were later interpolations added to a copy of the work from which the extant manuscripts originate; a feasible conjecture.

20. With occasional additions from a few other sources, and from his own personal information. He also added a few short sentences here and there (as in, for instance, p. 126 where he expresses his adverse opinion of the text without altering the text itself), and inserted the names of his own *shaykhs*, linking himself to the chains of transmission mentioned for the books in that index.

Apart from the adjustments referred to earlier, the notes presented in this volume have been left unchanged from the time of their original compilation. I, however, used my sabbatical leave in the fall of 2002 to update the bibliographical references in the light of recent publications in the field, and make some minor revisions. Wherever a manuscript has become available in printed version, all references are now to the printed edition. Some of the lost works which were originally cited through later works are now available in reconstructed volumes and some, but not all, of my references are changed to these reconstructed volumes. Better editions are now available for a number of sources used for this study. In some of these cases, especially where an older edition was too corrupt, as in the case of Ibn Ḥajar's *Lisān al-Mīzān*, or where a new edition offers the full, or at least a comparatively more extensive, text of the work, as in the cases of Balādhurī's *Ansāb al-ashrāf*, Ibn 'Asākir's *Ta'rīkh madīnat Dimashq*, and Ibn Sa'd's *Ṭabaqāt*, the references are changed to the new, better or more extensive edition. Such was also the case where the notes were taken from different editions of a work. The references are now all to a single, usually the most recent, edition. In a few instances, a different edition had to be used, but unless otherwise indicated the editions used are those cited in the Bibliography.

The term *Sunnī* is used throughout this work in its present day sense, a usage that post-dates the period covered here.

Unless otherwise specified, all dates are *hijrī* except for publication dates which can be either of the two eras: *hijrī* or Christian.

Finally, it is a pleasant duty to express my gratitude to Michael Cook for reading the entire text of this volume and for his many astute comments and corrections, and to Mohsen Ashtiany and Denise Soufi for their many valuable suggestions for improving the text.

I

'Alī and His Personal Associates

At the time of his death, the Prophet's only surviving child was his daughter, Fāṭima, whose own children included Ḥasan and Ḥusayn. 'Alī, one of the Prophet's closest associates since childhood and his son-in-law, was the head of this small family of the Prophet's offspring, known as the House of the Prophet.

Succession to the Prophet went to the most senior of his extended family, the tribe of Quraysh. The Prophet's daughter and grandchildren, now completely out of the limelight, must nevertheless have enjoyed the affection of the Muslims in Medina. Members of the Prophet's clan of the tribe of Quraysh, the Banū Hāshim, and a number of the clients of the House – former slaves manumitted by the Prophet and their children – and a few well-wishers, made up a small circle of associates of the House. There were a few among the disciples of the Prophet who had a special attachment to the House of the Prophet and kept this affection until the end of their lives. Salmān al-Fārsī, Abū Dharr al-Ghifārī, and Miqdād b. al-Aswad al-Kindī, three senior Companions, belonged to this camp. The Shī'a consider these Companions to be their first generation.

1: 'Alī b. Abī Ṭālib

Abū 'l-Ḥasan 'Alī b. Abī Ṭālib, the prophet's first cousin and son-in-law, the first Imām of the Shī'a and the fourth "Truly Guided" caliph of the Sunnīs (r. 35–40). Born in Mecca, ca. 600 AD, and raised by the Prophet, he was one of the Prophet's closest and most learned associates. He was assassinated in Kūfa in 40.

Biographical material about 'Alī can be found in very many sources, as well as many monographs and special chapters. For summaries of the material and lists of the main early sources for his biography, see the entries on him in the *Encyclopaedia of Islam*, 2nd edn., 1: 381–6 (L. Veccia Vaglieri) and *Encyclopaedia Iranica*, 1: 838–48 (I. K. Poonawala and E. Kohlberg).

1. *Qur'ānic recension*

'Alī is believed to have been the compiler of one of the early recensions of the Qur'ān.[1] His recension is said to have been chronologically arranged, that is, in the order in which the Qur'ān was revealed,[2] though the account that the sources[3] give of the arrangement of his codex does not support that assumption. It is also reported that his codex included additional exegetical material including information on the abrogated verses of the Qur'ān.[4] Shī'ite sources report that after the death of the Prophet, 'Alī presented this codex for official consecration, but it was rejected by other companions of the Prophet and he had to take it back home.[5] He is also one of the few original Readers of the Qur'ān whose

1. Ibn Sa'd 2: 338; Ibn Abī Shayba 6: 148; Ya'qūbī 2: 135; Ibn Abī Dāwūd: 10; *Kāfī* 8: 18; Ibn al-Nadīm: 30; Abū Hilāl al-'Askarī, *Awā'il* 1: 219–20; *Ḥilya* 1: 67; Ibn Juzayy 1: 4; Ibn Abī 'l-Ḥadīd 1: 27; Dhahabī, *Ma'rifat al-qurrā'* 1: 28.
2. Ibn Sa'd 2: 258; Dhahabī, *Ma'rifa* 1: 28; Suyūṭī, *Itqān* 1: 216.
3. Ya'qūbī 2: 135–6; Shahrastānī, *Mafātīḥ* 1: 134–9 (quoting Muḥammad b. Khālid al-Barqī of the early 3rd century, presumably in his *Kitāb al-tanzīl* [Najāshī: 335]).
4. Suyūṭī, *Itqān* 1: 204.
5. Sulaym b. Qays: 72, 108; Ṣaffār: 193; *Kāfī* 2: 633; Bāqillānī: 107; Shahrastānī, *Mafātīḥ* 1: 120; *Iḥtijāj* 1: 107, 225–8; *Manāqib* 2: 42. It should be noted that a report in 'Abd al-Razzāq 4: 6–7 and Bukhārī 2: 277 (attested partially also in Aḥmad 1:141, and with variations in Ibn Abī Shayba 15: 227; 'Uthmān al-Dārimī, *al-Radd 'alā Bishr*: 130; Ibn 'Asākir 39: 266) states that 'Alī, reacting to the public complaint against 'Uthmān's tax officials, offered 'Uthmān the text of the Prophet's guidelines to tax collectors and asked him to instruct his tax collectors to follow it. 'Uthmān, however, rejected that and said he did not need it. 'Alī therefore had to take it back. The similarities with the account quoted above are striking (see further below, footnote 48).

Reading has been preserved.[6] A number of alleged differences between his reading and the current standard version of the Qur'ān are recorded in the sources.[7] A Sunnī expert on the text of the Qur'ān, Abū Ṭāhir 'Abd al-Wāḥid b. 'Umar al-Baghdādī al-Bazzāz (d. 349)[8] wrote a monograph on the reading of 'Alī.[9] Certain authors of works on Qur'ānic readings, however, suggest that the reading of 'Āṣim[10] as transmitted by Ḥafṣ,[11] that has long been the dominant standard version of the Qur'ān, is in fact the reading of 'Alī.[12] Ḥafṣ' reading is believed to have faithfully represented that of 'Āṣim with the single exception of one word.[13] 'Āṣim is quoted as having told Ḥafṣ that the reading he taught him was the one he had learnt from Abū 'Abd al-Raḥmān al-Sulamī,[14] who had received it from 'Alī.[15] 'Āṣim asserted that nowhere did he abandon the reading of Sulamī; Sulamī's reading in turn never deviated from that of 'Alī.[16] None of the variations attributed to 'Alī's codex is, however, attested in the 'Āṣim/Ḥafṣ reading. The Shī'ites did not recognize 'Āṣim's reading as that of 'Alī,[17] though some noted 'Āṣim's Shī'ite sympathies.[18] Sunnī polemics, however, use the idea that 'Alī's reading is known through Abū 'Abd al-Raḥmān al-Sulamī and that this latter's reading is not basically

6. Dhahabī, *Ma'rifa* 1: 42.
7. Ibn Jinnī records some 60 cases of these variant Readings in his *Muḥtasib*; they are scattered through the work but can be traced through the index of names at the end of the book 2: 506. Many of these and others are attested in other works, too, such as Sayyārī: 70 b; Ibn Abī Dāwūd: 53; Ibn al-Juḥām: 193; Ibn Khālawayh, *Badī*: 151; *Mabānī*: 103; *Manāqib* 3: 110 (quoting Abū 'l-Qāsim al-Kūfī in his *al-Radd 'alā ahl al-tabdīl*); also Jeffery: 185–92; *Mu'jam al-qirā'āt al-Qur'āniyya*, introduction: 15–16 and the sources named therein.
8. On whom see Ibn al-Nadīm: 35; Khaṭīb, *Ta'rīkh* 11: 7–8, and many other sources listed in the editors' footnotes to Dhahabī's *Siyar* 16: 21 and *Ta'rīkh* 25 (years 331–350): 424.
9. Najāshī: 247; *Fihrist*: 122.
10. 'Āṣim b. Abī 'l-Najūd al-Kūfī (d. 127), one of the seven Readers of the Qur'ān.
11. Ḥafṣ b. Sulaymān al-Kūfī (d. 180), a Reader of the Qur'ān and 'Āṣim's step-son and main student.
12. Ibn Mihrān, *Mabsūṭ*: 44, 46–47, 48, 51, 199; idem, *Ghāya*: 52; Ibn Ghalbūn 1: 61–62; Ibn al-Nadīm: 31; Abū 'l-'Alā' al-Hamadānī 1: 55; *Mabānī*: 103; Ibn al-Bādhish 1: 124; Dhahabī, *Ma'rifa* 1: 94.
13. Azharī: 99; Ibn Mihrān, *Mabsūṭ*: 56; idem, *Ghāya*: 53.
14. Abū 'Abd al-Raḥmān 'Abd Allāh b. Ḥabīb al-Sulamī (d. 73–74), a transmitter of *ḥadīth* and Reader of the Qur'an who taught it in the grand mosque of Kūfa for 40 years.
15. Abū 'l-'Alā' al-Hamadhānī 1: 55; Dhahabī, *Ma'rifa*: 92.
16. Ibn Mihrān, *Mabsūṭ*: 56. Elsewhere, however, this author quotes that 'Āṣim's other student, Abū Bakr b. 'Ayyāsh (d. 193) modified the reading of 'Āṣim in ten cases to make it conform completely with the Reading of 'Alī (ibid.: 440). See also Dhahabī, *Ma'rifa* 1: 27, 91, 92.
17. See especially Ibn Ṭāwūs, *Sa'd al-su'ūd*: 554.
18. 'Abd al-Jalīl al-Qazwīnī: 212–13, 238.

different from the standard reading of the text, to attack early Shī'ite arguments from reports suggesting that 'Alī had a variant recension of the Qur'ān.[19] One thus wonders if the identification of the reading of 'Alī with that of 'Āṣim/ Ḥafṣ was not originally meant for the same purpose and as a polemical strategy to disarm the Shī'ites in their sectarian debates with the Sunnīs.

2. *Kitāb 'Alī*

An early report asserts that 'Alī was once seen noting down on a parchment what he heard from the Prophet in his presence.[20] References to, and quotations from, a text believed to have been compiled by 'Alī from the statements of the Prophet are abundant in the material from the second century. According to a report, 'Aṭā' b. Abī Rabāḥ, the jurisconsult of Mecca in the early second century (d. 114), knew this text and had no doubt that it was actually 'Alī's compilation.[21] Some reports describe the text as a 70 cubit parchment scroll.[22] This is identical with a description given for a scroll called *al-Jāmi'a* mentioned in some other reports;[23] both were said to contain what people need in matters of lawfulness and unlawfulness and the laws of inheritance,[24] even monetary compensation for bodily bruises.[25] A similar description of the material, size and

19. Bāqillānī: 70, 378; *Mabānī*: 60. For the purpose of the argument, see Modarressi, "Early Debates on the Integrity of the Qur'ān": 24–28.
20. Ṣaffār: 163 (paragraph # 4, see also 160, para. # 31); 'Alī b. Bābawayh, *Imāma*: 174; Rāmhurmuzī: 601; Sam'ānī, *Adab al-imlā'*: 12, 13; Bulqaynī: 300.
21. Shāfi'ī, *Umm* 2: 126.
22. Ṣaffār: 142–6 (# 3, 5, 6, 7, 10, 11, 18, 19, 20, 21), 147–9 (# 1, 2, 5, 7, 14), 151 (# 2), 155 (# 10), 159 (# 26), all mentioning the measurement. That it was a parchment is mentioned in 142 (# 2), 147 (# 5). Others only mention it as a large scroll without giving the exact measurement, as in Najāshī: 360 (see also Ṣaffār: 148–9 [# 9, 12], 163 [# 3], 164 [# 6], 168 [# 24]), or that when wrapped it looked like a man's thigh (Ṣaffār: 165 [# 14]) or a camel's thigh (ibid.: 142 [# 2]; *Kāfī* 7: 94).
23. Ṣaffār: 142–46 (# 2, 4, 8, 9, 15, 22), 148–50 (# 8, 13, 16), 152–3 (# 3, 6), 157 (# 19), 160 (# 31); *Faqīh* 4: 419; *Khiṣāl*: 528. That this was a parchment is noted in Ṣaffār: 142 (# 2), 149 (# 13), 153 (# 6 where it is also mentioned that when wrapped it looked like a camel's thigh; also *Kāfī* 1: 241); *Kāfī* 1: 239, 241.
24. For the Book of 'Alī, see Ṣaffār: 142–6 (# 1, 3, 7, 11, 18), 148 (# 7), 149 (# 14), 154 (# 7), 164 (# 10), 166 (# 18); 'Ayyāshī 1: 25–6; *Kāfī* 1: 242. For the *Jāmi'a*, see Ṣaffār: 142–6 (# 4, 8, 9, 15, 22, 23), 148 (# 8), 150 (# 16), 152 (# 3), 157 (# 19), 161 (# 33); *Kāfī* 1: 239, 241.
25. For the Book of 'Alī, see Ṣaffār: 142–6 (# 3, 6, 10, 11, 16, 18, 19, 21), 147–48 (# 1, 6, 7, 11), 155 (# 10, 12), 159 (# 26), 164 (# 5), 166 (#18). For the *Jāmi'a*, see ibid.: 142–6 (# 2, 4, 8, 15, 22), 148 (# 8), 152 (# 3), 153 (# 6), 160 (# 31); *Kāfī* 1: 239, 241.

contents is also given for another text called *Muṣḥaf* (or *Kitāb*) *Fāṭima*.[26] The specific description which suggests that the text contained everything that people needed including monetary compensation for bruises is occasionally mentioned in connection with yet another text called the *Jafr*.[27] Both of the latter works were also believed to consist of ʿAlī's notes taken from the Prophet's dictation.[28] References to these last two texts, mostly in the case of the first[29] and totally in the case of the latter,[30] are, however, concerned with esoteric and apocalyptic matters. All these were supposed to be parts of the written heritage of the House of the Prophet that many early Shīʿites believed passed through the line of the Imāms,[31] providing them with the special knowledge that distinguished them from the rest of the community including the learned.[32] Whether or not all of this was a natural expansion of the single parchment report quoted in the opening of this discussion, as suggested by a contemporary author,[33]

---

26. Ṣaffār: 150–151 (# 1), 153 (# 5), 156 (# 14), 161 (# 33); *Kāfī* 1: 240; *Khiṣāl*: 528. See also *Kāfī* 3: 507. Contrary descriptions are given in Ṣaffār: 152–4 (# 3, 6), 157 (# 18), 158 (# 21), 159 (# 27); *Kāfī* 1: 240, 241. Compare also Ṣaffār: 152 (# 3), 153 (# 6), 157–8 (# 19), 161 (# 33); *Kāfī* 1: 239, 241 (# 5); *Khiṣāl*: 528 where the two works are categorically distiguished.
27. Ṣaffār: 155 (# 12), 156 (# 14); *Faqīh* 4: 419; *Khiṣāl*: 528. See also Ṣaffār: 156 (# 15), 160 (# 30), 161 (# 34) where it is described as containing what people need in matters of lawfulness and unlawfulness. The report in the *Faqīh* states that the text contains all knowledge.
28. For the *Muṣḥaf Fāṭima*, see Ṣaffār: 150–61 (# 5, 14, 19, 33; compare contrary accounts ibid.: 150–61, # 3, 18, 27). For the *Jafr*, see ibid.: 155–61 (# 10, 12, 15, 26, 30, 34).
29. See, for instance, Ṣaffār: 161 (# 32), 169 (# 3), 170 (# 7); ʿAlī b. Bābawayh, *Imāma*: 180; *Kāfī* 1: 241, 242, 8: 58. See also Ṣaffār: 158 (# 23) where it is said that the *Muṣḥaf* of Fāṭima was taken back (*qubiḍa*) after the death of Muḥammad al-Bāqir (d. 114–117).
30. See the article *Djafr* in the *Encyclopaedia of Islam*, 2nd edn., 2: 375–7 (T. Fahd).
31. Ṣaffār: 162–7 (# 1, 3, 7, 8, 9, 12, 17, 20); *Kāfī* 1: 276, 297–8; *Daʿāʾim* 1: 27, 2: 346–7; *Faqīh* 4: 189, 419; *Tahdhīb* 9: 176.
32. Ṣaffār: 142–6, 326–8; *Iḥtijāj* 2: 6–7.
33. This scenario assumes that the original story has developed in two directions: (a) in size, from a piece of parchment that ʿAlī filled in entirely, front and back as well as the margins (Ṣaffār: 163; Rāmhurmuzī: 601), the parchment being made of a sheep skin, neither large nor too small (Ṣaffār: 155 [# 12], 156 [# 14]), to a cow hide (*Kāfī* 1: 241, though this is denied in Ṣaffār: 156 [# 14]), to two parchments, one from a sheep and the other from a goat (Ṣaffār: 159 [# 26], but in *Faqīh* 4: 419 [also *Khiṣāl*: 528], it is the *Jafr* that is on a sheep skin and a goat skin), to a seventy cubit scroll (noted above), to a skin container made of cow hide with several books in it (ibid.: 156 [# 15], 160 [# 30], 161 [# 34]), to two skin containers full of books and other material (Ṣaffār: 151–4 [# 2, 9, 10, 12]); and (b) in content, from the prescription of the licit and illicit to prophecies and apocalyptics, first all attributed to the Book of ʿAlī, then another book was added for Fāṭima; then a third one as the *Jāmiʿa*, that at times was thought to be different from the *Kitāb ʿAlī* as noted above; then a fourth one as the *Jafr* (in fact, not one but two: a lesser and a greater [*Faqīh* 4: 419; *Khiṣāl*: 528]); then a text on which the names of

the ʿUthmāniyya counter-acted by quoting ʿAlī as categorically denying that he received anything particular from the Prophet except for a folio, as tiny as the size of a finger,[34] with three brief sentences he had heard from the Prophet,[35] recorded and placed in the sheath of ʿAlī's sword.[36] The text of these brief sentences is quoted in many variants.[37] As

---

all Shīʿites were recorded so that the Imāms could recognize their own followers (Ṣaffār: 170–72), again of the size of a camel's thigh (ibid.: 173 [# 10]), and at times together with another text on which the names of all enemies of the Imāms until the Day of Resurrection were recorded (*Faqīh* 4: 419; *Khiṣāl*: 528; the two texts were in fact given to the Prophet on his Night Journey and were passed by him to ʿAlī [Ṣaffār: 192]); then another text with the names of all future rulers (ibid.: 169 [# 5]; Ibn Samka: 184–5), though the list of the future rulers was at times said to have been in the *Kitāb ʿAlī* (Ṣaffār: 169 # 1; *Maqātil*: 142) or in the *Kitāb* or *Muṣḥaf* of Fāṭima (Ṣaffār: 169[# 3, 7]; *Kāfī* 1: 242) and at times the names of the Prophets were thought to be in the same text as well (Ṣaffār: 169 [# 4, 6]); then two texts, one for the names of the Prophets and the other for those of the kings (ibid.: 169 [# 2]; *Kāfī* 1: 242 [# 7]. *Daʿāʾim* 2: 347 suggests that ʿAlī gave his two sons by Fāṭima, Ḥasan and Ḥusayn, "the Book of Qurʾān and the Book of Knowledge, and a confidential testament in which he wrote for them the names of all the kings of the world, the duration of the world, and the names of those who will call to God [*duʿāt*, presumably meaning the Imāms] until the Day of Resurrection"). On another front, while the mainstream Shīʿites were content with the book of ʿAlī as an earthly text, the Extremists identified it with the heavenly "hidden book" mentioned in the Qurʾān 56: 78 (Nuʿmānī: 327). A possible parallel may be worth noting: a report in *Kāfī* 1: 530; *Kamāl*: 295; Ibn ʿAyyāsh: 16, 17 suggests that the most prominent rabbi of Medina at the time of ʿUmar had in his possession a book that was dictated by Moses and copied by Aaron. A well known quotation from the Prophet, known among the Shīʿa as *Ḥadīth al-Manzila*, states that ʿAlī was to the Prophet all that Aaron was to Moses except that ʿAlī, unlike Aaron, was not a prophet.

34. *Ḥilya* 4: 164.
35. The esoteric Shīʿites, in turn, wasted no time in coming up with their own contribution and asserted that each letter of those sentences was in fact a code that could open one thousand full chapters of knowledge (Ṣaffār: 307–8; *Kāfī* 1: 296; *Khiṣāl*: 649).
36. Fazārī: 260; Ṭayālisī 1: 90, 154; Ḥumaydī 1: 172–3; ʿAbd al-Razzāq 9: 263, 10: 99; Ibn Abī Shayba 9: 293; Aḥmad 1: 79, 81, 100, 118, 119, 122, 126, 142, 151; Ibn Zanjawayh: 441–42; Bukhārī 4: 289; Muslim: 995–9, 1147; Ibn Māja: 887; Tirmidhī: 4: 6. A variant locates the record in the sheath of the Prophet's sword, found after his death by the public (ʿAlī b. Jaʿfar: 292; Shāfiʿī, *Musnad* 2: 97 [see also Ibn Zanjawayh: 442; *Maḥāsin*: 105; *Kāfī* 7: 275; *Faqīh* 4: 98; Bayhaqī 8: 26]; Ibn Abī ʿĀṣim, *Diyāt*: 36) or by ʿAlī in particular (*Maḥāsin*: 17–18; Abū Yaʿlā 1: 277; Bayhaqī 8: 324). A report in Ibn ʿAdī: 1408 suggests that it was ʿAlī b. al-Ḥusayn Zayn al-ʿĀbidīn who brought out the document from the sheath of the Prophet's sword. Yet another report (Ibn Saʿd 5: 78) ascribes the whole matter to ʿAlī's son, Muḥammad Ibn al-Ḥanafiyya who said that ʿAlī's family did not inherit anything from the Prophet except the Qurʾān (sic) and a folio that Ibn al-Ḥanafiyya kept in the sheath of his own sword with the same text ascribed in other reports to that of ʿAlī's. This was Ibn al-Ḥanafiyya's response to the supporters of Mukhtār al-Thaqafī (d. 67) who suggested that Ibn al-Ḥanafiyya had a special knowledge.
37. Rifʿat Fawzī ʿAbd al-Muṭṭalib has collected most of these variations in a booklet entitled *Ṣaḥīfat ʿAlī b. Abī Ṭālib ʿan Rasūl Allāh*. See also Miyānajī 2: 106–30, 154–56, 176–77 for a similar display of these variants. See also the editors' footnotes to Ṭayālisī 1: 90–91, 152; Abū Yaʿlā 1: 282–3; Aḥmad (Beirut, 1995) 2: 36–7, 52, 265, 268, 286, 304,

usual,[38] some could not see even that much in the sheath of 'Alī's sword and transferred it to the sheath of 'Umar's.[39]

The book of 'Alī was thought to have been in the possession of 'Alī Zayn al-'Ābidīn,[40] Muḥammad al-Bāqir,[41] and Ja'far al-Ṣādiq.[42] The latter two frequently quoted from it, though some of the quotations of Ja'far al-Ṣādiq were through his father.[43] Later Imāms also occasionally quoted the book.[44]

305, 428–9. For a possible factual error in the most popular version of that text, see the editor's footnote to Muslim: 995–8 (whence Aḥmad [Beirut, 1995] 2: 52).

38. See Modarressi, "Early Debates on the Integrity of the Qur'ān": 19–21. For the polemic purpose of the citations in question, see, for instance, Ḥākim 4: 153; Ibn Ḥajar, *Fatḥ* 1: 182, 4: 74. This purpose can be further attested by versions of the citation where 'Alī swears by God that he did not receive from the Prophet anything he did not share with others except for those brief sentences (Fazārī: 220; Ṭayālisī 1: 90; 'Abd al-Razzāq 10: 100, 11: 449; Ḥumaydī 1: 172–3; Shāfi'ī, *Umm* 6: 33, 7: 292; Ibn Abī Shayba 9: 293; Aḥmad 1: 79, 81, 100, 102, 119, 142; Ibn Shabba: 1166; Bukhārī 4: 289; see also Ibn Abī Shayba 6: 566; Aḥmad 1: 108; Muslim: 1967; 'Abd Allāh b. Aḥmad: 217 where 'Alī gets angry when asked if the Prophet told him anything [special]), or says that whoever claims that he received anything else from the Prophet is a liar (Ibn Abī Shayba 14: 198; Aḥmad 1: 81; Muslim: 995; 1147; Tirmidhī 4: 6; 'Abd Allāh b. Aḥmad: 218–19; Abū Ya'lā 1: 228). The point is also confirmed by reports where 'Abd Allāh b. Saba', whom Sunnī sources hold responsible for the founding of the Shī'ite school, is brought into the picture as 'Alī tells him that the Prophet did not privilege 'Alī with anything special that the Prophet kept it secret from others and that you (i.e. Ibn Saba') are a liar (Ibn Abī 'Āṣim, *Sunna* 2: 674–5; 'Abd Allāh b. Aḥmad: 231; Abū Ya'lā 1: 349–50). It is further attested by the fact that some reports also try to put the words into the mouth of Mālik al-Ashtar, a close disciple of 'Alī whom the Shī'ites profoundly admired but the 'Uthmāniyya especially disliked as they believed he was among those who killed 'Uthmān (a report refrains from even mentioning his name in the present context and refers to him as "someone that the transmitter mentioned" [see, for instance, Ibn Ḥazm 10: 353]), having him run to 'Alī to inform him that the community has become disunited by what they hear, so he, i.e. 'Alī, should tell them if he has received any special "testament" from the Prophet. To which question 'Alī responds that the Prophet did not privilege him with anything beyond what others received, except for that short text (Nasā'ī 6: 335, 8: 56; Ṭabarānī, *Awsaṭ* 5: 267 [see also Aḥmad 1: 119, 122, 5: 127–8, whence Abū Dāwūd 4: 180–81]; Abū Ya'lā 1: 462; Ḥākim 2: 141; Bayhaqī 8: 194. [Cf. 'Abd al-Razzāq 11: 449; Aḥmad 1: 142–3, 148; Ibn Shabba: 1166–7; Abū Ya'lā 1: 282; Bayhaqī 8: 29]).
39. 'Abd al-Razzāq 4: 9; Bayhaqī 4: 90.
40. *Kāfī* 8: 163 (cf. ibid. 8: 131).
41. Ṣaffār: 165; Najāshī: 966 (see also *Tahdhīb* 1: 142; 'Abd Allāh b. Ḥamza, *'Iqd*: 93).
42. Kashshī: 376 (see also *Kāfī* 3: 397). Following the hereditary line of the Imāmate, it was natural for some people to think that the book should have passed from Ja'far al-Ṣādiq to his son and successor, Mūsā al-Kāẓim ('Abd Allāh b. Ja'far: 317; Nu'mānī: 327). According to one version of a report in Ṣaffār: 166–7, however, Ja'far al-Ṣādiq is quoted as saying that he had buried the Book of 'Alī out of caution (lest it fell into the hands of the government?).
43. Zayd al-Zarrād: 3–4 (whence *Ma'ānī*: 1–2); 'Abd al-Razzāq 4: 532; 'Abd Allāh b. Ja'far: 92 (quoting "a book of 'Alī"); *Faqīh* 3: 416 (also *'Ilal* 2:188; *Tahdhīb* 7: 481); Ibn Ḥazm 7: 102–3.
44. E.g. *Kāfī* 5: 452 quoting Mūsā al-Kāẓim; Irbilī 3: 136 quoting Muḥammad al-Jawād; Mas'ūdī, *Murūj* 5: 82–3 quoting 'Alī al-Hādī.

The vast majority of the quotations are legal injunctions, though later a few esoteric reports are also attributed to it. In a few cases, the citation quotes something that the Prophet or 'Alī did or did not do,[45] a sentence that normally could not have been dictated by the first and copied by the second. It must be noted that in the first centuries, there existed some texts that the partisans of 'Alī compiled about his virtues (*faḍā'il*) or from his statements and acts, in many cases as quotations from him. References to this genre are also found in general biographical works.[46] Citations from the "Book of 'Alī" which describe his acts may thus actually refer to works in this latter genre.

Here is a list of the citations from The Book of 'Alī in early sources:[47]

I LAW

On prayer:

- Shāfi'ī 2: 126
- Ṣaffār: 165
- *Kāfī* 3: 397 (quoting "a book dictated by the Prophet")
- Ibid. 3: 175
- *Tahdhīb* 2: 23, 251
- Ibid. 2: 102
- Ibid. 2: 243
- Ibid. 3: 28 (see also ibid. 1: 142)

On fasting:

- *Tahdhīb* 4:158

45. See *Tahdhīb* 10: 108 where it is quoted from the Book of 'Alī that the Prophet did not amputate more than one hand and one foot as a punishment for theft (even for persistent criminals); *Maḥāsin*: 273 (also *Kāfī* 7: 176; *Faqīh* 4: 75) quoting the Book of 'Alī describing 'Alī's practice in criminal punishment. Also *Tahdhīb* 8: 82 where the Prophet's conversation with a woman, and *Kāfī* 2: 666 (also 5: 31, quoting "a book by 'Alī") where the text of a Prophetic rescript addressed to the Emigrants and Helpers (Meccans and Medinese among the first generation of the Muslims), are quoted.
46. See the entries on Khilās b. 'Amr al-Hajarī al-Baṣrī (Ibn Abī Ḥātim, *Jarḥ* 3: 402 [*ṣuḥuf 'an 'Alī*], 402–3 [*kitāb 'an 'Alī*]; idem, *Marāsīl*: 55; 'Uqaylī 2: 29; *Mizān* 1: 658; Mizzī 8: 365) and Abū Hārūn al-'Abdī (d. 134) (Yaḥyā b. Ma'īn 4: 146 [read: *hādhihi Ṣaḥīfat al-Waṣī* as in all other sources]; 'Uqaylī 3: 314; Ibn Abī Ḥātim, *Jarḥ* 6: 364; Ibn 'Adī: 1732; Ibn Ḥibbān, *Majrūḥīn* 2: 177).
47. Many of these citations are collected in Miyānajī, *Makātīb al-Rasūl* 2: 135–313, a few also in Jalālī, *Tadwīn al-sunna*: 64–70 and Muṣṭafā Qaṣīr al-'Āmilī, *Kitāb 'Alī*: 23–38. The passages are listed in the order in which they are expected to appear in a reconstructed volume.

On pilgrimage to Mecca:

- Bazanṭī, *Nawādir*: 33 (also *Tahdhīb* 5: 152)
- *Kāfī* 4: 340 (also *Faqīh* 2: 338; *ʿIlal* 2: 94 [*fī Kitāb jaddī*])
- *Kāfī* 4: 368 (also *Tahdhīb* 1: 329)
- *Kāfī* 4: 389–90 (two variants, also *Tahdhīb* 5: 355 [and 357 with variations])
- *Kāfī* 4: 390 (also *Tahdhīb* 5: 344)
- *Kāfī* 4: 534
- Ibn Ḥazm 7: 102–3 (quoting ʿAbd al-Razzāq)

On holy war:

- *Kāfī* 2: 666, 5: 31(*fī kitāb li-ʿAlī* in the second case)

On prohibitions:

- Ḥusayn b. Saʿīd, *Zuhd*: 39 (also *Kāfī* 2: 347; *ʿIqāb*: 261 [repeated at 270–71]; *Khiṣāl*: 124)
- ʿAyyāshī 1: 223 (also *ʿIqāb*: 278)
- *Kāfī* 2: 71–2
- Ibid. 2: 278–9
- Ibid. 5: 541 (also Ibn Bābawayh, *Amālī*: 385; *ʿIlal* 2: 271; *ʿIqāb*: 301; cf. *Kāfī* 2: 374 where a longer version of the same report is attributed in a different transmission to *Kitāb Rasūl Allāh*)
- Ibn Bābawayh, *Amālī*: 509–18 (also *Faqīh* 4: 3–18)
- *ʿIlal* 2: 160–61 (also *Khiṣāl* 1: 273)

On property:

- ʿAlāʾ b. Razīn: 153 (whence *Faqīh* 3: 452)
- ʿAyyāshī 2:25 (also *Kāfī* 1: 407, 5: 279–80)

On marriage and divorce:

- Aḥmad b. ʿĪsā 3: 51
- Aḥmad b. Muḥammad b. ʿĪsā: 79 (also *Tahdhīb* 7: 432), 87 (also *Kāfī* 5: 452)
- *Faqīh* 3: 416 (also *ʿIlal* 2: 188; *Tahdhīb* 7: 481, 490)
- *Tahdhīb* 8: 82

On dietetics:

- ʿAlī b. Jaʿfar: 115 (also *Kāfī* 6: 219, 220 [with variations]; *Tahdhīb* 9: 2, 4, 5 [also 6])

- ʻAbd al-Razzāq 4: 532 (also Bayhaqī 9: 258)
- ʻAyyāshī 1:294, 295 (also *Kāfī* 6: 202, 207)
- *Kāfī* 3: 9 (also *Tahdhīb* 1: 227 [also 9: 86 with variations])
- *Kāfī* 6: 232
- Ibid. 6: 246
- Ibid. 6: 255
- *Faqīh* 3: 330

On arbitration:

- *Kāfī* 7: 414–15 (two variants)

On inheritance:

- Ṣaffār: 165
- *Kāfī* 7: 77
- Ibid. 7: 119
- Ibid. 7: 136
- *Faqīh* 4: 283(cf. *Tahdhīb* 9: 308)
- *Maʻānī*: 217 (also *Tahdhīb* 9: 211)
- *Tahdhīb* 9: 325–6

Numerous other quotations are attributed to a text on the law of inheritance (*Ṣaḥīfat al-farāʼiḍ*),[48] also believed to have been compiled by ʻAlī from the dictation of the Prophet. This was said to be a part of the

48. It was noted above that a report in ʻAbd al-Razzāq 4: 6–7 (also Aḥmad 1: 141; Ibn Abī Shayba 15: 227; Bukhārī 2: 277) suggested that ʻAlī offered a text that contained the orders of the Prophet on the topic of *farāʼiḍ* (here meaning religious taxes on livestock and agricultural products) to ʻUthmān but the latter rejected it. The numerous quotations from ʻAlī on the topic (ʻAbd al-Razzāq 4: 5–6, 7, 19, 22, 39, 75, 88, 89, 122, 133, 134; Ibn Abī Shayba 3: 117, 118, 122, 125, 127, 129, 132, 133, 136, 145, 219; Aḥmad 1: 92, 113, 145, 148; Abū Dāwūd 2: 99–101 and many other sources) may all go back to the same text which was allegedly issued by the Prophet but never actually sent out to tax collectors in his lifetime (Dārimī 1: 382–3; Abū Dāwūd 2: 98). A text similar in style that the Prophet is said to have issued for ʻAmr b. Ḥazm, his emissary and tax collector in Yemen, is, however, recorded in almost all the main collections of *ḥadīth*, albeit with some variations. A sentence cited by Khaṭṭābī 2: 176 from the text that ʻAlī allegedly offered to ʻUthmān but which was rejected by the latter is reported elsewhere to belong to a rescript that ʻAlī wrote to ʻUthmān b. Ḥunayf, his governor of Baṣra (Majd al-Dīn Ibn al-Athīr 2: 298 , but cf. 3: 392). On the other hand, a similar name, *Kitāb al-farāʼiḍ*, is also applied to another text attributed to ʻAlī on the monetary compensations for loss of life or bodily injuries (*Kāfī* 7: 330–43). All three texts which are said to have either been in the possession of ʻAlī or issued by him can reasonably go back to him, presumably as guidelines to his governors during his caliphate. The term *farāʼiḍ* in the general sense can also legitimately apply to all three subjects, though in later legal usage it is normally used in the sense of the law of inheritance.

Book of ʿAlī (*Kāfī* 7: 94 [read *fī Kitāb 'Alī* as in *Tahdhīb* 9: 271]) with a similar description of its size and shape (*Kāfī* 7: 94–5), or of the *Jāmiʿa* (Ṣaffār: 145; *Kāfī* 7: 125). Here is a list of citations from this text on the law of inheritance:

- *Kāfī* 7: 81 (where two conflicting accounts are given of the arrangement of the text).
- Ibid. 7: 93–4 (also *Daʿāʾim* 2: 369)
- *Kāfī* 7: 98 (also *Daʿāʾim* 2: 371)
- *Kāfī* 7: 112 (repeated at 113; also *Daʿāʾim* 2: 375)
- *Kāfī* 7: 126 (see also 7: 125; cf. Ṣaffār: 145 where the passage is cited from the *Jāmiʿa*)
- *Daʿāʾim* 2: 370
- Ibid. 2: 374
- Ibid. 2: 379
- *Tahdhīb* 9: 306
- Ḥurr al-ʿĀmilī, *Wasāʾil* 17: 493 (quoting the early fourth-century Shīʿite author, Ibn Abī ʿAqīl)

On the penal code:

- *Maḥāsin*: 273 (also *Kāfī* 7: 176)
- *Kāfī* 7: 201
- Ibid. 7: 214 (also 216 with variations)
- Ibid. 7: 316–7
- Ibid. 7: 313
- Ibid. 7: 318
- Ibid. 7: 329
- *Khiṣāl*: 539
- *Tahdhīb* 10: 108

II ETHICS

- Zayd al-Zarrād: 3–4 (also *Maʿānī*: 1–2)
- ʿAbd Allāh b. Jaʿfar: 92
- Ṣaffār: 147
- *Kāfī* 1: 41
- Ibid. 2: 71–2
- Ibid. 2: 136
- Ibid. 2: 259
- Ibid. 2: 484 (also 488 with variations)

- Ibid. 2: 666 (also *Tahdhīb* 6: 140)
- Ibn Hammām: 44
- Irbilī 3: 136

There is also a quotation in Ḥusayn b. Saʿīd, *Zuhd*: 44 on the proper etiquette for the treatment of slaves, ascribed to the "Book of the Messenger of God," presumably referring to the text in question.

III DOGMATICS AND VIRTUES (*FAḌĀ'IL*)

- Ṣaffār: 166–7
- Masʿūdī 5: 82–3
- *Khiṣāl*: 65–7
- Ibn al-Juḥām: 466 (also Ṭūsī, *Amālī* 2: 20)

IV TALES OF THE PROPHETS

- ʿAyyāshī 1: 27–9 (*fī kitāb min kutub 'Alī*; also ʿAlī b. Ibrāhīm 1: 36–41 [*fī Kitāb Amīr al-Mu'minīn*]; *'Ilal* 1: 100)
- ʿAyyāshī 2: 33–4 (also ʿAlī b. Ibrāhīm 1: 244–5; Ibn Ṭāwūs, *Sa'd*: 238–40 [quoting Ibn ʿUqda's *Tafsīr*])
- ʿAyyāshī 2: 129–36
- ʿAlī b. Ibrāhīm 1: 32–4
- Ibid. 1: 41
- *Kāfī* 8: 233

V ESOTERIC

- Ṣaffār: 169 (# 1; cf. # 3 and 7 where the account is ascribed to the Book of Fāṭima; also *Maqātil*: 208)
- *Kamāl*: 312–13 (also *'Uyūn* 1: 45–6 [the text is on pp. 40–45])
- Shādhān b. Jibrīl: 141–2
- *Manāqib* 4: 273
- *Dalā'il al-imāma*: 554–62 (also Ibn Ṭāwūs, *Malāḥim*: 168–71 [quoting a work of Yaʿqūb b. Nuʿaym, an early third-century author])

3. *Kitāb al-diyāt*[49]

A text attributed to ʿAlī on the monetary compensations for the loss of life or a limb, finger, eye, or any other part of the body, based on a rescript

49. *Kāfī* 7: 311

that he sent to his governors as a guideline.[50] In a few cases, this text is also referred to as *Kitāb 'Alī*[51] or *Kitāb al-farā'iḍ*.[52]

The full text of this book is quoted by Ibn Bābawayh in *Faqīh* 4: 75–92, by Ṭūsī in *Tahdhīb* 10: 295–308 (see also 10: 169, 245, 258, 267, 292), and later by Yaḥyā b. Sa'īd al-Ḥillī in his *al-Jāmi' li 'l-sharā'i'*: 605–24. A slightly different version is also quoted by Kulaynī in his *Kāfī* 7: 330–43 (see also 311, 324, 327, 363; see further, Miyānajī 2: 258–79). The material was also known to Zaydī (Aḥmad b. 'Īsā 4: 227) and Sunnī scholars ('Abd al-Razzāq 4: 5, 9: 280, 306, 316, 317, 323, 337–38, 343, 345, 358, 369, 371, 373, 380, 383; Ibn Abī Shayba 9: 134, 136, 142, 145, 147, 153, 155, 176, 178, 180, 188, 193, 213, 215–16, 224; Abū Dāwūd 2: 100–191; Ṭabarī, *Tafsīr* 5: 133; Dāraquṭnī 4: 177; Bayhaqī 8: 69, 74, 81, 85, 89, 96, 97, 98). The work is also published, under the name of its first well known transmitter, as *Diyāt Ẓarīf b. Nāṣiḥ,* in the collection of *al-Uṣūl al-sittat 'ashar* (Tehran, 1371): 134–48.

4. *Nahj al-balāgha*

Late in the third century, the number of sermons ascribed to 'Alī was around 400.[53] Half a century later, the number was said to be 480.[54] Several early transmitters of *ḥadīth* compiled registers of his sermons, including:

- Zayd b. Wahb al-Juhanī (late first century)[55]
- Mas'ada b. Ṣadaqa al-'Abdī (late second century)[56]
- Ismā'īl b. Mihrān al-Sakūnī (alive in 224)[57]
- Ṣāliḥ b. Abī Ḥammād al-Rāzī (mid-third century)[58]
- 'Abd al-'Aẓīm b. 'Abd Allāh al-Ḥasanī (d. 252)[59]

Others devoted chapters of their works to sermons, letters, and other statements quoted from 'Alī. They included early historians such as Muḥammad b. 'Umar al-Wāqidī (d. 207),[60] 'Alī b. Muḥammad al-Madā'inī

50. Ibid. 7: 330; *Faqīh* 4: 75.
51. E.g. *Tahdhīb* 10: 292.
52. E.g. *Kāfī* 7: 330.
53. Ya'qūbī, *Mushākala*: 12, 48.
54. Mas'ūdī 3: 172.
55. *Fihrist*: 72.
56. Najāshī: 415.
57. Ibid.: 27.
58. Ibid.: 198.
59. Ibid.: 247.
60. Abū Ghālib: 181.

(d. 225),[61] Aḥmad b. Muḥammad b. 'Abd Rabbih (d. 328),[62] and 'Abd al-'Azīz b. Yaḥyā al-Jalūdī (d. 332).[63] Yet others collected the texts of letters attributed to 'Alī, such as Ibrāhīm b. Muḥammad al-Thaqafī (d. 283).[64]

The earliest surviving work belonging to the first genre is the *Nahj al-balāgha*, a collection of selected sermons, letters and other statements attributed to 'Alī, compiled by the Sharīf al-Raḍī, Muḥammad b. al-Ḥusayn al-Mūsawī (d. 406) in 400.[65] Much of the contents of this work is attested in earlier sources, a few of which are mentioned in the work itself.[66] A number of works have recently assumed the task of documenting the passages cited in the *Nahj al-balāgha* through tracking down earlier sources where those passages are quoted from 'Alī. The most recent work in this genre is Riḍā Ustādī's *Madārik-i Nahj al-balāgha* (Qum, 1396). A recent edition of the *Nahj al-balāgha* (ed. Ja'far al-Ḥusaynī, Qum, 1419) also includes a section on the sources of its contents (pp. 591–621). In a few instances, passages attributed to other authorities in earlier sources are included in this work,[67] presumably on the basis of some other early sources that have not survived. Ibn Taymiyya and Dhahabī[68] have expressed doubts about the authenticity of much of the contents of the *Nahj al-balāgha*. Ibn Khallikān did the same in *Wafayāt* 3: 313, though elsewhere (ibid. 5: 8) he cited from the work with no qualms. Khaṭīb (*Jāmi'* 2: 161) rejects as spurious the eschatological sermons attributed to 'Alī, a few examples of which are included in the *Nahj al-balāgha*.

The *Nahj al-balāgha* is available in many editions and manuscripts dating from the fifth century onward. For a list of pre-tenth century manuscripts of the work, see 'Abd al-'Azīz al-Ṭabāṭabā'ī in *Turāthunā* (a quarterly published in Qum) 5: 25–102, 7–8: 13–36, 29: 7–25. A recent

---

61. Ibn al-Nadīm: 115.
62. Ibn 'Abd Rabbih 4: 166–81.
63. Parts of his *Musnad 'Alī* were devoted to 'Alī's sermons, poetry, letters and other statements. See the table of contents of the book in Najāshī: 240–42.
64. Najāshī: 17.
65. Ibid.: 398. See also Sharīf al-Raḍī, *Ḥaqā'iq*: 167; idem, *Majāzāt*: 39–40, 67, 199, 251, 391.
66. *Nahj al-balāgha*: 76, 353, 445, 464, 465, 541, 557.
67. For a few examples, see Ṣabrī Ibrāhīm al-Sayyid: 68–77, but there are others such as two statements about women, one (*Nahj al-balāgha*: 405, document 31) attributed in Ibn Qutayba, *'Uyūn* 4: 78–9 to Ibn al-Muqaffa', the other (*Nahj al-balāgha*: 105–6, sermon 80) ascribed, in a variant, by Sunnī authors to the Prophet (Aḥmad 2: 67, 374; Bukhārī 1: 85; Muslim: 86–7 [whence Abū Ḥayyān, *Baṣā'ir* 3: 74 ; Zamakhsharī, *Rabī'* 4: 279]).
68. *Mīzān* 3: 124; *Siyar* 17: 589–90. Generally speaking, false ascription to 'Alī was a widespread phenomenon, and that has continued to be true up to our time. A recent example is a text called *al-Munājāt al-ilāhiyyāt* (Tehran, 1386). It is well known to the scholars of the field that this text was forged early in the twentieth century.

work, *Nahj al-sa'āda fī mustadrak Nahj al-balāgha* by Muḥammad Bāqir al-Maḥmūdī (2nd edn., Tehran, 1998), attempts to collect statements, documents and poetry attributed to 'Alī that are not included in the *Nahj al-balāgha*.

Many commentaries have been written on this work during the course of the past ten centuries. For the early commentaries, see Uṭāridī in *Kāwushī dar Nahj al-balāgha*: 275–87. For others see Āghā Buzurg 14: 111–61; Ibn Yūsuf 2: 124–49. For a list of works written on the *Nahj al-balāgha* in Arabic and Persian, see Ustādī, *Kitābnāma-yi Nahj al-balāgha* (Tehran, 1359sh [1980–1981], reprinted in his *Chihil maqāla*: 351–98).

5. *Musnad*

As noted above, sermons and other administrative statements by 'Alī are collected in special volumes or chapters. There are also works which attempt to collect reports quoted from 'Alī on doctrinal, legal and ethical topics, many of which cite statements or acts of the Prophet. *Masānīd*, collections of *ḥadīth* that are organized on the basis of the first transmitter, rather than the more common subject arrangement, usually have a chapter devoted to reports quoted from 'Alī. Aḥmad 1: 75–160; Abū Ya'lā 1: 223–462; Ṭabarī, *Tahdhīb al-āthār*, the entire vol. 4; Ibn Kathīr, *Jāmi' al-masānīd* 19: 95–289, 20: 5–344, are a few examples. Most works cited or published as independent works under the title of *Musnad 'Alī* are, or seem to have been, parts of larger collections, including those by the following authors:

- Ya'qūb b. Shayba al-Baṣrī (d. 262),[69] in five volumes[70]
- Qāḍī Ismā'īl b. Isḥāq al-Jahḍamī al-Azdī (d. 282)[71]
- Muḥammad b. 'Abd Allāh al-Haḍramī al-Kūfī, known as Muṭayyan (d. 297)[72]
- Aḥmad b. 'Alī b. Shu'ayb al-Nasā'ī (d. 303)[73]
- Yaḥyā b. Muḥammad b. Ṣā'id al-Baghdādī (d. 318)[74]
- 'Abd al-Raḥmān b. 'Uthmān al-Tamīmī al-Dimashqī (d. 420)[75]

---

69. Najāshī: 451; *Fibrist*: 180.
70. Dhahabī, *Siyar* 12: 478.
71. Rūdānī: 354.
72. 'Abd al-'Azīz al-Ṭabāṭabā'ī, *Ahl al-Bayt*: 469–70. The work has survived in a manuscript printed in the form of scattered facsimile excerpts in Uzbak's *Musnad 'Alī b. Abī Ṭālib*.
73. Dhahabī, *Siyar* 10: 475, 12: 614, 14: 133; Ibn Ḥajar, *Tahdhīb* 1: 6.
74. Khaṭīb, *Ta'rīkh* 5: 19.
75. MS. *ḥadīth* 273, Ẓāhiriyya (*Cat. ḥadīth*: 360, *majāmī'* 1: 228).

– Jalāl al-Dīn 'Abd al-Raḥmān b. Abī Bakr al-Suyūṭī (d. 911)[76]

There are a number of recent works that attempt to collect all extant quotations from 'Alī. The most comprehensive are the *Musnad 'Alī b. Abī Ṭālib* by Yūsuf Uzbak (7 vols., Damascus and Beirut, 1995), which includes most of such quotations in Sunnī works of *ḥadīth*; and *Musnad al-Imām 'Alī* by Ḥasan al-Qapānchī (10 vols., Beirut, 2000) that includes 11,451 quotations in Shī'ite and Sunnī collections.

6. *Dīwān*

There are conflicting reports in the early sources as to whether 'Alī composed any poetry. In his *Musnad 'Alī*, 'Abd al-'Azīz al-Jalūdī (d. 322) devoted a chapter to the poetry attributed to 'Alī.[77] Later, several collections were made of this material, including:

- *Salwat al-Shī'a*, a collection of some 200 verses compiled by Abū 'l-Ḥasan 'Alī b. Aḥmad al-Fanjkirdī al-Naysābūrī (d. 513)[78]
- Anonymous, used by Kaydarī in his *Anwār al-'uqūl* (named below)
- *Dīwān 'Alī*, by Hibat Allāh b. 'Alī, Ibn al-Shajarī (d. 543), also used by Kaydarī in his *Anwār al-'uqūl*
- *al-Ḥadīqa al-anīqa*, by Quṭb al-Dīn Muḥammad b. al-Ḥusayn al-Kaydarī al-Bayhaqī (alive in 610), described by the author in his *Anwār al-'uqūl* as a collection of 'Alī's poems on ethical matters
- *Anwār al-'uqūl fī ash'ār Waṣī al-Rasūl*, also by Kaydarī, a collection of 506 poems attributed to 'Alī gathered from the sources named in the work and arranged in alphabetic order. An anonymous collection which has been published many times under the title of *Dīwān 'Alī* seems to be an adaptation of this latter work. The arrangement and material are to a great extent the same, but some poems and the chains of transmission are omitted[79]

Much of the poetry attributed to 'Alī in these works belongs to others. See Dānishpazhūh 5: 1108–24 and Ḥasanzāda 15: 306–13, 17: 62–5 for many examples.

---

76. Ed. Ḥāfiẓ 'Azīz Beg, Hyderabad, 1985. This is the section on *Musnad 'Alī* from the author's *Jāmi' al-aḥādīth* 15: 242–478, 16: 5–473.
77. Najāshī: 241.
78. There are many manuscripts of this work. See now Mihrīzī in *'Ulūm-i ḥadīth* 9 (1998): 206–8 for a list.
79. Āghā Buzurg 2: 431–4.

7. *Decisions*

The administrative practice, judicial decisions and executive orders of 'Alī during his caliphate were recorded by a number of his disciples including 'Ubayd Allāh b. Abī Rāfi', Ḥārith al-A'war, and possibly Aṣbagh b. Nubāta (see below). There are numerous references to collections of this genre in early sources.[80] The legal opinions ascribed to 'Alī in Sunnī works concerning various matters of rituals and law are recently collected by Muḥammad Rawwās Qal'ajī in a book called *Mawsū'at fiqh 'Alī b. Abī Ṭālib* (Damascus, 1983), a volume of his *Silsilat mawsū'āt fiqh al-salaf.*

2: Fāṭima al-Zahrā'

Fāṭima al-Zahrā', daughter of the Prophet and wife of 'Alī, and mother of Ḥasan and Ḥusayn, the second and third Imāms of the Shī'a. She is highly revered by the Shī'a as one of their Fourteen Infallibles that consist of the Prophet, Fāṭima, and the twelve Imāms. She died shortly after the death of her father in the year 11.

For a summary of the accounts of the early sources on Fāṭima, see the entry on her in the *Encyclopaedia of Islam*, 2nd edn., 2: 841–50 (L. Veccia Vaglieri) where a list is also given of some primary and secondary sources on her life. See also Denise L. Soufi, "The Image of Fāṭima in Classical Muslim Thought," Ph.D. dissertation, Princeton, 1997. For a list of other monographs on her, see 'Abd al-Jabbār al-Rifā'ī 5: 11–129.

1. *Muṣḥaf Fāṭima*

A work bearing this title is mentioned in numerous early Shī'ite reports, almost always with esoteric associations. A quotation from Ja'far al-Ṣādiq related that the *Muṣḥaf Fāṭima* contained the text of the will and testament of Fāṭima (Ṣaffār: 157 [# 16], 158 [# 21]; *Kāfī* 1: 241 [# 4]), but this would have meant a different and longer text than the very short one quoted from Muḥammad al-Bāqir in *Faqīh* 4: 244 as the will of Fāṭima. There are, however, other accounts of the authorship of the book. One report suggests that it was a collection of what the angel Gabriel had

80. E.g. Aḥmad, *'Ilal* 1: 346; Muslim: 13, 14.

related to her to comfort her after her father's death, and that it was her husband 'Alī who gathered the material together and wrote it down (Ṣaffār: 154 [# 6; see also 157, # 17]; *Kāfī* 1: 241 [# 5]). Another report concurs with most of this account, but without specifying the name of the angel (Ṣaffār: 157 [# 18]; *Kāfī* 1: 240 [# 2]). Yet other reports suggest that the book was dictated and revealed by God (Ṣaffār: 152 [# 3]; the reference is missing from the same report in *Kāfī* 1: 239; it is not clear whether the sentence was added to the text in Ṣaffār or edited out in the *Kāfī*), or dictated by the messenger of God and written down by 'Alī (Ṣaffār: 153 [# 5]). Another report tries to fuse the latter two accounts together by suggesting that the book was the word of God sent down to her, dictated by the messenger of God and written down by 'Alī (Ṣaffār: 156 [# 14]). *Biḥār* 26: 42 further suggests that the term "messenger of God" may refer to Gabriel and not the Messenger, i.e. the Prophet. Being dictated by the messenger of God and written down by 'Alī was, however, the standard formula to describe the Book of 'Alī, as noted above, where the phrase "messenger of God" was understood by all to refer to the Prophet.

There are also conflicting accounts about the nature of the contents of the book. All agree, however, that there was nothing from the Qur'ān in that book (Ṣaffār: 150–61 [# 1, 2, 3, 5, 8, 9, 14, 15, 17, 19, 27, 30, 33]; *Kāfī* 1: 239–40 [# 1, 3]; *Dalā'il*: 105), clearly an attempt to assert that even if revealed by God, the book was nevertheless not a part of the Prophetic message nor on a par with the Qur'ān (see especially Ṣaffār: 154–9 [# 9, 14, 17, 27]). As noted above, one account identified the text as the will and testament of Fāṭima. The Gabriel version, on the other hand, suggested that the book contained what the angel related to her on the situation of her father after death and what would happen to her offspring after her (Ṣaffār: 154 [# 6]; *Kāfī* 1: 241 [# 5]). A variant of this account that attributes the revelation of the book to an unnamed angel emphasizes that there was no material concerning *sharī'a* (*shay' min al-ḥalāl wa 'l-ḥarām*) in the book, rather some information about the future (Ṣaffār: 157 [# 18]; *Kāfī* 1: 240 [# 2]). Another report, however, expands the scope of the book and finds there whatever information people require for performing their religious duties, including even details of the penal code (Ṣaffār: 150–51 [# 1]; *Kāfī* 1: 240 [# 3]). As noted in the case of the Book of 'Alī, this latter description is also given for the two texts called *Jafr* and *Jāmi'a*. The actual references to the text usually deal with matters of divination and historical prophecy rather than religious duties. One, for instance, predicts that the Manicheans will re-appear in the year 128 as Ja'far al-Ṣādiq had found in the *Muṣḥaf* of Fāṭima (Ṣaffār: 157 [# 18]; *Kāfī* 1: 240 [# 2]). Another reports that he looked through the Book of Fāṭima where the names of all future kings were recorded but could not find the name of any of the Ḥasanids there (Ṣaffār: 169 [# 3, 5]; 'Alī b. Bābawayh, *Imāma*: 180; *Kāfī* 1: 242 [# 8]; a variant in Ṣaffār: 161 [# 32] and 170 [# 7] replaces *Banī 'l-Ḥasan* with *banī fulān* and gives them [a share in rulership] as small as the dust of a horseshoe), a clear reference to the claim of Muḥammad b. 'Abd Allāh al-Nafs al-Zakiyya who rose against the 'Abbāsid Manṣūr in 145. Another version of this report mentions al-Nafs al-Zakiyya by name, adding that not only the names of the kings but even those of all prophets and their legatees (*awṣiyā'*) are also recorded in that book (*Manāqib* 4: 249; also Ṣaffār: 169 [# 4, 6] where the title *Muṣḥaf Fāṭima* is replaced with "a book"). This does not accord with a report in Ṣaffār: 169 (# 2) and *Kāfī* 1: 242 (# 7) that reserves a separate book for each of the two categories, the prophets and the kings. A later and more esoteric description conveys an even stronger element of omniscience, asserting that the book contains all knowledge of the universe, and the past, present and the future of humanity, yet all of this forms the contents of only its first two folios (*Dalā'il*: 104–107).

This latter report also gives a glorious picture of the physical grandeur of the text in question (ibid.: 105). An earlier report only stated that the book was three times as big as the Qur'ān in size (Ṣaffār: 152 [# 3]; *Kāfī* 1: 239 [# 1]). There is also a small discrepancy concerning the text's whereabouts. While most reports speak of this book being available to Ja'far al-Ṣādiq and the Imāms after him (Ṣaffār: 150–58, 161 [# 1, 3, 5, 8, 15, 19, 32, 33]; *Kāfī* 1: 239–42 [# 1, 2, 3, 7, 8]), implying that it moves through the line of the Imāms from Fāṭima's offspring until it is received by the Mahdī (*Dalā'il*: 106), a single account maintains that the book was actually "taken back" after the death of the fifth Imām, Muḥammad al-Bāqir (Ṣaffār: 158 [# 23]). This latter idea is possibly a legacy of an early Shī'ite group who did not follow Ja'far al-Ṣādiq after his father (see *Biḥār* 74: 17; also Modarressi, *Crisis*: 54, n. 7). There are, however, indications that Ja'far al-Ṣādiq, who may have referred to this book on occasions, tried on others to imply that though he had seen the book in the past, he may not actually have owned it (*Kāfī* 3: 507). The above statement about the book being "taken back" may be in line with this last report.

As for the origin of the assumption that such a book existed, one author suggests a kind of natural expansion parallel to the line suggested in the case of the Book of 'Alī. There seems to have existed a belief among many early Imāmite Shī'ites in the late Umayyad period that the names of the Imāms from the offsping of Fāṭima and 'Alī were written on a tablet (*lawḥ*) which God had sent down to the Prophet who in turn had given it to Fāṭima (Nu'mānī: 62, 63; *Ikhtiṣāṣ*: 210–12; *Kamāl*: 308, 311, 313; *'Uyūn* 1: 42, 46, 47; *Ghayba*: 139, 144; see also Khazzāz: 196). Variants of the account identify the tablet as a folio (*ṣaḥīfa*) (*Kamāl*: 306–7, 312; *'Uyūn* 1: 40, 45) or a document (*kitāb*) (*Kamāl*: 312; *'Uyūn* 1: 45) dictated by the Prophet and written down by 'Alī. In many versions of this report, a post Occultation text is appended with a full list of the names of all twelve Imāms as the text of the Tablet or Folio (see, for instance, *Kāfī* 1: 527–8; Nu'mānī: 62–6; *Kamāl*: 307, 309–11; *'Uyūn*: 40–45; *Ikhtiṣāṣ*: 211–12; *Ghayba*: 144–6). The transition from the idea of a *ṣaḥīfa* to that of a *muṣḥaf* should have been a fairly smooth process.

Apart from the quotation on the re-emergence of the Manicheans mentioned above (Ṣaffār: 157; *Kāfī* 1: 240), there are a few other citations from the *Muṣḥaf Fāṭima* in the sources, including the following:

- *Kāfī* 3: 507 (on *zakāt*) quoting from the *Kitāb Fāṭima*
- Ibid. 8: 57–8 (on an addition to Qur'ān 70: 2, more in the form of a marginal gloss)
- *Biḥār* 30: 245 (on a different reading for Qur'ān 25: 28 [quoting *Ta'wīl al-āyāt*, though in the printed version of that work: 374, whence Ibn al-Juḥām: 193, the source appears as *Muṣḥaf 'Alī* instead of *Muṣḥaf Fāṭima*])

The last two references may seem to contradict the standard account that there was nothing Qur'ānic in that book. However, as noted above, this description was an attempt to prevent a possible misunderstanding that as a book revealed by God, it must be a complement to the Qur'ān. Thus, the description denies the existence of any material which can be regarded as an addition to the Qur'ān but not the inclusion of existing verses of the Qur'ān and the exegetical glosses upon them. The first quotation contradicts reports which state that nothing in the book was about *sharī'a* even if, as it seems, those reports also try to make a distinction between the nature of the Qur'ānic revelation and that of *Muṣḥaf Fāṭima*. However, the quotation goes well with other reports that describe the *muṣḥaf* as containing everything that people need for their religious duties.

2. *Musnad Fāṭima*

There are a good number of reports cited in the collections of *ḥadīth* on the authority of Fāṭima al-Zahrā' or on her life and virtues. There have been attempts to collect these in monographs:

- *Akhbār Fāṭima wa mansha'uhā wa mawliduhā*, by Abū 'Abd Allāh Muḥammad b. Zakariyyā b. Dīnār al-Jawharī al-Ghallābī al-Baṣrī (d. 298) (Najāshī: 347)
- *Faḍā'il Fāṭima*, by Abū 'l-Qāsim 'Abd Allāh b. Muḥammad b. 'Abd al-'Azīz al-Manī'ī al-Baghawī (d. 317) ('Abd al-'Azīz al-Ṭabāṭabā'ī, *Ahl al-Bayt*: 370)
- *Akhbār Fāṭima wa 'l-Ḥasan wa 'l-Ḥusayn*, by Abū Bakr Muḥammad b. Aḥmad al-Kātib al-Baghdādī, Ibn Abī 'l-Thalj (d. 325) (Najāshī: 382)
- *Akhbār Fāṭima*, by Abū 'Alī Aḥmad b. Muḥammad b. Ja'far al-Ṣūlī al-Baṣrī (alive in 353) (Najāshī: 233; *Fihrist*: 32), a large work (*Fihrist*: 32; whence *Ma'ālim*: 19), quoted in *Manāqib* 3: 331, 333, 337
- *Akhbār Fāṭima*, by Abū Ṭālib 'Ubayd Allāh b. Aḥmad b. Ya'qūb al-Anbārī (d. 356) (Najāshī: 233)
- *Akhbār al-Zahrā'*, by Ibn Bābawayh (d. 381), quoted in Ibn Ṭāwūs, *Yaqīn*: 157–60 (see further Kohlberg: 105–6) and Irbilī 2: 84–6 (as *Mawlid Fāṭima wa faḍā'iluhā wa tazwījuhā wa ẓulāmatuhā wa wafātuhā wa maḥsharuhā*; also Najāshī: 392 as *Kitāb mawlid Fāṭima*), 89–93, 98, 102–5, 127–8
- *Musnad sayyidat nisā' al-'ālamīn Fāṭima bint Rasūl Allāh*, by 'Alī b. 'Umar b. Aḥmad al-Dāraquṭnī (d. 385), quoted in 'Abd Allāh b. Ḥamza, *'Iqd*: 205, 220–22
- *Musnad Fāṭima*, by 'Umar b. Aḥmad b. Shāhīn al-Marrūdhī al-Baghdādī (d. 395) (Rūdānī: 360), published as *Faḍā'il Fāṭima* (ed. Muḥammad Sa'īd al-Ṭurayḥī, Beirut, 1985)
- *Juz' fī faḍā'il Fāṭima*, by al-Ḥākim Abū 'Abd Allāh Muḥammad b. 'Abd Allāh al-Naysābūrī (d. 405) (Dhahabī, *Ta'rīkh* 29 [years 401–420]: 132; whence Tāj al-Dīn al-Subkī 4: 166)
- *Al-Arba'īn fī faḍā'il al-Zahrā'*, by Abū Ṣāliḥ Aḥmad b. 'Abd al-Malik b. 'Alī al-Naysābūrī al-Mu'adhdhin (d. 470) (*Ma'ālim*: 25)
- *Musnad Fāṭima*, attributed to Ibn Rustam al-Ṭabarī (fifth century) in Ḥurr al-'Āmilī, *Ithbāt* 1: 58 and Hāshim al-Baḥrānī, *Maḥajja*: 28–46, 48, 107, 123, 168, 171, 191, 212 (also as *Manāqib Fāṭima wa wuldihā* in Hāshim al-Baḥrānī, *Madīna* 1: 328–9). This work is the same as the

Dalā'il al-imāma attributed to the same author (see the editor's introduction to this latter work: 38–9).

- *Faḍā'il al-Zahrā'*, by Abū Manṣūr Aḥmad b. 'Alī b. Abī Ṭālib al-Ṭabrisī (early sixth century) (*Ma'ālim*: 25)
- *Musnad Fāṭima wa mā warada fī fadlihā = al-Thughūr al-bāsima fī manāqib al-sayyida Fāṭima* (Ḥājī Khalīfa: 521), by Jalāl al-Dīn 'Abd al-Raḥmān b. Abī Bakr al-Suyūṭī (d. 911). The work contains 284 reports by or about Fāṭima (published, ed. Ḥāfiẓ 'Azīz Beg [Hyderabad, 1406] and Fawwāz Aḥmad Zamralī [Beirut, 1414])
- *Musnad Fāṭima al-Zahrā'*, by 'Azīz Allāh al-'Uṭāridī (Tehran, 1412)
- *Musnad Fāṭima al-Zahrā'*, by Ḥusayn Shaykh al-Islamī al-Tūysirkānī, (Qum, 1420)
- *Al-Kawthar*, by Muḥammad Bāqir al-Mūsawī (Qum, 1420). Published in seven volumes, the work includes 4,321 reports by or about Fāṭima

3: Abū Rāfi'

Abū Rāfi', originally a Copt, was a client/servant of the Prophet and, later in life, reportedly, head of the treasury of 'Alī. Not only he himself[81] but also his descendants for some generations[82] were widely recognized as reliable sources of information about the personal life of the Prophet. The family kept its ties with the House of the Prophet[83] and their transmissions attest to their Shī'ite sympathies.

Ibn Sa'd 4: 54–5; Ibn Hishām 2: 301–2; Aḥmad 6: 9; Ḥammād b. Isḥāq: 110; Balādhurī 1: 566–8; Ṭabarī 2: 261, 3: 170, 6: 180; Ibn Abī Ḥātim 2: 149; Ṭabarānī,

81. See, for instance, Ibn Sa'd 2: 283; Rūyānī 1: 463; Khaṭīb, *Taqyīd*: 91–2; Ṭūsī, *Amālī*: 468.
82. See, for instance, Ḥammād b. Isḥāq: 107–8; also Ibrāhīm al-Bayhaqī 2: 311 where Ḥajjāj sends after a member of the family of Abū Rāfi' to come and identify the sword and armor of the Prophet.
83. When Abū Rāfi' died, 'Alī personally assumed the guardianship of his orphans ('Abd al-Razzāq 4: 67; Shāfi'ī 7: 157; Abū 'Ubayd: 405; Ibn Abī Shayba 3: 149; Ibn Zanjawayh: 991; Bukhārī, *Kabīr* 1: 76; Aḥmad b. 'Īsā 2: 296). After the death of 'Alī, 'Ubayd Allāh, son of Abū Rāfi', declared himself a client of 'Alī's son and the Prophet's elder grandson, Ḥasan al-Mujtabā (Mubarrad 2: 437). Later, the family of Abū Rāfi' were considered to be clients of the 'Alīd Imāms, clearly by patrimony as descendants of the Prophet (see *Kāfī* 1: 487, 5: 339). The family was therefore a source of information about the personal life of the House of the Prophet as well (see, for instance, Aḥmad, *Faḍā'il* 1: 629–30; Ibn Shabba: 105, 106, 107, 111).

Kabīr 1: 307–9; Abū 'l-Faraj, *Aghānī* 4: 205–6; *Ḥilya* 1: 183–5; Mizzī 33: 301–2; Dhahabī, *Siyar* 2: 16 (and many other sources listed in the editor's footnote); Ibn Ḥajar, *Iṣāba* 7: 134–5; idem, *Tahdhīb* 12: 92–3.

He was originally a slave of ʿAbbās b. ʿAbd al-Muṭṭalib, the uncle of the Prophet, and was given to the Prophet as a gift and freed by him later. An account about a former slave of the Umayyad Saʿīd b. al-ʿĀṣ called Rāfiʿ (Ḥammād b. Isḥāq: 111; Balādhurī 1: 573; Ṭabarānī, *Kabīr* 5: 23; *Ḥilya* 1: 83) was erroneously attributed to Abū Rāfiʿ by Muṣʿab al-Zubayrī and Mubarrad 2: 436 (whence later works such as Ibn Qutayba, *Maʿārif*: 145–6; Ṭabarī 3: 170 and biographical sources). The mistake was corrected by Hishām b. Muḥammad al-Kalbī (Balādhurī 1: 483; whence Ibn Ḥajar, *Iṣāba* 7: 135–6).

That later in life he served as the treasurer of ʿAlī is reported by Ibn Abī Shayba 6: 458 and Najāshī: 4, 6 (see also Ibn Daʾb: 151; Qāḍī Nuʿmān, *Sharḥ* 1: 374; Ibn al-ʿAdīm: 4449). Ṭabarī 5: 156, as well as a report in ʿĀṣim b. Ḥumayd: 34, identify ʿAlī's treasurer as the son of Abū Rāfiʿ. This son is further identified in the latter report as the one who was ʿAlī's official scribe, i.e. ʿUbayd Allāh b. Abī Rāfiʿ (see below), but in Qāḍī Nuʿmān, *Sharḥ* 2: 20 and *Tahdhīb* 10: 151 (whence Warrām 2: 3–4) as ʿAlī b. Abī Rāfiʿ. Qāḍī Nuʿmān reports that this latter was both treasurer and keeper of the seal for ʿAlī.

His date of death is variously given as early as the time of ʿUmar (Bayhaqī 4: 107–8; see also ʿĀṣim b. Ḥumayd: 34) and as late as after Ḥasan al-Mujtabā's abdication and return to Medina in 41 (Ibn al-Juḥām: 98–9; Najāshī: 5–6; Ṭūsī, *Amālī*: 59). Ibn Ḥibbān (*Thiqāt* 3: 16–17; *Mashāhīr*: 37) and Dhahabī (*Siyar* 2: 16) give the date as 40. That he lived until the time of ʿAlī's caliphate is attested by the fact that his name appears among those who attended the battle of Ṣiffīn on ʿAlī's side (Ibn Abī Rāfiʿ, *Tasmiya*: 17, where it is also said that at the beginning of ʿAlī's caliphate he was 85). That he died in ʿAlī's lifetime is confirmed by reports that ʿAlī personally assumed the guardianship of his orphans. These reports do not accord with the date of 40 as they mention that ʿAlī used to pay *zakāt* from the property of the orphans of Abū Rāfiʿ until they reached the age of maturity. This implies that a number of years had lapsed between the death of Abū Rāfiʿ and that of ʿAlī. The reports also seem to imply that none of the children of Abū Rāfiʿ had yet reached the age of maturity to take care of the others, a point that does not go well with the above date as ʿUbayd Allāh, son of Abū Rāfiʿ, was an active member of the camp of ʿAlī from the first days of his caliphate.

1. *Kitāb Abī Rāfiʿ*

A good number of reports are quoted from Abū Rāfiʿ from or about the Prophet. Aḥmad 1: 8–10, 390–93; Rūyānī 1: 455–80, and Ṭabarānī, *Kabīr* 1: 307–33 devoted special sections to narratives from him (see also *al-Musnad al-jāmiʿ* 16: 217–40), but there are many others scattered in the sources. As a servant of the Prophet, his name was also popular with authors of wonder stories in later periods; they thus used it as their supposed authority for the narratives they ascribed to the Prophet (e.g. *Kamāl*: 224–8).

Najāshī: 6 names a book by Abū Rāfi' as *Kitāb al-sunan wa 'l-aḥkām wa 'l-qaḍāyā*, a text that Najāshī received through two partially different chains of transmission. Najāshī cites the opening sentence of the text on how 'Alī used to start his prayer. He then mentions the order of the text with sections devoted to prayer, fasting, pilgrimage to Mecca, alms-giving and judicial decisions. Ṭabarānī, *Du'ā'*: 1030 and Khaṭīb, *Kifāya*: 472 quote Abū Rāfi' on how the Prophet used to start his prayer, on the basis of a written record that Abū Rāfi' handed to[84] the transmitter of the account. Given the many transmissions from 'Ubayd Allāh, the son of Abū Rāfi', quoting 'Alī and describing the way the Prophet started his prayer (e.g. Ṭabarānī, *Du'ā'*: 1026–29), it is clear that Shī'ite and Sunnī sources refer to the same text, presumably one that the son of Abū Rāfi' put together about the practices of 'Alī (see below).[85] Omission of the word *ibn* and, hence, misattribution of material quoted by the son of Abū Rāfi' to the father was a common error (e.g. 'Abd al-Razzāq 3: 179–80, # 5231–2), already detected by Bayhaqī 4: 107–8 and others in other cases. Ṭūsī clearly notes the point and does not ascribe any work to Abū Rāfi'.

2. *Akhbār Abī Rāfi'*

Ibn Shahrāshūb (*Manāqib* 2: 14–15, 41, 59, 180, 237, 3: 78, 124) quotes from a book by the Zaydī scholar Abū 'l-Qāsim 'Abd al-'Azīz b. Isḥāq al-Kūfī, Ibn al-Baqqāl (d. 363)[86] called *Kitāb akhbār Abī Rāfi'*. In accordance with the topic of Ibn Shahrāshūb's work, the examples quoted all deal with virtues of the House of the Prophet.

84. Cf. Ṭabarānī, *Kabīr* 1: 314 where the formula *waqa'a ilayya kitābun* (a text came down to me) appears in the same narrative instead of *dafa'a ilayya kitāban* (he handed me a text). The context as well as Khaṭīb's quotation, which is on the basis of a partially different chain of transmission, confirms the latter formula which presents Abū Rāfi' as offering the text to the transmitter.

85. The point can be further strengthened by the fact that unlike 'Ubayd Allāh who was the official scribe of 'Alī, there seems to be no evidence to suggest that Abū Rāfi' was able to read and write.

86. For him see Khaṭīb, *Ta'rīkh* 10: 458–9; *Rijāl*: 432–3; *Lisān* 4: 378–9; Sezgin 1: 568.

4: Ibn Abī Rāfiʻ

ʻUbayd Allāh b. Abī Rāfiʻ, son of the Prophet's servant named above, was ʻAlī's assistant and official scribe during his caliphate. He accompanied ʻAlī in the course of his caliphate and afterwards continued to work as the official scribe for his son, Ḥasan al-Mujtabā, when he assumed the caliphate after his father's death in 40.

Naṣr b. Muzāḥim: 471; Ibn Saʻd 4: 55, 5: 215; Ḥumaydī 1: 177; Bukhārī 3: 349; Muslim: 1941; ʻIjlī: 316; Abū Dāwūd 2: 252; Tirmidhī 2: 38, 5: 333; Ibrāhīm b. Hāshim, *Qaḍāyā Amīr al-Muʼminīn*: 61; Balādhurī 1: 573; Ibn Qutayba, *Maʻārif*: 145; Ibn Ḥibbān, *Ṣaḥīḥ* 14: 424; Mubarrad 2: 436; Abū Yaʻlā 1: 315, 316; Ṭabarī 3: 170, 6: 180; Ibn Abī Ḥātim 5: 307; *Kāfī* 7: 371; Jahshiyārī: 14; Qāḍī Nuʻmān, *Sharḥ* 2: 16; *Faqīh* 3: 25; Dāraquṭnī, *Muʼtalif*: 223; Najāshī: 4; Bayhaqī, *Dalāʼil*: 16; Ṭūsī, *Amālī*: 729; *Fihrist*: 107; *Rijāl*: 71; Khaṭīb, *Jāmiʻ* 1: 263; idem, *Taʼrīkh* 10: 304; Ibn ʻAsākir 45: 502; Ibn Ṭāwūs, *Kashf*: 173–4 (quoting Kulaynī's *Rasāʼil al-Aʼimma*; see also Sulaym b. Qays: 193); Mizzī 19: 34–5 (and the many other sources listed in the editor's footnote). See also *Nahj al-balāgha*: 530.

For his presence during various events and wars of ʻAlī's troubled caliphate see, for instance, Ibn Abī Shayba 14: 595; Muslim: 749; Fasawī, *Sunna*: 392 (whence Khaṭīb, *Taʼrīkh* 10: 305); Nasāʼī, *Khaṣāʼiṣ*: 309–10; Ājurrī: 31; Ibn Ḥibbān, *Ṣaḥīḥ* 9: 46; Bayhaqī 8: 171; Ibn Abī ʼl-Ḥadīd 7: 37; see further his signature on various documents of the period as noted below.

For his attachment to, and continuing to work as the official scribe for, Ḥasan al-Mujtabā, see Mubarrad 2: 437; Abū Ṭālib, *Ifāda*: 53. With the abdication of Ḥasan and his return to Medina, ʻUbayd Allāh too retreated to that city and lived there, presumably for the rest of his life (see Muḥammad b. Sulaymān 1: 507). Mubarrad 2: 436 and Ibn Qutayba, *Maʻārif*: 143 report that he was lashed for calling himself a client of the Prophet by ʻAmr b. Saʻīd b. al-ʻĀṣ, who was appointed governor of Medina by Yazīd I (r. 60–64), in the year 60. Ṭabarī 3: 170 identifies the victim as Rāfiʻ without further specification. As noted above in the entry on Abū Rāfiʻ, this whole episode pertains to a different person who was a former slave of the governor's father, and not to any member of the family of Abū Rāfiʻ.

ʻUbayd Allāh's signature as the official scribe or witness appears at the end of many documents of ʻAlī's caliphate. Examples include:

1. ʻAlī's letter of Ṣafar, 36 to the people of Egypt concerning the appointment of Qays b. Saʻd b. ʻUbāda as their governor (Thaqafī: 210–11; Ṭabarī 4: 548–9)
2. His letter to ʻUthmān b. Ḥunayf, his governor in Baṣra, when approaching that town in 36 (around the beginning of Jumādā I) for what came to be the battle of the Camel (Ibn Abī ʼl-Ḥadīd 9: 312–13 quoting Abū Mikhnaf Lūṭ b. Yaḥyā [d. 157], presumably in his *Kitāb al-jamal*)

3. His letter of Jumādā I, 36 from Baṣra to the people of Kūfa informing them of the atrocities committed by the rebels, including what they did to the governor of Baṣra (Mufīd, *Jamal*: 398–9)
4. His letter to the governor of Kūfa informing him of his victory at the battle of the Camel in mid-Jumādā I, 36 (Ṭabarī 4: 542)
5. His letter of Jumādā I, 36 to the people of Medina giving an account of the battle of the Camel and stating that he was setting out for Kūfa (Mufīd, *Jamal*: 395–6)
6. His letter of Rajab, 36 to the people of Kūfa (ibid.: 403–40)
7. His letter of Sha'bān, 36 to Ash'ath b. Qays, governor of Azerbaijan (Ibn Maytham 4: 350–51)
8. His letter of 1 Ramaḍān, 36 to Muḥammad b. Abī Bakr, appointing him as the governor of Egypt (Thaqafī: 224–5; Ṭabarī 4: 556; Ibn Shu'ba: 176)
9. His rescript for the Christians of Najrān dated 10 Jumādā II, 37 (Abū Yūsuf: 74)
10. His letter of Dhū 'l-Qi'da, 37 to 'Abd Allāh b. 'Abbās, his governor of Baṣra (Naṣr b. Muzāḥim: 105)
11. His letter of the year 37 to Mikhnaf b. Sulaym, his governor of Iṣfahān and Hamadān (ibid.: 104–5)
12. His letter of the year 39 to 'Awsaja b. Shaddād (Thaqafī: 115–16)
13. 'Alī's will concerning his property dated 10 Jumādā I, 36 (Ibn Shabba 1: 225–8), 37 ('Abd al-Razzāq 7: 288), or 39 (Ibn Abī 'l-Dunyā, *Maqtal*: 51–5 [partially repeated at 55–6]; Aḥmad b. 'Īsā 2: 313–15). 'Ubayd Allāh is quoted as saying that 'Alī was assassinated only four months and thirteen days after he wrote this will. That sets the date of the document as Jumādā I, 40. 'Ubayd Allāh is one of the two witnesses to the will; the document was in 'Alī's own handwriting (Ibn Abī 'l-Dunyā, *Maqtal*: 48). (See also *Kāfī* 7: 49–51 and *Tahdhīb* 9: 146–8 where the date is given as 10 Jumādā, 37 and the signatures of the witnesses are missing)
14. 'Alī's last will to his son, Ḥasan al-Mujtabā, that he dictated on his death bed on 20 Ramaḍān, 40 (Ibn Abī 'l-Dunyā, *Maqtal*: 45–7; see also Fasawī 2: 811)

'Ubayd Allāh also copied the letter that 'Alī sent to Mu'āwiya before the start of the battle of Ṣiffīn (Naṣr b. Muzāḥim: 471).

For an example of 'Ubayd Allāh's poetry, see Khwārazmī, *Manāqib*: 204–5 (read *'Ubayd Allāh* for *'Abd Allāh*).

1. *Kitāb Ibn Abī Rāfi'*

As noted above, the book attributed by Najāshī: 6 to Abū Rāfi' with the title *Kitāb al-sunan wa 'l-aḥkām wa 'l-qaḍāyā* seems to belong to this person's son, 'Ubayd Allāh. According to Najāshī, the book began with a description of how 'Alī started his prayer (see also the Zaydī Aḥmad b. 'Īsā 1: 108–9). Sunnī sources quote a long report on the authority of

'Ubayd Allāh quoting 'Alī describing the Prophet's prayer. It begins with a description of how the Prophet started his prayer. But it is most likely that the account is actually a description of 'Alī's prayer, as Shī'ite sources assert. It has been suggested that, as a general rule, the Sunnī tradition presumes that whatever a companion of the Prophet has said in matters of religion should represent a statement or action of the Prophet as there is no room for a personal opinion of a Companion in Divine matters.[87] It is likely that the same mentality influenced some later transmitters of the report of Ibn Abī Rāfiʿ to depict 'Alī as the transmitter, rather than the protagonist in the story.[88]

The work included chapters on prayer, fasting, pilgrimage to Mecca, alms-giving and judicial decisions (Najāshī: 6). Ṭūsī (*Fihrist*: 107) ascribes a book on the judicial decisions of 'Alī, *Kitāb qaḍāyā Amīr al-Mu'minīn 'alayh al-salām*, to 'Ubayd Allāh that should have been identical with the last section of the work mentioned by Najāshī. The chains of transmission given by the two authors are identical at the early stages; both are related

87. See Ṣubḥī al-Ṣāliḥ, *Mabāḥith fī 'ulūm al-Qur'ān*: 143 and the sources named therein. There are too many examples of acting upon that presumption in the sources to be quoted here. Here are a few representative examples in the specific case of 'Alī: (1) Ibn Abī Shayba 12: 482 quotes Abū Isḥāq al-Sabī'ī from Ḥārith al-A'war who transmitted from 'Alī on the merits of being prepared to fight in the path of God. Ibn Abī Ḥātim, *'Ilal* 1: 315 and Ṭabarānī, *Awsaṭ* 1: 131, 2: 40, through the same transmitters, have 'Alī citing that statement from the Prophet. (2) Tirmidhī 2: 280, 5: 168, 169 quotes two versions of a statement explaining a word in the Qur'ān; in one version (5; 169; also Ṭabarī, *Tafsīr* 1: 69, 70), the statement is quoted as being 'Alī's own; in the other (2: 280, 5: 168), he transmits it from the Prophet. (3) 'Abd al-Razzāq 3: 17, 56, 58 quotes 'Alī in # 4625 and 4775 (on the call to prayer), but 'Alī from the Prophet in # 4626 and 4783 (also Ṭayālisī 1: 116; Ibn Abī Shayba 2: 241, 286; Aḥmad 1: 77, 88, 89, 98, 111, 115; Ibn Māja: 363). (4) Dāraquṭnī 2: 103 quotes 'Alī on religious taxes on working cows. Ibn Zanjawayh: 845 has 'Alī quote the same from the Prophet. Abū Dāwūd 2: 100; Ṭabarānī, *Ṭiwāl*: 145 and Bayhaqī 4: 93, 99, 106, 136, 137 explain how this discrepancy occurred as the transmitter explicitly says that he received the report as a quotation from 'Alī but believed that 'Alī should have been quoting it from the Prophet. See also 'Abd al-Razzāq 4: 34 (from 'Alī), 4: 33, 34, 89 ('Alī from the Prophet); Ibn Abī Shayba 3: 118 (from 'Alī), 3: 117, 118 ('Alī from the Prophet). (5) Ibn Abī Shayba 1: 247; Ṭabarānī, *Du'ā'*: 1061 (on the authority of Ḥārith al-A'war); and Bayhaqī 2: 96 quote what 'Alī used to say in prayer. In Ṭabarānī, *Du'ā'*: 1052–4 and Sahmī: 380, 'Alī quotes that from the Prophet. (6) Ibn Abī Shayba 1: 352 (from 'Alī), cf. Ṭabarānī, *Awsaṭ* 5: 214 and Abū Nu'aym, *Ḥilya* 10: 114 ('Alī from the Prophet). (7) 'Abd al-Razzāq 4: 282; Shāfi'ī 7: 176; Ibn Abī Shayba 3: 65 ('Alī on fasting on Fridays), cf. Ibn al-Jawzī, *'Ilal*: 550 ('Alī quoting the same from the Prophet).

88. At least in one example, the point is explicitly attested: In 'Abd al-Razzāq 2: 100 (also Ibn Abī Shayba 1: 370, 373; Bayhaqī 2: 168), Ibn Abī Rāfiʿ relates that 'Alī used to recite certain chapters of the Qur'ān in different cycles of his prayer. Taḥāwī, *Sharḥ Ma'ānī al-āthār* 1: 206, however, suggests that 'Alī must be quoting this from the Prophet.

by the Kūfan 'Alī b. [Muḥammad b.] al-Qāsim al-Kindī,[89] from Muḥammad, son of 'Ubayd Allāh b. Abī Rāfi', from his father, 'Ubayd Allāh.

Najāshī: 6–7 ascribes a separate book on religious rituals and other sections of law, with a different opening sentence, to a second son of Abū Rāfi' called 'Alī whom Najāshī identifies as the scribe of 'Alī b. Abī Ṭālib. He alleges that the book was very popular among the 'Alīds. Although a son of Abū Rāfi' called 'Alī is mentioned in the sources,[90] Najāshī's identification of this son as the scribe of 'Alī casts doubt on the accuracy of his account.[91] He does not mention 'Ubayd Allāh, whose holding of that position in 'Alī's administration is well documented in Shī'ite and Sunnī sources, as an author. Ṭūsī, on the other hand, does not make any reference to 'Alī b. Abī Rāfi' (except as father of a disciple of 'Alī Zayn al-'Ābidīn, in *Rijāl*: 47) or a book compiled by him, an unusual omission if 'Alī b. Abī Rāfi' had a book as popular with the 'Alīds as Najāshī claims.[92]

It cannot be completely ruled out that the source where Najāshī obtained information on the alleged work by 'Alī b. Abī Rāfi' was not entirely clear on the true identity of 'Ubayd Allāh b. Abī Rāfi', possibly confusing him with 'Ubayd Allāh, son of 'Alī b. Abī Rāfi', whose name Najāshī mentioned as transmitter of this latter work (Najāshī: 7, lines 6–7). This confusion is not an isolated case. Ibn 'Asākir 45: 502 quotes the *Tasmiyat man shahida ma' 'Alī* of 'Ubayd Allāh b. Abī Rāfi', a work related by the author's son Muḥammad (see below). Ibn 'Asākir received this text

89. On him see *Lisān* 5: 74 and the sources named in the editor's footnote.

90. Maḥāmilī: 263; Ibn Ḥajar, *Iṣāba* 5: 67; also as father of two transmitters of *ḥadīth*, Ḥasan and 'Ubayd Allāh, and as grandfather of their descendants, several of whom were transmitters of *ḥadīth*, too.

91. It should be noted that the last link in the chain of transmission given for the alleged book of 'Alī b. Abī Rāfi' in Najāshī: 7, lines 2–4, is clearly corrupt as it reads: "*ḥaddathanī Abū Muḥammad 'Abd al-Raḥmān ibn Muḥammad ibn 'Ubayd Allāh ibn Abī Rāfi '-wa kāna kātib Amīr al-Mu'minīn alayh al-salām- annahu kāna yaqūl..*" Since this transmitter was not a disciple of 'Alī and Najāshī does not try to suggest him as the author of the work, the original sentence in the source that Najāshī used most likely read: "*ḥaddathanī Abū Muḥammad 'Abd al-Raḥmān ibn Muḥammad ibn 'Ubayd Allāh ibn Abī Rāfi' 'an abīh 'an jaddih 'Ubayd Allāh b. Abī Rāfi' – wa kāna kātib Amīr al-Mu'minīn alayh al-salām – annahu kāna yaqūl ...*" The middle part was clearly missed by the copyist of the copy Najāshī used, jumping from one mention of the name of 'Ubayd Allāh b. Abī Rāfi' to the other by haplography, a most frequent visual error when copying manuscripts.

92. Dāraquṭnī, *Ḍu'afā'*: 147 falls victim to the same confusion in his entry on Muḥammad b. 'Ubayd Allāh b. Abī Rāfi' "who related from his father, 'Ubayd Allāh". The latter, Dāraquṭnī notes, was "not the companion of 'Alī. That was 'Ubayd Allāh b. 'Alī b. Abī Rāfi'."

through three chains of transmission. The first chain goes back to the transmitter, Muḥammad b. 'Ubayd Allāh b. 'Alī b. Abī Rāfi' who quoted it "from his father: 'Ubayd Allāh b. Abī Rāfi' who was the scribe of 'Alī." This is clearly wrong as the one who was 'Alī's scribe would be the uncle of this transmitter's father and not his father. A later transmitter has tried to correct this by removing *b. 'Alī* from the middle of a third chain of transmission of the same material. Qāḍī Nu'mān, *Sharḥ* 2: 330 attributes a story about a legal case adjudicated by 'Alī that appears elsewhere on the authority of Muḥammad b. 'Ubayd Allāh b. Abī Rāfi' from his father (see, for instance, Ibn al-Qayyim, *Ṭuruq*: 67) to Muḥammad b. 'Abd (sic) Allāh b. 'Alī b. Abī Rāfi'. The confusion about 'Ubayd Allāh b. 'Alī b. Abī Rāfi' due to the name he had in common with his uncle was a common phenomenon,[93] as also seen in the chains of transmission of numerous reports[94] and indicated by his biographers. This is also most likely the cause of the misidentification of the authorship of the Book of Ibn Abī Rāfi' and of the true official scribe of 'Alī in Najāshī's account. Ṭūsī obviously noted the confusion and did not fall into the trap.

Here is a list of quotations that belong or are likely to belong to this work:

DESCRIPTION OF WHAT 'ALĪ (IN SHĪ'ITE NARRATION) OR THE PROPHET (IN SUNNĪ TRANSMISSION) RECITED BEFORE, DURING, AND AFTER PRAYER:

Ṭayālisī 1: 120–30; 'Abd al-Razzāq 2: 79, 163; Shāfi'ī 1: 91; Ibn Abī Shayba 1: 231, 248; Aḥmad, *Faḍā'il*: 695–6; idem, *Musnad* 1: 94, 102–3; Muslim: 534–6; Abū Dāwūd 1: 201–2; Tirmidhī 5: 422–5; Aḥmad b. 'Īsā 1: 108–9; Ṭabarānī, *Du'ā'*: 1027–30, 1043–4, 1052–4, 1063–4. The account appears in many other sources, too. For most of those, see Uzbak: 2019–47.

93. Towards the end of his section on 'Alī b. Abī Rāfi', Najāshī mentions two alternative chains of transmission of that work. The second actually belongs to a different work by Ḥārith al-A'war (Najāshī: 7, line 18 himself notes the difference between the two works). The first goes back to Muḥammad b. 'Umar b. 'Ubayd Allāh b. Muḥammad, a descendant of 'Alī b. Abī Ṭālib, who related the work from his father who quoted it from his father (Najāshī: 7, lines 12–13). This part is identical with the chain of authority of a report quoted in Ibn Sa'd 3: 15–16 (whence Ibn 'Asākir 42: 69) from 'Ubayd Allāh b. Abī Rāfi' citing 'Alī, presumably a part of his book on 'Alī's statements. It thus seems that the alleged book of 'Alī b. Abī Rāfi' was in fact a section of 'Ubayd Allāh's *Kitāb al-sunan wa 'l-aḥkām wa 'l-qaḍāyā*. The fact that apparently only one book was known to the 'Alīds as the Book of Ibn Abī Rāfi' (as understood from Najāshī: 7, lines 9–10; see also Ṣaffār: 165) further confirms the above conclusion.

94. For a further example, see Mizzī 28: 329.

(Ibn Māja: 335 cites a part of this narrative on the authority of Abū Rāfi' from 'Alī).

ON HOW THE PROPHET PRAYED AS NARRATED BY 'ALĪ:

Aḥmad 1:93 (also Bukhārī, *Raf' al-yadayn*: 23; Ibn Māja: 280; Abū Dāwūd 1: 198–9, 202–3)

ON HOW 'ALĪ PRAYED:

1. 'Abd al-Razzāq 2: 100 (also Ibn Abī Shayba 1: 370, 373; Bukhārī, *Khayr al Kalām*: 35; Fasawī 1: 419)
2. 'Abd al-Razzāq 3: 179–80 (also Aḥmad 2: 430; Muslim: 877; Ibn Māja: 1118; Tirmidhī 1: 524; Ṭūsī, *Amālī*: 647)

OTHER NARRATIVES ON PRAYER:

1. Aḥmad 6: 9, 391
2. Aḥmad b. 'Īsā 1: 210
3. Bazzār 1: 353
4. Ḥākim 2: 392 (also Bayhaqī 2: 279)
5. Najāshī: 7
6. Ṭabarānī, *Awsaṭ* 2: 57 (whence Khaṭīb, *Ta'rīkh* 4: 255; also Bazzār 1: 240 and partially in Aḥmad 1: 80, 120; Dārimī 1: 348; 'Uthmān al-Dārimī, *Jahmiyya*; 34)
7. Ḥākim 1: 239 (also Taḥāwī, *Ma'ānī* 1: 209; Bayhaqī, *Qirā'a*: 92)

DESCRIPTION OF THE PROPHET'S PILGRIMAGE TO MECCA AS NARRATED BY 'ALĪ:

Shāfi'ī 2: 97 (also Ibn Abī Shayba 14: 417; Aḥmad 1: 72, 76, 81, 156; Azraqī 2: 55; Ibn Māja: 1001; Fākihī 1: 389, 2: 51, 4: 322, 5: 37; Tirmidhī 2: 221–3)

OTHER NARRATIVES ON THE PILGRIMAGE:

1. Ibn Abī Shayba 4: 64
2. Ṭabarī, *Tahdhīb, Ibn 'Abbās*: 224–5
3. Aḥmad 1: 121
4. Bayhaqī 4: 329

OTHER LEGAL MATTERS:

Sale: Aḥmad b. 'Īsā 3: 183
Marriage: Bayhaqī 7: 111
Divorce: Aḥmad b. 'Īsā 3: 100

Slaves: Ibid. 4: 203
Penal code: Ibid. 4: 203 (two reports), 216

JUDICIAL DECISIONS:

1. Qāḍī Nu'mān, *Sharḥ* 2: 330–31 (see also Wakī' 1: 95–7 where the account is quoted from a different transmitter)
2. Ibn al-Qayyim, *Ṭuruq*: 67–8

RELIGIOUS ETHICS:

1. Abū Dāwūd 4: 354 (also Abū Ya'lā 1: 345; Abū Ṭālib, *Amālī*: 344)
2. Abū 'l-Shaykh, *Akhlāq al-Nabī*: 62, 80 (also Baghawī, *Sharḥ al-sunna* 5: 180)

ON THE QUR'ĀN:

Ḥākim 3: 237

ON VIRTUES (*FAḌĀ'IL*):

- Ḥumaydī 1: 177–8 (also Ibn Abī Shayba 12: 154, 14: 384; Aḥmad 1: 79; Bukhārī 2: 249, 3: 349–50; Muslim: 1941–2; Tirmidhī 5: 533)
- Ibn Sa'd 1: 99
- Ibid. 3: 15–16 (also Muḥammad b. Sulaymān 1: 364–5; Abū Ṭālib: 75; Ṭabrisī, *I'lām*, 190–91; Ibn 'Asākir 42: 69)
- Ibn Abī Shayba 14: 595 (also 'Āṣimī 1: 431; Ibn 'Asākir 42: 534)
- Aḥmad, *Faḍā'il*: 657 (also Muḥammad b. Sulaymān 1: 485–6, 491, 495, 2: 536; Ṭabarānī, *Kabīr* 1: 318; *Irshād* 1: 87)
- Aḥmad, *Musnad* 1: 81 (also Ibn 'Adī: 1060)
- Muslim 2: 749 (also Fasawī 1: 391; Nasā'ī, *Khaṣā'iṣ*: 309–10)
- Bazzār 3: 213 (also Muḥammad b. Sulaymān 1: 395; Ibn 'Adī: 2126)
- Muḥammad b. Sulaymān 1: 262, 285, 286 (also Ṭabarānī, *Kabīr* 1: 320 [# 922]; Ḥākim 3: 183 [cf. Ibn al-Juḥām: 286])
- Muḥammad b. Sulaymān 1: 284, 395, 397 (also Ibn Abī 'l-Ḥadīd 13: 228)
- Muḥammad b. Sulaymān 1: 433–4 (also Ṭabarānī, *Kabīr* 1: 319 [# 949])
- Muḥammad b. Sulaymān 1: 236
- Ibid. 1: 310
- Ibid. 1: 474
- Ibid. 1: 489
- Ibid. 1: 392 (cf. Ibn al-Juḥām: 391)
- Rūyānī 1: 461 (also Ṭabarānī, *Kabīr* 1: 321; Abū Nu'aym, *Mā nazal*: 62–3; Najāshī: 4–5)

- Ibn al-Juḥām: 203–4 (also Ibn 'Asākir 42: 49–50)
- Furāt: 527–8.
- Ṭabarānī, *Kabīr* 1: 315 (# 931)
- Ibid. 1: 319 (# 946)
- Ibid. 1: 319 (# 948)
- Ibid. 1: 320 (# 951)
- Ibid. 1: 319–20 (# 950; also idem, *Akhbār al-Ḥasan*: 66)
- *Irshād* 1: 73–4
- Ṭūsī, *Amālī*: 463–72
- Ḥaskānī 2: 233
- Ṭabrisī, *I'lām*: 187
- Abū Ṭāhir al-Silafī: 376
- Ibn 'Asākir 42: 141 (see also 'Ayyāshī 2: 127)

2. *Tasmiyat man shahida ma'a 'Alī ḥurūbah min al-Muhājirīn wa 'l-Anṣār*

A list of the companions of the Prophet and other notables who fought in the three wars during the caliphate of 'Alī on his side; one of the earliest examples of the works of its genre (see Jalālī, *Tasmiyāt*: 52–68 for a list of some one hundred similar works in this genre from early periods). *Fihrist*: 107 names it as *Tasmiyat man shahida ma'Amīr al-Mu'minīn alayhi 'l-salām al-Jamal wa-Ṣiffīn wa-Nahrawān min al-Ṣaḥāba raḍiya 'llāh 'anhum*. Ibn 'Asākir 45: 502 quotes it as *Tasmiyat man shahida ma'Amīr al-Mu'minīn 'Alī b. Abī Ṭālib min Quraysh wa 'l-Anṣār wa-min muhājirī al-'Arab*. Ṭabarānī, *Kabīr* 2: 146, 259, 288, 3: 223–4, 273, 276, 4: 14, 30, 197, 199 (twice), 203, 217, 5: 35, 60, 69 (twice) (whence Ibn Ḥajar in the corresponding entries of his *Iṣāba*) quotes it as *Tasmiyat man shahida ma' 'Alī min aṣḥāb Rasūl Allāh*. Ibn al-Athīr, *Usd al-ghāba* 1: 266, 267, 270, 2: 24, 61, 78, 123, 128, 162, 171, 220 quotes it as *Kitāb 'Ubayd Allāh b. Abī Rāfi' fī tasmiyat man shahida ma' 'Alī* (1: 266), *Siyar 'Ubayd Allāh b. Abī Rāfi' fī tasmiyat man shahida Ṣiffīn ma' 'Alī* (1: 270), *Tasmiyat man shahida ma' 'Alī ḥurūbah* (2: 220), *Man shahida ma' 'Alī min al-Ṣaḥāba* (2: 171), *Tasmiyat man shahida ma' 'Alī min aṣḥāb Rasūl Allāh* (2: 123), and the like (but wrongly ascribing the work to its first transmitter, the author's son Muḥammad, in 2: 128, 162, 171). (See also Haythamī, *Majma' al-zawā'id* 7: 245.)

The full text of this work has survived in Qāḍī Nu'mān, *Sharḥ al-akhbār* 2: 16–36. Additional material about the persons named, including the author himself (ibid. 2: 20), has been inserted into the work by later transmitters. These insertions can easily be detected.

5: Rabīʿa b. Sumayʿ

Rabīʿa b. Sumayʿ, a tax collector for ʿAlī.

Kāfī 3: 539; Najāshī: 7–8.

Najāshī: 7–8 (whence Sezgin 1: 525) ascribed to this person a book on the *zakāt* taxes of livestock. This was a text of a detailed executive order that ʿAlī wrote for him when he dispatched him on a mission as a tax collector. The word *kitāb* here did not therefore mean a book as Najāshī assumed, but rather a document of which Rabīʿa was only the recipient and transmitter (much of the discussion in Muḥammad Taqī al-Tustarī 4: 354 on the nature of the book of Rabīʿa b. Sumayʿ is thus irrelevant). A part of this document is preserved in *Kāfī* 3: 539–40 (whence *Tahdhīb* 4: 95) where the name of the recipient/ transmitter appears in the printed version as *Zamʿa b. Subayʿ* on the basis of some manuscripts. At least one good manuscript of the *Kāfī* has *Rabīʿa* for *Zamʿa*, another has *Subayʿ* without the dot under the Arabic equivalent of "b" (Miyānajī 1: 450–51). Thus, it seems that the *Kāfī*'s record of the names most probably agreed with that found in Najāshī.

6: ʿAlī Zayn al-ʿĀbidīn

Abū ʾl-Ḥasan ʿAlī b. al-Ḥusayn Zayn al-ʿĀbidīn, known also as *Sajjād* among the Shīʿa, grandson of ʿAlī and Fāṭima and the fourth Imām of the Imāmite Shīʿites. He was the most respected member of the House of the Prophet in his time. Born in Medina where he also lived all his life, he died in 94.

For a summary of Sunnī and Shīʿite biographical material on him, see the entries on him in the *Encyclopaedia Iranica* 1: 849–50 (W. Madelung) and the *Encyclopaedia of Islam*, 2nd edn., 11: 481–3 (E. Kohlberg), both with select bibliographies at the end. For fuller lists, see the editors' footnotes in Dhahabī, *Taʾrīkh* 6 (years 91–100): 431–2 and Mizzī 20: 382; also ʿAbd al-Jabbār al-Rifāʿī 8: 157–249.

1. *Al-Ṣaḥīfa al-kāmila*

As can be gathered from his two epithets, Zayn al-'Ābidīn was noted for his asceticism and devoutness. Many sayings of his on the topic of *zuhd* (e.g. *Kāfī* 8: 14–17; Ibn Shu'ba: 249–52, 272–4; *Biḥār* 78: 128–62) as well as prayer and worship are recorded. Ja'far al-Ṣādiq once offered a disciple the text of a supplication by Zayn al-'Ābidīn that was recorded on the folios of an old notebook (*awrāq min ṣaḥīfa 'atīqa*) (Ṭūsī, *Amālī*: 15–18). Some 54 lengthy or short texts of supplications for general purposes or specific occasions are collected in a volume known as *al-Ṣaḥīfa al-kāmila*. This book is regarded with immense respect by present day Imāmite Shī'ites, though its popularity does not go back more than four centuries (*Biḥār* 110: 43, 60–61).

The book begins with a story about the origins of its own composition. The story has a chain of transmission which begins in the mid-sixth century and goes all the way back to the early second (variants of this *isnād* with different names in the lower part that appear in a few manuscripts start in the late fourth or early fifth centuries). The story, however, speaks of "a supplication," not of a book of many supplications. Only at the very end of the story, a sentence seemingly appended later breaks the order and speaks of 64 supplications that are contained in the volume (the known copies of the *Ṣaḥīfa* usually have 54 supplications at most). Najāshī: 426 and *Fihrist*: 170–71 also mention a single supplication as *Du'ā' al-ṣaḥīfa*, not a collection. It is therefore likely that the volume started with a single supplication, introduced by a story and chain of transmission that only referred to that one text, and was supplemented by other texts in later periods. There are many differences between the various manuscripts of this work, both in the number of supplications they cover and in the wording of each text, as also noted by scholars of the past (Shānachī: 23, 37–8, quoting the early twelfth century bio-bibliographer, 'Abd Allāh al-Afandī al-Iṣfahānī in his *al-Ṣaḥīfa al-thālitha*). The earliest dated manuscript known of this work, if the date is authentic (MS. 12405/2 Raḍawī, Mashhad, dated 416, published by Kāẓim Mudīr Shānachī, Mashhad, 1413) contains only 38 supplications. MS. 53 Sufism, Grand Mosque, Ṣan'ā', copied ultimately from a manuscript with a transmission chain dated Ṣafar 367 (*Cat.*: 374) ends with supplication no. 42 in the most current version, though the arrangement of the supplications may be different in this manuscript. The text offered by Ja'far al-Ṣādiq to his disciple from the old *ṣaḥīfa* is supplication # 49 in the present day standard version of *al-Ṣaḥīfa al-Sajjādiyya*.

Among the texts included in this work, some contain stylistic features and phrasing befitting the time and the character of Zayn al-'Ābidīn as depicted in biographical sources. There is also a text on *zuhd* attributed to him whose first transmitter found it in a *ṣaḥīfa*, here presumably meaning a sheet of paper or parchment as against oral transmission (*Kāfī* 8: 14), and is therefore called the *Ṣaḥīfat 'Alī b. al-Ḥusayn fī 'l-zuhd*. The full text of this *ṣaḥīfa* is quoted in *Kāfī* 8: 14–17.

Ever since the collection found its current shape in the mid-sixth century, numerous supplements and commentaries have been written for and on this work. For lists of both, see Āghā Buzurg 14: 345–59; Sezgin 1: 528; 'Alī Naqī Munzawī 1: 158–61; Shānachī: 32–7, 42–4. For some of the oldest manuscripts of the work, see Shānachī: 23–4, 28–9. For some of its many editions, see ibid.: 31–2.; 'Abd al-Jabbār al-Rifā'ī 8: 220–23. It has been translated into English (William C. Chittick, trans., *The Psalms of Islam*, London, 1988).

There have been attempts to collect all the texts of supplication attributed to Zayn al-'Ābidīn in a single work, the most recent of these attempts being Jawād al-Qayyūmī al-Iṣfahānī's *Ad'iyat al-Imām Zayn al-'Ābidīn* in two volumes (Qum, 1419) with 267 texts documented in 2: 781–840, and Muḥammad Bāqir al-Muwaḥḥid al-Abṭaḥī al-Iṣfahānī's *al-Ṣaḥīfa al-Sajjādiyya al-jāmi'a* (Qum, 1411) with 270 texts.

2. *Risāla ilā ba'ḍ aṣḥābih = Risālat al-ḥuqūq*

The text of a letter on the duties that one has towards God, religion, the ruler, oneself, as well as other human beings. The first transmitter of the text, Abū Ḥamza al-Thumālī (d. 148–150), refers to it as the epistle of Zayn al-'Ābidīn to one of his disciples (Ibn Shu'ba: 255; *Khiṣāl*: 564), but Najāshī: 116 calls it *Risālat al-ḥuqūq*. The full text of this epistle is quoted in Ibn Shu'ba: 255–72, and with variations in Ibn Bābawayh, *Amālī* 451–6; *Faqīh* 2: 618–26; *Khiṣāl*: 564–70 (whence *Biḥār* 74: 2–21; the text was also attested, at least partially, in Kulaynī's *Rasā'il al-A'imma* as quoted by Ibn Ṭāwūs, *Falāḥ*: 287). It is also published separately (Baghdad, 1369; Tehran, 1402), and recently in Muḥammad Riḍā al-Ḥusaynī al-Jalālī, *Jihād al-Imām al-Sajjād* (Qum, 1418): 255–96. There is a similar, but shorter, text attributed to Zayn al-'Ābidīn's son, Zayd, as a letter he wrote on the same topic (full text in *'Ulūm al-ḥadīth* [a quarterly published in Qum] 6: 225–56). One of the two texts is an abridgement or expanded version of the other.

3. Kitābuh ilā Muḥammad b. Muslim al-Zuhrī

The text of a lengthy letter of rebuke and advice that Zayn al-'Ābidīn reportedly wrote to the late Umayyad traditionist, Ibn Shihāb al-Zuhrī (d. 124). Zuhrī was a student and admirer of Zayn al-'Ābidīn (Ibn Sa'd 5: 165, 166; *'Ilal* 1: 219; *Ḥilya* 3: 135; Ibn 'Asākir 41: 370, 372–3, 376; Mizzī 20: 386), whom he described as the most excellent of the Hāshimids and the most learned person he had ever seen (Ibn Sa'd 5: 166; Fasawī 1: 544; Abū Zur'a al-Dimashqī: 536; Ibn Abī Ḥātim 6: 179; *'Ilal* 1: 220; *Ḥilya* 3: 136; Ibn 'Asākir 41: 366, 371, 398; Mizzī 20: 386, 388). He is also one of the chief transmitters from Zayn al-'Ābidīn (see 'Uṭāridī, *Musnad* 2: 451). The letter that appears in Ibn Shu'ba: 274–7 (whence *Biḥār* 78: 131–5) has a noticeable late Umayyad flavor.

4. Dīwān

A collection of some 150 lines of poetry ascribed to Zayn al-'Ābidīn. It is available in numerous manuscripts (Āghā Buzurg 9: 431; Sezgin 1: 526–7; it is already known that the copy date of 298 in a manuscript assumed to be the oldest copy of the work is a fake) and a number of editions. There is, however, no evidence to support the ascription of this collection of poetry to Zayn al-'Ābidīn. It has even been suggested that both style and content point to a different time and composer. None of the lines of poetry quoted from Zayn al-'Ābidīn in early sources (see *Biḥār* 46: 51, 81, 82–7, 91, 97–8, 146) appears in this volume.

5. Musnad

Najāshī: 242, 395 mentions two works as *Akhbār 'Alī b. al-Ḥusayn*, one by the Baṣran historian, 'Abd al-'Azīz b. Yaḥyā al-Jalūdī (d. 332), probably a chapter of a larger work; another by the traditionist Muḥammad b. 'Umar al-Ji'ābī (d. 335), most likely an independent work. These would have been collections of reports by and about Zayn al-'Ābidīn quoted in the Sunnī tradition. The entry on Zayn al-'Ābidīn in Ibn 'Asākir's *Ta'rīkh madīnat Dimashq* 41: 360–416 also serves the same purpose. A recent work by 'Azīz Allāh al-'Uṭāridī: *Musnad al-Imām al-Sajjād*, in two volumes (Tehran, 1379 sh [2000–01]), attempts to collect similar material in the Shī'ite tradition.

7: Muḥammad al-Bāqir

Abū Ja'far Muḥammad b. 'Alī al-Bāqir, the fifth Imām of the Imāmite Shī'ites, was a highly respected scholar of the Qur'ān, *ḥadīth* and religious law in his time. Born in Medina in 56 or 57, he lived all his life there and had a large circle of students, disciples and admirers. He was the first to formulate much of what were to become the fundamental doctrines of Imāmite Shī'ism. As the most distinguished member of the House of the Prophet, he was regarded by the pro-'Alīd circles in Iraq as their spiritual leader with the hope that, some day, he may try to challenge the Umayyads and establish a moral government. This he never ventured. He died in 114 or 117.

For a summary of the biographical material on him, see the entry on him in the *Encyclopaedia of Islam*, 2nd edn., 7: 397–400 (E. Kohlberg) with a list of the main sources at the end. For fuller lists, see the editors' footnotes in Dhahabī, *Ta'rīkh* 7 (years 101–120): 462 and Mizzī 26: 136–7; also 'Abd al-Jabbār al-Rifā'ī 8: 251–77.

For reference to him as the most distinguished member of the House of the Prophet in his own time, see Mubarrad 4: 119 (also Ṭabarī 7: 569–70; Ibn 'Abd Rabbih 5: 82–3); Dhahabī, *Ta'rīkh* 7 (years 101–120): 462–3. For the attachment of the Pro-'Alīd Iraqis to him, see Ibn 'Asākir 54: 279 where the caliph Hishām b. 'Abd al-Malik (r. 105–125) refers to him as "the one the people of Iraq are in love with"; also 'Alī b. Ibrāhīm 2: 284 where some people describe Muḥammad al-Bāqir to Hishām as "the Prophet of the People of Kūfa" (see also *Kāfī* 1: 342). For the political expectations, see Sa'd b. 'Abd Allāh: 75; *Kāfī* 1: 342, 536, 8: 80, 341; Ibn Samka: 169: Nu'mānī: 167–8, 169, 215, 216, 237; *Kamāl*: 325; Ibn 'Asākir 54: 291.

1. *Tafsīr al-Qur'ān / Tafsīr al-Bāqir*

A commentary on the Qur'ān attributed to Muḥammad al-Bāqir (Ibn al-Nadīm: 36 [who has it as the first on the list of early Qur'ānic commentaries]; Najāshī: 170; *Fihrist*: 72; *Ma'ālim*: 52; Ibn Ṭāwūs, *Sa'd*: 23–4, 245–9. This latter author had a copy of at least the first five parts of the work which he described and quoted in the pages noted [see further Kohlberg: 339]). This was in fact a collection of reports that Muḥammad al-Bāqir's pupil Abū 'l-Jārūd Ziyād b. al-Mundhir quoted from him on the meaning of Qur'ānic passages. The work is partially extant (see section II below, no. 13, the entry on Abū 'l-Jārūd). 'Abd Allāh b. Ḥamza, *'Iqd*: 312 quoted from a book of *tafsīr* that was related from Muḥammad al-Bāqir by three of his disciples, including Abū Ḥamza al-Thumālī but was different from what was commonly available in 'Abd Allāh b. Ḥamza's time as *Tafsīr al-Bāqir.* The chain of transmission he mentions is the same as the one given by Najāshī: 114–15 for the *Tafsīr* of Abū Ḥamza (see section III below, no. 201).

2. *Al-Manāsik*

A quotation from Muḥammad al-Bāqir's son, Ja'far al-Ṣādiq, in 'Ayyāshī 1: 252–3 states that "before Abū Ja'far [Muḥammad al-Bāqir] the Shī'ites did not know [the right way to perfom] the rituals of the pilgrimage to Mecca [*ḥajj*] ... until he emerged and performed the pilgrimage for them, explaining to them how to do it ..." There is a treatise on the rituals of *ḥajj* that Abū 'l-Jārūd Ziyād b. al-Mundhir quoted from Muḥammad al-Bāqir. The full text of this treatise is quoted in Aḥmad b. 'Īsā 2: 356–67 (with some extra material inserted by the author of that work in between, ibid. 2: 360–62, 365, 367; there are also other quotations from Muḥammad al-Bāqir on the topic, ibid. 2: 368–72, with the same chain of transmission as the treatise, that may also have belonged to that work). The treatise was published in Baghdad, 1342, but attributed to 'Alī Zayn al-'Ābidīn on the basis of a manuscript with a chain of transmission through Abū Khālid 'Amr b. Khālid al-Wāsiṭī (see section III below, no. 42) to Zayd b. 'Alī. The editor, however, thought that Zayd had related the text from his father, Zayn al-'Ābidīn, on the strength of a reference in *Fihrist*: 179 where a *Kitāb al-manāsik* by the latter is mentioned. The above report in 'Ayyāshī, however, may confirm the attribution of the treatise to Muḥammad al-Bāqir. In addition, the overwhelmingly ethical tone of the many quotations from 'Alī Zayn al-'Ābidīn on the topic of *ḥajj* ('Uṭāridī, *Musnad* 2: 225–38) is distinctly different from the pure legal language of this text. Ibn 'Adī: 1561 (whence *Lisān* 3:39) also refers to the text on the rituals of *ḥajj* quoted from Muḥammad al-Bāqir and notes that a variant of the same text is quoted from his son, Ja'far al-Ṣādiq (see also Ibn 'Adī: 556, 557). This clearly refers to a lengthy text quoted through a number of Sunnī *isnād*s from Ja'far al-Ṣādiq in Ṭayālisī 3: 246–9; Ibn Abī Shayba, *al-juz' al-mafqūd*: 377–81; Aḥmad 3: 320–21; Dārimī 2: 44–9; Muslim: 886–92; Ibn Māja: 1022–7; Abū Dāwūd 2: 182–6; Abū Ya'lā 4: 23–6; Ibn Ḥibbān, *Ṣaḥīḥ* 9: 250–56 and many other sources where this text is quoted in full or part (see the editors' footnotes to Ṭayālisī 3: 244–50 and Aḥmad [Beirut, 1995] 22: 328–31 for detailed lists).

II

Kūfan Shī'ism in the Umayyad Period

If we accept the historical accounts of the early Islamic period as authentic, the origins of Shī'ism go back to the early part of the fourth decade of the Islamic calendar and the city of Kūfa, and it remains basically a Kūfan phenomenon for most of the of Umayyad period.[1]

It began like this: A group of Kūfan people become unhappy with the policies of the governor of their city who was appointed by the third caliph, 'Uthmān. A small section of the youth, led by Mālik b. al-Ashtar al-Nakha'ī, start to speak publicly against the governor and the caliph who has sent him. The governor reports them to the caliph and, on his instructions, banishes them to Syria where Mu'āwiya is the ruler. He sends them to Ḥimṣ. Later, the group flees from Ḥimṣ back to Kūfa, removes the government representative and takes control of the administration of the city. The caliph submits to their demands and appoints a governor of their choice to the city. Dissatisfaction with the caliph's policies, however, continues. A group of Kūfans travel to Medina and join others who have come to complain about the caliph's policies.

1. The Ḥijāz, generally speaking, was never a Shī'ite land. Some reports suggest that during the late Umayyad period, only four Shī 'ites lived in Mecca (Kashshī: 246, 389) and fewer than twenty in Mecca and Medina combined (Ibn Abī 'l-Ḥadīd 4: 104). The Ḥusaynid branch of the House began to find followers in the land of Persia late in that period; a few already lived in Khurāsān (Ibn Samka: 204). At the outset, however, and for some time to come, Mesopotamia (ibid.: 169; *Kāfī* 2: 242) and, in particular, Kūfa (Ṣaffār: 77 [whence Ibn Qūlawayh: 314; *Thawāb*: 114]; *Bishārat al-Muṣṭafā*: 134) remains the main focal point where Shī'ite populations were concentrated.

All eyes are now on 'Alī as the alternative to restore government to its former style and revert to previous policies. The Kūfans join his camp. When 'Uthmān is killed, those Kūfans are seen among 'Alī's close associates from the very beginning of his caliphate. With their support, 'Alī suppresses the revolt of Baṣra and then moves to and settles in Kūfa, which remains his seat of government until the end of his rule. The first civil war breaks the unity of the Muslim community, dividing it into supporters of 'Alī and his opponents, who come to be identified as supporters of 'Uthmān. The division continues for almost a century before it becomes more complex in nature.

For this whole period, Kūfa is the center of the supporters of 'Alī's cause, though it takes different shapes as time goes by. When the camp of 'Alī is defeated by Mu'āwiya and hopes are dashed, a few partisans of 'Alī remain active and uncompromising. Such are Rashīd (or Rushayd) al-Hajarī and 'Amr b. al-Ḥamiq, as well as Ḥujr b. 'Adī and his associates, all of whom are killed by Mu'āwiya's men. Others seem to have followed Ḥasan al-Mujtabā in his decision to make peace with Mu'āwiya, and although remaining loyal to 'Alī's cause, do not participate in any political activity or resort to any veneration of the person of 'Alī. These are the ones for whom the ethico-religious nature of 'Alī, as represented by his personal and administrative conduct, and a deep affection for his descendants are all that matters.[2] For yet another group, nostalgic memories give way to apocalyptic expectations that one day 'Alī will return. Affection now turns into veneration. Then hopes are directed towards the family, an 'Alīd instead of 'Alī himself. A hasty plan to set up a counter government under Ḥusayn's leadership is promptly crushed. A group of the partisans of 'Alī sacrifice their lives in a suicidal revolt to keep the memory of Ḥusayn alive. A local rebel succeeds in briefly establishing an independent government under the slogan of revenge for the blood of Ḥusayn. It names Muḥammad b. al-Ḥanafiyya, another son of 'Alī, as its spiritual leader. Not all surviving partisans of 'Alī are accounted for in this episode. As time goes on and 'Alī Zayn al-'Ābidīn, the sole surviving son of Ḥusayn, gets seniority in the House, attention and affection are directed towards him, and then to his son, Muḥammad al-Bāqir. Imāmite Shī'ism is born.

Kūfan Shī'ism was far from being a monolithic phenomenon, and this remained true for two more centuries to come. Though it began as an

---

2. See Ṭabarī 6: 11, 13.

anti-'Uthmān movement, complaints soon spread to the first two caliphs. Many Kūfan Shī'ites now believe that history took a wrong turn immediately after the death of the Prophet when his powerful tribe of Quraysh decided to take the matter into their own hands, thereby blocking 'Alī's legitimate right to succession. The caliphate of 'Uthman and, later, the rule of the Umayyads were nothing but the logical conclusion of that earlier wrong turn. Nostalgic, oppressed, and suppressed for a lengthy period of time, one branch of Kūfan Shī'ism was inevitably forced into a populist and predominantly political mould with strong esoteric tendencies. There are ample references to this branch in the reports from Ja'far al-Ṣādiq.[3] Another, similarly well attested branch, was better educated, and more receptive to the world outside the Shī'ite circles, which in the late Umayyad period had reportedly some fifty thousand members in Kūfa.[4] Like other divergent Islamic tendencies, some of the Shī'ite trends of the time may have appeared crude and lacking in sophistication. But gradually with the passage of time, and through the teachings of Muḥammad al-Bāqir, Shī'ism began to exhibit its religious spirit and create a discourse to articulate its tenets and aspirations.

---

3. E.g. Kashshī: 301.
4. See *Ṣifāt*: 203; *Bishārat al-Muṣṭafā*: 163.

1: Maytham al-Tammār

Maytham b. Yaḥyā, the date seller, a client of the Banū Asad and a resident of Kūfa. He was a devout and outspoken partisan of 'Alī, for whose cause he was executed by the Umayyad governor of Kūfa, late in 60.

Barqī: 34, 43; *Kāfī* 2: 220; Kashshī: 9, 78–87; *Irshād* 1: 323–5; *Rijāl*: 96, 105; Ibn Abī 'l-Ḥadīd 2: 291–4 (quoting Thaqafī's *Ghārāt* [the reference is missing from the surviving manuscripts and, hence, printed versions of that work]); Mizzī 3: 309 (and the footnote); Ibn Ḥajar, *Iṣāba* 6: 238, 316–18 (quoting the Shī'ite al-Mu'ayyad b. al-Nu'mān in his *Manāqib*). The early historian, Hishām b. Muḥammad b. al-Sā'ib al-Kalbī (d. 204–206) wrote a monograph on the killing of Maytham and two other disciples of 'Alī (Najāshī: 435). There are also recent monographs on him. See 'Abd al-Jabbār al-Rifā'ī 6: 421–2.

As one of the earliest martyrs of the Shī'ite cause who was singled out and crucified by the Umayyad governor in order to intimidate the Shī'ites of Kūfa and suppress their rallying in support of the 'Alīds a few days before the expected arrival of Ḥusayn, Maytham has enjoyed the affection and reverence of the Shī'ites throughout history. The account of his martyrdom is quoted in several versions, all couched in a hagiographical style, but converging and sharing much when narrating the events of his final ordeal. His tomb in Kūfa remains a sacred shrine for the Shī'ites up to our time (for a description of the shrine, see Ḥirz al-Dīn 2: 340–44; Murād 1: 35–47).

Maytham was the head of a learned Shī'ite family from the late first to the mid-third centuries, and a number of his descendants and offspring were transmitters of *ḥadīth*. These include his sons ('Imrān,[5] Shu'ayb,[6] Ṣāliḥ,[7] Ya'qūb,[8] 'Alī,[9] Muḥammad,[10] and possibly Ismā'īl[11] and Ḥamza[12]), grandsons (four through

---

5. Kashshī: 81, 82, 114; Najāshī: 292; *Rijāl*: 118, 256. See also 'Uqaylī 3: 306; Ṭabarānī, *Awsaṭ* 4: 171 (whence Ibn 'Asākir 42: 329).
6. Barqī: 51 (delete the editor's added "*Ya'qūb*" and read *Shu'ayb b. Maytham* for *Ya'qūb b. Shu'ayb b. Maytham* as also required by generational sequence); *Rijāl*: 224.
7. Barqī: 59; Kashshī: 80, 115; *Rijāl*: 138, 225 (see also 'Alī b. Ibrāhīm 2: 388; Ibn Qūlawayh: 258; Ibn 'Asākir 42: 356, 361; Ibn al-Mubārak, *Zuhd*: 261).
8. Ṭūsī, *Amālī*: 406.
9. Ibn al-Mashhadī: 149.
10. Ibn Ḥajar, *Iṣāba* 7: 241.
11. Ibn al-Mashhadī: 349 (cf. Ibn Qūlawayh: 452 where the same report is related from an unnamed son of Maytham).
12. Kashshī: 80. Cf. ibid.: 81–2 where Ibn Faḍḍāl, an early authority on Shī'ite transmitters of *ḥadīth*, suggests that the name *Ḥamza* as a transmitter of the report in Kashshī: 80–81 is a corruption of *'Imrān*. In Suyūṭī, *La'ālī* 1: 378, *'Imrān b. Maytham* is corrupted to *'Amr b. Maytham*.

his son, Shu'ayb: Ibrāhīm,[13] Isḥāq,[14] Ismā'īl[15] and Ya'qūb,[16] as well as others: Ḥassān b. Ṣāliḥ,[17] 'Alī b. Muḥammad,[18] Yūnus b. 'Imrān[19] and Yūsuf b. 'Imrān[20]), great-granchildren ('Ammār,[21] Muḥsin,[22] Muḥammad b. Ya'qūb b. Shu'ayb,[23] Ḥasan b. Ismā'īl b. Shu'ayb,[24] 'Alī b. Ismā'īl b. Ṣāliḥ, [25] and Kulthum bint Yūsuf b. 'Imrān[26]), and later descendants (Ismā'īl b. Ḥasan b. Ismā'īl b. Shu'ayb,[27] Aḥmad b. Ḥasan b. Ismā'īl b. Shu'ayb,[28] Muḥammad b. Ḥasan b. Ziyād,[29] and Ibrāhīm b. al-Naḍr[30]) and dependents (e.g. Abān b. 'Umar al-Asadī [alive in 148] who married into the family[31]). A great-grandson of his, 'Alī b. Ismā'īl b. Shu'ayb al-Maythamī,[32] was a well known Shī'ite theologian in the early third century.

Kitāb Maytham

The biographical sources do not mention that Maytham had compiled a book. However, a son of his, Ṣāliḥ, quotes from a *Kitāb Maytham* (Ṭūsī, *Amālī*: 148–9) and another, Ya'qūb, from the book, or books, of his father (ibid.: 405–6; see also Ibn al-Juḥām: 465).[33] It is therefore possible that a register of 'Alī's sayings existed in the family and was believed to have been written by Maytham. A number of reports by Maytham from 'Alī in

---

13. Ibn Qūlawayh: 140–41; *Rijāl*: 157; also Barqī: 81 (read *al-Maythamī* for *al-Taymī*).
14. *Rijāl*: 162.
15. Ibid.: 160.
16. Najāshī: 450; *Fihrist*: 180; *Rijāl*: 149, 323, 345.
17. *Maḥāsin*: 395.
18. 'Ayyāshī 1: 194; Ibn Ḥajar, *Iṣāba* 7: 241.
19. *Kāfī* 4: 270.
20. Kashshī: 83; *Kāfī* 2: 146.
21. 'Ayyāshī 1: 359 who quotes him as *'Ammār b. Maytham* transmitting a report from Ja'far al-Ṣādiq. The man should have been a grandson of Maytham given the time period.
22. 'Ayyāshī 1: 137; *Kāfī* 2: 76; *Tahdhīb* 2: 73–4.
23. *Tahdhīb* 4: 171; also *Faqīh* 2: 170 (read *Muḥammad b. Ya'qūb b. Shu'ayb 'an abīh* for *Muḥammad b. Ya'qūb 'an Shu'ayb 'an abīh*).
24. *Maḥāsin*: 479–80.
25. Ṭabarī 7: 597, 601, 626.
26. Barqī: 146.
27. *Kāfī* 4: 31.
28. Kashshī: 468; Najāshī: 74; *Fihrist*: 22; *Rijāl*: 332.
29. Najāshī: 363.
30. Ibn Bisṭām: 124.
31. Najāshī: 10; *Rijāl*: 164.
32. Najāshī: 251; *Fihrist*: 87; *Rijāl*: 362.
33. A contemporary author claims that Abū Ja'far al-Ṭabarī in his *Bishārat al-Muṣṭafā* "states in many cases that I found such and such in the Book of Maytham al-Tammār" (Jalālī, *Tadwīn*: 243; see also ibid.: 141 where the book of Maytham is also said to have been extant until the 7th century on the ground that the said scholar had cited directly from the work). I have not come across a single example of such a statement in the book, at least in its printed versions.

early sources, related by Maytham's descendants, may therefore go back to that register if it ever existed. They include the following:

- Thaqafī: 413–15 (with a reference to a pilgrimage to Jerusalem, not a common practice of Maytham's time unless that reference was added later; see also Ibn Abī Shayba 2: 374, 12: 208 where there is a reference to the same account albeit on a different authority)
- *Kāfī* 7: 186–7 (also *Tahdhīb* 10: 9–11). The quotation has, however, an anti-Kaysānī tone in the last sentence that dates the report to a few decades after Maytham, unless this last sentence was added later, not an impossible scenario
- Furāt: 55–6
- *'Iqāb*: 261
- Ṭūsī, *Amālī*: 309 (also Ibn 'Asākir 42: 278)
- Ṭabrisī, *Majma'* 30: 75 (quoting 'Ayyāshī's *Tafsīr* in the section that has not survived)
- Ibn al-Mashhadī: 149–53 (also Shahīd I, *Mazār*: 283–8)
- Ibn Ḥajar, *Iṣāba* 7: 242 quoting a Shī'ite author in his work in support of the idea that Abū Ṭālib, the father of 'Alī, was a Muslim. The work that Ibn Ḥajar quotes on 7: 236–42 is different from Fakhār b. Ma'add's *al-Ḥujja 'alā 'l-dhāhib ilā takfīr Abī Ṭālib* that has survived. The quotation appears in the *Iṣāba* with a chain of transmission going back to 'Alī b. Muḥammad b. Mtym (sic) from his father, from his ('Alī b. Muḥammad's) grandfather who heard 'Alī. *Mtym* is a corruption for *Maytham* as is attested by the fact that Ibn Ḥajar also refers to this quotation in Maytham's biography (ibid. 6: 318). The transmitter is the same 'Alī b. Muḥammad b. Maytham whom 'Ayyāshī 1: 194 quotes as a transmitter from Ja'far al-Ṣādiq

In common with some other well known names among the disciples of 'Alī, Maytham's name was also used in later periods to document esoteric and apocalyptic material as transmissions from 'Alī, as in the following examples:

- Khaṣībī: 125–6, 148–50
- Ibn Bābawayh, *Amālī*: 189–90 (also *'Ilal* 1: 217–18)
- Ibn Abī 'l-Fawāris: 90–96 (also Shādhān b. Jibrīl: 2–5)
- *Biḥār* 54: 344–6

None of these last citations is reported through any member of Maytham's family.

2: Ḥārith al-A'war

Abū Zuhayr Ḥārith b. 'Abd Allāh al-Hamdānī, the one eyed, a prominent Kūfan *tābi'ī* known for his knowledge of religion, law and arithmetic. An associate of 'Alī, he remained a committed supporter of 'Alī's cause throughout his life. He died in Kūfa in 65.

Almost every biographical dictionary for transmitters of *ḥadīth* has an entry on Ḥārith. For lists of many of these, see the editors' footnotes to Mizzī 5: 244–53 and Dhahabī, *Ta'rīkh* 5 (years 61–80): 89–90.

Ḥārith was from Hamdān, a tribe of Yemen, many of whose members were among the staunchest supporters of 'Alī during his caliphate. According to the genealogical line of descent in Ibn al-Kalbī, *Nasab*: 520–21 (whence Ṭabarī, *Dhayl*: 662 and others), Ḥārith was from the Ḥawthī clan of Hamdān. *Khārifī* in Bukharī, *Awsaṭ* 1: 282; idem *Kabīr* 2: 273, and many later sources must have been a corruption of *Ḥawthī* as Khārif was a different clan of Hamdān (Ibn al-Kalbī, *Nasab*: 521). *Khārifī* has in turn been corrupted in *Rijāl*: 60 to *Ḥāliqī*. Either *Ḥawthī* or *Khārifī* has been further corrupted to *Jurjānī* in a report quoted in Sahmī: 260 (in which also read *taqiyya* for *thiqa* as in the *Musnad al-Firdaws* [Uzbak: 454]). This latter corruption seems to have persuaded a contemporary of Yaḥyā b. Ma'īn (d. 233) to suggest that Ḥārith might have been of Persian origin (Mizzī 5: 245).

Ḥārith was one of the ten-member group of Kūfans who rebelled against 'Uthmān's governor in Kūfa and took over the city (Ibn Sa'd 5: 24; Balādhurī 2: 339–40). For his attachment to 'Alī, see further Naṣr b. Muzāḥim: 121; Pseudo-Nāshi': 22; Thaqafī: 302, 479; Fasawī 2: 617, 624; *Khiṣāl*: 334; *Nahj al-balāgha*: 459–60 (letter # 69); Mufīd, *Amālī*: 4, 271, 351; Ibn Ṭāwūs, *Kashf*: 174.

On his date of death, Ṭabarī, *Dhayl*: 663 suggests that the year 65 is not precise; more accurately, Ḥārith died during the time of 'Abd Allāh b. Yazīd al-Anṣārī who was governor of Kūfa on behalf of 'Abd Allāh b. al-Zubayr (r. 64–73). This Anṣārī was governor of Kūfa from Friday 22 Ramaḍān 64 to Thursday 25 Ramaḍān 65 (Ṭabarī, *Ta'rīkh* 5: 560, 622) and performed in person the funeral rites for Ḥārith ('Abd al-Razzāq 3: 498).

The biographers agree on the point that Ḥārith was a very knowledgeable and learned person. But there is disagreement about the extent of his reliability. There are two recent monographs on the subject by the Moroccan scholar 'Abd al-'Azīz b. Muḥammad b. al-Ṣiddīq al-Ḥusaynī al-Ghumārī (d. 1418): *al-Bāḥith 'an 'ilal al-ṭa'n fī 'l-Ḥārith* (2nd edn.: Qum, 1420 [in *'Ulūm al-ḥadīth* 5: 307–60]) and *Bayān nakth al-nākith al-muta'addī bi-taḍ'īf al-Ḥārith* (2nd edn.: Qum, 1420 [in *'Ulūm al-ḥadīth* 6: 257–93]).

1. *Kitāb / Ṣaḥīfa*

A report in Ibn Sa'd 6: 209 and Rāmhurmuzī: 370 asserts that Ḥārith purchased sheets and brought them to 'Alī who wrote on them "much knowledge" for him. Another in *Kāfī* 1: 141 and *Tawḥīd*: 31 has Ḥārith record a sermon by 'Alī and later quote it to a transmitter from his own written record. That transmitter was Abū Isḥāq 'Amr b. 'Abd Allāh al-Sabī'ī al-Hamdānī (d. 126–129),[34] who allegedly married Ḥārith's widow and thus gained access to his "books."[35] There are also numerous references in the early sources to the *Kitāb* or *Ṣaḥīfa* of Ḥārith al-A'war, a collection of records he took from the statements and acts of 'Alī in Kūfa. Abū Isḥāq al-Sabī'ī, who quotes Ḥārith extensively on what 'Alī said or did, is generally thought to have received only four reports from Ḥārith orally,[36] and all his many other transmissions are said to be from the book of Ḥārith.[37] The reports of two other late first-century transmitters, Khilās b. 'Amr al-Hajarī al-Baṣrī and 'Abd al-A'lā b. 'Āmir al-Tha'labī al-Kūfī, from 'Alī are also suspected to have been from the same book.[38] Possibly because of the similarity of the contents,[39] Najāshī identified the book that he too received through Abū Isḥāq al-Sabī'ī as a variant of the book of Ibn Abī Rāfi'.[40] Here is a list of some of the passages that are recorded in the sources on the authority of Abū Isḥāq al-Sabī'ī, from Ḥārith, from 'Alī:

I ON THE QUR'ĀN[41]

1. Aḥmad 1: 91 (also Abū Ya'lā 1: 302; Ibu 'Adī: 1320 [see also 'Ayyāshī 1: 3]; also a variant in Ṭabarānī, *Awsaṭ* 2: 29; idem, *Saghīr* 2: 78 [cf. Ibn Abī Shayba 10: 482; Dārimī 2: 435; Tirmidhī 5: 29–30 where the same report is quoted from Ḥārith through a different transmitter])
2. Ibn Māja: 1158, 1169 (also Quḍā'ī 1: 51 [with a variation])
3. Ibn Abī Shayba 10: 529, 13: 286 (also Dārimī 2: 442, 443; Ibn Qutayba, *'Uyūn* 2: 131 [all with variations])

---

34. For him see Mizzī 22: 102–13 and the many sources listed in the editor's footnotes.
35. Dhahabī, *Siyar* 5: 398 quoting Aḥmad b. Ḥanbal.
36. Bukhārī, *Awsaṭ* 1: 282; Abū Dāwūd 1: 239; Nasā'ī, *Khaṣā'iṣ*: 84; Ibn Abī Ḥātim 1: 132.
37. 'Ijlī: 366.
38. For Khilās, see Ājurrī 2: 145 (*yuḥaddithu 'an ṣaḥīfat al-Ḥārith al-A'war*), and for 'Abd al-A'lā, see Ibn Abī Ḥātim 6: 26 (*waqa'a ilayh kitāb al-Ḥārith al-A'war*; see also Fasawī 2: 818).
39. See Bayhaqī 2: 33 for an example.
40. See Najāshī: 7.
41. Both here and in the entry on Aṣbagh b. Nubāta, the passages are listed in the order they would be expected to appear in a reconstructed volume.

4. Ibn al-Mundhir, *Tafsīr* (Uzbak: 419)
5. ʿAbd al-Razzāq 7: 505
6. Ṭabarānī, *Awsaṭ* 7: 310
7. Ibn Kathīr 1: 606
8. *Ḥilya* 7: 136 (also Khaṭīb, *Taʾrīkh* 6: 248 [with a fuller text])
9. *Firdaws* (Uzbak: 415)
10. Ṭabarī, *Tafsīr* 2: 81
11. Ibn Abī Shayba 2: 504, 505 (also Ṭabarī, *Tafsīr* 2: 554; Dānī, *Muktafā*: 188)
12. Ṭabarī, *Tafsīr* 7: 18, 21 (also Ibn Abī Ḥātim, *Tafsīr*: 1192; cf. Saʿīd b. Manṣūr: 1547 where the passage is cited on the authority of *Shaʿbī* from Ḥārith)
13. Ibn Abī Shayba, *al-juzʾ al-mafqūd*: 439 (also Tirmidhī 2: 280; Ṭabarī, *Tafsīr* 10: 169)
14. ʿAlī b. Ibrāhīm 2: 276 (two reports)
15. Thaʿlabī, *al-Kashf wa ʾl-bayān*, under Qurʾān 39: 63 (Uzbak: 414)
16. Ṭabarī, *Tafsīr* 24: 35 (also Abū Nuʿaym, *Ṣifat al-janna* 2: 132)
17. Kalābādhī, *Baḥr* (Uzbak: 394)
18. Ibn al-Mubārak, *Raqāʾiq*: 107 (also ʿAlī b. Ibrāhīm 2: 287–8 [with a much longer text]; Bayhaqī, *Shuʿab* 7: 56)
19. Ibn Abī Ḥātim, *Tafsīr*: 3288 (whence Ibn Kathīr 6: 248)
20. Ibn Abī Shayba 2: 524 (also Ṭabarī, *Tafsīr* 26: 180)
21. Thaʿlabī, *al-Kashf wa ʾl-bayān*, under Qurʾān 51: 1 (Uzbak: 416)
22. Ṭabarī, *Tafsīr* 27: 169
23. Ibid. 30: 129
24. Ibn Abī Shayba 3: 203 (Ṭabarī, *Tafsīr* 30: 319)
25. Nuʿmānī: 304–5

II DOGMATICS

1. Abū Yaʿlā 1: 400 (also Ibn Abī Ḥātim, *ʿIlal* 2: 146; Ibn ʿAdī: 821; Dāraquṭnī, *Muʾtalif*: 627)
2. *Ḥilya* 3: 73 (read *Sufyān ʿan Abī Isḥāq* for *Sufyān b. Abī Isḥāq*)
3. *Kāfī* 1: 141–2 (also *Tawḥīd*: 31–4)
4. Thaqafī 1: 111–12 (also *Tawḥīd*: 184)
5. Bayhaqī 10: 204 (see also Ibn Abī Ḥātim 1: 245; Ibn ʿAdī: 604)
6. Ibn ʿAsākir 42: 512–13
7. Ibn al-Jawzī, *ʿIlal*: 150
8. *ʿIqāb*: 252
9. Ṭabarānī, *Awsaṭ* 7: 128 (also idem, *Ṣaghīr* 2: 93; Khaṭīb, *Talkhīṣ*: 795)

10. *Firdaws* (Uzbak: 418)
11. Ṭabarī, *Tafsīr* 24: 35–6
12. Ibn 'Adī: 2150

III LAW

Ritual purity:

1. Ibn Abī Shayba 1: 26 (also Dāraquṭnī 1: 78–9; Bayhaqī 1: 12)
2. Tirmidhī 1: 95
3. Ṭabarānī, *Du'ā*: 977
4. Ibn 'Adī: 2348
5. Ibn Abī Shayba 1: 100 (also Ibn Māja: 139; Ibn Abī Ḥātim, *'Ilal* 1: 56)
6. Aḥmad b. 'Īsā 1: 16
7. 'Abd al-Razzāq 1: 117
8. Ibn Abī Shayba 1: 160 (also Ṭabarī, *Tafsīr* 5: 114; Bayhaqī 1: 221)
9. 'Abd al-Razzāq 1: 242, 244 (also Ibn Abī Shayba 1: 160, 2: 433; Dāraquṭnī 1: 186; Aḥmad b. 'Īsā 1: 70; Bayhaqī 1: 232, 233)
10. Ṭabarī, *Tafsīr* 6: 126
11. Ibn Abī Shayba 1: 36 (also Aḥmad 1: 77; Ibn Māja: 133)
12. 'Abd al-Razzāq 1: 340 (also Ibn Abī Shayba 1: 104; Bazzār 1: 162 [with variations]; see also Aḥmad 1: 90)
13. Ibn Abī Shayba 1: 65 (also Ṭabarī, *Tahdhīb, 'Alī*: 217)
14. Ibn al-Mundhir, *Awsaṭ* (Uzbak: 422)
15. 'Abd al-Razzāq 1: 263 (also Ibn Abī Shayba 1: 71)
16. Ibn Abī Shayba 1: 139
17. Ibn Abī Shayba 1: 81
18. 'Abd al-Razzāq 1: 230, 284 (also Ibn Abī Shayba 1: 81)
19. 'Abd al-Razzāq 1: 277 (also Ibn Abī Shayba 1: 76)
20. Ibn Abī Shayba 1: 76
21. Ṭabarī, *Tahdhīb, 'Alī*: 277
22. Ibn 'Adī: 1308
23. Shāfi'ī 7: 153 (also Ibn Abī Shayba 2: 45)
24. 'Abd al-Razzāq 1: 302 (also Ibn Abī Shayba 1: 93; Dārimī 1: 215–16)
25. Rāfi' b. 'Āṣim (Uzbak: 424)
26. 'Abd al-Razzāq 3: 407 (also Ibn Abī Shayba 3: 269)
27. Ibn Abī Shayba 3: 235
28. Ibn al-Mundhir, *Awsaṭ* (Uzbak: 423)
29. Aḥmad b. 'Īsā 1: 48

Prayer:

1. Ṭabarānī, *Awsaṭ* 7: 301 (also idem, *Ṣaghīr* 2: 52; Ṭabrisī, *Majma'* 12: 231)
2. *Firdaws* (Uzbak: 405)
3. Bayhaqī 2: 33
4. Aḥmad b. 'Īsā 1:115, 116
5. Ibn Abī Shayba 1: 372 (see also 'Abd al-Razzāq 2: 100)
6. Ibn Abī Shayba 1: 247 (also Ṭabarānī, *Du'ā*: 1061; Sahmī: 338; Bayhaqī 2: 96 [with variations])
7. 'Abd al-Razzāq 2: 187 (also Ibn Abī Shayba 2: 534; Ṭabarānī, *Du'ā*: 1075)
8. Shāfi'ī 7: 153 (also Ibn Abī Shayba 1: 295; Aḥmad b. 'Īsā 1: 127–8; Bayhaqī 2: 143)
9. Ibn Abī Shayba 1: 258 (on *sujūd* in general)
10. Ibid. 1: 258 (on the proper manner of *sujūd* for men)
11. 'Abd al-Razzāq 3: 138 (also Ibn Abī Shayba 1: 269 [on the proper manner of *sujūd* for women]; Bayhaqī 2: 222)
12. Ibn Abī Shayba 1: 284
13. Ṭayālisī 1: 150 (also 'Abd al-Razzāq 2: 144–5 [see also 2: 141–2, 184, 267]; Aḥmad 1: 146; 'Abd b. Ḥamīd 1: 121; Bazzār 1: 265; partially also in Ibn Abī Shayba 1: 285, 2: 71, 414, 434, 437; Ibn Māja: 289, 310; Abū Dāwūd 1: 239; Tirmidhī 1: 315; Aḥmad b. 'Īsā 1: 290; Ṭabarānī, *Awsaṭ* 3: 12, and many other works)
14. 'Abd al-Razzāq 2: 240 (also Ibn Abī Shayba 1: 305 [with variations])
15. Aḥmad 1: 96, 104, 5: 88 [with variations] (also Abū Ya'lā 1: 384)
16. Ibn al-Mundhir, *Awsaṭ* (Uzbak: 421)
17. Aḥmad b. 'Īsā 1: 139, 142
18. Ibn Abī Shayba 2: 316
19. Ibn Abī Shayba 2 305 (also Bayhaqī 2: 698 [with variations])
20. 'Uqaylī 1: 55 (also Ibn 'Adī: 2679; *Ḥilya* 7: 183)
21. Ibn Abī Shayba 2: 464 (also Aḥmad b. 'Īsā 1: 187 [repeated in 1: 180]; Bazzār 1: 328)
22. 'Abd al-Razzāq 2: 507
23. Bazzār 1: 325
24. Ibn Abī Shayba 2: 489
25. 'Abd al-Razzāq 2: 126
26. Ibn Abī Shayba 2: 276
27. 'Abd al-Razzāq 2: 29
28. Ibid. 2: 305 (also Ibn Abī Shayba 2: 26 [with variations])

29. 'Abd al-Razzāq 2:122 (also Shāfi'ī 7: 153; Ibn Abī Shayba 1: 397)
30. 'Abd al-Razzāq 2: 338 (also Qāḍī Nu'mān, *Īḍāḥ*: 109b; Dāraquṭnī 1: 156; Bayhaqī 2: 256 [all with variations])
31. Qāḍī Nu'mān, *Īḍāḥ*: 110a
32. Ibn Abī Shayba 2: 64
33. 'Abd al-Razzāq 2: 352 (also Aḥmad b. 'Īsā 1: 225; Dāraquṭnī 1: 185; Bayhaqī 1: 234 [Qāḍī Nu'mān, *Īḍāḥ*: 89a-b, 85a and Ibn 'Adī: 316 offer a fuller text of this report])
34. Bayhaqī 2: 298
35. 'Abd al-Razzāq 2: 208
36. Ibn Abī Shayba 2: 324
37. 'Abd al-Razzāq 3: 463 (two variants)
38. Bazzār 1: 249
39. 'Abd al-Razzāq 3: 301; 8: 167 (see also ibid. 8: 168; Ibn Abī Shayba 2: 101; Bayhaqī 3: 179; Aḥmad b. 'Īsā 1: 188)
40. 'Abd al-Razzāq 3: 210
41. Ibn Abī Shayba 2: 104 (also Aḥmad b. 'Īsā 1: 195 [with variations])
42. Ibn Abī Shayba 2: 111 (also Ibn Abī Ḥātim, *'Ilal* 1: 198)
43. Ibn al-Ja'd: 770 (# 2015)
44. Ibn Abī Shayba 2: 278
45. Ṭabarānī, *Awsaṭ* 4: 224–5 (also Bayhaqī 3: 295)
46. Aḥmad b. 'Īsā 1: 187
47. 'Abd al-Razzāq 3: 297 (also Ibn Abī Shayba 2: 180 [with variations]; Bayhaqī 3: 295)
48. 'Abd al-Razzāq 3: 366 (also Ibn Abī Shayba 2: 160; Dāraquṭnī 2: 44; Bayhaqī 3: 283 [all with variations])
49. 'Abd al-Razzāq 3: 289, 299 (also Ibn Abī Shayba 2: 163; variants of the same text also in Ibn Māja: 411; Tirmidhī 1: 535; Aḥmad b. 'Īsā 1: 188; Bayhaqī 3: 281, 311)
50. Ibn Abī Shayba 2: 182
51. Ibid. 2: 173
52. Aḥmad b. 'Īsā 1: 187
53. Ibid. 1: 188
54. Ibid. 1: 189
55. Ibn Abī Shayba 3: 307
56. Ṭayālisī 1: 116 (also 'Abd al-Razzāq 3: 17, 56, 58; Ibn Abī Shayba 2: 241, 286; Aḥmad 1: 77, 88, 89, 98, 111, 115; Ibn Māja: 363)
57. Aḥmad 1: 89 (also 'Abd b. Ḥamīd 1: 121; Tirmidhī 1: 475; Abū Ya'lā 1: 356; Qāḍī Nu'mān, *Īḍāḥ*: 130a-b [all with variations])

58. Ibn al-Qaysarānī, *Ṣafwa* (Uzbak: 421; the text appears on p. 189 of the Beirut, 1995 edition of that work without *isnād*)
58. Ṭabarānī, *Awsaṭ*: 330
59. Aḥmad 1: 86
60. Abū Nu'aym, *Akhbār Iṣbahān* 1: 213
61. Ibn Abī Shayba 2: 523 (also Ṭabarī, *Tafsīr* 26: 180–81)
62. Ibn 'Adī: 704
63. 'Abd al-Razzāq 1: 498 (also Dāraquṭnī 1: 40; Bayhaqī 3:57)
64. Qāḍī Nu'mān, *Īḍāḥ*: 71b
65. Khaṭīb, *Ta'rīkh* 1: 283 (also Ibn al-Jawzī, *'Ilal*: 966)
66. 'Abd al-Razzāq 2: 501
67. Ibn Abī Shayba 2: 81, 82 (also Ṭabarānī, *Awsaṭ* 3: 241–2; idem, *Ṣaghīr* 1: 105 [all with variations])
68. Ibn al-Ja'd: 769
69. Ibid.: 770 (# 2016)
70. *Miṣbāḥ*: 316 (also Ibn Ṭāwūs, *Jamāl*: 91, 104–5)
71. Shahīd I, *Arba'īn*: 316
72. Ibn Ṭāwūs, *Iqbāl* 1: 459–60
73. Aḥmad, *Faḍā'il*: 616 (also Tirmidhī 5: 482–3; Nasā'ī, *'Amal*: 609; idem, *Khaṣā'iṣ*: 82)
74. Ibn Bābawayh, *Amālī*: 674–5 (also *Thawāb*: 199)
75. Ṭabarānī, *Du'ā'*: 1436
76. Ibid.: 1599
77. Ibn Abī Ḥātim 1: 179
78. Abū Dāwūd 4: 427
79. Ṭabarānī, *Awsaṭ* 7: 334
80. Ibn Abī Shayba 7: 405, 8: 47, 10: 313, 423 (also Aḥmad 1: 76; 'Abd b. Ḥamīd 1: 120; Tirmidhī 5: 527; Ṭabarānī, *Du'ā'*: 1319–20; Ṭūsī, *Amālī*: 638)
81. Ṭabarānī, *Du'ā'*: 1225–6 (also Ibn al-Najjār 2: 48)
82. Ibn Abī Ḥātim, *'Ilal*; 360 (also Ibn 'Asākir, *Arba'īn*: 63, whence *Biḥār* 76: 293–4; cf. Tirmidhī 5: 443 and the many Sunnī sources listed in the editor's footnote, and Ṭūsī, *Amālī*: 515, where Abū Isḥāq al-Sabī'ī quotes the same report from 'Alī through a different transmitter)
83. Ibn Bisṭām: 37
84. Ibid.: 17–18

Fasting:

1. Aḥmad b. 'Īsā 2: 317
2. Ibn Abī Shayba 3: 68 (also Ṭabarī, *Tahdhīb, Ibn 'Abbās*: 765 [with variations])
3. Abū Ya'lā 1: 346 (also Ibn Abī Ḥātim, *'Ilal* 1: 247; Ṭabarānī, *Awsaṭ* 9: 76–7; Bazzār 1: 494 [all with variations])
4. Dhahabī, *Tadhkira*: 612
5. Ibn Abī Shayba 3: 173
6. Ibid. 3: 81
7. 'Abd al-Razzāq 4: 242 (also Ibn Abī Shayba 3: 34; Bayhaqī 4: 259 [all with variations])
8. 'Abd al-Razzāq 4: 216 (also Ibn Abī Shayba 3: 38, 39; Bayhaqī 4: 215 [with variations])
9. Ibn al-Jawzī, *'Ilal*: 550–51; parts of this report are also quoted in Ibn Abī Shayba 3: 44, 94 (cf. Shāfi'ī 3: 65, 7: 176; 'Abd al-Razzāq 4: 256, 282; Ibn Abī Shayba 3: 65 where Abū Isḥāq al-Sabī'ī quotes the same report from Ḥārith through an intermediary)
10. Ṭabarānī, *Awsaṭ* 5: 254
11. Ibn Abī Shayba, *al-juz' al-mafqūd*: 30
12. Ibid. 3: 56 (also Ibn 'Abd al-Barr, *Tamhīd* 7: 207)
13. 'Abd al-Razzāq 4: 274 (also Ibn Abī Shayba 3: 28 [with variations])
14. Ibn Ḥazm 5: 194
15. Dāraquṭnī 2: 200

Alms-giving:

1. Yaḥyā b. Ādam: 150 (also Ibn Abī Shayba 3: 139)
2. Ṭayālisī 1: 115 (also Ḥumaydī 1: 81; Abū 'Ubayd, *Amwāl*: 463; Ibn Abī Shayba 3: 152; Saḥnūn 1: 244; Aḥmad 1: 121, 132, 146; Ibn Zanjawayh: 945, 1019, 1061; 'Abd b. Ḥamīd 1: 119; Ibn Māja: 570, 580; Abū Dāwūd 2: 99–101, 136; Aḥmad b. 'Īsā 2: 267; Abū Ya'lā 1: 256, 436; Ṭabarānī, *Ṭiwāl*: 144–6; Dāraquṭnī 2: 92, 103; Bayhaqī 4: 93, 95, 99, 106, 136, 137)
3. Dāraquṭnī 2: 149 (also Ḥākim 1: 411)
4. Ṭayālisī 1: 146 (also 'Abd al-Razzāq 11: 106; Aḥmad 1: 96, 115)
5. Yaḥyā b. Ādam: 116 (read *'an Ḥārith wa 'Āṣim* for *'an Ḥārith aw 'Āṣim*, as in all similar cases)

Pilgrimage to Mecca:

1. Tirmidhī 2: 166 (also Ṭabarī, *Tafsīr* 4: 16–17; Sahmī: 391; 'Uqaylī 4: 348; Ibn 'Adī: 2580)
2. Ṭayālisī 1: 148 (# 148, also Ibn Abī Shayba 4: 105, 10: 367; Ṭabarānī, *Du'ā'*: 1200–201; Bayhaqī 5: 79)
3. Ibn Ḥazm 5: 151
4. Ibn Abī Shayba, *al-juz' al-mafqūd*: 398
5. Ibid.: 175 (cf. ibid. 2: 26; 'Abd al-Razzāq 2: 305)
6. Ṭabarī, *Tafsīr* 10: 64

Holy war:

1. Ibn Abī Shayba 12: 482 (also Ibn Abī Ḥātim, *'Ilal* 1: 315)
2. 'Uqaylī 4: 451 (also Ṭūsī, *Amālī*: 383–4 [read *Yūsuf b. Isḥāq 'an Abī Isḥāq 'an al-Ḥārith* for *Yūsuf b. Isḥāq b. Abī Isḥāq 'an al-Ḥārith*]; Khaṭīb, *Mūḍiḥ* 2: 261 [combining a similar text to that of 'Uqaylī with # 1 above])
3. 'Abd al-Razzāq 3: 547, 5: 277
4. Ibn 'Adī: 2149–50 (also Quḍā'ī 2: 215; Ibn 'Asākir 18: 81–2)

Property:

1. Ibn Abī Ḥātim, *'Ilal* 1: 390 (also Ibn 'Adī: 498; Bayhaqī, *Shu'ab* 2: 88)
2. Abū Ya'lā 2: 401
3. Fākihī 3: 50 (also *Faqīh* 3: 267; *Tahdhīb* 7: 162)
4. Aḥmad 1: 85, 93
5. 'Abd al-Razzāq 8: 124
6. Thaqafī 1: 111–112
7. Shāfi'ī 7: 167

Marriage and divorce:

1. *Kāfī* 5: 326
2. Ibn 'Adī; 1532 (also Sahmī: 257)
3. 'Abd al-Razzāq 7: 270
4. Ibn Abī Shayba 4: 224
5. Abū 'Ubayd, *Nāsikh*: 124 (also Bayhaqī 7: 306 [read *Abū Isḥāq al-Sabī'ī 'an al-Ḥārith* for *Abū Isḥāq 'an al-Sha'bī 'an al-Ḥārith*])
6. Ibn Abī Shayba 5: 198
7. Aḥmad b. 'Īsā 3: 92
8. Ibid. 3: 95
9. Ibid. 3: 112

Dietary:

1. Ibn Abī Shayba 8: 87
2. Dāraquṭnī 4: 274
3. 'Uqaylī 2: 324, 4: 123

Inheritance:

1. Ibn Abī Shayba 11: 372
2. Ṭayālisī 1: 148 (also 'Abd Al-Razzāq 10: 249; Shāfi'ī 4: 29; Ibn Abī Shayba 10: 160, 11: 402; Aḥmad 1: 79, 131, 144; Dārimī 2: 368; Ibn Māja: 906, 915; Tirmidhī 3: 600–01, 623; Ṭabarī, *Tafsīr* 4: 280–81; *Tahdhīb* 9: 326, 327)
3. 'Abd al-Razzāq 10: 287 (see Ibn Abī Shayba 11: 250 [with variations])
4. Abū Ya'lā 2: 297 (also Ibn 'Adī: 1889)
5. Ibn Abī Shayba 11: 258
6. Dāraquṭnī 4: 68 (also Bayhaqī 6: 253)
7. 'Abd al-Razzāq 10: 251
8. Ibn Ḥazm 9: 305
9. Ibn Abī Shayba 11: 149 (also Ibn 'Adī; 2511 [with a much longer text])
10. 'Abd al-Razzāq 9: 66 (also Ibn Abī Shayba 11: 202)
11. Ibn Abī Shayba 11: 155
12. Ibid. 11: 157
13. Ibn Ḥazm 9: 321

Penal code:

1. 'Abd al-Razzāq 10: 199
2. Dāraquṭnī 3: 177
3. Ibn Abī Ḥātim, *'Ilal* 1: 459

IV VIRTUES (*FAḌĀ'IL*)

1. *Kamāl*: 237 (also Bazzār 3: 221)
2. Mufīd, *Amālī*: 318
3. Ṭabarānī, *Awsaṭ* 1: 220 (also *Thawāb*: 186; Bayhaqī, *Shu'ab* 2: 216)
4. Ibn al-Juḥām: 135
5. Abū Nu'aym, *Mā nazal*: 276
6. Ṭabarānī, *Awsaṭ* 3: 371–2
7. Ibn Kathīr 2: 564–5
8. Ṭūsī, *Amālī*: 353 (also Khaṭīb, *Talkhīṣ*: 308–9; Ibn 'Asākir 42: 385)

9. ʿUqaylī 2: 22 (also Ibn ʿAsākir 42: 331)
10. Ibn ʿAsākir 42: 360
11. Ṭūsī, *Amālī*: 248, 633 (also Ibn ʿAsākir 70: 113)
12. Aḥmad, *Faḍāʾil*: 613 (also Ibn ʿAsākir 42: 337)
13. *Bishārat al-Muṣṭafā*: 166
14. Ibn Qutayba, *Maʿārif*: 210
15. *Manāqib* 2: 306 (quoting Ibn ʿUqda's *Dalāʾil*)
16. Suyūṭī, *Laʾālī* 1: 334
17. Mufīd, *Amālī*: 271
18. Ṭabarānī, *Awsaṭ* 7: 127–8 (also Abū Nuʿaym, *Akhbār Iṣbahān* 1: 100)
19. Ibn ʿAsākir 13: 195
20. Ṭabarānī, *Akhbār al-Ḥasan*: 75 (also idem, *Kabīr* 3: 47)
21. Ṭabarānī, *Akhbār al-Ḥasan*: 56–7 (also idem, *Kabīr* 3: 36)
22. Abū Ṭālib: 92
23. Ibn ʿAsākir 24: 460–61 (also Kalābādhī, *Baḥr*: 87)
24. Abū Nuʿaym, *Akhbār Iṣbahān* 2: 361
25. Ibid. 1: 172
26. Dāraquṭnī 3: 80 (also Bayhaqī, *Shuʿab* 7: 359; Ṭūsī, *Amālī*: 473 [both with longer texts]; Khaṭīb, *Faqīh* 1: 32; Quḍāʿī 1: 203)

V ETHICS

1. *Ḥilya* 2: 35 (also Ibn ʿAsākir 13: 254–5 [with a fuller text]; partially also in Ibn Ḥibbān, *Majrūḥīn* 2: 306; Quḍāʿī 1: 78, 2: 38, 39; Ibn ʿAdī 1: 52; cf. Ibn Shuʿba: 225–6 [without *isnād*]; *Maʿānī*: 244, 245, 247, 256, 258 [quoting Aṣbagh b. Nubāta from Ḥārith])
2. Ṭūsī, *Amālī*: 457–8)
3. Quḍāʿī 1: 232
4. ʿUqaylī 3: 135
5. Khaṭīb, *Faqīh* 2: 160
6. *Firdaws* (Uzbak: 427)
7. Aḥmad 1: 88–9 (also Dārimī 2: 275–6; Ibn Māja: 461; Tirmidhī 4: 453; Ṭūsī, *Amālī*: 478, 634–5; partially also in Ibn Abī Shayba 3: 235, 8: 435)
8. Ibn Abī Shayba 8: 502 (also Ṭabarānī, *Awsaṭ* 5: 349; idem, *Duʿāʾ*: 1683–4 [with variations])
9. Ibn Abī Shayba 8: 497
10. Ṭabarānī, *Awsaṭ* 7: 155 (also idem, *Duʿāʾ*: 1690)
11. Ṭūṣī, *Amālī*: 516
12. Ibn ʿAdī: 798

13. Ibn Abī Ḥātim, *'Ilal* 2: 212 (also Ṭabarānī, *Awsaṭ* 5: 364; Bayhaqī 10: 235)
14. Khaṭīb, *Ta'rīkh* 3: 186
15. Abū Nu'aym, *Akhbār Iṣbahān* 1: 178
16. Ibn 'Adī: 520; Bayhaqī, *Shu'ab* 6: 493
17. Ibn 'Asākir 13: 31, 14: 30
18. Ṭūsī, *Amālī*: 458
19. *Khiṣāl*: 124
20. Khaṭīb, *Taqyīd*: 89
21. Aḥmad al-Dīnawarī 2: 103 (also Khaṭīb, *Kifāya*: 262)
22. Ibn 'Adī: 473 (whence Sahmī: 211)
23. *Firdaws* (Uzbak: 402; also Suyūṭī, *La'ālī* 2: 375)
24. *Firdaws* (Uzbak: 399–400; also Ibn al-Jawzī, *'Ilal*: 709)
25. 'Abd al-Razzāq 10: 458
26. Bayhaqī, *Shu'ab* 1: 493–4
27. Ibn Abī Shayba 8: 120
28. *Firdaws* (Uzbak: 419)
29. Khaṭīb, *Muttafiq*: 1844
30. Ibn 'Adī: 2677
31. 'Uqaylī 4: 187 (also Ibn 'Adī: 2410)
32. Rāmhurmuzī: 499 (also Bazzār 2: 100, 430; Ṭabarānī, *Awsaṭ* 5: 330 [with variations])
33. Ṭabarānī, *Awsaṭ* 7: 128 (also idem, *Ṣaghīr* 2: 93; Khaṭīb, *Talkhīṣ*: 795)
34. *Firdaws* (Uzbak: 427, # 276)
35. Ibn 'Adī: 1778
36. *Kāfī* 2: 316 (also *Khiṣāl*: 43)
37. Ibn Bābawayh, *Amālī*: 295–6 (also *Ma'ānī*: 231 [read *'Āṣim b. [Abī] Ḍamra wa 'l-Ḥārith* for *'Āṣim b. [Abī] Ḍamra 'an al-Ḥārith*])[42]
38. Ibn Bābawayh, *Amālī*: 505
39. *Khiṣāl*: 15
40. Ibid.: 45–6
41. Ṭabarānī, *Awsaṭ* 2: 352 (also idem, *Ṣaghīr* 1: 30; Ṭūsī, *Amālī*: 405)

42. 'Āṣim is not attested to have ever related from Ḥārith (Mizzī 13: 497–8). Sabī'ī, in particular, is quoted as saying that 'Āṣim never related anything to him from anyone other than 'Alī (ibid. 13: 497, though this may not exclude citations from 'Alī through an intermediary). The chain of transmission of the report in question should therefore read as Sabī'ī from 'Āṣim *and* Ḥārith, as in numerous other cases (e.g. Saḥnūn 1: 244; Ibn Zanjawayh: 945, 1061; Abū Dāwūd 2: 99, 100; Tirmidhī 2: 8–9; Ṭabarānī, *Ṭiwāl*: 144–5; Dāraquṭnī 2: 103; Bayhaqī, *Shu'ab* 2: 216; idem, *Sunan* 4: 93, 95, 99, 106, 136, 137).

42. Ibn ʿAsākir 18: 81–2 (partially also in Ibn ʿAdī: 2149; Suyūṭī, *Laʾālī* 2: 455)
43. *Firdaws* (Uzbak: 410)
44. Ibid. (Uzbak: 417)
45. *Kāfī* 5: 516
46. ʿAbd al-Razzāq 11: 402 (also Bazzār 4: 151)
47. Ibn ʿAbd al-Barr, *Jāmiʿ*: 985
48. Ibn Ḥibbān, *Majrūḥīn* 3:67 (also Khaṭīb, *Taʾrīkh* 13; 411)
49. Aḥmad 1: 67, 89, 93 (also ʿAbd b. Ḥamīd 1: 122)
50. Ṭabarānī, *Akhbār al-Ḥasan*: 111–14 (also *Maʿānī*: 245, 247, 256, 258 where a few passages from this long text are cited from Ḥārith through a different transmitter)

VI MISCELLANEOUS

1. Ibn ʿAdī: 2149
2. Abū Muḥammad al-Samarqandī, *Dhikr mā fī hādhihi ʾl-umma min al-abdāl* (Uzbak: 410)
3. *Firdaws* (Uzbak: 409)
4. Ibid. (Uzbak: 383–4; see also Dhahabī, *ʿUluww*: 45; for a revised version of this report, see Ayyūbī, *Manāhil al-silsila*: 75)

VII LATER CONTRIBUTIONS

Like some other well known chains of transmission, Abū Isḥāq from Ḥārith from ʿAlī was a convenient way for latecomers to authenticate their own contributions. It also served as a convenient recourse in sectarian debates for the ʿUthmāniyya to rebuff the Shīʿites by putting an anti-Shīʿite creed into the mouth of ʿAlī through Ḥārith, who was nevertheless identified by all Sunnī authorities as a staunch Shīʿite. What follows is a partial list of narratives of the above two categories, which in all likelihood did not go back to the Book of Ḥārith.

Pro-ʿUthmānī

1. Dhahabī, *Siyar* 3: 144 (other sources quote this report from Shaʿbī, a transmitter well known for his pro-Umayyad tendencies, indicating that *Sabīʿī* in the above-mentioned source is most likely corrupt; see Ibn Abī Shayba 15: 293; ʿAbd Allāh b. Aḥmad: 223; Ibn ʿAsākir 59: 151).
2. Bayhaqī 1: 305 (cf. Aḥmad 1: 103, 129; Abū Yaʿlā 1: 335; Bayhaqī 1: 304, all quoting the same report from Sulamī from ʿAlī)

3. Aḥmad, *Faḍāʾil* 1: 308 (also Ibn ʿAsākir 30: 377, 44: 204)
4. Ibn ʿAsākir 39: 128
5. Ibn ʿAdī: 498 (also Ibn ʿAsākir 42: 33)
6. Khaṭīb, *Taʾrīkh* 10: 192
7. Abū ʾl-ʿArab: 108
8. Ibn Saʿd 3: 114 (also Ibn Abī Shayba 12: 113; Aḥmad 1: 76, 95, 107, 108; Ibn Māja: 49; Fasawī 2: 534; Tirmidhī 6: 139–40)
9. Aḥmad, *Faḍāʾil* 1: 434
10. *Firdaws* (Uzbak: 404)
11. Ibid. (Uzbak: 380; also Ibn ʿAsākir 23: 462)
12. Ibn Abī Shayba 1: 19 (also Ṭabarī, *Tafsīr* 6: 128; Bayhaqī 1: 71 [with an addition])
13. Aḥmad al-Dīnawarī 8: 294–5 (also Ibn ʿAsākir 30: 118)

Pro-Shīʿite

To be sure, later Shīʿites have also used the same link to authenticate some of their own contributions. An example is a report with the full list of the twelve Imāms in Ibn Shādhān: 23–4 (whence Khwārazmī, *Maqtal*: 145; see also *Biḥār* 26: 316 [quoting Ibn al-Juḥām through Ḥasan b. Sulaymān's *Tafḍīl al-aʾimma ʿalā ʾl-anbiyāʾ*]; also *Manāqib* 1: 292 and Ibn Ṭāwūs, *Ṭarāʾif* 1: 256 where *Abū Isḥāq ʿan al-Ḥārith wa Saʿīd ʿan ʿAlī* is corrupted to *Abū Ishāq b. al-Ḥārīth ʿan Saʿīd ʿan ʿAlī* and *Abū Isḥāq b. al-Ḥārith wa Saʿīd ʿan ʿAlī*, respectively). It is not unlikely that a text did originally exist but was later added to and updated, a common enough procedure in many other similar instances.

VIII OTHERS

There are also a number of reports which the sources quote on the authority of Abū Isḥāq al-Sabīʿī who quotes them from Ḥārith from ʿAlī through an intermediary, signifying normal verbal transmission rather than quotation from a written record. Examples are as follows:

1. Sabīʿī, from ʿAbd Allāh b. Murra, from Ḥārith: Shāfiʿī 3: 165, 7: 176 (also ʿAbd al-Razzāq 4: 256, 282; Ibn Abī Shayba 3: 65)
2. Sabīʿī, from Karīm, from Ḥārith: ʿUqaylī 4: 11
3. Sabīʿī, from ʿAbd Allāh b. al-Ḥārith, from Ḥārith: Dhahabī, *ʿUluww*: 45

As noted above, quotations from ʿAlī by Khilās b. ʿAmr al-Hajarī al-Baṣrī and ʿAbd al-Aʿlā b. ʿĀmir al-Thaʿlabī al-Kūfī are also suspected to have been from the book of Ḥārith. Uzbak: 849–63, 1967–76 supplies a total of sixty narratives of this nature by Khilās (but there are still others as in Aḥmad b. ʿĪsā 3: 192) and some twenty by ʿAbd al-Aʿlā.

2. *Kitāb al-masāʾil allatī akhbara bihā Amīr al-Muʾminīn al-Yahūdī*

(*Fihrist*: 111). This is a Kūfan Shīʿite sectarian pamphlet, most likely from the Umayyad period, in the form of a register of answers given by ʿAlī to questions posed to him by the head of the Jewish community (of Kūfa?) after the battle of Nahrawān. According to the chain of transmission mentioned in *Fihrist*: 111, the work is quoted by ʿAmr b. Abī ʾl-Miqdām, an early second century transmitter, on the authority of Abū Isḥāq al-Sabīʿī from Ḥārith. The full text of this pamphlet has survived in *Khiṣāl*: 365–82.

3: Aṣbagh b. Nubāta

Abū ʾl-Qāsim Aṣbagh b. Nubāta al-Tamīmī al-Ḥanẓalī al-Mujāshiʿī, a close associate and a member of the elite force of ʿAlī in Kūfa. He lived to an old age.

Ibn al-Kalbī, *Jamhara*: 205; Naṣr b. Muzāḥim: 406, 442–3; Pseudo-Nāshiʾ: 22; Ibn Saʿd 6: 247; Khalīfa b. Khayyāṭ, *Taʾrīkh*: 184; Yaḥyā b. Maʿīn 2: 41; Bukhārī, *Kabīr* 2: 35; Fasawī 3: 39, 66, 190; Barqī: 36, 38; ʿUqaylī 1: 129–30; Ibn Abī Ḥātim 2: 319; Kashshī: 5, 98, 103, 221–2; Ibn Ḥibbān, *Majrūḥīn* 1: 173–4; Ibn ʿAdī: 398; Dāraquṭnī, *Muʾtalif*: 256; ʿĀṣimī 1: 276; Najāshī: 8; *Fihrist*: 37–8; *Rijāl*: 57, 93; Mizzī 3: 308–11 (and other sources named in the editor's footnote).

Ibn al-Kalbī gives Aṣbagh's full genealogical line of descent from Tamīm. Barqī: 38 identifies him as a Yemeni. Yemen was not a land of Tamīm. The *nisba* of *Tamīmī* was possibly corrupted to *Yamanī* in the author's source. That he was a member of ʿAlī's elite force is attested in Naṣr b. Muzāḥim: 443 and Kashshī: 5, 103. He was present with ʿAlī in battles of both the Camel (Qāḍī Nuʿmān, *Sharḥ* 2: 290) and Ṣiffīn (Naṣr b. Muzāḥim: 406, 442–3 where a three-line *rajaz* is assigned to him in the context of that battle). He is said to have carried a letter from ʿAlī to Muʿāwiya in the course of the exchange of messages that preceded the battle of Ṣiffīn (Khwārazmī, *Manāqib*: 205 where a three-line poem by Aṣbagh is also quoted).

That he lived into old age is reported in Kashshī: 221–2, Najāshī and *Fihrist*. A work is ascribed to him on the killing of Ḥusayn in 61, but the ascription is possibly wrong (see below). A report in Qāḍī Nu'mān, *Sharḥ* 2: 290 would imply that he lived until the time of Ḥajjāj in Kūfa (years 75–95).

For the Shī'ites, he was a loyal and pious disciple of 'Alī and a praiseworthy person. The Sunnīs, who did not have much problem with him as a person, nevertheless downgraded his transmission. Ibn Ḥibbān, *Majrūḥīn* 1: 173–4 explains the reason as Aṣbagh's zealous attachment to and love for 'Alī, a fact that made him quote what Ibn Ḥibbān describes as "calamities". Ibn Ḥajar, *Tahdhīb* 1: 316 too confirms that Aṣbagh's transmission was rejected because he was accused of *rafḍ*. 'Uqaylī 1: 129–30 accuses him of belief in *raj'a*, a point attested in, for instance, Ibn al-Juḥām: 212–13. Ibn 'Adī: 398 shows a more favorable attitude towards him. He thought the reason that Aṣbagh's transmissions were not accepted by the Sunnī authorities was the unreliability of those who quoted from him. "Should the transmitter from him happen to be a reliable person," Ibn 'Adī says, "there is no problem with his transmission in my opinion". This explains why, despite all the negative points made against Aṣbagh's transmission, later Sunnī scholars at times disqualified reports from him by finding fault in transmitters from him rather than directing their attacks at him personally, a point that was to puzzle the late Muḥammad Nāṣir al-Dīn al-Albānī in his *Silsilat al-aḥādīth al-ḍa'īfa* 2: 68.

A report in Muḥammad b. Sulaymān 2: 166 suggests that Aṣbagh, at least occasionally, kept written records of 'Alī's statements. Najāshī: 8 names Aṣbagh among the first Shī'ite authors of books. However, what Najāshī and *Fibrist*: 37–8 list as his works are simply two long documents and a long *ḥadīth* as follows:

1. 'Alī's alleged testament (*'ahd*) to his designated governor of Egypt, Mālik al-Ashtar. The text is preserved in the *Nahj al-balāgha* (letter 53).[43]
2. 'Alī's letter of advice (*waṣiyya*) to his son, Muḥammad Ibn al-Ḥanafiyya. The text is preserved in *Faqīh* 4: 384–92. *Kāfī* 5: 338, 510 quotes excerpts from a letter of advice said to have been written by 'Alī for his son Ḥasan, and notes that the same statements were quoted by Aṣbagh as parts of 'Alī's letter to his son Muḥammad. The text of 'Alī's letter to Ḥasan which has sentences in common with the one quoted by Aṣbagh is preserved in the *Nahj al-balāgha* (letter 31),[44] and earlier sources such as Ibn Shu'ba: 68–88; Kulaynī's *Kitāb al-rasā'il* and Ḥasan b. 'Abd Allāh al-'Askarī's *al-Zawājir wa 'l-mawā'iẓ* (both as quoted in Ibn Ṭāwūs, *Kashf*: 157–73). 'Askarī identified Aṣbagh's account as a variant of 'Alī's letter to Ḥasan (ibid.: 158).

---

43. *Nahj al-balāgha*: 426–45.
44. Ibid.: 391–406. For similarities, compare paragraphs on pp. 402, 404, 405 here with corresponding material ibid.: 384, 386, 392 (respectively).

3. A long report on the killing of Ḥusayn that the Shī'ite scholar, Abū Bakr Aḥmad b. 'Abd Allāh b. Jullīn al-Dūrī al-Warrāq (d. 377) quoted on the authority of Ibn 'Uqda through a chain of transmission that went back to Abū 'l-Jārūd (*Fihrist*: 38). There are a few reports on the topic quoted in early sources on the authority of Aṣbagh from 'Alī that may have been parts of that report, including the following:

   - Abū Nu'aym, *Dalā'il al-nubuwwa*: 211
   - Qāḍī Nu'mān, *Sharḥ* 2: 137

There are two quotations from his son, Qāsim b. Aṣbagh b. Nubāta, on the killing of Ḥusayn in Ṭabarī 5: 449–50 and *Maqātil*: 117–18 (the latter also in *'Iqāb*: 259–60 with a fuller text), both clearly parts of a longer account. One is tempted to suggest that the same account may have been erroneously attributed to Aṣbagh.

To the above list, two other items may be added:

1. *Khabar wafāt Salmān al-Fārsī*

A long report on the death of Salmān al-Fārsī in the form of an independent tract with a prologue and epilogue. This is an esoteric work, clearly a contribution by the Extremists of later periods. The full text of this tract is quoted on the alleged authority of Aṣbagh in Shādhān b. Jibrīl: 86–92.

2. *Kitāb Aṣbagh*

A large number of reports are cited in early sources on the authority of Aṣbagh citing 'Alī's statements and acts during his years as caliph. The volume of this body of material has persuaded some recent authors to think that, as in the case of Ḥārith al-A'war, there should have been in early centuries a notebook of reports from or about 'Alī attributed to Aṣbagh.[45] Though a part of this material may well go back to such a notebook if it ever existed, it is also plausible that in many of these quotations, his name was used by later transmitters simply as a convenient way to document material in an unbroken chain of transmission to the time of 'Alī. The chief "transmitter" from him, Sa'd al-Iskāf, was a

45. See Khu'ī 3: 225.

professional preacher/storyteller (Kashshī: 215), and "Sa'd from Aṣbagh from 'Alī" was also as popular a link in later times as "Sabī'ī from Ḥārith from 'Alī."

Here is a list of reports from or about 'Alī,[46] recorded in the sources on the authority of Aṣbagh:

I ON VIRTUES

(a) the virtues of 'Alī

i. in the Qur'ān

1. Furāt: 50
2. *Kāfī* 1: 428 (also 'Alī b. Ibrāhīm 2: 148–9)
3. *Manāqib* 3: 80 (also *Ta'wīl al-āyāt*: 759–60)
4. 'Ayyāshī 1: 212 (also Ḥaskānī 1: 178)
5. *Manāqib* 3: 85
6. Ibn al-Juḥām: 109
7. Ibid.: 212–13
8. Ibid.: 213
9. Ibid.: 281
10. Furāt: 253 (see also *Manāqib* 3: 93)
11. Ḥaskānī 1: 198
12. Ṣaffār: 497 (also Furāt: 142–3; Ḥaskānī 1: 263 [with variations])
13. 'Ayyāshī 1: 14 (also Ibn al-Juḥām: 318)
14. 'Alī b. Ibrāhīm 2: 417
15. Ibn al-Juḥām: 471
16. Ḥaskānī 2: 405 (also Suyūṭī, *La'ālī* 1: 192)

ii. from the Prophet

1. Ṭūsī, *Amālī*: 309 (also Ibn 'Asākir 42: 378)
2. Ibn 'Asākir 42: 168
3. *Kamāl*: 669
4. Muḥammad b. Sulaymān 1: 207 (also 'Āṣimī 2: 195–7, 214)
5. Muḥammad b. Sulaymān 2: 427
6. Ibid. 2: 485
7. Abū Ṭālib: 73
8. Ibn Bābawayh, *Amālī*: 450

---

46. Almost everything quoted from Aṣbagh is either from or about 'Alī. There are only a very few exceptions to this rule, such as in 'Abd al-Razzāq 3: 574 (from Fāṭima); Khazzāz: 223, and Abū Ṭālib: 376 (both from Ḥasan al-Mujtabā from the Prophet).

9. Ibid.: 731
10. Ibn Shādhān: 63
11. Ibn Shādhān: 71–2 (also Ibn Ṭāwūs, *Yaqīn*: 244–5)
12. *Maḥāsin* 1: 291 (also Ṭūsī, *Amālī*: 181; Ḥaskānī 1: 517)
13. *Manāqib* 2: 237
14. Ṭūsī, *Amālī*: 223
15. *Manāqib* 3: 67
16. Ḥaskānī 2: 232 (also Khwārazmī, *Manāqib*: 325)
17. Khaṭīb, *Ta'rīkh* 13: 122 (also Ibn 'Asākir 42: 327–8; Ibn Ṭāwūs, *Yaqīn*: 149–50)
18. Ibn Ṭāwūs, *Ṭarā'if* 1: 147 (quoting Ibn Mardawayh's *Manāqib*)
19. Ṭūsī, *Amālī*: 406
20. Ṣaffār: 51
21. Ibn Bābawayh, *Amālī*: 563
22. Ibid.: 564
23. Khazzāz: 132
24. *Mīzān* 1: 271
25. Ibn al-Athīr, *Usd* 5: 205 (also Ibn Ḥajar, *Iṣāba* 7: 161 [quoting Ibn 'Uqda's *Kitāb al-muwālāt*])

iii. by 'Alī himself

1. Qāḍī Nu'mān, *Sharḥ* 1: 152, 168 (also *Manāqib* 3: 208 [from Ṭabarī in his work on the *Ḥadīth al-Walāya*])
2. Ibn Bābawayh, *Amālī*: 702 (also *Faqīh* 4: 419–20)
3. Ibn Bābawayh, *Amālī*: 77
4. Ibid.: 92
5. *Manāqib* 3: 62
6. Muḥammad b. Sulaymān 1: 392, 395 (also 'Āṣimī 2: 390–91)
7. 'Āṣimī 2: 417–20
8. Irbilī 2: 32
9. Ibn Bābawayh, *Amālī*: 422–5 (also *Tawḥīd*: 305–8)
10. Qāḍī Nu'mān, *Sharḥ* 1: 192
11. *Khiṣāl*: 643, 644, 651
12. Kashshī: 221–2

iv. by others

1. Ibn Bābawayh, *Amālī*: 724
2. Muḥammad b. Sulaymān 2: 15
3. *Manāqib* 2: 56

(b) the virtues of his family

1. Ḥibarī: 44 (also 'Ayyāshī 1: 9; *Kāfī* 2: 627; Furāt: 46–8 [with variations]; Qāḍī Nu'mān, *Sharḥ* 2: 353 [like Furāt])
2. Ibn al-Juḥām: 317
3. Muḥammad b. Sulaymān 2: 166
4. Ṣaffār: 111
5. Ibid.: 268
6. Furāt: 394–5
7. Ibid.: 285–6
8. *Manāqib* 2: 104
9. Ibid. 3: 373–5
10. 'Ayyāshī 2: 229 (also *Kāfī* 1: 217; 'Alī b. Ibrāhīm 1: 86)
11. Khaṭīb, *Talkhīṣ*: 111
12. Ibn al-Juḥām: 478
13. Ibid.: 151
14. Ibid.: 181 (also Furāt: 278; Ḥaskānī 1: 524)
15. *Kāfī* 1: 450 (also Furāt: 112–13 [with variations]; Qāḍī Nu'mān, *Sharḥ* 1: 124; partially also in Ṭabarānī, *Kabīr* 3: 151; Ḥākim 3: 192)
16. Ibn Qūlawayh: 115
17. Abū 'Ubayd, *Amwāl*: 525
18. Ibn Bābawayh, *Amālī*: 755
19. *Manāqib* 3: 326–7
20. *Kamāl*: 174–5
21. Fakhār b. Ma'add: 106

(c) the virtues of the Shī'a

1. 'Ayyāshī 2: 124
2. Furāt: 293
3. Ibid.: 311–12
4. Ibid.: 155
5. Muḥammad b. Sulaymān 2: 297 (also *Irshād* 1: 42)
6. Muḥammad b. Sulaymān 1: 404 (also Ṭūsī, *Amālī*: 228)
7. Ibn Bābawayh, *Ṣifāt*: 171
8. Ḥusayn b. Sa'īd, *Mu'min*: 16 (also Ṭūsī, *Amālī*: 409–10)
9. Nu'mānī: 209–10
10. Mufīd, *Amālī*: 3–7
11. Ṭūsī, *Amālī*: 650
12. Ṣaffār: 21–2

(d) the *faḍā'il* of Kūfa

1. Ibn Sa'd 6: 86 (also Ṭabarī, *Ta'rīkh* 4: 59 [with variations])
2. *Ghayba*: 473 (quoting Faḍl b. Shādhān's work on *Ghayba*)
3. Qāḍī Nu'mān, *Sharḥ* 2: 416–17 (also Ṭūsī, *Amālī*: 51)
4. Ibn Qūlawayh: 72
5. Naṣr b. Muzāḥim: 126–7
6. Ibn Bābawayh, *Amālī*: 298 (also *Faqīh* 1: 231–2)

(e) miscellaneous

1. *Ikhtiṣāṣ*: 221–2
2. *Firdaws* (Uzbak: 99; also Ibn 'Asākir 44: 196)

II ON THE LIFE OF 'ALĪ AND THE EVENTS OF HIS CALIPHATE

(a) the battle of the Camel

1. Furāt: 111–13 (also Qāḍī Nu'mān, *Sharḥ* 1: 124; partially also in *Kāfī* 1: 450)
2. 'Ayyāshī 1: 200
3. Mufīd, *Kāfi'a*: 31
4. Ibid.: 34
5. 'Ayyāshī 1: 136
6. Qāḍī Nu'mān, *Sharḥ* 2: 290
7. *Manāqib* 2: 98
8. *Ma'ānī*: 168
9. Ibn Abī 'l-Ḥadīd 1: 248–9 (quoting Abū Mikhnaf's *Kitāb al-Jamal*)
10. Ibid. 1: 263 (quoting Abū Mikhnaf, *op. cit.*)

(b) the battle of Ṣiffīn

1. 'Abd al-Karīm b. Ṭāwūs: 23
2. Kashshī: 98 (also Qāḍī Nu'mān, *Sharḥ* 2: 12; Ḥākim 3: 402; Sharīf al-Raḍī, *Khaṣā'iṣ*: 53)
3. Kashshī: 103 (also *Ikhtiṣāṣ*: 65)
4. Ibn 'Asākir 42: 474
5. *Ikhtiṣāṣ*: 181
6. Naṣr b. Muzāḥim: 159–60
7. Ibid.: 322–3 (also Furāt: 70; Mufīd, *Amālī*: 167)

(c) the battle of Nahrawān

1. *Tawḥīd*: 225

2. Abū 'l-Shaykh, *Akhlāq al-Nabī*: 133
3. Ibn Ṭāwūs, *Faraj*: 105–7
4. Abū Ṭālib: 146

(d) **'Alī's assassination**

1. Abū Mikhnaf, *Maqtal Amīr al-Mu'minīn* (*Biḥār* 42: 261–3; also *Irshād* 1: 12 [with variations])
2. *'Ilal* 1: 166
3. Muḥammad b. Sulaymān 2: 37
4. Qāḍī Nu'mān, *Sharḥ* 1: 165–6, 2: 435 (also 'Uqaylī 3: 130; Abū 'l-'Arab; 101 [with a fuller version]; *Manāqib* 3: 313; Ibn 'Asākir 47: 480 [with variations in most])
5. Abū 'l-'Arab: 95 (also Ibn 'Asākir, 42: 555)
6. *Irshād* 1: 14
7. *Manāqib* 2: 271 (from Ṣafwānī's *Kitāb al-iḥan wa l-miḥan*)
8. Abū Nu'aym, *Akhbār Iṣbahān* 2: 60
9. Mufīd, *Amālī*: 351–3

(e) **his conduct in Kūfa**

1. Naṣr b. Muzāḥim: 5
2. *Kāfī* 3: 493
3. 'Ayyāshī 1: 14
4. Abū 'Ubayd, *Amwāl*: 86 (also Ibn Zanjawayh : 253; Bayhaqī 6: 150 [both with variations]; partially also in Aḥmad b. 'Īsā 3: 190)
5. Aḥmad b. 'Īsā 3: 194
6. *Firdaws* (Uzbak: 102)
7. *Makārim al-akhlāq*: 129 (from Ibn Bābawayh's *Zuhd Amīr al-Mu'minīn*; partially also in *Manāqib* 2: 97)
8. Saḥnūn 2: 52 (also Ibn Ḥazm 7: 325; Ibn al-Qayyim, *Aḥkām*: 36; idem, *Ṭuruq*: 69)
9. Qāḍī Nu'mān, *Sharḥ* 2: 361 (also Ibn Bābawayh, *Amālī*: 357–8)
10. Ṣaffār: 306 (also *Khiṣāl*: 644–5)
11. Naṣr b. Muzāḥim: 231
12. Abū Nu'aym, *Akhbār Iṣbahān* 1: 45
13. Ibn al-Juḥām: 297–8
14. Ibn 'Asākir 42: 523
15. 'Ayyāshī 2: 285
16. *Maḥāsin*: 352 (also 'Alī b. Ibrāhīm 2: 281; Ibn Bābawayh, *Amālī*: 597; *Faqīh* 2: 272–3)

17. Kashshī: 127
18. ʿAyyāshī 1: 360–61 (cf. Shāfiʿī 7: 154; Abū Yaʿlā 1: 322; Bazzār 4: 93)

(f) his judicial decisions

There are a relatively large number of reports from Aṣbagh on ʿAlī's judicial decisions, both from his time as caliph and before. The mid-third century Shīʿite scholar Ibrāhīm b. Hāshim al-Qummī included most of this material in his *Qaḍāyā Amīr al-Muʾminīn* which has survived. A contemporary author tries to identify this as a work of Aṣbagh related by Ibrāhīm.[47] The book as it stands cannot be by Aṣbagh as it also includes much material quoted from authorities other than him. It lacks part of what has been quoted from Aṣbagh in other sources or, more significantly, quotes them on different authorities.

Here is a list of reports quoted from Aṣbagh on ʿAlī's judicial decisions:

1. *Qaḍāyā Amīr al-Muʾminīn*: 27 (also *Kāfī* 7: 265)
2. *Faqīh* 3: 20–22 (also *Qaḍāyā*: 34–7 [from a different transmitter]; Ibn al-Qayyim, *Ṭuruq*: 89–91 [with no *isnād*])
3. *Faqīh* 3: 24 (also *Qaḍāyā*: 33 [from a different transmitter])
4. Ibn al-Qayyim: 69–70 (also *Manāqib* 2: 363 [with variations and without *isnād*])
5. *Qaḍāyā*: 124–5 (see also *Manāqib* 2: 358 where a different version of this is quoted, with no *isnād*, as ʿAlī's answer to a question from the king of Rūm)
6. *Qaḍāyā*: 53–4 (also Qāḍī Nuʿmān, *Sharḥ* 2: 325–7; *Irshād* 1: 213)
7. *Qaḍāyā*: 60–63 (also *Kāfī* 7: 372–3; Ibn al-Qayyim: 71–2; *Faqīh* 3: 24–7 [with variations and from a different transmitter])
8. Ibn al-Qayyim: 96–7 (also *Kāfī* 7: 294 [on a different authority]; *Faqīh* 3: 27 [with variations and without *isnād*])
9. *Qaḍāyā*: 44–5 (also *Kāfī* 7: 323 [with variations]; *Faqīh* 3: 19–20 [from a different transmitter])
10. *Qaḍāyā*: 45–6 (also Ibn al-Qayyim: 73)
11. *Faqīh* 4: 31–2 (also *Qaḍāyā*: 77–8 [a shorter version from a different transmitter])
12. *Faqīh* 4: 32–3 (also *Qaḍāyā*: 74–6 [from a different transmitter])
13. *Qaḍāyā*: 48 (also Ibn al-Qayyim: 74–5; also *Kāfī* 4: 288 where it is quoted from Ibrāhīm b. Hāshim but with an *isnād* to Aṣbagh

47. Jalālī, *Tadwīn*: 140.

different from that in the *Qaḍāyā* [this may cast doubt on the validity of the ascription of the latter work to Ibrāhīm b. Hāshim]; *Faqīh* 3: 30–31 quoting from the ultimate transmitter in the *isnād* of the *Kāfī*)
14. *Faqīh* 4: 169–70
15. *Qaḍāyā*: 47–8 (also Ibn al-Qayyim: 74)
16. *Qaḍāyā*: 49
17. Ibid.: 49
18. Ibid.: 46 (also Ibn al-Qayyim: 73)
19. Ibid.: 48–9 (also Ibn al-Qayyim: 77)
20. Ibn al-Qayyim: 77–8 (also *Qaḍāyā*: 51–2; *Kāfī* 7: 159 [both from a different transmitter])
21. *Faqīh* 3: 28 (also *Tahdhīb* 6: 232)
22. *Faqīh* 3: 7 (also *Tahdhīb* 2: 96)
23. *Faqīh* 3: 95 (also *Tahdhīb* 6: 209 [with variations and from a different transmitter])
24. Ibn al-Qayyim: 97

III 'ALĪ'S SAYINGS

(a) sermons

1. Ibn Bābawayh, *Amālī*: 422–5 (and partially at 196–7; see also *Tawḥīd*: 305–8)
2. Abū Ṭālib: 185 (also Ibn 'Asākir 42: 495–6)
3. *Kāfī* 2: 49–50
4. Ibid. 2: 338
5. Ibid. 5: 150
6. Ibid. 8: 360–62
7. Thaqafī: 501–503
8. Mufīd, *Amālī*: 234–5 (also Ṭūsī, *Amālī*: 10–11)
9. Sharīf al-Murtaḍā, *Inqādh*: 241–2 (also Ḥimmaṣī 1: 193–4; Ibn Abī 'l-Ḥadīd 18: 227–8 [quoting Abū 'l-Ḥusayn al-Baṣrī's *Ghurar*]; see also the editor's introduction to Jishumī, *Risālat Iblīs*: 5–6)
10. Nu'mānī: 27–8
11. Damīrī 1: 111 (quoting Ibn al-Najjār)

(b) on the Qur'ān

1. Ṭayālisī 2: 642 (also Ṭabarī, *Tafsīr* 27: 185; Abū Nu'aym, *Ṣifat al-janna* 3: 229)

2. Ṭabarānī, *Akhbār al-Ḥasan*: 157–8 (also idem, *Kabīr* 3: 93; whence Abū Nu'aym, *Akhbār Iṣbahān* 1: 45)
3. 'Ayyāshī 1: 138 (also 'Alī b. Ibrāhīm 1: 85–6)
4. 'Ayyāshī 1: 217
5. Ibid. 2: 32–3
6. Ibid. 2: 285
7. Ibid. 2: 351
8. *Kāfī* 2: 624–6
9. Ṭabarī, *Tafsīr* 14: 95
10. Abū Nu'aym, *Ṣifat al-janna* 1: 38
11. Ṭabarī, *Tafsīr* 22: 93
12. *Ma'ānī*: 225
13. 'Alī b. Ibrāhīm 2: 238
14. Ibid. 2: 106
15. Ibid. 2: 276
16. Fākihī 2: 42
17. *Qaḍāyā*: 120–23 (also Ṣaffār: 449–50; *Kāfī* 2: 281–4)
19. Thaqafī: 183–7
20. *Ma'ānī*: 315
21. Abū Ṭālib: 269 (also Bayhaqī, *Faḍā'il al-awqāt*: 254; idem, *Shu'ab* 3: 337–8; 'Abd al-Ṣamad b. 'Asākir, *Faḍl Ramaḍān* [Uzbak: 96], all with variations)
22. Bayhaqī, *Shu'ab* 4: 148
23. Ibn Ḥibbān, *Majrūḥīn* 1: 177 (also Ḥākim 2: 537; Bayhaqī, *Sunan* 2: 75; Ṭūsī, *Amālī*: 377; Khaṭīb, *Ta'rīkh* 14: 422)

(c) on rituals and law

1. Naṣr b. Muzāḥim: 146 (partially also in 'Abd al-Razzāq 1: 7)
2. Ibn Abī 'l-Dunyā, *Shukr*: 19 (also Bayhaqī, *Shu'ab* 4: 113)
3. *Kāfī* 3: 173
4. Ibn 'Adī: 1188 (cf. Ibn al-Jawzī, *Mawḍū'āt* 3: 225 and *Mīzān* 2: 124 where 'Alī quotes this from the Prophet)
5. Ibn Qūlawayh: 535 (also 'Āṣimī 2: 74; *Jāmi' al-akhbār*: 58 [with variations])
6. Aḥmad b. 'Īsā 1: 118
7. 'Uqaylī 3: 227 (also *Tahdhīb* 2: 314 [with variations])
8. *Tahdhīb* 2: 38
9. Ibn Bābawayh, *Amālī*: 327
10. *Qaḍāyā*: 48

11. Bayhaqī, *Sunan* 3: 281
12. Ibn al-Rāzī, *ʿArūs*: 168
13. *Kāfī* 3: 42 (also *ʿIlal* 1: 270)
14. *Faqīh* 1: 423
15. ʿAbd al-Qādir al-Jīlānī, *Ghunya* 2: 63
16. Ibn Bābawayh, *Amālī*: 474 (also *Khiṣāl*: 409–10; *Thawāb*: 46; Ṭūsī, *Amālī*: 432; *Tahdhīb* 3: 249)
17. *Maʿānī*: 140
18. ʿAbd al-Razzāq 2: 236 (also *Ḥilya* 7: 123 [with variations])
19. *Firdaws* (Uzbak: 97, # 23)
20. Aḥmad b. ʿĪsā 2: 345
21. Ṭūsī, *Amālī*: 173
22. Abū Muḥammad al-Khallāl, *Amālī* (Uzbak: 105)
23. *Tahdhīb* 4: 272
24. *Kāfī* 5: 54
25. Ibid. 5: 9
26. ʿAbd al-Razzāq 6: 50; 10: 367 (also Abū Yaʿlā 1: 273, 278; cf. Naṣr b. Muzāḥim: 146 where the passage is quoted through a different transmitter)
27. *Faqīh* 4: 19
28. Ibn ʿAdī: 1684
29. *Maḥāsin*: 439 (also *Kāfī* 6: 318)
30. *Maḥāsin*: 612 (see also *Faqīh* 1: 120–21)
31. Aḥmad b. ʿĪsā 4: 263 (also Bayhaqī 10: 212)
32. Aḥmad b. ʿĪsā 4: 261 (also *Tahdhīb* 10: 95)
33. *Tahdhīb* 10: 130

(d) on ethics

1. *Firdaws* (Uzbak: 97 [# 24])
2. *Khiṣāl*: 231–5 (also Ibn Shuʿba: 164; cf. *Kāfī* 2: 50–51; *Nahj al-balāgha*: 473–4; Khaṭīb, *Mūḍiḥ* 1: 223 [also his *Taʾrīkh* 1: 222]; Ṭūsī, *Amālī*: 37–8; Ibn ʿAsākir 42: 514–15 where the same statement is quoted from ʿAlī on a different, or rather no, authority)
3. Ibn Bābawayh, *Amālī*: 640–41
4. *Tawḥīd*: 337
5. Ibid.: 369
6. Bazzār 2:85
7. *Kāfī* 5: 317 (also Ibn Bābawayh, *Amālī*: 678; *Khiṣāl*: 360; *ʿIqāb*: 305; *Firdaws* [Uzbak: 93]; Ibn al-Najjār, *Dhayl* 3: 137)

8. *'Ilal* 2: 208 (also *Thawāb*: 47–8, 61)
9. *Tawḥīd*: 372
10. *Maḥāsin*: 118 (*Kāfī* 2: 340)
11. *Faqīh* 3: 167
12. *Khiṣāl*: 113
13. *Maḥāsin*: 191 (also *Kāfī* 1: 10–11; Ibn Bābawayh, *Amālī*: 770; *Khiṣāl*: 102)
14. *Maḥāsin*: 345
15. *Khiṣāl*: 217
16. Ibid.: 426–7
17. *'Iqāb*: 310
18. *Kāfī* 2:90
19. *Mishkāt al-anwār*: 54
20. *Kāfī* 6: 50
21. Khaṭīb, *Faqīh* 2: 113
22. Ḥākim 4: 321
23. *Khiṣāl*: 505–6
24. Aḥmad b. 'Īsā 4: 263 (also Ibn Qūlawayh, *Kitāb*: 145; Ibn 'Asākir 50: 321, 322; partially also in Ibn Abī 'l-Dunyā, *Dhamm al-malāhī* [Uzbak: 90])
25. *'Ilal* 1: 77
26. Abū Ṭālib: 419–20
27. Ibn Bābawayh, *Amālī*: 713–14
28. Ṭūsī, *Amālī*: 453–4, 511 (also Khaṭīb, *Ta'rīkh* 14: 239; *Firdaws* [Uzbak: 90]; Ibn al-Dubaythī, *Dhayl*: 183)
29. Ibn Bābawayh, *Faḍā'il al-ashhur*: 91–2
30. Ibn Abī Ḥātim 1: 492 (also Bazzār 3: 362; Dūlābī: 100; 'Uqaylī 1: 54; Ibn 'Adī: 255; Bayhaqī, *Ādāb*: 357)
31. *Maḥāsin*: 316
32. 'Uqaylī 2: 120 (also Ṭabarānī, *Awsaṭ* 9: 127)
33. Ṭūsī, *Amālī*: 163–4
34. Ḥusayn b. Sa'īd, *Zuhd*: 47–8 (see also *Nahj al-balāgha*: 492–3)
35. Abū Ṭālib: 372–3
36. *Ma'ānī*: 245, 247, 256, 257–8 (see also Ṭabarānī, *Akhbār al-Ḥasan*: 111–14 for the full text of this report, albeit on a different authority)
37. 'Abd al-Qādir al-Jīlānī, *Ghunya* 1: 184 (read *al-Aṣbagh b. Nubāta* for *al-Aṣbagh 'an banātih*)

(e) miscellaneous

1. 'Alī's answers to the questions of Ibn al-Kawwā':[48] *Qaḍāyā*: 105–6; 'Ayyāshī 1: 41–2, 2: 339, 341–9; Ṣaffār: 143, 146; 'Alī b. Ibrāhīm 2: 106–7; Furāt: 143–4; Qāḍī Nu'mān, *Sharḥ* 2: 343–4; *Tawḥīd*: 282; Sharīf al-Raḍī, *Khaṣā'iṣ*: 87; *Iḥtijāj* 1: 337–40, 385–8 (see also Thaqafī: 178–83)
2. Thaqafī: 187–9 (also *Qaḍāyā*: 101–3)
3. *Ma'ānī*: 42 (from Muḥammad b. al-Ḥanafiyya)
4. *Kāfī* 8: 157
5. Ibid. 5: 338
6. *Manāqib* 2: 56
7. Ibn Bābawayh, *Amālī*: 395–6 (also *Khiṣāl*: 331–2; *Ma'ānī*: 46–7; *Tawḥīd*: 237)
8. Karājikī, *Kanz*: 179 (also Yāqūt, *Mu'jam al-buldān* 1: 116)
9. Ibn 'Asākir 6: 237
10. Ibid. 6: 185
11. *Maḥāsin*: 481
12. Ibn Bisṭām: 35
13. Sharīf al-Raḍī, *Khaṣā'iṣ*: 48–9
14. *Kāfī* 2: 624–6
15. Ibn Fahd, *'Udda*: 293
16. Ibn Māja: 1152
17. Ibn 'Adī: 1187
18. *Khiṣāl*: 228–9

(f) eschatology

1. Khazzāz: 146–51
2. *Kamāl*: 303

---

48. He is identified as 'Abd Allāh b. 'Amr al-Yashkurī, an Arab genealogist, who later joined the Khārijites in their rebellion against 'Alī and was killed in the battle of Nahrawān. See Ibn Abī Shayba 15: 325; Ibn Durayd, *Ishtiqāq*: 340; Ibn Qutayba, *Ma'ārif*: 535; Ibn al-Nadīm: 102; Ḥākim 3: 146; Ibn 'Asākir 27: 96–107 (see also Naṣr b. Muzāḥim: 295, 502). Apart from the sources mentioned above which quote parts or all of his questions from 'Alī, with 'Alī's responses to them, on the authority of Aṣbagh, many other early works quote parts of these with a different, or no, authority. See for instance, Ibn Isḥāq: 184; 'Abd al-Razzāq 5: 29; Ibn Abī Shayba 4: 169; Azraqī 1: 49, 52; Bukhārī, *Adab*: 260, 434; Bazzār 2: 166; Ṭabarī, *Ta'rīkh* 1: 52; idem, *Tafsīr* 13: 221, 15: 49, 16: 8, 34, 26: 184, 27: 16–17; Ṭaḥāwī, *Ma'ānī* 2: 350; Nu'mānī: 268, 312; Abū Ya'lā 1: 311; Khaṭṭābī 2: 179; Ḥākim 2: 352, 466; *Ḥilya* 4: 365; Bayhaqī 7: 376; Ibn 'Abd al-Barr, *Jāmi'* 1: 140; Khaṭīb, *Faqīh* 2: 187; idem, *Ta'rīkh* 12: 62.

3. Nu'mānī: 248
4. Ibid.: 278
5. *Kamāl*: 302, 303
6. Ibid.: 280
7. Ibid.: 669
8. Ibid.: 259–60 (also *Ikhtiṣāṣ*: 223–4; *Qiṣaṣ*: 367)
9. Khazzāz: 132–3
10. Ibid.: 223
11. *Kāfī* 1: 338 (also Khazzāz: 220)
12. Nu'mānī: 318
13. Jubā'ī, *Majmū'a*: 179–0 (also *Biḥār* 60: 223)
14. *Biḥār* 100: 234–5 (quoting 'Alī b. 'Abd al-Ḥamīd al-Nīlī's *Surūr ahl al-īmān*)
15. *Biḥār* 52: 272–5 (quoting the above-mentioned work of Nīlī)
16. Abū Nu'aym, *Dalā'il al-nubuwwa*: 211
17. Qāḍī Nu'mān, *Sharḥ* 2: 137

(g) esoteric

1. Sharīf al-Raḍī, *Khaṣā'iṣ*: 58
2. Bursī: 135
3. Ibn Bābawayh, *Amālī*: 294
4. Ṭūsī, *Amālī*: 283
5. *Ikhtiṣāṣ*: 307
6. Ṣaffār: 262
7. *Ikhtiṣāṣ*: 181–3
8. *Manāqib* 2: 260–61
9. Ibid. 4: 52
10. Ibid. 2: 269
11. *Kharā'ij*: 219
12. Shādhān b. Jibrīl: 172–3 (see also *Biḥār* 34: 267–9 where the same account is ascribed to the *Kharā'ij*)
13. Bursī: 92–3
14. *Biḥār* 42: 53–5

4: Kumayl b. Ziyād

Kumayl b. Ziyād b. Nahīk al-Nakhaʿī, a close disciple of ʿAlī and a nobleman and leading notable in the community of Kūfa. He was among the first Kūfans who publicly spoke out against ʿUthmān and his policies, and were consequently banished from Kūfa to Ḥimṣ in Syria by the order of the caliph in the year 33 or shortly after. Later, Kumayl joined the camp of the followers of ʿAlī in Medina and was among his close associates from the very first days of his caliphate. He was later appointed by ʿAlī as governor of Hīt, a strategic region to the north of Kūfa, where Kumayl successfully repelled an early foray by Mu'āwiya's troops into Iraq. He served as a commander with ʿAlī at the battle of Ṣiffīn. Later in his life, he joined the revolt of ʿAbd al-Raḥmān b. Muḥammad b. al-Ashʿath against Ḥajjāj in the year 82. He was executed by Ḥajjāj in the same year, or a year later, at the age of 90 for his part in the rebellion, as well as his activities against ʿUthmān half a century before and his continued devotion to ʿAlī.

Ibn Saʿd 6: 217; Khalīfa b. Khayyāṭ, *Ṭabaqāt*: 335–6; idem, *Ta'rīkh*: 288; Bukhārī, *Kabīr* 7: 243; ʿIjlī: 398; Barqī: 38; Balādhurī 2: 339–40, 5: 131, 150, 159; Ibn Aʿtham 4: 48, 7: 141–3; Ṭabarī, *Dhayl*: 663–4; idem, *Ta'rīkh* 4: 318–26, 403–4, 446, 6: 350; Ibn Durayd: 242; Ibn Abī Ḥātim 7: 995; Abū 'l-ʿArab: 204–5; Ibn Ḥibbān, *Majrūḥīn* 2: 221; idem, *Thiqāt* 5: 341; Masʿūdī, *Tanbīh*: 275; Dāraquṭnī, *Mu'talif*: 198; *Irshād* 1: 327; Ibn Ḥazm, *Jamhara*: 390; *Rijāl*: 80, 95; Ibn Mākūlā 7: 176; Ibn ʿAsākir 50: 247–57; Mizzī 24: 218–23; Dhahabī, *ʿIbar* 1: 95; idem, *Mīzān* 3: 415; idem, *Mughnī* 2: 533; idem, *Ta'rīkh* 3 (years 11–40): 430–31, 6 (years 81–100): 176–8; Ibn Kathīr, *Bidāya* 9: 46–7; Ibn Ḥajar, *Iṣāba* 5: 65–4; idem, *Tahdhīb* 8: 447–8.

He is described by most earlier authorities on the transmitters of *ḥadīth* as reliable and pious. In the revolt of Ibn al-Ashʿath, he was a senior member of the regiment of the *Qurrā'* (the Reciters of the Qur'ān, at least by then), a group renowned for their faith and piety (Ṭabarī 6: 350).[49] A number of mainly later Sunnī authorities criticize him for his excessive love for ʿAlī or, in other words,

49. According to Balādhurī 5: 150, the group existed, and Kumayl was a member of it, back in the time of ʿUthmān. Naṣr b. Muzāḥim: 208, 246 mentions them in the context of the battle of Ṣiffīn. The group was, in general, anti-Umayyad as attested by an Umayyad statement against them in Aḥmad 2: 175, 4: 151; Ibn Qutayba, *Gharīb* 1: 453; ʿUqaylī 1: 274; Ṭabarānī, *Kabīr* 17: 179, 305. For later non-political comments against them, see Sulamī, *Ṭabaqāt*: 11 (whence Dhahabī, *Siyar* 8: 389–90; idem, *Ta'rīkh* 12 [years 181–190]: 342–3). See further the references given, though not necessarily the opinions expressed, in the entry on them in the *Encyclopaedia of Islam*, second edn. 5: 499–500 (T. Nagel), and the recent studies named there.

for his Shī'ite sympathies. Shī'ite sources unanimously praise him (see Khu'ī 14: 128–9).

For his early activities as a member of the anti-'Uthmān camp of Kūfa and his subsequent exile to Ḥimṣ, see Ibn Sa'd 5: 24; Balādhurī 5: 131, 150, 159; Ṭabarī 4: 318, 322, 326 (also 403 where a report claims that Kumayl later went to Medina in an early, unsuccessful attempt on 'Uthmān's life); Ibn 'Asākir 50: 247. Kumayl's name appears among the close aides of 'Alī early in his caliphate. He was, for instance, 'Alī's envoy to 'Abd Allāh, son of the former Caliph 'Umar, sent to persuade him to join 'Alī for what became known as the battle of the Camel (Ṭabarī 4: 446).

For his appointment as governor of Hīt and his repulsion of the Syrian troops, see Balādhurī 2: 339–40; Ibn A'tham 4: 48 (and its sixth century Persian translation: 714–16 with a much fuller account). The texts of two letters of 'Alī to Kumayl as governor of Hīt are preserved, one in reprimand (Balādhurī 2: 339; *Nahj al-balāgha*: 450–51 [letter 61]), the other in admiration (Ibn A'tham, Persian: 716).

For his participation in Ibn al-Ash'ash's revolt, see Ṭabarī, *Dhayl*: 663–4; idem, *Ta'rīkh* 6: 350; Abū 'l-'Arab: 204–5.

For the year he was killed by Ḥajjāj, most early authorities of biographical material on Kumayl suggest the year 82 (see the citations in Ibn 'Asākir 50: 257; Mizzī 24: 222; Ibn al-'Imād 1: 335), though Ṭabarī 6: 365 (whence Ibn al-Athīr, *Kāmil* 4: 481–2) lists it among the events of the following year, a more plausible date as the revolt was suppressed by Ḥajjāj in the middle of the latter. Yaḥyā b. Ma'īn is said to have suggested the year 84 (Ibn 'Asākir 50: 257; Mizzī 24: 222) or 88 (Ibn Ḥajar, *Tahdhīb* 8: 448). Ṣafadī 24: 370 gives the date as around the year 90.

His age at the time of death is given as 100 by Ibn Kathīr (*Bidāya* 9: 46); most others have it as 90 but Madā'inī (as quoted by Ibn 'Asākir 50: 257 and Mizzī 24: 222) as 70. Ibn Ḥajar, *Tahdhīb* 8: 448 ascribes this to Yaḥyā b. Ma'īn, too. This latter must have been a corruption of *tis'īn* to *sab'īn*, very common in Arabic script, as an old age is also implied by several remarks of Ḥajjāj, Kumayl himself, and others, both before and after his capture by the government (see Ṭabarī 4: 404; Ibn A'tham 7: 142; Abū 'l-'Arab 204–5; Fasawī 2: 481; *Irshād* 1: 327; Ibn 'Asākir 50: 256; Ibn Ḥajar, *Iṣāba* 5: 654).

There is a tomb in Kūfa that the Shī'a identify and visit as that of Kumayl (see the description in Ḥirz al-Dīn 2: 219–20). This identification, however, does not seem to go back more than two centuries. The first author to mention the tomb, in the late thirteenth century (Khwānsārī 6: 66), noted that it had been found, built upon, and become a place of visitation "in these recent times".

There is a post-mortem aspect of Kumayl's character to be noted here, that is, as a symbolic figure in medieval Islamic Sufi literature. As mentioned above, Kumayl is described by many of his biographers as pious and devout. That, plus the pitiful story of his killing at a very old age because of his attachment to 'Alī, naturally generated a great deal of sympathy for him and later created an aura of holiness around him. Already at the time of his killing, a poet mourns him and blames Ḥajjāj for the cruel act (Ṭabarī, 4: 404). Later, some Muslim mystics saw him as one of the main channels of esoteric light of the House of the Prophet and came up with a chain of authority for their ceremonial Sufi robe, known as *khirqa*, that went through Kumayl to 'Alī and then to the Prophet. This seems to have started in the sixth century. The earliest major figure in Sufism whom I have found to claim the authority for his robe through Kumayl is Najm al-Dīn Kubrā (d. 618) who mentions this in a certificate he issued for a student on 4 Shawwāl 598 (Ḥāfiẓ Ḥusayn 2: 306–8). After Najm al-Dīn, many Sufi orders and major mystics who trace the authority for their robe through him have Kumayl as one of their last links in the chain of authority linking them to 'Alī and the Prophet (see Ḥaydarkhānī [1989]: 18–22, 30–38, 53–8 where the names of many orders and more than thirty sources are listed; also Haydarkhānī [1992]: 58–60; a few examples: Bākharzī: 27; Simnānī, *Manāẓir*: 136; idem, *Tadhkira*: 153; Ḥaydar al-Āmulī, *Jāmi'*: 223–4, 614; idem, *Muḥīṭ* 1: 521–2; idem, *Naṣṣ*: 218, 222–3; Asīrī: 350).

Ibn Ḥibbān, who lists Kumayl among the reliable transmitters of *ḥadīth* in his *Thiqāt* 5: 341, blames him for his excessive love for 'Alī in *Majrūḥīn* 2: 221 and reports that he quoted "complicated" statements (*mu'ḍalāt*) from 'Alī including miracles. None of this genre seems to have survived in Sunnī literature with the possible exception of his alleged statement at the time of his execution that 'Alī had told him that Ḥajjāj would be his killer (Ibn Ḥajar, *Iṣāba* 5: 654; also *Irshād* 1: 327). There are in fact only a few quotations in the collections of *ḥadīth* on the authority of Kumayl, a fact which goes well with Ibn Ḥajar's description of him in *Tahdhīb* 8: 448 as *qalīl al-ḥadīth*. They include the following:[50]

1. Ibn Hishām, *Tījān*: 180
2. Aḥmad 2: 309, 520, 524 (read *Kumayl* for *Khyl*), 535 (also Nasā'ī, *'Amal*: 358; whence Ibn 'Asākir 50: 248 and others)
3. Balādhurī 5: 173
4. Qāḍī Nu'mān, *Sharḥ* 1: 209
5. Ṭabarānī, *Awsaṭ* 2: 153 (see also Daylamī, *Irshād* 2: 35–6 for what seems to be a paraphrase of the same report)
6. Ibn Shu'ba: 196–7
7. Ḥākim 3: 317
8. *Nahj al-balāgha*: 513 (*ḥikam*: 257)
9. Bayhaqī, *Dalā'il* 5: 341(whence Ibn 'Asākir 69: 202–3)
10. Abū Ṭālib: 213

50. There is also a quotation from Kumayl in Muttaqī 9: 577 (citing Sa'īd b. Manṣūr's *Sunan*). Bukhārī, *Kabīr* 1: 230–31, however, has the transmitter as Kuhayl by whom he should have meant Kuhayl al-Fazārī, who he named in the same work 7: 238.

11. Ibn 'Asākir 50: 251
12. Daylamī, *A'lām*: 95
13. Fayḍ, *Kalimāt*: 77–8 (also 'Ināthī: 222–3; Ṭurayḥī 4: 115–16; see also *Biḥār* 58: 84–5 where the author notes that the quotation in question is not attested in any early *ḥadīth* work and that its ascription to Kumayl is obviously spurious)

With the exception of no. 7, all of these quotations are from 'Alī. There are also reports by others that quote what 'Alī said to Kumayl, though Kumayl himself does not narrate them or his reports have not survived:

1. Mas'ūdī 3: 175
2. Mufīd, *Amālī*: 283
3. Quḍā'ī, *Dustūr*: 117–18
4. Daylamī, *A'lām*: 265
5. Idem, *Irshād* 2: 35–6

Apart from the above, Kumayl is known as the ultimate authority for a number of texts quoted from 'Alī. They are:

1. Ḥadīth Kumayl

This report that starts with a reference to hearts as containers (*al-qulūbu aw'iya*) is a long and eloquent text on the merits of true religious knowledge. It is quoted, with certain variations, in many Sunnī and Shī'ite sources. Examples are as follows:

Thaqafī 1: 148–54; Ya'qūbī 2: 205–6; Muḥammad b. Sulaymān 2: 95–6; Ibn 'Abd Rabbih 2: 212–13; Nu'mānī: 136; Ibn Shu'ba: 169–71; *Kamāl*: 289–94; *Khiṣāl*: 186–7; Nahrawānī 3: 331–2, 4: 135–7; Abū Hilāl al-'Askarī, *Dīwān* 1: 143–4; *Nahj al-balāgha*: 495–7 (*ḥikam*: 147); Mufīd, *Amālī*: 247–50; *Irshād* 1: 227–8; Abū Ṭālib: 139; *Ḥilya* 1: 79–80; Quḍā'ī, *Dustūr*: 70–72; Khaṭīb, *Faqīh* 1: 50; idem, *Ta'rīkh* 6: 379; Ṭurṭūshī: 121–2; Ibn Ḥamdūn 1: 67–8; Ibn 'Asākir 50: 251–5; Ibn al-Jawzī, *Ṣifa* 1: 127–8; Mizzī 24: 220–22; Muttaqī 10: 262–4 (quoting other early sources). Parts of, or references to, this text can also be found in works as early as Ibn Qutayba, *'Uyūn* 2: 120; Ibn Qiba, *Naqḍ*: 189, and many others.

What made this text of special interest to the Shī'a was a sentence that said that the earth would never be devoid of individuals who stand as proof of God, bear the knowledge of truth and, as such, represent God on the earth. Most Shī'ite and many Sunnī (e.g. Ibn 'Abd Rabbih 2: 213;

Nahrawānī 3: 331–2; Quḍā'ī, *Dustūr*: 71–2; Ibn 'Asākir 50: 255; Muttaqī 10: 263–4; see also Abū Hilāl, *Dīwān* 1: 143–4) versions of the text include here a clause that these bearers of truth can be manifest and well known or afraid and subdued (*maghmūr*). Writing in the first half of the third century, Jāḥiẓ (*Ḥayawān* 2: 269) names a certain heretical group he calls the *Kumayliyya* who held that there is always a need for an Imām, whether active or silent, whom the people can turn to in person. Thus the *Kumayliyya*, Jāḥiẓ tells us, did not allow Imāmate by proxy – that the Imām be absent and someone else act on his behalf[51] – a point at issue at some stages of the 'Abbāsid revolution. This seems to refer to the statement in question and indicate how early Shī'ites understood the clause on "manifest or subdued". Later, the Imāmites reinterpreted the word *maghmūr*, formerly understood as subdued and non-active, to mean hidden, and used the text in their sectarian debates with their opponents. In response to a criticism by a Zaydī opponent who questions why the Imāmites, who persistently argued that there should always be a visible and existent Imām, now believe in a hidden one, Ibn Qiba (late third–early fourth century) writes: "The Imāmites have always maintained that the Imām is either visible and in the open or hidden and concealed ... If there were not on that point anything other than the report of Kumayl b. Ziyād, it would suffice" (*Naqḍ*: 187; for later argument with this text for that purpose, see, for instance, Nu'mānī: 25; *Kamāl*: 289–94).

2. *Waṣiyyat Amīr al-Mu'minīn*

This is a long text containing ethical advice that 'Alī allegedly gave to Kumayl on manners of social behavior. The text is related in two versions, a shorter one by the mid-fourth century author, Ibn Shu'ba:

51. Jāḥiẓ makes the above statement to explain a reference in a poem by the late 2nd century blind poet, Abū 'l-Sarī Ma'dān al-Shumayṭī (Sezgin 2: 454) on the heresies of the various sects of Shī'ites in his time (for the poem see Charles Pellat in *Oriens* 16 [1963]: 99–109 and *Arabica* 42 [1975]: 300–302; Josef van Ess in *Der Islam* 47 [1971]: 245–51; Wadād al-Qāḍī in *Studia Islamica* 78 [1993]: 37–9) in which he condemned Kumayl and his followers for their heretical opinions. The opinions mentioned are those of a group called by the authors of heresiographical works the *Kāmiliyya*; so the word *Āl Kumayl* in the poem is most probably a pejorative form for their name. Later, Qāḍī 'Iyāḍ (*Shifā*: 1072) also used the same diminutive form to refer to the same group as a pejorative name as explained by some commentators on the work (Qārī 4: 510; see also Zabīdī 8: 104), though others dispute this point and think that the diminutive form may have been a misspelling or misreading by the author or, alternatively, the first copyist of his work (Khafājī 4: 510). Ma'dān's poem has therefore nothing to do with our Kumayl, and Jāḥiẓ's reference to the no proxy doctrine seems misplaced.

171–6, and a longer one, with much additional, harshly worded, sectarian material scattered in the text, by the mid-sixth century Abū Ja'far al-Ṭabarī (*Bishārat al-Muṣṭafā*: 25–31). The first version, which seems to be older, includes two references to engaging in *jihād* under an unjust *imām* and to publicizing the secrets of the House of the Prophet, both matters of special concern in the late-Umayyad period. The second version speaks of the twelve prisoners of Hell, a later Umayyad Shī'ite concept (see below, under Sulaym b. Qays al-Hilālī), but divides them into two groups, six from among the ancients and six from the late-comers. This reference, nevertheless, seems to belong to a period before the Imāmite Shī'ites ended up with the number 12 for their own Imāms. A paragraph in this latter version condemns excessive religiousity, stating that extreme love for rituals will tempt a person towards the false *imāms*. This may indicate an Extremist provenance for this version (see Modarressi, *Crisis*: 35, note 101).

3. *Du'ā' Kumayl*

A long text quoted on the authority of Kumayl as the religious supplication that 'Alī taught him (*Miṣbāḥ*: 844–50; Ibn Ṭāwūs, *Iqbāl* 3: 331–8). This is a very popular supplication among the Shī'a who recite it on Thursday nights. Many commentaries are written on this text. For a list, see Āghā Buzurg 13: 258–9; also 'Abd al-Jabbār al-Rifā'ī 6: 50–52, 53, 56, 91.

4. *Ḥadīth "Ma 'l-ḥaqīqa?"*

A text with the tone and terminology of the mystic school of Muḥyī 'l-Dīn Ibn 'Arabī (d. 638) that surfaced in the seventh century as 'Alī's response to Kumayl's inquiry about the nature of truth. The text, a very popular one in Shī'ite Sufism since then, is quoted, without any formal chain of transmission, in Sufi literature (e.g. Ḥaydar al-'Āmulī, *Jāmi'*: 170; idem, *Naṣṣ*: 440), and whence in some anthologies (e.g. *Jung-i Mahdawī*: 136–7; Bahā' al-Dīn al-'Āmilī 2: 219–20) and late biographical works (e.g. Khwānsārī 6: 62). Numerous monographs have been written during the past eight centuries as commentaries on this alleged "*ḥadīth*." For lists of many of these, see Āghā Buzurg 13: 196–8; Dānishpazhūh 3: 461–4; Munzawī 2: 1331 (see also Ḥājī Khalīfa 2: 1041). It should be borne in mind that in the school of Ibn 'Arabī, mystical knowledge can be received directly (i.e. *ex nihilo*) through revelation, rather than by formal transmission through a chain of authorities. Ibn ʿArabī's own *Fuṣūṣ al-ḥikam* is, in fact, a prime example of this phenomenon (see his introduction to the book: 47). It seems therefore unnecessary to look any further for a possible earlier source for the text in question.

5: Zayd b. Wahb

Abū Sulaymān Zayd b. Wahb al-Juhanī al-Kūfī, a senior *tābiʿī* and a prolific transmitter of *ḥadīth*. He converted to Islam during the lifetime of the Prophet, though he never met him, and was an active member of the Muslim community after his death. He was also an active member of the camp of ʿAlī, at least from the time the latter assumed the caliphate in 36, and fought on his side in all the battles between him and his opponents. As an eyewitness, Zayd is one of the main sources for the chronology of the events of those wars. Not having been a known member of the anti-ʿUthmān camp, he has not been accused of Shīʿite heresy by Sunnī authors on the transmitters of *ḥadīth*. He may not have been an anti-ʿUthmān figure, but his anti-ʿUthmānī tendency is attested in some of his reports. Various dates are given for his death, but there seems to be a general agreement that he died after 80. Year 96 is the latest suggested.

Ibn Saʿd 6: 160; Khalīfa b. Khāyyāṭ, *Ṭabaqāt*: 364; idem, *Taʾrīkh*: 288; Bukhārī, *Kabīr* 3: 407; Muslim, *Kunā* 1: 370; ʿIjlī: 171; Fasawī 2: 768–71, 3: 118; Barqī: 38; Abū Zurʿa al-Dimashqī: 676–7; Yaʿqūbī 2: 241, 282; Dūlābī: 598; Ibn Abī Ḥātim 3: 574; Ibn Ḥibbān, *Thiqāt* 4: 250; *Fihrist*: 72; *Rijāl*: 64; Khaṭīb, *Taʾrīkh* 8: 440–42; Ibn ʿAbd al-Barr, *Istīʿāb* 2: 559; Ibn al-Athīr, *Usd* 2: 242; Mizzī 10: 111–13 (and other sources named in the editor's footnote).

For his activities before ʿAlī's period, see especially Ibn Saʿd 6: 160. For his presence in battles on ʿAlī's side and his authority as an eyewitness on the events of ʿAlī's caliphate, see Ṭaḥāwī, *Maʿānī* 3: 212 (preparations for the battle of the Camel); Naṣr b. Muzāḥim: 234, 242–3, 249–50, 450 (battle of Ṣiffīn); ʿAbd al-Razzāq 10: 147 (also Ibn Abī Shayba 15: 117, 311, 320; Muslim: 748); Khaṭīb, *Taʾrīkh* 8: 441 (battle of Nahrawān); Ibn Abī ʾl-Dunyā, *Maqtal*: 61 (ʿAlī's assassination and death); Ṭabarī 5: 13–14, 14–15, 16, 18–19, 25, 39, 45, 84, 90–91 (quoting Abū Mikhnaf). For his anti-ʿUthmānī tendency, see Fasawī 2: 768–70 (whence Mīzān 2: 107). He appears as the ultimate transmitter for a number of reports on the virtues of ʿAlī as, for instance, in Ibn Abī Shayba 12: 62; Ibn

Bābawayh, *Amālī*: 560; *Irshād* 1: 80–85 (also *Manāqib* 3: 123–4); Abū Nuʿaym, *Mā nazal*: 31 (also Ḥaskānī 1: 63; *Manāqib* 3: 52); Ḥaskānī 2: 302 (also Ibn Abī 'l-Ḥadīd 13: 225–6), 348 (also Ibn ʿAsākir 42: 362). He is also quoted as a source for material on the Companions ʿAmmār b. Yāsir and Abū Dharr al-Ghifārī (see, for instance, Naṣr b. Muzāḥim: 326–28; Fasawī 2: 770; Ibn Abī 'l-Ḥadīd 3: 53, 8: 261), both much loved by the Shīʿa but disliked by the ʿUthmāniyya. Like some other disciples of ʿAlī, Zayd's name was used by later contributors of Shīʿite eschatology who attributed some of their own thinking and pronouncements to him as transmissions from ʿAlī. An example of this genre appears in Ibn ʿAyyāsh: 31; another in *Iḥtijāj* 2: 10–11. A similar attempt is made by contributors of material in the other camp who use Zayd's name to ascribe anti-Shīʿite statements to ʿAlī. Examples can be found in Fazārī: 327 (also *Ḥilya* 7: 201; Khaṭīb, *Kifāya*: 376); Shāfiʿī 7: 151 (whence Bayhaqī 1: 287); Ibn ʿAsākir 29: 7, 44: 214–15.

Kitāb khuṭab Amīr al-Mu'minīn

A collection of sermons by ʿAlī given on Fridays, days of religious festivals (*Fiṭr* and *Aḍḥā*) and other occasions (*Fihrist*: 72). Ibn Shahrāshūb (*Manāqib* 2: 47) reports that the then extant *Kitāb khuṭab Amīr al-Mu'minīn* of Ismāʿīl b. Mihrān al-Sakūnī (Najāshī: 27) was based on Zayd b. Wahb's material. The numerous quotations in the sources of sermons of ʿAlī on the authority of Zayd b. Wahb fit this work. The chain of transmission that *Fihrist*: 72 mentions for the book is identical with the one that accompanies most of the sermons of ʿAlī quoted from Zayd b. Wahb in Naṣr b. Muzāḥim's *Waqʿat Ṣiffīn* and other works. Examples of the sermons are as follows:

- *Miṣbāḥ*: 380–83 (also *Faqīh* 1: 427–32 where the text appears without attribution to Zayd; this is a sermon ʿAlī gave on a Friday)
- *Khiṣāl*: 400–401 (also *Tawḥīd*: 278–9)
- Naṣr b. Muzāḥim: 225 (where his name is corrupted to *Yazīd*; also Ṭabarī 5: 13–14), 232 (also Ṭabarī 5: 14–15), 256 (also Ṭabarī 5: 25), 391 (also Ṭabarī 5: 45)
- Ṭabarī 5: 84, 90–91
- Nasāʾī, *Khaṣāʾiṣ*: 317–22 (also Ibn Abī Shayba 15: 117, 311, 320; Ibn Qutayba, *ʿUyūn* 1: 164)

There are also many shorter statements and conversations between ʿAlī and others in battles and elsewhere quoted in the sources on the authority of Zayd b. Wahb. Some of these passages too may have originally belonged to the same work. Examples are as follows:

- Ṭayālisī 1: 133 (also Aḥmad, *Faḍā'il*: 542–3; idem, *Musnad* 1: 91; idem, *Zuhd*: 165; partially also in Ibn Abī Shayba 13: 282; Ibn Abī 'l-Dunyā, *Tawāḍu'*: 168), 150 (also Ibn Abī Shayba 8: 165; Aḥmad 1: 90–91, 97, 153; Bukhārī 3: 489, 4: 85; Muslim: 1645)
- 'Abd al-Razzāq 10: 147 (also Aḥmad 1: 91; Muslim: 748; 'Abd Allāh b. Aḥmad: 272)
- Naṣr b. Muzāḥim: 249–50 (also Ṭabarī 5: 18–19), 326–7 (also Ṭabarī 5: 39–40), 450
- Ibn Abī Shayba 9: 437 (also Dārimī 2: 391)
- Ṭaḥāwī, *Ma'ānī* 1: 490 (also Ibn Abī 'l-Ḥadīd 4: 76 [quoting Ibrāhīm b. Dīzīl (d. 281) in his *Kitāb Ṣiffīn*])
- Mufīd, *Majālis* 2: 80 (also *Manāqib* 3: 120)
- *Ḥilya* 1: 147
- Khaṭīb, *Ta'rīkh* 8: 441 (cf. Nasā'ī, *Khaṣā'iṣ*: 317)

Naṣr b. Muzāḥim and Ṭabarī quote Zayd through Abū Mikhnaf, who usually (e.g. Ṭabarī 5: 13–14, 14–15, 16, 18–19, 25, 39–40, 45, 84) quotes Zayd through the Kūfan transmitter and poet, Mālik b. A'yan al-Juhanī[52] (see also Ibn Abī Ḥātim 8: 206). Ṭūsī also received Zayd's book through Abū Mikhnaf, from Abū Manṣūr[53] al-Juhanī, from Zayd (*Fihrist*: 72; the *isnād* is also attested in a report in *Khiṣāl*: 400–401 and *Tawḥīd*: 278–9). The long quotation from Mālik b. A'yan in *Kāfī* 5: 39–42 containing several sermons of 'Alī, clearly in the style of a book, is in all likelihood from Zayd's book and may represent the original style of that work.

6: Sulaym b. Qays al-Hilālī

Sulaym b. Qays al-Hilālī, allegedly a Kūfan disciple of 'Alī who escaped from Kūfa eastward when Ḥajjāj cracked down on the pro-'Alīd elements in Kūfa. He went into hiding in the town of Nawbandagān in Iran's southern province of Fārs where he later died while Ḥajjāj (d. 95) was still in power. It is, however, obvious that such a person never existed and that

52. On him see Barqī: 56, 65; *Rijāl*: 145, 302. Two examples of his poetry are quoted in Marzubānī: 366 [whence *Irshād* 2:157–8; Ibn 'Asākir 54: 274; *Manāqib* 4: 277–8; Dhahabī, *Siyar* 4:404], one in praise of Muḥammad al-Bāqir, the other an elegy on Ja'far al-Ṣādiq (but *Rijāl*: 302 states that Mālik died while Ja'far al-Ṣādiq was still alive).
53. Mālik b. A'yan's *kunya* is given by Ibn Bābawayh (*Mashyakha*: 440) as *Abū Muḥammad*. This may be a corruption of *Abū Manṣūr* or vice versa.

the name is only a pen name used for the sole purpose of launching an anti-Umayyad polemic in the troublesome later years of that dynasty.

Barqī: 35, 41, 43, 49; Kashshī: 104–5; Ibn al-Nadīm: 275; *Ikhtiṣāṣ*: 3, 8; Ibn al-Ghaḍā'irī: 63–4, 118–19; Najāshī: 8; *Fihrist*: 81; *Rijāl*: 66, 94, 101, 114, 136. There is also an entry on him in the *Encyclopaedia of Islam*, 2nd edn., 9: 818–19 (M. Djebli).

All of the sources named above rely for their information on the introductory note in the beginning of the Book of Sulaym. Early in the fifth century, Ibn al-Ghaḍā'irī (d. 411) quoted the Shī'ite scholars as saying that this Sulaym was unknown and that there was no mention of him in any text or report (Ibn al-Ghaḍā'irī: 63). Two and a half centuries later, Ibn Abī 'l-Ḥadīd was told by a contemporary Shī'ite scholar that this name had no matching body and that there never was such a person as Sulaym b. Qays al-Hilālī (Ibn Abī 'l-Ḥadīd 12: 217). As will be noted below, a prominent recent Shī'ite scholar too agrees with these points.

Kitāb Sulaym b. Qays al-Hilālī

This is the oldest surviving Shī'ite book and one of the rare examples of works surviving from the Umayyad period. The original core of the work which is preserved to a great extent in the current version is definitely from the reign of Hishām b. 'Abd al-Malik (r. 105–25), almost certainly from the final years of his reign when the long-established Umayyad hegemony was already under threat from troubles concerning his succession. There are repeated references in the work to the twelve unjust rulers who usurped the leadership of the Muslim community after the Prophet: the first two caliphs, 'Uthmān, Mu'āwiya, his son Yazīd, and "seven members from the offspring of al-Ḥakam b. Abī 'l-'Āṣ, the first of them being Marwān" (*Kitāb Sulaym*: 110, 174, 175, 205; see also 136, 170, 200). From among the Shī'ite Imāms, only the first five are mentioned by name, and it is said that the Imāmate will continue in the descendants of Muḥammad b. 'Alī b. al-Ḥusayn (al-Bāqir) (ibid.: 206; see also 168). Likewise, it is stated that the "masters of Paradise" among the descendants of 'Abd al-Muṭṭalib were the Prophet, 'Alī, his brother Ja'far, their uncle Ḥamza, Ḥasan and Ḥusayn, Fāṭima, and the Mahdī (ibid.: 217; see *Kāfī* 1: 450, 8: 49–50 for other similar statements from the period; these statements obviously predate the formulation of the Imāmite theory that considers the Imāms to be more excellent than anyone other than the prophets, including Ja'far and Ḥamza, a theory already present by early 'Abbāsid period). The hope was that one of the offspring of Fāṭima (*Kitāb Sulaym*: 140), more specifically a descendant of Ḥusayn (ibid.: 175), would overthrow the Umayyad government. The Shī'ites at the time were reckoned to be only seventy thousand.[54] The book focuses only on Kūfa, describing the situation of the Shī'ites there in some detail (ibid.: 180–82), a clear indication that the book is from that city, and possibly also suggesting that Shī'ism had not yet spread beyond that region in any noticeable way.

The language of the book is eschatological, depicting some of the historical events of the first century of Islam as seen through a Shī'ite perspective in the form of prophecies from the Prophet and 'Alī. In common with books of this nature up to our time, the prophecies have been updated in two or three stages in later periods by the insertion of words or sentences here and there. There is thus a reference in two passages of the book to the black banners from the East that would bring the Umayyad caliphate to an end (ibid.: 157, 175). The reference is obviously an updating and does not necessarily point to a Hāshimite Shī'ite sympathy, as the book has a clear 'Alīd, pro-Ḥusaynid provenance. There is also a reference to twelve (sic) Imāms from among the descendants of 'Alī who would succeed him (ibid.: 217–18). The relevant passage is inserted in a paragraph that describes how God looked at the people of the earth and selected from among them the Prophet and 'Alī as his chosen ones. (This follows the statement about the masters of Paradise noted above). The passage then continues by asserting that God then took a second glance (at the earth) and chose, after the Prophet and 'Alī, twelve legatees of the descendants of the Prophet[55] to be the elect of his community in each generation. The style itself identifies this last line as a later insertion, obviously added after the number of the Imāms was finally determined early in the fourth century. This addition was of course a careless slip as the contributor had failed to note that it would raise the number of the Imāms, when we include 'Alī himself, to thirteen. Najāshī: 330 reports that a fourth century Shī'ite author, in a book he wrote for a Zaydī patron and in order to please him, used this passage to argue that Zayd b. 'Alī, the eponym of Zaydī Shī'ism, was also an Imām, adding his name to the list of the Imāmites' twelve Imāms. This was the only report on the number of the Imāms in the version of the *Kitāb Sulaym* available to the historian Mas'ūdī in the early fourth century (see his *Tanbīh*: 198–9).

54. See also *Ṣifāt*: 203; *Bishārat al-Muṣṭafā*: 163. A report in *Biḥār* 10: 220, however, quotes Abū Ḥanīfa telling Ja'far al-Ṣādiq that more than ten thousand people in Kūfa "cursed the companions of the Prophet".
55. Read *min ahl baytī* for *wa ahl baytī* as also in the Qum, 1995 edition of the work: 857.

However, soon after that when Nu'mānī wrote his *Kitāb al-ghayba* around 340, there was at least one copy of the *Kitāb Sulaym* with many further references inserted here and there on the final number of the Imāms. The sentences were now more carefully drafted to avoid the problems caused by the former passage. These appear in the printed versions of the work too (*Kitāb Sulaym*: 62, 109, 125, 136, 151, 166, 167, 168, 201, 207). These references made the book a major source for the Imāmites' argument that the Twelfth Imām lived in occultation (see Nu'mānī: 101–102).

According to the introductory note at the beginning of the work, the book was entrusted by its original author to Abān b. Abī 'Ayyāsh, a *ḥadīth* transmitter who was then very young. Abān in turn gave the work to another transmitter two months before his own death. The book is one written by commoners for commoners. It is a display of primitive, unsophisticated beliefs among the rank and file of the Shī'ites of Kūfa during the late Umayyad period with clear residues of the usual Kaysānī exaggerations on the virtues of the House of the Prophet. It also refers to the Umayyad positions on some of the matters discussed. Many such popular, unsophisticated Shī'ite lines of interpretation and belief were later transformed and developed by the Shī'ite rationalists of the fourth and fifth centuries. Later Shī'ite scholars therefore had problems with the ideas expressed in the book as well as a number of factual errors in it (see Mufīd, *Taṣḥīḥ*: 149, stating that the book is unreliable and that corrupt material has been incorporated into it). However, the text being such an old and persistently popular book among the Shī'ites, and its chain of transmission up to the first alleged transmitter, Abān b. Abī 'Ayyāsh, being conventionally held to be strong, some Shī'ite scholars of the early centuries and later times thought that Abān, who was generally known as an unreliable transmitter, may have been responsible for the corrupt material (see Ibn al-Ghaḍā'irī 1: 36, 63, 118–19, also emphasizing that the book is undoubtedly a fake and that Abān is the one suspected of the forgery [also quoted in Ibn al-Muṭahhar, *Muhannā'iyya*: 124]; Ibn Dāwūd: 178, 414, repeating Ibn al-Ghaḍā'irī's remarks). A prominent recent Shī'ite scholar, while confirming that the book is a fake, holds that this forgery "was done for a good purpose" and that its maker piled up all sorts of data, some well known, others incorrect, but in general aimed to serve a purpose. He also supports the idea that the book is late Umayyad, before the number of the "unjust" caliphs went beyond twelve, "as it prophesied that the right [to rule] would then be restored to those entitled to it. This, however, never came to pass as the number of the "usurpers" increased and the right did not return to those legitimately entitled to it" (Abū 'l-Ḥasan al-Sha'rānī 2: 373–4). It should thus be concluded that one or more of the early transmitters came across this book and related it by *wijāda* (as against *samā'*, that is, direct hearing of the material from the author). Meanwhile, someone also added the story about the genesis of the book. The text is, at any rate, older than two months before Abān b. Abī 'Ayyāsh's death, which was in 138.

Owing to the fact that a number of insertions were made in the book, there are variations among its different manuscripts, as described by Āghā Buzurg 2: 152–9. Fortunately, later accretions seem always to have been in the form of insertions and additions rather than replacements and alterations.[56] The old core is therefore preserved in most of the manuscripts, even at the cost of obvious contradictions. Some of these variations are noted in the editions of the book: a number of Najaf editions; Beirut, 1407; Qum, 1415 (the one used here is Najaf: Ḥaydariyya, n.d., 236 pp.).

7: Jābir al-Ju'fī

Jābir b. Yazīd b. al-Ḥārith al-Ju'fī, a prominent traditionist of Kūfa in the late Umayyad period. He was considered to be one of the main sources of

56. As noted above, even the reference to twelve descendants of 'Alī (rather than eleven) has not been altered in most manuscripts; instead others with correct figures have been added here and there. Another example is on pp. 84–7 where the division of the community into seventy-three groups, as mentioned in a well known quotation from the Prophet, is noted. The text tries to establish that all partisans of 'Alī, even those who do not know the exact identity of the Imām of their own age, belong to the one group that will be saved on the Day of Judgment. One should side with the 'Alīds and believe in their right even if the hard times make it difficult to ascertain who the Imām among the 'Alīds is. There is a well-attested 'Abbāsid version of this idea from the late Umayyad period. Among the pro-'Alīds, the idea arose because of the Ḥasanids' ambitions and their dispute with the Ḥusaynids over the leadership of the House of the Prophet (see Modarressi, *Crisis*: 53). The Jārūdī Zaydīs adopted this as their fundamental doctrine, but Imām Ja'far al-Ṣādiq condemned it (Nu'mānī: 133–5), and the idea is not attested any further in the Ḥusaynid branch whose teachings informed what later came to be known as Imāmite Shī'ism. ('Abd Allāh b. Abī Ya'fūr [d. 131] is among those who report Ja'far al-Ṣādiq's condemnation of this doctrine.) In the present text, however, a passage has been inserted in the middle of that discussion, without tampering with its argument, asserting that among the seventy-three groups thirteen profess the love for the House of the Prophet, yet still twelve of them will end up in hell and only one will be saved (*Kitāb Sulaym*: 84).

religious knowledge in his day. Many of the distinguished scholars of the early 'Abbāsid period studied with him and transmitted *ḥadīth* from him as a learned and reliable transmitter, though disagreeing with his Shī'ite beliefs. He died in 128.

Almost all Sunnī and Shī'ite biographical works on the transmitters of *ḥadīth*, as well as most general biographical dictionaries, have entries on Jābir al-Ju'fī. For a summary of this material and a list of the main sources on him, see the entry in the *Encyclopaedia of Islam*, 2nd edn., supplement: 232–3 (W. Madelung). See also Sezgin 1: 307. A late fourth century Shī'ite scholar of Baghdad, Aḥmad b. Muḥammad b. 'Ubayd Allāh al-Jawharī, known as Ibn 'Ayyāsh (d. 401) wrote a monograph on him entitled *Akhbār Jābir al-Ju'fī* (Najāshī: 86).

There is a point mentioned about Jābir in heresiographical works on which Jābir's biographers are silent. Several works on heresiography (including Abū 'l-Ḥasan al-Ash'arī 1: 73; 'Abd al-Qāhir al-Baghdādī, *Farq*: 44, 232; Ibn Ḥazm, *Fiṣal* 5: 44; Nashwān al-Ḥimyarī: 168; Shahrastānī 1:73) name him as the second head of the Mughīriyya (on whom see the entry *al-Mughīriyya* in the *Encyclopaedia of Islam*, 2nd edn. 7: 347–8 [W. Madelung]), a branch of Shī'ite Extremism founded by Mughīra b. Sa'īd al-Bajalī (d. 119). After Muḥammad al-Bāqir, however, the Mughīriyya supported the claims of the Ḥasanid branch of the House and later joined the camp of Muḥammad b. 'Abd Allāh b. al-Ḥasan al-Nafs al-Zakiyya, while Jābir seems to have remained faithfully attached to the Ḥusaynid branch, more specifically to Muḥammad al-Bāqir's son, Ja'far al-Ṣādiq. A report in Kashshī: 192 certainly confirms this latter point but at the same time may allude to some, possibly earlier, relations between Jābir and Mughīra b. Sa'īd (see also Ibn Abī Shayba 1: 47).

On his date of death, the most reliable accounts suggest the years 128 and 132. A report in Nawbakhtī: 51 and Sa'd b. 'Abd Allāh: 43 asserts that after the death of 'Abd Allāh b. Mu'āwiya al-Ṭālibī in 129 or 131, a group of his followers developed Extremist ideas and claimed that Jābir al-Ju'fī too held the same views. The language of the account may suggest that Jābir was already dead by that time and thus confirm 128 as his death date.

Jābir was an extremely prolific transmitter of *ḥadīth*. Some of his biographers describe him as a major fount of religious knowledge (*min aw'iyat al-'ilm*) (Dhahabī, *Ta'rīkh* 8 [years 121–140]: 59). Tirmidhī 1: 248, 6: 233 says that were it not for Jābir, Kūfa (a major center of *ḥadīth* in the second century) would be devoid of *ḥadīth*. He had heard *ḥadīth* from many masters of the science, but it was from the Imām Muḥammad al-Bāqir that Jābir received most of his knowledge: some seventy thousand *ḥadīth*s (Muslim: 20), many thousands of which he never shared with others (Fasawī 2: 715; for variants of this quotation, see *Kāfī* 8: 157; Kashshī: 194; *Ikhtiṣāṣ*: 66–7). He is alleged to have studied with the Imām for 18 years

(Ṭūsī, *Amālī*: 296). His transmission has the clear stamp of the populist branch of late Umayyad Kūfan Shī'ism: exaggeration about 'Alī and his descendants, now mostly directed towards the Ḥusaynid branch, esoteric, hostile towards the caliphs before 'Alī and, of course, the 'Uthmāniyya, and awaiting a turn in the tide of events in favor of the House of the Prophet.

On this last point, there are many reports on his authority on the concept of the *Mahdī*, most of which sound genuine and reflect the aspirations and expectations of the Shī'ite community in the late Umayyad period. Some of the reports speak of a revolutionary figure (that is, *Qā'im*, but even *Manṣūr* [a messianic figure for the Iraqi Shī'ites of the Umayyad period], as in *Irshād* 1: 37)[57] from the House of the Prophet who will rise up and take revenge for them from the Umayyads (Furāt: 399; 'Ayyāshī l: 292). Others regret that no revolt against Hishām b. 'Abd al-Malik would succeed (*Kāfī* 8: 394–5; Irbilī 2: 350 quoting 'Abd Allāh b. Ja'far al-Ḥimyarī's *Dalā'il*) or wait for the black banners to come to Kūfa and take the oath of allegiance to the *Mahdī* who should have just declared himself in Mecca (Nu'aym b. Ḥammād: 241; *Ghayba*: 452). In general, however, most of the reports genuinely represent the hopes and expectations of the time (see, for instance, Nu'mānī: 311–12 where the assumption is that Muḥammad al-Bāqir would be the *Qā'im*), though some later contributions, often in the form of one or two added words or sentences, are also easily detectable. Here are some examples of reports quoted on the authority of Jābir on the concept of the *Qā'im*:

- Nu'aym b. Ḥammād: 241
- 'Ayyāshī 1: 64–6, 244–5, 292
  2: 76
- *Kāfī* 1: 264, 307
  8: 394–5
- Ibn al-Juḥām: 295
- Nu'mānī: 200–201, 237–8, 251, 279–82, 302, 311–12, 332
- *Kamāl*: 286, 330, 394, 648, 653, 673
- *Irshād* 1: 37
  2: 180–81, 374–5, 383, 386
- *Ghayba*: 187, 339, 441–2, 445–6, 452, 470, 471
- Ṭabrisī, *Majma'* 27: 136
- *Kharā'ij* (quoted in *Biḥār* 52: 336)

57. For later use of this concept among the Yemeni Ismā'īlīs, see Qāḍī Nu'mān, *Iftitāḥ*: 32 with a reference to the same quotation mentioned above.

- *Manāqib* 1: 281
- *Ta'wīl al-āyāt*: 732–3, 734–6, 792

It was, however, the flavor of esoterism and exaggeration in some of Jābir's transmissions that attracted most attention. This was also what made him so popular to Extremist Shī'ites, who considered him one of their highest ranking forerunners, and as fully initiated into the mysteries of the gnostic knowledge and superhuman nature of the Imāms. This is clearly what is intended by reports which suggest that he could not share so much of his knowledge with others, and that he was instructed by the Imāms not to reveal parts of what he had heard from them to the common people (see, for instance, *Kamāl*: 253) or, alternatively, was advised to put his head in a well in the desert and disclose some of those "secrets" only to the well (*Kāfī* 8: 157; Kashshī: 194). A report in Kashshī: 485 of clear Extremist provenance asserts that the knowledge of the Imāms eventually ended up in four persons, namely Salmān al-Fārsī, Jābir (that most likely means Jābir al-Ju'fī, not Jābir b. 'Abd Allāh al-Anṣārī as Khu'ī 4: 15 suggests), al-Sayyid al-Ḥimyarī and Yūnus (presumably the Extremist Yūnus b. Ẓabyān [on him see Kashshī: 363–5] who appears as the transmitter from Jābir in, for instance, *Kamāl*: 253, not the non-Extremist Yūnus b. 'Abd al-Raḥmān as appears in Kashshī). Another report equates the rank of Jābir before the Imāms with that of Salmān al-Fārsī before the Prophet, and the rank of the Extremist Dāwūd b. Kathīr al-Raqqī with that of the Companion Miqdād b. al-Aswad al-Kindī (*Ikhtiṣāṣ*: 216). In the material contributed by the Extremists, as attested by the use of their terminology, Jābir is called the "doorkeeper" of the Imām Muḥammad al-Bāqir (see Ibn Abī 'l-Thalj: 33; Ibn Hammām, *Anwār*: 44; *Dalā'il al-Imāma*: 217; Yūsuf b. Ḥātim: 603 [whence later works such as Kaf'amī, *Miṣbāḥ*: 611; al-Qummī al-Mashhadī, *Kāshif*: 86; Ibn al-Ṣabbāgh: 211; Tāj al-Dīn al-Ḥusaynī: 96]), thus conveying the idea that he was initiated into gnostic knowledge. The Extremists even ascribe miraculous qualities and powers to Jābir (for which see the sources named in the entry on him in the *Encyclopaedia of Islam* mentioned above; for some of the miracles ascribed to him, see Kashshī: 195–8; also Ja'far al-Haḍramī: 80; *Manāqib* 4: 187). Some early authors (e.g. Ibn Rusta: 219) therefore identify him as an Extremist.

There are many reports on the authority of Jābir on the miracles of the Prophet and the Imāms that may well be original and authentically reflect the mind of the branch of Kūfan Shī'ism that Jābir represented. Many of these accounts are so creative that even some early transmitters, as well as later authors, who do not feel uncomfortable with miracles term them *aʿājīb* or *gharāʾib* (see, for instance, Ṣaffār: 238; *Biḥār* 26: 17, 30: 300). Here is a list of some of the more interesting ones which appear in the works of mainstream Imāmite Shīʿites, especially those with a pro-*Mufawwiḍa* attitude:[58]

- Ṣaffār: 97, 350, 354–5, 357, 376, 397 (repeated at 399), 404–5
- *Kāfī* 1: 396
- Kashshī: 14–15
- *Kamāl*: 253–4
- *Ikhtiṣāṣ*: 272, 299, 302–3, 315 (repeated at 317)
- Ḥusayn b. ʿAbd al-Wahhāb: 78–83
- *Manāqib* 1: 450
  2: 266–7
  4: 140–41, 183
- *Dalāʾil al-imāma*: 92, 103–104, 212, 220, 224–6, 242, 269
- *Kharāʾij*: 246, 259–60, 275–6, 605–5, 754–5, 810 (also *Biḥār* 47: 99)

Parts of this material have parallels in the works of the sectarian, heretical Extremists who were expelled from the mainstream of Imāmite Shīʿism, such as Khaṣībī: 128–9, 160, 216, 218, 226–32, 239–40. There are also materials quoted from Jābir in the works of the Extremists that are not attested in the works of the mainstream Imāmite Shīʿites as, for instance, ibid.: 41–3, 70–73, 124, 153. There are also purely esoteric ideas ascribed in the works of the Extremists to Jābir on the pre-existence of human souls as shadows and on cyclical history that, in all likelihood, are of later origin.[59] The same is clearly true of reports that give the full list of the twelve Imāms (e.g. Nuʿmānī: 93–4; *Kamāl*: 253–4, 256–7, 311; Khazzāz: 53–6, 246–8; *Ghayba*: 139, 149; Ibn ʿAyyāsh: 30–32), though in most cases, material of this latter genre appears in the form of additions to existing texts (in fact, the most common form of forgery appears to have been introducing spurious material into older texts, rather than fabricating an entirely new text *ex nihilo* and disguising it as an old document).[60] There are

58. For similar material in the works of other Shīʿite groups, see for instance the Zaydī Muḥammad b. Sulaymān 2: 192.
59. On this point in general, see *Kāfī* 8: 254; Kashshī: 297, 299.
60. See, for instance, *Manāqib* 1: 282, a direct quotation from a work by Jābir, where the names of the Imāms after Muḥammad al-Bāqir are clearly added, since the original text struggles to prove even the truth of the Imāmate of Muḥammad al-Bāqir. See also *Kamāl*: 256–7.

also other prophecies about future events as, for instance, in 'Ayyāshī 1: 64–6 (whence Nu'mānī: 279–82; *Irshād* 2: 372–3, foretelling the infighting within the 'Abbāsid family and a number of other events); *Maqātil*: 524 (predicting the revolt of Abū 'l-Sarāyā in the year 199); Ibn Bābawayh, *Amālī*: 119 and *'Uyūn* 2: 257 (foretelling the burial of 'Alī al-Riḍā in Ṭūs); *Kharā'ij*: 754–5 (also Khaṣībī: 128–9, and a variant in Kashshī: 198, where Jābir predicts the digging of the water canal of Kūfa in the time of the 'Abbāsid Manṣūr). There are also reports that do not tally with well known historical facts. One, for instance, shows Muḥammad al-Bāqir during his Imāmate sending Jābir al-Ju'fī to bring the Companion Jābir b. 'Abd Allāh al-Anṣārī to the Imām's presence to give his testimony on a matter (*Kharā'ij*: 589–93). That Companion had died long before. Fake ascription to Jābir was by no means unusual; Nawbakhtī: 51 names a certain 'Abd Allāh b. al-Ḥārith who spread Extremist ideas which he ascribed to Jābir, apparently shortly after his death (see also Sa'd b. 'Abd Allāh: 43).

The main reason that Jābir fell out of favor with Sunnī authorities was reportedly[61] his belief in the doctrine of *raj'a*, the idea that 'Alī and his oppressed offspring will one day come back to the world to take revenge on their enemies. This idea, with its clear pre-Islamic and Saba'ī/Kaysānī post-Islamic parallels, was apparently a popular concept among many Kūfan Shī'ites of the time and is attested in Jābir's transmission as well ('Ayyāshī 2: 257, 326 [also Nu'mānī: 332; *Ikhtiṣāṣ*: 257–8; *Ghayba*: 478–9]; Ḥasan b. Sulaymān: 18, 26, 29, 37–8, 39; see also 'Alī b. Ibrāhīm 1: 25). A report in Ibn 'Asākir 54: 284 seems to exonerate Jābir from that belief as it quotes him as saying that no one in the House of the Prophet ever held that doctrine. The report is, however, an example of the widespread traditional tactic of rebutting an idea by attributing a statement against it to one of its well known adherents. He is also charged with maintaining that 'Alī was the "beast of the earth" mentioned in the Qur'ān 27: 82 as one of the signs to be manifested by God on the Day of Doom.[62] The idea is a part and parcel of the doctrine of *raj'a* (see Ibn al-Juḥām: 223) and is accounted for in surviving reports from Jābir (e.g. ibid.: 211, 215). The hostility against the early caliphs which was a dominant feature of a branch of Kūfan Shī'ism is also well attested in Jābir's reports, though

---

61. See, for instance, Muslim: 20; Fasawī 2: 715–16.
62. For the history of the idea, see Ibn Sa'd 3: 28; Balādhurī 2: 360; 'Uqaylī 2: 63; *Mīzān* 2: 52.

again there are others to the contrary (e.g. Ṭabarānī, *Awsaṭ* 7: 322; *Ḥilya* 3: 184–5 [whence Ibn ʿAsākir 54: 286]), basically attempting to rebut the Shīʿa, not to exonerate Jābir.

Whatever Jābir's actual responsibility for the esoteric material ascribed to him, it made later Shīʿite scholars, including some as prominent as the Shaykh al-Mufīd (d. 413), suspicious not only of his reports but even of the actual status of his personal belief (Najāshī: 128; see also Ibn al-Muṭahhar, *Khulāṣa*: 35; Ibn Dāwūd: 433–4). Suspicions about his transmissions reportedly existed among the Shīʿa from a very early time (see Ṣaffār: 238, 459; Kashshī: 192; *Ikhtiṣāṣ*: 204). Shīʿite scholars of *ḥadīth* also noted that most of the transmitters from Jābir were generally considered unreliable, and rendered most citations from him "weak", regardless of his own situation. However, much of the material ascribed to him is perfectly coherent in form and matter and can be said to reflect the attitude and diction of one section of Kūfan Shīʿism at the time. Looked at in this way, it may serve as a valuable register of the beliefs and discourse of an early, unsophisticated, popular Kūfan creed in the Umayyad period.

Jābir was among the few early authorities of *ḥadīth* who used to record in writing what he would hear (Khaṭīb, *Taqyīd*: 109). As is well known, this was against the practice of many of his colleagues in this generation.[63] There is, however, a report quoted on his authority against writing on the basis that it distracts people from the Qur'ān (Ibn Abī Shayba 9: 52), not an altogether convincing argument coming from someone who claimed to have received seventy thousand *ḥadīth*s from one of his teachers alone. Another report in Fasawī 3: 13 depicts Jābir as being dismayed that two of his pupils were recording what they heard from him. However, the students themselves understood the objection to be about who records, not the act of recording itself.

Jābir had many students some of whom could have heard as many as ten thousand *ḥadīth*s from him. This was in fact the number of the *ḥadīth*s that the prominent judge of Kūfa, Sharīk b. ʿAbd Allāh al-Nakhaʿī (d. 157) said he had received from Jābir (*Mīzān* 2: 220). Some of Jābir's pupils indeed recorded their hearings from him. Yaḥyā b. Saʿīd al-Qaṭṭān (d. 198) received a scroll from a teacher on which transmissions from Jābir were recorded (Fasawī 2: 156). Aḥmad b. Ḥanbal was seen copying the

---

63. See Michael Cook, "The Opponents of the Writing of Tradition in Early Islam", *Arabica* 44 [1997]: 437–530.

notebook of *ḥadīth* that Zuhayr (d. 173), another student of Jābir, had made from his transmissions (Ibn Rajab, *Sharḥ 'Ilal al-Tirmidhī* 1: 385–6). One of the surviving early works of Shī'ite *ḥadīth*, the *Kitāb Ja'far b. Muḥammad b. Shurayḥ al-Ḥaḍramī*, is basically a notebook of what the transmitter Ḥumayd b. Shu'ayb heard from Jābir, with only a few reports from others toward the end, including one or two from Jābir but through a different transmitter. Ṭūsī mentions two works by 'Amr b. Abī 'l-Miqdām, a transmitter from Jābir, the contents of one of which he quoted entirely from Jābir (*Fihrist*: 111). Both works have survived (*Khiṣāl*: 364–82; *Iḥtijāj* 1: 192–210) and both represent material heard in its entirety from Jābir. Another surviving example is the *Kitāb ṣifat al-janna wa 'l-nār* of Sa'īd b. Janāḥ al-Kūfī (Najāshī: 191) that is quoted in full in *Ikhtiṣāṣ*: 345–65. The section on the description of Hell (pp. 359–65) is entirely from Jābir, most probably from his *Tafsīr*, with only four short quotations from others at the very end.

Najāshī: 129 names eight works by Jābir, none of which has survived, but quotations from some are found in later works, and there is an abundance of material on the topics of the works, related through the chains of transmission mentioned by Najāshī, a sign that the citations should almost certainly be from the relevant work. Najāshī: 287 also mentions that 'Amr b. Shimr (or Shamir) al-Ju'fī, one of the main transmitters from Jābir, added extra material to the books of Jābir, and thus some of the works are also attributed to 'Amr. That, Najāshī adds, has confused the situation. However, as will be seen under *Kitāb Ṣiffīn* in the list below, 'Amr's contributions seem to have been in the form of additions, without ascription of the new material to Jābir and with no apparent tampering with the original material. At the end of his list, Najāshī: 129 notes that there are other works ascribed to Jābir that are actually forged. This seems to refer to treatises contributed by the Extremists such as the one quoted in full in Khaṣībī: 226–32 and *Biḥār* 26: 8–17. Najāshī specifies a text attributed to Jābir as the letter of Abū Ja'far (Muḥammad al-Bāqir) to the people of Baṣra. Muḥammad Taqī al-Tustarī 2: 543 correctly notes that this letter is in fact from Abū Ja'far II (Muḥammad al-Jawād), quoted by the Extremist Muḥammad b. Sinān al-Zāhirī (d. 220) as mentioned in *Fihrist*: 131. Tustarī blames Najāshī for the confusion, but the confusion may have been in the *isnād* mentioned in a copy of that text that Najāshī or his source had seen.

Here is a list of the works of Jābir, beginning with those listed by Najāshī:

1. *Kitāb al-tafsīr*

Najāshī and Ṭūsī (*Fihrist*: 45) received this book through different chains of transmission. There is also a reference to the *tafsīr* of Jābir in Kashshī: 192 that may refer to the whole work or, alternatively, to an interpretation by Jābir of a certain verse of the Qur'ān. That Jābir was noted both for his knowledge of and interest in the interpretation of the Qur'ān is also attested by a report in *Ḥilya* 3: 181 where, in a visit to Muḥammad al-Bāqir together with a group of people, the Imām turns to him and asks him what the scholars of Iraq have to say about the meaning of a certain Qur'ānic verse. A report in Muslim: 20–21 (also Fasawī 2: 715–16 and others) shows people asking Jābir about the meaning of verses of the Qur'ān (see further 'Alī b. Ibrāhīm 1: 25).

The book seems to have been a fairly well known work in its field. The title of the entry on Jābir in *Ikhtiṣāṣ*: 204 reads: "Jābir b. Yazīd al-Ju'fī, author of the *Tafsīr*." Khaṣībī: 18 and *Manāqib* 1: 281–2 (whence, though not so acknowledged, 'Alī b. al-Muṭahhar: 85–6; Yūsuf b. Ḥātim: 792), 2: 168–9, 188 directly cite from the work. These citations are short passages. There are, however, two lengthy citations from Jābir in *Kāfī* 8: 379–81 and Sa'īd b. Janāḥ's *Ṣifat al-janna wa 'l-nār*: 359–65 that in all likelihood are from the work in question and seem to convey the original style of the book, something which is hard to discern in the short citations. *Ta'wīl al-āyāt*: 528–9, 734–9 has two additional similar citations with the same style and flavor. The last citation that covers verses 11 through the end of chapter 74 of the Qur'ān (*Sūrat al-Muddaththir*; Jābir's commentary on verses 8–10 of this chapter appears ibid.: 732–3) begins as follows: "it is related/ mentioned (*jā'a*) in the *Tafsīr Ahl al-Bayt* that the transmitters (*rijāl*) quoted from 'Amr b. Shimr/Shamir, from Jābir b. Yazīd, from Abū Ja'far [Muḥammad al-Bāqir] that ..." (ibid.: 734). This may indicate that the *Tafsīr* of Jābir was known as *Tafsīr Ahl al-Bayt*. Āghā Buzurg 4: 262 mentions a seventh-century manuscript with a similar title that he saw in a private collection in Tehran.

There are many quotations on Qur'ānic commentary from Jābir in Sunnī and Shī'ite works of *tafsīr* and *ḥadīth*; most of them in all probability go back to this work. Here is a partial list:

- Ja'far al-Ḥaḍramī: 63, 66, 70, 74
- Ṭayālisī 2: 462 (also Ṭabarī 27: 185; Ṭabarānī, *Kabīr* 7: 40; Abū Nu'aym, *Ṣifat al-janna* 3: 229)
- Sa'īd b. Janāḥ: 356–8, 359–65

- 'Abd al-Razzāq, *Muṣannaf* 3: 370–71
- Idem, *Tafsīr* 1: 479
- Ḥusayn b. Sa'īd, *Zuhd*: 53
- *Maḥāsin*: 151, 152, 224, 227 (# 156), 249–50, 252, 299, 300
- Fākihī 4: 275 (also Ṭabarī, *Ta'rīkh* 1: 276)
- Ṣāliḥ b. Aḥmad 2: 48
- Ibn Hāni' 2: 212
- Ibn Abī 'l-Dunyā, *Hamm*: 94
- Ṣaffār: 55–6, 70, 76, 193, 208–9, 213, 294, 354–5, 357, 446–9
- 'Ayyāshī 1: 11, 12, 26–9, 39–41, 41–2, 48, 49, 50, 59, 61, 64–6, 67, 72, 86, 98, 101, 102, 103, 141, 165–6, 171, 185, 187, 194, 196, 197–8, 202, 206, 227, 244–5, 326, 330, 351–2, 366, 388
  2: 41, 50, 52, 76, 84, 86, 95–6, 103, 107, 120, 123, 142–3, 184, 188, 204, 208, 211, 228, 235, 240–1, 242, 248–9, 256–7, 257–8, 280, 290, 304, 317, 326, 350, 351
- Muḥammad b. Sulaymān 1: 130, 194
- Wakī' 1: 42
- Ṭabarī, *Tafsīr* 1: 241, 261
  2: 46, 186
  3: 337 (read *Jābir 'an Āmir*, for *Jābir b. Āmir* as also noted in the editor's footnote 2)
  5: 181, 216
  6: 44, 129
  8: 57
  9: 79
  12: 15
  23: 86
  24: 86–7
- Idem, *Ta'rīkh* 1: 266, 269 (two conflicting accounts), 276, 329
- Ibn Khuzayma, *Juz'* (Uzbak: 1755)
- Ibn Abī Ḥātim, *Tafsīr*: 923, 1119
- *Kāfī* 1: 38, 173, 218–19, 226, 230, 416, 417, 418, 424, 451
  2: 93 (part of 'Ayyāshī 2: 188; Ibn Hammām: 63; Ibn Ṭāwūs, *Sa'd*: 242 quoting the *Tafsīr* of Ibn 'Uqda), 601, 609, 649
  3: 231–4, 259
  6: 466
  8: 60, 90, 312–13, 344–5, 379–81
- Furāt: 54, 73–5, 93, 105, 106, 132, 146, 228–30, 241, 260, 282, 291, 298, 325, 329, 364, 366, 369, 399–400, 408–9, 453–4, 465, 467, 468, 509, 583–4

- Ibn al-Juḥām: 101, 102, 129, 145, 149, 151, 152, 154, 194–5, 211, 215, 218, 234, 236, 242, 245–6, 257, 275, 294, 295, 296, 301, 303, 318, 319–20, 323, 324, 337–8, 351, 357, 366, 376, 377, 402, 410, 411, 413–14, 427–8, 431–2, 451, 474, 475–6
- Ibn Hammām: 63
- Nu'mānī: 131–2, 251
- 'Alī b. Ibrāhīm 1: 27–8, 36–41, 339–41, 361, 369–70
  2: 14, 27–8, 65–6, 104, 110–11, 165–6, 255, 297–8, 391, 407, 421
- Ṭabarānī, *Awsaṭ* 6: 18
- Idem, *Kabīr* 7: 40 (two reports), 9: 143
- Ibn al-Sunnī: 209–10 (partially also in Ṭabarānī, *Kabīr* 1: 108; Ibn Kathīr, *Tafsīr* 1: 526)
- Ibn 'Adī: 1780
- *Faqīh* 3: 58
- *'Ilal* 1: 98–100, 117–18
- *Kamāl*: 253–4, 256–7, 394
- *Khiṣāl*: 132, 652
- *Ma'ānī*: 58–62, 63, 104–5, 167, 228, 400–401
- *Ṣifāt*: 202–3
- *Tawḥīd*: 66–7, 159, 277
- *Ikhtiṣāṣ*: 18, 23, 128–30, 278, 302–3, 332, 334
- Tha'labī, *al-Kashf wa 'l-bayān* (Uzbak: 1375; also cited from Tha'labī in Ibn Biṭrīq, *Khaṣā'iṣ*: 225, 229)
- Abū Ṭālib: 418
- *Ḥilya* 3: 181, 190
- Ṭūsī, *Amālī*: 232–3, 255, 272, 346
- Ḥaskānī 1: 39, 76, 357–8, 363–4, 397–8, 420–22, 434–6, 457, 469, 491–2, 583
  2: 164, 175, 182–3, 309, 368, 383, 388, 389, 430, 460–62, 464–6
- Ibn al-Maghāzilī: 267
- Ṭabrisī, *Majma'* 1: 336
  2: 65, 138, 162
  4: 245
  10: 157, 159
  13: 168
  14: 77
  19: 189
  23: 130
  27: 136

29: 39, 51
30: 75

- *Qiṣaṣ*: 35–40, 76–7, 190–91, 220, 246, 247
- *Manāqib* 1: 281, 282–3, 284
  2: 29, 168–9, 188, 266–7
  4: 178
- 'Abd Allāh b. Ḥamza, *Shāfī* 3: 108
- *Dalā'il al-imāma*: 53, 92
- *Mishkāt al-anwār*: 99
- *Ta'wīl al-āyāt* (other than those quoted from Ibn al-Juḥām and other sources mentioned above): 193, 363–4, 397–9, 504–6, 528–9, 531, 550, 609, 716, 732–3, 734–6, 792, 807–8, 829–30

2. *Kitāb al-faḍā'il*

Most of the passages listed in the previous section on the *Kitāb al-tafsīr* also fit the topic of this work, for the main thrust of Jābir's commentary on the Qur'ān was to prove that every praise and laudatory comment found there was directed towards 'Alī, his descendants and their followers and that their enemies were the butt of all Qur'ānic condemnations. What follows is a list of those quotations from Jābir on the virtues, mainly, though not exclusively, of the House of the Prophet and their Shī'ites, which are not in the form of commentary on the Qur'ān:

- Ja'far al-Haḍramī: 60–65
- Ṭayālisī 2: 106 (also Ibn Sa'd 1: 112; 'Abd al-Razzāq 7: 494; Ibn Abī Shayba 3: 379; Aḥmad 4: 283; Rūyānī 1: 247)
- 'Abd al-Razzāq 1: 346, 347
- Ibn Sa'd 3: 18, 19, 21, 22
  5: 248
  6: 257
  8: 24
  Ḥusayn: 38
- Aḥmad, *Faḍā'il*: 682, 764, 792
- Idem, *Musnad* 1: 232 (also Luwayn: 110)
- Fasawī 1: 539
- Tirmidhī 1: 247
  6: 151

- *Maḥāsin*: 134, 168, 171, 186, 227 (# 157), 387
- Ibn Abī 'l-Dunyā, *Faḍā'il Ramaḍān*: 46–8
- Idem, *Ikhwān*: 177
- Idem, *'Iyāl*: 210
- Balādhurī 2: 134
- Bazzār 3: 102
- Ṣaffār 3, 4, 5, 8, 15–16, 21, 49, 75, 90, 95, 104, 110, 117, 144, 182, 188, 193, 208, 209, 289, 299, 300, 309–10, 376, 397, 399, 413–14, 415, 447, 454
- Muḥammad b. Sulaymān 1: 297, 350, 394, 478, 480, 522
  2: 58–9, 60–61, 107, 192, 232–3, 286, 287
- Ṭabarī, *Ta'rīkh* 4: 209, 285, 500
- 'Uqaylī 2: 312
- *Kāfī* 1: 307, 396, 442, 443, 460, 467
  2: 74, 235
  8: 18–30, 70–72, 159, 170–73, 336, 394–5
- Kashshī: 193–4
- *Maqātil*: 50, 130, 524
- Ṭabarānī, *Akhbār al-Ḥasan*: 58, 62
- Idem, *Awsaṭ* 4: 187
  7: 332
- Idem, *Kabīr* 3: 36
  11: 118, 239
- Rāmhurmuzī: 601
- Ibn 'Adī: 542, 1549, 1780
- Ibn Bābawayh, *Amālī*: 60, 73–4, 78, 341, 408–9, 472, 770–71
- Idem, *Faḍā'il al-Shī'a*: 274
- *'Ilal* 1: 127, 172, 135, 175, 222, 223
- *'Iqāb*: 248
- *Kamāl*: 279, 286, 311, 330, 648, 653, 673
- *Khiṣāl*: 76, 147, 217–18, 219–20, 360, 429, 516, 581, 584, 650
- *Ṣifāt*: 200–201
- *Tawḥīd*: 21, 138
- Mufīd, *Amālī*: 74, 76–8 (repeated at 345–7), 118, 214, 215, 217, 311
- Idem, *Masārr*: 56–7 (whence *Miṣbāḥ*: 801)
- *Irshād* 1: 37, 41–2, 75, 143, 160, 180–81
- *Ikhtiṣāṣ*: 26, 224, 280, 299, 315, 317
- Ibn Shādhān: 169
- Abū Ṭālib: 87–8, 148

- Abū Nu'aym, *Faḍīlat al-'ādilīn*: 111–13
- *Ḥilya* 3: 182, 184, 185
  4: 185
- 'Āṣimī 2: 227
- Ṭūsī, *Amālī*: 79–80, 84, 232–3, 273, 296, 431, 735–6
- Khaṭīb, *Mūḍiḥ* 1: 80
- Idem, *Muttafiq*: 967–8
- Idem, *Talkhīṣ*: 231, 762
- Khuzā'ī: 63
- *Qiṣaṣ*: 229–30, 254–5, 262, 288
- *Manāqib* 2: 288, 364, 368
  3: 68, 78, 110, 232, 251, 325
  4: 167, 185, 188, 206
- Ibn 'Asākir 14: 170
  42: 141–2, 242, 333, 367, 396, 487
  54: 281, 284, 286
- 'Abd Allāh b. Ḥamza, *Shāfī* 1: 103
- Idem, *'Iqd*: 91–2
- *Bishārat al-Muṣṭafā*: 12–13, 14–15, 17–18, 49, 63, 65–6, 92, 110, 113, 148, 161–2, 189, 193
- Ibn Abī 'l-Ḥadīd 4: 104, 105, 108
  16: 29, 211
- Ibn Ṭāwūs, *Iqbāl* 2: 37–8
- Daylamī, *A'lām*: 119, 451, 461
- Ibn Ḥajar, *Iṣāba* 1: 38
- *Biḥār* 15: 23
  68: 42 (quoting Faḍl Allāh b. Maḥmūd's *Riyāḍ al-janān*)

There are many citations of this genre on Jābir's authority in the works of the Extremists that are normally couched in their own idiosyncratic language. At times, however, the citations are possibly taken from the works of mainstream Shī'ites as in the case of the following few examples:

- *Kitāb al-haft*: 192
- Khaṣībī: 377–8
- Maḥmūd bi-'Amrih: 2–4

3. *Kitāb al-Jamal*

Relevant quotations:

- Ṭabarī 4: 500, 512
- Ibn al-Juḥām: 472
- Ṭabarānī, *Awsaṭ* 4: 18
- *'Ilal* 2: 242 (also *Khiṣāl*: 650)
- *Khiṣāl*: 49
- Mufīd, *Amālī*: 295–8 (whence Ṭūsī, *Amālī*: 70–72 with variations)
- Idem, *Kāfi'a*: 14–15, 18–19, 24–5, 31–2
- Murtaḍā, *Shāfī* 4: 344 (whence Ṭūsī, *Talkhīṣ* 3: 135)
- *Kharā'ij*: 97
- *Manāqib* 3: 203
- Ibn Abī 'l-Ḥadīd 4: 104 (possibly)
  14: 11–13

4. Kitāb Ṣiffīn

The bulk of the material of this work has survived in Naṣr b. Muzāḥim's *Waq'at Ṣiffīn*: 156–7, 167, 169–70, 174–83, 202–3, 204–7, 221–2, 230, 236–46, 250, 272–3, 293–5, 295–6, 298–9, 301–2, 313–15, 315–17, 340, 343–9, 371–2, 457–62, 478–82, 500, 504–8, 554–9. All of these quotations (with the exception of pp. 295–6) are from Jābir on the authority of 'Amr b. Shimr/ Shamir, who is the transmitter of the book in Najāshī: 129. There are also numerous citations from 'Amr ibid.: 170–72, 231, 274–5, 327, 339, 342–3, 353–62, 367–9, 433–9, 473–6, 477–8, 524–7 which he narrates either from other authorities that he names or without mentioning his source. These must be among the extra material that 'Amr added to Jābir's work, as noted by Najāshī.

Other material quoted from Jābir on the battle of Ṣiffīn can be found in the following works:

- Thaqafī: 42–3, 124–5 (read *Jābir al-Ju'fī* for *Sālim al-Ju'fī* as also noted in the editor's footnote 3 on p. 124)
- *Kāfī* 8: 352–60
- Khaṣībī: 124
- Ibn Bābawayh, *Amālī*: 490–91
- *Ikhtiṣāṣ*: 81–2
- Ibn 'Asākir 59: 136–7
- Ibn Abī 'l-Ḥadīd 2: 195
- Ḥasan b. Sulaymān: 29

Also possibly the following passages on the aftermath of the battle:

- Ṭabarī 5: 63–4, 92
- Ibn Abī 'l-Ḥadīd 6: 75

5. *Kitāb al-Nahrawān*

A lengthy text made up of 'Alī's answers to questions posed to him by the head of the Jewish community (of Kūfa?) on his return from Nahrawān (*Khiṣāl*: 364–82) may have belonged to this book. There is also a text of a sermon allegedly given by 'Alī on his return from Nahrawān to Kūfa that Ibn Bābawayh quotes from Jābir in *Ma'ānī* 58–60 with a lengthy commentary by Jābir himself (*Ma'ānī*: 60–62) that is obviously taken from a book by him. This too may have been taken from the work in question.

6. *Kitāb maqtal Amīr al-Mu'minīn*

Relevant quotations:

- Ibn Abī 'l-Dunyā, *Maqtal*: 33–5, 45–8, 61, 73, 88, 90–91
- Abū 'l-'Arab: 82–3 (read *Jābir al-Ju'fī*, as in the Riyadh, 1984 edition of this work: 100–101, for *Ḥātim al-Ju'fī*)
- *Kāfī* 1: 298–9
- Ibn Bābawayh, *Amālī*: 396–7
- *Khiṣāl*: 364–82
- *Irshād* 1: 24–5
- Ṭūsī, *Amālī*: 595
- *Ghayba*: 194–5
- Ṭabrisī, *I'lām*: 202
- 'Abd al-Karīm b. Ṭāwūs: 51, 40–46 (whence Ibn al-Muṭahhar, *Dalā'il*: 847–8, 850)

Some of the quotations from Jābir on the conduct of 'Alī in Kūfa, his sermons and his judicial decisions may originally have belonged to this work too, as in the following examples:

- *Kāfī* 5: 151
  7: 216, 257
  8: 170–73
- Najāshī: 203
- *Manāqib* 1: 498

7. *Kitāb maqtal al-Ḥusayn*

This is in all likelihood the text quoted in full in *Biḥār* 30: 287–300. The author was told that the text was recorded in the *Dalāʾil al-imāma*, but it is not attested in any surviving manuscript of that work. There are also individual quotations from Jābir on the massacre at Karbalāʾ, including the following examples:

- Aḥmad, *Faḍāʾil*: 764
- *Maḥāsin* 1: 151
- ʿAyyāshī 2: 290, 326
- Ṭabarī 5: 449
- *Kāfī* 6: 452
- Nuʿmānī: 332 (also *Ikhtiṣāṣ*: 257–8; *Ghayba*: 478–9)
- Khaṣībī: 376–7
- ʿAlī b. Ibrāhīm 2: 297–8
- Ibn Bisṭām: 52
- *Maqātil*: 83, 85, 86, 87
- Ibn Qūlawayh: 114, 125–6, 148–9, 149–50, 162, 164, 183, 195–6, 281–2, 323, 375–7, 433–4
- *ʿIqāb*: 326–7
- *Ikhtiṣāṣ*: 255–8
- Ṭūsī, *Amālī*: 512 (partially also in Ibn Abī Shayba 15: 142 and Aḥmad 1: 98 without the phrase on the killing of Ḥusayn), 669
- *Kharāʾij* (as quoted in Ḥasan b. Sulaymān: 36–8; *Biḥār* 45: 80–82)
- *Qiṣaṣ*: 220
- ʿAbd al-Karīm b. Ṭāwūs: 43–6 (whence Ibn al-Muṭahhar, *Dalāʾil*: 848)
- Ḥasan b. Sulaymān: 29
- *Taʾwīl al-āyāt*: 651

8. *Kitāb al-nawādir*

Many of the numerous reports quoted from Jābir in Sunnī and Shīʿite sources fit the title of this work named by Najāshī. Possible candidates include a lengthy account of a plot against the Prophet (quoted in Khaṣībī: 77–82), the account of the attempts by Fāṭima al-Zahrāʾ to retain the possession of Fadak (quoted by Ibn Abī ʾl-Ḥadīd 16: 211–13; *Dalāʾil al-imāma*: 110–125), and many others.

9. *Kitāb ḥadīth al-Shūrā*

(*Fihrist*: 111). The full text of this treatise is quoted in *Iḥtijāj* 1: 320–36. The treatise lists the virtues of 'Alī that made him the most qualified to succeed the Prophet in the leadership of the Muslim community. The material is in the form of a direct speech by 'Alī, arguing with the members of the council set up by 'Umar at his deathbed to choose his successor. The text is quoted from Jābir by his main transmitter, 'Amr b. Shimr/Shamir, whose name is corrupted to *'Amr b. Maymūn* in *Fihrist*: 111. A similar text, *Khuṭbat al-Wasīla*, quoted by the same transmitter from Jābir as a sermon that 'Alī gave in Medina one week after the Prophet's death, is recorded in *Kāfī* 8: 18–30. Both of these texts are Shī'ite sectarian pamphlets. Their primitive style and arguments seem to point to an early date, not much later than the end of the Umayyad period.

10. *Aṣl/Kitāb*

Mentioned as *Aṣl* in *Fihrist*: 45, this is perhaps the same as the *Kitāb Jābir al-Ju'fī* that Abū Ghālib: 167 received through two different chains of transmission. Most of the many hundreds of reports quoted on the authority of Jābir in Sunnī (especially 'Abd al-Razzāq and Ibn Abī Shayba's *Muṣannafs*) and Shī'ite works on various topics of theology, ethics and law could have originally belonged to this notebook. For a list of those recorded in the four main collections of Shī'ite *ḥadīth*, see Khu'ī 4: 393–401. For many others that are scattered in other Shī'ite works, see *Fahāris Biḥār al-anwār* 8: 265–74.

Two representative examples are a lengthy account in *Kāfī* 2: 49–51 of the pillars of Islam and the nature of faith, and an even longer text in *Khiṣāl*: 585–8 on all cases where women have a legal status different from that of men.

8: Ibn Abī Ya'fūr

Abū Muḥammad 'Abd Allāh b. Abī Ya'fūr Wāqid al-'Abdī, a Kūfan client of the tribe of 'Abd al-Qays of Asad Rabī'a (hence the *nisba* 'Abdī), a Reciter of the Qur'ān in the grand mosque of Kūfa, and a close disciple of Imām Ja'far al-Ṣādiq. He was known in Kūfa for his piety and enjoyed the respect and recognition of the community. He died in 131.

Barqī: 71; Kashshī: 10, 161–2, 169, 172–3, 180, 246–50, 330, 427; Najāshī: 213; *Rijāl*: 230, 264. See also *Kāfī* 2: 172–3, 255, 3: 133, 7: 404.

The name of this transmitter's father is variously given as Wāqid or Waqdān (Ibn 'Adī: 490, quoting Ibn 'Uqda [also Najāshī: 213]).

Two reports in *Kāfī* 2: 255 and Kashshī: 247–8 indicate that he had poor health. Kashshī: 246 reports that Ibn Abī Ya'fūr died in the year of the plague during the time of Imām Ja'far al-Ṣādiq. That was the year 131 (Ibn Sa'd 6: 32, 7: 190, 226 [see also 7: 180, 182, 187]; Khalīfa b. Khayyāṭ, *Ta'rīkh*: 603; Mubarrad, *Ta'āzī*: 212; Ibn Qutayba, *Ma'ārif*: 470 [also 471, 601]). Ṭabarī 7: 401 places the plague in 130, but he probably means the initial outbreak of the epidemic. Ibn Abī Ya'fūr was therefore not alive at the time of the death of Ja'far al-Ṣādiq in 148 to play any role in the succession of Mūsā al-Kāẓim against his brother, 'Abd Allāh b. Ja'far, whom Faṭḥite Shī'ites followed, as asserted by Nawbakhtī: 89 and Sa'd b. 'Abd Allāh: 88.

Kāfī 7: 404 (whence *Tahdhīb* 6: 278) cites a story according to which he was a neighbor of the Qāḍī Abū Yūsuf who once rejected Ibn Abī Ya'fūr's testimony as a witness on the grounds that he was a Shī'ite, but then accepted it when Ibn Abī Ya'fūr said he was afraid he could not qualify for that honor. This judge could not have been the same as Abū Yūsuf Ya'qūb b. Ibrāhīm al-Kūfī (d. 182), the chief judge of the 'Abbāsid empire in the second half of the second century, since he was only 17 years old when Ibn Abī Ya'fūr died, some 30 years before Abū Yūsuf became a judge. The story is a topos in Shī'ite literature; similar encounters and reactions are ascribed to Muḥammad b. Muslim al-Thaqafī (d. 150) (Kashshī: 162), Abū Kahmas (*Faqīh* 3: 75) and Fuḍayl Sukkara (ibid.) with Sharīk b. 'Abd Allāh al-Nakha'ī (d. 177), the judge of Kūfa from 153 on. As can be seen from the dates, the story does not even work for Muḥammad b. Muslim al-Thaqafī and Sharīk.

Ibn Abī Ya'fūr belonged to the more moderate branch of the Shī'ite community of Kūfa that opposed attribution of superhuman qualities to the Imāms. His transmissions, as well as statements of others about him, attest to that fact (see Modarressi, *Crisis*: 30–31). He was a source of religious knowledge for the Shī'ite community of Kūfa (Kashshī: 161–2). Some heresiographers mention a Shī'ite group called the *Ya'fūriyya* who existed, possibly in Kūfa as a report in Kashshī: 266 may imply, a few decades after Ibn Abī Ya'fūr's death, and held moderate positions on various theological and sectarian issues (Nawbakhtī: 65; Sa'd b. 'Abd Allāh: 69; Abū 'l-Ḥasan al-Ash'arī 1: 122). The above-mentioned report in Kashshī, however, seems to suggest that a group with that name never existed, and that the name referred to the views that Ibn Abī Ya'fūr advocated and not to any specific circle of followers.

Kitāb

A notebook of oral transmissions, related from Ibn Abī Ya'fūr by a number of Shī'ite transmitters including Thābit b. Shurayḥ al-Azdī al-Anbārī (Najāshī: 213). Quotations from Ibn Abī Ya'fūr, some through the said transmitter of this notebook (as, for instance, in *Tahdhīb* 7: 90), abound in Shī'ite works of *ḥadīth*. A list of well over one hundred of such quotations that appear in the four main collections of Shī'ite *ḥadīth* is given by Khu'ī 10: 416–19, 22: 349–54, and another of over two hundred, recorded mostly in other works, in *Fahāris Biḥār al-anwār* 9: 249, 10: 487–8. Much of this material may originally have belonged to the notebook in question.

9: Sālim b. Abī Ḥafṣa

Abū Yūnus Sālim b. Abī Ḥafṣa, a Kūfan client of the Banū 'Ijl. He was a Butrī Zaydī and, as such, anti-'Uthmān and anti-Umayyad. He quoted *ḥadīth* from Muḥammad al-Bāqir, but was not on good terms with Ja'far al-Ṣādiq and his followers. He died in 137.

Most Sunnī and Shī'ite biographical dictionaries of the transmitters of *ḥadīth* have entries on Sālim b. Abī Ḥafṣa. For Sunnī works, see the list in the editor's footnote to Mizzī 10: 133–4. For Shī'ite works, see Barqī: 54; Kashshī: 142, 230, 233–6; Najāshī: 188; *Rijāl*: 115, 136, 217. See also Shahrastānī 1: 81.

His father is known by his *kunya*. Khaṭīb, *Mūḍiḥ* 1: 298 notes that no one has specified the name of Abū Ḥafṣa. *Rijāl*: 115, however, reports that his father's name was *'Ubayd*, and Najāshī: 188 has him as *Ziyād*. One can only hope that the first account was not misinformed by a confusion of our transmitter with his Baṣran contemporary, Sālim b. 'Ubayd (on him see the sources named in the editor's footnote 1 to Mizzī 10: 163), and the second by a confusion with another Baṣran transmitter of this period, Sālim b. Dīnār (on him see Mizzī 10: 138–9 and the sources named in the editor's footnote 2 on p. 138) who has a report on Fāṭima al-Zahrā' in Abū Dāwūd 4: 62. Kashshī: 240 also has Sālim as *tammār*, date seller, but Muḥammad Taqī al-Tustarī 4: 608 suggests that this may be a corruption. *Tammār*, *Ziyād* and *Dīnār* can easily be corrupted and mistaken for one another in Arabic script.

There are yet other confusions in the biography of Sālim. Khaṭīb, *Mūḍiḥ* 1: 296 notes that Muslim confuses the brother of Sālim, Ibrāhīm b. Abī Ḥafṣa, with another transmitter called Ibrāhīm b. al-Muhājir al-Bajalī al-Kūfī and thus identifies Sālim's brother as Ibrāhīm b. Abī Ḥafṣa al-Bajalī, while this family were clients of the Banū 'Ijl, a clan of Rabī'a of 'Adnān, not of Bajīla which was of Kahlān. Further down in the discussion ibid. 1: 298, the text gives the *kunya* of Sālim as *Abū Qays*, which is clearly a corruption of *Abū Yūnus* as given by other biographers.

For the doctrines of the Butrīs who did not repudiate the caliphate of Abū Bakr and 'Umar, as against the Jārūdī Zaydīs and the Imāmites who considered 'Alī to be the immediate legitimate successor to the Prophet, see the entry on the group in the *Encyclopaedia of Islam*, second edn., supplement.: 129–30 (W. Madelung); also Nawbakhtī: 13, 57; Sa'd b. 'Abd Allāh: 10–11, 73. His anti-'Uthmān and anti-Umayyad tendencies are well attested by a report in Ṭabarī, *Dhayl*: 66 (cited also in Mizzī 10: 136, 137; *Mīzān* 2: 110 and other sources) and by other quotations from or about him. The antipathy between him and the followers of Ja'far al-Ṣādiq is well attested by several reports in *Kāfī* 2: 384, 403, 5: 350, 8: 100; Kashshī: 142, 230, 235; Mufīd, *Amālī*: 354 (the last one also in Ṭūsī, *Amālī*: 125, and partially in 'Ayyāshī 1: 152; *Kāfī* 4: 47; Kashshī: 233–4). See further Ṣaffār: 259, 509, 510.

The death date of 137 is given by Shī'ite sources. Sunnī sources (e.g. Dhahabī, *Kāshif* 1: 422; Ibn Ḥajar, *Tahdhīb* 3: 434; idem, *Taqrīb* 1: 279) give it as around the year 140.

Kitāb

Sālim's biographers point out that he transmitted little (e.g. Ibn Abī Ḥātim 4: 180; whence Mizzī 10: 135) and that his transmission was generally on the virtues of the House of the Prophet (Mizzī 10: 137–8). There are exceptions to that rule as, for instance, in Aḥmad, *Faḍā'il*: 168–9 (also Ibn Abī 'l-Dunyā, *Ṣifat al-janna*: 147, in praise of Abū Bakr and 'Umar); 'Abbād b. Ya'qūb: 17 (against Ṭalḥa, Zubayr, and 'Ā'isha); Bukhārī, *Adab*: 61 (on Qur'ān 55: 60); Ṭabarī, *Ta'rīkh* 1: 149 (on Qur'ān 7: 189–90 and the birth of Adam and Eve's first child); *Tawḥīd*: 457 (on theological debates on the nature of God); Mizzī 10: 134 (on Qur'ān 4: 80) and others. Generally speaking, however, most of Sālim's reports are indeed on the virtues of 'Alī and his two sons by Fāṭima. Najāshī: 188 mentions a *Kitāb* by Sālim that a Shī'ite scholar of the early third century related, apparently by *wijāda* rather than actual hearing of the material from a transmitter who may have heard it from the author himself. This could have been either Sālim's notebook of oral transmissions or, alternatively, a collection put together by a later transmitter from reports quoted on the authority of Sālim on the virtues of the House of the Prophet. It should have included, among others, the following:

(A) **ON THE PARTICULARITIES OF THE PROPHET:**

– *Kāfī* 1: 442

(B) **ON THE VIRTUES OF 'ALĪ:**

– Tirmidhī 6: 88–9 (also Muḥammad b. Sulaymān 2: 20)
– Muḥammad b. Sulaymān 1: 306, 319, 325, 462 (also Ḥākim 3: 51) 2: 342 (also Ibn 'Asākir 42: 473), 482 (partially also in *Manāqib* 3: 206)

- Ṭabarānī, *Kabīr* 2: 186 (also Ḥaskānī 2: 326)
- *Khiṣāl*: 644
- Ṭūsī, *Amālī*: 251 (also Ḥaskānī 2: 81)
- Ḥaskānī 1: 139
- *Manāqib* 2: 72

(C) ON THE VIRTUES OF ḤASAN AND ḤUSAYN, AND OTHER MEMBERS OF THE HOUSE:

- Ibn Sa'd, *Ḥasan*: 46 (also Muḥammad b. Sulaymān 2: 235, 243), 89 (also Abū Zur'a al-Dimashqī: 588)
- Muḥammad b. Sulaymān 2: 112, 236, 238, 482
- Ṭabarānī, *Akhbār al-Ḥasan*: 75–7
- *Irshād* 2: 132

10: Abān b. Taghlib

Abū Sa'īd Abān b. Taghlib b. Rabāḥ al-Raba'ī al-Bakrī al-Jurayrī, a Kūfan client of the Banū Jurayr, a clan of Bakr b. Wā'il of Rabī'a. A prominent member of the Shī'ite community and a head of its Imāmite branch in Kūfa, he was a well known and respected scholar of his time in a number of disciplines, including Arabic grammar, lexicography and literature as well as Qur'ān, *ḥadīth* and religious law. He was especially known as an authority on the recitation of the Qur'ān. He studied with many of the prominent scholars of the time, and above all with Ja'far al-Ṣādiq, from whom he reportedly received some thirty thousand *ḥadīth*s. Shī'ites and Sunnīs alike consider him a reliable transmitter of *ḥadīth*. His transmissions represent the more moderate and sophisticated branch of Kūfan Shī'ism. He died in 141.

Almost all Sunnī and Shī'ite biographical dictionaries of the transmitters of *ḥadīth*, as well as many general biographical works, have entries on Abān. Subḥānī 2: 17 and Shabistarī 1: 25–6 offer lengthy lists of many of the major sources. The most informative accounts about him in Sunnī tradition are in Mizzī 2: 6–8 and Ibn Ḥajar, *Tahdhīb* 1: 93–4, and in Shī'ite tradition in Muḥammad Taqī al-Tustarī 1: 97–107.

There are a few discrepancies between the sources on some of Abān's biographical details. His *kunya* is given as *Abū Sa'īd* (corrupted to *Abū Sa'd* in Ibn Khālawayh, *I'rāb* 1: 258 and later works such as Ibn al-Jazarī 1: 4; Mizzī 2: 6;

Ṣafadī 5: 300 and the works of Dhahabī [*Siyar* 6: 308; *Ta'rīkh* 9 (years 141–160): 55] and Ibn Ḥajar [*Tahdhīb* 1: 93; *Taqrīb* 1: 50]) in most accounts; a few mention *Abū Umayya* (corrupted to *umayma* in Ibn al-Jazarī 1: 4) as an alternative. The first is attested in reports where he is addressed as *Abū Saʿīd* by others (e.g. by Jaʿfar al-Ṣādiq in *Maʿānī*: 66). Everyone knows him as a Kūfan, but Qālī 2: 79 thought he was one of the pietists of Baṣra. Barqī: 50, 63 and *Mashyakha*: 435 give his *nisba* as *Kindī* (also in *Ikhtiṣāṣ*: 249), indicating that he might have been an Arab from the tribe of Kinda, many of whose members lived in Kūfa at the time. But this goes against all the other cited sources.

His prominent position as a head of the Shīʿite community is mentioned in some reports from the period (e.g. Ibn Qūlawayh: 546 where Jaʿfar al-Ṣādiq calls him "*min ru'asā' al-Shīʿa*"). He was greatly respected by Jaʿfar al-Ṣādiq, as attested by numerous reports, and accompanied him on a pilgrimage to Mecca (*Kāfī* 1: 267, 2: 171 [also Aḥmad b. ʿĪsā 4: 341 with variations], 3: 440, 4: 398; Nuʿmānī: 313; Ibn Bābawayh, *Amālī*:141). He was also with Jaʿfar al-Ṣādiq when the latter came to Kūfa (Ibn Qūlawayh: 83). That Abān related thirty thousand *ḥadīth*s from him is mentioned by Najāshī: 12. In a different report (ibid.: 13; Kashshī: 331), Jaʿfar al-Ṣādiq tells a disciple that Abān has heard "much *ḥadīth*" from him. Sunnī scholars (named in Ibn Ḥajar, *Tahdhīb* 1: 94) describe him as a pious man who was the preacher of the Shīʿite community in Kūfa. A number of reports assert that he used to sit in the grand mosque of Kūfa and receive people, many of them non-Shīʿites, who would come to him with their questions on religious matters (*Maḥāsin:* 181; *Kāfī* 2: 520; Kashshī: 330; see also Najāshī: 12). His student Sufyān b. ʿUyayna (d. 198) praised him for eloquency and oratory (Ibn Ḥajar, *Tahdhīb* 1: 94). Ibn Khālawayh, *Badīʿ*: 56 reports that he was a teacher by profession. According to a report in Mufīd, *Mutʿa*: 15 (also *Khulāṣat al-Ījāz*: 58), he was wealthy and once ransomed his reputation with ten thousand *dirham*s when cheated by a woman whom he had approached in Mecca for a *mutʿa* marriage (his interest in the topic is also attested by reports in *Kāfī* 5: 455, 458–9 where he asks Jaʿfar al-Ṣādiq about the details of that type of contract). Fasawī 2: 467 quotes a story that a high ranking government official passed by a group that included Abān. Everyone stood up in respect save Abān. When asked why, he responded that he did not want to debase the Qur'ān. This certainly indicates that the group were engaged in recitation of the Qur'ān at the time.

The sources are unanimous in praising him for his knowledge and trustworthiness, though most also note his open and passionate Shīʿism (see especially ʿUqaylī 1: 37 for comments by Abān's contemporaries among the ʿUthmāniyya of Kūfa). Ibn ʿAdī: 380 identifies him as a well known [scholar] of Kūfa. Abū Nuʿaym describes him as one of those at the top of their ranks (*ghāyatan min al-ghāyāt*) (Ibn Ḥajar, *Tahdhīb* 1: 94; see also Najāshī: 11). That he was an authority on Arabic lexicography is confirmed by reports in literary sources of what he had heard from the Arabs of the desert who provided the yardstick for correct and eloquent Arabic (see, for instance, Jāḥiẓ, *Bayān* 4: 72–3 quoting Aṣmaʿī [also Qālī 2: 79 quoting the same from Ibn al-Anbārī, with variations]; Ibn Ṭayfūr, *Balāghāt*: 62 [two stories, both from Aṣmaʿī; Aṣmaʿī also quotes other examples of good Arabic from Abān; see, for instance, Bayhaqī, *Shu'ab* 6: 341]; Muḥammad b. Dāwūd, *Zahra*: 474; see also Ibn Abī Ḥātim 2: 297; Najāshī: 10; *Fibrist*: 17). His mastery in Arabic grammar that has been pointed out by many of his biographers (e.g. Ibn 'Adī: 380; Ibn al-Jazarī 1: 4; Suyūṭī, *Bughya* 1: 404) is confirmed by a report from Sufyān b. 'Uyayna who describes how he was corrected by Abān (Ibn 'Adī: 380), and by another in Kashshī: 276 where it is said that he defeated his opponent in an argument on Arabic. Other reports demonstrate his interest and knowledge in Arabic poetry for which he is also praised (Najāshī: 11). Examples can be found in Ibn Abī 'l-Dunyā, *Iṣlāḥ al-māl*: 363 (whence Ibn 'Asākir 50: 246) where Abān quotes a poem that Kumayl recited to him in a conversation and in Abū Nu'aym, *Shu'arā'*: 28–9 (about Farazdaq). A long report in Ibn Ḥibbān, *Sīra*: 71–6 (also Abū Nu'aym, *Dalā'il al-nubuwwa*: 237–41; Bayhaqī, *Dalā'il* 2: 422) further shows his knowledge of Arab genealogy (see also *Mīzān* 2: 107 for a mention of him as a source for biographical data on transmitters of *ḥadīth*).

Many of his biographers describe him as *qāri'* or *muqri'*, Reader of the Qur'ān (e.g. Ibn Ḥibbān, *Mashāhīr*: 259; Najāshī: 10, 11; *Fihrist*: 17, 18; Dāraquṭnī, *Mu'talif*: 306; Ibn al-Athīr, *Kāmil* 5: 508; Dhahabī, *Ta'rīkh* 9 [years 141–160]: 55; idem, *Siyar* 6: 308; Mizzī 20: 146). Dhahabī, *'Ibar* 1: 192 describes him as the well known Reader (*al-qāri' al-mashhūr*). He was a formal Reader of the Qur'ān whose Reading is noted in many sources and partially preserved. He read Qur'ān with four teachers, including 'Āṣim and A'mash. In fact, he was one of only three who read the entire text of the Qur'ān with the latter (Ibn al-Jazarī 1: 4). Kisā'ī (d. 189), one of the chief seven Readers of Qur'ān, read it with him (Ibn Mihrān, *Mabsūṭ*: 72; 'Abd al-Karīm al-Ṭabarī: 120). As is clear from his work on the topic, he was also an authority on the interpretation of the Qur'ān (on his interest in, and involvement with, this topic, see further Furāt: 104, 108, 151, 239).

It is not known how old Abān was when he died. Ibn Mihrān, *Mabsūṭ*: 72 relates that Kisā'ī felt proud that he had met and studied with the masters of the older generation of Kūfa such as Abān b. Taqhlib and Ibn Abī Laylā (d. 148), the judge of the town for 33 years, who died a few years after Abān at the age of 74. This specifies the generation to which Abān belonged. Abān himself is quoted (*'Ilal* 1: 221) as saying that he saw 'Alī Zayn al-'Ābidīn (d. 95). There are a number of reports that suggest that Abān even heard from Zayn al-'Ābidīn (e.g. *Kāfī* 6: 236; *Faqīh* 4: 204). He is thus identified as a disciple of 'Alī Zayn al-'Ābidīn by Kashshī (as cited by Najāshī: 10 from Kashshī's original work, though the reference does not appear in the surviving abridgement of his book); Najāshī: 10, and Ṭūsī (*Rijāl*: 109; *Fihrist*: 17), a distinction that requires him to be at least a teenager at the time. This sets his birthdate at about the same time as Ibn Abī Laylā (b. 74) and Ja'far al-Ṣādiq (b. 80). In a report quoted in *Kāfī* 3: 440, Ja'far al-Ṣādiq tells Abān and his companions that they are young while Ja'far is old. That statement should therefore be understood as being addressed to other members of the group, rather than Abān who should have been the same age as Ja'far al-Ṣādiq if not older. Abān predeceased Ja'far al-Ṣādiq who was deeply grieved by his death (Kashshī: 330, whence Najāshī: 10 and *Fihrist*: 17). The assertion by Nawbakhtī: 89 and Sa'd b. 'Abd Allāh: 89 that Abān supported Mūsā al-Kāẓim as the true successor to Ja'far al-Ṣādiq when the latter died cannot be upheld.

A number of works by Abān b. Taghlib are mentioned by Ibn al-Nadīm: 276; Najāshī: 11; *Fihrist*: 17–18. Ibn 'Adī: 380 (whence Mizzī 2: 7; Ibn Ḥajar, *Tahdhīb* 1: 93 and others) also refers to his "reports and written works." Ibn 'Adī mentions that the Sunnīs had no problem with his transmissions as there was nothing heretical in them. Indeed they generally represent the more moderate, non-Extremist trend of Kūfan Shī'ism that, though profoundly Shī'ite and pro-'Alīd, was not much influenced by the esoteric ideas conventionally identified with Saba'ī/ Kaysānī Shī'ism. That moderate trend, as clear as it is in Abān's transmissions, did not, however, discourage later transmitters from ascribing to him a fair share of reports that "predicted" the exact number of the Imāms,[64] or spoke about the wonders of the past,[65] present,[66] and future;[67] esoteric reports about Salmān, a standard Extremist favorite,[68] and the Imāms,[69] or on a *jinnī* who paid a visit to 'Alī to inform him of the killing of his own child[70] and the like. Some of the general, non-esoteric, eschatological quotations from him on the coming of the expected savior, however, sound genuine as they reflect the persisting hope of the Shī'ites for a change in their favor in the future. Such can be the case with a report in *Maḥāsin* 1: 87 (also *Kāfī* 3: 503; *Faqīh* 2: 11; *Thawāb*: 221). Others may reflect the worries of the community at the time, such as a report in Nu'mānī: 298–9 that predicts that when the banner of truth appears, everyone will curse it because of so much hurt and harm that they have previously suffered from former claimants of the House. Another,

64. *Miṣbāḥ*: 337–8 (the original text might have been genuine but the passage with the names of the twelve Imāms was later added); *Khiṣāl*: 475 (also *Kamāl*: 262; whence Khazzāz: 46, 245–6). This latter, however, seems to be a case of confusion between Abān b. Taghlib and Abān b. 'Abī 'Ayyāsh as the ultimate authority for the report is Sulaym b. Qays for whom the latter was the sole transmitter. The citation must have given originally the name as Abān without further identification, and a later transmitter must have misidentified him as Abān b. Taghlib.
65. *Iḥtijāj* 2: 180–1; *Biḥār* 14: 270–71, 445–7.
66. *Khiṣāl*: 489–90 (whence *Iḥtijāj* 2: 250–53; partially also in Ṣaffār: 401; whence *Ikhtiṣāṣ*: 318–19).
67. Ṭabarānī, *Ṣaghīr* 1: 245; 'Ayyāshī 2: 254; Nu'mānī: 313–15, later updated to the text ibid.: 310–11 (also Ibn Qūlawayh 233–5; *Kamāl*: 671–2; *Khiṣāl*: 649); *Kharā'ij*: 860.
68. *Ikhtiṣāṣ*: 221–2.
69. Ṣaffār: 274, 277, 283; *Kharā'ij*: 615–16; Ḥasan b. Sulaymān, *Mukhtaṣar* (as quoted in *Biḥār* 53: 66).
70. Bursī: 91–2.

obviously post-Mūsā al-Kāẓim, Wāqifite report advises the Shīʿites to remain as they were after their Imām disappears (that is, to continue to recognize him as the true Imām) until their sun rises again (*Kamāl*: 349).

1. *Qur'ānic Reading/Kitāb al-qirā'a*

Both Najāshī: 11 and *Fihrist*: 17–18 note that Abān had a particular Reading of the Qur'ān that was well known among the Readers. Najāshī's account makes it clear that this reading was recorded in the form of a text that both he and Ṭūsī received through a chain of transmitters they name. This should be the same as *Kitāb al-qirā'āt* (sic, possibly *qirā'a*) named by Ibn al-Nadīm: 276.

Parts of the reading of Abān b. Taghlib are preserved in the sources. Najāshī quotes the opening sentence of the text. Other surviving parts of the text identify where his readings differed from the standard, including those in the cases of the following Qur'ānic verses:[71]

- 3: 95 (Ibn Khālawayh, *Badīʿ*: 21; Ibn Jinnī, *Muḥtasib* 1: 165)
- 5: 60 (Ibn Jinnī 1:214)
- 8: 35 (Ibn Jinnī 1: 278–9)
- 9: 30 (Naḥḥās 2: 210)
- 9: 123 (Naḥḥās 2: 240; Ibn Khālawayh, *Iʿrāb* 1: 258)
- 12: 31 (Ibn Jinnī 1: 339)
- 18: 1–2 (Ibn Khālawayh, *Badīʿ*: 78)
- 20: 124 (Ibn Khālawayh, *Badīʿ*: 90; Ibn Jinnī 2: 60)
- 23: 116 (Ibn Khālawayh, *Badīʿ*: 99)
- 26: 51 (Ibn Jinnī 2: 127)
- 28: 57 (Ibn Khālawayh, *Badīʿ*: 113, Ibn Jinnī 2: 153)
- 38: 84 (Dānī, *Muktafā*: 486)
- 56: 79 (Ibn Khālawayh, *Badīʿ*: 151)

Most of these instances are now cited in *Muʿjam al-qirāʾāt al-Qurʾāniyya* 2: 752, 223, 448, 3: 52, 166, 4: 118, 228, 312, 5: 29, 276 from numerous sources. However, where a variant reading is ascribed to Abān quoting ʿĀṣim, this refers to a different person: Abān b. Yazīd b. Aḥmad al-Baṣrī al-ʿAṭṭār, a younger contemporary of Abān b. Taghlib who was also a grammarian, a student of ʿĀṣim and a transmitter of his reading (see Ibn

---

71. There is also a report on his authority in ʿAlī b. Ibrāhīm 2: 349 where he quotes a variant reading from ʿAlī for Qurʾān 56: 82.

al-Jazarī 1: 4). A number of recent authors have confused the two Abāns and misidentified the transmitter from 'Āṣim with Abān b. Taghlib who, while also a student of 'Āṣim, had an independent reading.

2. *Tafsīr gharīb al-Qur'ān*

This book is mentioned by Najāshī: 11 and *Fihrist*: 17 (as *Kitāb al-gharīb fī 'l-Qur'ān*). It seems to be the same as the *Kitāb ma'ānī 'l-Qur'ān* in Ibn al-Nadīm: 276 who describes it as a small book (*laṭīf*). Najāshī: 11 cites the opening sentence of the text. *Fihrist*: 17 notes that the book explains the uncommon words of the Qur'ān by quoting parallels in Arabic poetry. The passage quoted from Abān in Ṭabrisī, *Majma'* 15: 81 on Qur'ān 17: 75 is therefore undoubtedly from this work as it fits the description perfectly.

There are other quotations from Abān on the meaning of various words of the Qur'ān that may well go back to the same work, including his comments on the following verses:

- 5: 3 (A long section in *Khiṣāl*: 451–2; also, though not so attributed, in 'Alī b. Ibrāhīm 1: 161–2)
- 5: 4 ('Ayyāshī 1: 295; *Kāfī* 6: 204)
- 5: 97 ('Ayyāshī 1: 346)
- 8: 30 (Ṭabrisī, *Majma'* 9: 137)
- 9: 101 (Ṭabrisī, *Majma'* 10: 130)
- 13: 29 ('Ayyāshī 2: 212)
- 33: 33 (Ibn 'Asākir 14: 137)
- 42: 52 (Ṣaffār: 455)
- 100: 2 (Khaṭīb, *Sābiq*: 116)

There are also many other quotations from Abān on various Qur'ānic passages, many of which are on the virtues of 'Alī and the House of the Prophet. The latter presumably belonged to Abān's *Kitāb al-faḍā'il*, but some of the others that do not belong to the genre of *faḍā'il* may originally have been parts of the work in question. They include the following:

- Muslim: 114–15 (also Ṭabarī, *Tafsīr* 7: 255; whence Ibn Ḥibbān, *Ṣaḥīḥ* 1: 414–15; Ṭabarānī, *Awsaṭ* 6: 337; idem, *Ṣaghīr* 2: 68; Khaṭīb, *Ta'rīkh* 5: 299) (possibly on Qur'ān 2: 233)
- *Kāfī* 7: 40 (# 3; also *Ma'ānī*: 217) (on 2: 260)
- *Kāfī* 7: 40 (# 1–2; also *Faqīh* 4: 204; *Ma'ānī*: 217) (possibly on 2: 229 or 4: 20)

- 'Ayyāshī 1: 174–5 (also *Kāfī* 8: 337) (on 3: 49)
- Nu'mānī: 320 (on 3: 179)
- Ṭabarānī, *Ṣaghīr* 1: 75 (on 4: 41)
- 'Ayyāshī 1: 261–2 (on 4: 84)
- Ibid. 1: 272 (on 4: 102)
- Ṭabarī, *Tafsīr* 7: 255 (also Ibn 'Adī: 380) (on 6: 82)
- 'Ayyāshī 2: 13 (on 7: 31)
- Ibid. 2: 48 (also *Kāfī* 1: 546; *Faqīh* 2: 44–5) (on 8: 1)
- Ibn Abī 'l-Dunyā, *Mawt*: 54 (possibly on 8: 50 or 32: 11)
- Ibn Bābawayh, *Amālī*: 319–24 (on 12: 50–101)
- *Kamāl*: 671 (on 15: 76)
- *Maḥāsin* 1: 179 (on 21: 101)
- Ibn Abī 'l-Dunyā, *Tahajjud*: 471 (on 40: 18)
- Khaṭīb, *Mūḍiḥ* 2: 420 (possibly on 56: 79)
- 'Ayyāshī (quoted in Ṭabrisī, *Majma'* 30: 239; also *Kāfī* 2: 267) (on 58: 22)
- *'Iqāb*: 247 (on 88: 4)
- *Kāfī* 1: 447–8 (on chapter 105)

According to Najāshī: 12 and *Fihrist*: 17 (whence *Ma'ālim*: 27), Abān's book on *gharīb al-Qur'ān* was put together with similar works of two other pro-'Alīd scholars of Kūfa, the well known Muḥammad b. al-Sā'ib al-Kalbī (d. 146) and the less known 'Aṭiyya b. al-Ḥārith al-Hamdānī[72] in a volume by 'Abd al-Raḥmān b. Muḥammad al-Azdī al-Kūfī (whose name is erroneously given as Muḥammad b. 'Abd al-Raḥmān in Najāshī: 12, as noted by Muḥammad Taqī al-Tustarī 1: 103). He combined the texts of the three works under the relevant passages of the Qur'ān, clearly marking the agreements or particularities of the three works (*Fihrist*: 17). This book seems to be the same as the one quoted by Ibn Ṭāwūs in *Sa'd*: 36, 430–31 for a passage on Qur'ān 19: 28 (see further Kohlberg: 172–3).

3. *Kitāb al-faḍā'il*

(Najāshī: 11; *Fihrist*: 18). Quotations from Abān on the topic, many through the same chain of transmission mentioned by Najāshī and Ṭūsī, abound in Sunnī and Shī'ite collections of *ḥadīth*. They include the following:

- *Maḥāsin* 1: 33, 41, 181

72. For the Shī'ite sympathies of this scholar, see Ibn al-Muṭahhar, *Khulāṣa*: 127 quoting Ibn 'Uqda. See also Abū Ṭālib: 79–81; *Ta'wīl al-āyāt*: 261.

- Ibn Abī 'l-Dunyā, *Tawāḍu'*: 206
- Aḥmad b. 'Īsā 1: 209
  4: 341
- Ṣaffār: 49, 50–51, 52, 122, 307
- 'Ayyāshī 2: 100, 241, 287
- Ṭabarī, *Tafsīr* 7: 255
  20: 97
- Idem, *Tahdhīb, 'Alī*: 45
- *Kāfī* 1: 267
  2: 171–2, 191, 194, 352–3, 427, 520
  3: 197–8, 210–11, 212, 329
  4: 127, 222, 398
  5: 568
  8: 253
- Furāt: 90–91, 92, 106, 116, 134, 173, 201, 234, 274, 294, 320, 323, 557–8, 559
- Ibn al-Juḥām: 185, 216, 220, 222, 223, 278, 286, 372, 423, 452, 453, 473–5
- 'Alī b. Ibrāhīm 2: 117, 262
- Ṭabarānī, *Awsaṭ* 3: 371–2 (three reports)
  4: 171, 172
- Idem, *Du'ā'*: 903–4
- Idem, *Kabīr* 3: 371–2
  17: 225
- Idem, *Ṣaghīr* 1: 129
- Ibn Ḥibbān, *Ṣaḥīḥ* 12: 280
- Ibn 'Adī: 753 (also Khaṭīb, *Ta'rīkh* 7: 383), 2406
- Ibn Qūlawayh: 83–4, 171–2, 232–4, 546
- Ibn Bābawayh, *Amālī*: 88–9, 141, 187, 267, 343, 355, 433–4, 462, 589, 727–8, 737
- Idem, *Faḍā'il al-Shī'a* : 2
- *'Ilal* 1: 172–3, 221
- *Kamāl*: 221, 410
- *Ma'ānī*: 66
- *Thawāb*: 48, 54, 231
- Ibn Mardawayh, *Manāqib* (quoted in Ḥammū'ī, *Farā'id* 1: 270–72; Khwārazmī, *Manāqib*: 146–7; Ibn Ṭāwūs, *Ṭarā'if*: 24–6)
- Mufīd, *Amālī*: 112–13, 338
- *Ikhtiṣāṣ*: 23, 62–3, 284

- Tha'labī, *al-Kashf wa 'l-bayān*, on Qur'ān 3: 103 and 24: 36 (quoted in Ibn Biṭrīq, *Khaṣā'iṣ*: 79, 183 and *'Umda*: 350, 353)
- Abū Ṭālib: 32, 87
- Abū Nu'aym, *Akhbār Iṣbahān* (quoted in Suyūṭī, *Itqān* 4: 182)
- *Ḥilya* 3: 199–200
- 'Āṣimī 2: 31
- Ṭūsī, *Amālī*: 115, 188, 349, 636, 664–5
- *Miṣbāḥ*: 716, 841–2
- *Tahdhīb* 3: 91
- Wāḥidī, *Asbāb*: 363
- Ibn Shāhīn, *Targhīb*: 392
- Ḥaskānī 1: 169, 183, 344, 359, 374, 387, 425, 442, 495, 522, 533, 539, 563, 564, 569
  2: 74, 226, 330, 417–18, 431, 466
- Ṭabrisī, *Majma'* 4: 157
  19: 162
  30: 239
- Ibn 'Asākir 14: 137
  42: 264, 313, 329, 541
  54: 15, 275
- *Manāqib* 2: 231
  4: 77
- *Bishārat al-Muṣṭafā*: 118
- Ibn Ṭāwūs, *Muhaj*: 200–201
- Idem, *Yaqīn*: 11
- Kanjī: 186, 386–7 (quoting Ḥākim's *Ṭuruq Ḥadīth al-Ṭayr*)

4. *Kitāb Ṣiffīn*

This book is only mentioned by Najāshī: 11; he had not seen the book himself but was informed of its existence by Ibn al-Ghaḍā'irī who in turn quoted Ibn 'Uqda. The work was supposedly quoted by Sayf b. 'Amīra, a Shī'ite transmitter of *ḥadīth* whose transmission from Abān is attested elsewhere (e.g. *Kāfī* 2: 267, 6: 204; Ṭabarānī, *Awsaṭ* 3: 371–2 [three reports]). There is a long passage in *Bishārat al-Muṣṭafā*: 141–2 on some of the events that occurred at Ṣiffīn with the text of a sermon that 'Alī gave there, quoted on the authority of Abān but through a different transmitter. There is also a quotation from Abān on 'Alī's seemingly contradictory practices in the battles of the Camel and Ṣiffīn in *Kāfī* 3: 33 and Kashshī:

218. Abān, however, was not a historian. There is a long report, the size of a small treatise, on the events of the Saqīfa of the Banū Sā'ida, the place in Medina where Abū Bakr was declared caliph after the death of the Prophet. The report is quoted on the authority of Abān in *Iḥtijāj* 1: 186–203. This is basically a Shī'ite sectarian polemic which seems to have been in circulation in the Shī'ite community of Kūfa in the Umayyad period, and was later preserved in several different versions and through various chains of transmission. There are also other lengthy reports quoted on Abān's authority on other matters related to the events of the Saqīfa: the protest of Fāṭima al-Zahrā' (Ṭūsī, *Amālī*: 683–4) and a sermon by 'Alī called the *Shiqshiqiyya* where he talks, inter alia, about the Saqīfa (*'Ilal* 1: 144–6; *Ma'ānī*: 361–2). One is therefore tempted to suggest that the name *Ṣiffīn* in Najāshī may represent a slip of the pen or the tongue or a lapse of mind, by him or his informer, for *Saqīfa*, and that the reference is to that polemic treatise on the Shī'ite version of the events of the Saqīfa.

5. *Aṣl*

This work is mentioned in *Fihrist*: 18 and seems to be the one meant by Ibn al-Nadīm: 276, listing among Abān's works a *Kitāb [yu'addu] min al-uṣūl fī 'l-riwāya 'alā madhāhib* [possibly *madhhab*] *al-Shī'a*. Many of the numerous reports on legal and ethical matters quoted on the authority of Abān in Sunnī and Shī'ite works may originally have belonged to this notebook. For a list of most of these quotations in Shī'ite collections of *ḥadīth*, see Khu'ī 1: 403–8; *Fahāris* 8: 9, 249.

Ibn Idrīs, the Imāmite scholar of the late sixth century, quotes a large fragment of a text that he identifies as "the book of Abān b. Taghlib" in his *Mustaṭrafāt*: 39–44. The name *Abān* appears as the author at the very beginning of this text, but as is clear from the chains of transmission for the reports included, this Abān is a different person who must have lived in the middle of the third century, some one hundred years after Abān b. Taghlib (see further, Muḥammad Taqī al-Tustarī 1: 106).

11: Abū 'Ubayda al-Ḥadhdhā'

Abū 'Ubayda Ziyād b. 'Īsā, the shoemaker, a Kūfan client and a disciple of Muḥammad al-Bāqir, whom he once accompanied on a pilgrimage to Mecca, and Ja'far al-Ṣādiq. He died during the latter's lifetime; that is, in or before 148. He was a prolific transmitter of *ḥadīth* and, as can be gathered from his transmissions, a jurisconsult in his own community.

Barqī: 55, 66; Kashshī: 368–9; Najāshī: 170–71; *Rijāl*: 135, 208. See also Ḥusayn b-Sa'īd, *Mu'min*: 31; Abān al-Sindī: 564; *Maḥāsin*: 70, 263; 'Ayyāshī 1: 167; *Kāfī* 2: 179, 180, 4: 558, 5: 381; Ibn Hammām: 31; *Tahdhīb* 7: 365; *Ikhtiṣāṣ*: 83.

Najāshī cites the biographical material he found on this transmitter in earlier Shī'ite sources on the transmitters of *ḥadīth* where some data that relate to other early transmitters with the name *Ziyād* seem to have been misattributed to this person. A quotation from Sa'd b. 'Abd Allāh al-Ash'arī ibid.: 171 identifies our transmitter as Ziyād b. Aḥram (variantly, Akhram or Akhzam). *Rijāl*: 209 names a Ziyād b. Aḥmar al-'Ijlī al-Kūfī among the transmitters from Ja'far al-Sādiq who may be identical with this transmitter (assuming that one of the two names: *Aḥmar* and *Aḥram* is corrupt). The reference in *Rijāl* would thus suggest that Abū 'Ubayda was a client of the Banū 'Ijl of Bakr b. Wā'il.

Kitāb

The late third century Shī'ite biographer, Aḥmad b. 'Alī al-'Aqīqī, knew a notebook of *ḥadīth* by Abū 'Ubayda al-Ḥadhdhā' that the mid-second century transmitter, 'Alī b. Ri'āb had related from him (Najāshī: 171). The numerous quotations from Abū 'Ubayda on the authority of 'Alī b. Ri'āb in early Shī'ite sources may therefore be remnants extracted from this notebook. They include the following examples:

- Ḥusayn b. Sa'īd, *Zuhd*: 6–7, 51 (read *'an Abī 'Ubayda al-Ḥadhdhā'* as in *Maḥāsin*: 263 and *Kāfī* 2: 124), 56, 90–91 (read *'an Abī 'Ubayda al-Ḥadhdhā'* as in 'Alī b. Ibrāhīm 2: 259), 99, 100
- *Maḥāsin*: 205, 263, 635 (also *Kāfī* 6: 539–40)
- Ṣaffār: 153–4
- *Kāfī* 1: 42 (also 7: 409), 65, 241, 325 (partially also 2: 106), 348, 458
  2: 124, 208
  3: 82, 106, 328, 376
  4: 387, 388, 487
  5: 385, 408, 425 (also 445)
  6: 203, 208, 212, 539–40
  7: 110, 140 (also 298), 141 (also 344), 162, 259, 398
  8: 104–6, 182, 200

- 'Alī b. Ibrāhīm 1:127 (where the name of 'Alī b. Ri'āb is missing in this edition), 244–5 (also 'Ayyāshī 2: 33–4; Ibn Ṭāwūs, *Sa'd*: 118–19 [quoting Ibn 'Uqda's *Tafsīr*]), 365 (two citations)
  2: 259
- Ibn Qūlawayh: 77–8
- *Faqīh* 4: 42 (also *Tahdhīb* 10: 19)
- *Tahdhīb* 5: 14
  7: 463–4
  9: 396

Many of the quotations from Abū 'Ubayda in 'Ayyāshī (1: 84–5, 87–8, 167, 294, 335, 364, 2: 33–4, 129, 136, 143, 147, 154, 231), where the chains of transmission after the first transmitters are usually omitted in its current abridged version, may have been through 'Alī b. Ri'āb as attested for at least three of those citations ('Ayyāshī 1: 294 in *Kāfī* 6 : 203; 'Ayyāshī 1: 335 in *Kāfī* 8: 200; 'Ayyāshī 2: 33–4 in 'Alī b. Ibrāhīm 1: 244–5).

12: Sa'd al-Iskāf

Sa'd b. Ṭarīf al-Iskāf (the shoemaker), a Kūfan client of the Banū Ḥanẓala, a clan of Tamīm, and a transmitter of Sunnī and Shī'ite *ḥadīth*. He was a preacher/story teller (*qāṣṣ*) in the late Umayyad period, and this clearly helped his transmissions make their way into Sunnī literature in spite of the fact that he was publicly known as an advocate of 'Alī.

Bukhārī, *Kabīr* 4 : 59; 'Ijlī: 179; Nasā'ī, *Ḍu'afā'*: 130; Fasawī (who thought that Sa'd b. Ṭarīf and Sa'd al-Iskāf were two different persons) 3 : 38–9, 58, 64, 66; Barqī: 50; Kashshī: 214–15; Najāshī: 178; *Fihrist*: 76–7; *Rijāl*: 115, 136, 212; Mizzī 10: 271–2 (and many other sources listed in the editor's footnote).

'Uqaylī 2: 120, Ibn 'Adī 3: 1186 and later Sunnī biographical works identify this transmitter as a staunch Shī'ite. That he was a *qāṣṣ* is attested in a report from him in Kashshī: 215 and Najāshī: 178 (though in the latter, the word is corrupted to *qāḍī*). His date of death is unknown. Both Bukhārī, *Awsaṭ* 2: 49 and Dhahabī, *Ta'rīkh* 9 (years 141–160): 147 have him among those who died between the years 141 and 150. A report in Kashshī: 215 suggests that he was alive at the time of Ja'far al-Ṣādiq's death in 148 as it mentions that Sa'd "stopped" with Ja'far and did not follow anyone as his successor. This must have been a different person as it is not clear if Sa'd al-Iskāf was even a follower of Ja'far al-Ṣādiq. In contrast to a large number of citations from Muḥammad al-Bāqir, Sa'd's transmission from

Ja'far al-Ṣādiq is attested only in a single case (*Maḥāsin*: 590).[73] He also transmitted from other members of the House of the Prophet such as Zayd b. 'Alī[74] and Muḥammad b. 'Umar b. 'Alī b. Abī Ṭālib.[75] A couple of esoteric reports attributed to Sa'd al-Iskāf in Mufīd, *Mazār*: 192 (quoting Muḥammad b. Aḥmad b. Dāwūd al-Qummī's *Kitāb al-Ziyārāt*; also *Tahdhīb* 6: 106–7) and *Manāqib* 4: 222 (also *Kharā'ij*: 606–7) are most likely of later contribution as such an esoteric tone is not attested elsewhere in his transmissions.

Sa'd al-Iskāf is the source for a large number of reports in Sunnī and Shī'ite collections of *ḥadīth*. He is the main transmitter from Aṣbagh b. Nubāta from, or about, 'Alī. Consistent with his profession as a *qāṣṣ*, his other transmissions are generally in the field of religious ethics. There are occasional exceptions such as the material that Naṣr b. Muzāḥim: 5, 98–100, 126–7, 167, 303–4 quotes from him on the events of Ṣiffīn (the last citation sounds as if it is taken from a book by him as it begins with "Sa'd al-Iskāf said", with no *isnād* attached).

1. *Risālat Abī Ja'far ilayh*

This work, a letter from Imām Muḥammad al-Bāqir to Sa'd, is mentioned by Najāshī: 178. Muḥammad Taqī al-Tustarī 5: 47 suggests that Najāshī may have confused Sa'd al-Iskāf with Sa'd al-Khayr to whom *Kāfī* 8: 52–7 ascribes the texts of two letters written by Muḥammad al-Bāqir. This latter, Sa'd b. 'Abd al-Malik, a descendant of 'Abd al-'Azīz b. Marwān, brother and the original heir-apparent of the caliph 'Abd al-Malik (*Ikhtiṣāṣ* : 85), was an Umayyad partisan of the 'Alīds' cause.

Kāfī 2: 596–8 also quotes the text of a long statement supposed to be by Muḥammad al-Bāqir to Sa'd al-Iskāf on the merits of the Qur'ān, followed by a set of questions and answers between Sa'd and the Imām that is intended to prove the excellence of the House of the Prophet. This is a second century Shī'ite polemical tract, different in style and tone

73. There is also an esoteric report ascribed to Ja'far al-Ṣādiq on the authority of Sa'd al-Iskāf in Mufīd, *Mazār*: 192 (also *Tahdhīb* 6: 106–7), but the ascription sounds spurious as noted above. A report in *Tahdhīb* 6: 229 on the authority of *Sa'd* from Ja'far al-Ṣādiq may not be by Sa'd al-Iskāf. It is quoted from *Sa'd* by [Ibn] Abī 'Umayr, an occasional transmitter from Sa'd al-Iskāf (e.g. *Kāfī* 3: 164) but more frequently from others of the same name (see Khu'ī 8: 48–9, 94, 14: 426, 22: 282). A citation by Sa'd attributed to Ja'far al-Ṣādiq in *Ma'ānī*: 343 is ascribed to Muḥammad al-Bāqir in *Khiṣāl*: 112 and seems to originally have been part of a longer report cited in *Ma'ānī*: 314 (as well as *Maḥāsin*: 4 and *Khiṣāl*: 84) or from a text in *Kāfī* 2: 668, both from Muḥammad al-Bāqir.

74. Ḥusayn b. Sa'īd, *Zuhd*: 101; Abū Nu'aym, *Ṣifat al-janna* 3:247 (also Khaṭīb, *Ta'rīkh* 1: 266).

75. Ṣaffār: 50.

from other transmissions of Saʿd, but probably presented at the time as a letter from the Imām to him. It is possibly to this text that Najāshī refers.

2. *Kitāb*

Saʿd's notebook of *ḥadīth*, related from him by various transmitters (*Fihrist*: 76). Apart from his citations from ʿAlī through Aṣbagh, the Shīʿites were particularly interested in Saʿd's transmissions from Muḥammad al-Bāqir that should have formed a major component of Saʿd's notebook. Examples include the following:

- Ḥusayn b. Saʿīd, *Muʾmin:* 15–16
- Idem, *Zuhd*: 22, 66
- Ibn Shabba: 132
- *Maḥāsin*: 4, 40, 60, 393, 590, 616
- Ṣaffār: 24, 48, 56, 74, 97, 100, 391–2, 414, 496–7 (also 499, 500 with variations)
- Aḥmad b. ʿĪsā 4: 367
- ʿAyyāshī 1: 25, 86, 101, 171, 203–4, 384
  2: 18, 267 (repeated at 268), 326; also Ṭabrisī, *Majmaʿ* 30: 131 (quoting from the lost section of ʿAyyāshī)
- Muḥammad b. Sulaymān 1: 429
  2: 537–8
- *Kāfī* 1: 208, 394 (and a variant at 395; esoteric, most likely a later contribution)
  2: 330–31, 570–71 (read *ʿan Abī Jaʿfar* as in *Tahdhīb* 2: 117 and *Faqīh* 1: 471), 601 (read *ʿan Abī Jaʿfar* as in ʿAyyāshī 1: 25), 612 (also Ibn Bābawayh, *Amālī*: 115; *Maʿānī*: 147; *Thawāb*: 129), 668
  3: 111, 164 (two reports), 165
  4: 46, 69–70, 254–5
  5: 119 (repeated at 520), 147, 161, 521
  6: 54, 326, 400
  7: 352, 405
- Furāt: 257–8, 364
- Ibn al-Juḥām: 402 (read *Saʿd b. Ṭarīf* [as in *Taʾwīl al-āyāt*: 715] for *Sālim b. Ṭarīf*)
- Alī b. Ibrāhīm 2: 346
- Qāḍī Nuʿmān, *Sharḥ* 1: 228
  2: 409–10, 415–16

- Ibn Qūlawayh: 146
- *Faqīh* 4: 61
- *Khiṣāl*: 84, 112, 118–19, 448 (cf. *Thawāb*: 52, 53 and *Tahdhīb* 2: 283, 284 for variants of this text; see further *Faqīh* 1: 293)
- *Ma'ānī*: 35–6, 164, 314, 373, 395
- *Irshād* 1: 87
- *Ḥilya* 3: 183 (two reports)
- Ḥaskānī 1: 79, 436, 2: 309
- Ibn 'Asākir 14: 198
  21: 412 (read *Sa'd* for *Abī Sa'd*)
  42: 53–4
- Ḥasan b. Sulaymān: 93–4
- *Biḥār* 43: 201 (quoting Hāshim b. Muḥammad's *Miṣbāḥ al-anwār*)

13: Abū 'l-Jārūd

Abū 'l-Jārūd Ziyād b. al-Mundhir al-Hamdānī al-Khārifī, the blind, a Kūfan Shī'ite scholar and leader of the Jārūdī branch of Zaydī Shī'ism. A disciple of Muḥammad al-Bāqir in his time, he later joined Zayd b. 'Alī in revolt against the Umayyads and separated his path from the followers of Ja'far al-Ṣādiq.

For a summary of biographical material and a list of the main sources on Abū 'l-Jārūd, see the entries on him in the *Encyclopaedia Iranica* 1: 327–8 (W. Madelung) and van Ess, *Theologie* 1: 254–7. For the doctrines of Jārūdī Zaydism, see the latter 1: 257–68.

Dhahabī, *Ta'rīkh* 9 (years 141–160): 140–41 has Abū 'l-Jārūd among those who died between the years 140–150 and Bukhārī, *Awsaṭ* 2: 112 among those who died between 151–160. These are clearly random guesses as there is basically little, if anything, known about him after the last years of the Umayyad period.[76]

A large number of reports are quoted on the authority of Abū 'l-Jārūd in Sunnī and Shī'ite works. A report in Ibn Abī Ḥātim 3: 546 refers to 'Abū 'l-Jārūd's books, which, according to this source, he burnt late in life.

76. Two reports in Ibn al-Nadīm: 226–7 suggest a major change in Abū 'l-Jārūd's position, both in terms of religiosity and in doctorial belief, later in life. This may go well with the report in Ibn Abī Ḥātim 3: 546 which suggests that he burnt his books before his death, as cited above.

1. *Tafsīr al-Qu'rān*

This work, also known as *Tafsīr al-Bāqir*, is mentioned by Ibn al-Nadīm: 36; Najāshī: 170; *Fihrist*: 72; Ibn 'Adī: 1048 and others. Both Najāshī and Ṭūsī received the book through a chain of transmission that goes back to Abū Sahl Kathīr b. 'Ayyāsh al-Qaṭṭān, a transmitter from Abū 'l-Jārūd who was reportedly alive until the end of the second century and later in life joined the revolt of Abū 'l-Sarāyā (Sarī b. Manṣūr al-Shaybānī) in the years 199–200 (*Fihrist*: 72). It has partially survived in a work known as *Tafsīr 'Alī b. Ibrāhīm al-Qummī* that incorporates the bulk of the material from Abū 'l-Jārūd's *Tafsīr* from the beginnings of chapter 3 of the Qur'ān to the end, always clearly marked (for a list of this material, see now Bar-Asher: 244–7, and for an analysis see ibid.: 46–56). The chain of transmission in this work also ends up with the same transmitter, Kathīr b. 'Ayyāsh ('Alī b. Ibrāhīm 1: 102 [the first citation from Abū 'l-Jārūd], 198, 224, 271). A copy of the work in its original form was still available in the mid-seventh century to Ibn Ṭāwūs who describes and quotes from its first five parts in his *Sa'd al-su'ūd*: 245–9 (see further Kohlberg: 339). Material on interpretation of verses of the Qur'ān, in most cases presumably from the same work, is also cited in many early works, many times through the same transmitter of the book (e.g. Ibn al-Juḥām: 170, 188, 196, 243–4, 261, 287, 403; Ibn Bābawayh, *Amālī*: 186). Examples include the following:

- Ḥibarī: 44
- Aḥmad b. 'Īsā 4: 333, 334 (two reports)
- 'Ayyāshī 1: 9, 17, 86, 154, 225, 233, 234, 283, 288–9, 380
  2: 101, 218, 315 (also Ṭabrisī, *Majma'* 23: 167 ; *Manāqib* 4: 179, both quoting from the missing part of 'Ayyāshī's work)
- Muḥammad b. Sulaymān 1: 171
  2: 382, 414–15
- Ṭabarī, *Tafsīr* 3: 300
  30: 265
- *Kāfī* 8: 289
- Furāt: 79, 90, 119, 187, 188, 246, 277, 278, 325, 347, 395–7, 419–20, 496–7, 534
- Ibn al-Juḥām 109–10, 170, 180, 188, 196, 207–8 (three reports), 216, 217, 230, 232, 243–4, 261, 281–2, 287, 302, 352, 379, 382, 403
- Ibn 'Adī: 1048

- Ibn Bābawayh, *Nuṣūṣ* (quoted in *Biḥār* 13: 178)
- Ḥaskānī 1: 59, 254–5, 357–8, 366–8, 386, 388, 409, 569
  2: 82–3, 183, 284, 357, 421
- Ṭabrisī, *Majma'* 5: 206–7
  23: 167
- *Manāqib* 2: 16, 104
  3: 98, 202–3
  4: 2–3, 116, 129, 130, 179
- *Ta'wīl al-āyāt*: 401

2. *Aṣl*

Abū 'l-Jārūd's notebook of *ḥadīth*, related from him by Kathīr b. 'Ayyāsh al-Qaṭṭān (*Fihrist*: 72) who, as noted above, also related this author's *Tafsīr*. Most of the quotations from Abū 'l-Jārūd in the Imāmite and Zaydī collections of *ḥadīth* on legal and ethico-religious matters, some indeed through Kathīr b. 'Ayyāsh (e.g. Aḥmad b. 'Īsā 3:25; Ibn Bābawayh, *Amālī*: 394–5; *Ma'ānī*: 101–2, 45–6; *Tawḥīd*: 236) seem to go back to this notebook. In Zaydī sources, however, Abū 'l-Jārūd is mostly cited on the authority of Muḥammad b. Bakr al-Arḥabī al-Kūfī (d. 171, as in *Rijāl*: 278), and in Imāmite works through Muḥammad b. Sinān al-Ẓāhirī (d. 220) who should have quoted Abū 'l-Jārūd via an intermediary or directly from his notebook. Ibn al-Ghaḍā'irī: 61 reports that in his time the Imāmites too preferred Arḥabī's transmissions to those by Muḥammad b. Sinān, though very few examples of Arḥabī's transmissions have survived in Imāmite works (as, for instance, in *Kāfī* 2: 624–6).

Here is a very incomplete list of citations from Abū 'l-Jārūd in some Zaydī and Imāmite works of *ḥadīth*:

- 'Abbād b. Ya'qūb: 16
- *Maḥāsin*: 4, 5, 103, 104, 157, 160, 251, 264, 269, 271, 388, 400, 415, 447, 454, 495, 511, 547, 579, 584, 601, 612, 643
- Aḥmad b. 'Īsā 1: 34 (two reports), 37, 41, 42 (two reports), 47, 48, 50, 55, 62, 64, 67 (two reports), 68, 75, 77, 82, 92 (two reports), 100, 106, 108, 110, 129, 130, 136 (two reports), 147 (two reports, in the second read *'an Muḥammad b. Bakr 'an Abī 'l-Jārūd* for *'an Muḥammad b. Abī 'l-Jārūd*), 153, 157, 159, 164, 168, 171, 174–5 (four reports), 180 (two reports), 184, 201 (three reports), 202 (four reports), 203, 204, 215 (three reports, in the last two read *'an Muḥammad b. Bakr 'an Abī*

'l-Jārūd as above), 226, 227–8 (three reports), 229–30 (four reports), 232, 233, 236, 240, 242, 244, 245, 246, 247 (two reports), 248
2: 287, 354, 356–70 (Muḥammad al-Bāqir's treatise on the rituals of *ḥajj*, related by Yaḥyā b. Sālim al-Farrā' from Abū 'l-Jārūd), 370–72 (14 reports), 425 (by 'Abd Allāh b. al-Mughīra)
3: 18, 25 (by Kathīr b. 'Ayyāsh al-Qaṭṭān), 31, 32, 41, 42, 47, 131, 173
4: 323 (by Ibrāhīm al-Shaybānī; whence Abū 'Abd Allāh al-Shajarī, *Faḍl*: 44–6), 334 (two reports)[77]

- Ṣaffār: 21, 84, 85, 111, 148 (also 149, 163, 164, 168 with variations), 218–19, 377, 407, 421, 489, 492 (also 494 with variations)
- Muḥammad b. Sulaymān 1: 205, 358, 392, 2: 162, 164, 552, 554
- *Kāfī* 1: 11, 41, 60, 194–5, 221, 290, 303–4, 532, 534
  2: 21–2, 86, 90, 126, 143, 189–90, 600
  3: 121, 164, 173, 222, 226, 506
  4: 256, 354, 362, 365, 433, 465
  5: 123, 420
  6: 246, 264, 270, 349–50, 390, 412, 445, 447–8, 467, 477, 545
  7: 39, 272
  8: 86, 263, 289, 317–18
- Kashshī: 5, 103, 106, 113–14, 124–5, 231–2
- Furāt: 151
- Nuʿmānī: 154, 179, 182, 183, 191–3 (three reports), 194–6 (three reports), 229, 238 (two reports), 242, 274, 315, 322 (also 323 with variations)
- *Maqātil*: 18, 127, 130
- Qāḍī Nuʿmān, *Īḍāḥ*: 48b, 48b–49a, 50a, 102b, 110b, 115b
- Ibn Qūlawayh: 106, 151–2, 451, 489–90 (also *Thawāb*: 114)
- Ibn Bābawayh, *Amālī*: 61, 65, 85, 191, 202–3 (two reports), 228–9, 235, 278, 315–16, 380, 394–5, 434, 698–700, 705
- Idem, *Faḍā'il al-ashhur*: 123–4
- *Faqīh* 1: 152, 253, 260
  2: 360, 459
  3: 534
  4: 171, 180
- *'Ilal* 2: 37, 272
- *'Iqāb*: 255, 271–2, 279, 288, 309, 310, 320, 327

77. With the exception of those specified, all above citations are by Muḥammad b. Bakr al-Arḥabī al-Hamdānī (see ibid. 1: 37).

- *Kamāl*: 304, 670
- *Khiṣāl*: 113, 132, 171, 194–5, 200, 219, 292, 397–8, 409–10, 477–8 (on the tablet that came down to Fāṭima al-Zahrā' with the names of the twelve Imāms on it, a report that according to Mufīd in his monograph against the followers of Abū 'l-Jārūd [*al-Masā'il al-Jārūdiyya*: 35] they ridicule), 499, 554–63, 640
- *Ma'ānī*: 45–6, 95, 188, 222, 262, 298, 299
- *Tawḥīd*: 165, 236, 288, 383–4, 457
- *Thawāb*: 26, 27, 114, 131, 231
- Mufīd, *Kāfi'a*: 25–6, 31, 34, 40, 41–2
- *Irshād* 2: 172, 384
- Murtaḍā, *Nāṣiriyyāt*: 64
- Ṭūsī, *Amālī*: 142, 317, 426, 456–7, 501, 600–602, 623
- *Ghayba*: 139 (a revised text), 427, 441, 474
- *Tahdhīb* 2: 191, 337
  4: 164, 262, 317
  6: 46
  8: 5, 147
- Ḥaskānī 2: 79
- *Bishārat al-Muṣṭafā*: 16, 18, 32, 59–60, 69, 73, 185 (two reports)

Parts of this material have found their way into Sunnī sources too. Examples are as follows:

- Yaḥyā b. Ma'īn 2: 180
- Tirmidhī 4: 241
- Bazzār 2: 146–7 (whence Ibn Shāhīn, *Nāsikh*: 188–9 [also 190, 191 with variations])
- Abū Ya'lā 1: 347
- Ṭabarānī, *Akhbār al-Ḥasan*: 116–17
- Ibn 'Adī: 1047–8 [twelve reports]
- Khaṭīb, *Talkhīṣ*: 600
- Ibn 'Asākir 42: 60, 168, 333, 468
- Ibn al-Jawzī, *'Ilal* 1: 150

III

The Period of Persecution (136–198)

The 'Abbāsid revolution brought an end to the long established anti-Hāshimid rule of the Umayyads in Damascus. The seat of the caliphate now moved for a brief period to the largely, though by no means exclusively, pro-Shī'ite Kūfa. For a few years immediately before and after the revolution, the Shī'a, who were still basically concentrated in Kūfa and to a much lesser degree in some other regions of Iraq, enjoyed a time of relative calm and peace. The power struggle between the 'Abbāsids and the Ḥasanid branch of the 'Alīds soon changed this situation. Under Manṣūr, the second 'Abbāsid ruler (r. 136–158), the persecution of the 'Alīds resumed and then continued in full force to the end of the reign of his grandson, Hārūn al-Rashīd (r. 170–193).

The Shī'ite community witnessed a number of tragedies that revived for them the memories of similar disasters in the Umayyad period. At first, the Ḥasanid branch of the House of the Prophet lost many members to the brutal, ruthless suppression of Manṣūr, resulting in the revolts and subsequent massacres of such figures as Ibrāhīm b. 'Abd Allāh b. al-Ḥasan in Baṣra and his brother Muḥammad b. 'Abd Allāh al-Nafs al-Zakiyya in Medina, both in 145, their cousin Ḥusayn b. 'Alī b. al-Ḥasan, Ṣāḥib Fakhkh, in 169, and the younger brother of al-Nafs al-Zakiyya, Yaḥyā b. 'Abd Allāh b. al-Ḥasan in 175. Next, the Ḥusaynids, represented by the Imāms Ja'far al-Ṣādiq and Mūsā al-Kāẓim and their followers, suffered severe persecution culminating in the death of the latter in prison under Harūn in 183. Internally, Imāmite Shī'ism experienced splits and divisions caused by the schism of followers of the Extremist Abū 'l-Khaṭṭāb Muḥammad b. Abī Zaynab al-Asadī in ca. 138,[1] of the Faṭḥites who followed 'Abd Allāh al-Afṭaḥ as the Imām after the death of his father Ja'far al-Ṣādiq in 148, and later recognized Mūsā al-Kāẓim only as successor to 'Abd Allāh and not to his father Ja'far, and of the Wāqifites who after the death of Mūsā al-Kāẓim in 183 denied his death, suggesting that he had gone into occultation to reappear in a future time as the one who establishes the rule of justice on earth. External persecution and internal splits, the two main features of the Imāmite community in this period, continued until the last years of the century when the civil war brought Ma'mūn (r. 198–218) to the caliphate and he, in turn, appointed Imām 'Alī al-Riḍā as successor to the throne.

The list that follows this introductory note includes the Imāmite authors who lived during the first seventy years or so of 'Abbāsid rule but in most probability did not survive into the third century. It also includes a number of non-Imāmite authors of this period, whether Sunnīs or Zaydīs, certain works of whom were considered by later Imāmites as parts of their own heritage. Most of these were transmitters of *ḥadīth* who frequented the house of Ja'far al-Ṣādiq and quoted *ḥadīth* from him; but the Imāmites rarely, if at all, saw them after that time, though some lived into the early years of the third century. The list also includes those among the first generation of the Wāqifites whose dates of death are unknown and about whom there is no information after the period covered in this section. Some of them, too, may have lived into the early years of the following century.

---

1. A report from this period in Irbilī 3: 197 that speaks of the time when the Shī'ite community split (read *ḥīn ikhtalaf al-Shī'a*) seems to refer to this schism.

1: Abān al-Aḥmar

Abū 'Abd Allāh Abān b. 'Uthmān al-Aḥmar, a client of Bajīla and a prominent scholar of general Arabic literature and history. He lived in both Kūfa and Baṣra at different times, and was a transmitter from Ja'far al-Ṣādiq and his disciples.

Barqī: 99; Kashshī: 352, 375; 'Uqaylī 1: 37–8; Ibn Ḥibbān, *Thiqāt* 8: 131; Najāshī: 13; *Fihrist*: 18–19; *Rijāl*: 164; *Mīzān* 1:10; *Lisān* 1: 35–6.

Yāqūt, *Irshād* 1: 39 citing Ṭūsī's *Fihrist* (whence Suyūṭī, *Bughya* 1: 405) identifies this scholar as *Abān b. 'Uthmān b. Yaḥyā b. Zakariyyā al-Lu'lu'ī*. The reference does not appear in the *Fihrist*, nor does it seem correct as Yaḥyā b. Zakariyyā al-Lu'lu'ī is a late third century scholar whom Ṭūsī mentions in a separate entry in that work: 179. *Maḥāsin*: 72 calls him Abān b. 'Uthmān al-Aḥmar *al-Tamīmī*, a *nisba* not attested for Abān elsewhere. Abān's student, Muḥammad b. Sallām al-Jumaḥī in his *Ṭabaqāt*: 211, 414 calls him Abān *al-A'raj*. This may be a corruption of the epithet *al-Aḥmar* mentioned in all other sources.

There is a conflict of reports about Abān's town of origin. Kashshī: 352 reports that he was a Baṣran by origin who lived in Kūfa. Najāshī: 13 and *Fihrist*: 18, on the other hand, have him as a Kūfan who lived in both Baṣra and Kūfa at different times. *Ma'ālim*: 27 says that he was a Kūfan who resided in Baṣra. Barqī: 99 calls him *a Kūfan*, an expression said by Muḥammad Taqī al-Tustarī 1: 13 to normally refer to the place of origin (as against *the Kūfan* which indicates one's place of residence; but this assumption needs further investigation). There were certainly more Bajalīs in Kūfa, their first adopted home after they moved up from their original lands in Arabia during the caliphate of 'Umar (Ṭabarī 3: 471); there was a special district of the city named after them (Kaḥḥāla 1: 65).

Both Najāshī and *Fihrist* note that scholars of Baṣra such as Abū 'Ubayda Ma'mar b. al-Muthannā (d. 209) and Abū 'Abd Allāh Muḥammad b. Sallām (al-Jumaḥī, d. 232) quoted him in their works as an authority on Arab poetry, genealogy and historic battles. *Ma'ālim*: 27 erroneously combines parts of these names and asserts that Abū 'Ubayd Qāsim b. Sallām (al-Harawī, d. 224) studied with Abān. Jāḥiz, *Bayān* 2: 50–55 quotes five sermons from 'Alī on the authority of Ma'mar b. al-Muthannā (see ibid. 51: *qāla Abū 'Ubayda*, 55: *wa bi-hādhā 'l-isnād*), including one on the virtues of the House of the Prophet with strong Shī'ite overtones. Wilferd Madelung[2] suggests that Ma'mar may have actually quoted those, or at least some of them, from Abān. Muḥammad b. Sallām quotes Abān in his *Ṭabaqāt fuḥūl al-shu'arā'*: 45, 87, 211, 213, 316, 322, 375, 406, 414, 422, 423, 458.

2. In his article "Abū 'Ubayda Ma'mar b. al-Muthannā as a historian," in the *Journal of Islamic Studies* (Oxford) 3 (1992): 47–56.

Kashshī: 352 reports that Abān became a *Nāwūsī*, a group that after the death of Ja'far al-Ṣādiq did not recognize anyone as his successor and thus separated from the overwhelming majority of his followers who eventually accepted one or the other of his sons as the next Imām. Recent Shī'ite authors (such as Muḥammad Taqī al-Tustarī 1: 114–16) have argued against the authority of that report but none of their arguments is sufficiently convincing.

Kashshī: 375 says that Abān was among the younger generation of the disciples of Ja'far al-Ṣādiq (d. 148). Shī'ite sources do not give a date of death for Abān but *Lisān* 1: 36 gives the year 200. The round figure suggests a random dating. The same source also cites an unspecified work, most likely Ibn Abī Ṭayy's *Ta'rīkh al-Shī'a*, that praised Abān's phenomenal memory for being so retentive as to enable him to quote verbatim (read *yarwī lanā*) his own work (from memory) without adding a single word to it.

1. *Kitāb al-mubtada' wa 'l-mab'ath wa 'l-maghāzī wa 'l-wafāt wa 'l-Saqīfa wa 'l-ridda*

(Najāshī: 13; *Fihrist*: 18). This was a work on the life of the Prophet, with a chapter on the creation of man and the history of the prophets before Muḥammad. The many quotations from Abān by later authors on those topics seem all to be taken from this work. That includes Ya'qūbī who specifies in his *Ta'rīkh* 2: 6 that he quotes from Abān from Ja'far al-Ṣādiq. Sezgin 1: 278 erroneously identifies Ya'qūbī's source as Abān, son of the caliph 'Uthmān, who is conventionally believed to be the first author of a work on the life of the Prophet, written for the future Umayyad caliph, Sulaymān b. 'Abd al-Malik, in the year 82. This latter Abān is clearly unlikely to have been Ya'qūbī's source, since Ya'qūbī's source quotes from Ja'far al-Ṣādiq who was born in the year 80.

The book was still available in the early sixth century to Ṭabrisī who quoted a large part of it in his *I'lām*: 82–139 (with isolated citations from other sources in between). Recently, Rasūl Ja'farīyān has taken that section, supplemented it with a number of other citations from Abān on the life of the Prophet, and published it all in a volume under its original title as it appears in Najāshī and the *Fihrist*. He has, however, missed a lengthy citation from Abān in Bayāḍī 2: 79–83 on the events of the Saqīfa, that must have formed the bulk of the material of that chapter of the work, and a short passage in Ibn Qūlawayh: 42 (repeated at 44, 45, 46).

2. *Aṣl / Kitāb*

Abān's notebook of *ḥadīth*, related from him by a number of transmitters including Ḥasan b. 'Alī al-Washshā' and Muḥassin b. Aḥmad al-Qaysī (Abū Ghālib: 165; Najāshī: 39; *Fihrist*: 19; *Lisān* 1: 36). Aḥmad b. Muḥammad b. Abī Naṣr al-Bazanṭī related all works by Abān (Najāshī: 13). The transmitter Ibn Abī 'Umayr (d. 217) heard Abān quoting from his own book (*Lisān* 1: 36).

Several hundred quotations from Abān in later Shī'ite works of *ḥadīth*, listed in Khu'ī 1: 125–38, 162–9, 371–403, 408–37 and *Fahāris* 8: 7–8, 10–11, many through the same transmitters (see Khu'ī 2: 485, 600–601, 4: 497, 5: 283–4, 326–7, 14: 193–5, 416–17, 23: 165), may go back to this notebook.

2: 'Abbād b. Ṣuhayb

Abū Bakr 'Abbād b. Ṣuhayb al-Tamīmī al-Kulaybī al-Yarbū'ī, a prolific Sunnī transmitter of *ḥadīth* with pro-Mu'tazilite and Shī'ite sympathies. A Baṣran by origin but Kūfan by residence, he transmitted *ḥadīth* from Ja'far al-Ṣādiq, among others, and is said to have died in or around the year 202.

Barqī: 74; Kashshī: 391–2; Najāshī: 293; *Fihrist*: 120; *Rijāl*: 142, 243. For Sunnī sources, see the list in the editor's footnote to *Lisān* 3: 666–7 (Ibn 'Adī: 1652–3 and *Mīzān* 2: 367 have the most detailed accounts).

In Shī'ite sources, material about this scholar seems to have been confused with that on an earlier scholar of Baṣra, 'Abbād b. Kathīr (see Muḥammad Taqī al-Tustarī 5: 643–4, 653–6 for details; for a further possible example of that confusion apart from those mentioned in this work, see *'Ilal* 2: 113).

'Abbād's Shī'ite sympathies are reflected in his transmissions on the virtues of 'Alī and the rest of the House of the Prophet (e.g. Aḥmad, *Faḍā'il*: 658; Ḥusayn b. 'Abd al-Wahhāb: 46–7; Ḥaskānī 1: 181–2, 357, 457). He met various notables of the House and heard from them (see, for instance, 'Ayyāshī 1: 91 where he cites to Mūsā al-Kāẓim an opinion of 'Abd al-Allāh b. al-Ḥasan; *Khiṣāl*: 360 [read *'Abbād* for *'Attāb* as in *Biḥār* 43: 210] where he quotes from 'Īsā b. 'Abd Allāh b. Muḥammad b. 'Umar b. 'Alī).

The date of, or around, 202 for his death appears in Bukhārī, *Kabīr* 6: 43, but Ibn 'Adī: 1652 (whence *Lisān* 3: 667, 669) quotes it from the same author as after 200 or around 212. Either date may signify that 'Abbād lived to an old age if his transmission from authorities such as Jābir al-Ju'fī (as in Furāt: 241; whence

Ḥaskānī 1: 457) who were active early in the second century was through direct hearing.

Ibn ʿAdī: 1653 notes that ʿAbbād had a number of notebooks from his transmissions.

Kitābuh ʿan Abī ʿAbd Allāh

His notebook of transmissions from Jaʿfar al-Ṣādiq (Najāshī: 293; *Fihrist*: 120). Ṭūsī received this notebook through the transmitter Ḥasan b. Maḥbūb (d. 224), and the overwhelming majority of quotations from ʿAbbād in Shīʿite works of *ḥadīth* are cited on the authority of this transmitter. Most Sunnī and Zaydī citations from ʿAbbād are, however, through a different transmitter, Muḥammad b. ʿUmar al-Māzinī al-Baṣrī.

ʿAbbād's quotations from Jaʿfar al-Ṣādiq include the following:

- Aḥmad, *Faḍāʾil*: 658 (also Ibn Bābawayh, *Amālī*: 248–9)
- *Maḥāsin*: 293
- Aḥmad b. ʿĪsā 4: 333–4
- ʿAyyāshī 1: 235
- Muḥammad b. Sulaymān 1: 359 (also Ṭūsī, *Amālī*: 504–5), 460 (repeated in 2: 230)
- *Kāfī* 1: 49
  2: 276
  3: 547
  5: 28, 238, 524 (also *ʿIlal* 2: 252)
  6: 163 (repeated in 7: 212), 215
  7: 208, 239
- Ibn Hammām: 45, 66 (also *Khiṣāl*: 127)
- Furāt: 343, 452–3
- Ibn al-Juḥām: 365
- ʿAlī b. Ibrāhīm 2: 389
- Abū ʾl-Faraj, *Aghānī* 7: 277
- *ʿIlal* 1: 92–5, 153, 170, 184
- *Khiṣāl*: 127, 189, 511–14
- Ibn Shādhān: 35
- Abū Ṭālib: 148, 434
- Ṭūsī, *Amālī*: 647–8 (three reports, with the same *isnād*)

- *Tahdhīb* 3: 166
  7: 331
  9: 38, 170
  10: 144
- Ḥaskānī 1: 357
- *Manāqib* 3: 331
- *Bishārat al-Muṣṭafā*: 162 (read *'an Ja'far 'an abīh 'an 'Alī b. al-Ḥusayn*, as in many other cases, for *'an 'Alī b. al-Ḥusayn*)
- Mizzī 18: 82 (whence Suyūṭī, *La'ālī* 1: 35)
- *Biḥār* 92: 306–25

3: Al-'Abdī al-Khazzāz

'Abd al-'Azīz b. 'Abd Allāh al-'Abdī, the furrier, a Kūfan client of the Banū 'Abd al-Qays from Asad Rabī'a and a transmitter from Ja'far al-Ṣādiq.

Barqī: 75; Najāshī: 244; *Rijāl*: 239, 265.

A report in *Kharā'ij*: 636 (whence Irbilī 2: 403) quotes this transmitter (the name of whose profession is given here as *qazzāz*, the silk seller, rather than *khazzāz*, the furrier) explaining how he held Extremist ideas about the divine nature of the Imāms but Ja'far al-Ṣādiq advised him against them (cf. Ṣaffār: 236 where the story is ascribed to this person's son, Ismā'īl, with additional and most probably later accretions that go against the intent of the report). That the man had some Extremist tendencies can also be detected in his report in *Tawḥīd*: 152 and is possibly the reason why Najāshī: 244 considers him "weak."

Kitāb

His notebook of *ḥadīth*, related by a number of transmitters, including Ḥasan b. Maḥbūb (Najāshī: 244). Apart from a few examples where the author's son Ismā'īl (*Kāfī* 3: 560, 562), possibly a second son, Muḥammad (ibid. 6: 345), and others (e.g. *Maḥāsin*: 31 [whence *Kāfī* 2: 519]) quote from him, all quotations from this author in later works are through Ḥasan b. Maḥbūb, as in the following examples:

- *Maḥāsin*: 277, 497 (also *Kāfī* 6: 340), 500 (also *Kāfī* 6: 333), 540
- Ṣaffār: 207 (also *Kāfī*: 214; see also Ibn al-Juḥām: 231 where the same passage is quoted through a different transmitter from 'Abd al-'Azīz)

- *Kāfī* 1: 375–6 (whence Nu'mānī: 132–3; see also 'Ayyāshī 1: 135)
  2: 319 (also *Thawāb*: 201), 320 (also *Khiṣāl*: 88 [read *Sahl b. Ziyād 'an Ḥasan b. Maḥbūb* as in *Kamāl*: 338, 411; see also Khu'ī 8: 342]), 449
  3: 133–4, 192
  4: 126, 379
  5: 306, 392
  7: 197–8, 208, 306 (also *Faqīh* 4: 126–7)
- Kashshī: 43
- Ibn Bābawayh, *Amālī*: 329 (also *Thawāb*: 57)
- *Faqīh* 4: 309–10
- *'Ilal* 2: 161 (also *'Iqāb*: 277; *Khiṣāl*: 273–4)
- *Kamāl*: 338 (a revised text; repeated at 411)
- *Tawḥīd*: 152
- *Tahdhīb* 8: 207
- Ibn Ṭāwūs, *Falāḥ*: 202–3

4: 'Abd al-Ghaffār al-Jāzī

'Abd al-Ghaffār b. Ḥabīb al-Ṭā'ī al-Jāzī, an Iraqi transmitter from Ja'far al-Ṣādiq.

Najāshī: 247; *Fihrist*: 122; *Rijāl*: 241, 435

Najāshī explains that the *nisba* of this transmitter refers to a village in Mesopotamia called *Jāziya*. Muḥammad Taqī al-Tustarī 6: 195, however, suggests that the correct form of the *nisba* should be *Jārī* as no *Jāziya* is mentioned by either Yāqūt or Sam'ānī, while numerous *Jārīs* are named in the sources. This is certainly not a good argument.

Kitāb

His notebook of *ḥadīth*, related by a number of transmitters including Naḍr b. Shu'ayb (Najāshī: 247; *Fihrist*: 122) who quotes this author at times through an intermediary (*Faqīh* 4: 213). With a single exception (*Tahdhīb* 7: 291), all quotations from 'Abd al-Ghaffār al-Jāzī in Shī'ite works of *ḥadīth* are through Naḍr b. Shu'ayb as in the following examples:

- Ṣaffār: 16 (whence *Kāfī* 2: 3), 178, 193–4, 290 (read *Naḍr b. Shu'ayb 'an 'Abd al-Ghaffār* as in *Biḥār* 43: 330), 321, 328, 513–14 (two reports)

- *Kāfī* 5: 99
- Ibn Bābawayh, *Faḍā'il al-ashhur*: 96
- *Faqīh* 4: 213
- *Ma'ānī*: 137, 138, 200
- *Tahdhīb* 1: 128 (read *Naḍr b. Shu'ayb* [as in *Istibṣār* 1: 114] for *Naḍr b. Suwayd 'an Shu'ayb*)
  5: 258, 467 (partially also at 369)

5: Abū Maryam

Abū Maryam 'Abd al-Ghaffār b. al-Qāsim b. Yaḥyā b. Qays b. Qahd al-Anṣārī, a Kūfan scholar of *ḥadīth* in the first half of the second century and a transmitter known to both Sunnī and Shī'ite communities of his time. He transmitted from the Imāms Muḥammad al-Bāqir and Ja'far al-Ṣādiq, among others.

Yaḥyā b. Ma'īn 2: 367; Bukhārī, *Kabīr* 6: 122; Barqī: 52, 64; Ṭabarī, *Dhayl*: 680; Ibn Abī Ḥātim 6: 53–4; ' Uqaylī 3: 100–102; Ibn Ḥibbān, *Majrūḥīn* 2: 143; Ibn 'Adī: 1964–5; Najāshī: 246–7; *Fihrist*: 188–9; *Rijāl*: 118, 140, 241; *Lisān* 4: 412–14 (and other sources named in the editor's footnote).

His genealogy as given above follows Ibn 'Adī: 1964. Najāshī: 246 and *Rijāl*: 241 have him as 'Abd al-Ghaffār b. al-Qāsim b. Qays b. Qays b. Qahd. The first Qays should be a corruption of Yaḥyā or vice versa.

Sunnī authors, while admiring his knowledge of *ḥadīth* and its transmitters, blame him for strong Shī'ite sympathies, reflected especially in his reports against 'Uthmān, and describe him as an unreliable transmitter. Shu'ba b. al-Ḥajjāj (d. 160), a well known mid-second century scholar of *ḥadīth*, studied with and transmitted from him. Ibn Abī Ḥātim 6: 54 (whence *Mīzān* 2: 640) identifies Abū Maryam as a leader of the Shī'ite community. Ibn 'Adī: 1965 and others (e.g. Ibn 'Asākir 30: 359) call him an Extremist Shī'ite. This clearly refers to his anti-'Uthmān transmissions (e.g. 'Uqaylī 3: 102; Ibn Ḥibbān, *Majrūḥīn* 2: 143). 'Uqaylī 3: 102 indicates that his objectionable transmissions belong to a later period in his life, and that scholars such as Shu'ba had studied with him before that period. 'Uqaylī (whence *Mīzān* 2: 641) praises Abū Maryam for his knowledge of the authorities of *ḥadīth*, and makes it clear that the Sunnī authorities considered him unreliable because of his beliefs, not because of deficiencies in his transmission.

Notwithstanding his Shī'ite sympathies, he used to travel to Damascus at times and frequent the princely court of the Umayyad Ibrāhīm b. al-Walīd (d. 132), as mentioned by himself in a report that appears in a revised version in Khazzāz: 251. In this report, he also complains to Muḥammad al-Bāqir that he has already reached an old age waiting all his life for the *Qā'im* to arise (ibid.: 252). The report clearly belongs to later years of Muḥammad al-Bāqir's life early in the second century.

As for his personal conduct, a report in *Kāfi* 6: 410 asserts that he used to drink *nabīdh*, a mild alcoholic beverage that many of the jurists of Iraq considered to be licit in moderation. There were also members of the Shī'ite community who thought drinking *nabīdh* was permissible (ibid. 6: 411; Kashshī: 201). Abū Maryam's drinking habit is also attested in 'Uqaylī 3: 102.

Dhahabī suggests that Abū Maryam should have lived until around 160 as some of those who transmitted from him are known to have been born around the middle of the second century and could not have reached the age of learning before the aforementioned date. This argument is correct if they had actually heard from Abū Maryam, as Dhahabī assumes to have been the case.

1. *Kitāb al-ṣalāt*

(*Fihrist*: 189). A fair number of quotations from this author on the topic of prayer in later works of *ḥadīth* may go back to this work. Examples are as follows:

- Aḥmad b. 'Īsā 1: 257
- 'Ayyāshī 1: 243
- Wakī' 3:16
- *Kāfī* 1: 450 (also *Tahdhīb* 1: 296)
  3: 219, 305, 421
- *Tahdhīb* 1: 416
- Abū 'Abd Allāh al-Shajarī, *Adhān*: 74

2. *Kitāb*

His notebook of *ḥadīth*, related by a number of Shī'ite transmitters (Najāshī: 247; *Fihrist*: 189). There are close to two hundred quotations from Abū Maryam in Imāmite Shī'ite works of *ḥadīth*, many of which in all likelihood are taken from this notebook. For lists see Khu'ī 10: 56, 22: 211–15; *Fahāris* 9: 286–7, 10: 298. There are also a good number of quotations from him in Sunnī sources, mostly on the virtues of 'Alī but also on legal and ethical topics. Here are a few examples:

- Bazzār 2: 105–6 (also Muḥammad b. Sulaymān 1: 370–71; Ṭabarī, *Tafsīr* 19: 121–2; idem, *Tahdhīb, 'Alī*: 62–3; idem, *Ta'rīkh* 2: 319–21), 290 (also Abū Nu'aym, *Akhbār Iṣbahān* 2: 47)
- Ibn Abī 'l-Dunyā, *Maqtal Amīr al-Mu'minīn*: 36

- Wakīʿ 3: 11
- ʿUqaylī 3: 101 (see also Ibn al-Juḥām: 224–5 for a Shīʿite version of this report)
- Ṭabarānī, *Ṣaghīr* 1: 120–21
- Ibn ʿAdī: 534 (read *'an Abī Maryam*, as ibid.: 1965 and *Mīzān* 1: 376, for *'an Ibn Abī Maryam*), 843, 1964–5 (five reports)
- Ibn Mardawayh, *Juz'*: 238
- Abū Nuʿaym, *Ma'rifa*: 88
- *Ḥilya* 4: 375–6 (whence Bayhaqī, *Sunan* 9: 126; idem, *Shu'ab* 7: 484 [read *Abū Maryam* for *Abū Mirthad*])
- Ibn ʿAsākir 30: 359
  42: 187–8, 491
- Suyūṭī, *La'ālī* 1: 408

Quotations from this author appear also in Zaydī and Ismāʿīlī sources, as in the following instances:

- Naṣr b. Muzāḥim: 217–18
- Aḥmad b. ʿĪsā 1: 257
  2: 266
  3: 112, 122
- Muḥammad b. Sulaymān 1: 189, 288, 325
  2: 102, 167, 202, 251, 379, 407, 408, 449, 538
- Qāḍī Nuʿmān, *Īḍāḥ*: 15a, 21b
- Idem, *Sharḥ* 2: 286–8

6: Karrām al-Khathʿamī

ʿAbd al-Karīm b. ʿAmr b. Ṣāliḥ, known as Karrām, a Kūfan client of Khathʿam and a distinguished member of the Shīʿite community of Kūfa in his time. He transmitted from Jaʿfar al-Ṣādiq and Mūsā al-Kāẓim, and was among the leaders of the Wāqifites after the death of the latter.

Barqī: 75, 117; Kashshī: 555; Ibn al-Ghaḍā'irī: 114; Najāshī: 245; *Fibrist*: 109; *Rijāl*: 239, 339; *Ghayba*: 54, 63–64.

According to Ibn al-Ghaḍā'irī, Karrām's name was popular among the Extremists who reproduced much of his transmissions in their own works. A few esoteric reports in Shīʿite works of *ḥadīth* (e.g. *Kāfī* 8: 232–3 [partially also in

Ṣaffār: 353–4; *Ikhtiṣāṣ*: 301]; see also Ṣaffār: 20; *Ikhtiṣāṣ*: 286) may represent remnants of that material.

Most of his biographers note that he was a Wāqifite, a staunch one as understood from *Rijāl*: 339. This fact, however, did not discourage a later transmitter from upgrading one of Karrām's reports to "predict" that the number of the Imāms would be twelve (*Kāfī* 1: 534). The older version of the report (ibid. 4: 141) does not include the clause about the twelve Imāms.

Kitāb

His notebook of *ḥadīth*, related by a number of Shīʿite transmitters, including ʿUbays b. Hishām al-Nāshirī and Aḥmad b. Muḥammad b. Abī Naṣr al-Bazanṭī (Najāshī: 245; *Fihrist*: 109; *Rijāl*: 339). There are a large number of quotations from Karrām in Shīʿite works of *ḥadīth*, overwhelmingly on the authority of these two transmitters of this notebook – sometimes one or the other, sometimes both together (as, for instance, in *Ghayba*: 425–6; compare also *Tahdhīb* 5: 483 where a text appears as quoted from Karrām by ʿUbays, with *Istibṣār* 2: 260, where the same text is quoted from Karrām on the authority of Bazanṭī). For well over one hundred quotations from him in the four main works of Shīʿite *ḥadīth*, see the lists in Khuʾī 10: 59–61, 68–70, 408–14, 14: 111–12, 371–2 (more than half of these on the authority of Bazanṭī alone); for another hundred or so, mainly in other Shīʿite works, see *Fahāris* 9: 288–90, 10: 9.

7: ʿAbd Allāh b. Ayyūb

ʿAbd Allāh b. Ayyūb b. Rāshid al-Zuhrī, a seller of clothing made by Jhāts. Most likely a Kūfan, he lived in the middle and latter half of the second century, and reportedly transmitted from Jaʿfar al-Ṣādiq. He is said to have had esoteric tendencies.

Najāshī: 221; *Fihrist*: 104, 105.

Najāshī is the one who identifies this transmitter as *Bayyāʿ al-Zuṭṭī*, a seller of clothing made by the Indian Jhāts (*al-thiyāb al-Zuṭṭiyya*, for which see Ibn Manẓūr, *Lisān* 7: 308; Zabīdī 5: 146). He was, most likely, a son of Ayyūb b. Rāshid, a Kūfan cloth seller and a transmitter from Jaʿfar al-Ṣādiq (*Rijāl*: 163). Ayyūb's transmission from that Imām is attested in *Kāfī* 1: 69, 3: 505, 6: 415, 7: 198–9. In this last instance, Ayyūb quotes from Jaʿfar al-Ṣādiq through an intermediary who was also a seller of clothing made by Jhāts. This strengthens the likelihood that this Ayyūb was the father of our transmitter who belonged to the same professional circle. That 'Abd Allāh's father was a transmitter of *ḥadīth* is further confirmed by a report in Ṣaffār: 166 where 'Abd Allāh quotes from Ja'far al-Ṣādiq with his own father as the intermediary.

Rijāl: 231 names an 'Abd Allāh b. Ayyūb, a Kūfan client of the Banū Asad, among the transmitters from Ja'far al-Ṣādiq. Ibn al-Ghaḍā'irī: 79 mentions an 'Abd Allāh b. Ayyūb al-Qummī about whom he knew nothing except that he was quoted by the Extremists in their works. There is also a report in *Kāfī* 1: 31–3 on the authority of 'Abd Allāh b. Ayyūb al-Ash'arī who should have lived late in the second century. Almost all Ash'arid transmitters from the Imāms were from the branch of the tribe that emigrated from Kūfa to Qum, reportedly late in the first century. Muḥammad Taqī al-Tustarī 6: 260 suggests that there was possibly a single 'Abd Allāh b. Ayyūb whose *nisba* was variously given. It is true that a corruption involving *Asadī* and *Ash'arī*, and even those and *Zuhrī*, cannot be ruled out in Arabic script. The accusation of holding esoteric beliefs that Najāshī mentions in the case of our transmitter, on the other hand, goes well with Ibn al-Ghaḍā'irī's report on the popularity of 'Abd Allāh b. Ayyūb al-Qummī with the Extremists. Two reports quoted from our transmitter in Ṣaffār: 131, 429 qualify as what many Shī'ite scholars of the third and fourth centuries considered esoteric. However, there is certainly more than one 'Abd Allāh b. Ayyūb involved here. Ibn al-Ghaḍā'irī obviously refers to a name mentioned in a Nuṣayrī text recorded in Maymūn al-Ṭabarānī, *Majmū' al-a'yād*: 133 as Abū Muḥammad 'Abd Allāh b. Ayyūb al-Qummī from whom the text quotes a long story about the merits of the Nuṣayrī feast of the Ninth of Rabī' I (ibid.: 133–43). However, if one takes this report seriously, this Qummī should have lived in the mid-third century as a close disciple of 'Alī al-Hādī (ibid.: 134–7, 143). There is also a post 'Alī al-Riḍā report in *Kāfī* 1: 346–7 and *Kamāl*: 536–7 from a transmitter named 'Abd Allāh b. Ayyūb, who should have lived around the middle of the 3rd century. In addition, there are a number of reports in Sunnī sources quoting 'Abd Allāh b. Ayyūb, from his father, from Muḥammad al-Bāqir (alternatively, from his father, from his grandfather, from Ḥasan al-Mujtabā). This Abū Bakr 'Abd Allāh b. Ayyūb b. Abī 'Ilāj, the rope seller, was a transmitter from Mosul (see the entry on him and examples of his transmission in Ibn 'Adī: 1527; also *Lisān* 3: 729 and the many other sources listed in the editor's footnote; see also Ibn al-Jawzī, *Mawḍū'āt* 1: 401; Suyūṭī, *La'ālī* 1: 383).

Kitāb / Kitāb nawādir

(Najāshī: 221; *Fihrist*: 104, 105). Apart from the reports mentioned above and a few others, in all of which this author transmits from Ja'far al-Ṣādiq through an intermediary (e.g. Ṣaffār: 166 ; *Khiṣāl*: 9, also 61 where the ultimate authority for the report is Ḥasan al-Mujtabā), he may be the same as the 'Abd Allāh b. Ayyūb who was the principal transmitter of the *Kitāb al-diyāt*, a lengthy text of 'Alī's executive order to his governors on the monetary compensation for various acts of mayhem, including mutilation and injuries. The full text of this executive order has survived (see above, the entry on 'Alī).

8: Ibn Bukayr

Abū 'Alī 'Abd Allāh b. Bukayr b. A'yan, a member of the originally Byzantine family of Āl A'yan of Kūfa (see no. 234 below) and a prominent Shī'ite jurist and *mutakallim.* He transmitted from Ja'far al-Ṣādiq and joined the Faṭḥites after his death, following his eldest surviving son, 'Abd Allāh, rather than Mūsā al-Kāẓim, as his successor.

Barqī: 71; Sa'd b. 'Abd Allāh: 89; Nawbakhtī: 79, 112; Kashshī: 345, 375; Abū Ghālib: 114; Ibn al-Nadīm: 243, 276; Ghaḍā'irī: 192; Najāshī: 222; *Fibrist*: 106; *Rijāl*: 230. See also *Ghayba*: 56.

Abū 'l-Ḥasan al-Ash'arī 1: 112 mentions the opinion of 'Abd Allāh b. Bukayr, alongside other Shī'ite theologians of the mid-second century, on the question of *istiṭā'a* (that is, whether man's capability to act precedes or coincides with the act itself). There is a quotation on this topic from him in *Tawḥīd*: 347. An example of his personal opinion based on independent legal judgment (*ra'y*) on a matter of the law of divorce is quoted in *Kāfī* 6: 77–8 and is discussed and criticized by later Shī'ite scholars (see, for instance, *Tahdhīb* 8: 35–6; also Najafī, *Jawāhir* 32: 129–31). That he was among the prominent Shī'ite jurists of his time is also mentioned in Kashshī: 345, 375; Abū Ghālib: 114; Nawbakhtī: 112. His opinions and interpretations were known in the Shī'ite community of his time and were at times quoted to the Imāms (e.g. *Ma'ānī*: 266–7 [also *'Uyūn* 1: 310–11]; see also *Kashshī*: 144). He was a prolific transmitter (Abū Ghālib: 114), a fact well attested by the amount of reports quoted on his authority in Shī'ite works of *ḥadīth*.

1. *Kitāb*

His notebook of *ḥadīth*, related by a large number of Shī'ite transmitters including Ḥasan b. 'Alī b. Faḍḍāl (d. 224) (Kashshī: 516; Ibn al-Nadīm: 243; Abū Ghālib: 171; Najāshī: 222 [see also 125]; *Fibrist*: 106). Faḍl b. Shādhān al-Naysābūrī, the prominent Shī'ite scholar of the third century, heard the notebook from the same transmitter (Kashshī: 516). Two fragments of this notebook have survived in 'Abd Allāh b. Ja'far: 167–74 (nos. 613–41) and Ibn Idrīs, *Mustaṭrafāt*: 137–9. The work was still available in the mid-seventh century to Ibn Ṭāwūs who quoted from it in his *Kashf al-maḥajja*: 125 (see further Kohlberg: 219).

There are many quotations from 'Abd Allāh b. Bukayr in Shī'ite works of *ḥadīth*, mainly on the authority of Ḥasan b. 'Alī b. Faḍḍāl. For lists of over seven hundred of these in the four main collections of Shī'ite *ḥadīth*, see Khu'ī 10: 126–30, 420–32, 22: 160–69, 363–78. For lists of many others quoted in other collections, see *Fahāris* 8: 239–40, 9: 198.

2. *Musnad 'Abd Allāh b. Bukayr b. A'yan*

A work by Ibn 'Uqda, Aḥmad b. Muḥammad b. Sa'īd al-Kūfī (d. 333), clearly a collection of the reports that the author received on the authority of Ibn Bukayr. The work is mentioned in Najāshī: 94 and *Fihrist*: 29. The three quotations from 'Abd Allāh b. Bukayr through Ibn 'Uqda in Nu'mānī: 264, 301 should have been among the components of the work in question.

9: 'Abd Allāh b. Ghālib

Abū 'Alī 'Abd Allāh b. Ghālib b. al-Hudhayl al-Asadī, a Kūfan Shī'ite poet and jurist of the mid-second century and a transmitter from Muḥammad al-Bāqir and Ja'far al-Ṣādiq.

Barqī: 64; Kashshī: 339; Najāshī: 222; *Rijāl*: 141–2, 233.

For possible examples of his poetry, see Ibn Qūlawayh: 210; *Ghayba*: 49. His father (see Khu'ī 13: 219–20), Abū 'l-Hudhayl Ghālib b. al-Hudhayl, a client of the Banū Asad, was also a poet and a transmitter from Muḥammad al-Bāqir and Ja'far al-Ṣādiq (*Rijāl*: 142, 267). His brother, Isḥāq b. Ghālib, also a transmitter from Ja'far al-Ṣādiq, was a poet too (Najāshī: 72; *Rijāl*: 162; see also *Lisān* 1: 562, misattributing his information to Kashshī).[3]

As for his distinction as a jurist mentioned by Najāshī, see, for instance, *Kāfī* 7: 347.

3. He was also the author of a notebook of *ḥadīth*, related by Ṣafwān b. Yaḥyā and others (Najāshī: 72). Examples of quotations from him in later works, some through the same transmitter, include Ḥusayn b. Sa'īd, *Zuhd*: 33 (also *Kāfī* 4: 2; *Thawāb*: 169; *Khiṣāl*: 48), 47 (also 'Ayyāshī 2: 89–90; *Kāfī* 2: 412): *Maḥāsin*: 98 (also *'Iqāb*: 242); *Kāfī* 1: 203–5 (an elegent text on the Shī'ite conception of the Imāmate, narrated as a sermon of Ja'far al-Ṣādiq's but most likely composed by Isḥāq on the basis of the Imām's teachings; another part of this text appears ibid. 1: 244–5; another part from the beginning of the text appears in Ṣaffār: 412–13; the text in *Tawḥīd*: 44–5 [also *'Ilal* 1: 114] is also most likely a part of the same work, clearly from its very beginning), 2: 321(also Ibn Bābawayh, *Amālī*: 274), 602; *Tahdhīb* 4: 190–91.

Kitāb

His notebook of *ḥadīth,* related by many transmitters including Ḥasan b. Maḥbūb (Najāshī: 222). The following quotations from ʿAbd Allāh b. Ghālib on the authority of the same transmitter may thus go back to the notebook in question:

- *Maḥāsin*: 155 (whence Ṣaffār: 33; *Kāfī* 1: 215), 295
- ʿAyyāshī (without the name of the transmitter from ʿAbd Allāh, as usual)
  1: 59–60
  2: 164
- *Kāfī* 2: 230–31 (also 2: 47 where *ʿAbd Allāh* is corrupted to *ʿAbd al-Malik*), 265
  3: 188
  4: 15
  5: 514
  7: 347
  8: 72–6, 244–5, 336
- Ibn Bābawayh, *Amālī*: 593–6, 633 (also *Thawāb*: 232; *Tahdhīb* 1: 303–4)
- *ʿIlal* 2: 276
- Ibn Bisṭām: 35 (read *Ḥasan b. Maḥbūb* for *Muḥammad b. Maḥbūb*)
- *Tahdhīb* 10: 151–2
- *Manāqib* 2: 287

10: Al-Armanī

Abū ʾl-Ḥakam ʿAbd Allāh b. al-Ḥakam al-Armanī, a transmitter from Jaʿfar al-Ṣādiq, who was accused of holding Extremist views about the Imāms. He seems to have lived into the last years of the second century.

Najāshī: 225; Ibn al-Ghaḍāʾirī: 81; *Fihrist*: 101–2 (see also *Rijāl*: 437).

His *kunya* is attested in *Kāfī* 1: 313, 316, 317 (cf. ibid. 1: 358, 366). For his being alive until the late second century, see *Kāfī* 1: 315, a quotation from him that speaks of four years after the death of Hārūn al-Rashīd (d. 193) and of the birth of Muḥammad al-Jawād (b. 195).

Kitāb

His notebook of *ḥadīth*, related by Abū 'Imrān Mūsā b. Ranjawayh al-Armanī (Najāshī: 225; *Fihrist*: 101–2). The following quotations from 'Abd Allāh b. al-Ḥakam in Shī'ite works of *ḥadīth* are all on the authority of the same transmitter:

- Ṣaffār: 144
- *Kāfī* 1: 358–67 (read *Muḥammad b. Ḥassān 'an Mūsā b. Ranjawayh*, as in Najāshī: 225 and *Fihrist*: 101–2, for *Muḥammad b. Ranjawayh*, or possibly *'an Abī Muḥammad b. Ranjawayh*, as in *Tahdhīb* 8: 293 [cf. *Kāfī* 7: 460])[4]
  2: 616–17 (also Ibn Bābawayh, *Amālī*: 328)
  3: 493
  7: 460
- *Faqīh* 3: 52–3 (also *Tahdhīb* 6: 367), 307 (also *Tahdhīb* 10: 177–8), 308, 383 (for the *isnād*, see also ibid. 4: 515)
- *'Iqāb*: 309
- *Tahdhīb* 10: 153–4, 269
- Ibn Ṭāwūs, *Jamāl*: 278 (read *Ranjawayh* for *Zanjawayh*)

11: Abū Muḥammad al-Ja'farī

Abū Muḥammad 'Abd Allāh b. Ibrāhīm b. Muḥammad b. 'Alī b. 'Abd Allāh b. Ja'far b. Abī Ṭālib, a historian of the House of the Prophet and a transmitter from Ja'far al-Ṣādiq and Mūsā al-Kāẓim.

Najāshī: 216; Ibn 'Inaba: 43, 50.

A quotation from this transmitter in *Kāfī* 1: 313–16 speaks of four years after the death of Hārūn al-Rashīd (d. 193) and of the birth of Muḥammad al-Jawād (b. 195). The report, if authentic, indicates that he was alive until the very last years of the century.

---

4. The *kunya* of Mūsā b. Ranjawayh is given as Abū 'Imrān in Najāshī and *Fihrist*. That, as is well known to students of Muslim biography, is the *kunya* by default for anyone named Mūsā and does not exclude a filial *kunya*.

1. *Kitāb khurūj Muḥammad b. ʿAbd Allāh wa maqtalih*

On the unsuccessful rebellion of al-Nafs al-Zakiyya in 145 (Najāshī: 216). The full text of this treatise is preserved in *Kāfī* 1: 358–66.

2. *Kitāb khurūj Ṣāḥib Fakhkh wa maqtalih*

On the unsuccessful rebellion of Ḥusayn b. ʿAlī Ṣāḥib Fakhkh in 169 (Najāshī: 216). Najāshī received this work through the transmitter Bakr b. Ṣāliḥ. A large portion of this treatise, from its beginning on, is quoted through the same transmitter, Bakr b. Ṣāliḥ al-Rāzī, in Aḥmad b. Sahl al-Rāzī, *Akhbār Fakhkh*: 132–47 (with a couple of insertions from other sources in between). The name of the author, however, appears here as *ʿAbd Allāh b. Muḥammad b. Ibrāhīm*, with the insertion of additional names in the genealogical line of descent from Jaʿfar b. Abī Ṭālib. Two fragments of the work are also quoted in *Kāfī* 1: 366–7. The first, a conversation between the Ṣāḥib Fakhkh and Mūsā al-Kāẓim, is also attested in the section quoted by Aḥmad b. Sahl al-Rāzī: 135 (though with variations). The second is an exchange of letters between Mūsā al-Kāẓim and Yaḥyā b. ʿAbd Allāh al-Ṭālibī, the younger brother of al-Nafs al-Zakiyya who participated in the rebellion of the Ṣāḥib Fakhkh but survived the massacre at Fakhkh and began his own rebellion whose events are recorded along with those of Fakhkh in the same volume by Aḥmad b. Sahl, and most likely by our author as well.

3. *Kitāb waṣiyyat Mūsā b. Jaʿfar*

This treatise, containing the text of the will of Mūsā al-Kāẓim and what happened between ʿAlī al-Riḍā and his brothers after the death of their father, is also quoted in *Kāfī* 1: 316–19 (also *ʿUyūn* 1: 33–7 with variations) with the closing formula of the treatise on p. 319. The text is in support of ʿAlī al-Riḍā's rightful succession to his father. Another lengthy text, with the same *isnād* and purpose in mind, quoted just before the aforementioned text in *Kāfī* 1: 313–16 (also ʿAlī b. Bābawayh, *Imāma*: 215–18; *ʿUyūn* 1: 23–6), also seems originally to have been a part of the work in question.

4. *Aṣl*

Najāshī: 216 notes that this author had a number of books, though he only names two of them. Numerous quotations from 'Abd Allāh b. Ibrāhīm al-Ja'farī in Shī'ite works of *ḥadīth*, mostly, though not exclusively, through Bakr b. Ṣāliḥ, may indicate that he had a notebook of miscellaneous reports as well. Examples include the following:

- *Maḥāsin*: 369 (also *Kāfī* 2: 532), 370, 425, 553, 555 (whence *Kāfī* 6: 359–60), 592, 642
- Ṣaffār: 198 (with two errors in the genealogy of 'Abd Allāh)
- *Kāfī* 1: 387–8
- *'Uyūn* 1: 279 (also *Khiṣāl*: 392)
- Ṭūsī, *Amālī*: 455–6

12: Ibn al-Qaddāḥ

'Abd Allāh b. Maymūn b. al-Aswad, the arrow maker, a Meccan client of the Banū Makhzūm, a clan of Quraysh. A servant of Ja'far al-Ṣādiq, he transmitted from him and, occasionally, other early authorities of *ḥadīth*. He was known to both Shī'ite and Sunnī circles of transmission of *ḥadīth*.

Bukhārī, *Kabīr* 5: 206; Barqī: 71; Fasawī 2: 195–6; Nasā'ī, *Ḍu'afā'*: 150; 'Uqaylī 2: 302; Ibn Abī Ḥātim 5: 172; Kashshī: 246, 389; Ibn Ḥibbān, *Majrūḥīn* 2: 21; Ibn al-Nadīm: 275; Mufīd, *Amālī*: 134; Najāshī: 213–14; *Fihrist*: 103; *Rijāl*: 231; *Mīzān* 2: 512, and other sources listed in the editor's footnote to Mizzī 16: 198–9.

The name of this transmitter's grandfather is given in Sunnī sources as *Dāwūd* and in Shī'ite sources as *Aswad*, one possibly a corruption of the other, but the latter goes better with *Maymūn*, if we assume a slave origin. 'Abd Allāh was a client of the descendants of Ḥārith b. 'Abd Allāh b. Abī Rabī'a al-Makhzūmī ('Uqaylī 2: 302; Ibn 'Adī: 1504; Mizzī 16: 199), a Meccan *tābi'ī* who served as governor of Baṣra for 'Abd Allāh b. al-Zubayr (r. 64–73). The same should have naturally been the case with 'Abd Allāh's father, Maymūn al-Qaddāḥ (on him see Barqī: 59, 66; Najāshī: 213; *Rijāl*: 120, 145, 309). *Rijāl*: 309, however, identifies Maymūn as a client of the Banū Hāshim. That may have been a corruption or slip of pen. After all, Ṭūsī himself indentifies Maymūn as a client of the Banū Makhzūm ibid.: 145. Both Maymūn and his son were, however, servants of the Imāms, Maymūn of Muḥammad al-Bāqir (*Kāfī* 1: 400) and 'Abd Allāh of Ja'far al-Ṣādiq (Ibn 'Adī: 1504; see also *Kāfī* 6: 443), and this may have been behind Ṭūsī's assumption in *Rijāl*: 309.

The sectarian affiliation of Ibn al-Qaddāḥ is, however, unclear. None of his Sunnī biographers ascribe a Shīʿite sympathy to him. Majlisī (*Biḥār* 84: 242) indicates that the contents of his reports in most cases reveal a Sunnī tendency. Kashshī: 389 reports on the authority of a transmitter who may have met Ibn al-Qaddāḥ late in his life (see ʿAbd Allāh b. Jaʿfar: 20) that he was a philo-Zaydī (the expression used here is *tazayyud*, for the meaning of which see Jishumī, *Jalāʾ*: 128). Ṭūsī in *Tahdhīb* 5: 230 suggests that in a specific case, Ibn al-Qaddāḥ attributed the opinion of ʿAbd Allāh b. al-Ḥasan, who was much favored by the early Zaydīs as their most senior supporter from among the members of the House of the Prophet, to Jaʿfar al-Ṣādiq. This may indicate that Ibn al-Qaddāḥ was close to Zaydī circles. Abū ʾl-ʿAlāʾ al-Maʿarrī in his *Ghufrān*: 407–8 quotes the Shīʿites as saying that ʿAbd Allāh b. Maymūn al-Qaddāḥ, a member of the Arab tribe of Bāhila, was a prominent disciple of Jaʿfar al-Ṣādiq and transmitted much from him but then apostatized (*irtadda*). Maʿarrī cites some senior Shīʿite scholar(s) who told him that the Shīʿa, when quoting Ibn al-Qaddāḥ, specified that they heard him at his best, i.e. before he apostatized (*qabla ʾan yartadd*). He then quotes two pieces of poetry allegedly by Ibn al-Qaddāḥ against Jaʿfar al-Ṣādiq. Our Ibn al-Qaddāḥ was, however, not an Arab from Bāhila but a client of the Banū Makhzūm. The sources say nothing about his alleged apostasy. The word *yartadda* may have been a corruption of *tazayyada*, although the first line of the first piece of poetry quoted by Maʿarrī, if interpreted literally, implies disbelief in the hereafter. At any rate, the report, if it actually refers to our person, confirms the suspicion that Ibn al-Qaddāḥ was at least not an Imāmite Shīʿite later in his life. There is in fact a curious and unusual practice followed by a transmitter from Ibn al-Qaddāḥ, most likely the same transmitter who reported in Kashshī: 389 that Ibn al-Qaddāḥ was a philo-Zaydī: he gives the date at which he heard a report from him (ʿAbd Allāh b. Jaʿfar: 20). This may confirm Maʿarrī's assertion about the concern of the Shīʿa for the timing of Ibn al-Qaddāḥ's reports. Nevertheless, apart from occasional quotations of his reports through Imāmite chains of transmission, the name of Ibn al-Qaddāḥ does not appear in Zaydī sources. However, in most of his reports in Sunnī works, Jaʿfar al-Ṣādiq is depicted as quoting, directly or through his father, from early authorities of Sunnī *ḥadīth*. This is certainly a non-Imāmite practice. Furthermore, in many, if not most, of the reports recorded on his authority in Shīʿite works other than the *Kāfī*, he refers to Jaʿfar al-Ṣādiq using his first name, in contrast to the Imāmites' well established habit of referring to him by his *kunya*. If one assumes the use of the Imām's first name to be his original, unedited style, that too indicates that he was not an Imāmite Shīʿite. One may also be tempted to think that the variation in referring to the Imām between *kunya* and first name may signify different stages in this transmitter's life. But some of these reports are quoted on the authority of the same transmitters in different works, one mentioning the Imām with his first name, another with his *kunya* (cf. for instance, *Kāfī* 2: 523 with Ibn Ṭāwūs, *Falāḥ*: 376). This confirms the hypothesis of later editing as noted above. The suspicion of a non-Shīʿite provenance can further be confirmed by some of his transmissions (e.g. *Kāfī* 6: 19).

Ibn al-Nadīm: 238 and Ismā'īlī sources (for a list, see the editor's note in Juwaynī, *Jahāngushā* 3: 341–2) name an 'Abd Allāh b. Maymūn al-Qaddāḥ, a disciple of Ja'far al-Ṣādiq, as the originator of the Qarmatian doctrine. The biographical specifications they ascribe to that person (see the entries on him in the *Encyclopaedia of Islam*, 2nd edn., 1: 48 [S. M. Stern] and *Encyclopaedia Iranica* 1: 182–3 [H. Halm]) do not agree with the corresponding material in Sunnī and Shī'ite sources on Ibn al-Qaddāḥ. It is, however, possible that the ambiguities about our Ibn al-Qaddāḥ encouraged Ismā'īlī esoterism to turn him into a legendary figure. There is also a good possibility that there was a person with a similar name that early Ismā'īlī authors confused with our Ibn al-Qaddāḥ, assuming him to be a disciple of Ja'far al-Ṣādiq, though the Ismā'īlī account of his life and activities requires him to have lived in the latter part of the third century and to have died after 261.

Ibn al-Qaddāḥ seems to have lived into the late second century. A transmitter states that he heard him in the year 198 ('Abd Allāh b. Ja'far: 20). This point is also confirmed by the generation to which the transmitters from him belonged, though there is naturally the possibility that those transmitters may have quoted from the works, not from the author. The year 180 given by Ziriklī 4: 141 as the date of the death of Ibn al-Qaddāḥ does not seem to come from an authoritative source.

Najāshī: 214 mentions that Ibn al-Qaddāḥ had a number of books that Najāshī received through the transmitter Ja'far b. Muḥammad b. 'Ubayd Allāh (al-Ash'arī, as in *Maḥāsin*: 34, 439 [against the suggestion in Khu'ī 4: 100 that this transmitter has never been identified anywhere as *Ash'arī*]). Najāshī names two of Ibn al-Qaddāḥ's works:

1. *Kitāb mab'ath al-Nabī wa akhbārih*

Nothing seems to have survived from this work.

2. *Kitāb ṣifat al-janna wa 'l-nār*

A report in 'Abd Allāh b. Ja'far: 24–5 as well as a few others (e.g. *Kāfī* 5: 537) fit within the title of this work. The passage in 'Abd Allāh b. Ja'far: 24–5 (reported on different authorities also in Sunnī works of *ḥadīth* such as Ibn Abī 'Āṣim, *Sunna* 1: 248–9; Ṭabarānī, *Kabīr* 8: 153) speaks of God's declaration concerning the people of paradise and hell. The brief texts of God's declarations on both groups begin as follows: *Bism Allāh al-Raḥmān al-Raḥīm. Kitāb min al-Raḥmān al-Raḥīm fī ahl al-Janna/ fī ahl al-nār.* One only hopes that this initial formula did not mislead an early author of Shī'ite bio-bibliographical material into assuming that the text in front of him was the beginning of a book on the topic.

3. *Kitāb*

His notebook of *ḥadīth* (Ibn al-Nadīm: 275; Abū Ghālib: 166; *Fihrist*: 103), in three parts (*ajzā'*), according to Abū Ghālib al-Zurārī who received the work through the scholar Ḥasan b. 'Alī b. Faḍḍāl. Ṭūsī received the work through three different *isnād*s that went back to (1) the above-mentioned Ja'far b. Muḥammad b. 'Ubayd Allāh named by Najāshī, (2) 'Abd Allāh b. al-Ṣalt al-Qummī, and (3) Ibrāhīm b. Hāshim al-Qummī. Ibn Bābawayh quotes Ibn al-Qaddāḥ in the *Faqīh* through this last transmitter (*Mashyakha*: 500), who at times quotes our author through the first transmitter, Ja'far b. Muḥammad b. 'Ubayd Allāh (e.g. *Ṣaffār*: 148; *Kāfī* 4: 153; *Khiṣāl*: 650 [as explained below]); this may always have been the case even where the name of the intermediary is not mentioned in the *isnād*.

Quotations from 'Abd Allāh b. Maymūn al-Qaddāḥ by the above-mentioned four transmitters of this notebook include the following examples:

- Muḥammad b. 'Alī b. Maḥbūb: 94 (also Ibn Ṭāwūs, *Falāḥ*: 376, quoting another passage from the same source [see idem, *Muḥāsaba*: 14])
- *Maḥāsin*: 9, 15–16 (two reports), 34–5, 38–9, 84 (also Ibn Bābawayh, *Amālī*: 573; *'Iqāb*: 276), 96 (also *'Iqāb*: 242), 106, 112, 229, 254, 260–61 (read *al-Ash'arī* for *Ibn al-Ash'ath*), 293–4 (two reports), 362, 409, 435, 443, 448, 452, 560, 561 (three reports), 576, 577
- Ṣaffār: 3, 7, 134, 148 (read *Ja'far b. Muḥammad 'an 'Abd Allāh b. Maymūn*, as ibid.: 164 where the text is repeated, for *Ja'far b. Muḥammad b. 'Abd Allāh b. Maymūn*), 297, 310, 503
- *Kāfī* 1: 34, 40, 48
  2: 79, 90, 102, 114, 152, 183, 293, 297, 327, 378, 436, 444, 462, 467, 468, 471 (two reports), 473, 475, 487, 492 (two reports), 495, 498–9, 523, 539–40, 569, 610, 645, 647, 657, 659, 664
  3: 22, 69, 124, 246, 262–3, 428, 488
  4: 7, 27, 29, 51, 153 (read *Ja'far b. Muḥammad b. 'Ubayd Allāh* for *Ja'far b. 'Abd Allāh*), 272, 347, 412, 527
  5: 24, 46, 95, 165, 312, 327, 328, 329, 368, 474,494, 495, 497, 503, 516, 523–4, 537, 541, 542, 550
  6: 19, 40, 47 (two reports), 266, 285, 290, 297, 309, 315, 317, 322, 331, 336, 350, 354, 361, 370, 376, 384, 386 (two reports), 387, 435, 439, 443, 445, 447, 448, 457, 467, 469 (two reports), 476, 492, 495 (two reports), 512, 528, 533, 534, 543, 550
  8: 306, 475

- 'Alī b. Ibrāhīm 2: 398–9
- Ibn Qūlawayh: 453
- Ibn Bābawayh, *Amālī*: 116 (also *Thawāb*: 159–60), 714 (also *Khiṣāl*: 293)
- *Faqīh* 2: 342
  3: 69, 300, 353, 384, 436, 573
  4: 130
- *'Ilal* 1: 277
  2: 25, 33, 215, 270, 277
- *'Iqāb*: 270, 275
- *Khiṣāl*: 4, 134, 225, 287, 295, 321, 338, 439, 650 (read *'an 'Alī b. Ibrāhīm 'an abīh* as in the editor's footnote)
- *Ma'ānī*: 152
- Abū Ṭālib: 318, 415–16 (read *Ja'far b. Muḥammad [b. 'Ubayd Allāh]*, as in the author's source: *Maḥāsin*: 293, for *Ja'far b. 'Abd Allāh al-Muḥammadī*)
- *Tahdhīb* 2: 195
  3: 80–82 (two reports), 244–5, 256, 293, 319 (read *Ja'far b. Muḥammad b. 'Ubayd Allāh* [as in *Istibṣār* 1: 477] for *Ja'far b. Muḥammad 'an 'Ubayd Allāh*)
  4: 300
  5: 239, 454, 472
  6: 153
  9: 262–3, 295, 423
  10: 222, 268–9 (read *Ja'far b. Muḥammad b. 'Ubayd Allāh* for *Ja'far b. Muḥammad 'an 'Ubayd Allāh*)
- Ibn Ṭāwūs, *Fatḥ*: 147–8

'Abd Allāh b. Ja'far al-Ḥimyarī quotes a fragment of 24 reports from Ibn al-Qaddāḥ through a single transmitter in his *Qurb al-isnād*: 19–28 (# 66–74, 77–91). The transmitter, Muḥammad b. 'Īsā, should be the same as the one who occasionally quotes from Ibn al-Qaddāḥ through Ḥasan b. 'Alī b. Faḍḍāl (e.g. *Kāfī* 4: 51), and that may have been the case here, too.

In the Sunnī tradition, Ibn 'Adī: 1504–6 quotes some thirteen reports on his authority, eight from Ja'far al-Ṣādiq (from his father, from Jābir b. 'Abd Allāh [# 1–7] and Anas b. Mālik [# 8]), and five directly from 'Abd Allāh b. 'Umar, Jābir or Anas. His quotations from the last three should have been through intermediaries as those three preceded him by two generations. He actually quotes from both 'Abd Allāh b. 'Umar (Ṭabarī, *Tafsīr* 1: 13) and Ibn 'Abbās (Ibn Ḥibbān, *Majrūḥīn* 2: 21) through two intermediaries. Some of his quotations from Ja'far al-Ṣādiq recorded by Ibn 'Adī are cited in other early Sunnī works, too. One, for instance, on the unsuitability of fasting for a traveler (Ibn ʻAdī: 1505) appears also in Ṭabarī, *Tahdhīb, Ibn ʻAbbās* 1: 124 and Abū Nuʻaym, *Ḥilya* 3: 202; another on God's predetermination (Ibn ʻAdī: 1504) in Tirmidhī, *Jāmiʻ* 4: 22; a third on the Prophet's habit of wearing his ring on his right hand (Ibn ʻAdī: 1504) in Tirmidhī, *Shamāʼil*: 151; Ibn Qutayba, *ʻUyūn* 1: 302; ʻUqaylī 2: 302 (also *ʻIlal* 1: 152). Other examples of quotations from Jaʻfar al-Ṣādiq by ʻAbd Allāh b. Maymūn al-Qaddāḥ in Sunnī sources include the following:

- Aḥmad 5: 122
- Ibn Qutayba, *ʻUyūn* 1: 302 (also Aḥmad al-Dīnawarī 2: 422–3, 8: 39; Ibn ʻAsākir 42: 445)
- Ṭabarānī, *Kabīr* 23: 411
- Abū ʼl-Shaykh, *Amthāl*: 86 (part of *Kāfī* 2: 659)
- Lālikāʼī: 782–3 (also Ismāʻīl al-Tamīmī: 24–5)
- Sahmī: 324
- Khaṭīb, *Taʼrīkh* 13: 300
- Dhahabī, *Siyar* 18: 258–9 and *Tadhkira*: 1158

A report in Ṭabarī, *Taʼrīkh* 5: 63–4 (partially repeated at 92) citing some of ʻAlī's decisions after Ṣiffīn, related by an ʻAbd Allāh b. Maymūn, may belong to our author, too (cf. *Tahdhīb* 6: 153). There is also a quotation from him with a Sunnī chain of transmission in Ibn Bābawayh, *Amālī*: 348–9 (partially also in *Kamāl*: 392).

4. *Ifādat al-baṣīr li-kull rāmī mubtadiʼ aw māhir niḥrīr*

This is a treatise on archery by a certain ʻAbd Allāh b. Maymūn, available in MS 5144, Chester Beatty, copied in 1085 in 155 folios (*Cat.* 7: 48–9). Ziriklī 4: 141 ascribes this work to Ibn al-Qaddāḥ, obviously in connection with Ibn al-Qaddāḥ's profession as an arrow maker, but the work clearly belongs to a much later period.

13: Ibn Muskān

Abū Muḥammad ʻAbd Allāh b. Muskān, a Kūfan client of the Banū ʻAnaza, of Asad Rabīʻa, a prominent Shīʻite jurist of his time and a prolific transmitter of *ḥadīth*. He was a contemporary of Jaʻfar al-Ṣādiq and Mūsā al-Kāẓim, and died before the death of the latter in 183.

Barqī: 71; Kashshī: 375, 382–3; *Mashyakha*: 461–2; Najāshī: 214–15; *Fihrist*: 196 (ed. Sprenger; the reference is missing from the Najaf edition of this source normally used in the present work); *Rijāl*: 264; Ibn Mākūlā: 257 (quoting Ibn Faḍḍāl). See also Muḥammad Taqī al-Tustarī 6: 608–15.

1. *Kitāb fī 'l-imāma*

Related by Muḥammad b. Sinān al-Zāhirī (Najāshī: 214). It is very likely that the word *imāma* in the title of this work is a corruption of *a'imma*, and that the work in question is a text of biographical information about the Prophet and the Imāms that Kulaynī received through the same transmitter from Ibn Muskān, quoting six excerpts from it, all in identical style and with the same chain of transmission, in *Kāfī* 1: 461–2 (on Ḥasan al-Mujtabā; also in *Maqātil*: 76–7), 463 (on Ḥusayn), 468 (on 'Alī Zayn al-'Ābidīn), 472 (on Muḥammad al-Bāqir), 475 (on Ja'far al-Ṣādiq), and 486 (on Mūsā al-Kāẓim). The last excerpt has proved problematic as it speaks of Mūsā al-Kāẓim's death in 183 when neither Ibn Muskān nor his authority for the material in this text, Abū Baṣīr, lived that long. Contrary to what Muḥammad Taqī al-Tustarī 6: 610 suggests, this excerpt cannot be dismissed as a misattribution to Ibn Muskān because it is clearly part of that longer text. It seems therefore more likely that a later transmitter, possibly Muḥammad b. Sinān who is the immediate transmitter from Ibn Muskān (and who may also be responsible for two similar paragraphs on 'Alī al-Riḍā and Muḥammad al-Jawād in *Kāfī* 1: 492, 497),[5] updated the information. Another excerpt from the same text appears in the abridged version of Ibn Hammām, *Anwār*: 21–2 (read *'an Ibn Sinān* [i.e. Muḥammad b. Sinān] for *'an 'Abd Allāh b. Sinān*[6]) on the Prophet; a second appears in *Dalā'il al-imāma*: 79 (repeated at 134, read *Ibn Sinān* as in *Biḥār* 43: 9, 170, most likely in the form of *wa 'bn Sinān*) on Fāṭima al-Zahrā'.[7]

---

5. The date mentioned in the latter paragraph, shortly before the end of 220, further points to a later transmitter in the *isnād* for that date. According to Najāshī: 328, Muḥammad b. Sinān himself died in 220. Updating of biographical material by later transmitters was a common practice in early centuries.
6. The latter, a senior contemporary of Ibn Muskān, was not a transmitter from Ibn Muskān nor a *shaykh* of Aḥmad b. Muḥammad b. 'Īsā al-Ash'arī al-Qummī who quotes from Ibn Sinān both the excerpt here as well as the entire text as in Najāshī: 214.
7. The latter excerpt is also quoted on the authority of Ibn Hammām, possibly also from the original version of his *Anwār*, though the reference does not appear in the surviving abridgement of that work.

The above suggestion on the correct title and topic of the work is based on the assumption that a book by a figure as prominent as Ibn Muskān on a topic as fundamental as the Imāmate could hardly have been missed by Ṭūsī who does not mention it, while it was not only known but actually received by his contemporary, Najāshī. For a short text on the lives of the Imāms, however, opinions may vary whether to call it a book or not. This may have been the reason behind Ṭūsī's failure to name the present text as an independent work of Ibn Muskān.

There are also other biographical reports on the Imāms quoted in the sources on the authority of Ibn Muskān, many by Muḥammad b. Sinān. It is not entirely improbable that some of these passages may originally have belonged to the same text, too. Here are some examples:

- *Maḥāsin*: 612
- 'Ayyāshī 1: 261
  2: 41
- *Kāfī* 1: 264–5, 446, 452–3
  6: 448–9, 487, 500
  8: 163–4, 203–4, 378–9
- Kashshī: 111–12
- Ibn Qūlawayh: 163, 169–71, 216, 257, 263–4 (reported through other chains of transmission at 266, 279–80, 281–2), 275, 290, 309 (repeated at 318), 311, 351–2, 488–9
- *Thawāb*: 171
- *Manāqib* 4: 163, 223–4
- Ibn Ṭāwūs, *Muhaj*: 260

There are also many citations in early Shī'ite sources from Ibn Muskān on matters related to the topic of *Imāma*, many through the same transmitter. If Ibn Muskān did have a work on this topic as Najāshī indicates, many of these citations would fit the title of that work, including the following examples:

- *Maḥāsin*: 99, 143, 144, 145, 146, 156, 158, 162, 164, 182–3, 185, 186, 198, 200, 231, 246, 259–60, 272, 290, 299–300, 612
- Ṣaffār: 36, 44–5, 53–4 (also Ibn Qūlawayh: 116; Ibn Bābawayh, *Amālī*: 285, 772), 64, 74, 84, 107–8, 116, 136 (repeated at 137 through two other *isnāds*), 137, 144–5, 171–2, 174, 175–6, 177, 178, 188, 217 (also Ibn al-Juḥām: 404), 230, 260–61, 292, 306–7 (also *Khiṣāl*: 644), 315,

322, 325, 328, 331, 336, 344, 345, 346, 362–5 (a text reported through six partially different *isnāds*), 380, 382, 389–90, 399–400, 473, 480, 519, 520, 23

- 'Ayyāshī 1: 13, 323
  2: 41
- 'Alī b. Bābawayh, *Imāma*: 161, 178, 211
- *Kāfī* 1: 53, 178, 225, 235, 258 (repeated with two different *isnāds*), 270, 273, 275, 286–8 (two reports), 310, 376, 390, 399, 402 (the last passage of a work as indicated by the ending clause), 415
  3: 132–3
  8: 58, 146, 163–4, 296
- Kashshī: 120, 315–16, 323, 360
- Furāt: 429–30
- Ibn al-Juḥām: 167, 233, 235–6, 311, 404, 463
- Nu'mānī: 321 (two reports)
- 'Alī b. Ibrāhīm 1: 44, 72, 73, 74, 106, 129, 194, 210, 214–15, 247, 248, 316–17, 324, 366
  2: 73, 84–5, 160, 239, 290, 357, 367
- *'Ilal* 1: 171, 187–8, 190, 196–7
- *Kamāl*: 203–4, 232, 262 (revised, also in *'Uyūn* 1: 52; *Khiṣāl*: 475), 344, 410
- *Khiṣāl*: 324
- *Ikhtiṣāṣ*: 82, 287–8, 288–9, 307–8, 310, 317–18, 331
- Mufīd, *Amālī*: 45, 184, 279, 328

2. *Kitāb fī 'l-ḥalāl wa 'l-ḥarām*

Mentioned by Najāshī: 214 who also points out that the bulk of the contents of this book is quoted from the mid-second century scholar, Muḥammad b. 'Alī b. Abī Shu'ba al-Ḥalabī (no. 147 below). Ibn Muskān is in fact the principal transmitter of Ḥalabī's book on what is lawful and unlawful. The book was organized in chapters, apparently according to subject matter. Both Najāshī: 325 and *Mashyakha*: 427 received Ḥalabī's book through Ibn Muskān. The contribution of Ibn Muskān seems to consist of copying Ḥalabī's work and supplementing it with some other relevant transmissions on legal matters of his own. Most legal quotations from Ḥalabī on the authority of Ibn Muskān in early sources should therefore have been parts of the work in question. They include the following examples:

- *Maḥāsin*: 324, 612
- Aḥmad b. Muḥammad b. ʿĪsā: 128–9, 163–4
- ʿAyyāshī 1: 70–71
- *Kāfī* 1: 415
  2: 355
  3: 6, 37, 39, 45, 59–60, 89 (read *Ṣāfwān ʿan Ibn Muskān ʿan Muḥammad al-Ḥalabī*; see Burūjirdī, *Tajrīd asānīd al-Kāfī*: 93–4), 185, 331, 337–8, 403, 440, 441, 473, 517 (repeated through a different *isnād* at 518), 525, 554–5
  4: 91, 108, 310, 513, 561
  5: 244, 247, 265, 284, 384, 443
  6: 126 (two reports of the same text), 182, 187, 191, 207, 212–13, 414
  7: 112 (two reports of the same text), 230, 278, 442, 451–2
- Ibn Bisṭām: 62, 108, 114
- Ibn Qūlawayh: 351–2
- *Faqīh* 2: 53, 137, 366, 398, 459
  3: 207, 209–10, 217, 226, 284, 289, 317, 479
  4: 65, 310
- *Kamāl*: 344
- *Tahdhīb* 1: 23, 138, 147, 240, 259, 265, 361, 406
  2: 54, 68–9, 150–51, 158, 160, 168, 174, 190, 226, 234, 248, 269–70, 305, 332, 368, 369
  3: 68–9, 200, 228, 242, 268, 311
  4: 32, 81, 108, 124, 156, 262, 264, 308, 323
  5: 70, 109, 113, 161, 210, 312 (partially also at 309), 326, 332, 337
  6: 380
  7: 28, 36 (two reports), 41, 54, 55–6, 93–4, 99–100, 102, 106, 119, 122, 154, 195, 205, 289, 296, 321
  8: 116, 122, 217–18 (two reports), 253, 270, 295
  9: 32–3 (three reports), 43, 56, 113, 133, 306, 308 (two reports), 386
  10: 111

It is not very difficult to identify and locate much of the extra material that Ibn Muskān added to Ḥalabī's book. Quotations from Ibn Muskān from authorities other than Ḥalabī, quoted from Ibn Muskān through the same chains of transmission as for material he quoted from Ḥalabī, abound in early collections of Shīʿite *ḥadīth*. At times, those from others are quoted immediately after (e.g. *Kāfī* 3: 338; *Tahdhīb* 2: 270) or within a few lines (e.g. *Tahdhīb* 5: 161, 7: 93–4) of those from Ḥalabī, or are merged with them (e.g. *Kāfī* 2: 355 [read *wa 'l-Ḥalabī* for *aw al-Ḥalabī*]; *Tahdhīb* 2: 150–51). In these last instances, it may have been Ibn Muskān himself who added to Ḥalabī's text only the name of the other transmitter to indicate that the report was also attested through another channel. Alternatively, he may have cited a passage from another authority after an identical passage in Ḥalabī's book. Later transmitters of the book may, however, have put the relevant passage under the two names as there was no point in repeating the identical text. For many examples of this latter genre quoted in the *Kāfī*, see Burūjirdī, *Tajrīd asānīd al-Kāfī*: 92–5, 227, 283, 291–2, 332, 633–4, 699. For those quoted in the *Tahdhīb*, see idem, *Tanqīḥ asānīd al-Tahdhīb*: 6, 67, 134, 173, 190–92, 218–20, 259, 344, 353–4, 630–31, 635.

3. Kitāb

His notebook of *ḥadīth* (*Fihrist*: 196 [ed. Sprenger]), extending well beyond the field of the lawful and unlawful that formed the bulk of the material of the previous work. Ibn Muskān is in fact responsible for close to one thousand reports in the four main collections of Shī'ite *ḥadīth* (as listed in Khu'ī 10: 329–30, 498–509, 23: 31–3, 284–313), and for many others in other works (as listed in *Fahāris* 9: 241–2, 10: 305–6).

14: Al-Baṭal

'Abd Allāh b. al-Qāsim b. al-Ḥārith al-Haḍramī, known as al-Baṭal, a Baṣran by origin who was a disciple of the prominent Shī'ite scholar of Kūfa, Mu'āwiya b. 'Ammār al-Duhnī (d. 175), but later developed Extremist tendencies and disassociated himself from Duhnī. He joined the Wāqifites after the death of Mūsā al-Kāẓim.

Kashshī: 326; Ibn al-Ghaḍā'irī: 78; Najāshī: 226; *Fihrist*: 106; *Rijāl*: 341. See also *Kāfī* 1: 258, 536, 8: 206; *Ma'ānī*: 111.

The full name of this transmitter appears as above in Ṣaffār: 398; Ibn Qūlawayh: 197; *Ikhtiṣāṣ*: 316. Najāshī, Ibn al-Ghaḍā'irī and *Fihrist*: 106 have separate entries on 'Abd Allāh b. al-Qāsim al-Ḥārithī, whom Ibn al-Ghaḍā'irī identifies as a Baṣran known as al-Baṭal, and 'Abd Allāh b. al-Qāsim al-Ḥaḍramī, whom Ibn al-Ghaḍā'irī identifies as a Kūfan, *Rijāl*: 341 as a Wāqifite, and Najāshī as al-Baṭal. Najāshī and Ibn al-Ghaḍā'irī identify both 'Abd Allāh b. al-Qāsims as

Extremists as does Kashshī with the one person he has of that name. Muḥammad Taqī al-Tustarī 6: 555–6 seems correct in suggesting that the two names refer to a single person.

His Wāqifite tendency is attested by a report in *Ghayba*: 422 and 471 with a clear reference to Mūsā al-Kāẓim as the *Qā'im*. Another report by him in Ṣaffār: 150 (read *Mūsā b. Sa'dān 'an 'Abd Allāh b. al-Qāsim* as in *Biḥār* 26: 33 as well as all other cases where this *isnād* appears) fixes the number of the Imāms at seven. The report in *Ghayba*: 139 that predicts that the Imāms will be twelve with 'Abd Allāh b. al-Qāsim in its chain of transmission is obviously an updated text, regardless of his involvement. His Extremist tendencies are well attested in many, if not most, of his transmissions and by the character of many of his masters and transmitters as, for instance, in the case of his direct (e.g. *Maḥāsin*: 89; *Kāfī* 1: 343, 473; *Kamāl*: 349; *Ghayba*: 164) and indirect (e.g. Ṣaffār: 138; *Kāfī* 1: 224–5; *'Iqāb*: 249; *Ta'wīl al-āyāt*: 868–9 quoting Ibn Bābawayh; see also Kashshī: 326) quotations from Mufaḍḍal al-Ju'fī. On Extremist Wāqifites, see Kashshī: 477–9.

Kitāb

His notebook of *ḥadīth*, related by a number of transmitters including Muḥammad b. Khālid al-Barqī, 'Abd Allāh b. 'Abd al-Raḥmān al-Aṣamm and Muḥammad b. al-Ḥusayn b. Abī 'l-Khaṭṭāb (Najāshī: 226; *Fihrist*: 106 [both in their two entries on this author]). The last transmitter, however, usually quotes 'Abd Allāh b. al-Qāsim through Mūsā b. Sa'dān al-Ḥannāṭ, and that may have been the case even where Ibn Abī 'l-Khaṭṭāb sounds as if he quotes directly from 'Abd Allāh b. al-Qāsim. Examples of quotations from this author by the above-mentioned transmitters of this notebook include the following:

- *Maḥāsin*: 89 (also *'Iqāb*: 249), 137–8, 150, 286 (a fuller version of the previous text [p. 150]; whence *Kāfī* 2: 46)
- Ṣaffār: 49, 66, 141, 150 (read *Mūsā b. Sa'dān 'an 'Abd Allāh b. al-Qāsim* as in *Biḥār* 26: 33), 188, 241–2, 270–71, 351, 394, 401, 403, 408, 414–15 (also *'Ilal* 1: 158), 432, 456, 499
- *Kāfī* 1: 195, 209, 231, 258, 387, 529–30, 536–7
  2: 46, 104, 123–4, 138, 239–40, 335, 422
  3: 124, 237, 431 (read *Muḥammad b. al-Ḥasan b. Shammūn 'an 'Abd Allāh b. 'Abd al-Raḥmān* as in all similar cases)
  4: 3, 27, 365, 581–2
  5: 298, 498, 513
  6: 25
  7: 442 (also *Ma'ānī*: 389; *Faqīh* 3: 373)
  8: 206, 212–15

- Kashshī: 378–9
- Ibn al-Juḥām: 184–5, 225–6, 267, 363, 461
- Nuʿmānī: 310–11
- ʿAlī b. Ibrāhīm 1: 335
- Ibn Qūlawayh: 133–4 (partially also at 136), 140–41, 219–20, 231–2 (and a fuller version at 353–4), 350 (also in Ibn Bābawayh, *Amālī*: 737)
- *ʿIlal* 2: 189
- *ʿIqāb*: 249, 280
- *Kamāl*: 349
- *Khiṣāl*: 204–5, 264–5
- *Maʿānī*: 111, 143
- *Thawāb*: 167
- Mufīd, *Mutʿa*: 42–3
- Ṭūsī, *Amālī* (as quoted in *Biḥār* 97: 54)
- *Ghayba*: 422 (repeated with a fuller version at 471; see also 474)
- *Tahdhīb* 3: 176, 187–8 (in both, read *Aḥmad b. Muḥammad ʿan abīh* as in all similar cases)
  4: 122
  6: 74
  7: 267–8
- Ṭabrisī, *Iʿlām*: 367–9 (quoted from Kulaynī, but the reference is missing in *Kāfī* 1: 529–30)
- *Qiṣaṣ*: 189 (read *Mūsā b. Saʿdān* as in *Biḥār* 75: 95)

Ibn Ṭāwūs, *Faraj*: 92–3 quotes a lengthy report that he found in the *Kitāb* of ʿAbd Allāh b. al-Qāsim al-Ḥaḍramī (see further Kohlberg: 219).

15: Ibn Sinān

ʿAbd Allāh b. Sinān, a Kūfan client of Quraysh and a controller of the government treasury in Kūfa during the reign of the ʿAbbāsids Manṣūr and Mahdī. He was a transmitter from Jaʿfar al-Ṣādiq and a prominent member of the Shīʿite community of his time.

Yaḥyā b. Maʿīn 3: 489; Barqī: 71; ʿUqaylī 2: 263; Ibn Abī Ḥātim 5: 68–9; Kashshī: 410–11; Ibn ʿAdī: 1560–61; Najāshī: 214; *Fihrist*: 101; *Rijāl*: 264, 339; Khaṭīb, *Taʾrīkh* 13: 466; *Mīzān* 2: 436–7, and many other sources listed in the editors' footnotes to Dhahabī, *Taʾrīkh* 12 (years 181–90): 209 and *Lisān* 4: 38.

Shī'ite sources identify this transmitter as a client of Quraysh (Barqī: 71; Kashshī: 411; *Rijāl*: 264), more specifically of the Banū Hāshim clan (Najāshī: 214), though there was a disagreement as to whether he belonged to its Ṭālibid or 'Abbāsid branch. Some Sunnī sources, however, identify him as *Zuhrī* (Ibn 'Adī: 1560; *Mīzān* 2: 436; *Lisān* 3: 297), referring to the Banū Zuhra b. Kilāb, a clan of Quraysh.[8] This, however, seems to be a corruption of *Zāhirī*, as in 'Uqaylī 2: 263, which according to Najāshī: 328 signified a relation to, or clientage of, Khuzā'a. Najāshī: 214 identifies our transmitter as a son of Sinān b. Ṭarīf. *Rijāl*: 283 names an 'Abd Allāh, son of Sinān b. Ṭarīf al-Hāshimī and his brother, Muḥammad, among the transmitters from Ja'far al-Ṣādiq. There is a Muḥammad b. Sinān al-Zāhirī who was a younger comtemporary of, and transmitter from, 'Abd Allāh b. Sinān (Najāshī: 328). It is not clear whether the two transmitters are related to each other or whether the similarities in names have led to misidentification and confusion.

Barqī: 71; Kashshī: 411, and *Rijāl*: 264 (in which read *khazā'in* for *jaysh*) report that 'Abd Allāh b. Sinān was a state treasurer in the reigns of Manṣūr and Mahdī. According to Najāshī: 214, he continued to hold that office under Hādī and Hārūn al-Rashīd. Khaṭīb, *Ta'rīkh* 9: 469 (also *Talkhīṣ*: 350) reports that 'Abd Allāh b. Sinān held that position jointly with Jarrāḥ b. Malīḥ al-Ru'āsī, the father of the Kūfan scholar Wakī' (d. 197), who is known to have served in the government treasury at Kūfa (see Ziriklī 8: 117 and the sources named) earlier in the 'Abbāsid period (Khaṭīb, *Ta'rīkh* 13: 468, certainly before the middle of the second century while Sulaymān b. Mihrān al-A'mash [d. 148] was still alive), and in the state treasury in Baghdad in the reign of Hārūn al-Rashīd (Ibn Sa'd 6: 265 and the many other sources listed in the editor's footnote to Mizzī 4: 517), possibly until he died some time after 175 (Khalīfa b. Khayyāṭ, *Ṭabaqāt*: 397): 176 as in Mizzī 4: 520, or 186 as in *Mīzān* 1: 390. According to Yaḥyā b. Ma'īn 3: 489 (whence Khaṭīb, *Ta'rīkh* 9: 469), Ibn Sinān too later moved to Baghdad and settled in the district known as *Qaṭī'at al-Rabī'*, so called in attribution to Rabī' b. Yūnus, Ibn Abī Farwa (d. 169), who received that district as a land grant from Manṣūr. How long Ibn Sinān continued as Jarrāḥ's co-treasurer is not clear. It is, however, reported that he was poor later in life after his good days in the period of Manṣūr (Ibn Hammām: 45).

Though a transmitter of insignificant contribution to Sunnī tradition (Ibn 'Adī: 1561), 'Abd Allāh b. Sinān was a prolific transmitter of Shī'ite *ḥadīth* and an authority on the teachings of the Imāms in the Shī'ite community of his time (see *Kāfī* 1: 51–2). He authored a number of books that were related from him by groups of Shī'ite transmitters (Najāshī: 214), including the following:

---

8. Cf. Ibn Mākūlā 4: 451 and Khaṭīb, *Talkhīṣ*: 350, where 'Abd Allāh b. Sinān b. Abī Sinān al-Zuhrī, a transmitter from his father, is distinguished from our 'Abd Allāh b. Sinān.

1. *Kitāb 'amal yawm wa layla*

(Najāshī: 214 [noting that the work was alternatively known as *Kitāb al-ṣalāt*]; *Fihrist*: 101). Surviving works of this genre, such as the one by Ṭūsī, are on the obligatory and supererogatory daily prayers. The following quotations from 'Abd Allāh b. Sinān in early collections of Shī'ite *ḥadīth* may therefore have belonged to this work:

- Ḥasan b. Maḥbūb: 81 (also *Thawāb*: 196; Ibn Ṭāwūs, *Falāḥ*: 297)
- *Maḥāsin*: 84 (also Ibn Bābawayh, *Amālī*: 573–4; *'Iqāb*: 276), 639
- 'Ayyāshī 1: 127–8 (also 'Alī b. Ibrāhīm 1: 79)
  2: 320
- *Kāfī* 2: 585
  3: 280, 322, 413, 414, 415, 420, 428, 449
- Ibn Bābawayh, *Amālī*: 462 (also *Thawāb*: 194), 586, 638
- *Faqīh* 1: 489
- *'Ilal* 2: 18, 19, 38
- *Kamāl*: 351–2
- *Khiṣāl*: 7 (also *Thawāb*: 63), 393, 460, 499
- *Thawāb*: 172
- Ṭūsī, *Amālī*: 214
- *Miṣbāḥ*: 363–4
- *Tahdhīb* 2: 28, 39, 51, 53, 56, 66, 67, 79, 89, 116, 136, 257, 276
  3: 4–5, 13, 25, 85, 86, 131, 235–6, 274, 280, 282
- Ibn Ṭāwūs, *Jamāl*: 157–8, 274, 275 (see also 277)
- Shahīd I, *Dhikrā* 2: 373
- Jubā'ī, *Majmū'a* (quoted in *Biḥār* 86: 217–18)

2. *Kitāb al-ṣalāt al-kabīr*

(Najāshī: 214). Parts of the large amount of material quoted from 'Abd Allāh b. Sinān in later works of *ḥadīth* on non-daily prayers may have originated from this work. They include the following examples:

- Zayd al-Narsī: 45
- Ḥasan b. Maḥbūb: 81 (two reports), 86–7, 90 (whence *Maḥāsin*: 18; 'Ayyāshī 1: 48)
- Bazanṭī, *Nawādir*: 29 (two reports, one also in *Tahdhīb* 2: 28)
- Muḥammad b. 'Alī b. Maḥbūb: 96
- *Maḥāsin*: 48, 315–16 (also *Kāfī* 3: 454), 318, 429

- 'Ayyāshī 2: 318
- 'Uqaylī 2: 263
- *Kāfī* 3: 207, 266, 274, 286–7, 295–6, 309, 314, 317 (two reports), 318, 333, 342, 355, 370, 371, 376, 387, 401–2, 404–5, 424, 449, 454, 468, 488
- Ibn Bisṭām: 109–10, 117
- Ibn Bābawayh, *Amālī*: 366 (also *Ma'ānī*: 117–18)
- *Faqīh* 1: 109, 163, 223–4, 256, 266, 287, 346, 387, 407, 439–40, 564, 566, 568–9
- *'Ilal* 1: 284
  2: 16, 21
- *Thawāb*: 35, 59, 62, 103 (two reports)
- *Miṣbāḥ*: 782–7
- *Tahdhīb* 1: 254, 390, 401, 404, 407, 427
  2: 6, 13–14, 50, 59–60, 61, 70, 131, 147, 222, 265, 270 (also Ibn Ṭāwūs, *Muḍāyaqa*: 342–3 where the passage is quoted from Ḥusayn b. Sa'īd's *Kitāb al-ṣalāt*), 287, 291, 299, 313, 343, 350, 355, 359, 361, 365, 366
  3: 12–13, 25, 35, 64–6, 69, 128, 136, 160, 176, 178, 199, 216, 231, 236, 241, 242, 256, 257, 295, 308, 315
- Ṭabrisī, *Majma'* 30: 155, 207
- Abū Ṭālib: 215
- *Makārim al-akhlāq*: 130, 135 (two reports)
- Ibn Ṭāwūs, *Ghiyāth*: 8
- Idem, *Iqbāl* 1: 49–51, 475

3. *Kitāb fī abwāb al-ḥalāl wa 'l-ḥarām*

This book is mentioned by Najāshī: 214 who calls it *Kitāb fī sā'ir al-abwāb min al-ḥalāl wa 'l-ḥarām*, and it is probably the same as the *Kitāb* mentioned by Abū Ghālib: 183, and Ṭūsī in *Fihrist*: 101 and *Rijāl*: 339. The work must have contained 'Abd Allāh b. Sinān's transmissions on legal topics, close to one thousand examples of which are quoted in the four main collections of Shī'ite *ḥadīth*, and many others in other early Shī'ite works. For the list of those in the Four Books, see Khu'ī 10: 203–9, 454–78, 22: 186–91, 392–404; for others, see *Fahāris* 9: 71–3, 214–16.

4. *Nawādir*

This is mentioned by Abū Ghālib: 183 as part of 'Abd Allāh b. Sinān's larger notebook of *ḥadīth*. Parts of the quotations from this transmitter on non-legal issues, many of them listed in Khu'ī and *Fahāris* as noted above, may originally have belonged to this work.

16: Ibn Ṭalḥa al-Nahdī

'Abd Allāh b. Ṭalḥa al-Nahdī, an 'Arab Kūfan Shī'ite and a transmitter from Ja'far al-Ṣādiq.

Barqī: 72; Najāshī: 224; *Rijāl*: 232. See also *Kāfī* 2: 172, 232–3 (a clearly late Umayyad report); *Tahdhīb* 6: 35.

Kitāb

His notebook of *ḥadīth*, related by the late second-century scholar 'Alī b. Ismā'īl al-Maythamī (Najāshī: 224). Ja'far b. Muḥammad b. Shurayḥ al-Haḍramī quotes a fragment of eighteen reports in his *Kitāb*: 74–7 on the authority of 'Abd Allāh b. Ṭalḥa that may have been taken from the work in question. Other quotations from our author, some through 'Alī b. Ismā'īl al-Maythamī (e.g. Ḥusayn b. Sa'īd, *Zuhd*: 36), include the following:

- Ḥusayn b. Sa'īd, *Zuhd*: 36, 44–5
- *Maḥāsin*: 584 (also *Kāfī* 6: 240)
- Ṣaffār: 253 (also *Kāfī* 8: 232), 458–9
- 'Ayyāshī 1: 43 (repeated at 68)
- *Kāfī* 2: 510 (also Ibn Bābawayh, *Amālī*: 337; idem, *Faḍā'il al-ashhur*: 86, 111), 620
  4: 64 (also Ibn Bābawayh, *Amālī*: 645; idem, *Faḍā'il al-ashhur*: 121–2; *Thawāb*: 75)
  7: 147, 229, 247, 293 (two reports)
  8: 272
- Ibn Bābawayh, *Amālī*: 247–8, 682
- *Ma'ānī*: 241
- Ṭūsī, *Amālī*: 677
- *Tahdhīb* 6: 21, 35
  10: 4, 292

17: Ibn Waḍḍāḥ

Abū Muḥammad ʻAbd Allāh b. Waḍḍāḥ, a Kūfan client and an associate of the prominent Imāmite *ḥadīth* transmitter of Kūfa, Abū Baṣīr Yaḥyā b. al-Qāsim al-Asadī (d. 149–50).

Najāshī: 215; *Fihrist*: 193; *Rijāl*: 340.

A report in *Ghayba*: 44 may suggest that this transmitter joined the Wāqifites later in life. He is certainly different from Abū Muḥammad ʻAbd Allāh b. al-Waḍḍāḥ al-Kūfī al-Lu'lu'ī, a Sunnī transmitter and a *shaykh* of Tirmidhī, Yaʻqūb b. Iṣḥāq al-Fasawī and many others, who died in 250 (Mizzī 16: 266–7 and the sources listed in the editor's footnote). Quotations from this latter transmitter also appear in Shīʻite works (e.g. Furāt: 408–9).

Najāshī: 215 noted that this transmitter composed a number of books, of which Najāshī knew only one:

1. *Kitāb al-ṣalāt*

Related from the author by the prominent Wāqifite scholar ʻAlī b. al-Ḥasan al-Ṭāṭarī, most of the material of this book was quoted by the author from his above-mentioned master, Abū Baṣīr (Najāshī: 215). Quotations from this author on matters related to prayer, some on the authority of the same transmitter, include the following few examples:

- *Kāfī* 3: 478
- *Tahdhīb* 2: 141, 259

2. *Kitāb al-tafsīr*

(*Fihrist*: 193). There is a long quotation from this author in ʻAlī b. Ibrāhīm 2: 47 on Qur'ān 18: 110 and several other verses that may originally have belonged to this work.

18: Al-Kāhilī

Abū Muḥammad ʻAbd Allāh b. Yaḥyā al-Kāhilī, an Arab Kūfan Shīʻite and a transmitter from Jaʻfar al-Ṣādiq and Mūsā al-Kāẓim. He was particularly close to the latter and died during his lifetime, before 182.

Barqī: 71; Kashshī: 401–2, 434–5, 447–8; Najāshī: 221–2; *Fihrist*: 102; *Rijāl*: 341. See also *Kāfī* 3: 491, 4: 506; *Faqīh* 1: 178.

Barqī notes that this transmitter was from the Banū Kāhil, a clan of Asad Khuzayma. Najāshī, however, quotes the prominent genealogist Muḥammad b. 'Abd al-Raḥmān al-'Abdī, known as Ibn 'Abda, author of a book on the Banū Asad (Ibn al-Nadīm: 118), to the effect that the man was in fact from the tribe of the Banū Tamīm. The *nisba* of *Kāhilī* may therefore signify that the man lived in the district of the Banū Kāhil in Kūfa. A quotation from this transmitter in Ibn al-Mashhadī: 122, in the chapter on the mosque of the Banū Kāhil in Kūfa, describes how Ja'far al-Ṣādiq said his dawn prayer in that mosque.

Kashshī quotes a report that Mūsā al-Kāẓim asked 'Alī b. Yaqṭīn, a high ranking Shī'ite official of the early 'Abbāsid administration (no. 38 below), to protect Kāhilī and his family. Henceforth, Kāhilī received regular payments from 'Alī b. Yaqṭīn, including an annual grant to go on pilgrimage to Mecca. According to ibid.: 448, Kāhilī died during the lifetime of 'Alī b. Yaqṭīn (d. 182) and Mūsā al-Kāẓim.

Kitāb

His notebook of *ḥadīth*, related by a number of transmitters including Aḥmad b. Muḥammad b. Abī Naṣr al-Bazanṭī (Najāshī: 222; *Fihrist*: 102). A fragment of this notebook quoted on the authority of this transmitter has survived into our time and is published in the collection of *al-Uṣūl al-sittat 'ashar*: 114–16. This fragment consists of thirteen reports (see further Kohlberg, *Uṣūl*: 155). Many other quotations from Kāhilī appear in Shī'ite collections of *ḥadīth*; most of them should go back to the original, complete version of this notebook. For lists of many of these, see Khu'ī 10: 379, 381, 390, 23: 134–5; *Fahāris* 9: 231, 248–9, 10: 7.

19: Al-Rassān

'Abd Allāh b. al-Zubayr, the rope seller, a Kūfan client of the Banū Asad who joined Zayd b. 'Alī in his revolt against the Umayyad Hishām b. 'Abd al-Malik in 122. He later joined, and survived, the revolt of Muḥammad b. 'Abd Allāh al-Nafs al-Zakiyya in 145. He was a transmitter from Ja'far al-Ṣādiq, among others, and was also known to Sunnī and Zaydī scholars of *ḥadīth*, specially as the father of Abū Aḥmad al-Zubayrī (d. 203), a *Shaykh* of Aḥmad b. Ḥanbal and many others and a respected scholar of Sunnī *ḥadīth*.

'Ijlī: 256; Abū Zur'a al-Rāzī: 496; Barqī: 91; Ibn Abī Ḥātim 5: 56; Kashshī: 338; Ibn Ḥibbān, *Thiqāt* 8: 345; *Maqātil*: 290; Ibn Bābawayh, *Amālī*: 416; Najāshī: 220; *Rijāl*: 234; Khaṭīb, *Talkhīṣ*: 20; *Lisān* 4: 17 (and other sources listed in the editor's footnote).

Mizzī 25: 476 has this transmitter as 'Abd Allāh b. al-Zubayr b. 'Umar b. Dirham al-Aslamī, the client of the Banū Asad. *Aslamī* in Mizzī's source was most likely a corruption of *Asadī*, as being a client of the Banū Asad does not go well with the *nisba* of *Aslamī*, which refers to the Arab tribe of the descendants of Ilyās b. Muḍar, an ancestor of the Prophet.

Rope selling seems to have been the family business of this transmitter. Both he (Kashshī: 338; Khaṭīb, *Talkhīṣ*: 20, editor's footnote) and his brother Fuḍayl[9] (Kashshī: 338; Ibn Bābawayh, *Amālī*: 416; Khaṭīb, *Talkhīṣ*: 20) are described as *rassān*. 'Abd Allāh's son, Abū Aḥmad, is also said to have been a *ḥabbāl* who sold ropes (Mizzī 25: 480; Dhahabī, *Siyar* 9: 531).

That he survived both Zayd's and al-Nafs al-Zakiyya's revolts is attested by a report in *Maqātil*: 290. A narrative in Ibn Bābawayh, *Amālī*: 416 reports that he received financial aid from Ja'far al-Ṣādiq after the revolt of Zayd was suppressed. The narrative is also quoted in Kashshī: 338 (whence Mufīd, *Irshād* 2: 173) with a confusing additional word.

'Ijlī: 256 and Ibn Ḥibbān, *Thiqāt* 8: 345 included this man among reliable transmitters of *ḥadīth*, while Ibn Abī Ḥātim 5: 56 and Abū Zur'a al-Rāzī: 496 considered him unreliable. For examples of his non-Shī'ite transmissions, see Ṭabarī 6: 161; Ibn Ḥibbān, *Thiqāt* 8: 345 (the latter, a report by this man from 'Abd Allāh b. Sharīk who met Muḥammad al-Bāqir on a pilgrimage to Mecca, appears also in Kashshī: 125–6 with a longer text; there is also an updated version of a Shī'ite report that our transmitter quotes on the authority of 'Abd Allāh b. Sharīk in *Kamāl*: 317).

For his son, Abū Aḥmad Muḥammad b. 'Abd Allāh al-Zubayrī, see Mizzī 25: 476–81; Dhahabī, *Ta'rīkh* 14 (years 201–210): 353–5, and the many sources listed in the editors' footnotes to these two entries. 'Abd Allāh's other son, Ḥasan, was also a transmitter of *ḥadīth*, as was Abū Aḥmad's son, Ṭāhir. Both Abū Aḥmad ('Ijlī: 406; see also Ibn 'Asākir 42: 142) and Ḥasan (Khaṭīb, *Ta'rīkh* 5: 402) were pro-'Alīd; Ḥasan, in fact, is said to have been among the leaders of the pro-'Alīd trend among the Sunnī *ḥadīth* transmitters of his time (ibid.) as his father was (Khaṭīb, *Talkhīṣ*: 20). None, however, was an Imāmite (see, for instance, Mizzī 22: 355).

Kitāb al-nawādir

A collection of his transmissions from Ja'far al-Ṣādiq, related from the author by 'Abbād b. Ya'qūb al-Rawājinī (d. 250) (Najāshī: 220). Quotations in Imāmite and Zaydī sources from Ja'far al-Ṣādiq on the authority of

9. A transmitter of *ḥadīth* (see Khu'ī 13: 326–7; *Fahāris* 9: 546), he is the author of the *Tasmiyat man qutila ma'a 'l-Ḥusayn min wuldih wa ikhwatih wa shī'atih* (ed. Muḥammad Riḍā al-Ḥusaynī, Qum, 1406 [in *Turāthunā* 2: 125–60]).

'Abd Allāh b. al-Zubayr, some through the same transmitter (e.g. Aḥmad b. 'Īsā 2: 428), should originally have been parts of this notebook. Examples include the following:[10]

- Aḥmad b. 'Īsā 2: 428
- Ibn Bābawayh, *Amālī*: 141
- *Tahdhīb* 1: 414

20: 'Abd al-Malik al-Khath'amī

'Abd al-Malik b. Ḥakīm al-Khath'amī, a Kūfan Shī'ite and a transmitter from Ja'far al-Ṣādiq and Mūsā al-Kāẓim.

Najāshī: 239–40; *Fihrist*: 110.

Kitāb

His notebook of *ḥadīth*, related by his nephew Ja'far b. Muḥammad b. Ḥakīm (Najāshī: 239–40; *Fihrist*: 110). This notebook has survived on the authority of the same transmitter, and is published in the collection of *al-Uṣūl al-sittat 'ashar*: 98–101 (see further Kohlberg, *Uṣūl*: 155).

21: 'Abd al-Malik al-Nakha'ī

'Abd al-Malik b. 'Utba al-Nakha'ī, the moneychanger, a Kūfan Imāmite and a transmitter from Ja'far al-Ṣādiq and Mūsā al-Kāẓim.

Najāshī: 239; *Rijāl*: 238.

Kitāb

His notebook of *ḥadīth*, mentioned by both Najāshī and Ṭūsī. *Fihrist*: 110, copying its source as usual, mentions a *Kitāb* by 'Abd al-Malik b. 'Utba

10. This is by no means a comprehensive list as some of my notes on this author are missing.

al-Hāshimī, a Meccan descendant of Abū Lahab, uncle of the Prophet. Najāshī: 239 corrects that assumption, noting that the *kitāb* known in his time, and related by a number of transmitters, as the *Kitāb* of 'Abd al-Malik b. 'Utba belongs to this Kūfan moneychanger and not to the Meccan Hāshimid. The misattribution seems to have been old, caused possibly by a mistake by one of the earlier authors of lists of Shī'ite transmitters of *ḥadīth*. Misled by that early misinformation, some later transmitters already misidentified the notebook, at times adding the *nisba* of *al-Hāshimī* to the name of the author when transmitting material from it. A principal transmitter of the notebook, 'Alī b. al-Ḥakam, was himself a Kūfan client of Nakha' and affiliated with the moneychangers of the city (Kashshī: 570). Even in some of his transmissions, all received through the same chain of transmitters, the Hāshimid *nisba* is added to the name of 'Abd al-Malik, possibly by a later transmitter. There is, however, ample evidence in these quotations to clearly identify the author of the notebook. In one example (*Kāfī* 5: 245), 'Abd al-Malik tells the Imām in detail about what moneychangers do, clearly an explanation from someone from within the profession. In others, quoted from him through different transmitters (*Kāfī* 5: 307; *Tahdhīb* 7: 115), he tells the Imām in detail about what he personally does as a moneychanger. In yet another report in *Tahdhīb* 7: 188–9, 'Abd al-Malik explains that he had previously consulted the Sunnī jurists of Kūfa about an issue of moneychanging, but that Ja'far al-Ṣādiq later advised him contrary to what they had said. Similar indications can be found in quotations from 'Abd al-Malik in *Kāfī* 5: 206 and *Tahdhīb* 7: 59, 189 [two reports]. It was most probably because of material of this nature that Najāshī noticed that the notebook must belong to 'Abd al-Malik b. 'Utba, the Kūfan moneychanger, not the Meccan Hāshimid.

Here is a list of quotations from this author on the authority of 'Alī b. al-Ḥakam in two of the main works of Shī'ite *ḥadīth*:

- *Kāfī* 2: 673–4
  3: 548 (read *Aḥmad 'an 'Alī b. al-Ḥakam* as in all similar cases), 551
  4: 116 (also *Faqīh* 2: 134), 127 (also *'Ilal* 2: 70), 134, 279
  5: 206, 245
- *Tahdhīb* 1: 372, 436
  7: 59 (repeated at 81, 238), 189 (two reports)

Material quoted by other transmitters, or without a chain of transmission, but most probably from this notebook, includes the following:

- *Kāfī* 5: 307
- *Faqīh* 2: 252–3
- *Tahdhīb* 7: 115, 188–9

22: 'Abd al-Mu'min al-Anṣārī

Abū 'Abd Allāh 'Abd al-Mu'min b. al-Qāsim al-Anṣārī, a Kūfan Shī'ite transmitter of *ḥadīth* and brother of the better known Abū Maryam 'Abd al-Ghaffār b. al-Qāsim (no. 5 above). He was a transmitter from Muḥammad al-Bāqir and Ja'far al-Ṣādiq, and died in 147 at the age of 81.

Barqī: 51, 64; 'Uqaylī 3: 92; Ibn al-Nadīm: 275; Najāshī: 249; *Fihrist*: 122; *Rijāl*: 142, 241; *Lisān* 4: 481–2 (and the sources listed in the editor's footnote). See further Ṣaffār: 46–7; *Ikhtiṣāṣ*: 279.

He was certainly a Shī'ite, as attested by his many reports on the virtues of 'Alī and his descendants. He does not, however, seem to have been an Imāmite in the later, more developed sense of the word. This point is confirmed by his transmissions from Muḥammad al-Bāqir, from Jābir b. 'Abd Allāh al-Anṣārī, from the Prophet (e.g. Mufīd, *Amālī*: 66–7, 165). This is a well known *isnād* in Sunnī and Zaydī *ḥadīth* but not particularly favored, in non-sectarian issues, by the Imāmites who prefer to emphasize the hereditary aspect of the knowledge of the House.

Kitāb

His notebook of *ḥadīth*, related by a number of transmitters including Sufyān b. Ibrāhīm b. Mazyad al-Azdī (Ibn al-Nadīm: 275; Najāshī: 249; *Fihrist*: 122). This transmitter (on whom see *Rijāl*: 220) is also known to Sunnī biographers as a transmitter from 'Abd al-Mu'min (*Mīzān* 2: 164–5; *Lisān* 3: 52). He is commonly known as Ḥarīrī with reference to his profession as *bayyā' al-ḥarīr*, silk seller (Ṭūsī, *Amālī*: 232). The *nisba* is corrupted in Najāshī: 249 to *Ḥārithī* and in numerous *isnād*s to *Jarīrī* / *Jurayrī*.

Quotations from this author in later works through Sufyān b. Ibrāhīm, representing in all likelihood the notebook in question, include the following examples:

- 'Uqaylī 3: 306 (also Ṭabarānī, *Awsaṭ* 4: 171; Ibn Shāhīn, *Sunna*: 156; Abū Nu'aym, *Faḍā'il al-khulafā'*: 62–3; Ibn 'Asākir 42: 329)

- *Maḥāsin*: 485 (also *Kāfī* 6: 332)
- Ibn al-Juḥām: 275 (read *'Abd al-Mu'min* for *'Abd Allāh* as in *Ta'wīl al-āyāt*: 512; also Ṣaffār: 55–6 and *Kāfī* 1: 212 where the same report is quoted from 'Abd al-Mu'min through a different transmitter)
- Ṭabarānī, *Awsaṭ* 4: 172
- *Khiṣāl*: 445
- 'Āṣimī 1: 500 (also Ṣaffār: 310, where the report is quoted from 'Abd al-Mu'min through a different transmitter)
- Ṭūsī, *Amālī*: 232, 255
- *Ghayba*: 180, 472–3 (clearly from 'Abd al-Mu'min, but his name is either missing or corrupted in the *isnād*)
- *Bishārat al-Muṣṭafā*: 118
- Ibn Ṭāwūs, *Yaqīn*: 194 (quoting Abū Isḥāq al-Thaqafī's *Kitāb al-ma'rifa*)

Other quotations from the author, many most likely from this notebook and all on the virtues of 'Alī and his descendants as well as matters of religious ethics, but not theology or law, include the following examples:

- Ḥusayn b. Sa'īd, *Zuhd*: 45–6
- *Maḥāsin*: 11 (also *Khiṣāl*: 349–50), 33–4
- Ṣaffār: 46–7, 56, 310, 512
- 'Uqaylī 3: 92
- *Kāfī* 1: 154, 214 (see Ṣaffār: 46–7)
  8: 131 (also Ṭūsī, *Amālī*: 693), 234 (also *Khiṣāl*: 139 and a longer version at 152)
- *Faqīh* 2: 115–16 (also *Ma'ānī*: 336)
- *'Ilal* 1: 80
- *Khiṣāl*: 349–50, 571
- Mufīd, *Amālī*: 66–7, 165
- Ṭūsī, *Amālī*: 483

23: Ibn al-Ḥajjāj

Abū 'Alī 'Abd al-Raḥmān b. al-Ḥajjāj, seller of *Shāpūrī* clothing, a Kūfan client of Bajīla who moved to Baghdad. He was a prominent Shī'ite jurist and a close disciple of Ja'far al-Ṣādiq and Mūsā al-Kāẓim. He lived into the late second century and died in Medina during the Imāmate of 'Alī al-Riḍā.

Barqī: 74, 117; *Maḥāsin*: 70; *Kāfī* 4: 558; Kashshī: 441–2; *Mashyakha*: 447; Najāshī: 237–8; *Fihrist*: 108; *Rijāl*: 236, 339; *Ghayba*: 61, 71, 348.

He is identified by his biographers as *Bayyā' al-Sāburī* after his profession as seller of *Shāpūrī* clothing. This was made of a thin, transparent gauze, mentioned in *ḥadīth* (e.g. 'Abd Allāh b. Aḥmad b. Ḥanbal, *Sunna* 1: 313, 338) and Arabic poetry of the early Islamic period (see the examples in Zabīdī 3: 253) as a symbol of delicacy. *Sāburī* was also the name of a fine Kūfan date (Ibn Qutayba, *'Uyūn* 1: 220; *Kāfī* 6: 348; Zabīdī 3: 253) but that is not what is meant here (see further Sam'ānī 7: 4; Ibn Ḥajar, *Tabṣīr*: 712). The pronunciation of the name is given by the lexicographers as *Sābirī* and by Sam'ānī as *Sābarī*. The Persian origin of the name, however, suggests *Sāburī* and this most likely was the common pronunciation of the word in the early times.

Ibn al-Ḥajjāj was close to 'Alī b. Yaqṭīn (no. 38 below), the high ranking Shī'ite official in the early 'Abbāsid administration who sponsored Ibn al-Ḥajjāj's annual trips to Mecca for the *ḥajj* (Kashshī: 435; see also 431). These annual trips provided the opportunity for Ibn al-Ḥajjāj not only to hear from the Imāms but also to carry messages to and fro between them and their followers in Iraq (ibid.: 265–6, 269–71, 279, 431). A report in Kashshī: 431, has him carrying a large amount of funds to Mūsā al-Kāẓim. *Ghayba*: 349, possibly referring to a variant of the same report, suggests that Ibn al-Ḥajjāj was in fact a financial agent (*wakīl*) of Ja'far al-Ṣādiq. The institution of financial agency for the Imāms did not exist at the time of this Imām (see Modarressi, *Crisis*: 13).

Najāshī reports that Ibn al-Ḥajjāj was accused of Kaysānī tendencies but that he later returned to the true path. The context clearly shows that the word *Kaysāniyya* is a misnomer for *Wāqifiyya*. *Ghayba*: 71 has him among the prominent disciples of Mūsā al-Kāẓim who after his death held that he was alive but later recognized 'Alī al-Riḍā as his successor. A report ibid.: 61 confirms Ibn al-Ḥajjāj's earlier position on that matter. He died during the Imāmate of 'Alī al-Riḍā, according to the latter source. That he was alive until 183 is also required by a report in *Kāfī* 1: 308.

Ibn al-Ḥajjāj was a prominent jurist of the Shī'ite community in his time and was recognized as such by members of that community (see *Kāfī* 4: 391). Based on evidence from his own transmission, he had a good knowledge of the opinions of the Sunnī jurists of Iraq, their language and their methods of legal reasoning. Ja'far al-Ṣādiq occasionally asked him about what the jurists of Iraq had said on various matters of law. His transmissions, predominantly legal in nature, demonstrate a legalist mind preoccupied with details of cases and their legal implications. Examples are too numerous to cite, but a few can be given: *Kāfī* 5: 200, 6: 163, 409–10 [partially repeated at 417], 7: 26–7, 61–2, 130–31, 137, 165–6, 182, 278–9, 280–81, 385–6; *Tahdhīb* 7: 21–2, 155. In *Kāfī* 7: 26–7, Ja'far al-Ṣādiq challenges him to a legal debate on the basis of analogical reasoning (*qiyās*), a method most popular at the time among the Sunnī jurists of Iraq but disapproved by Ja'far al-Ṣādiq himself. In *Kāfī* 4: 234, Ibn al-Ḥajjāj reminds the Imām that he himself reasoned by analogy in response to Ibn al-Ḥajjāj's question, to which the Imām answered that he wanted to make it easy for Ibn al-Ḥajjāj to understand the argument. He had also studied with some of the Sunnī jurists of

Iraq, for at times he quotes what he had heard from them (e.g. *Kāfī* 7: 280–81, 427–8). Ja'far al-Ṣādiq encouraged him to get in touch with the people and scholars of Medina in order for them to know that the Shī'ite community had scholars of his rank (Kashshī: 442). He was, however, not familiar with theological debates and language, as attested by a report in Kashshī: 279.

Kitāb

Related from the author by a large number of transmitters including his prominent student,[11] Ṣafwān b. Yaḥyā al-Bajalī (d. 210), himself a seller of *Shāpūrī* clothing by profession, and Ibn Abī 'Umayr (Abū Ghālib: 163, 172; Najāshī: 238; *Fihrist*: 108; *Rijāl*: 339), this was a book organized in chapters according to subject matter, as attested by Najāshī's reference to its *kutub* ("books," as chapters devoted to separate subjects in a book are traditionally often called). Abū Ghālib mentions two different books by Ibn al-Ḥajjāj that may refer to different versions of the same work as related by different transmitters. The overwhelming majority of close to five hundred quotations from Ibn al-Ḥajjāj in Shī'ite works of *ḥadīth*, listed in Khu'ī 9: 318–22, 526–38 and *Fahāris* 8: 330, 9: 263, are from the same two transmitters and seem to represent the material of the book in question.

The main characteristics of the book can be identified through the vast body of surviving material. The book was in the dialogue form ("I said ... he said ... ") found in the legal works of the late second to early third centuries (e.g. *Kāfī* 2: 278–9, 385–6, 401–2, 3: 398, 500, 4: 234, 300–301, 391, 5: 132, 169, 200, 246–7, 251, 252, 254, 255, 385–6, 427, 478, 6: 86, 163, 7: 26–7, 61–2, 130–31, 137, 165–6, 278–9, 280–81, 385–6; *Tahdhīb* 5: 346, 6: 384, 7: 49, 105, 469, 8: 157, 9: 360 [also in the *Kāfī* but with a fuller text here], 10: 108). It frequently used the expressions "*a-ra'ayta?*", "*a-tarā?*" and the like, also typical of the legal works of that period. The author at times noted the differences of opinion between the Shī'ite and Sunnī schools (e.g. *Kāfī* 3: 532, where he inserted a comment in the middle of a report on the obligatory alms [*zakāt*] on camels that "this is a difference between us and other people"). At times, he first quoted the Sunnī opinion on a topic, following it with a ruling from Ja'far al-Ṣādiq on the Shī'ite side (e.g. *Kāfī* 7: 280–81). The book was not all in direct narrative form, as he occasionally added his own comments and prefatory remarks (e.g. Aḥmad b. Muḥammad b. 'Īsā: 67 [also *Kāfī* 6: 160

---

11. *Rijāl*: 236.

where the editor has added the sentence *'an Abī 'Abd Allāh* between brackets as he erroneously thought it was missing from the text]). It seems that the book also had a section on legal documents, again a common phenomenon in early works on Islamic law. Copies of the wills and deeds of charitable endowments of 'Alī and Ja'far al-Ṣādiq which the author requested and received from Mūsā al-Kāẓim (*Kāfī* 7: 49–54), as well as the text in *Kāfī* 7: 39, were most likely parts of this section of the book.

For a lengthy citation which represents some of these characteristics of the book, see *Kāfī* 4: 300–301 (where only the phrase *fa-sa'altu 'amman ma'anā min al-nisā'* on p. 301, l. 4 is changed to *fa-sa'ala 'Abd al-Raḥmān 'amman ma'anā* ... [proper editorial procedure would require *'amman ma'ahu*] in order to mark the end of the former passage and prevent a confusion about who is now speaking). For some other representative paragraphs, see *Maḥāsin*: 214; 'Ayyāshī 2: 94; *Kāfī* 5: 309–10, 6: 409–10, 7: 373–4, 409, 427–8; *Faqīh* 3: 511.

24: Ibn Kathīr al-Hāshimī

'Abd al-Raḥmān b. Kathīr al-Hāshimī, a Kūfan client of Abū 'l-Faḍl 'Abbās b. Muḥammad b. 'Alī b. 'Abd Allāh b. al-'Abbās (d. 186, brother of the caliph Manṣūr and governor of Syria in his time and of Mesopotamia in the time of Hārūn al-Rashīd). 'Abd al-Raḥmān was a transmitter from Ja'far al-Ṣādiq, with clear esoteric tendencies.

Barqī: 67; Kashshī: 452; Najāshī: 234–5; *Fihrist*: 108–9; *Rijāl*: 237.

The information on the clientage of 'Abd al-Raḥmān is given above as in Najāshī. In a number of reports in Ibn Bābawayh, *Amālī*: 649; *Thawāb*: 31; *Tahdhīb* 1: 53, the man is described as client of Muḥammad b. 'Alī, presumably father of the above-mentioned 'Abbās and Manṣūr and founder of the 'Abbāsid *da'wa*. This certainly does not contradict Najāshī's account. In some reports (e.g. 'Ayyāshī 1: 62; Ibn Qūlawayh: 237), however, this transmitter has been identified as client of *Abū Ja'far*; this should mean either the same 'Abbāsid Muḥammad b. 'Alī, as *Abū Ja'far* was a default *kunya* for those named *Muḥammad*, or Abū Ja'far al-Manṣūr, the caliph, who would be this transmitter's patron by heredity. A complimentary clause of "*peace be upon him!*" in front of *Abū Ja'far* in Ibn Qūlawayh: 237 shows that a later transmitter or copyist thought Muḥammad al-Bāqir was meant. That is the understanding of Ibn al-Ghaḍā'irī: 77, too, at least as his text now stands.

That the man held esoteric tendencies is widely attested in his transmissions. He was a transmitter from Mufaḍḍal al-Ju'fī who was well known as a source of esoteric material. Najāshī reports that the Shī'ite scholars of his time knew 'Abd al-Raḥmān as a forger of *ḥadīth*.

1. *Kitāb faḍl sūrat Innā anzalnāh / Kitāb thawāb Innā anzalnāh*

(Abū Ghālib: 175; Najāshī: 235, 257). A report in 'Alī b. Ibrāhīm 2: 351 clearly belongs to this work. The work has possibly survived in a redaction by a later transmitter of esoteric material, Ḥasan b. al-'Abbās b. al-Ḥarīsh al-Rāzī (on him see Ibn al-Ghaḍā'irī: 51–2; Najāshī: 60–61; *Fihrist*: 53) as quoted by Ṣaffār: 222–4 and *Kāfī* 1: 242–53 (updated). *Kāfī* 1: 242 and later sources assume that Ibn al-Ḥarīsh quoted this redaction from Muḥammad al-Jawād. Ṣaffār: 222, 223, however, quotes Ibn al-Ḥarīsh as reporting that he showed "the treatise" to Muḥammad al-Jawād who confirmed its authority. There are two long paragraphs in Ṣaffār: 224–5 on the topic of this work, both quoted from Ja'far al-Ṣādiq on the authority of an unspecified Shī'ite transmitter. The second of those two paragraphs asserts that the angels who used to visit the Prophet on the Night of Destiny came down to 'Alī after his death. *Kharā'ij*: 778–9 has this latter paragraph as quoted from 'Abd al-Raḥmān b. Kathīr. Both paragraphs should therefore originally have been part of 'Abd al-Raḥmān's work on the topic. The first of the two, on the *Taymī* (Abū Bakr) and *'Adawī* ('Umar) also appears in the text attributed to Ibn al-Ḥarīsh in *Kāfī* 1: 249. This may suggest that the treatise that Ibn al-Ḥarīsh allegedly showed to Muḥammad al-Jawād was the work in question, and that Ibn al-Ḥarīsh's is at most a redaction of 'Abd al-Raḥmān's work.

2. *Kitāb Fadak*

(Najāshī: 235)

3. *Kitāb ṣulḥ al-Ḥasan*

(Najāshī: 235). The full text of this treatise is preserved in Ṭūsī, *Amālī*: 561–7, related through the same chain of transmission as mentioned by Najāshī.

4. *Kitāb al-aẓilla*

(Abū Ghālib: 175; Najāshī: 235, 257). Najāshī describes this as a corrupt and esoteric book. It should have been in the same line as the *Kitāb al-haft wa 'l-aẓilla*, attributed to Mufaḍḍal al-Ju'fī (but probably a work of Muḥammad b. Sinān al-Zāhirī), which is extant and published. A long quotation from 'Abd al-Raḥmān in *Kāfī* 4: 191–4 may originally have belonged to the work in question. The quotation explains, among other matters, how the exact location of the Ka'ba was decided, by the order of Gabriel, according to the shadow cast by a cloud on that specific location.

5. *Kitāb*

His notebook of *ḥadīth*, related like his other works by his nephew 'Alī b. Ḥassān b. Kathīr (*Fihrist*: 108–9). Many quotations by this transmitter from 'Abd al-Raḥmān that do not relate to the topics of his other works probably belonged to the notebook in question, including the following examples:

- *Maḥāsin*: 45–6 (also Ibn Bābawayh, *Amālī*: 649; *Thawāb*: 31–32; also *Kāfī*
  3: 70–71 through a transmitter other than the author's nephew), 348–9
- Ṣaffār: 17, 40, 45, 71, 78, 105 (also *Kāfī* 1: 192), 206, 212–13, 214, 253, 280–81, 344, 358, 420, 427, 480 (also *Kāfī* 1: 275), 490, 517
- 'Ayyāshī[12] 1: 41, 62 (read *'an 'Abd al-Raḥmān* for *'Umar ibn 'Abd al-Raḥmān*), 128, 162, 201, 211, 281, 366–7
  2: 105
- *Kāfī* 1: 185, 192, 210, 213, 217, 229, 275, 340, 368 (whence Nu'mānī: 198, 243), 413, 414–15 (two reports), 420–21 (three reports), 423–4 (two reports), 425 (also *Ma'ānī*: 299), 426
  2: 65
  5: 337–8, 374–5, 467, 503 (a variant also in Ḥaskānī 1: 450–51), 510, 537
  6: 345, 391 (whence Ibn Qūlawayh: 212), 464, 521 (two reports)

---

12. As already noted several times, quotations in the surviving abridged version of this source usually appear without the name of the second transmitter. In the present case, however, they seem to have been through the author's nephew as attested, for instance, in the case of 'Ayyāshī 1: 162, which is quoted through 'Alī b. Ḥassān in *Kāfī* 1: 414.

- Kashshī: 193–4, 225–6
- Furāt: 398–9
- Ibn al-Juḥām: 458
- Nu'mānī: 173, 198 (two reports, one repeated at 243)
- 'Alī b. Ibrāhīm 2: 131, 234, 286, 319, 332, 351, 385–6, 395, 426, 429, 441
- *Maqātil*: 464
- Ibn Qūlawayh: 74–6, 237–8
- *Faqīh* 1: 524 (see *Mashyakha*: 474; also *Khiṣāl*: 242)
- *'Ilal* 1: 112
  2: 7, 160 (the first sentence of the report also at 79; an abridged version also in *Faqīh* 3: 561–2; *Khiṣāl*: 364), 111, 195, 196, 220
- *Tahdhīb* 1: 54
  6: 37–8
- Ibn 'Asākir 54: 275 (whence Dhahabī, *Siyar* 4: 404)
- Fakhār b. Ma'add: 4–5
- Ibn Ṭāwūs, *Falāḥ*: 451
- Idem, *Jamāl*: 155
- 'Abd al-Karīm b. Ṭāwūs: 77–8
- Ḥasan b. Sulaymān: 16–17
- *Ta'wīl al-āyāt*: 843–4, 855 (where the name of the transmitter from 'Abd al-Raḥmān is missing)
- *Biḥār* 100: 247

25: 'Abd al-Raḥmān al-'Arzamī

Abū Muḥammad 'Abd al-Raḥmān b. Muḥammad b. 'Ubayd Allāh al-Fazārī al-'Arzamī, a Kūfan transmitter of *ḥadīth* with mild Shī'ite sympathies and member of a well known family of *ḥadīth* transmitters. He transmitted from Ja'far al-Ṣādiq, among others, and this is how the Shī'ite scholars became interested in him. He is said to have died in 180.

Ibn Abī Ḥātim 5: 282; Ibn Ḥibbān, *Thiqāt* 7: 9; Dāraquṭnī, *Ḍu'afā'*: 119; Najāshī: 237; *Fihrist*: 108; *Rijāl*: 237; *Lisān* 4: 291–2 (and other sources listed in the editor's footnote).

On the family origin and the significance of the *nisba* of *'Arzamī*, see Mizzī 18: 323; Sam'ānī 4: 178, 9: 271 (and the references in the editor's footnote 6). On 'Abd al-Raḥmān's father, Muḥammad (d. 155), a poet and *ḥadīth* transmitter, see Mizzī 26: 41–5 and the many sources listed in the editor's footnote. Numerous other members of the family are also mentioned in Sunnī biographical dictionaries of the transmitters of *ḥadīth*, including the uncle of this transmitter's father, 'Abd al-Malik b. Abī Sulaymān Maysara (d. 145), the most prominent *ḥadīth* transmitter of the family (Mizzī 18: 322–9 and the sources listed in the editor's footnote), 'Abd al-Raḥmān's two brothers, Isḥāq and Ḥasan (Dāraquṭnī, *Ḍu'afā'*: 119), his own son, Muḥammad (Yaḥyā b. Ma'īn 2: 529; Ibn Abī Ḥātim 6: 320), and others (Sam'ānī 9: 274; Ibn 'Adī: 2116).

On his mild Shī'ite sympathies, see, for instance, *Kāfī* 4: 47. His son, Muḥammad, also had Shī'ite sympathies as attested by a report in Ibn Bābawayh, *Amālī*: 105–6 (with an abridged version ibid.: 188–9; *Khiṣāl*: 293).

Kitāb

A notebook of *ḥadīth*, related, among others, by Yūsuf b. al-Ḥārith al-Kumandānī (Najāshī: 237; *Rijāl*: 427). The notebook contained 'Arzamī's transmissions from Ja'far al-Ṣādiq, many of which are recorded in later works on the authority of the said Kumandānī through the same chain of transmission mentioned in *Rijāl*: 427. Examples include the following:

- 'Abbād b. Ya'qūb: 18, 19 (also *Tahdhīb* 1: 316)
- *Maḥāsin*: 263 (whence *Kāfī* 2: 126–7; *'Ilal* 1: 112), 458–9, 617
- Ṣaffār: 185
- Aḥmad b. 'Īsā 4: 218
- 'Ayyāshī 1: 93
- Muḥammad b. Sulaymān 2: 155
- *Kāfī* 1: 463–4
  2: 18, 59, 91, 126–7
  4: 47, 364
  5: 225, 371–2, 549
  6: 19, 277, 294, 383, 470
  7: 47, 199–200 (two variants of the same report)
  8: 218–19 (also 'Alī b. Ibrāhīm 2: 276), 271 (also *'Ilal* 2: 133; *Ma'ānī*: 385)
- *'Ilal* 2: 83
- *Khiṣāl*: 62, 132–3
- *Tawḥīd*: 338–9, 368
- Ṭūsī, *Amālī*: 559–60
- *Tahdhīb* 3: 40, 160 (and a variant at 244), 194–5
  10: 116, 275

26: ʿAbd al-Ṣamad al-ʿUrāmī

ʿAbd al-Ṣamad b. Bashīr al-ʿUrāmī al-ʿAbdī, a Kūfan client of the Banū ʿAbd al-Qays of Asad Rabīʿa and a transmitter from Jaʿfar al-Ṣādiq.

Barqī: 75; Najāshī: 248–9; *Fihrist*: 122; *Rijāl*: 241.

Kitāb

His notebook of *ḥadīth*, related by a number of transmitters including ʿUbays b. Hishām al-Nāshirī (Najāshī: 249; *Fihrist*: 122). There are quite a few quotations from ʿAbd al-Ṣamad b. Bashīr in Shīʿite works of *ḥadīth*, many through ʿUbays and some, as in the case of a lengthy report in ʿAyyāshī 1: 143–4, in the style of quotation from a book. Here is a list:

– Ḥusayn b. Saʿīd, *Zuhd*: 37 (also *Kāfī* 2: 157), 83 (also *Kāfī* 3: 134)
– Ṣaffār: 169 (also *Kāfī* 1: 242; *ʿIlal* 1: 197), 192, 209 (two reports), 361 (read *ʿan ʿUbays b. Hishām ʿan ʿAbd al-Ṣamad b. Bashīr ʿan ʿAbd Allāh b. Sulaymān* as in *Ikhtiṣāṣ*: 306 citing Ṣaffār; part of this correction applies to *Kāfī* 1:438–9 as well), 377–8, 387, 493
– ʿAyyāshī 1: 143–4, 157–60, 200
 2: 128
– *Kāfī* 1: 108 (also *Tawḥīd*: 145), 298, 544
 2: 437, 656
 4: 566–7
 5: 92, 509
 6: 314
 7: 200 (also *Tahdhīb* 10: 52, with a variant in 10: 62)
 8: 255, 317
– Kashshī: 298–9
– Ibn al-Juḥām: 258 (a variant also in Qāḍī Nuʿmān, *Sharḥ* 1: 236–7)
– Nuʿmānī: 261–2
– ʿAlī b. Ibrāhīm 1: 209
-- *Faqīh* 3: 207–8 (also *Tahdhīb* 7: 35)
 4: 23
– *ʿUyūn* 1: 28
– Ibn Shādhān: 137

- Ṭūsī, *Amālī:* 650
- *Tahdhīb* 5: 29, 72–3
  9: 100
  10: 121
- *Dalā'il al-imāma*: 228–9
- Ibn Ṭāwūs, *Falāḥ*: 472
- Ḥasan b. Sulaymān: 94

27: Aḥmad al-Aḥmasī

Abū 'Alī Aḥmad b. 'Ā'idh b. Ḥabīb, a Kūfan client of Aḥmas, a clan of Bajīla, and an associate of the Shī'ite transmitter of *ḥadīth*, Abū Khadīja Sālim b. Mukram (no. 187 below). He lived in Baghdad and was a seller of sesame oil by profession.

Kashshī: 362; *Mashyakha*: 514; Najāshī: 98–9; *Rijāl*: 126, 155.

'Ā'idh b. Ḥabīb, father of this transmitter, was known to Sunnī (see Mizzī 14: 95–8 and the many sources listed in the editor's footnote), Zaydī (e.g. Aḥmad b. 'Īsā 3: 53, 132) and Imāmite scholars of *ḥadīth*. Barqī: 112 identifies him as 'Ā'idh b. Ḥabīb al-Bajalī al-Aḥmasī, a Kūfan seller of clothing made in Herat. The man appears with that professional affiliation (*bayyā' al-Harawī*) in the chain of transmission of a report in *Kāfī* 6: 46. Ṭūsī, however, suggests that 'Ā'idh b. Ḥabīb and his family were Arabs from the tribe of the Banū 'Abs (*Rijāl*: 262, also 132, 134, 155, 185, 203) and that 'Ā'idh al-Aḥmasī, seller of clothing made in Herat, was a different transmitter from this period called 'Ā'idh b. Nubāta whose name appears as a transmitter from Ja'far al-Ṣādiq in Ṭabrisī, *I'lām*: 268 (citing Muḥammad b. Aḥmad b. Yaḥyā al-Ash'arī's *Nawādir al-ḥikma*). However, Sunnī sources identify the same 'Ā'idh b. Ḥabīb, father of Aḥmad, as both *'Absī* and *Bayyā' al-Harawī* (see Mizzī 14: 95 and the sources named). He is known to them as the brother of Rabī' b. Ḥabīb al-'Absī (also mentioned in *Rijāl*: 134, 203), a transmitter from the prominent Imāmite scholar of Kūfa, Zurāra b. A'yan, among others, and a staunch Shī'ite (*Mīzān* 2: 363) and, according to some Sunnī authorities, a Zaydī (Yaḥyā b. Ma'īn 2: 290; Abū Zur'a al-Rāzī: 385; 'Uqaylī 3: 411).

The overwhelming majority of quotations from Aḥmad b. 'Ā'idh in Shī'ite works of *ḥadīth* are quoted by him from Abū Khadīja Sālim b. Mukram, a fact that confirms the biographers' accounts of Aḥmad's association with the latter.

As for profession, he is identified as *ḥallāl* by Najāshī: 99 who, in the entry on a different transmitter of the same profession, Aḥmad b. 'Umar al-Ḥallāl, defines the job as the selling of sesame oil (ibid.: 99).

Kitāb

His notebook of *ḥadīth*, related by Ḥasan b. ʿAlī al-Washshāʾ, among others (Najāshī: 99; also *Mashyakha*: 514). Almost all quotations from Aḥmad b. ʿĀʾidh in Shīʿite works of *ḥadīth* are on the authority of this transmitter. Here is a list:

- *Maḥāsin*: 181 (also *Kāfī* 2: 520), 448 (also *Kāfī* 6: 292–3; cf. *Maḥāsin*: 431), 457 (also *Kāfī* 6: 271–2)
- Ṣaffār: 9 (also *Khiṣāl*: 123, and partially in *Kāfī* 1: 34), 31 (also *Kāfī* 1: 208), 482 (also *Kāfī* 1: 260; Irbilī 2: 351 [quoting ʿAbd Allāh b. Jaʿfar al-Ḥimyarī's *Kitāb al-dalāʾil*]), 496
- *Kāfī* 1: 46, 180, 190, 205, 276, 376, 416, 464, 535
  2: 138, 162–3 (two reports), 304, 339
  3: 138, 549
  4: 59, 188–9, 341, 362, 511
  5: 137, 218, 309
  6: 24, 32, 347, 455–6, 486–7, 546 (two reports)
- Kashshī: 217–18
- Ibn Qūlawayh: 122, 130–32, 266–7, 276–7, 298
- *Faqīh* 3: 2–3, 18
  4: 336
- *ʿIlal* 2: 85
- *ʿIqāb*: 313 (cf. *Maḥāsin*: 108–9), 318
- *Maʿānī*: 201, 247–8
- *Thawāb*: 137
- *Ghayba*: 437
- *Tahdhīb* 2: 309
  4: 137

28: Ibn Rizq

Aḥmad b. Rizq al-Bajalī al-Ghumshānī, a Kūfan Shīʿite from the mid-second century.

Najāshī: 98; *Fibrist*: 35–6; *Rijāl*: 155.

Kitāb

His notebook of *ḥadīth*, related from him by a number of transmitters including 'Alī b. al-Ḥasan b. Faḍḍāl who received it through the transmitter 'Abbās b. 'Āmir al-Qaṣabānī from the author (Najāshī: 98; *Fihrist*: 35). A fragment of this notebook, consisting of 19 reports related by Ibn Faḍḍāl from 'Abbās b. 'Āmir from the author, is quoted by Ṭūsī in his *Amālī*: 671–6 (the first report in this fragment is also cited in Ṣaffār: 75 and *Kāfī* 1: 437). Most of the reports are about the virtues of the House of the Prophet and the Shī'ites, but they also include a few citations on religious law and ethics. There are a few other quotations from this author, related by the same chain of transmission, in other Shī'ite works of *ḥadīth*, as in *Kāfī* 4: 542 and Ibn Qūlawayh: 218–19. There are also citations which appear without, or with a different, *isnād* as in *Tahdhīb* 1: 303 and *Ghayba*: 188.

29: 'Alā' al-Nahdī

Abū 'l-Qāsim 'Alā' b. al-Fuḍayl b. Yasār, a Baṣran member or client of the Banū Nahd and a transmitter from Ja'far al-Ṣādiq.

Barqī: 78; Najāshī: 298; *Fihrist*: 113; *Rijāl*: 247.

Najāshī: 298 and *Rijāl*: 247 identify this transmitter as a client of the Banū Nahd. Najāshī, however, identifies his father, Abū 'l-Qāsim Fuḍayl b. Yasār al-Nahdī, as a pure 'Arab (Najāshī: 309) and does not describe his other son, Qāsim (ibid.: 313) nor the latter's son, Muḥammad (ibid.: 362) as clients. Barqī: 63; *Mashyakha*: 441, and *Rijāl*: 269 identify Fuḍayl b. Yasār as a Kūfan client of the Banū Nahd (corrupted in Barqī to Banū Nahīk) who moved to Baṣra. Barqī thus does not find it contradictory to describe Fuḍayl as a Baṣran (ibid.: 52) but 'Alā' as a Kūfan (ibid.: 78).

Kitāb

His notebook of *ḥadīth*, related by Muḥammad b. Sinān al-Zāhirī (Najāshī: 298; *Fihrist*: 113). Almost all quotations from 'Alā' b. al-Fuḍayl in Shī'ite works of *ḥadīth* are through this transmitter. Here is a partial list:

- *Maḥāsin*: 273, 372, 430, 434
- 'Ayyāshī (without the name of the second transmitter, as usual)
  1: 86–7
  2: 208, 352

- *Kāfī* 2: 87, 173 (repeated at 637), 260, 652
  6: 189
  7: 198, 262, 280, 282, 291, 298, 312, 351
- Ibn Bābawayh, *Amālī*: 702
- *Faqīh* 2: 488
  4: 272
- *Khiṣāl*: 159
- *Tawḥīd*: 328
- *Tahdhīb* 1: 415
  3: 263, 303–4
  5: 90, 473
  6: 142
  10: 61

30: 'Alā' al-Qallā'

'Alā' b. Razīn al-Qallā' (maker of *sawīq*, a food product made from parched grain flour), a Kūfan client of Thaqīf and a transmitter from Ja'far al-Ṣādiq. He was an associate and student of the prominent Imāmite jurist of Kūfa, Muḥammad b. Muslim b. Rabāḥ (d. 150).

Barqī: 77; Najāshī: 298; *Fihrist*: 112–13; *Rijāl*: 247.

That he was a client of Thaqīf is mentioned by both Najāshī and Ṭūsī in his *Rijāl*. His teacher, Muḥammad b. Muslim b. Rabāḥ, was also a client of Thaqīf. Najāshī, however, reports that the genealogist Muḥammad b. 'Abd al-Raḥmān al-'Abdī, known as Ibn 'Abda and author of a book on the Banū Asad, identified the man as a client of Yashkur, a clan of Asad Rabī'a.

Kitāb

Related from the author by a number of transmitters (Abū Ghālib: 148, 182–3; Najāshī: 39, 298; *Fihrist*: 112–13), this was a book organized in chapters according to subject matter, as understood[13] from Najāshī's reference to it as *kutub* (ibid.: 298). Ṭūsī (*Fihrist*: 112–13) reported that there were four versions of this book as related by four different transmitters. There are close to one thousand quotations from 'Alā' b. Razīn

13. See the entry on Ibn al-Ḥajjāj (# 23 above).

in Shī'ite works of *ḥadīth*, listed in Khu'ī 11: 161–5, 169–71, 178, 449–68 and *Fahāris* 9: 341–2, mainly through the four transmitters named by Ṭūsī. With few exceptions, his transmissions are uniformly from his teacher, Muḥammad b. Muslim. A fragment of the book in question has survived and is published in the collection of *al-Uṣūl al-sittat 'ashar*: 150–57. Ibn Ṭāwūs quotes from the book of 'Alā' b. Razīn in his *Ghiyāth*: 9 (see further Kohlberg: 221).

31: Ibn 'Abd al-'Azīz

'Alī b. 'Abd al-'Azīz, a Kūfan transmitter from Ja'far al-Ṣādiq.

Mashyakha: 517; Najāshī: 276; *Rijāl*: 141, 246, 266.

As attested by his transmissions, this transmitter was a Shī'ite, and possibly a client of Azd (see *Kāfī* 6: 199). Ṭūsī (*Fihrist*: 95–6) identifies this transmitter with the judge, 'Alī b. 'Abd al-'Azīz al-Fazārī, better known as 'Alī b. Ghurāb (d. 184)[14] who likewise transmitted from Ja'far al-Ṣādiq, among others.[15] Ṭūsī was apparently influenced by a comment in a report related by Ibn 'Uqda (Ibn Ḥajar, *Tahdhīb* 7: 372–3) on the identity of an 'Alī b. 'Abd al-'Azīz whose name appears in the *isnād* of this report.[16] Obvious differences in the characteristics of their transmissions and the character of the transmitters from them leave no doubt that these are two different persons.[17]

---

14. On this scholar, see Ibn Sa'd 6: 273; Barqī: 77; *Fihrist*: 95–6; *Rijāl*: 245, 266; Mizzī 21: 90–96 (and the many sources listed in editor's footnote). Ibn Sa'd 6: 273 states that he died early in 184 in Kūfa. This is accepted by all later biographers. Khalīfa b. Khayyāṭ, *Ṭabaqāt*: 402, however, suggests the year 204.
15. For his Shī'ite sympathies, see Ibn al-Junayd: 169; Ibn Ḥibbān, *Majrūḥīn* 2: 105; Khaṭīb, *Ta'rīkh* 12: 46; idem, *Kifāya*: 207; Mizzī 21: 93; Ibn Ḥajar, *Tahdhīb* 7: 372. On his affection for Ja'far al-Ṣādiq in particular, see Ibn Bābawayh, *Amālī*: 315 and *'Ilal* 1: 224 (attested in *Faqīh* 4: 411 and *Ma'ānī*: 250, 291).
16. See further Ibn 'Adī: 1848–9; Khaṭīb, *Mūḍiḥ* 2: 276; Mizzī 21: 55.
17. The two transmitters named were also distinct from yet another transmitter with the same name who quotes from 'Alī al-Riḍā in Khaṭīb, *Ta'rīkh* 1: 255 (cf. *Khiṣāl*: 179 and *'Uyūn* 1: 227, where the same transmitter quotes the passage in question from 'Alī al-Riḍā through Abū 'l-Ṣalt 'Abd al-Salām b. Ṣāliḥ [d. 236]). Ibn Bābawayh quotes other reports from this transmitter in *Khiṣāl*: 69, 70, 206. In *Ma'ānī*: 211, 272, 273, 275–7, 277–84, 302–3, 303–4, 320, 321–2, 326, there are many quotations by this person from Abū 'Ubayd Qāsim b. Sallām (d. 224) on the meaning of some uncommon words used in a number of *ḥadīths*. This was Abū 'l-Ḥasan 'Alī b. 'Abd al-'Azīz b. Marzubān b. Sābūr al-Baghawī, a student of Abū 'Ubayd and later resident of Mecca who died in 286. He communicated with the *shaykh* of Ibn Bābawayh in writing. The same was the case with Ibn Abī Ḥātim who received some transmissions of Abū 'Ubayd through this 'Alī b. 'Abd al-'Azīz in writing (Ibn Abī Ḥātim 6: 196).

Kitāb

A notebook of *ḥadīth*, related from the author by a number of transmitters (Najāshī: 276; *Fihrist*: 95–6). A notebook is also assigned to 'Alī b. Ghurāb in Ibn al-Nadīm: 275 (whence *Rijāl*: 245), listing it among Shī'ite collections of reports from their Imāms. Ṭūsī, who identifies our author with the latter, names three chains of transmission to the notebook of 'Alī b. 'Abd al-'Azīz in *Fihrist*: 95–6, two Imāmite, and presumably to the work in question, and one through the Zaydī Naṣr b. Muzāḥim who is known as a transmitter from 'Alī b. Ghurāb to Sunnī biographers (Mizzī 21: 55). A number of quotations in early collections of Shī'ite *ḥadīth*, some through the Imāmite *isnād*s mentioned by Ṭūsī, should represent the notebook in question. Examples are as follows:

- *Maḥāsin*: 69, 163, 289 (partially also in *Kāfī* 4: 62–3; Ibn Bābawayh, *Faḍā'il al-ashhur*: 122)
- Ṣaffār: 397
- 'Ayyāshī 1: 190
- *Kāfī* 3: 428
  4: 241, 330, 414
  5: 84
  8: 238
- *Faqīh* 3: 157
  4: 411, 516
- *Ṣifāt*: 214–15
- *Tahdhīb* 1: 232
  2: 340
- *Qiṣaṣ*: 143–5

Shī'ite quotations[18] supposedly from 'Alī b. Ghurāb include the following, some of which may likewise belong to our author:

- Aḥmad b. 'Īsā 1: 123
  4: 288
- *Kāfī* 4: 12 (partially repeated in 5: 72)
- Furāt: 173, 512
- 'Alī b. Ibrāhīm 2: 390

18. For examples of his Sunnī transmissions, see Ibn Māja: 349, 826–7, 1031; Nasā'ī 5: 177, 8: 362, 402–3; Ibn 'Adī: 1848–9 (nine reports). See also Khaṭīb, *Mūḍiḥ* 2: 274–6; *Mīzān* 3: 149–50.

- *Faqīh* 3: 71–2
  4: 411
- *'Ilal* 1: 166
- *Ma'ānī*: 250, 291 (cf. Ibn Bābawayh, *Amālī*: 315 [also *'Ilal* 1: 223–4] according to which these two quotations in *Ma'ānī* should have been from Ḥafṣ b. Ghiyāth (d. 194), not 'Alī b. Ghurāb; this can further be confirmed by Ṭūsī, *Amālī*: 581; the ultimate transmitter from 'Alī b. Ghurāb in *Ma'ānī*: 250 is in fact one whose transmission from Ḥafṣ b. Ghiyāth is attested in *Ma'ānī*: 325 and *Kāfī* 3: 119)
- Ṭabarānī, *Kabīr* 1: 79–80 (whence Ibn 'Asākir 39: 463, quoted on the authority of 'Alī b. Ghurāb *al-Muḥāribī*; an authority on the biography of transmitters of *ḥadīth* suggested that the *nisba* of *Muḥāribī* for this transmitter was an error [Mizzī 21: 91] as 'Alī b. Ghurāb was in fact a client of Fazāra, not of the Banū Muḥārib).[19]
- Khaṭīb, *Mūḍiḥ* 2: 275, 276

32: Al-Baṭā'inī

Abū 'l-Ḥasan 'Alī b. Abī Ḥamza Sālim al-Baṭā'inī, a Kūfan client of the Anṣār and a transmitter from Ja'far al-Ṣādiq and Mūsā al-Kāẓim. He was a cloth seller by profession who lived in Baghdad where he represented Mūsā al-Kāẓim as his financial agent. He was a founder of Wāqifism, reportedly the first to suggest that Mūsā al-Kāẓim did not die and to oppose 'Alī al-Riḍā's claim to the succession. He died during the lifetime of 'Alī al-Riḍā, reportedly while the latter was in Marw in the years 201–2.

Barqī: 76, 117; Kashshī: 403–6, 443–6, 463–5; Ibn al-Ghaḍā'irī: 83; Najāshī: 249–50; *Fihrist*: 96–7; *Rijāl*: 245, 339. See also 'Abd Allāh b. Ja'far: 347, 351–2; *Ghayba*: 55, 56, 63–5, 67, 69, 70, 224, 352.

---

19. It is not, however, clear if the transmitter of this report is the same Fazārī. In early Islamic times, tribal affiliation was used as an often readily available and convenient marker to draw a distinction between two or more persons who shared the same name and father's name. Thus it helped to prevent possible confusion among two or more persons and misapprehension that they were all one and the same person. Later biographers, however, do not always appear cognizant of this and falsely assume that different tribal affiliations for persons with otherwise identical names merely imply differences of opinion on the tribal affiliation of a single person, and thus fail to consider the possibility that they may be dealing with two or more persons, rather than just one. We shall come across many instances of such misleading assumptions in this work.

This man was an associate and guide of the prominent Imāmite transmitter of *ḥadīth*, Abū Baṣīr Yaḥyā b. al-Qāsīm al-Asadī, the Blind (d. 149–150). Most of the transmissions of Baṭā'inī are indeed from Abū Baṣīr.

That he was a leader of the Wāqifites is mentioned in most of the biographical sources named above. Ibn al-Ghaḍā'irī: 83 and *Ghayba*: 67 identified him as the founder of Wāqifism. Imāmite sources offer a financial basis for his and his colleagues' refusal to recognize 'Alī al-Riḍā as successor to his father. A report suggests that when Mūsā al-Kāẓim died, Baṭā'inī had some thirty thousand *dīnārs* in his possession as the financial agent of the Imām, a fortune which he decided to keep for himself (see Modarressi, *Crisis*: 62). A statement quoted from 'Alī al-Riḍā in 'Abd Allāh b. Ja'far: 351–2 suggests a more doctrinal motive for Baṭā'inī's decision, a point that may also apply to some other leaders of the movement (see Kashshī: 467, end of paragraph # 887). His well known doctrinal viewpoint, nevertheless, did not discourage later upgrading of a report transmitted by him, to "predict" the exact number and present the accurate list of the twelve Imāms (*Kamāl*: 258–9).

His profession is mentioned in a report in Ṣaffār: 172 (read *Ibn Abī Ḥamza* for *Abī Ḥamza* as in *Biḥār* 47: 66). That he died while 'Alī al-Riḍā was in Marw is noted in a report in *Manāqib* 4: 337.

1. *Kitāb al-tafsīr*

(Najāshī: 250). According to Najāshī, most of the material of this work was quoted from Abū Baṣīr, a point well attested in what has survived from the work. Judging by a number of long and short excerpts from this work in its original style (*Kāfī* 1: 421, 431–2, 435–6, 8: 184, 381; 'Alī b. Ibrāhīm 2: 47, 57, 434–9; *Kamāl* 17–18) the work had the same style and flavour as the earlier Shī'ite *tafsīrs* of Jābir al-Ju'fī (e.g. *Kāfī* 8: 379–81) and Abū Ḥamza al-Thumālī (e.g. 'Ayyāshī 1: 168, 2: 152), and those of the next generation such as the ones by this author's son, Ḥasan b. 'Alī b. Abī Ḥamza (e.g. *Kāfī* 2: 5–6) and Ḥasan b. Maḥbūb (e.g. ibid. 1: 432–5).

The following is a partial list of material quoted from this author on *tafsīr*, almost all of which must have belonged to the work in question:

- Ḥusayn b. Sa'īd, *Zuhd*: 24, 31, 62–3, 92–3 (four reports), 99
- *Maḥāsin*: 166–7, 623
- Ṣaffār: 65, 110, 429, 463–4
- 'Ayyāshī 1: 19, 74 (cf. *'Ilal* 2: 164), 220, 266, 278, 301, 339
  2: 2, 16, 44, 46, 73, 158, 166, 176, 225–6 (cf. *Kāfī* 3: 239–40), 278, 293, 321, 353
- *Kāfī* 1: 219, 414, 418–19, 421, 431–2, 435–6
  2: 151, 270–71, 334

3: 503
5: 119
6: 139, 406
8: 179–81, 184, 187–9, 290–91, 337–8, 381

- Ibn al-Juḥām: 234, 253 (read *Ibn Abī Ḥamza* for *Abī Ḥamza* as in the editor's footnote and *Ta'wīl al-āyāt*: 469), 273, 286, 289
- Nu'mānī, *Ghayba*: 51–2, 240, 241, 251, 269, 316
- Idem, *Tafsīr*: 3
- 'Alī b. Ibrāhīm 1: 199
  2: 40, 46–47 (two reports), 48, 55, 57, 57–8, 63, 154, 198, 344, 408, 415, 416, 422, 423, 427, 434–9
- Ibn Qūlawayh: 134
- *'Ilal* 1: 30, 48
  2: 122–3
- *'Iqāb*: 323
- *Kamāl*: 17–18 (repeated at 340–41), 325–6, 357, 417, 670, 673
- *Khiṣāl*: 160, 531 (read *'Alī b. Abī Ḥamza*)
- *Ma'ānī*: 132, 162, 174, 349, 368, 369 (read *Ibn Abī Ḥamza* for *Abī Ḥamza*; see *Biḥār* 24: 215), 392
- *Tawḥīd*: 20, 117, 356
- *Thawāb*: 130, 132 (two reports), 133, 136, 143–4 (two reports), 145, 146–7, 150 (two reports), 151, 152
- Mufīd, *Amālī*: 196
- Ibn Ṭāwūs, *Muhaj*: 379 (quoting Ṣaffār in his *Faḍl al-du'ā'*)
- *Ta'wīl al-āyāt*: 435, 496–7, 808, 844–5

A juxtaposition of 'Ayyāshī 2: 225–6 with *Kāfī* 3: 239–40, of 'Ayyāshī 1: 118 with *Maḥāsin*: 229, of 'Ayyāshī 2: 2, 46 (repeated at 73), 166 with *Thawāb*: 132 (two reports), 166, and of numerous similar examples, reveals that much of the material quoted in 'Ayyāshī's *Tafsīr* on the authority of Abū Baṣīr was in fact received through 'Alī b. Abī Ḥamza, though the latter's name does not appear in the surviving abridged version of 'Ayyāshī's work where the names of the second transmitters are usually omitted. Here is a list of the quotations from Abū Baṣīr in 'Ayyāshī, many of which in all likelihood originally formed a part of the work in question:[20]

20. Some of that material is, however, known not to be related through 'Alī b. Abī Ḥamza. An example is a passage in 'Ayyāshī 2: 259 that appears in Ibn Ṭāwūs, *Sa'd*: 234 on the authority of 'Abd Allāh b. Ḥammād from Abū Baṣīr.

1: 10, 11, 49–50, 51, 52, 63, 69–70, 76, 78, 79, 81, 83–4, 85, 90–91, 95, 100, 102, 103, 106, 111, 113, 114, 115, 116, 117, 118, 122, 123, 125–6, 129–30,132, 133, 134, 139, 140, 142–3, 144, 148–9, 151, 161, 162, 164–5, 172, 192–3, 194, 195, 196, 222–3, 225, 227–8, 232–3, 234, 241, 242, 249–51, 254, 256, 268, 281, 295, 303, 304, 313, 317, 322, 325, 326, 330, 337, 353, 362, 364, 366, 367, 370, 371, 376, 377, 380, 383, 388
2: 2, 9, 12, 13, 26–7, 31, 37, 40, 40, 42, 44, 46, 48, 51, 61–2, 71, 73, 74–5, 83, 86, 87, 90, 109, 112, 118, 122, 126, 136, 150–51, 154–5, 156, 159, 160, 178–9, 181, 184, 190–91, 196, 199, 212–13, 223–4, 225–6, 239–40, 241, 243, 244–7, 248, 252, 259, 261, 263, 265, 269–70, 277, 280, 283, 284–5, 286, 288, 292, 302, 303, 305, 317, 320, 321, 325, 327, 336, 339–40, 350

There are also many quotations from Baṭā'inī in the context of Qur'ānic verses without mention of a Qur'ānic passage, or, alternatively, in a different context but using a Qur'ānic formula. Some of this material too may have originally belonged to the work in question, as in the following examples:

- Ḥusayn b. Sa'īd, *Zuhd*: 89, 91
- *Maḥāsin*: 229 (also 'Ayyāshī 1: 118 where the name of 'Alī b. Abī Ḥamza as the second transmitter is missing), 314, 535
- Ṣaffār: 205
- 'Ayyāshī 2: 115
- *Kāfī* 1: 385–7, 442–3, 616
  2: 195, 203, 617 (and a variant at 618–19)
  4: 157
  6: 206, 207, 486
- Ibn Bābawayh, *Amālī*: 242–3, 312 (also *Ma'ānī*: 94)
- *'Ilal* 1: 16 (two reports), 115, 116
- *Qiṣaṣ*: 59 (two reports), 129–31 (cf. 'Ayyāshī 2: 176; Ṭūsī, *Amālī*: 414)

2. *Kitāb jāmi' fī abwāb al-fiqh*

Mentioned by Najāshī: 250 who also names two other books by this author as *Kitāb al-ṣalāt* and *Kitāb al-zakāt*, this was clearly a collection of the author's transmission on religious law organized according to subject matter. The other two books would thus seem to have been parts of the same comprehensive work.

Most of the several hundred quotations from this transmitter in the four main works of Imāmite *ḥadīth*, listed in Khu'ī 11: 227–31, 487–500,

22: 229–30, are on legal topics and fit the title of this work, including many on prayer and religious alms, topics of the two separate works named by Najāshī.

3. Aṣl / Kitāb

His notebook of *ḥadīth*, related by Ibn Abī 'Umayr and Ṣafwān b. Yaḥyā (*Fihrist*: 96–7; *Rijāl*: 339). The notebook must also have contained much of the non-legal material quoted from the author in Shī'ite works of *ḥadīth* through these two transmitters and others. For a list of these citations, see *Fahāris* 8: 228, 469, 9: 391–2.

33: Ibn 'Aṭiyya al-Ḥannāṭ

'Alī b. 'Aṭiyya al-Aṣamm, the wheat seller, a Kūfan client and a transmitter from Ja'far al-Ṣādiq and his disciples.

Barqī: 77, 116, 120; Kashshī: 367; *Mashyakha*: 472; Najāshī: 46; *Fihrist*: 97; *Rijāl*: 141, 246, 266, 339.

There are some ambiguities about the Arab tribe of which this transmitter was a client (see Muḥammad Taqī al-Tustarī 7: 516–18 for details) and his profession. He is a wheat seller (*ḥannāṭ*) in *Mashyakha*: 472; Najāshī: 46; *Fihrist*: 97; *Rijāl*: 180, and this is attested in a report by the man himself in *Kāfī*: 5: 182. This was after all his family business (Najāshī: 46). *Kāfī* 8: 330 and *Ikhtiṣāṣ*: 201, however, quote from an 'Alī b. 'Aṭiyya *al-Zayyāt* (the oil seller).[21] *Ikhtiṣāṣ*: 201 further reports that the man was known as *Bawwāb*. Kashshī: 367; Najāshī: 46, and *Rijāl*: 180, 195 (also Ibn Qūlawayh: 348) name a Ḥasan b. 'Aṭiyya al-Daghshī al-Muḥāribī Abū Nāb, a cloth seller (Barqī: 106) whom they identify as a brother of 'Alī b. 'Aṭiyya. Najāshī and *Rijāl* have *Abū Nāb* as the *kunya* of Ḥasan, but Kashshī: 367 seems to imply that it was a family title for the brothers, though some manuscripts of Kashshī, mentioned in the editor's footnote, agree with the former two sources. Nonetheless, the orthographic similarity of *Abū Nāb*, *al-bawwāb*, and *al-zayyāt* in Arabic script is striking.

He is attested at least once in Mecca (*Tahdhīb* 5: 263) and Medina (*Kāfī* 2: 98).

21. The same is also quoted from Ṣaffār's *Baṣā'ir* in *Biḥār* 25: 49, but in the *isnād* of the relevant passage in the printed version of Ṣaffār: 446 the name appears without any epithet. It seems that in the manuscript of the work used in *Biḥār*, the sentence *'Alī b. 'Aṭiyya 'an 'Alī b. Ri'āb* (as in *Kāfī* 1: 389) was corrupted to *'Alī b. 'Aṭiyya al-Zayyāt*.

Kitāb

His notebook of *ḥadīth*, related by Ibn Abī 'Umayr (*Fihrist*: 97).[22] The following quotations from our author on the authority of the same transmitter seem to originate from this notebook:

- *Maḥāsin*: 462
- *Kāfī* 1: 83 (also *Tawḥīd*: 105)
  2: 98, 300, 673
  3: 283 (also 4: 98 where the name of the transmitter from our author is missing)
  5: 149, 182
  6: 469
- *Tahdhīb* 5: 263, 308
  6: 337
  10: 59–60

34: 'Alī b. Ḥassān

'Alī b. Ḥassān b. Kathīr al-Hāshimī, a client of the 'Abbāsid 'Abbās b. Muḥammad b. 'Alī (d. 186, brother of the caliph Manṣūr) and a transmitter of esoteric material in the late second century.

Kashshī: 451–2; Ibn al-Ghaḍā'irī: 77; Najāshī: 251; *Fihrist*: 98.

Najāshī mentions in the entries on this transmitter and his uncle 'Abd al-Raḥmān b. Kathīr that they were clients of the 'Abbāsids. Ibn al-Ghaḍā'irī identifies 'Alī b. Ḥassān as a client of Abū Ja'far (Muḥammad) al-Bāqir. This is wrong, as explained in the entry on 'Abd al-Raḥmān b. Kathīr (no. 24 above).

He is described by Kashshī as both a liar and a Wāqifite, and by Najāshī and Ibn al-Ghaḍā'irī as an Extremist of corrupt doctrine.

Tafsīr al-bāṭin

Najāshī: 251 and Ibn al-Ghaḍā'irī: 77 mention this work, the former describing it as entirely esoteric and the latter as a book which has

22. Ibn Bābawayh quotes this author in *Faqīh* 1: 500, 2: 480 through 'Alī b. Ḥassān (*Mashyakha*: 472). Other quotations from this author through that transmitter include Ṣaffār: 446 (also *Kāfī* 1: 389); *'Ilal* 2: 213; *Qiṣaṣ*: 53 (cf. *Kāfī* 6: 513).

nothing to do with Islam. Later works obviously did not quote the most radical material of the book, but there are still many quotations from 'Alī b. Ḥassān in the field of *tafsīr*, some of which certainly measure up to Najāshī's description. Examples include the following:

- Ṣaffār: 40, 45, 71, 78, 206, 358, 427
- 'Ayyāshī[23] 1: 41, 128, 162, 201, 211, 281, 366–7
  2: 105
- *Kāfī* 1: 185, 196–8 (possibly), 210, 213, 217, 275, 413, 414–15 (two reports), 418, 420–21(three reports), 422–3 (two reports), 425 (also *Ma'ānī*: 299), 426
  2: 407 (possibly)
  4: 191–4
  5: 503 (cf. Ḥaskānī 2: 450–51)
  6: 513
- Kashshī: 192
- Furāt: 398–9
- Ibn al-Juḥām: 458
- Nu'mānī: 198 (repeated at 243)
- 'Alī b. Ibrāhīm 1: 165, 167
  2: 131, 234, 286, 319, 332, 351, 385–6, 390, 426, 429, 441
- Ibn Qūlawayh: 74–6
- *Faqīh* 3: 561- 2 (also *'Ilal* 2: 160; *Khiṣāl*: 364)
- *'Ilal* 1: 119, 195, 196
- *Tawḥīd*: 329–30 (and possibly 458)
- *Ta'wīl al-āyāt*: 843–4, 855

Two excerpts in *Kāfī* 1: 420–21 and 426 seem to represent the original structure of the work.

35: Ibn Ri'āb al-Ṭaḥḥān

Abū 'l-Ḥasan 'Alī b. Ri'āb, the miller, a Kūfan client and a prominent transmitter from Ja'far al-Ṣādiq, Mūsā al-Kāẓim, and their disciples.

Barqī: 76; Kashshī: 585; Mas'ūdī 4: 28; Ibn al-Nadīm: 275; Najāshī: 250; *Fibrist*: 87; *Rijāl*: 246; Ibn Mākūlā 4: 5. See also van Ess 1: 382–3.

---

23. See above, the entry on 'Abd al-Raḥmān b. Kathīr.

Barqī identifies this transmitter as a client of Jarm, a clan of Quḍā'a, but *Rijāl*: 246 as a client of the Banū Sa'd. Najāshī mentions both, explaining that it is the Banū Sa'd b. Bakr of Hawāzin that is meant here.

On his prominence in his time as a transmitter of *ḥadīth*, see Kashshī: 585. Mas'ūdī 4: 28, who calls him one of the eminent scholars of the Shī'a, reports that he had a brother, Yamān b. Ri'āb, who was among the prominent scholars of the Khārijites.[24] The two brothers would meet once every year for three days, debate over their sectarian discord, and then separate, without exchanging any fraternal compliments.

1. *Kitāb al-waṣiyya wa 'l-imāma*

Related from the author by Ḥasan b. Maḥbūb (Najāshī: 250), this was clearly on the topic of the Imāmite concept of the Imāmate by designation and will. There are numerous quotations from 'Alī b. Ri'āb on the topic of the Imāmate in general and on 'Alī being the designated Imām and the executor of the will of the Prophet in particular, almost all related by Ḥasan b. Maḥbūb. Those of the latter category and some of the other most likely originated from the work in question. Here is a list:

- Ṣaffār: 89 (also *Kāfī* 1: 437–8 [partially also at 436]; Ibn al-Juḥām: 321), 113 (also *Kāfī* 1: 256–7), 124–5, 142, 153–4 (also *Kāfī* 1: 241), 354, 518 (also 'Alī b. Ibrāhīm 2: 61; Ibn al-Juḥām: 144), 519
- *Kāfī* 1: 261–2, 281, 333, 348
  7: 171
- Ibn al-Juḥām: 487–8
- Nu'mānī: 43, 128–9, 250
- 'Alī b. Ibrāhīm 1: 365
  2: 66–7
- *Kamāl*: 18 (repeated at 336), 328, 416, 481, 648
- Ṭūsī, *Amālī*: 642–3
- *Ghayba*: 68, 332
- *Bishārat al-Muṣṭafā*: 85–6
- Ibn Ṭāwūs, *Sa'd*: 238–40

---

24. On him see Abū 'l-Ḥasan al-Ash'arī 1: 197–8, 200; Ibn al-Nadīm: 233; Dāraquṭnī, *Mu'talif*: 1052; Najāshī: 307; *Fibrist*: 124; Ibn Mākūlā 4: 5–6; *Mīzān* 4: 460, and other sources listed in the editor's footnote to *Lisān* 7: 521 (Dāraquṭnī and Ibn Mākūlā identify him as a Khurāsāni). See further Cook, *Early Muslim Dogma*: 98–9; van Ess 2: 599-600.

2. *Kitāb al-diyāt*

On monetary compensations for injuries inflicted upon a fellow human being, this work was also related from the author by Ḥasan b. Maḥbūb (Najāshī: 250). The following quotations from 'Alī b. Ri'āb on the topic, almost all through the same transmitter, may well go back to this work:

- 'Abd Allāh b. Ja'far: 165 (also *Kāfī* 7: 351, 353)
- *Kāfī* 7: 141, 285, 288 (two reports), 294–5 (two reports, one also in *'Ilal* 2: 229), 300, 305–6 (two reports), 310 (three reports), 328, 344, 357
- *Faqīh* 4: 108, 109, 110, 121
- *Tahdhīb* 10: 182, 195, 196, 215–16

3. *Aṣl / Kitāb*

'Alī b. Ri'āb's large (*Fihrist*: 87) notebook of *ḥadīth*, related by Ḥasan b. Maḥbūb (Abū Ghālib: 182; *Fihrist*: 87; also Ibn al-Nadīm: 275) who is the transmitter of the overwhelming majority of the over five hundred citations from Ibn Ri'āb in later works, listed in Khu'ī 12: 18–25, 285–95, 22: 174–78, 380–86 and *Fahāris* 8: 545–6, 9: 395. 'Abd Allāh b. Ja'far: 163–7 quotes a fragment of 17 reports from Ibn Ri'āb through Ḥasan b. Maḥbūb that may originally have been parts of this notebook (cf. Kashshī: 585).

36: Ibn Abī Arāka

'Alī b. Shajara b. Maymūn b. Sanjār, the arrowhead maker, a Kūfan client and a member of a Shī'ite family of transmitters of *ḥadīth*. He was a transmitter from Ja'far al-Ṣādiq.

Barqī: 77; Najāshī: 275; *Fihrist*: 94, 95; *Rijāl*: 266, 339.

His father, Shajara, and uncle, Bashīr, as well as brother, Ḥasan, and a cousin, Isḥāq b. Bashīr, were transmitters from Muḥammad al-Bāqir and Ja'far al-Ṣādiq. Abū Arāka was either the *kunya* of our transmitter's grandfather, Maymūn (*Rijāl*: 127, 224) or the family's great-grandfather (Najāshī: 275). Barqī: 38 and *Rijāl*: 86 name a Kūfan transmitter from 'Alī as Abū Arāka al-Bajalī.[25] There are

25. See also Bukhārī, *Kabīr* 9: 31 (erroneously as 'Abū Rāka); Ibn Abī Ḥātim 9: 336; Ibn Ḥibbān, *Thiqāt* 5: 584. For examples of his transmissions from 'Alī, see Naṣr b. Muzāḥim: 274; Ḥusayn b. Sa'īd, *Zuhd*: 5: 23 (also Ibn 'Abī 'l-Dunyā, *Tahajjud*: 271–2;

discrepancies about the Arab tribe of which this family was a client. *Rijāl*: 127, 169, 224 (whence *Lisān* 2: 59) identifies different members of the family as clients of the Banū Wābish, a clan of Qays 'Aylān, of 'Adnān. *Rijāl*: 266, 339, however, describes our transmitter, 'Alī b. Shajara, as a *Shaybānī*. *Lisān* 2: 41 claims that both Ṭūsī and Kashshī have called 'Alī's uncle, Bashīr al-Nabbāl, a *Shaybānī* too, but this is not attested in our copies of these works. Shaybān was a clan of Bakr b. Wā'il, of 'Adnān. Najāshī: 275, on the other hand, identifies this transmitter as a client of Kinda, a tribe of Kahlān, whose name is mentioned in a report by this transmitter in *Kāfī* 3: 493. If the Abū Arāka al-Bajalī named by Barqī and Ṭūsī was in fact the grandfather or great-grandfather of our transmitter, that further complicates the situation, as Bajīla is a different tribe of Kahlān.

Arrowhead making seems to have been the family business of our transmitter, as various members of the family are described as *nabbāl* (e.g. Kashshī: 369; Najāshī: 275; *Rijāl*: 127, 169, 224; also in the *isnād*s of numerous reports).

Kitāb

His notebook of *ḥadīth*, related by a number of transmitters including Ḥasan b. 'Alī b. Faḍḍāl and Ḥasan b. Muḥammad b. Samā'a (Najāshī: 275; *Fihrist*: 94, 95). Quotations from 'Alī b. Shajara, some on the authority of these two transmitters, include the following examples:

- Ḥusayn b. Sa'īd, *Zuhd*: 56, 61, 74
- *Maḥāsin*: 159, 173
- *Kāfī* 3: 170, 174, 345, 493
  4: 82
  5: 168, 278
  8: 107
- Ibn Qūlawayh: 146–7
- *Tawḥīd*: 459–60
- *Thawāb*: 155
- *Tahdhīb* 2: 251–2
- *Qiṣaṣ*: 276–7 (read *'an 'ammih Bashīr al-Nabbāl* for *'an 'ammih 'an Bashīr al-Nabbāl*)

Ibn 'Adī: 275; Mufīd, *Amālī*: 196–7; *Ḥilya* 1: 76; Khaṭīb, *Mūḍiḥ* 2: 296–7); Ṣaffār: 149; Ibn 'Adī: 1878; *Ikhtiṣāṣ*: 78–9.

37: Ibn 'Uqba

Abū 'l-Ḥasan 'Alī b. 'Uqba b. Khālid, the cloak seller, a Kūfan client of the Banū Asad and a transmitter from Ja'far al-Ṣādiq and Mūsā al-Kāẓim.

Barqī: 77; Kashshī: 344; Najāshī: 271; *Fihrist*: 90; *Rijāl*: 245, 266.

His profession is mentioned in *Kāfī* 2: 438 (where he is called *Bayyā' al-Aksiya*). Ṭūsī, *Amālī*: 680 has him as *'Alī b. 'Uqba b. Bashīr*. That does not go well with other sources unless *Bashīr* was the name of a great-grandfather.

He is attested in Medina at least once during the lifetime of Mūsā al-Kāẓim (*Kāfī* 3: 321).

Kitāb

His notebook of *ḥadīth*, related by a number of transmitters including Ḥasan b. 'Alī b. Faḍḍāl and 'Abd Allāh b. Muḥammad al-Ḥajjāl (Najāshī: 271; *Fihrist*: 90). Almost all of the well over one hundred quotations from this author in Shī'ite works of *ḥadīth* are through the first transmitter; only a few are through the second and a very few by others. Here is a partial list:

- *Maḥāsin*: 91–2, 109, 161–2, 162–3, 167, 170, 173 (two reports), 174, 175–6, 182, 198, 201 (also 'Ayyāshī 2: 137; *Tawḥīd*: 414–15), 223, 392
- Ṣaffār: 308, 482
- 'Ayyāshī 1: 371
  2: 34 (also *'Ilal* 1: 66), 79
- *Kāfī* 1: 69, 166, 391–2
  2: 78, 95, 144, 166, 171, 175, 179, 213–14, 257, 293, 302, 303–4, 310, 352, 366, 422, 438, 487 (read *'an Tha'laba wa 'Alī b. 'Uqba* as, for instance, ibid. 2: 638, 665, 8: 84), 616, 627, 638, 665
  3: 119, 128–9, 169, 173, 179, 225, 255, 321, 400, 505, 515–16
  4: 39, 213, 322, 397, 418
  5: 109, 149–50 (two reports), 229, 297, 327, 366–7, 438, 559
  6: 159, 251–2, 386, 436, 449, 460, 490, 401, 494, 539
  7: 12, 44, 57, 271, 394, 396 (three reports), 417, 429–30 (cf. ibid. 7: 44)
  8: 80–81, 84–5, 101, 129–31 (two reports), 295
- Kashshī: 31–2, 231, 292–3, 344, 345, 417–18
- Nu'mānī: 43, 200, 318
- 'Alī b. Ibrāhīm 1: 27–8, 29, 133

- Ibn Qūlawayh: 425, 494
- Ibn Bābawayh, *Amālī*: 287, 379, 420, 640 (also *Tawḥīd*: 401)
- *'Ilal* 1: 66, 70–71
  2: 190
- *'Iqāb*: 321
- *Khiṣāl*: 132, 263, 544, 648
- *Ma'ānī*: 193, 242, 255–6, 379
- *Thawāb*: 40, 161
- Mufīd, *Amālī*: 193, 194–5, 354
- *Irshād* 2: 384–5
- *Ikhtiṣāṣ* 202–3 (see also Kashshī: 163–4 where the *isnād* should read *'an Ḥasan b. Faḍḍāl 'an 'Alī b. 'Uqba 'an Abī Kahmas*)
- Ṭūsī, *Amālī*: 646, 680–82 (four reports), 692–5 (nine reports)
- *Tahdhīb* 1: 153, 320, 398, 447, 448, 459
  2: 227, 358
  4: 14
  6: 209–10, 241, 247, 284 (two reports)
  7: 4, 392, 461
  9: 194
  10: 195
- *Qiṣaṣ*: 269
- Ibn Ṭāwūs, *Falāḥ*: 76

Ṭūsī quotes a fragment of twelve reports in his *Amālī*: 680–82 and 692–5 through a single chain of transmission to 'Alī b. 'Uqba. This may have been taken from the notebook in question.

38: Ibn Yaqṭīn

Abū 'l-Ḥasan 'Alī b. Yaqṭīn b. Mūsā, a Kūfan client of the Banū Asad and resident of Baghdad. Son of a chief organizer of the 'Abbāsid revolution, he was born in 124 in Kūfa and appointed in 168 by the caliph Mahdī as his chief of staff and in 169 by the caliph Hādī as the keeper of the caliphal seal. He remained a high ranking official of the 'Abbāsid government for the rest of his life until his death in 182. He was a loyal follower of, and a fairly prolific transmitter from, Mūsā al-Kāẓim.

Barqī: 117; Ṭabarī 8: 167, 168, 170, 189, 221; Jahshiyārī: 124–5, 132; Mas'ūdī 4: 181–2; Kashshī: 430–37; Ibn al-Nadīm: 279; Najāshī: 273; *Fihrist*: 90–91; *Rijāl*: 340.

On his father, Yaqṭīn b. Mūsā, see Ziriklī 8: 207 and the sources cited. Originally a weaver,[26] he joined the 'Abbāsid movement from an early date, certainly before the revolt of Zayd b. 'Alī in the year 122 (Ibn Samka: 231; see also Jahshiyārī: 125 [read *wa kāna Yaqṭīn min wujūh al-du'āt*]; Ibn al-Nadīm: 279), and was reportedly the one who arranged for the Saffāḥ to assume leadership of the movement (Ibn Kathīr, *Bidāya* 10: 188). After the victory of the revolution, he served in various positions as a close and trusted confidant of the 'Abbāsid caliphs (see, for instance, Ṣābī: 381–2). In 137, the caliph Manṣūr sent him on a mission to Abū Muslim (Ṭabarī 7: 482–3; see also Khaṭīb, *Ta'rīkh* 11: 438). In 158, he was among the few close associates of Manṣūr who placed his corpse in its resting place (Ṭabarī 8: 61). In 161, Mahdī put him in charge of an extensive improvement of the pilgrimage route from Baghdad to Mecca (ibid. 8: 161; see also ibid. 8: 150), a position he held until 171. In 167, Mahdī appointed him to oversee a project to enlarge the grand mosque in Mecca (ibid. 8: 165; see also 'Ayyāshī 1: 185–6). In 169, he carried the head of the 'Alīd Ḥusayn b. 'Alī Ṣāḥib Fakhkh who had revolted against the 'Abbāsids but was defeated and killed, to Hādī (Ṭabarī 8: 303; see also ibid. 8: 199). In 178, he was sent to Ifrīqiya to persuade the rebel 'Abdawayh to return to obedience (ibid. 8: 256). He died in 185, three years after his son, 'Alī, in Baghdad (ibid. 8: 273, but Ibn Kathīr, *Bidāya* 10: 188, perhaps erroneously, has his death among the events of 186). He was not a follower of the Imāms nor a sympathizer of the 'Alīds (*Kāfī* 1: 369 [whence Nu'mānī: 295; cf. *'Ilal* 2: 268], further confirmed by *Kāfī* 2: 13). At the time of Zayd b. 'Alī's revolt, Yaqṭīn was already a person deeply committed to the 'Abbāsids and left Kūfa with the local head of their movement, Abū Salama al-Khallāl (d. 132) in order to avoid supporting Zayd. They returned after the revolt was suppressed and Zayd was killed (Ibn Samka: 231). Ibn al-Nadīm: 279 (whence *Fihrist*: 91) makes a gross mistake in assuming that he was a follower of the Imāms. Ibn al-Nadīm clearly transfers some information about 'Alī b. Yaqṭīn to his father. Yaqṭīn was a committed veteran of the 'Abbāsid cause, so much so that his son, 'Alī, worried that a curse possibly uttered by Ja'far al-Ṣādiq upon those who brought the 'Abbāsids to power may fall on Yaqṭīn and his descendants (*Kāfī* 2: 13; also Kashshī: 435–6 where the text of the report is corrupt). His four sons, however, were all followers of Mūsā al-Kāẓim[27] as later generations of his descendants also seem to have been.[28]

---

26. Abū 'l-Faraj, *Aghānī* 14: 364. Cf. Kashshī: 230 who says that Yaqṭīn, a client of the Banū Asad, was a spice seller, possibly on the basis of a lampoon, also quoted by Abū 'l-Faraj, where there is a mention of *abzār* of Yaqṭīn, a word that in this context may have a meaning other than spice.
27. Kashshī: 427, where the names of the sons appear as 'Alī, 'Ubayd (also mentioned in Ṭabarī 8: 199; Ibn al-Nadīm: 279; *Tahdhīb* 7: 456; he was the grandfather of the prominent Imāmite scholar of mid-third century, Abū Ja'far Muḥammad b. 'Īsā b. 'Ubayd al-Yaqṭīnī), Khuzayma and Ya'qūb (mentioned also in *Tahdhīb* 6: 412).
28. *Tahdhīb* 7: 456. See also Jāḥiẓ, *Bayān* 3: 345 where he reports that some of the descendants of Yaqṭīn are Imāmite Shī'ites and quotes a poem about this.

For 'Alī b. Yaqṭīn's high rank in the 'Abbāsid court, see Ṭabarī 8: 168, 170, 221; Jahshiyārī: 132; Mas'ūdī 4: 181–2 (see also 'Abd Allāh b. Ja'far: 305). At his death, the heir apparent Muḥammad al-Amīn led the funeral prayer over his corpse (Ibn al-Nadīm: 279 [whence Ṭūsī, *Fihrist*: 91]).

The date of 180 mentioned for the death of 'Alī b. Yaqṭīn in Kashshī: 430 is most likely erroneous. His sons, Ḥasan and Ḥusayn, were among Imāmite scholars of the next generation and transmitters from the Imāms. He also had a son named 'Īsā (*Tahdhīb* 7: 456).

1. *Kitāb mā su'ila 'anhu 'l-Ṣādiq min umūr al-malāḥim*
2. *Kitāb munāẓaratih [ma'] al-shākk bi-ḥaḍrati Ja'far*

These two works are mentioned by Ibn al-Nadīm: 279 (copied with minor modifications in Ṭūsī, *Fihrist*: 91) as belonging to 'Alī b. Yaqṭīn. Neither of the two were known to the Shī'ite biographers or authors of the books of *ḥadīth*. The topic of neither book seems to fall within the province of 'Alī b. Yaqṭīn. The closest that he ever got to the first title dealing with eschatological reports from Ja'far al-Ṣādiq is a single report in *'Ilal* 2: 268 in which 'Alī asks Mūsā al-Kāẓim why the apocalyptic predictions for the Shī'ites have not come true. The second title is even more problematic as 'Alī is nowhere described as a *mutakallim* or debater.

It seems that Ibn al-Nadīm may have misattributed a book by Yūnus b. 'Abd al-Raḥmān, a prominent Shī'ite scholar of the late second century, to 'Alī b. Yaqṭīn. Yūnus was a client of 'Alī b. Yaqṭīn and a student of Hishām b. al-Ḥakam, the well known Shī'ite *mutakallim* of the time. Yūnus quoted theological debates of Ja'far al-Ṣādiq and Hishām b. al-Ḥakam (e.g. *Kāfī* 1: 72; *Tawḥid*: 270–75). Ibn al-Nadīm most probably came across the second title in the list of works of Hishām b. al-Ḥakam as a record of his debate with a sceptic in the presence of Ja'far al-Ṣādiq, put together by Yūnus, client of 'Alī b. Yaqṭīn.[29] A slip or, alternatively, a corrupt copy might have made Ibn al-Nadīm think the book was put together by 'Alī b. Yaqṭīn himself. The book may therefore have been the same as the long text of Hishām's debate with a Catholic priest recorded on the authority of Yūnus in *Tawḥīd*: 270–75, or a similar text.[30]

---

29. *Mawlā 'Alī b. Yaqṭīn* as in Kashshī: 487, 491, 498; Najāshī: 446; *Rijāl*: 346, 378.
30. In fact, another item on the list of Hishām's works in Najāshī: 433 is compiled by his other student, 'Alī b. Manṣūr, from Hishām's statements.

3. *Kitāb masāʾil Abī ʾl-Ḥasan Mūsā b. Jaʿfar*

ʿAlī b. Yaqṭīn's notebook of answers to his questions by Mūsā al-Kāẓim, related by a number of transmitters including Aḥmad b. Muḥammad b. Khālid al-Barqī and Aḥmad b. Hilāl, both of whom quote it from the author's son, Ḥasan (Najāshī: 273; *Fibrist*: 91). Many quotations from this author in later works are recorded on the authority of Barqī (see Khuʾī 5: 316–19), and occasionally Aḥmad b. Hilāl (e.g. *Tahdhīb* 8: 157),[31] from Ḥasan. It thus seems that a book with the same title attributed by Najāshī: 45 and *Fibrist*: 48 to Ḥasan b. ʿAlī b. Yaqṭīn was at best a redaction of the book in question. Barqī is mentioned as the main transmitter of Ḥasan's book too.

The many quotations by ʿAlī b. Yaqṭīn from Mūsā al-Kāẓim in Shīʿite works of *ḥadīth* most probably belonged to this work, including the following:

- Aḥmad b. Muḥammad b. ʿĪsā: 87, 104 (see the editor's footnote)
- Ṣaffār: 316, 317
- ʿAyyāshī 1: 47
- *Kāfī* 1: 369
  2: 13
  3: 18, 46, 155, 168, 192, 435, 518, 539, 547–8
  4: 312, 380, 524
  5: 110, 112, 292, 452, 540
  6: 36, 406, 412 (two reports), 502
  7: 46
- Ibn Bisṭām: 87 (read *ʿan Abī ʾl-Ḥasan Mūsā*)
- Ibn Bābawayh, *Amālī*: 459–60 (also *ʿUyūn* 1: 79; Ibn Ṭāwūs, *Muhaj*: 43–5 with an appendix)
- *Faqīh* 1: 114, 267, 271, 415, 446, 451
  2: 36, 39, 222, 524
  3: 67, 176, 251
  4: 209, 304
- *ʿIlal* 1: 67 (also *Maʿānī*: 353)
  2: 59, 268
- *Tawḥīd*: 352–3, 460
- *Thawāb*: 169, 203

---

31. A misunderstanding by Khuʾī 12: 236–7 and Muḥammad Taqī al-Tustarī 7: 619–20 of the words *Aḥmad b. Hilāl ʿanhu* in *Fibrist*: 91 should thus be corrected.

- *ahdhīb* 1: 19, 111–12 (two reports), 142, 147, 221–2, 237, 271
  2: 32, 76, 103, 143, 157, 166, 187, 211, 235 (repeated at 307), 279, 296, 340, 374
  3: 7, 8, 12, 36, 209, 212–13 (four variants of a report), 246–7 (two reports), 267, 277, 296, 298
  4: 228
  5: 108, 127, 128, 131, 142, 173, 241, 430, 440
  6: 255
  7: 22, 80, 92
  8: 157–8, 244, 253, 261, 289, 382, 460
  9: 126–7, 137, 243, 330
- *Makārim al-akhlāq*: 190
- Ibn Ṭāwūs, *Ghiyāth*: 7

39: ʿAmmār al-Thawbānī

ʿAmmār b. Marwān, the furrier, a Kūfan client of the descendants of Thawbān b. Sālim al-Yashkurī and a transmitter from Jaʿfar al-Ṣādiq and Mūsā al-Kāẓim.

Ibn al-Ghaḍā'irī: 74; Najāshī: 191; *Fihrist*: 117; *Rijāl*: 252.

Mashyakha: 498 names an ʿAmmār b. Marwān *al-Kalbī* who is not mentioned by the biographers of the transmitters of *ḥadīth* but is quoted by Ibn Bābawayh in *Faqīh* 2: 142, 274 and *Khiṣāl*: 329–30 (see also ibid.: 290). The passage in *Faqīh* 2: 142 is quoted in *Kāfī* 4: 129, through a similar *isnād*, from *Muḥammad* b. Marwān (al-Kalbī) who is named in *Rijāl*: 144 as a transmitter from Muḥammad al-Bāqir. This prompts Khu'ī 12: 259 to suggest that there may never have been an *ʿAmmār* b. Marwān al-Kalbī and that Ibn Bābawayh's assumption to the contrary may have been caused by a confusion or corruption. However, Ibn Bābawayh is not alone in this matter as *Maḥāsin*: 358[32] quotes our transmitter as ʿAmmār b. Marwān al-Kalbī.

Kitāb

His notebook of *ḥadīth*, related by Muḥammad b. Sinān al-Zāhirī (Najāshī: 191; *Fihrist*: 117) who is the ultimate authority for some one

32. This is in the context of a citation which belongs to our transmitter as indicated by its *isnād*. The same report is quoted in *Kāfī* 2: 669 from an unqualified *ʿAmmār b. Marwān*.

hundred quotations from this author in Shī'ite works of *ḥadīth*. For lists of these quotations, see Khu'ī 12: 256–8, 371–3; *Fahāris* 9: 450.

40: 'Ammār al-Sābāṭī

Abū 'l-Faḍl 'Ammār b. Mūsā al-Sābāṭī was a Kūfan client who lived in Ctesiphon and a transmitter from Ja'far al-Ṣādiq and Mūsā al-Kāẓim. He was a Faṭḥite who acknowledged the Imāmate of Mūsā al-Kāẓim after 'Abd Allāh al-Afṭaḥ, but as a successor to 'Abd Allāh and not to Ja'far al-Ṣādiq as the mainstream Imāmites held. Some Faṭḥites joined other Shī'ite sects when 'Abd Allāh died without leaving an heir, but many joined the rank of the followers of Mūsā al-Kāẓim with the same understanding as 'Ammār and are, thus, identified by the early heresiographers as the 'Ammāriyya after our transmitter, who was clearly the most notable among them. He was noted for his wealth as well as for his learning in religious law.

Barqī: 94, 117; Kashshī: 253–4, 406, 504; Najāshī: 290; *Fihrist*: 117; *Rijāl*: 251, 340. See also *Kāfī* 5: 467 (also Mufīd, *Mut'a*: 69).

Barqī says that this transmitter was a Kūfān originally from Ctesiphon. *Rijāl*: 340 reverses the order and identifies him as a Kūfan by origin who lived in Ctesiphon. The latter seems to be correct as indicated by the fact that the principal transmitter from him, Maṣdaq b. Ṣadaqa, and the transmitter from the latter in the following generation were both from Ctesiphon. At other times, he is quoted by unnamed, unspecified residents of that town (e.g. Kashshī: 253) or, more specifically, of Sābāṭ (e.g. *Kāfī* 3: 501, repeated in 4: 27), a district of Ctesiphon (Yāqūt, *Mu'jam* 3: 166), where 'Ammār must have also lived.

On the 'Ammāriyya of the Faṭḥites, see Kashshī: 266 (citing the first Islamic heresiographical work ever written, that of Ibn al-Muq'ad, from the reign of the 'Abbāsid Mahdī [r. 158–169]), 284; Abū 'l-Ḥasan al-Ash'arī 1: 99; Nawbakhtī: 79; Sa'd b. 'Abd Allāh: 89; 'Abd al-Qāhir al-Baghdādī: 62 (see also Nashwān al-Ḥimyarī: 164).

On his wealth see *Kāfī* 3: 501 (repeated in 4: 27).

Despite the fact that he was a staunch Faṭḥite, the Imāmites generally consider him a reliable transmitter (Najāshī: 290; *Tahdhīb* 7: 101; Muḥaqqiq, *'Izziyya*: 65), though Ṭūsī at times contradicts himself on this point (cf. *Tahdhīb* 7: 101 with *Istibṣār* 1: 372). Much of his legal transmission, however, does not go well with the established positions of Imāmite law and may represent a different trend in the early days of that school. Muḥammad Taqī al-Tustarī 8: 19–31 provides a list of most of these disparities, some of which were even brought to the attention of the Imāms in their times (e.g. *Kāfī* 3: 362).

Kitāb

His notebook of *ḥadīth*, related by a late second-century transmitter from Ctesiphon, Maṣdaq b. Ṣadaqa (Najāshī: 290; *Fihrist*: 117). Ṭūsī describes this as a large, good and reliable notebook (*Fihrist*: 117). The notebook was still available in the late seventh century to Ibn al-Muṭahhar who quoted from it in his *Mukhtalaf* 8: 310. Ibn Ṭāwūs quotes from the notebook in *Ghiyāth*: 4 through an unspecified work of Ṭūsī (see further Kohlberg: 124).

The overwhelming majority of some five hundred quotations from this author in Shī'ite works of *ḥadīth*, listed in Khu'ī 12: 246, 260, 263–4, 272–3, 370–84, 23: 101 and *Fahāris* 9: 447–51, are on the authority of the same transmitter.

41: Al-Ḥulwānī

Abū 'Uthmān 'Amr b. Jumay' al-Azdī, a mid-second century Baṣran Sunnī transmitter of *ḥadīth* with Shī'ite sympathies. He lived in Baghdad where he held a *ḥadīth* transmission session in a mosque. In different periods in his life, he served as a judge in Ḥulwān and Ray. He transmitted *ḥadīth* from Ja'far al-Ṣādiq, among others.

Fasawī 3: 39; Barqī: 92 (read *Azdī* for *'Abdī*); 'Uqaylī 3: 264; Ibn Abī Ḥātim 6: 224; Ibn 'Adī: 1764–5; Kashshī: 390; Najāshī: 288; *Fihrist*: 111; *Rijāl*: 142, 251; *Lisān* 5: 295–6 (and other sources listed in the editor's footnote).

His *kunya* appears as *Abū 'Uthmān* in Shī'ite sources and as *Abū al-Mundhir* in Ibn 'Adī: 1764. Other Sunnī sources mention both (see *Mīzān* 3: 251, *Lisān* 5: 295). Sunnī sources identify him as the judge of Ḥulwān (*Kirmān* in Nasā'ī, *Ḍu'afā'*: 184 is almost certainly corrupt). Shī'ite sources, on the other hand, know him as the judge of Ray (Najāshī: 288; *Rijāl*: 251).

Nuskha / Kitāb

His notebook of *ḥadīth* (Najāshī: 288; *Fihrist*: 111), related, among others, by Yūnus b. 'Abd al-Raḥmān in Imāmite tradition (*Fihrist*: 111, as for instance in *Maḥāsin*: 8, 11, 443, 445; *Kāfī* 2: 83; *Ma'ānī*: 302), and 'Abd Allāh b. Dāhir al-Rāzī among the Zaydīs (see Aḥmad b. 'Īsā and Abū Ṭālib in all cases listed below). The Imāmites were especially interested in his transmissions from their own Imāms. Here is a list of some of this author's quotations from the Imāms, particularly from Ja'far al-Ṣādiq, that made up the bulk of the material of this notebook:[33]

- *Maḥāsin*: 8, 54, 241 (also *Tawḥīd*: 313; *Ma'ānī*: 11 [read *'Amr b. Jumay'* as in *Biḥār* 90: 218]), 443, 445 (two reports)
- Aḥmad b. 'Īsā 1: 116
  3: 8–9 (two reports), 165, 188
  4: 268, 333, 334, 338, 340, 347, 349, 356 (two reports), 358 (two reports), 362–3 (five reports)
- 'Ayyāshī 1: 25, 120
- 'Uqaylī 3: 264 (from Ḥasan al-Mujtabā through intermediaries; also Ibn 'Adī: 1764; however, *Mīzān* 3: 251 [whence *Lisān* 5: 296], quoting 'Uqaylī, has 'Amr transmitting this passage from Ja'far al-Ṣādiq)
- *Kāfī* 2: 83, 87, 114, 233 (read *Azdī* for *'Abdī*), 442, 445, 467, 604, 621
  3: 369, 504
  5: 34, 72 (also *Thawāb*: 215), 147 (two reports), 325, 569
  6: 297, 300, 539
- Ibn 'Adī: 1764–5 (five reports from 'Alī, one the same as 'Uqaylī 3: 264, another also in Abū Nu'aym, *Akhbār Iṣbahān* 1: 157)
- Ibn Bābawayh, *Amālī*: 561
- *Faqīh* 3: 71, 272
- *'Ilal* 1: 7
- *'Iqāb*: 265
- *Kamāl*: 236–7
- *Khiṣāl*: 480–81
- *Ma'ānī*: 200 (also Bayhaqī, *Shu'ab* 1: 223), 300–302 (four reports), 344–5
- *Thawāb*: 16, 131
- Abū Ṭālib: 145, 168 (also *Mīzān* 3: 251), 238, 365–6, 377
- *Ḥilya* 3: 196–7
- Abū 'Abd Allāh al-Shajarī, *Adhān*: 70
- Ṭūsī, *Amālī*: 497
- *Tahdhīb* 3: 201
  4: 191, 198

33. There are also quotations from this author on the virtues of 'Alī that he quoted on the authority of A'mash, Ibn Abī Laylā, and others. For a few examples of these, as well as other citations from him in the Shī'ite works, see Aḥmad, *Faḍā'il*: 628 (whence Ibn 'Asākir 42: 43, 313); *Maḥāsin*: 11; Ibn Bābawayh, *Amālī*: 367–9; *Khiṣāl*: 449; *Thawāb*: 16; Ḥaskānī 2: 184 (also Ibn 'Asākir 56: 36).

– *Firdaws* (Uzbak: 2215)
– Ibn al-Najjār 2: 62

42: Abū Khālid al-Wāsiṭī

Abū Khālid ʿAmr b. Khālid al-Wāsiṭī, a Kūfan client of the Banū Hāshim who later moved to Wāsiṭ. He was a Zaydī, best known as the ultimate transmitter of the works of Zayd b. ʿAlī, including his *Majmūʿ*, *Manāsik*, and *Tafsīr gharīb al-Qurʾān*.[34]

Yaḥyā b. Maʿīn 2: 442; Aḥmad, *ʿIlal* 1: 246, 2: 558, 3: 16, 128; Bukhārī, *Kabīr* 6: 328; Fasawī 1: 700, 2: 395, 3: 436; Barqī: 52; Nasāʾī, *Ḍuʿafāʾ*: 185; ʿUqaylī 3: 268; Ibn Abī Ḥātim 6: 230; Kashshī: 231–2, 390; Ibn Ḥibbān, *Majrūḥīn* 2: 76; Dāraquṭnī, *Ḍuʿafāʾ*: 133; Ibn ʿAdī: 1774–8; Ibn al-Nadīm: 275; Najāshī: 288; *Rijāl*: 142; Mizzī 21: 603–7 (and the many other sources listed in the editor's footnote). See also Madelung: 54–7.

His grandfather was a client of ʿAqīl b. Abī Ṭālib, the brother of ʿAlī (Fasawī 1: 700). Kashshī: 232 notes that he lived in the neighborhood of Masjid Simāk in Kūfa, a mosque originally built in the time of ʿUmar in the district of the Banū Naṣr b. Quʿayn, as the biggest mosque of the Banū Asad in Kūfa (Abū ʾl-Faraj, *Aghānī* 11: 251). This was later known as Masjid al-Ḥawāfir and the district was that of the ironsmiths of the town (Ibn al-Mashhadī: 120). In fact, Simāk's grandfather was the first ironsmith of the town (Balādhurī, *Futūḥ*: 348). The Umayyad poets Uqayshir (d. 80) and Akhṭal (d. 90) composed poems about this mosque, one a lampoon, the other in praise (Abū ʾl-Faraj, *Aghānī* 11: 251; Balādhurī, *Futūḥ*: 348). The mosque was named after Simāk b. Makhrama b. Ḥumayn al-Asadī (Balādhurī, *Futūḥ*: 348; Ibn Abī Ḥātim 4: 279; Ibn Mākūlā 2: 534; Fīrūzābādī 1: 718; see also *Kāfī* 3: 490; *Khiṣāl*: 301), head of the anti-ʿAlī faction of Kūfa during ʿAlī's time. He sided with Muʿāwiya, had to leave Kūfa for Raqqa, and fought with ʿAlī's commander, Mālik al-Ashtar (Naṣr b. Muzāḥim: 12, 146; Thaqafī: 323–5; Balādhurī, *Futūḥ*: 348). Later, he was one of the ʿUthmāniyya of Kūfa who testified against Ḥujr b. ʿAdī, the prominent partisan of ʿAlī, in 51 in a plot to bring about his execution by Muʿāwiya (Abū ʾl-Faraj, *Aghānī* 17: 146). According to the legend, ʿAlī did not pray in this mosque (ibid. 11: 251), and it was later renovated in celebration for the killing of Ḥusayn (Thaqafī: 484; also *Kāfī* 3: 490; *Khiṣāl*: 301; Ṭūsī, *Amālī*: 169). As late as the fourth century, the Shīʿites of Kūfa still avoided this mosque, and the district around it was predominantly populated by the ʿUthmāniyya (Abū ʾl-Faraj, *Aghānī* 11: 251).

The district could not tolerate ʿAmr's Shīʿite sympathies for ever. Ibn ʿAdī: 1774 quotes the Kūfan Wakīʿ b. al-Jarrāḥ (d. 197) saying that ʿAmr b. Khālid was

34. See Sezgin 1: 552–7, 559.

in their neighborhood, but when it became clear that he was a liar (an obvious reference to his transmission of pro-'Alīd material), he had to move to Wāsiṭ. The Khaṭīb's assumption in *Mūḍiḥ* 2: 288 that the man was a Wāsiṭī who lived in Kūfa may thus be inaccurate.

With a few exceptions,[35] all transmissions by this author are from Zayd b. 'Alī and Muḥammad al-Bāqir.

Kitāb

(Ibn al-Nadīm: 275 [whence Ṭūsī, *Fihrist*: 189]; Najāshī: 288). Najāshī, who knows this author as a transmitter from Zayd b. 'Alī, describes this work as a large book, related from the author by the historian Naṣr b. Muzāḥim al-Minqarī. He seems to refer to the *Majmū'* of Zayd b. 'Alī, also published as *Musnad al-imām Zayd*, which is compiled from his transmissions by 'Amr b. Khālid and quoted from the latter by Naṣr b. Muzāḥim through Ibrāhīm b. al-Zibriqān (Zayd b. 'Alī: 50). Quotations of the material of this work, normally through its other chief transmitter, Ḥusayn b. 'Alwān al-Kalbī, abound in Sunnī, Zaydī and Imāmite works of *ḥadīth*. There is other material quoted from this author in later works,[36] including quotations from Muḥammad al-Bāqir, as in the following examples:

- Baḥshal: 193 (also *Mīzān* 3: 258)
- Aḥmad b. 'Īsā 1: 18, 23, 31, 43, 50, 55, 61, 62, 63, 65, 75, 81, 145, 148, 149, 172, 185, 198, 209, 226, 244, 309, 320, 336, 343, 390, 392, 401, 404
  2: 339
  3: 90, 103, 120, 122, 132, 169
  4: 268
- *Kāfī* 2: 75–6
  3: 393
  4: 92
- Kashshī: 231–2 (also Ibn Bābawayh, *Amālī*: 415)

---

35. 'Abd al-Razzāq 2: 350 (whence Fasawī 1: 700) Ibn 'Adī: 1776–8 (twelve reports); Ibn Bābawayh, *Amālī*; 563, 681 (also *Thawāb*: 68–9); *Kamāl*: 280 (updated, also *'Uyūn* 1: 64); *Thawāb*: 76; Ṭūsī, *Amālī*: 632; Khaṭīb, *Mūḍiḥ* 2: 288–91; Ibn Ṭāwūs, *Falāḥ*: 252–8; *Mīzān* 3: 258.
36. These quotations are also on the authority of Ḥusayn b. 'Alwān or, alternatively, Naṣr b. Muzāḥim, with Ibrāhīm b. al-Zibriqān as the intermediary (e.g. Ṭūsī, *Amālī*: 489) or without (as in Naṣr b. Muzāḥim, *Waq'at Ṣiffīn*: 134; Aḥmad b. 'Īsā 3: 120, 122, 4: 374; Ibn Bābawayh, *Amālī*: 136–7 [also *Khiṣāl*: 429]; Khaṭīb, *Faqīh* 1: 45; *Bishārat al-Muṣṭafā*: 128; Ibn Ṭāwūs, *Falāḥ*: 252–8).

- Abū Ṭālib: 275
- Bayhaqī 9: 283
- Ṭūsī, *Amālī*: 585
- *Tahdhīb* 8: 310
- *Firdaws* (Uzbak: 682; whence Ibn al-Jawzī, *'Ilal*: 933)
- Ṭabrisī, *Majma'* 23: 153 (from 'Ayyāshī; cf. Ḥaskānī 2: 177)

43: Abū 'Abd Allāh al-Ju'fī

Abū 'Abd Allāh 'Amr b. Shimr (or Shamir) b. Yazīd al-Ju'fī, a Kūfan Arab transmitter of *ḥadīth* who was known to both the Sunnī and Shī'ite communities of the city. He was a transmitter from Ja'far al-Ṣādiq and Jābir al-Ju'fī.

Yaḥyā b. Ma'īn 2: 446; Bukhārī, *Kabīr* 6: 344; Barqī: 92; Nasā'ī, *Ḍu'afā'*: 185; 'Uqaylī 3: 275; Ibn Abī Ḥātim 6: 239–40; Ibn Ḥibbān, *Majrūḥīn* 2: 75; Ibn 'Adī: 1779–82; Ibn al-Ghaḍā'irī: 74; Abū Nu'aym, *Ḍu'afā'*: 118; Najāshī: 287; *Fihrist*: 112; *Rijāl*: 141, 250; *Lisān* 5: 309–11 (and the many other sources listed in the editor's footnote).

Ibn 'Adī: 1779 reports on the authority of the *mu'adhdhin* Ḥusayn al-Ju'fī that 'Amr b. Shimr/Shamir was the *imām* of the mosque for thirty years. That should have been the Masjid Ju'fī of Kūfa, outside of the city wall (Warrām: 304) and a popular haunt for the Arab Shī'ites of the city (Thaqafī: 484 [read *nās min al-'Arab min awliyā'inā* as in Ṭūsī, *Amālī*: 168]). As a Shī'ite base in Kūfa, it was considered among the blessed mosques of the city (Ibn al-Mashhadī: 149–53), though some reports state that the truly hallowed one, which clearly had significance for the local Shī'ites in the late Umayyad period, was the old mosque of the Ju'fī that was destroyed in the course of time (*Kāfī* 3: 490; *Khiṣāl*: 301). A report in *Manāqib* 4: 187 confirms that the latter mosque was already in ruins before the end of the Umayyad period.

Some Sunnī biographical works identify this transmitter as a Shī'ite (e.g. Ibn Ḥibbān, *Majrūḥīn* 2: 75). Others accuse him of fabricating *ḥadīth* for the Shī'a (see *Mīzān* 3: 269). Despite his transmission of Jābir al-Ju'fī's radical Shī'ite material and texts such as his *Kitāb ḥadīth al-Shūrā* (see above, section II, # 7, the entry on Jābir al-Ju'fī), 'Amr does not seem to have been a radical Shī'ite himself. A report by him in Ibn 'Asākir 54: 286 condemns those people in Iraq who claim they love the Family of the Prophet but show disrespect towards Abū Bakr and 'Umar (see further Ibn 'Adī: 1780–81: 'Uqaylī, *Ḍu'afā'* 3: 276; Khaṭīb, *Mūḍiḥ* 1: 80, 2: 295–7).

Kitāb

(*Fihrist*: 112). As noted in the entry on Jābir al-Ju'fī, 'Amr was the chief transmitter of the works of Jābir to which he added extra material. Some of these works were therefore ascribed to him, too (Najāshī: 287). The work in question is certainly different from the revised versions of the works of Jābir, most likely his own notebook that should have also included the material that 'Amr related from authorities other than Jābir. Numerous quotations from that material can be found in Sunnī and Zaydī works of *ḥadīth*, but more frequently in Imāmite sources. For lists see Khu'ī 13: 108, 398–403; *Fahāris* 9: 478–9.

44: Ibn Abī 'l-Miqdām

Abū Muḥammad 'Amr b. Abī 'l-Miqdām Thābit b. Hurmuz was a Kūfan client of the Banū 'Ijl, a clan of Bakr b. Wā'il, and a transmitter of Sunnī and Shī'ite *ḥadīth*. He related from Muḥammad al-Bāqir and Ja'far al-Ṣādiq, among others, and died in 172.

Ibn Sa'd 6: 267; Bukhārī, *Kabīr* 6: 319; Muslim: 16; Abū Dāwūd 1: 77; Barqī: 52, 63; Ibn Abī Ḥātim 6: 223; Kashshī: 392; Ibn al-Ghaḍā'irī: 73, 111; Najāshī: 290; *Rijāl*: 141, 248, 265, and other sources listed in the editors' footnotes to Mizzī 21: 553–9 and Dhahabī, *Ta'rīkh* 11 (years 171–180): 279.

Sunnī sources usually accuse this transmitter of extreme Shī'ite sympathies (Ibn Sa'd 6: 267; Abū Dāwūd 1: 77; Ibn Abī Ḥātim 6: 223), even as extreme as cursing the "predecessors" (Muslim: 16; 'Uqaylī 3: 262). Aḥmad b. Ḥanbal reported that this man used to specifically curse 'Uthmān, but others testified that he had said that all the companions of the Prophet, save four, apostatized after his death ('Uqaylī 3: 261; Ājurrī 3: 212 [here: "save five"]),[37] a well attested theme in early Kūfan Shī'ism. His reports in Shī'ite sources confirm his strong Shī'ite sympathies[38] and that he identifed himself more with the Shī'ites in spite of his relations with Sunnī circles of transmission of *ḥadīth* of Kūfa in his time (as attested in 'Ayyāshī 1: 216). His father, Thābit b. Hurmuz, was a transmitter

37. The statement is attested in a report quoted from him in *Ikhtiṣāṣ*: 6 (but here, it is "save three") in an account of the events of the Saqīfa of the Banū Sā'ida where Abū Bakr was appointed as the caliph. For Ibn Abī 'l-Mīqdām's other reports in condemnation of that action, see 'Ayyāshī 1: 200, 2: 66–8; *Kāfī* 8: 270.

38. See, for instance, 'Ayyāshī 1: 200, 2: 66–8; *Kāfī* 8: 212–14; *Khiṣāl*: 364–82. See also his comment about Ja'far al-Ṣādiq in Ibn 'Adī: 556.

from ʿAlī Zayn al-ʿĀbidīn (Najāshī: 116; Mizzī 4: 380–81 [and the many sources listed in the editor's footnote]; Najāshī credits him with a register [*nuskha*] of his transmissions from that Imām) and Muḥammad al-Bāqir (see, for instance, ʿAbbād b. Yaʿqūb: 15–17 [four reports]; *Kāfī* 3: 188; *Khiṣāl*: 444 [also *Ṣifāt*: 198–9, repeated at 202]; Abū ʿAbd Allāh al-Shajarī, *Adhān*: 28–9).

The year 172 is given as his date of death on the authority of ʿAbbād (b. Yaʿqūb al-Rawājinī) in Bukhārī, *Awsaṭ* 2: 104; idem, *Kabīr* 6: 319. Ibn Saʿd 6: 267 does not mention a specific year but asserts that he died during the reign of Hārūn al-Rashīd (r. 170–193).

1. *Kitāb al-masāʾil allatī akhbara bihā Amīr al-Muʾminīn al-Yahūdī*

This book is mentioned in *Fihrist*: 111 as a work of ʿAmr b. Abī ʾl-Miqdām, though in a wrong entry (see Muḥammad Taqī al-Tustarī 8: 144). The work, clearly a late Umayyad Shīʿite polemic that ʿAmr received through two authorities on *ḥadīth*, has survived in *Khiṣāl*: 364–82.

2. *Kitāb*

His notebook of *ḥadīth* described by Najāshī: 290 as a small book related from him by ʿAbbād b. Yaʿqūb al-Rawājinī. A fragment of eleven reports from ʿAmr is quoted in the surviving version of ʿAbbād b. Yaʿqūb's notebook: 15–17, clearly from the work in question. In fact, with an additional quotation ibid.: 18, quotations from Ibn Abī ʾl-Miqdām make up twelve out of the total of eighteen reports of the surviving version of ʿAbbād's notebook. Other citations from this author through ʿAbbād that must originally have belonged to the work in question include the following:

- Muḥammad b. Sulaymān 1: 288, 328 (two reports), 384, 385, 477, 511 2: 366, 367 (also Ibn ʿAdī: 1773), 390, 402, 404, 405, 409
- *Maqātil*: 51–67, 67–9
- Ibn ʿAdī: 1772, 1773
- Ibn Qūlawayh: 196, 450–51, 454
- Ibn Bābawayh, *Amālī*: 203
- Ibn Shādhān: 49–50
- Ṭūsī, *Talkhīṣ al-Shāfī* 3: 48

45: Abū Ḍamra

Abū Ḍamra Anas b. 'Iyāḍ al-Laythī, a Medinese Arab from the Banū Layth b. Bakr b. 'Abd Manāt and a Sunnī transmitter of *ḥadīth* who transmitted from Ja'far al-Ṣādiq,[39] among others. He lived long and died late in the second century.

Ibn Sa'd 5: 502; Yaḥyā b. Ma'īn 2: 43; Khalīfa b. Khāyyāṭ, *Ṭabaqāt*: 276; Bukhārī, *Kabīr* 2: 33; Fasawī 1: 190; Abū Zur'a al-Dimashqī: 277, 415; Ibn Abī Ḥātim 2: 289; Ibn Ḥibbān, *Mashāhīr*: 226; idem, *Thiqāt* 6: 76; Najāshī: 106; *Fihrist*: 39; *Rijāl*: 165, and the many other sources listed in the editor's footnote to Dhahabī, *Ta'rīkh* 13 (years 191–200): 112.

His brother, Abū 'l-Ḥasan Jalaba b. 'Iyāḍ was also a transmitter from Ja'far al-Ṣādiq and author of a notebook of *ḥadīth*, related from him by Hārūn b. Muslim al-Anbārī al-Kātib (Najāshī: 128; *Fihrist*: 186) who seems to have received it from the author through an intermediary (see *'Ilal* 2: 216). All surviving quotations from this author are through the same transmitter as in *'Ilal* 2: 216 (two reports), 250; *Kamāl*: 221; *Khiṣāl*: 103; *Ikhtiṣāṣ*: 63; Ibn Ṭāwūs, *Iqbāl* 2: 279–82.

On Abū Ḍamra's date of death, Ibn Ḥibbān (*Mashāhīr*: 226; *Thiqāt* 6: 76) suggests the year 180, but Bukhārī, *Kabīr* 2: 33 and Fasawī 1: 190 opt for the year 200. The round figures may indicate that they are approximate.

Kitāb

His notebook of *ḥadīth* from Ja'far al-Ṣādiq and others, related by a number of transmitters (Najāshī: 106; *Fihrist*: 39). Examples of his transmission from Ja'far al-Ṣādiq include the following:

- Ibn Sa'd 1: 18, 50
  2: 178, 198–9, 211, 218, 227, 228
  8: 19, 338–9
- *Maḥāsin*: 636
- Ibn Abī 'l-Dunyā, *Ahwāl*: 30
- Aḥmad b. 'Īsā 1: 108, 134, 182

---

39. A statement by a non-Shī'ite contemporary of this transmitter, suggests that there were doubts about Abū Ḍamra's direct transmission from Ja'far al-Ṣādiq (Fasawī 1: 190). The language of the passage is, however, ambiguous and the main reservation might have concerned not the actual transmission by Abū Ḍamra from Ja'far al-Ṣādiq but the method of transmission of knowledge in the House of Imāmate: whether it followed the normal pattern of transmission of *ḥadīth* at the time or a more esoteric "knowledge of the House" pattern as the Shī'ites maintained.

2: 361, 384, 389
3: 34, 119, 124, 161
4: 211, 324, 331, 347, 352

- *'Ilal* 2: 35
- Khaṭīb, *Ta'rīkh* 3: 358
- Ibn Abī 'l-Ḥadīd 2: 311

His non-Shī'ite transmissions are at times attested in Shī'ite works too. See, for instance, Khazzāz: 223 (updated); *Tahdhīb* 4: 315, 6: 175 (partially through Najāshī's *isnād* to the notebook).

46: 'Anbasa al-'Ābid

'Anbasa b. Bijād al-'Ābid, a Kūfan client of the Banū Asad and a transmitter from Ja'far al-Ṣādiq. The biographers praise him as both virtuous and learned.

Barqī: 101; Kashshī: 372; Najāshī: 302; *Fihrist*: 120; *Rijāl*: 140, 261.

Ḥilya 3: 198 (also Lālikā'ī 1: 145) quotes a statement from Ja'far al-Ṣādiq on the authority of 'Anbasa al-Khath'amī whom he describes as *min al-akhyār*. The same statement appears in *Ḥilya* 3: 184 on the authority of 'Anbasa b. *Makhlad* (sic, clearly a corruption for *bijād*) al-'Ābid.

Kashshī says that 'Anbasa *kān khayran fāḍilan*. The last word is corrupted in Najāshī where it is said of the man that he *kān qāḍiyan*.

Kitāb

His notebook of *ḥadīth*, related by Ṣafwān b. Yaḥyā and 'Abd al-Raḥmān b. Muḥammad b. Abī Hāshim (Najāshī: 302; *Fihrist*: 120). Quotations from this author in later works, some through the same two transmitters, include the following examples:

- *Maḥāsin*: 171 (also Ḥaskānī 2: 388, 389), 293 (whence *Kāfī* 2: 427), 531 (whence *Kāfī* 6: 345)
- Ṣaffār: 147, 165, 168–9 (also *Kāfī* 8: 395; *Maqātil*: 208)
- 'Abd Allāh b. Ja'far: 163
- *Kāfī* 2: 100, 301 (also Ibn Bābawayh, *Amālī*: 503; *Ḥilya* 3: 184, 198; see also *Kāfī* 8: 141 for another possible report by this transmitter on a related subject), 347, 483, 664, 665

4: 91
7: 65 (also Ibn Qūlawayh, *Kitāb*: 146; Ibn Bābawayh, *Amālī*: 355)
8: 260 (also Ibn al-Juḥām: 357), 394–5

- Kashshī: 245
- Ibn Bābawayh, *Amālī*: 309 (also *Kamāl*: 74)
- *'Ilal* 2: 69
- *Ikhtiṣāṣ*: 279–80
- *Tahdhīb* 2: 275, 353
- Ibn Abī 'l-Ḥadīd 2: 202

47: Asbāṭ Bayyā' al-Zuṭṭī

Abū 'Alī Asbāṭ b. Sālim, seller of clothing made by Jhāts, a Kūfan client of Kinda and a transmitter from Ja'far al-Ṣādiq.

Barqī: 109; Najāshī: 106; *Fihrist*: 38–9; *Rijāl*: 166. See also *Kāfī* 5: 199; *Faqīh* 3: 350.

Kitāb / Aṣl

His notebook of *ḥadīth*, related by a number of transmitters including Ibn Abī 'Umayr (Najāshī: 106; *Fihrist*: 38–9). Quotations from this author in later works, some through the same transmitter, include the following examples:

- *Maḥāsin*: 179
- Ṣaffār: 55, 205, 355 (also *Kāfī* 1: 218), 451, 456 (repeated at 458 [also *Kāfī* 1: 273]; the passage ibid.: 55 is another part of this report)
- 'Ayyāshī 1: 57, 235, 236, 247
  2: 317
- *Kāfī* 1: 192, 207, 218 (two variants), 273
  2: 470
  3: 255, 505
  4: 12
  5: 75, 131 (two variants), 199
  6: 6, 388, 413, 521
  8: 302
- Ibn al-Juḥām: 356–7

- *Faqīh* 3: 350
- *'Ilal* 1: 87
- Ṭūsī, *Amālī*: 694
- *Ghayba*: 476
- *Tahdhīb* 7: 4
- *Qiṣaṣ*: 59–60

48: 'Āṣim al-Ḥannāṭ

Abū 'l-Faḍl 'Āṣim b. Ḥumayd, the wheat seller, a Kūfan client of the Banū Ḥanīfa, a clan of Bakr b. Wā'il, and a prolific transmitter of *ḥadīth* known to both the Shī'ite and Sunnī traditions. He was a transmitter from Ja'far al-Ṣādiq and his disciples. He lived and died in Kūfa.

Barqī: 111; Ibn Abī Ḥātim 6: 342; Kashshī: 367; Ibn Shāhīn, *Thiqāt*: 219–20; Najāshī: 301; *Fihrist*: 120; *Rijāl*: 262, and other sources listed in the editors' footnotes to Mizzī 13: 482 and Dhahabī, *Ta'rīkh* 13 (years 191–200): 240.

An early Sunnī authority identifies 'Āṣim as the most reliable among the Shī'ites of Kūfa (see Mizzī 13: 482).

Kitāb

His notebook of *ḥadīth*, related by various transmitters (Abū Ghālib: 148; Najāshī: 301; *Fihrist*: 120; *Rijāl*: 408). A version of this notebook has survived and is published in *al-Uṣūl al-sittat 'ashar*: 21–41 (see further Kohlberg, *Uṣūl*: 152). This must be a fragment of the original notebook, as over five hundred other quotations from this author have survived in Shī'ite works of *ḥadīth*, overwhelmingly through those specified by Najāshī and Ṭūsī as transmitters of this notebook. For lists of these quotations, see Khu'ī 9: 178, 181–4, 471–82; *Fahāris* 9: 163–5. Examples of his transmissions in Sunnī sources include the following:

- *Ḥilya* 1: 79–80 (whence Khaṭīb, *Faqīh* 1: 50; Ibn 'Asākir 50: 252–3, 253–4; see also Muḥammad b. Sulaymān 2: 94–6)
- 'Āṣimī 1: 182
- Bayhaqī, *Dalā'il* 5: 341 (read *'Āṣim b. Ḥumayd 'an al-Thumālī* as in Ibn 'Asākir 69: 203)
- Khaṭīb, *Talkhīṣ* 1: 383

49: ʿĀṣim al-Kūzī

Abū Shuʿayb ʿĀṣim b. Sulaymān al-Kūzī, the shoemaker, a Baṣran Sunnī transmitter of *ḥadīth* with some Shīʿite sympathies. He transmitted from Jaʿfar al-Ṣādiq, among others.

ʿUqaylī 3: 337; Ibn ʿAdī: 1877–9; Najāshī: 301; *Rijāl*: 262; *Lisān* 3: 640–41 (and other sources listed in the editor's footnote).

The biographers identify this transmitter as Baṣran. Najāshī: 184 describes his nephew, Sulaymān b. Samāʿa, as a Kūfan. There is some ambiguity about the tribal affiliation of ʿĀṣim. There seem to have been three clans known as Banū Kūz, one belonging to the Banū Ḍabba, one to Asad Khuzayma, and a local tribe in Baṣra (Ibn Naṣir al-Dīn 7: 372). Ibn ʿAdī: 1877 and others attribute him to the Baṣran tribe. Najāshī: 301 hesitates whether the man belonged to the Kūz of the Banū Ḍabba or of Asad Khuzayma, though he identifies his nephew categorically as *Ḍabbī (*ibid: 184). To complicate the situation even further, others add the *nisba*s of *Tamīmī* (*Lisān* 3: 640) and *ʿAbdī* (Ibn ʿAdī: 1877). Samʿānī 11: 167 strings together these contradictory accounts and describes him as "*al-Tamīmī al-Kūzī al-ʿAbdī*, a Baṣran."

The profession of shoemaking is mentioned for him in the *isnād* of a report in *Lisān* 3: 642. His above-mentioned nephew was also a shoemaker (Najāshī: 184).

Kitāb

His notebook of *ḥadīth*, related by the author's nephew Sulaymān b. Samāʿa (Najāshī: 301). The following quotations from this author in Shīʿite works of *ḥadīth* are all through the same transmitter:

- *Kāfī 2: 164*
  5: 324
  6: 19, 33
- *ʿIqāb*: 300
- *Maʿānī*: 265
- *Tahdhīb* 3: 281

The following passages may be from the same author as well:[40]

- Ḥusayn b. Saʿīd, *Zuhd*: 103
- ʿAyyāshī 2: 23–4 (read *Baṣrī* for *Miṣrī*), 326

---

40. Another Shīʿite quotation from him appears in *Mīzān* 2: 352. For examples of his Sunnī transmissions, see Ibn ʿAdī: 1877–9 where fourteen such reports are quoted.

- Ibn Bābawayh, *Amālī*: 659–60
- Idem, *Faḍā'il al-ashhur*: 64–5

50: Akhū Udaym

Ayyūb b. al-Ḥurr al-Ju'fī, seller of clothing made in Herat, known among transmitters of *ḥadīth* as the Brother of Udaym. He was a Kūfan client and a transmitter from Ja'far al-Ṣādiq.

Barqī: 84; *Mashyakha*: 518; Najāshī: 103; *Fihrist*: 16–17; *Rijāl*: 166, 331

Barqī and Najāshī identify him as a Ju'fī. Najāshī specifies that he was a client of this tribe. Ṭūsī, however, describes him as a client of Ṭarīf (*Rijāl*: 331). The latter may possibly refer to a specific person named Ṭarīf from the tribe of Ju'fī and not to the Khazrajī clan of that name. In *isnād*s, Ayyūb is usually identified as *Akhū Udaym* (e.g. Barqī: 151, 160; Ṣaffār: 523; *Kāfī* 2: 520, 4: 303, 5: 78; also in Najāshī and *Mashyakha*) and *Bayyā' al-Harawī* (*Maḥāsin*: 26, 276; *Kāfī* 5: 78 [where the epithet may refer to either Ayyūb or his brother Udaym, as it reads *'an Ayyūb akhī Udaym Bayyā' al-Harawī*]), that is, seller of clothing made in Herat (see Zabīdī 10: 410). For his brother, Udaym b. al-Ḥurr, see below, no. 207.

Kitāb

His notebook of *ḥadīth*, related by Aḥmad b. Muḥammad b. Khālid al-Barqī (Najāshī: 103; *Fihrist*: 16–17), who quoted it from the author through intermediaries (see *Mashyakha*: 518). Quotations from this author in later Shī'ite works of *ḥadīth*, mainly through the same transmitter, include the following examples:

- Ḥusayn b. Sa'īd, *Zuhd*: 85 (also Ṣaffār: 523)
- *Maḥāsin*: 26, 146, 149, 151, 154, 160, 199, 201, 219 (whence *Kāfī* 2: 215), 220–21 (also 'Ayyāshī 1: 9), 234, 285 (whence *Kāfī* 2: 38), 392, 395, 405, 483 (whence *Kāfī* 6: 328)
- Ṣaffār: 30, 204, 205 (repeated at 206), 479 (also 'Ayyāshī 2: 15), 523
- 'Ayyāshī 1: 15, 169, 256
- *Kāfī* 1: 69, 185, 213, 269, 286–8
  2: 38, 179–80, 215–16, 310, 406, 519 (repeated at 520)
  3: 213, 255
  4: 303, 306, 310 (also *Ma'ānī*: 242), 407, 427
  5: 78, 120

6: 328, 490
7: 17, 125
- Kashshī: 243–4
- *'Ilal* 2: 60
- Ṭūsī, *Amālī*: 248 (repeated at 633), 670, 694
- *Tahdhīb* 1: 350
5: 168
6: 300
7: 357
8: 153
9: 229

51: Burayd al-'Ijlī

Abū 'l-Qāsim Burayd b. Mu'āwiya al-'Ijlī, a leading scholar in the Imāmite community of Kūfa in the first half of the second century. He was a disciple of, and transmitter from, Muḥammad al-Bāqir and Ja'far al-Ṣādiq, and was also known to Sunnī transmitters of *ḥadīth*. He died in 150.

Barqī: 57, 65; Kashshī: 10, 135, 137, 138, 148, 169, 170, 185, 238, 240; Najāshī: 112; *Rijāl*: 128, 171; Dāraquṭnī, *Mu'talif*: 172; Ibn Mākūlā 1: 227–8; Khaṭīb, *Talkhīṣ* 1: 509–10; *Lisān* 2: 18.

Kashshī's account of this scholar contains some specific details. He was a leader of the Imāmite community of Kūfa (p. 169), one of the most eminent disciples of, and transmitters from, Muḥammad al-Bāqir (pp. 10, 137, 170), and one of the four most favored by Ja'far al-Ṣādiq (pp. 135, 185, 238). The Extremist, esoteric Shī'ites at the time, represented by Abū 'l-Khaṭṭāb and his followers, disliked these four, who were looked upon by the Imāmite community of Kūfa as the true representatives of the Imām, a position that the Extremists tried to claim for themselves (p. 138). Burayd agreed with Zurāra b. A'yan (d. 148–149) on the theological question of *istiṭā'a* (pp. 148, 240).

Kitāb

His notebook of *ḥadīth*, related by 'Alī b. 'Uqba b. Khālid al-Asadī (Najāshī: 112)[41] and, as attested by the volume of his citations from this

41. For examples of his transmission from our author, see *Kāfī* 5: 327, 7: 12, 57, 8: 79–80; *Tahdhīb* 7: 399.

author (as demonstrated in Burūjirdī, *Tajrīd asānīd al-Kāfī* 1: 265–6), by ʿUmar b. Udhayna. There are close to four hundred quotations from this author in Shīʿite works of *ḥadīth*, listed in Khuʾī 3: 503–10 and *Fahāris* 8: 210–11, overwhelmingly through the latter transmitter.

52: Ibn Farqad

Dāwūd b. Abī Yazīd Farqad, the perfumer, a Kūfan client of the descendants of Abū al-Sammāl al-Asadī (no. 101 below) and a transmitter from Jaʿfar al-Ṣādiq and Mūsā al-Kāẓim.

Barqī: 88, 115; Kashshī: 345–6; Najāshī: 158–9; *Fihrist*: 68; *Rijāl*: 201, 336.

Kitāb

His notebook of *ḥadīth*, related by a large number of Shīʿite transmitters (Najāshī: 158, 159; *Fihrist*: 68; *Rijāl*: 336). Quotations from this author, many through those specified in the aforementioned works as transmitters of this notebook, abound in Shīʿite works of *ḥadīth*, including some two hundred listed in Khuʾī 7: 92–4, 117–18, 398–9, 404–8 and *Fahāris* 8: 514, 516.

53: Ibn al-Ḥuṣayn

Dāwūd b. al-Ḥuṣayn, a Kūfan client of the Banū Asad and a transmitter from Jaʿfar al-Ṣādiq and Mūsā al-Kāẓim. He joined the Wāqifites after the death of the latter.

Najāshī: 159–60; *Fihrist*: 68; *Rijāl*: 202, 336. See also *Mashyakha*: 466.

Kitāb

His notebook of *ḥadīth*, related by a number of Shīʿite transmitters including ʿAbbās b. ʿĀmir al-Qaṣabānī (Najāshī: 160; *Fihrist*: 68). A fair number of quotations from this author are recorded in Shīʿite works of *ḥadīth*, predominantly through the same transmitter, as in the following examples:

- *Kāfī* 4: 83
  5: 191
  6: 45 (also *Faqīh* 3: 304–5), 400
- *'Ilal* 2: 16
- *Tahdhīb* 3: 56–7 (repeated at 281)
  4: 328
  5: 419
  7: 318
  8: 147–8
  9: 106, 157 (two reports), 160, 193, 397

54: Ibn Sirḥān

Dāwūd b. Sirḥān, the perfumer, a Kūfan client and transmitter from Ja'far al-Ṣādiq.

Barqī: 88; Najāshī: 159; *Fibrist*: 68–9; *Rijāl*: 202. See also Kashshī: 368–9.
For his profession as a perfumer, see *Faqīh* 3: 226–7 (also *Tahdhīb* 7: 139).

Kitāb

His notebook of *ḥadīth*, related from him by a large number of Shī'ite transmitters including Aḥmad b. Muḥammad b. Abī Naṣr al-Bazanṭī (d. 221), Muḥammad b. Abī Ḥamza,[42] and 'Abd al-Raḥmān b. Abī Najrān[43] (Abū Ghālib: 159, 164; Najāshī: 159; *Fihrist*: 69; also *Mashyakha*: 468). Abū Ghālib: 153, 164 had a copy of the notebook read with 'Abd al-Raḥmān b. Abī Najrān in Baghdad in 227. Abū Ghālib read the book with his teacher, who related it through an intermediary from Ibn Abī Najrān in 299, and made a copy for himself from it in 348 on paper (implying that the old copy was on parchment). The overwhelming majority of close to one hundred surviving quotations from Dāwūd b. Sirḥān are on the

42. For an example of his transmission from this author, see Furāt: 426.
43. His transmission from our author is attested in Ṣaffār: 169–70 [read *wa Muḥammad b. Sinān*]; *Tahdhīb* 1: 378.

authority of the first said transmitter of this notebook, Aḥmad b. Muḥammad b. Abī Naṣr al-Bazanṭī, as in the following examples:

- Aḥmad b. Muḥammad b. ʿĪsā: 77 (also *Kāfī* 5: 407), 109 (also *Kāfī* 5: 426), 132 (also *Kāfī* 5: 354)
- *Kāfī* 2: 14, 250, 375
  3: 158
  4: 101, 176, 178, 218, 368
  5: 265, 384 (also *Tahdhīb* 7: 364 with an addition), 393, 437, 471
  6: 90, 167, 475 (two reports)
  7: 350, 392
- *Faqīh* 1: 422
  3: 93, 97, 99, 226–7
  4: 111
- Ibn Bābawayh, *Amālī*: 480
- *Khiṣāl*: 252
- *Tahdhīb* 1: 185
  2: 285
  6: 195, 212, 276, 389
  7: 424

55: Abū Mālik al-Ḥaḍramī

Abū Mālik Ḍaḥḥāk al-Ḥaḍramī, a Kūfan Arab and a transmitter from Mūsā al-Kāẓim. He was a *mutakallim* and an associate of the prominent Shīʿite theologian Hishām b. al-Ḥakam.

Ibn al-Nadīm: 226; Najāshī: 205; *Rijāl*: 227.

That this scholar was an associate of Hishām b. al-Ḥakam is attested in *Kāfī* 1: 410; Kashshī: 278. Early works of *kalām* regard him as a prominent Shīʿite theologian and quote some of his views (e.g. Abū ʾl-Ḥasan al-Ashʿarī 1: 111, 112, 118, 2: 178, 200; ʿAbd al-Qāhir al-Baghdādī, *Farq*: 52; idem, *Uṣūl al-dīn*: 260; Ibn Ḥazm, *Fiṣal* 4: 158; for details, see now van Ess 1: 348–9). Masʿūdī 4: 237 quotes his statement about love at the court of the vizier, Yaḥyā b. Khālid al-Barmakī (d. 190), though he misidentifies him as a Khārijite (see also ibid. 4: 28). For his anti-Extremist positions on the question of Imāmate, see *Kāfī* 1: 410; Kashshī: 247.

He was also a transmitter of *ḥadīth*. Examples of his transmissions can be found in Ṣaffār: 465; *Kāfī* 6: 206, 412, 8: 108; Kashshī: 247; Nuʿmānī: 268–9; Ibn Bābawayh, *Amālī*: 565; *Faqīh* 3: 384; *Tahdhīb* 2: 302; 3: 209, 8: 59.

Kitāb fī 'l-tawḥīd

(Najāshī: 205). Some of the theological opinions quoted from Abū Mālik in early works of *kalām* may have been taken from this work. They include his opinions about the will of God (Abū 'l-Ḥasan al-Ash'arī 1: 111, 2: 178), man's capacity to act (ibid. 1: 112), man's knowledge (ibid. 1: 118), and God's punishment of children ('Abd al-Qāhir al-Baghdādī, *Uṣūl:* 260).

56: Dharīḥ al-Muḥāribī

Abū 'l-Walīd Dharīḥ b. Muḥammad b. Yazīd al-Muḥāribī, a Kūfan Arab and a transmitter from Ja'far al-Ṣādiq.

Barqī: 109; Kashshī: 372–4; Najāshī: 163; *Fihrist*: 69; *Rijāl*: 203.

He is Dharīḥ b. Muḥammad b. Yazīd in Najāshī, but Dharīḥ b. Yazīd b. Muḥammad in *Mashyakha*: 510. A report in *Tahdhīb* 3: 72 confirms Najāshī's account.

He seems to have been well known in the Shī'ite community of Kūfa in his time (Kashshī: 373; *Faqīh* 3: 190), and to have had an esoteric tendency (see *Kāfī* 4: 549; Kashshī: 193, 373; *Ikhtiṣāṣ*: 71).

Kitāb / Aṣl

Dharīḥ's notebook of *ḥadīth*, related by a number of Shī'ite transmitters including Ja'far b. Bashīr al-Bajalī (d. 208), Ibn Abī 'Umayr and 'Abd Allāh b. al-Mughīra (Najāshī: 163; *Fihrist*: 69; also *Mashyakha*: 510). Other transmitters of the notebook included 'Abd Allāh b. Jabala (d. 219), as suggested by his comment at the end of a report in Kashshī: 373, and Ṣafwān b. Yaḥyā, as attested by the volume of his quotations from Dharīḥ.

A version of the notebook, related by Muḥammad b. al-Muthannā al-Ḥaḍramī, has survived and is published in the *Aṣl* of the latter transmitter in *al-Uṣūl al-sittat 'ashar*: 83–93, the entire contents of which is quoted from Dharīḥ, with the exception of only three reports at the end (pp. 92–3) and a sentence added to a report by Dharīḥ from someone else's transmission (p. 91). Most of the citations from Dharīḥ in other Shī'ite collections of *ḥadīth* are attested in this work. Quotations from Dharīḥ by other specified transmitters of this notebook include the following examples:

- Ṣaffār: 310 (also *Khiṣāl*: 649), 414, 484–5
- *Kāfī* 2: 100
  3: 167, 276, 440
  4: 268, 290, 398
  5: 72 (two versions of the same text), 88
  6: 50
  8: 375
- Kashshī: 40, 110, 372–3
- *Faqīh* 4: 168–9
- *'Ilal* 2: 85–6
- *Kamāl*: 230
- Mufīd, *Amālī*: 18–19
- Ṭūsī, *Talkhīṣ al-Shāfī* 3: 50
- *Tahdhīb* 1: 465
  2: 33, 246, 253–4, 257, 284
  3: 241, 309
  5: 403
  6: 198

57: Ibn Abī Manṣūr

Durust b. Abī Manṣūr Muḥammad al-Wāsiṭī, a transmitter from Ja'far al-Ṣādiq and Mūsā al-Kāẓim. He joined the Wāqifites after the death of the latter.

Barqī: 117, 118; Kashshī: 556; Najāshī: 162; *Fihrist*: 69; *Rijāl*: 203, 336.

An account in *Maḥāsin*: 551 and *Kāfī* 6: 355–6 indicates that Durust had affiliations with Mufaḍḍal al-Ju'fī, head of an Extremist tendency in the Shī'ite community of Kūfa in his time. The name *Durust* in that account, however, seems to be a corruption of someone else's name as attested in *Maḥāsin*: 552.

Kitāb

His notebook of *ḥadīth*, related by a number of transmitters including Ibn Abī 'Umayr and 'Alī b. al-Ḥasan al-Jarmī al-Ṭāṭarī who quoted the book through his uncle (Najāshī: 162; *Fihrist*: 69). A fragment of this notebook has survived and is published in *al-Uṣūl al-sittat 'ashar*: 158–69 as *Mā wujid min Kitāb Durust b. Abī Manṣūr*, quoted from the author by 'Ubayd Allāh

b. 'Abd Allāh al-Wāsiṭī al-Dihqān (Durust: 160), whose principal transmitter was Abū Ja'far Muḥammad b. 'Īsā b. 'Ubayd al-Yaqṭīnī (Najāshī: 231; *Fihrist*: 107). In Shī'ite works of *ḥadīth*, there are still many other quotations from Durust on the authority of Dihqān, mostly through Yaqṭīnī, that are not attested in the surviving fragment. More are quoted from Durust by others. Here is a list of citations from Durust by the said three transmitters:

(A) **YAQṬĪNĪ FROM DIHQĀN FROM DURUST:**

- *Maḥāsin*: 193, 373, 398 (also *Khiṣāl*: 93), 403, 447, 467, 472, 481, 488, 532, 539–40, 545, 547, 557 (two reports), 563, 564 (also Ibn Bābawayh, *Amālī*: 476; *'Ilal* 2: 220; *Khiṣāl*: 63–4), 590, 622 (also *Khiṣāl*: 92), 628, 631 (these passages also appear in *Kāfī* 6: 269, 306, 316, 319–20, 325, 331, 349, 352, 362, 373, 377, 538, 540)
- *Kāfī* 5: 162
6: 353, 366, 373, 478, 546
- *Khiṣāl* 9, 221, 264, 422–3, 481 (also *Thawāb*: 34)
- *Tahdhīb* 6: 362
7: 163[44]

(B) **DIHQĀN (QUOTED BY OTHERS) FROM DURUST:**

- Ja'far b. Muḥammad b. Sinān: 127 (two reports; read *'Ubayd Allāh* for *'Abd Allāh*)
- *Maḥāsin*: 631 (also *Kāfī* 6: 538)
- Ṣaffār: 447–9
- *Kāfī* 1: 23, 32 (also Ibn Bābawayh, *Amālī*: 340; *Ma'ānī*: 141; see also Ja'far b. Muḥammad b. Sinān: 127), 48
2: 487, 507, 623 (also *Thawāb*: 153)
3: 213
4: 28 (also *Khiṣāl*: 258; *Ma'ānī*: 141)
5: 74, 549 (also *'Ilal* 2: 239), 554
6: 353, 488, 495–6 (see *Khiṣāl*: 481; *Thawāb*: 34)
- Ibn Bābawayh, *Amālī*: 92, 636
- *'Ilal* 2: 217–18 (also *Ma'ānī*: 150–51)
- *Khiṣāl*: 103, 287
- *Ma'ānī*: 390 (two reports; read *'Ubayd Allāh* for *'Abd Allāh*)

---

44. Possibly also ibid. 1: 366 (also *'Ilal* 1: 266; *'Uyūn* 2: 82) and 7: 162 where Yaqṭīnī quotes Durust without an intermediary. It is not, however, certain that the missing link was Dihqān as in a very few cases Yaqṭīnī also quoted Durust through others (e.g. *'Ilal* 1: 71; *Ikhtiṣāṣ*: 22).

- *Tawḥīd*: 411–12 (presumably also 339, 343, 365 where 'Alī b. Ma'bad appears as if quoting Durust directly; he quotes Durust through Dihqān in Ṣaffār: 447; *Kāfī* 5: 549; *'Ilal* 2: 239; *Qiṣaṣ*: 138)
- *Thawāb*: 230 (also 159 where 'Alī b. Ma'bad quotes Durust directly)
- *Qiṣaṣ*: 138

(C) IBN ABĪ 'UMAYR FROM DURUST:

- *Maḥāsin*: 235 (also *Kamāl*: 665)
- *Kāfī* 2: 156, 308 (also *'Iqāb*: 263), 315 (also *Khiṣāl*: 25), 482
  6: 397
  7: 82, 120

(D) ṬĀṬARĪ FROM DURUST:

- *'Ilal* 1: 13
  2: 168
- *Tahdhīb* 5: 139, 298, 308, 337, 351, 358–9, 403

58: Faḍl al-Baqbāq

Abū 'l-'Abbās Faḍl b. 'Abd al-Malik al-Baqbāq, a Kūfan client and a transmitter from Ja'far al-Ṣādiq. He was a notable in the Shī'ite community of Kūfa and seems to have been close to the Imām.

Barqī: 91; Kashshī: 336–7; Najāshī: 308; *Rijāl*: 268.

On his close association with Ja'far al-Ṣādiq, see Kashshī: 336; Mufīd, *Ṣāghāniyya*: 72 (quoting Ḥusayn b. Sa'īd's *Kitāb al-nikāḥ*).

Kitāb

His notebook of *ḥadīth*, related by Dāwūd b. al-Ḥuṣayn (Barqī: 91; Najāshī: 308), who was a companion of Baqbāq (Najāshī: 159). Quotations from Baqbāq by the same transmitter include the following examples:

- *Kāfī* 2: 94
  4: 175, 176
  5: 376, 396, 479
  6: 476–7
  7: 140, 279

- Ibn al-Juḥām: 338
- *Faqīh* 3: 96 (also *Tahdhīb* 6: 209–10), 311 (also *Tahdhīb* 7: 157 with an addition), 451 (also *Tahdhīb* 7: 348)
- *Tahdhīb* 3: 164–5 (repeated at 226–7; see also *Faqīh* 1: 398), 233, 325
  9: 397
- Muḥaqqiq, *Mu'tabar* 2: 283 (quoting Bazanṭī's *Jāmi'*)

The main transmitter from Baqbāq is, however, the scholar Abān b. 'Uthmān al-Aḥmar, for whose many quotations from Baqbāq see the lists in Khu'ī 13: 464, 21: 401–3.

59: Ibn Abī Qurra

Abū Muḥammad Faḍl b. Abī Qurra al-Tamīmī al-Tiflīsī al-Sahandī (the latter referring to a region in Azerbaijan called Sahand), a Kūfan in origin who later moved to Armenia. He was a transmitter from Ja'far al-Ṣādiq.

Barqī: 91; Ibn al-Ghaḍā'irī: 84; Najāshī: 308; *Fihrist*: 125; *Rijāl*: 269. See also 'Alī b. Ibrāhīm 2: 372; *Mashyakha*: 518–19.

Kitāb

His notebook of *ḥadīth*, related by Sharīf b. Sābiq al-Tiflīsī (Najāshī: 308; *Fihrist*: 125; see also *Mashyakha*: 481, 518–19). Almost all quotations from this author in later works are through the same transmitter, including the following:

- *Maḥāsin* 107 (whence *Kāfī* 5: 553)
- *Kāfī* 1: 39
  2: 322, 373, 477, 524, 663 (also *Ma'ānī*: 164; also Bazanṭī, *Jāmi'*: 62–3 without naming the transmitter from Faḍl)
  4: 45
  5: 74 (two reports), 121, 149, 318–19
  6: 3–4, 49
- Nu'mānī: 211
- Ibn Bisṭām: 124
- Ibn Bābawayh, *Amālī*: 704

- *Faqīh* 3: 163
- *'Ilal* 1: 119
- Abū Ṭālib: 331
- Ṭūsī, *Amālī*: 46–7 (read *Faḍl b. Abī Qurra* for *Faḍl b. 'Abd al-Malik*; see also *Qiṣaṣ*: 188–9)
- Ibn 'Asākir 42: 242

A number of other instances can be added to the above where the name of Sharīf al-Tiflīsī does not currently appear as the transmitter from Faḍl:

- 'Ayyāshī 1: 283
  2: 154
- 'Alī b. Ibrāhīm 2: 372–3
- Khaṭīb, *Ta'rīkh* 3: 94 (also Ṣarīfīnī: 101)

60: Faḍl al-Kātib

Faḍl b. Yūnus al-Baghdādī al-Kātib, was a Kūfan client who resided in Baghdad and was a government official under Hārūn al-Rashīd. He joined the Wāqifites after the death of Mūsā al-Kāẓim.

Barqī: 122; Kashshī: 500; Najāshī: 309; *Fihrist*: 125; *Rijāl*: 342.

1. *Ḥadīth al-Faḍl b. Yūnus al-Kātib*

(Abū Ghālib: 175). This seems to be the account of a visit that Mūsā al-Kāẓim once paid this person (Kashshī: 500; a somewhat different version of this story is reported in *Maḥāsin*: 450–51; *Kharā'ij*: 368 offers a very different variant that misattributes the story to 'Alī al-Riḍā). Details of what Mūsā al-Kāẓim said or did during that visit are recorded by Faḍl in a report quoted in *Maḥāsin*: 425, 430, 431, 451, 559–60 (whence *Kāfī* 6: 291, 304, 377–8).

2. *Kitāb*

His notebook of *ḥadīth*, related by Ḥasan b. Maḥbūb and Ibn Abī 'Umayr (Najāshī: 309; *Fihrist*: 125 [read *Ibn Abī 'Umayr wa 'l-Ḥasan b. Maḥbūb*]).

Quotations from this author through the same two transmitters include the following examples:

- Ḥasan b. Maḥbūb: 84–5 (whence Mufīd, *Amālī*: 210–11; *Ikhtiṣāṣ*: 343)
- ʿAbd Allāh b. Jaʿfar: 312–14 (a fragment of three reports; in the *isnād* of the first, read *ʿan al-Faḍl b. Yūnus al-Kātib* as in *Tahdhīb* 1: 445; the second is also in *Kāfī* 3: 102; the third is also in *Faqīh* 2: 431 and partially in *Kāfī* 4: 266 [also 304 with a different *isnād*]; the fragment seems to have been taken from Ḥasan b. Maḥbūb's *Kitāb al-mashyakha*)
- ʿAyyāshī 2: 232 (without the name of the transmitter from Faḍl, as usual; read *Faḍl b. Yūnus* for *Faḍl b. Mūsā*)
- *Kāfī* 2: 579 (also 2: 73 with variations and through a different transmitter)
  4: 371 (read *Aḥmad b. Muḥammad ʿan Ḥasan b. Maḥbūb* as in *Tahdhīb* 5: 465 and as in a similar *isnād* in *Kāfī* 4: 304)
- Ibn Bābawayh, *Amālī*: 714–16 (also *ʿIlal* 2: 89–90 and *Tawḥīd*: 253–4 through other transmitters)
- *Faqīh* 3: 416
- *Tahdhīb* 9: 348

61: Ibn ʿIyāḍ

Abū ʿAlī Fuḍayl b. ʿIyāḍ b. Masʿūd al-Tamīmī al-Yarbūʿī al-Marwazī, a well known Sunnī ascetic of Kūfan origin. Born in Khurāsān in 105, he moved, later in life, to Kūfa and then to Mecca where he stayed until his death in 187. He transmitted *ḥadīth* from Jaʿfar al-Ṣādiq, among others.

Most biographical dictionaries have entries on this scholar. For a long list of many of these, see the editor's footnote to Dhahabī, *Taʾrīkh* 12 (years 181–190): 332–3. For his transmission from Jaʿfar al-Ṣādiq, see Mizzī 23: 282; Dhahabī, *Siyar* 8: 373, and their sources.

Nuskha ʿan Abī ʿAbd Allāh / Kitāb

A small register of this author's transmissions from Jaʿfar al-Ṣādiq, related by the Baṣran Sulaymān b. Dāwūd al-Minqarī (Najāshī: 310). Quotations by Fuḍayl b. ʿIyāḍ from Jaʿfar al-Ṣādiq, all recorded through the same transmitter, include the following:

- ʿAyyāshī 1: 360 (as attested in *Maʿānī*: 252–3; ʿAlī b. Ibrāhīm 1: 200–201), 370 (possibly)
- *Kāfī* 2: 307, 461
  4: 290 (also in ʿAyyāshī 2: 77)
  5: 9–10 (also *Khiṣāl*: 240; Ibn al-Rāzī, *Ghāyāt*: 190; cf. *Tahdhīb* 6: 124), 108
- *Faqīh* 2: 488 (another part of the report in ʿAyyāshī 2: 77 and *Kāfī* 4: 290; the full text in *Maʿānī*: 296)
- *ʿIlal* 2: 100
- *Maʿānī*: 245 (also Ibn Shuʿba: 371–2)

62: Fuḍayl al-Aʿwar

Abū Muḥammad Fuḍayl b. ʿUthmān al-Anbārī, the one eyed, the goldsmith, a Kūfan client of the Banū Murād and a transmitter from Muḥammad al-Bāqir and Jaʿfar al-Ṣādiq.

Barqī: 52, 91; Najāshī: 308 (as *Faḍl* b. ʿUthmān); *Fibrist*: 126; *Rijāl*: 143, 268, 269.

Kitāb

His notebook of *ḥadīth*, related by a number of transmitters, including Ibn Abī ʿUmayr and Ṣafwān b. Yaḥyā (Najāshī: 308; *Fihrist*: 126 [cf. Najāshī: 276]; also *Mashyakha*: 436). Examples of quotations from Fuḍayl by the same two transmitters include the following:

- *Maḥāsin*: 394
- Ṣaffār: 259 (repeated at 510; also Kashshī: 235–6)
- *Kāfī* 1: 115 (also *Tawḥīd*: 314), 397
  2: 62
  3: 36
- *Tawḥīd*: 457
- *Tahdhīb* 1: 58 (repeated at 79–80)

Most quotations from Fuḍayl are, however, through other transmitters. See the lists in Khuʾī 13: 308–10, 325, 330–31, 342, 470–71; *Fahāris* 9: 546, 547.

63: Fuḍayl al-Nahdī

Abū 'l-Qāsim Fuḍayl b. Yasār, a Kūfan client of the Banū Nahd who moved to Baṣra. A transmitter from Muḥammad al-Bāqir and Ja'far al-Ṣādiq and a distinguished member of the Shī'ite community of his time, he died during the lifetime of Ja'far al-Ṣādiq, thus in or before 148.

Bukhārī, *Kabīr* 7: 122; Barqī: 52, 63 (read *Banī Nahd* for *Banī Nahīk*); Kashshī: 212–14, 311; Ibn Abī Ḥātim 7: 76; Ibn Ḥibbān, *Thiqāt* 7: 315; *Mashyakha*: 441; Najāshī: 309–10; *Rijāl*: 143, 269. See also *Tahdhīb* 3: 27.

Najāshī: 309 mentions *Abū Miswar* as an alternative for the *kunya* of this transmitter. Ibn Samka: 31 has him as *Abū Ja'far* al-A'raj al-Qāri'. Kashshī: 238 counts him as one of the six most learned among the older generation of the disciples of Muḥammad al-Bāqir and Ja'far al-Ṣādiq. He was also known to Sunnī scholars of *ḥadīth* as a Shī'ite (*Lisān* 5: 482) transmitter from Muḥammad al-Bāqir. Two of his sons, 'Alā' and Qāsim, were also among the transmitters of *ḥadīth* (Najāshī: 298, 313, 362; *Rijāl*: 247, 272, 366), as was his son-in-law, 'Abd al-Raḥmān b. Abī 'Abd Allāh al-Baṣrī (Kashshī: 311; *Rijāl*: 236).

Kitāb

His notebook of *ḥadīth*, related by a number of transmitters including Ḥammād b. 'Īsā al-Juhanī (d. 209) (Najāshī: 309–10), who apparently quoted it from the author through the transmitter Rib'ī b. 'Abd Allāh al-Hudhalī who was a close associate of Fuḍayl (Najāshī: 167). The following quotations from this author in Shī'ite works of *ḥadīth* are through Ḥammād quoting Rib'ī:

- Muḥammad b. 'Alī b. Maḥbūb: 110
- Ṣaffār: 511
- 'Ayyāshī 2: 217
- *Kāfī* 2: 89, 281
- Ibn Qūlawayh: 171, 172 (a variant also at 488)
- *Tawḥīd*: 127–8, 327
- *Ghayba*: 195–6

In Qāḍī Nu'mān, *Īḍāḥ*: 54a (quoting Abū Dharr Aḥmad b. al-Ḥusayn b. Asbāṭ's *Kitāb al-ṣalāt*), Ḥammād quotes from Fuḍayl without an intermediary, though there may have been one whose name is missing in the text. There are also a good number of other quotations from Fuḍayl that Ḥammād quotes through Ḥarīz b. 'Abd Allāh al-Sijistānī or, less frequently, through Ibrāhīm b. 'Umar al-Yamānī, as in the following examples:

- *Maḥāsin*: 262 (also *Kāfī* 2: 125)
- *Kāfī* 1: 222
  2: 151, 269
  3: 280, 294–5, 363, 418, 453, 509 (partially also at 497–8)
  4: 153
  5: 279
- Kashshī: 16, 53–4
- *Faqīh* (see *Mashyakha*: 425) 3: 477
  4: 284, 308
- *Tahdhīb* 2: 332, 379
  3: 69–70
  4: 73 (two reports)

The overwhelming majority of the close to three hundred quotations from Fuḍayl, listed in Khu'ī 13: 338–41, 471–7 and *Fahāris* 9: 547–8, are, however, through other transmitters.[45]

64: Ghālib al-Minqarī

Ghālib b. 'Uthmān, an oculist and Kūfan client of the Banū Minqar, a clan of Tamīm.[46] A late second century transmitter who related *ḥadīth* from

45. His son-in-law, 'Abd al-Raḥmān b. Abī 'Abd Allāh, quoted some 700 reports from him (Ibn Dāwūd: 222). A notebook by a student of Fuḍayl, Abū Ismā'īl al-Baṣrī, who seems to have transmitted exclusively from this scholar, is mentioned in *Fihrist*: 188. The notebook was related from Abū Ismā'īl by Ibn Abī 'Umayr as also attested in *Kāfī* 2: 104, 167, 655 (read *'an Abī Ismā'īl* in the last two), 5: 148, 6: 271; Kashshī: 214 (read *'an Abī Ismā'īl*); *Thawāb*: 48 (read *'an Abī Ismā'īl*).
46. According to Najāshī: 305, this person might have actually been a client of the Kūfan family of Āl A'yan, who were in turn clients of the Banū Shaybān, not Tamīm. There was a Ghālib b. 'Uthmān al-Hamdānī al-Mish'ārī (d. 166 at the age of 78), a Kūfan Zaydī poet (see *Maqātil*: 228–9 [also Ṭabarī 7: 545–6], 304–5, 384–5, 385–6), and a transmitter from Ja'far al-Ṣādiq (Najāshī: 305; *Rijāl*: 267; for examples of his transmissions, see Aḥmad b. 'Īsā 4: 313 [also Muḥammad b. Sulaymān 1: 460]; Ibn al-Juhām: 262–3; Furāt: 318 [read *Hamdānī* for *Nahdī*]; Ibn 'Asākir 42: 487; Ibn Ṭāwūs, *Iqbāl* 3: 86; possibly also Kashshī: 5 from *Ghiyāth* al-Hamdānī, possibly a corruption of *Ghālib*), and probably author of the notebook quoted by Ibn Ṭāwūs, *Iqbāl* 3: 86 through Abū 'l-'Abbās Aḥmad b. Naṣr b. Sa'd's *Kitāb al-rijāl*. The *nisba* of *Mish'ārī* for this person refers to a clan of the tribe of Hamdān (Zabīdī 3: 305). The *nisba* of *Minqarī* for Ghālib b. 'Uthmān, the oculist, may thus represent a corruption of *Mish'ārī* by someone who confused the two persons.

the disciples of Ja'far al-Ṣādiq and Mūsā al-Kāẓim, he reportedly joined the Wāqifites after the death of the latter.

Najāshī: 305; *Fihrist*: 123–4; *Rijāl*: 267.

Kitāb

His notebook of *ḥadīth*, related by Ḥasan b. 'Alī b. Faḍḍāl (Najāshī: 305; *Fihrist*: 123–4). The following quotations from this author are recorded in Shī'ite works of *ḥadīth* on the authority of the same transmitter:

- *Maḥāsin*: 39 (whence *Kāfī* 2: 498), 562, 576 (read *Ghālib b. 'Uthmān* for *Ghālib b. 'Īsā*)
- *Kāfī* 2: 110, 147
  3: 21, 115, 236–7, 242
  5: 121–2, 512
  6: 468
  8: 79–80
- Kashshī: 364
- Ibn Bābawayh, *Amālī*: 408 (also *Faqīh* 4: 400; *Mawā'iẓ*: 115; *Thawāb*: 192)
- *'Ilal* 2: 105
- *Tahdhīb* 1: 13, 449
  2: 319
  3: 292

65: Ghiyāth b. Ibrāhīm

Abū Muḥammad Ghiyāth b. Ibrāhīm al-Tamīmī al-Dārimī al-Asbadhī, a Baṣran Butrī Zaydī who lived in Kūfa. He was a transmitter from Ja'far al-Ṣādiq.

Najāshī: 305; *Fihrist*: 123; *Rijāl*: 142, 268, 435.

He is identified in Najāshī and *Rijāl*: 268 as *Usayyidī*, with reference to a clan of Tamīm. Muḥammad Taqī al-Tustarī 8: 354 suggests that *Usayyidī* is a corruption of *Asbadī*, referring to another clan of Tamīm. He argues with a report in *Faqīh* 3: 146 (also in the *isnād* of another report in *Thawāb*: 219) where this transmitter appears as *Dārimī* (also *Tahdhīb* 8: 228 [read *Dārimī* for *Dārī* as in

Istibṣār 4: 6; see also *Tahdhib* 1: 431 where this transmitter is identified as *Rizāmī*, most likely also a corruption of *Dārimī*]). *Asbadīs* were descendants of Zayd b. 'Abd Allāh b. Dārim, as noted by Sam'ānī 1: 195–6, and were as such Dārimīs but not *Usayyidīs*, who belonged to a different branch of Tamīm (ibid. 1: 254).

There is an Abū 'Abd al-Raḥmān Ghiyāth b. Ibrāhīm al-Nakha'ī al-Kūfī, a transmitter of the same period with certain Shī'ite sympathies (see, for instance, 'Āṣimī 2: 264 [also Ibn 'Asākir 42: 223]; Khaṭīb, *Ta'rīkh* 12: 323; possibly also Muḥammad b. Sulaymān 2: 231 [also Ibn 'Asākir 13: 116]) who is mentioned in most Sunnī biographical dictionaries of the transmitters of *ḥadīth* (many of which are listed in the editors' footnotes to Dhahabī, *Ta'rīkh* 10 [years 161–170]: 388–90 and *Lisān* 5: 421–2). It is not clear whether the two are the same, so that *nakha'ī* might be a misidentification or a corruption of *tamīmī*, or, alternatively, if some of the transmissions of the one are not misattributed to the other because of a common name.

For his transmission from other 'Alīds, see, for instance, Abū 'Abd Allāh al-Shajarī, *Adhān*: 84.

1. *Jāmi'/ Kitāb / Kitāb mubawwab fī 'l-ḥalāl wa 'l-ḥarām*

A book on the licit and illicit organized in chapters (Najāshī: 305), related by a number of transmitters including Ismā'īl b. Abān b. Isḥāq al-Azdī al-Warrāq (d. 216) and Muḥammad b. Yaḥyā al-Khazzāz (Abū Ghālib: 165; Najāshī: 305; *Fihrist*: 123, 154; see also *Mashyakha*: 490). Qāḍī Nu'mān calls it *Jāmi'* and quotes from it through Ismā'īl (b. Abān) in his own *Īḍāḥ*: 64b. Ibn Shahrāshūb (*Ma'ālim*: 89) mentions it as *Jāmi'a*, a corruption of *Jāmi'* or vice versa. Ibn Ṭāwūs knows it as *Kitāb* and quotes from it in his *Falāḥ*: 166 (see further Kohlberg: 222–3).

The Zaydī Muḥammad b. Manṣūr al-Murādī received the work through Muḥammad b. Rāshid from Ismā'īl b. Abān from the author.[47] He quotes the work extensively through this chain of transmission as in the following examples:

Aḥmad b. 'Īsā 1: 17, 74, 79, 80, 237
2: 267, 308 (whence Abū Ṭālib: 264)
3: 7, 32 (two reports), 28, 33 (three reports), 35, 38, 42 (two reports), 46, 49, 79 (two reports), 90 (where the name of Ghiyāth is missing), 95, 97 (two reports), 98, 106, 112, 116, 117 (two reports), 139, 145, 146, 151, 175
4: 212, 217–18, 226 (three reports), 227, 228, 239, 240, 495 (three reports)

---

47. See also Abū 'Abd Allāh al-Shajarī, *Adhān*: 72, 84.

The Imāmites too quote Ghiyāth at times through Ismāʿīl b. Abān as in *Faqīh* 3: 511; *Thawāb*: 237; Ibn Shādhān: 143–4 (also Qāḍī Nuʿmān, *Īḍāḥ*: 26a, 64b, 71a, 83a, 88b [two reports], 96a [without the name of the transmitter from him in this last case]). The overwhelming majority of the many quotations from Ghiyāth in the Imāmite collections of *ḥadīth* are, however, through the other main transmitter of his book, Muḥammad b. Yaḥyā al-Khazzāz, as in the following examples:

- Muḥammad b. ʿAlī b. Maḥbūb: 98, 105
- *Maḥāsin*: 113 (also *ʿIqāb*: 317), 115, 398 (also *Kāfī* 6: 273), 434 (two reports, both also in *Kāfī* 6: 293), 491 (also *Tahdhīb* 4: 199), 636 (also *Kāfī* 6: 542)
- *Kāfī* 2: 315, 647, 648–9
  3: 332, 538 (two reports)
  4: 9, 13, 69 (from Muḥammad b. Yaḥyā *al-Khathʿamī* [also in *Maʿānī*: 315] who seems to be the same as Muḥammad b. Yaḥyā al-Khazzāz who quotes this passage in *Faqīh* 2: 172–3 [see *Mashyakha*: 490]; see further Muḥammad Taqī al-Tustarī 9: 650), 112, 244, 363–4, 408, 434, 503
  5: 49, 59, 103, 164, 177, 184, 191, 242–3, 278, 381, 488, 535, 536–7, 560 (two reports)
  6: 44, 47, 200 (from Muḥammad b. Yaḥyā *al-Khathʿamī*; the passage is quoted from Muḥammad b. Yaḥyā *al-Khazzāz* in *Tahdhīb* 6: 398), 213–14, 229–30, 245, 255–6, 258, 273, 293 (two reports, one also in Ibn Bābawayh, *Amālī*: 374; *Thawāb*: 219), 296 (repeated at 318), 385, 464, 542
  7: 230–31, 338, 454
- Ibn Bābawayh, *Amālī*: 432 (also *Maʿānī*: 185–6)
- *Faqīh* 3: 70–71 (two reports), 97–8, 99, 150, 264, 265, 487
  4: 143
- *ʿIlal* 2: 171 (also *Tahdhīb* 9: 19), 184, 231 (also *Tahdhīb* 10: 40)
- *Maʿānī*: 366
- Mufīd, *Amālī*: 66, 211–12
- *Tahdhīb* 1: 162, 266, 295, 353, 464
  2: 326 (repeated at 357), 371
  3: 235, 256, 269
  4: 214 (read *Muḥammad b. Yaḥyā* for *Muḥammad b. ʿAlī*), 275
  5: 442
  6: 195 (repeated at 212), 196, 256–7, 299
  7: 76, 221, 238, 273, 410–11, 426, 432–3, 435
  8: 21, 228, 319 (where the name of Khazzāz is missing)

10: 80, 136 (read *Aḥmad ʿan Muḥammad b. Yaḥyā* as in the Tehran, 1316 lithograph edition of this work), 143, 150, 224 (partially also at 7: 221), 261 (two reports), 293

2. *Maqtal Amīr al-Muʾminīn*

A work on the killing of ʿAlī, related from the author by Zayd b. ʿUmar (*Fihrist*: 123). Khaṭīb (*Mūḍiḥ* 1: 276; *Taʾrīkh* 1: 153–4) quotes two passages from a text that the transmitter Ajlaḥ b. ʿAbd Allāh al-Kindī (d. 145) compiled on the basis of the information he received from Jaʿfar al-Ṣādiq, Zayd b. ʿAlī, ʿAbd Allāh b. al-Ḥasan and his son Muḥammad, in which he listed the companions of the Prophet who participated in the wars of ʿAlī on his side (*tasmiyat man shahida maʿ ʿAlī min aṣḥāb Rasūl Allāh*). Khaṭīb's chain of transmission to that text goes through the scholar Ibn ʿUqda, to Jaʿfar b. Muḥammad al-Khashshāb, to his father, to Zaydān b. ʿUmar, to Ghiyāth b. Ibrāhīm, to Ajlaḥ. Ṭūsī's chain of transmission to Ghiyāth's *Maqtal* also goes from Ibn ʿUqda to Zayd (sic) b. ʿUmar but through different intermediaries (see *Fihrist*: 123). The text mentioned by Khaṭīb may have been a part of Ghiyāth's *Maqtal*, or, alternatively, this latter could be the same text as mentioned by Khaṭīb, but wrongly categorized and misattributed by Ṭūsī or his source.

There are a number of quotations from Ghiyāth on the virtues of ʿAlī that may have belonged to this work should it ever have existed with a larger frame of reference than that described by the Khaṭīb. Examples are as follows:

- Ibn al-Juḥām: 337
- Ibn Bābawayh, *Amālī*: 341–2 (also *Kamāl*: 241)
- *Kamāl*: 240 (also *Maʿānī*: 90–91; *ʿUyūn*: 57 [updated])
- Ibn Shādhān: 143–4
- ʿĀṣimī 2: 264 (possibly; also Ibn ʿAsākir 42: 223)
- Khaṭīb, *Taʾrīkh* 12: 323 (possibly)

66: Ibn al-Bakhtarī

Ḥafṣ b. al-Bakhtarī, a Kūfan client who lived in Baghdad and was a transmitter from Jaʿfar al-Ṣādiq and Mūsā al-Kāẓim.

Barqī: 96; Najāshī: 134; *Fihrist*: 61; *Rijāl*: 190, 335.

According to Najāshī, he was accused of lacking religiosity by the members of the influential Kūfan Shī'ite family of the Āl A'yan who alleged that he was a chess player, a charge that Najāshī suggests was motivated by a personal grudge.

Kitāb / Aṣl

His notebook of *ḥadīth*, related by a number of transmitters including Ibn Abī 'Umayr (Najāshī: 134; *Fihrist*: 61). There are over two hundred quotations from this author in Shī'ite works of *ḥadīth*, listed in Khu'ī 6: 132–4, 360–66 and *Fahāris* 8: 202, 443, almost all through the same transmitter. The notebook was available to Ibn Ṭāwūs who quotes from it in his *Ijāzāt*: 44 (see further Kohlberg: 223).

67: Ḥafṣ al-Qāḍī

Abū 'Umar Ḥafṣ b. Ghiyāth b. Ṭalq b. Mu'āwiya al-Nakha'ī, a Kūfan jurist and *ḥadīth* transmitter who was appointed by Hārūn al-Rashīd as the judge of the eastern half of Baghdad in 177, a position he held for two years. He was then appointed as the judge of Kūfa and served in that position for 13 years. He died in 194 at the age of 77.

For long lists of biographical sources which have entries on this judge, see the editors' footnotes to Mizzī 7: 56 and Dhahabī, *Ta'rīkh* 13 (years 191–200): 152–3. The most informative account of him is that of Khaṭīb, *Ta'rīkh* 8: 188–200.

Notwithstanding his anti-Imāmite rhetoric, some of which are recorded in the sources, he had certain pro-'Alī sympathies as attested by his transmissions on the virtues of 'Ali[48] and was a transmitter of *ḥadīth* from Ja'far al-Ṣādiq and a number of Imāmite scholars such as Abū Ḥamza al-Thumālī (See Mizzī 7: 57). He was also a main source of material from 'Alī on legal matters in Sunnī tradition.[49]

Ḥafṣ was born in 117 (Mizzī 7: 69). Ṭūsī's assumption that he met Muḥammad al-Bāqir (*Rijāl*: 133) is therefore wrong. Ḥafṣ, in fact, always quotes Muḥammad al-Bāqir through intermediaries as in Ibn Abī Shayba 1: 126; Dārimī

48. Fasawī 3: 192 (whence Ibn 'Asākir 42: 298); Ibn Abī 'l-Dunyā, *Ṣamt*: 554–5; Ibn al-Juḥām: 328; Khazzāz: 110–111; *Manāqib* 3: 326 (on Fāṭima al-Zahrā').

49. 'Abd al-Razzāq 1: 340; Shāfi'ī 7: 165 (also Ibn Abī Shayba 7: 263); Ibn Abī Shayba 1: 15, 101, 102, 110, 127, 180, 181 (also Abū Dāwūd 1: 42), 194, 3: 300, 303, 307, 4: 370, 392, 5: 175, 6: 420 (repeated in 12: 333; a variant also in Bayhaqī 9: 141), 7: 263, 10: 48, 82, 134, 138 (repeated in 12: 274), *al-juz' al-mafqūd*: 94; Bukhārī, *Kabīr* 1: 414; Idem, *Ṣaḥīḥ* 4: 331; Tirmidhī 1: 191; 'Abd Allāh b. Aḥmad: 219; Aḥmad b. 'Īsā 4: 228; Ṭabarānī, *Ṣaghīr* 1: 143–4; Dāraquṭnī 1: 89, 286 (also Bayhaqī 1: 87 and 2: 31 respectively).

1: 71 (also Ibn Abī 'l-Dunyā, *Ṣamt*: 296); *Kāfī* 3: 114 (also *Ḥilya* 3: 134). In addition to Ja'far al-Ṣādiq, he appears as a transmitter from Mūsā al-Kāẓim in *Kāfī* 2: 606; *Ma'ānī*: 343; *Tahdhīb* 6: 377, but the first and the last are attributed to Ja'far al-Ṣādiq in *Thawāb*: 157 and *Kāfī* 8: 144, respectively.

Yaḥyā b. Ma'īn reports that Ḥafṣ quoted some three to four thousand *ḥadīths* in Kūfa and Baghdad from memory, without using any written record (Khaṭīb, *Ta'rīkh* 8: 195). However, he recorded what he had heard from his teachers in writing as there are numerous references in biographical narratives to his *kitābs* (see, for instance, Ibn Abī Ḥātim 3: 186; Mizzī 7: 61, 62). His son, 'Umar (d. 222), himself a *ḥadīth* transmitter, presented to a colleague the notebook that his father made of his own transmissions from A'mash (Khaṭīb, *Ta'rīkh* 8: 197). He also had a notebook of reports he had heard from Ja'far al-Ṣādiq. It was this material that made Shī'ite scholars interested in this transmitter.

Kitābuh 'an Ja'far b. Muḥammad

A notebook of some one hundred and seventy reports that Ḥafṣ had heard from Ja'far al-Ṣādiq, related from the author by a number of transmitters including his above-mentioned son, 'Umar (Najāshī: 135). Sunnī sources too quote some of Ḥafṣ' transmissions through the same son (e.g. Bukhārī, *Adab*: 216; idem, *Ṣaḥīḥ* 4: 331; Muslim: 892–3; Fasawī 3: 192; Ibn Abī 'l-Dunyā, *Ṣifat al-nār*: 56). Ṭūsī (*Fihrist*: 61; see also *Rijāl*: 425), who received the notebook through a common link with Najāshī from Ḥafṣ's son, refers to the son as *Muḥammad* (also *Tahdhīb* 1: 302). This seems to be an error on his part as no son of that name related from Ḥafṣ in Sunnī tradition either (see Mizzī 7: 59). Ibn Bābawayh quotes Ḥafṣ in *Faqīh* simultaneously through three different chains of transmission, indicating transmission from a written record; two of these chains go back to the transmitter Sulaymān b. Dāwūd al-Minqarī (*Mashyakha*: 473). The overwhelming majority of quotations from Ḥafṣ in Shī'ite collections of *ḥadīth* are through this latter transmitter.

Quotations from Ja'far al-Ṣādiq recorded in Sunnī and Shī'ite works on the authority of Ḥafṣ, all obviously deriving from the notebook in question, include the following:

(A) **SUNNĪ WORKS:**

- 'Abd al-Razzāq 1: 340 (also Ibn Abī Shayba 1: 101–2)
- Ibn Sa'd, *Ḥusayn*: 35

- Ibn Abī Shayba 1: 64 (whence Ibn Māja: 191), 110, 127
  2: 187, 455
  5: 379, 380, 396
  6: 237, 570
  7: 137
  12: 424 (also *Kāfī* 5: 12)
  Al-juz' al-mafqūd: 305, 345
- Bukhārī, *Kabīr* 1: 414
  2: 286
- Muslim: 886–93 (also Abū Dāwūd 2: 187)
- Ibn Shabba 1: 171 (also *Kāfī* 5: 278)
- Abū Dāwūd 3: 195 (also Tirmidhī 2: 162 and others)
- Ibn Abī Dāwūd: 178
- Ṭabarānī, *Kabīr* 23: 351
- Sulamī, *Ādāb*: 73 (quoting Ibn Shabba)
- Abū Nu'aym, *Ma'rifa*: 1970
- Bayhaqī 9: 304
- Ibn Ḥazm 7: 61 (quoting Ibn Abī Shayba)
- *Firdaws* (Uzbak: 667 [also Ibn al-Jazarī, *Asnā*: 93–4], 699 [read *Ḥafṣ b. Ghiyāth* for *Ja'far b. Ghiyāth*])
- Ibn 'Asākir 42: 553
- Ibn al-Jazarī, *Asnā*: 108–9

(B) **ZAYDĪ WORKS:**

- Aḥmad b. 'Īsā 2: 267, 372, 434
  3: 38 (two reports), 168
  4: 204, 205, 228
- Muḥammad b. Sulaymān 2: 80

(C) **IMĀMITE WORKS:**

- *Maḥāsin*: 47, 328 (also *'Ilal* 2: 127), 439–40
- 'Ayyāshī 1: 48 (also 324–5, 385, 2: 85)
  2: 179–80
- Kāfī 1: 35 (also Ṭūsī, *Amālī*: 47, 167), 46 (two reports), 47 (two reports)
  2: 77, 88–9, 128, 148 (repeated in 8: 143; also Mufīd, *Amālī*: 274–5) 263, 319 (also Ṭūsī, *Amālī*: 208), 628–9 (also Ibn Bābawayh, *Amālī*: 119; idem, *Faḍā'il al-ashhur*: 87)
  3: 421–2, 430

5: 10–12 (also, in full or part, in ʿAyyāshī 1: 324, 2: 85; ʿAlī b. Ibrāhīm 2: 320–21; *Khiṣāl*: 274–6), 28–29, 44
6: 473
7: 387, 457
8: 143–4 (five reports), 128–9
– ʿAlī b. Ibrāhīm 1: 29 (read *Ḥafṣ b. Ghiyāth* for *Jaʿfar b. Ghiyāth*), 200, 242–3
2: 114, 146, 159, 320–21
– Ibn Bābawayh, *Amālī*: 676–7 (two reports, the second also in *ʿIqāb*: 295–6)
– *Faqīh* 1: 508, 524
3: 435
– *Khiṣāl*: 386 (partially also at 394), 407
– *Maʿānī*: 30 (also *Tawḥīd*: 327), 156, 220, 256, 325
– *Tawḥīd*: 116 (read *ʿan Ḥafṣ b. Ghiyāth* for *ʿan Ḥafṣ aw ghayrih*), 120, 416 (also *Thawāb*: 161)[50]
– *Thawāb*: 157 (see also *Kāfī* 2: 606 where the passage is attributed to Mūsā al-Kāẓim)
– Ṭūsī, *Amālī*: 581
– *Tahdhīb* 1: 177, 253–4
3: 21–2, 195, 248
4: 333
6: 146–7, 151–2
7: 180–81
10: 155
– *Qiṣaṣ*: 184, 230
– *Manāqib* 4: 73–4

The fragment quoted in *Tahdhīb* 3: 21–2 represents the original style of the work. A large section of the work was on holy war (*siyar*, corrupted in *Tahdhīb* 6: 145 to *sīra* and in *Kāfī* 5: 44 to *sunan*). It began with the paragraph quoted in *Kāfī* 5: 44 and *Tahdhīb* 6: 145–6, with other parts scattered in those two works (*Kāfī* 5: 10–12, 28–9, 32–4; *Tahdhīb* 4: 115–16, 6: 136–7, 142, 144, 145–6, 146–7, 151–2, with parallels in *Maḥāsin*: 327–8; ʿAyyāshī 1: 48, 324–5, 385, 2: 85; ʿAlī b. Ibrāhīm 2: 320–21; *Faqīh* 4: 319; *Khiṣāl*: 276). Another section on ethics can be reconstructed from scattered quotations in *Kāfī* 2: 88–9, 148, 263, 317, 319, 452, 456–7, 8: 128–9,

50. The text ascribed to Ḥafṣ in some manuscripts of the *Tawḥīd*, printed in a footnote in the Tehran, 1387 edition of the work: 397–9, is a clear forgery.

143, 144 and Ibn Bābawayh, *Amālī*: 764–5 (also *Maḥāsin*: 224; *Khiṣāl*: 41, 119; *'Iqāb*: 263; Mufīd, *Amālī*: 274–5, 329).

68: Abū Wallād al-Ḥannāṭ

Abū Wallād Ḥafṣ b. Sālim, the wheat seller, a Kūfan client of the Banū Makhzūm and a transmitter from Ja'far al-Ṣādiq and Mūsā al-Kāẓim.

Barqī: 96; Najāshī: 135; *Fibrist*: 62; *Rijāl*: 197 (see also *Kāfī* 5: 290).

Barqī: 96 and *Fibrist*: 62 have him as a client of Ju'fī. Najāshī also quotes this from one of his sources, but the information may relate to a different person with the same *kunya* and profession as our transmitter (see further Muḥammad Taqī al-Tustarī 3: 580–81).

Kitāb / Aṣl

His notebook of *ḥadīth*, related by Ḥasan b. Maḥbūb (Najāshī: 135; *Fibrist*: 62; also *Mashyakha*: 465, 469). There are close to one hundred quotations from this author in Shī'ite works of *ḥadīth*, listed in Khu'ī 6: 137, 22: 68–9, 222–4 and *Fahāris* 8: 444, 10: 451,[51] almost all through the same transmitter.

69: Ḥafṣ al-'Amrī

Ḥafṣ b. Sūqa, a Kūfan client of the descendants of 'Amr b. Ḥurayth al-Makhzūmī (d. 85) and a transmitter from Ja'far al-Ṣādiq and his disciples.

Barqī: 96; Najāshī: 135; *Fibrist*: 62; *Rijāl*: 196.

The account just given of this transmitter's clientage follows Najāshī. He also names two brothers of this transmitter, Ziyād and Muḥammad, who both transmitted from Muḥammad al-Bāqir and Ja'far al-Ṣādiq. Ṭūsī (*Rijāl*: 114) also names the two, but identifies Ziyād b. Sūqa as a client of Jarīr b. ' Abd Allāh al-Bajalī (ibid.: 135, 208; on Jarīr b. 'Abd Allāh, see below, no. 114), and Muḥammad b. Sūqa, whom he calls *al-Marḍī al-Khazzāz*, as a man of Bajīla and

51. For a further example in a non-Imāmite work, see Abū Ṭālib: 444.

transmitter from Ja'far al-Ṣādiq (ibid.: 285). This Muḥammad seems to be the same as the Abū Bakr Muḥammad b. Sūqa al-Kūfī al-'Ābid named by the Sunnī biographers (see Mizzī 25: 333–6 and the sources listed in the editor's footnote) as a transmitter from Muḥammad al-Bāqir and further described as *al-Raḍī* (ibid. 23: 334) and *Khazzāz* (ibid. 23: 335). He is, however, identified as a *Ghanawī*, that is, a descendant or client of Ghanī b. Ya'ṣur of Qays 'Aylān.

Kitāb / Aṣl

A small notebook of *ḥadīth*, related from the author by Ibn Abī 'Umayr (Najāshī: 135; *Fihrist*: 62). It must have included the following small number of transmissions of this author:

- *Kāfī* 4: 103
  5: 202
  7: 462
- *Tahdhīb* 7: 414 (repeated at 461)
  5: 155

70: Ḥakam al-A'mā

Abū Muḥammad Ḥakam b. Miskīn, the blind, a Kūfan client of Thaqīf and a transmitter from Ja'far al-Ṣādiq.

Barqī: 98; Najāshī: 136; *Fihrist*: 62; *Rijāl*: 197.

Najāshī gives Ḥakam's *kunya* as noted above. *Mashyakha*: 453–4 has it as *Abū 'Abd Allāh*.

The man was blind as mentioned by all the sources named above. A report in *Manāqib* 4: 232 that quotes Ḥakam as saying that he personally saw something may not therefore be accurate, except in a figurative sense.

Kitāb / Aṣl

A notebook of *ḥadīth*, related by a number of transmitters including Ibn Abī 'Umayr, Ḥasan b. Maḥbūb,[52] and Muḥammad b. al-Ḥusayn b. Abī 'l-Khaṭṭāb (Abū Ghālib: 182; *Fihrist*: 62). The last transmitter, Ibn Abī

---

52. *Fihrist*: 62 (read *wa 'l-Ḥasan b. Maḥbūb* for *'an al-Ḥasan b. Maḥbūb* [see Muḥammad Taqī al-Tustarī 3: 600]).

'l-Khaṭṭāb (d. 262), a main transmitter from this author, must have received this notebook and numerous other works he quotes via our author (see *Mashyakha*: 441, 452, 453–4, 464, 466, 496, 498, 499, 518, 522, 562) through intermediaries. In Ṣaffār: 477, he quotes Ḥakam through 'Alī b. Asbāṭ, a frequent transmitter from our author (see Khu'ī 6: 370–74; also *Maḥāsin*: 275–6; Ibn Bisṭām: 103; *Khiṣāl*: 63). Ibn Bābawayh quotes directly from the *Kitāb* of Ḥakam b. Miskīn in *Faqīh* 1: 441.

Quotations from this author in Shī'ite works of *ḥadīth* on the authority of the above-mentioned transmitters include the following examples:

- *Maḥāsin*: 275–6, 470
- Ṣaffār: 57, 76 (also *Kāfī* 1: 413; Ibn al-Juḥām: 253), 276–7, 477
- *Kāfī* 1: 274–5
  2: 191–2
  3: 31 (also *'Ilal* 1: 273), 115 (also *Thawāb*: 229), 455, 467
  4: 73–4
  5: 19, 467, 492 (two reports, one repeated at 493)
  6: 79
  7: 190–91 (two reports of the same text), 205–7 (two reports of the same text)
  8: 262–3
- Ibn Qūlawayh: 180, 215 (also Ibn Bābawayh, *Amālī*: 200), 217–18, 264
- Ibn Bābawayh, *Amālī*: 496, 682 (also *Thawāb*: 69)
- *Faqīh* 3: 454
- *'Ilal* 2: 32
- *'Iqāb* 251, 273 (see also *Maḥāsin*: 80 where the same text is reported from Ḥakam through a different transmitter)
- *Kamāl*: 301–2 (also *Khiṣāl*: 476–7; *'Uyūn* 1: 52–4)
- *Khiṣāl*: 63, 139–40, 411 (read *Ḥakam b. Miskīn* for *Ḥasan b. Miskīn*), 485 (read *Ḥakam* as in the previous case), 554–63
- *Tahdhīb* 1: 27
  2: 19, 149, 182, 316, 332, 335
  3: 20–21, 223, 281
  4: 197
  6: 365
  7: 162–3
  8: 301 (read *A'mā* for *A'shā*; cf. *Kāfī* 1: 413, 3: 467, 5: 556)
  10: 23, 66
- *Qiṣaṣ*: 178

Najāshī: 136 names three other works by this author as *Kitāb al-waṣāyā*, *Kitāb al-ṭalāq*, and *Kitāb al-ẓihār*. These works seem to have been unavailable to the authors of Shī'ite works of *ḥadīth* as, with a single exception (*Kāfī* 6: 79 on a question of divorce), nothing is quoted from Ḥakam on these topics in later works.

71: Ibn Abī Ṭalḥa

Ḥammād b. Abī Ṭalḥa, seller of Shāpūrī clothing, a Kūfan Shī'ite who transmitted from the disciples of Ja'far al-Ṣādiq.

Barqī: 71; Najāshī: 144; *Rijāl*: 194.

Kitāb

His notebook of *ḥadīth*, related by a number of transmitters including Aḥmad b. Abī Bishr (Najāshī: 144) and Muḥammad b. Sinān al-Zāhirī as attested by his numerous citations from this author. Examples of quotations from this author by these two transmitters include the following:

- Ṣaffār: 272
- *Kāfī* 1: 537
  2: 209
  4: 281
  5: 101
  8: 237
- Nu'mānī: 308–9
- *Tahdhīb* 2: 252
  4: 143–4
  6: 189

72: Ḥammād al-Nāb

Ḥammād b. ʿUthmān al-Nāb, a Kūfan client and a transmitter from Jaʿfar al-Ṣādiq and Mūsā al-Kāẓim. He was a prolific transmitter of *ḥadīth* and noted in the Shīʿite community for his knowledge. He died in Kūfa in 190.

Barqī: 70, 117; Kashshī: 372, 375; Najāshī: 143; *Fihrist*: 60–61; *Rijāl*: 186, 334, 354.

There are disagreements over a number of biographical details of this transmitter. See Muḥammad Taqī al-Tustarī 3: 648–51 for details.

Kashshī: 375 counts this transmitter as one of the six most learned among the younger generation of the disciples of Jaʿfar al-Ṣādiq.

Kitāb

His notebook of *ḥadīth*, related by a number of transmitters including Ibn Abī ʿUmayr, Ḥasan b. ʿAlī al-Washshāʾ, Ḥasan b. ʿAlī b. Faḍḍāl, and Muḥammad b. al-Walīd al-Khazzāz (Najāshī: 143; *Fihrist*: 60–61; *Rijāl*: 334). Ibn Ṭāwūs quotes from this work in his *Ghiyāth*: 6, 9 and *Malāḥim*: 119–20 (see further Kohlberg: 223). There are close to two thousand quotations from this author in Shīʿite collections of *ḥadīth*, mainly through the above-mentioned transmitters of this notebook. For lists see Khuʾī 6: 189–198 (cf. Muḥammad Taqī al-Tustarī 3: 652–3), 216–23, 374–422; *Fahāris* 8: 452–4, 456–7.

73: Ḥamza al-Shaybānī

Ḥamza b. Ḥumrān b. Aʿyan, a Kūfan client of the Banū Shaybān and member of the prominent Shīʿite family of the Āl Aʿyan (see below, no. 234). He was a transmitter from Muḥammad al-Bāqir and Jaʿfar al-Ṣādiq.

Barqī: 100; *Kāfī* 6: 154; *Mashyakha*: 512; Abū Ghālib: 114, 132; Najāshī: 140; *Fihrist*: 64; *Rijāl*: 132, 190.

Ḥamza was a son of Ḥumrān b. Aʿyan, an eminent Shīʿite scholar of the first half of the second century (on whom see Khūʾī 6: 255–6; Muḥammad Taqī al-Tustarī 4: 13–22), named also in the Sunnī tradition as a transmitter of *ḥadīth* and expert on the text of the Qurʾān (see the many sources listed in the editor's footnote to Mizzī 7: 306–7).

Kitāb

His notebook of *ḥadīth*, related by a number of transmitters including Ṣafwān b. Yaḥyā (Najāshī: 140; *Fihrist*: 64). There are close to one hundred quotations from this author in Shī'ite works of *ḥadīth*, listed in Khu'ī 6: 267–8, 454–6 and *Fahāris* 8: 464–5, some through the specified transmitters of this notebook.[53]

74: Ḥanān al-Ṣayrafī

Ḥanān b. Sadīr b. Ḥakīm b. Ṣuhayb, the moneychanger, a Kūfan client of Azd and a prominent member of the Shī'ite community of Kūfa. He was a transmitter from Ja'far al-Ṣādiq and Mūsā al-Kāẓim. He joined the Wāqifites when the latter died, and lived to a very old age.

Barqī: 111, 117; Kashshī: 296, 555; Najāshī: 146; *Fihrist*: 64; *Rijāl*: 193, 334. He was also known to Sunnī scholars of *ḥadīth*. See Ibn Abī Ḥātim 3: 299; Ibn Ḥibbān, *Thiqāt* 8: 219; Dāraquṭnī, *'Ilal* 5: 184; idem, *Mu'talif*: 430–31, and other sources listed in the editor's footnote to *Lisān* 2: 695.

The *kunya* of *Abū 'l-Faḍl* is mentioned in his entry in Najāshī as if it belongs to him. It actually belongs to his father (see Barqī: 65; Kashshī: 210; *Thawāb*: 238 [also Mufīd, *Amālī*: 195]; *Ghayba*: 45; *Rijāl*: 114, 223). For his Azdī clientage, see Kashshī: 592.

Najāshī mentions the exact location of this transmitter's shop in the market of Kūfa, in the area in front of the entrance to the grand mosque among the cloth sellers.

Zaydī (e.g. Aḥmad b. 'Īsā 3: 120) and Sunnī (e.g. Dāraquṭnī, *Mu'talif*: 430, 431; Ibn 'Asākir 20: 148–9 [also Ibn Bābawayh, *Amālī*: 412–13; Mufīd, *Amālī*: 126], 62: 306 [read *Ḥanān* for *Ḥassān*]) sources also quote from him.

For his pro-Wāqifite transmission, see *Ghayba*: 45, 50, 53, 58, all quoted from 'Alī b. Aḥmad al-'Alawī al-Mūsawī's *Kitāb fī nuṣrat al-Wāqifa*. This author, a mid-third century scholar, and some other transmitters from that period directly quote from Ḥanān, a fact that may support Najāshī's report that Ḥanān lived to a very old age.[54]

---

53. Here are a few examples: Ḥusayn b. Sa'īd, *Zuhd*: 8; Ṣaffār: 482 (also Kulaynī, *Rasā'il* as quoted in Ibn Ṭāwūs, *Luhūf*: 56–7); *Kāfī* 3: 266 (also *Tahdhīb* 2: 238).
54. There is also the possibility that these transmissions were from Ḥanān's works and not through actual hearing of the material from him.

1. *Kitāb fī ṣifat al-janna wa 'l-nār*

(Najāshī: 146). The first sentence of the work quoted by Najāshī is the same as the opening sentence of the *Kitāb ṣifat al-janna wa 'l-nār* of Sa'īd b. Janāḥ that has survived (*Ikhtiṣāṣ*: 345–65). There is a long report quoted from Ḥanān on the topic (*Thawāb*: 238 [partially also at 180]; Mufīd, *Amālī*: 177–8) with an opening sentence similar to the one in Sa'īd b. Janāḥ's work but with a different text and not substantial enough to have been an independent treatise. Najāshī, or his source, may have confused the two texts.[55] Sa'īd b. Janāḥ quotes the first half of his work (pp. 345–56) through a transmitter from "one of our colleagues." This cannot refer to the long report by Ḥanān as the two texts differ considerably in their language.

2. *Kitāb*

Ḥanān's notebook of *ḥadīth*, related by a number of transmitters including Ibn Abī 'Umayr, Ḥasan b. Maḥbūb, Muḥammad b. 'Īsā b. 'Ubayd al-Yaqṭīnī, Ibrāhīm b. Hāshim al-Qummī (*Mashyakha: 428; Fihrist*: 64 [read *wa 'l-Ḥasan b. Maḥbūb* for *'an al-Ḥasan b. Maḥbūb* as also suggested by Muḥammad Taqī al-Tustarī 4: 68]), and possibly Muḥammad b. Ismā'īl b. Bazī' (see Burūjirdī, *Tajrīd*: 619). Abū Ghālib: 167, 168 received two copies of this notebook, one related from the author by Muḥammad b. Bakr b. Janāḥ, the other by 'Abd Allāh b. Ja'far al-Ḥimyarī through two transmitters from Qum, Muḥammad b. 'Abd al-Ḥamīd and 'Abd al-Ṣamad b. Muḥammad,[56] who related the work from the author. Ḥimyarī quotes two fragments of this notebook through the last two transmitters in his *Qurb al-isnād*: 96–101 (12 reports) and 123–5 (6 reports). *Maḥāsin*: 524 (whence *Khiṣāl*: 144), 538, 580 quotes Ḥanān through "a group of our colleagues", indicating citation from a work.

---

55. It is also possible, though not very likely, that the two names *Sa'īd* and *Janāḥ* were corrupted in a copy of Sa'īd b. Janāḥ's work that Najāshī or his source received. Someone might therefore have reversed the order of the two names to give what he thought was the correct order. This is similar to what happened to a manuscript of Abū Ṭālib Yaḥyā b. al-Ḥusayn al-Hārūnī's *al-Di'āma fī tathbīt al-imāma*, on which basis the book was published as the *Nuṣrat madhāhib al-Zaydiyya* by the Ṣāḥib b. 'Abbād (ed. Nājī Ḥasan, Beirut, 1981). Corruption of the personal names of Ḥanān and Sadīr on the other hand, was a frequent phenomenon. See Ibn Ḥajar's comments in *Lisān* 2: 304, 351 (on *Mīzān* 1: 449, 487); see also the editors' footnotes to *Lisān* 2: 695 and Dāraquṭnī, *Mu'talif*: 430.

56. Ibn Bābawayh also received the notebook through this transmitter, among others (*Mashyakha*: 428).

Most of the close to two hundred quotations from Ḥanān in Shīʿite works of *ḥadīth*, listed in Khuʾī 6: 302–5, 464–70 and *Fahāris* 8: 477–8, are through the above-mentioned transmitters of this notebook.

75: Ḥārith al-Naṣrī

Abū ʿAlī Ḥārith b. al-Mughīra, a Kūfan Arab from the descendants of Naṣr b. Muʿāwiya, a clan of Hawāzin, and a transmitter from Jaʿfar al-Ṣādiq.

Barqī: 59, 100; Kashshī: 337; Najāshī: 139; *Fihrist*: 65; *Rijāl*: 132, 191; *Lisān* 2: 290–91. See also *Maḥāsin*: 625; *Kāfī* 8: 158, 162; Ibn Bisṭām: 130, 134; Ṭūsī, *Amālī*: 318.

Barqī identified this transmitter as a Kūfan and Najāshī as a Baṣran. In a report in Kashshī: 337, the Kūfan Yūnus b. Yaʿqūb quotes Jaʿfar al-Ṣādiq advising a group of his visitors, most likely from Kūfa, to refer in religious matters to Ḥārith. Ḥārith's main transmitter, Ṣafwān b. Yaḥyā, and almost all other transmitters from him are also known Kūfans. The combination seems to suggest that either he was a Baṣran only by origin or that the word *Baṣrī* in Najāshī: 137 represents a corruption of *Naṣrī* in one of the author's sources.

Najāshī has him as a transmitter from Mūsā al-Kāẓim as well. A report in Kashshī: 337 may, however, indicate that Ḥārith died during Jaʿfar al-Ṣādiq's lifetime.

Kitāb

His notebook of *ḥadīth*, related by a number of Shīʿite transmitters including Ṣafwān b. Yaḥyā (Najāshī: 139; *Fihrist*: 65), who at times quotes Ḥārith through an intermediary (as in *Maḥāsin*: 219; Ibn al-Juḥām: 172–3; Ṣaffār: 480 (see also 65); Nuʿmānī: 242; *Tawḥīd*: 149). Ibn Bābawayh quotes Ḥārith in the *Faqīh* (e.g. 2: 442) through two transmitters simultaneously, Ibn Abī ʿUmayr and Yūnus b. ʿAbd al-Raḥmān (*Mashyakha*: 455). Elsewhere, Ibn Abī ʿUmayr too quotes Ḥārith through intermediaries (e.g. *Maḥāsin*: 259; Ibn Bābawayh, *Amālī*: 249), but Yūnus normally quotes him directly (e.g. Ṣaffār: 396, *Kāfī* 1: 223 [also *Kamāl*: 224]).

There are close to one hundred quotations from Ḥārith in Shīʿite works of *ḥadīth*, listed in Khuʾī 4: 462–4 and *Fahāris* 8: 318, 319, 321. The following are related by Ṣafwān:

- Ḥusayn b. Saʿīd, *Zuhd*: 73
- *Maḥāsin*: 219

- Ṣaffār: 323 (also Ibn al-Juḥām: 172–3; see also Ṣaffār: 321–2), 326–8 (also *Kāfī* 1: 264), 366–7, 480
- *Kāfī* 2: 484
  3: 276
  8: 158
- Nu'mānī: 242 (see also *Khiṣāl*: 200)
- *Tawḥīd*: 149

76: Ibn al-Aḥwal

Ḥārith b. Muḥammad b. al-Nu'mān, a Kūfan client of Bajīla and son of the prominent Shī'ite *mutakallim*, Abū Ja'far al-Aḥwal Ṣāḥib al-Ṭāq (no. 148 below).

Barqī: 100; Najāshī: 140; *Fihrist*: 64; *Rijāl*: 192; *Lisān* 2: 289–90.

Rijāl has his *kunya* as *Abū 'Alī* but *Lisān* as *Abū Muḥammad*. The latter, quoting 'Alī b. al-Ḥakam who in turn quoted Ḥasan b. Maḥbūb, reports that Ḥārith attended classes by the jurist Muḥammad b. al-Ḥasan al-Shaybānī (d. 189) who praised Ḥārith as an admirable character.

Kitāb / Aṣl

His notebook of *ḥadīth*, related by a number of Shī'ite transmitters including Ḥasan b. Maḥbūb (Najāshī: 140; *Fihrist*: 64). Quotations from this author in later works, mainly through the same transmitter, include the following examples:

- *Maḥāsin*: 180–81 (also Ibn Bābawayh, *Faḍā'il al-Shī'a*: 309–10), 350 (also *Kāfī* 4: 283)
- *Kāfī* 4: 122 (also *Faqīh* 2: 149)
  5: 380
  7: 234 (also *Faqīh* 4: 44), 314 (also *Tahdhīb* 10: 249)
  8: 156
- Ibn Bābawayh, *Amālī*: 381–2 (also *Faqīh* 4: 400; *Ma'ānī*: 196, and, partially, *Khiṣāl*: 153)
- *Faqīh* 4: 148 (also *Tahdhīb* 10: 233)
- *Thawāb*: 162

77: Ḥarīz al-Sijistānī

Ḥarīz b. ʿAbd Allāh al-Azdī al-Sijistānī, a Kūfan merchant trading in oil and a prominent Shīʿite jurist in the first half of the second century. He resided in Sijistān where he had a circle of followers. He became involved in armed struggle with the local Khārijites who dominated the region at the time, and was eventually killed by them.

Barqī: 103; Kashshī: 336, 383–5; Dāraquṭnī, *Mu'talif*: 356; *Ikhtiṣāṣ*: 207; Ibn Mākūlā 2: 86; Najāshī: 144–5; *Fihrist*: 62–3; *Rijāl*: 194; Khaṭīb, *Talkhīṣ*: 494; Yāqūt, *Muʿjam* 3: 191; *Lisān* 2: 347.

There are a number of discrepancies among the sources regarding biographical details of Ḥarīz. His *kunya* appears as *Abū Muḥammad* in Najāshī: 144, but as *Abū ʿAbd Allāh* in Kashshī: 385. Barqī and Kashshī: 385 state that he was an Arab, but *Rijāl*: 194 identifies him as a client of Azd. That he was an Azdī, whether by descent or as a client, seems to be a matter of agreement. ʿUqaylī 2: 240, however, describes a Baṣran that Sunnī sources identify as Ḥarīz's father as *ʿAwfī*. There were indeed two clans of the Banū ʿAwf among the Azd, one with members living in Baṣra (Ibn Ḥazm, *Jamhara*: 313, 358), but in the present context, *ʿAwfī* may well have been a corruption of *Kūfī*.

Shīʿite sources identify Ḥarīz as a Kūfan who would frequently travel to Sijistān for trade (Najāshī: 144), or moved to and resided in that region (Barqī: 103; Kashshī: 385; *Fihrist*: 62). That he was a Kūfan is confirmed by Ibn Abī Ḥātim 3: 289; Ibn Mākūlā 2: 86; *Lisān* 2: 347. Sunnī sources, however, identify him as a son of ʿAbd Allāh b. al-Ḥusayn al-Azdī, the judge of Sijistān, a transmitter of *ḥadīth* identified by most of his biographers as a Baṣran (Mizzī 14: 420–2 and the many sources listed in the editor's footnote) and accused by some of belief in the Shīʿite concept of *rajʿa* (Ajurrī, *Su'ālāt* [as quoted in Mizzī 14: 422; the passage is missing from the printed versions of that work]; *Mīzān* 2: 407–8; Ibn Nāṣir al-Dīn 2: 291).

That Ḥarīz got involved in armed struggle with the Khārijites in Sijistān is reported by Kashshī and Najāshī. Both also mention that he was reprimanded by Jaʿfar al-Ṣādiq for that action. Barqī and Kashshī report that Ḥarīz was killed in Sijistān. *Ikhtiṣāṣ*: 207 provides details of the story of his killing, together with his followers, by the Khārijites of the region.

That he was a prominent jurist of his time is further attested by two reports in Kashshī: 383–4, one describing a conversation between him and Abū Ḥanīfa on a number of legal issues, the other quoting the prominent Shīʿite scholar, Yūnus b. ʿAbd al-Raḥmān, praising Ḥarīz for his vast knowledge of religious law. Others describe Ḥarīz as one of the *mashāyikh al-Shīʿa* (Ibn al-Nadīm: 308; Dāraquṭnī, *Mu'talif*: 356; Khaṭīb, *Talkhīṣ*: 494; Ibn Nāṣir al-Dīn 2: 292).

Ḥarīz was a prolific transmitter of *ḥadīth*. Some one thousand five hundred reports are quoted on his authority in the four main collections of Shīʿite *ḥadīth* alone (Khuʾī 4: 253, 261, and the list at 467–96), with many more in other works (*Fahāris* 8: 337–338). Barqī reports that Ḥarīz wrote a number of works but does not provide any further details. Ibn al-Nadīm: 277; Najāshī: 145, and *Fihrist*: 63 name a number of these works. Both Najāshī and Ṭūsī, as well as other early scholars who mentioned these works (*Mashyakha*: 443–4; Abū Ghālib: 110) received them through the transmitter Ḥammād b. ʿĪsā al-Juhanī from the author. Close to one thousand quotations from Ḥarīz are recorded on the authority of the same transmitter in the four main works of Shīʿite *ḥadīth* (Khuʾī 6: 189, 231), with many more in other works.

1. *Kitāb Ḥarīz*

Ḥarīz's notebook of *ḥadīth*, mentioned in Ibn al-Nadīm: 275 and *Faqīh* 1: 3 as one of the main sources of the Shīʿite tradition by early authorities of that school. Abū Ghālib: 170 received the work in a copy which was in the handwriting of the scholar Ḥumayd b. Ziyād al-Dihqān (d. 310) who had received the work from the author through Ḥammād b. ʿĪsā. Other works of Ḥarīz were most likely composed out of the material of this comprehensive collection.

A fragment of this work is extant in Ibn Idrīs, *Mustaṭrafāt*: 71–5. All of the reports of this fragment deal, directly or indirectly, with the topic of prayer, but not a report that Ibn Ṭāwūs quotes from the Book of Ḥarīz in his own *Falāḥ*: 173, unless the latter was originally part of a larger statement whose other part dealt with a certain category of prayer.

2. *Kitāb al-ṣalāt*

(Ibn al-Nadīm: 277; Najāshī: 145; *Fihrist*: 63). This was Ḥarīz's larger work on the topic of prayer (Najāshī: 145). The entire contents of this work appear to have survived in later works, as the overwhelming majority of the huge number of quotations from Ḥarīz through Ḥammād deal with this topic. For a detailed list, see Khuʾī 4: 467–96.

3. *Kitāb al-ṣalāt*

Ḥarīz's shorter book on the topic (Najāshī: 145). This must have been the text that Ḥammād b. ʿĪsā had memorized (*Kāfī* 3: 311; Ibn Bābawayh,

Amālī: 498; *Faqīh* 1: 300).[57] The work must have contained statements from the Imāms on major aspects of the daily prayers.

4. *Kitāb al-zakāt*

(Ibn al-Nadīm: 277; *Fibrist*: 63). Najāshī: 142 credits Ḥammād with a *Kitāb al-zakāt*, the bulk of material of which was from Ḥarīz and only a small part from other authorities. This may mean that Ḥammād's book was basically a redaction of Ḥarīz's work. Alternatively, the book was all put together by Ḥammād from the material on the topic in Ḥarīz's notebook. Ibn Bābawayh seems to have used the work for the relevant material in his *Faqīh* (see *Mashyakha*: 443; for examples of the actual quotations, see *Faqīh* 2: 4–7, 9–10, 26, 50–51, but there is other material quoted in this source from Zurāra b. A'yan and others that may go back to the work in question as attested by parallel quotations in the *Kāfī*). There are numerous other quotations on the topic from Ḥarīz through Ḥammād in other early collections of Shī'ite *ḥadīth*, as in the following examples:

- 'Ayyāshī 2: 47 (also *Tahdhīb* 4: 132, 133 with variations)
- *Kāfī* 3: 496–7, 497–8, 504, 506, 509, 510, 512, 513, 514, 515, 516, 518 (two reports, the first also in *'Ilal* 2: 58), 520, 522, 523–4 (two reports), 525–6 (also *'Ilal* 2: 62–3), 528, 520–32 (five reports, the last one also in *Ma'ānī*: 327–8), 534–5 (two reports), 536–8 (two reports), 541 (three reports), 546 (two reports), 547, 548–9, 553–4 (five reports), 560 (two reports, the second also in *Ma'ānī*: 262), 564, 565, 566–7 (two reports), 568
  4: 13, 25, 49, 58
- 'Alī b. Ibrāhīm 2: 204
- *'Ilal* 2: 65 (two reports, the first also in *Tahdhīb* 4: 137–8)
- *Ma'ānī*: 246
- *Tahdhīb* 4: 9, 16, 40, 41, 51, 59, 61, 65, 66, 74, 77, 87, 92–3, 122, 147 (two reports)

---

57. That Ḥammād had memorized the Book of Ḥarīz on prayer is mentioned in the context of an alleged conversation between Ḥammād and Ja'far al-Ṣādiq in which the Imām blames Ḥammād for not being able to perform his prayers properly in spite of the fact that he had already reached the age of sixty or seventy. Ḥammād is said to have died in 209 aged over ninety ("seventy" in Kashshī: 317 is most probably corrupt). This puts his age at the time of death of Ja'far al-Ṣādiq at around thirty or so, a fact that may not go well with the above-mentioned statement. One may understand the statement as a reminder that younger people, if not corrected, will carry on with a habitual wrong practice into old age. However, this interpretation does not go well with the context.

A large portion of this work, cited by Ḥarīz from the two prominent Shī'ite jurists of the time, Zurāra b. A'yan and Muḥammad b. Muslim, displays the distinct language and structure of the law books of the second century. See especially the fragment quoted in *Kāfī* 3: 525–6 (also *'Ilal* 2: 62–3; see also *Tahdhīb* 4: 92–3). For other passages from the same fragment, see *Kāfī* 3: 496–7, 513, 520, 528, 530, 546, 547, 553–4 (three passages), 564, 565, 566–7, 568; *Faqīh* 2: 4–7.

5. *Kitāb al-ṣawm*

(Ibn al-Nadīm: 277; *Fihrist*: 63). The following quotations fit the title:

- *Maḥāsin*: 318 (whence *'Ilal* 2: 71)
- 'Ayyāshī 1: 90, 275 (also Ibn Qūlawayh, *Kitāb*: 146 without *isnād*)
- *Kāfī* 4: 62, 93 (also *Thawāb*: 105), 106, 118, 119, 146, 153
- *Faqīh* 2: 121 (also *Tahdhīb* 4: 271), 141, 183
- *Khiṣāl*: 508
- *Tahdhīb* 4: 151, 198, 203, 243, 244, 250, 254, 279, 298, 300, 331

6. *Kitāb al-nawādir*

(Ibn al-Nadīm: 277; Najāshī: 145; *Fihrist*: 63). Many of the quotations from Ḥarīz, specially those in matters of religious ethics, fit the title of this work. See *Fahāris* 8: 337–8 for a partial list.

78: Hārūn al-Ghanawī

Hārūn b. Ḥamza al-Ghanawī, the moneychanger, a Kūfan transmitter from Ja'far al-Ṣādiq.

Barqī: 85; Najāshī: 437; *Fihrist*: 176; *Rijāl*: 148, 318.

Hārūn's profession is given as moneychanger in Najāshī and *Tahdhīb* 8: 139. Ṣaffār: 420, however, has him as furrier.

Kitāb

His notebook of *ḥadīth* that later scholars received through the transmitter Yazīd b. Isḥāq al-Ghanawī, better know as Sha'ar (Abū

Ghālib: 166; Najāshī: 437; *Fihrist*: 176; see also *Mashyakha*: 472). Almost all surviving quotations from this author in later works are on the authority of the same transmitter, including the following examples:

- Ṣaffār: 50, 125, 205 (also *Kāfī* 1: 214), 207 (read *Yazīd Sha'ar* for *Yazīd b. Sa'd* as also noted in the editor's footnote)
- Kāfī 1: 214, 284 (also *Khiṣāl*: 117)
  3: 22, 163 (also *'Ilal* 1: 283), 442
  5: 84 (also *Faqīh* 3: 192 with an addition), 153, 281, 293, 297, 301
  6: 100–101
  7: 411, 431
- *Faqīh* 1: 507
  2: 441
- *Kamāl*: 232
- *Khiṣāl*: 423
- *Tahdhīb* 1: 238
  3: 286, 320
  4: 51, 160 (repeated at 165)
  5: 301, 379
  6: 284, 301
  7: 90, 206
  8: 122, 139
  9: 114, 181

79: Ibn al-Jahm

Hārūn b. al-Jahm b. Thuwayr b. Abī Fākhita, a Kūfan client of the Banū Hāshim and member of a well known Shī'ite family. He was a transmitter from Ja'far al-Ṣādiq and seems to have lived until late in the second century.

Barqī: 85; 'Uqaylī 4: 282; Najāshī: 438; *Fihrist*: 176; *Rijāl*: 318; *Mīzān* 3: 656; *Lisān* 7: 230–31. See also *Maḥāsin*: 304, 585.

His clientage of Quraysh through its clan of the Banū Hāshim was in a hereditary line from his great-grandfather, Abū Fākhita, who was a servant/client of Umm Hāni', daughter of Abū Ṭālib and sister of 'Alī. Hārūn's grandfather, Thuwayr, was a *tābi'ī* known for his Shī'ite sympathies (see Mizzī 4: 429–31 and the sources named in the editor's footnote [see also Najāshī: 118]; for examples of his Shī'ite transmissions, see Ibn Abī Shayba 3: 282; Ṭabarī, *Tafsīr* 2: 209; Furāt: 314; 'Alī b. Ibrāhīm 1: 165–6, 2: 252; Mizzī 20: 403). Hārūn's uncle, Ḥusayn, was also a transmitter and author of a notebook of *ḥadīth* (Barqī: 80; Najāshī: 55, 155; *Fibrist*: 59; *Rijāl*: 182, 196; *Lisān* 2: 511).[58]

Kitāb

His notebook of *ḥadīth*, related by the early third-century scholar Muḥammad b. Khālid al-Barqī (Najāshī: 438; *Fihrist*: 176) who seems to have received it through an intermediary as in Ṣaffār: 208 (also *Kāfī* 1: 230). Most of the quotations from this author in Shī'ite works of *ḥadīth* are through the same transmitter. They include the following examples:

- *Maḥāsin*: 4 (whence *Khiṣāl*: 84; *Ma'ānī*: 314), 208 (whence *'Iqāb*: 307), 220 (whence *Ma'ānī*: 154), 247, 248, 249–50, 304–5, 316, 356, 368–9, 393, 467, 584–5 (two reports, whence *Kāfī* 6: 268)
- Ṣaffār: 208 (also *Kāfī* 1: 230)
- *Kāfī* 2: 52, 98, 193–4 (cf. *'Iqāb*: 296 where the same report appears with a different *isnād*), 330–31 (also Ibn Bābawayh, *Amālī*: 325–6; *Khiṣāl*: 118–19), 331 (also *'Iqāb*: 322), 357, 422–3
  4: 15
  5: 86, 167, 528 (two reports)
  7: 203
- Ibn Qūlawayh: 535
- Ibn Bābawayh, *Amālī*: 92–3

80: Ibn Khārija

Abū 'l-Ḥasan Hārūn b. Khārija, the moneychanger, a Kūfan client of the Anṣār and a transmitter from Ja'far al-Ṣādiq.

Barqī: 85; Najāshī: 437; *Fihrist*: 176; *Rijāl*: 318 (see also 311). See also *Maḥāsin*: 56 (also 'Ayyāshī 2: 277; *Kāfī* 3: 491); *Kāfī* 3: 518 (also *'Ilal* 2: 58).

58. Ḥusayn b. Thuwayr's notebook was related from the author by the transmitter Khaybarī b. 'Alī al-Ṭaḥḥān (Najāshī: 55, 155; *Fihrist*: 59). Among the quotations from this author in Shī'ite works of *ḥadīth*, listed in Khu'ī 5: 207–8 and *Fahāris* 8: 348, 404, a few (e.g. *Kāfī* 1: 474, 3: 342, 5: 308; Ibn Qūlawayh: 166 [two reports], 253) are through the same transmitter (the last three passages are quoted from the author by Abū Sa'īd; this is the same as Khaybarī b. 'Alī al-Ṭaḥḥān [see *Kāfī* 1: 52]).

Kitāb

His notebook of *ḥadīth*, related by a number of transmitters including ʿAlī b. al-Nuʿmān and ʿUthmān b. ʿĪsā al-Ruʾāsī (Najāshī: 437; *Fihrist*: 176; also *Mashyakha*: 475). There are close to one hundred quotations from this author in Shīʿite works of *ḥadīth*, listed in Khuʾī 19: 224–5, 401–4 and *Fahāris* 10: 415, many through ʿAlī b. al-Nuʿmān (e.g. Ṣaffār: 516–17; *Kamāl*: 393; *Tahdhīb* 9: 82) and ʿUthmān b. ʿĪsā (e.g. *Maḥāsin*: 348, 598 [also *Maʿānī*: 144–5]; *Kāfī* 2: 143, 585, 646, 4: 467, 8: 241; *Khiṣāl*: 11). Those by Yaḥyā b. ʿImrān al-Ḥalabī (e.g. Ḥusayn b. Saʿīd, *Zuhd*: 105; *Kāfī* 2: 399, 3: 195, 235, 465, 4: 417, 8: 252, 316; ʿAlī b. Ibrāhīm 1: 86–91, 2: 370–71; Ibn Qūlawayh: 128) also seem to go back to this notebook.

81: Ibn al-Baṭāʾinī

Abū Muḥammad Ḥasan b. ʿAlī b. Abī Ḥamza al-Baṭāʾinī, a Kūfan client of the Anṣār and son of the author ʿAlī b. Abī Ḥamza al-Baṭāʾinī (no. 32 above). Like his father, he was a Wāqifite with clear esoteric tendencies.

Kashshī: 443, 552; Ibn al-Ghaḍāʾirī: 51; Najāshī: 36–7; *Fihrist*: 50, 51; *Maʿālim*: 35; *Lisān* 2: 433.

1. *Kitāb faḍāʾil al-Qurʾān*

(Najāshī: 37; *Fihrist*: 51). Najāshī received this work through the transmitter Ismāʿīl b. Mihrān al-Sakūnī. The entire text of this work appears to have survived, on the authority of the same transmitter, in Ibn Bābawayh's *Thawāb*: 130–58. Individual passages of this text appear also in other works such as ʿAyyāshī 1: 19 (also Ibn Ṭāwūs, *Muhaj*: 379 quoting Ṣaffār's *Faḍl al-duʿāʾ*); *Kāfī* 2: 620, 622 (two reports). A passage in Ibn Ṭāwūs, *Falāḥ*: 486 may have also belonged to this work although it does not appear among the excerpts quoted in the *Thawāb*.

2. *Tafsīr al-Qurʾān*

(Kashshī: 552). There is a good number of quotations from this author on *tafsīr*, some from his father, himself author of a work on *tafsīr*, but many from others. Here is a list of possible extracts from this work:

- *Kāfī* 1: 112 (also *Tawḥīd*: 190–91), 137
  2: 5–6, 195
  4: 190–91
  5: 127, 511, 530–31
  6: 206, 393–4 (read *'an Ḥasan b. 'Alī b. Abī Ḥamza* as ibid. 6: 514 that is a part of the same long passage), 406
  7: 262
- Furāt: 63–4, 534
- Ibn al-Juḥām: 289, and a passage on Qur'ān 37: 83 (quoted in *Ta'wīl al-āyāt*: 496–7 but missing in the reconstructed version of Ibn al-Juḥām's work)
- Nu'mānī, *Ghayba*: 51–2, 240, 241, 251, 269
- Idem, *Tafsīr*: 3–4
- 'Alī b. Ibrāhīm 2: 40–42, 46–7 (two reports), 48, 55, 56–7, 358–60, 370, 408–9, 415, 416, 422, 423, 427, 434–9
- Ibn Bābawayh, *Amālī*: 651
- *Ma'ānī*: 132, 392 (also 'Ayyāshī 2: 109)
- Ṭūsī, *Amālī*: 144

The long passage quoted in *Kāfī* 2: 5–6 seems to be in its original form.

3. Kitāb al-dalā'il

(Najāshī: 37; *Fihrist*: 51). Ṭūsī received this work through two different chains of transmission, including one through the transmitter Aḥmad b. Maytham, a grandson of the Kūfan Faḍl b. Dukayn al-Taymī (d. 219), who quoted it from the author (*Fihrist*: 51; see also *Rijāl*: 408 [read *Kitāb al-dilālāt* for *Kitāb al-dilāla*]). In *Fihrist*: 26, however, Ṭūsī mistakenly ascribes the work to Aḥmad b. Maytham himself (see further Muḥammad Taqī al-Tustarī 1: 664). A book entitled *Kitāb al-dalā'il* is also ascribed by Najāshī: 132 to the scholar Ḥumayd b. Ziyād al-Dihqān (d. 310) who according to *Rijāl*: 408 received Ibn al-Baṭā'inī's work through Aḥmad b. Maytham.

The work was available to Ibn Shahrāshūb (d. 588) who quoted several passages from it in his *Manāqib* 4: 182, 189, 226, 234, 243, always referring to it as *Dilālāt*. There are numerous other quotations from Ibn al-Baṭā'inī in Shī'ite sources that fit the title of this work, including the following examples:

- *Maḥāsin*: 89 (whence *'Iqāb*: 249)
- Ṣaffār: 346 (also *Kāfī*: 6: 223–4)

- ʿAyyāshī 2: 208 (as attested in Karājikī, *Kanz*: 36–7)
- *Kāfī* 1: 408–9
  2: 108 (repeated in 5: 75–6; also *Faqīh* 3: 162)
  6: 547 (also Ibn Qūlawayh: 198)
- Kashshī: 120–23 (two reports), 442–3, 445–6, 448
- Ibn al-Juḥām: 289
- Ibn Qūlawayh: 112–13, 201–2, 374–7 (partially also at 288, 433–4)
- Ibn Bābawayh, *Amālī*: 561
- *Faqīh* 4: 179–80 (a later contribution; also *Kamāl*: 259 [# 4]; *ʿUyūn* 1: 59; Khazzāz: 146, 259)
- *ʿIlal* 1: 176, 193–4, 221
- *Kamāl*: 258–9 (# 3, a revised text; also Khazzāz: 144–6)
- *Maʿānī*: 132, 392
- *Kharāʾij*: 821–2 (also Ḥasan b. Sulaymān: 112–13)
- *Biḥār* 61: 181 (quoting *Kitāb al-istidrāk*)

4. *Kitāb al-fitan / Kitāb al-malāḥim*

(Najāshī: 37). The book was available to Ibn Ṭāwūs who quoted a passage from an old copy of the work, which he found in the library of the shrine of Mūsā al-Kāẓim in Baghdad, in his own *Iqbāl* 3: 116–17 (see further Kohlberg: 245). There are quite a few quotations from this author in Shīʿite works of *ḥadīth* on the same topic. The long citation in Ibn Bābawayh, *Amālī*: 175–7 (partially repeated at 197) is definitely from this work. There are also a good number of passages quoted in Nuʿmānī: 194, 204, 211, 234–5 (two reports), 251, 253–7, 257, 259, 262–3 (two reports), 264, 267 269 that fit the topic perfectly and most likely belong to this work. This book was also related by Aḥmad b. Maytham (*Rijāl*: 408) and was possibly the one mistakenly ascribed to him in *Fihrist*: 26.

5. *Kitāb al-Qāʾim*

A smaller book (Najāshī: 37), clearly in comparision to no. 4 above, on the Shīʿite apocalyptic figure of the *Qāʾim*. A good number of quotations from the author on the topic, including some of those mentioned under no. 4 above, may have belonged to this work, as in the following examples:

- Ibn al-Juḥām: 289

- Nu'mānī: 200, 204, 234–5 (two reports), 239, 240, 241, 251, 253–7 (two reports), 262, 264, 267, 269, 272, 317, 320, 322
- *Kamāl*: 258–9 (two reports), 329, 345–6
- *Ghayba*: 420

6. *Kitāb al-ghayba*

7. *Kitāb al-raj'a*

These two works are also mentioned by Najāshī: 37. Some of the passages on the *Qā'im* mention the question of his occultation (e.g. *Kamāl*: 329, 345–6) and fit the topic of a *kitāb al-ghayba*. Others speak of the return of the Prophet and 'Alī (Nu'mānī: 234–5) or of the unjust caliphs of the past ('Alī b. Ibrāhīm 2: 416) and can legitimately belong to a work on the concept of *raj'a*.

8. *Kitāb faḍā'il Amīr al-Mu'minīn*

(Najāshī: 37). Relevant quotations:

- *Maḥāsin*: 89 (whence *'Iqāb*: 249)
- *Kāfī* 3: 492 (also *Thawāb*: 50)
- Ibn Bābawayh, *Amālī*: 442 (repeated at 768 with variations and an addition)
- Ṭūsī, *Amālī*: 144
- *Tahdhīb* 6: 34 (also 'Abd al-Karīm b. Ṭāwūs: 69–70)

9. *Kitāb al-ṣalāt*

(Najāshī: 37). Relevant quotations (on regular as well as supererogatory prayers):

- *Kāfī* 2: 478 (also *Thawāb*: 193), 492, 622 (also *Thawāb*: 155)
- Ibn Bābawayh, *Amālī*: 488–9, 651
- Idem, *Faḍā'il al-ashhur*: 92 (also Ṭūsī, *Amālī*: 497 with variations)
- *Tahdhīb* 1: 347
- Ibn Qūlawayh: 374–7 (partially also at 288, 433–4)
- Ibn Ṭāwūs, *Falāḥ*: 117–18, 119–20, 479–81 (read *Ḥasan b. 'Alī b. Abī Ḥamza* for *Ḥusayn* as also ibid.: 117, 118, 119, 502), 502–3
- Idem, *Jamāl*: 135

10. Kitāb al-mut'a
11. Kitāb al-farā'iḍ

(Najāshī: 37). There is no trace of the contents of these works in what has survived from Ibn al-Baṭā'inī. A book entitled *Kitāb al-mut'a* is ascribed in *Fihrist*: 26 to Aḥmad b. Maytham who related several other works of Ibn al-Baṭā'inī and was possibly mistakenly credited with authoring some of them, as noted above.

12. Kitāb

His notebook of *ḥadīth*, related by Aḥmad b. Maytham (*Fihrist*: 50). Apart from the quotations on topics that correspond to the titles of his previous works, the bulk of the remaining material from Ibn al-Baṭā'inī is on virtuous acts. It thus seems very likely that he also had a book on *faḍā'il al-a'māl* (possibly as *Kitāb al-nawādir*, a title ascribed to Aḥmad b. Maytham in *Fihrist*: 26 where some other works of Ibn al-Baṭā'inī are also misattributed), to which many of the following passages may have belonged:

- *Maḥāsin*: 205, 390, 602 (two reports)
- *Kāfī* 4: 152
  5: 330, 517
  6: 223–4, 546–7
  7: 430, 441
- Ibn Qūlawayh: 112, 201–2
- Ibn Bābawayh, *Amālī*: 116, 268, 473 (two reports), 552, 561, 646
- *'Ilal* 1: 42, 86
- *Tahdhīb* 6: 45

82: Ḥasan al-'Uranī

Ḥasan b. al-Ḥusayn al-Anṣārī al-'Uranī, a Kūfan of Medinese origin and a non-Imāmite Shī'ite. He was among the supporters of Yaḥyā b. 'Abd Allāh b. al-Ḥasan when the latter began his revolt against Hārūn al-Rashīd in 175.

Aḥmad b. Sahl al-Rāzī: 197 (whence Abū 'l-'Abbās al-Ḥasanī: 304); Ibn Abī Ḥātim 3: 7; Ibn Ḥibbān, *Majrūḥīn* 1: 238–9; Ibn 'Adī: 743–4; Najāshī: 51; *Mīzān* 1: 483–5; *Lisān* 2: 372–4. See also Ḥaskānī 1: 96, 384.

Kitāb 'an al-rijāl 'an Ja'far b. Muḥammad

Most of the surviving transmissions of Ḥasan al-'Uranī are on the virtues of 'Alī and the House of the Prophet. He worked, however, within Sunnī circles of *ḥadīth* transmission and generally heard and related to Sunnī transmitters of *ḥadīth*. What made Najāshī: 51 name him among the Imāmite authors was a notebook he had of what he received from Ja'far al-Ṣādiq through the latter's students. This should have been one of several similar notebooks where this author recorded material from different masters.

A good part of the notebook in question seems to have survived in later works, as in the following examples:

- Muḥammad b. Sulaymān 1: 159, 238 (partially also 2: 297), 460, 492
  2: 159, 160, 239, 296 (two reports), 517, 566–7
- *Kāfī* 3: 62
- Furāt: 49, 106, 606 (also Abū Nu'aym, *Mā nazal*: 285)
- Dāraquṭnī 2: 42–3
- Mufīd, *Amālī*: 319
- Ṭūsī, *Amālī*: 272 (also Ḥaskānī 1: 169)
- *Tahdhīb* 6: 396
- Ḥaskānī 1: 419
  2: 298
- Ibn 'Asākir 42: 311

83: Ibn Rāshid

Abū Muḥammad Ḥasan b. Rāshid, a Kūfan Shī'ite who resided in Baghdad. He was a client/servant of the 'Abbāsid Manṣūr and continued as an aide to his successors down to Hārūn al-Rashīd. He transmitted from Ja'far al-Ṣādiq and Mūsā al-Kāẓim.

Barqī: 78, 117; Ṭabarī 8: 355–6; Ibn al-Ghaḍā'irī: 49; *Fihrist*: 53–4.

Kitāb al-rāhib wa 'l-rāhiba

(Najāshī: 134; *Fihrist*: 53–4). The text of this work, an alleged conversation between Mūsā al-Kāẓim and a monk and a nun from Najrān in Yemen, is quoted in *Kāfī* 1: 481–4. The text ibid. 1: 478–81 is most likely a variant of the same.

84: Ibn Ḥayy

Abū 'Abd Allāh Ḥasan b. Ṣāliḥ b. Ḥayy al-Thawrī al-Hamdānī, a Kūfan Butrī Zaydī and a prominent jurist of Kūfa in his time. He died in 168 or 169.

Bibliographical material about this scholar can be found in many sources. For lists see the editors' footnotes to Mizzī 6: 177 and Dhahabī, *Ta'rīkh* 10 (years 161–170): 131. For a summary account of those sources on Ḥasan b. Ṣāliḥ and his views, see van Ess 1: 246–51.

Aṣl

Ḥasan b. Ṣāliḥ left a number of works listed by Ibn al-Nadīm: 227 (see also Ibn 'Adī: 729). He transmitted *ḥadīth* from Ja'far al-Ṣādiq and, through intermediaries, Muḥammad al-Bāqir, among others. That is how the Imāmites became interested in this scholar's notebook of *ḥadīth* that Ṭūsī received through the transmitter Ḥasan b. Maḥbūb (*Fihrist*: 50). The following quotations from Ḥasan b. Ṣāliḥ by that transmitter must therefore represent the notebook in question:

- *Maḥāsin*: 52 (also *Kāfī* 3: 478)
- 'Ayyāshī 2: 149 (as attested by *Kāfī* 4: 212–13 [partially repeated in 8: 283])
- *Kāfī* 3: 2
  5: 34, 409
  6: 80, 125, 182, 200–201
  7: 113–14, 143, 260, 289, 292, 306, 308, 327
- *Faqīh* 3: 189
- *Tahdhīb* 8: 176
  9: 194–5 (repeated at 216)
  10: 224

There are also other quotations by Ḥasan b. Ṣāliḥ from Ja'far al-Ṣādiq, as well as Muḥammad al-Bāqir through intermediaries, quoted on the authority of transmitters other than Ḥasan b. Maḥbūb. Here are a few examples:

- Ibn Abī Shayba 1: 9, 119, 126–7
- Aḥmad 1: 267
- 'Ayyāshī 2: 321
- Aḥmad b. 'Īsā 1: 139
  3: 32, 99, 126, 140–41, 167
- *Kāfī* 4: 486
- Ibn 'Adī: 557
- Ṭūsī, *Amālī*: 513 (repeated with a different *isnād* at 609–10)
- *Manāqib* 4: 249
- *Bishārat al-Muṣṭafā*: 86
- Ibn Abī 'l-Ḥadīd 4: 106

85: Ḥassān al-Jammāl

Abū 'Alī Ḥassān b. Mihrān b. al-Mughīra, the cameleer, a Kūfan client of the Banū Kāhil of Asad Khuzayma and a transmitter from Ja'far al-Ṣādiq.

Barqī: 80; Najāshī: 147; *Fihrist*: 64; *Rijāl*: 132, 193. See also *Kāfī* 4: 566.

He appears in *Maḥāsin*: 395 as Abū 'Alī Ḥassān b. Mihrān *al-Nakha'ī*. Further confusion about the tribal affiliation of this transmitter is reported in Najāshī: 147. Different tribal affiliation may at times refer to different persons, as noted above.

Kitāb

Ḥassān's notebook of *ḥadīth*, related by a number of Shī'ite transmitters (Najāshī: 147). The following quotations from Ḥassān al-Jammāl in Shī'ite works of *ḥadīth*, most of them related from him through an identical chain of transmission, may go back to this notebook:

- *Maḥāsin*: 391, 395 (two variants of the previous report)
- Ṣaffār: 61 (also *Kāfī* 1: 145), 171, 222, 294, 471
- *Kāfī* 2: 398, 455, 475
  4: 95 (read *Mihrān* for *Mukhtār* as in the following two cases), 156, 563, 566–7 (also Ibn al-Juḥām: 400; Qāḍī Nu'mān, *Sharḥ* 1: 240–41 with an addition in both)
  8: 87–8 (read *'an Sayf 'an Ḥassān* as in 4: 95, 156, 563)

- 'Alī b. Ibrāhīm 2: 204
- *Khiṣāl*: 519
- *Tahdhīb* 2: 272
- 'Abd al-Karīm b. Ṭāwūs: 79

86: Ḥātim al-Madanī

Abū Ismā'īl Ḥātim b. Ismā'īl al-Madanī, a Kūfan client who moved to Medina and lived there until the end of his life. He was a prominent Sunnī transmitter of *ḥadīth* in his time and a transmitter from Ja'far al-Ṣādiq, among others. He died in 187.

Almost all Sunnī biographical dictionaries of the transmitters of *ḥadīth* have entries on Ḥātim b. Ismā'īl. See the lists of many of them in the editors' footnotes to Mizzī 5: 187 and Dhahabī, *Ta'rīkh* 12 (years 181–190): 107.

Kitābuh 'an Ja'far b. Muḥammad

Ḥātim's biographers mention his notebook of *ḥadīth* as a sound and reliable work (see Mizzī 5: 190). What made Shī'ite scholars of *ḥadīth* interested in him was a notebook he had of his transmissions from Ja'far al-Ṣādiq (Najāshī: 147). The material of this notebook is widely quoted in later works. Examples include the following:

- Shāfi'ī, *Musnad*: 133 (also Bayhaqī 3: 122), 226, 509 (also Bayhaqī 6: 332), 532
- Ibn Sa'd 2: 179–80
  Ḥasan: 68, 69 (also Ibn Abī Shayba 5: 253), 73 (two reports, the first also in Tirmidhī 3: 353; *Kāfī* 6: 469; Ṭabarānī, *Akhbār al-Ḥasan*: 33)
- Ibn Abī Shayba 1: 48 (also Ibn Māja: 165), 153–4, 186
  3: 87, 257, 358 (also Nasā'ī 2: 422)
  4: 1, 95, 119, 144
  5: 22, 72, 81
  6: 285, 311 (repeated 11: 406)
  8: 15 (also *Maḥāsin*: 580; whence *Kāfī* 6: 383), 292 (also *Maḥāsin*: 617), 399, 548 (whence Aḥmad b. 'Īsā 4: 263)
  9: 236, 459, 470, 509, 528
  10: 165

14: 185
Al-juz' al-mafqūd: 119, 122 (read *Ḥātim* for *Jābir* in both cases), 319, 323, 377–81 (a lengthy report on the Prophet's pilgrimage to Mecca; also in Dārimī 2: 44–6; Muslim: 886–92; Ibn Māja: 1022–7; Abū Dāwūd 2: 182–6; Ibn Ḥibbān, *Ṣaḥīḥ* 9: 253–6, and many other sources)

- Muslim: 1445 (also Tirmidhī 3: 215)
- Ibn Māja: 355 (also Tirmidhī 1: 524)
- *Maḥāsin*: 427, 635
- Ibn Abī 'l-Dunyā, *Ahwāl*: 259
- Aḥmad b. 'Īsā 2: 268 (three reports)
  3: 92 (read *'an Ḥātim b. Ismā'īl* for *'an Ḥātim 'an Ismā'īl*), 119, 124, 161
  4: 216, 240, 288
- Nasā'ī 2: 206, 422
  8: 419
- *Kāfī* 4: 30 (also *Khiṣāl*: 133)
  5: 224
  6: 475, 476
- Abū 'Abd Allāh al-Shajarī, *Adhān*: 23–4 (through five different *isnād*s to Ḥātim, repeated at 63–9 through twelve other *isnād*s)
- Ibn Ḥazm 7: 381 (quoting Ibn Abī Shayba)
- Bayhaqī 2: 86
- Ṭūsī, *Amālī*: 401–402
- Ibn Abī 'l-Ḥadīd 2: 202

87: Hishām b. al-Ḥakam

Abū Muḥammad Hishām b. al-Ḥakam, seller of canvas, a client of Kūfan origin who grew up in Wāsiṭ and later moved to Baghdad. A close disciple of the Imāms Ja'far al-Ṣādiq and Mūsā al-Kāẓim, he was the most prominent Shī'ite *mutakallim* of his time, indeed of the entire three centuries of the history of the Shī'ite creed covered by the present work. He died in Kūfa in 179.

Biographical material about Hishām and accounts of his theological views appear in very many sources as well as numerous monographs in different languages. For an adequate summary of that material, see the entries on him in the *Encyclopaedia of Islam*, second edn., 3: 496–8 (W. Madelung) and van Ess 1: 349–79.

His profession as *bayyāʿ al-karābīs* is mentioned in *Mashyakha*: 437. That goes well with Rāghib, *Muḥāḍarāt* 3: 13 where it is said that Hishām and his Ibāḍī partner, ʿAbd Allāh b. Yazīd, were *sharīkān fī 'l-bazz*. For that partner, see the editor's introduction to Aḥmad b. Yaḥyā al-Nāṣir's *Kitāb al-najāt*: 4–9.[59] For Hishām's partnership with him, see Jāḥiẓ, *Bayān* 1: 46, 47; Masʿūdī 4: 28; *Kamāl*: 363. Masʿūdī narrates a story in which the Ibāḍī partner seeks the hand of the daughter of Hishām for his own son. Two other versions of the same story appear in *Kāfī* 5: 345 and Rāghib, *Muḥāḍarāt* 3: 13. The point that Hishām traded in clothing can further be confirmed by a report in *Kāfī* 5: 160–61 where he is depicted as selling *Shāpūrī* clothing on a specific occasion. The word *ḥarrār* in Masʿūdī 5: 21 (as well as *kharrāz* in a different instance ibid. 3: 194 of the Beirut, 1965 edition) may have therefore been a corruption of *bazzāz*. Other discrepancies in the biographical material on his life are discussed in the two references given in the previous paragraph.

Ibn al-Nadīm: 224 (whence Najāshī: 433; *Fihrist*: 175) gives a long list of Hishām's writings. Najāshī: 433 adds a few titles at the beginning and toward the end of the list. In one case, he explains that the work was actually put together by a student of Hishām from his statements. This seems to have been the case with at least two other items on Najāshī's list that contain records of Hishām's arguments on the topics of Divine unity and the Imāmate.

1. *Kitāb / Aṣl*

Hishām's notebook of *ḥadīth*, related by Ibn Abī ʿUmayr (Abū Ghālib: 177; Najāshī: 433; *Fihrist*: 175), a former student and disciple of Hishām (Ibn Bābawayh, *Amālī*: 731–2; also *ʿIlal* 1: 194–5; *Khiṣāl*: 215; *Maʿānī*: 133) who broke with him over a doctrinal dispute (*Kāfī* 1: 410). Most quotations from Hishām in Shīʿite works of *ḥadīth* are on the authority of the same transmitter. Here is a list:

- Aḥmad b. Muḥammad b. ʿĪsā: 61 (cf. *Kāfī* 7: 453), 87
- Muḥammad b. ʿAlī b. Maḥbūb: 96 (two reports)
- *Maḥāsin*: 83, 388, 393 (also *Kāfī* 2: 202–3), 394, 399 (also *Kāfī* 6: 280), 410 (also *Kāfī* 6: 280–81), 421(also *Kāfī* 6: 288), 504, 535 (also *Kāfī* 6: 347), 538 (also *Kāfī* 6: 348), 570–71, 608 (also *Khiṣāl*: 159), 609 (also *Kāfī* 6: 529), 610 (also *Kāfī* 6: 525), 621, 637 (also *Kāfī* 6: 542)

---

59. This work is a refutation of a book by the said ʿAbd Allāh b. Yazīd against the Muʿtazilites, named in Ibn al-Nadīm: 233. Ibn al-Nadīm also names a work by this author against the Shīʿites. For similar cases of friendship between the Shīʿites and their staunch opponents in the early periods, see *Kāfī* 3: 133; Jāḥiẓ, *Bayān* 1: 46; *Kamāl*: 510; *Ghayba*: 311 (see also Abū 'l-Faraj, *Aghānī* 7: 264–6).

- Ṣaffār: 365
- 'Ayyāshī 1: 311 (cf. *Qiṣaṣ*: 61)
- *Kāfī* 1: 13–20, 69, 128, 449
  2: 75, 109, 156, 191–2, 202–3, 264–5, 344, 474 (see also 315 [and 385–6, the latter seemingly an oral communication])
  3: 12, 209, 205, 368, 462–3, 506 (possibly also 249 [two reports])
  4: 51, 66, 128, 171 (see also 'Ayyāshī 1: 43; *Faqīh* 2: 77), 213 (also *'Ilal* 2: 104), 262 (two reports), 316, 327, 354, 412, 462, 470, 476, 477, 515
  5: 152, 160–61, 208, 219, 289, 333, 398
  6: 5, 6, 280–81 (two reports), 288, 341, 346, 347, 348, 382, 479, 483, 499, 521, 525, 529, 542
  7: 4 (repeated at 398–9 with variations), 22, 414 (read *Sa'd wa Hishām* as in *Tahdhīb* 6: 229), 453
  8: 163 (possibly)[60]
- Kashshī: 176, 202, 304, 310, 323, 349 (possibly also 233–4)
- Ibn Qūlawayh: 294–5 (repeated at 297), 312
- Ibn Bābawayh, *Amālī*: 319
- *Faqīh* 1: 443
  2: 31, 321, 352, 355, 386, 412, 478 (possibly also 599)
  3: 572–3 (also *'Ilal* 2: 178–9; *'Iqāb*: 306–7)
  4: 115
- *'Ilal* 1: 46–7, 49
- *Khiṣāl*: 392–3
- *Tawḥīd*: 134, 137 (repeated at 138), 250, 350–51
- Abū Ṭālib: 191
- *Tahdhīb* 1: 354, 376, 467
  2: 302, 333
  3: 284–5
  4: 158, 192, 331
  5: 491
  6: 229, 230 (possibly), 343
  7: 211
  9: 73(possibly)
- Ḥaskānī 1: 187

60. With the exception of 1: 13–20, 69, 4: 51, 66, 6: 341, 346, all above quotations are recorded in the *Kāfī* through an identical chain of transmission, indicating quotation from a book.

2. *Kitāb ʿilal al-taḥrīm wa ʾl-farāʾiḍ*

(Najāshī: 433 where *ʿilal al-taḥrīm* and *farāʾiḍ* appear, most likely erroneously, as titles of separate works). There are numerous quotations from Hishām on the topic of this work in later works that in all likelihood originated from this book. They include the following:

(A) **ON THE RATIONALE OF PROHIBITIONS:**

- *Maḥāsin*: 565 (whence *ʿIlal* 2: 219; also Ibn ʿAdī: 580)
- *ʿIlal* 2: 168
- *Iḥtijāj* 2: 238–9

(B) **ON THE RATIONALE OF OBLIGATIONS:**

- *Kāfī* 5: 363–4
- *ʿIlal* 1: 95
  2: 6–7, 22 (also *Faqīh* 1: 305), 24, 30 (also *Faqīh* 1: 272), 66 (also *Faqīh* 2: 73), 72

The large fragment quoted in *Kāfī* 5: 363–4 seems to represent the original structure of the work.

3. *Kitāb al-imāma*

4. *Kitāb al-waṣiyya wa ʾl-radd ʿalā man ankarahā*

These two seem to have been the main works by Hishām on the topic of the Imāmate. There are numerous references to his works (e.g. Ibn al-Haytham: 62) or work (e.g. ʿAbd al-Jabbār, *Mughnī* 20/1: 273; Abū Ṭālib, *Diʿāma*: 27) on that topic in early sources. Numerous statements quoted from Hishām on more general aspects of the topic (e.g. Ṣaffār: 35; ʿAyyāshī 1: 43, 58, 311; *Kāfī* 1: 262, 428; Ḥaskānī 1: 187; Ibn Ḥazm, *Fiṣal* 4: 172) fit the title of the first work, whereas those on the more specific question of the Imāmate through explicit designation (*naṣṣ*) and will (*waṣiyya*) (e.g. Ṣaffār: 414; ʿAyyāshī 1: 309–11; Ibn Ḥazm, *Fiṣal* 4: 169) may have originated from the second. A passage quoted from Hishām in Ibn Ḥazm, *Fiṣal* 4: 172, if taken from this latter work, indicates that it was written after the death of Jaʿfar al-Ṣādiq. The passage states that the Imām would become specifically known, without any need for a clear designation, if his brothers suffered from physical defects that disqualified them for the leadership of the Muslim community. This question arose after Ja'far al-Ṣādiq's death in debates between the followers of Mūsā al-Kāẓim and the Faṭḥites (see Kashshī: 282).

5. *Kitāb al-tadbīr*
6. *Kitāb al-majālis fī 'l-imāma*
7. *Kitāb al-majālis fī 'l-tawḥīd*

Najāshī: 433 defines the first work as a book on the question of the Imāmate put together by Hishām's student, 'Alī b. Manṣūr, from Hishām's statements on the topic. In the entry on 'Alī b. Manṣūr in Najāshī: 250, however, the book is named as *Kitāb al-tadbīr fī 'l-tawḥīd wa 'l-imāma*. It may thus be the same as the two titles added by Najāshī at the end of Ibn al-Nadīm's list of Hishām's works as *Kitāb al-majālis fī 'l-tawḥīd* and *Kitāb al-majālis fī 'l-imāma*, clearly records of Hishām's debates with his contemporaries over those topics, possibly put together by one or more of his students. The record of Hishām's debate with an Egyptian *Zindīq* in *Kāfī* 1: 72–4 (also *Tawḥīd*: 293–5) is in fact on the authority of the above-mentioned student. There are numerous other debates between Hishām and his contemporaries on the questions of the unity of God (e.g. Ibn Qutayba, *'Uyūn* 2: 153 [whence Ibn 'Abd Rabbih 2: 411–12]; *Kāfī* 1: 80–82, 128–9; *Tawḥīd*: 243–50, 270–75) and related matters (e.g. Mas'ūdī 5: 21–2), and of the Imāmate (e.g. Ibn Qutayba, *'Uyūn* 2: 150 [whence Ibn 'Abd Rabbih 2: 412]; *Kāfī* 1: 169–71 [also Kashshī: 271–3], 171–3; Kashshī: 258–63, 266; Mas'ūdī 5: 22–3 quoting Abū 'Īsā al-Warrāq in his *Kitāb al-majālis*; Mufīd, *Majālis* 1: 9, 25, 26–7, 54–5; *Ikhtiṣāṣ*: 96–8), all of which may originally have belonged to the works in question. Opinions ascribed to Hishām in law books on sectarian legal matters such as the invalidity of triple divorce (e.g. Ibn Qudāma, *Mughnī* 10: 327) may have been informed by material in Hishām's debates and works on the Imāmate and related topics.

8. *Kitāb al-dilāla 'alā ḥadath al-ajsām*

Such is the title of the work in Najāshī, though Ibn al-Nadīm and *Fihrist* have it as *Kitāb al-dilālāt 'alā ḥadath* (in *Fihrist*: *ḥudūth*) *al-ashyā'*.

9. *Kitāb al-radd 'alā 'l-Zanādiqa*

This may be the same as a long text quoted in *Iḥtijāj* 2: 197–200, 212–50 as a question and answer dialogue between a *Zindīq* and Ja'far al-Ṣādiq, related by Hishām (ibid. 2: 197). Parts of this text are also cited, through an identical *isnād*, in *Kāfī* 1: 80–81, 83–5, 108, 110, 168; *Tawḥīd*: 243–50 (also *Ma'ānī*: 8) on the authority of Hishām.

10. Kitāb al-radd 'alā aṣḥāb al-ithnayn

A few discussions by Hishām on the topic of this work are recorded in the sources, including two in *Kāfī* 1: 80–82, 128–9 (also *Tawḥīd*: 133).

11. Kitāb al-tawḥīd
12. Kitāb al-radd 'alā aṣḥāb al-ṭabā'i'
13. Kitāb al-radd 'alā Arasṭālīs fī 'l-tawḥīd
14. Kitāb al-shaykh wa 'l-ghulām

The topic of the last work is not defined in Ibn al-Nadīm's list, but Najāshī explains that it is *fī 'l-tawḥīd*. There are numerous quotations from Hishām on the topic, sometimes as transmissions from Ja'far al-Ṣādiq (e.g. *Tawḥīd*: 134, 137, 250), but mostly as citations from him in a style that indicates that they were taken from his works. Such is the case with a large fragment quoted from him in Shahrastānī, *Nihāya*: 217–18, another in *Kāfī* 1: 99–100, and a shorter citation in Ibn Ḥazm, *Fiṣal* 5: 193. There is a reference in Kashshī: 258 to Hishām's hostility toward the philosophers that can be confirmed by the title of no. 13 above.

15. Kitāb al-radd 'alā Hishām al-Jawālīqī

A refutation against the author's contemporary and fellow Shī'ite *mutakallim*, clearly on matters of divine body and form that divided the two (see *Kāfī* 1: 105–6; Kashshī: 279, 284–5; for more details, see Abū 'l-Ḥasan al-Ash'arī 1: 109, 115–18, 283, 2: 38, 199; Khayyāṭ: 6, 57 and many other sources). Their dispute was serious enough for the notables of the Shī'ite community to arrange a debate between the two to settle their differences (Kashshī: 279). Jawālīqī was, however, an admirer of Hishām (see especially *Tawḥīd*: 289; also Kashshī: 275–9 [the latter also in *Kāfī* 1: 171–3 where the name of Jawālīqī as the original transmitter is missing]).

16. *Kitāb [al-radd] 'alā Shayṭān al-Ṭāq*

A work against another contemporary and fellow Shī'ite *mutakallim* who held theological opinions different from those of Hishām on many questions (see, for instance, Abū 'l-Ḥasan al-Ash'arī 1: 111–12, 116, 118, 123, 291–2, 2: 38, 184; Ibn Ḥazm, *Fiṣal* 2: 269, 4: 158, 5: 39; Maqdisī, *Bad'* 5: 132).

17. *Kitāb al-mīzān*

As far as can be judged from the few surviving passages, this work discussed, either exclusively or inter alia, the differences of opinion among the Shī'a in the time of the author. Ibn Ḥazm quotes two passages from the work in his *Fiṣal*. The first, 4: 157 (whence Subkī, *Fatāwā* 2: 567), quotes the opinion of Ḥasan b. Ṣāliḥ b. Ḥayy on the question whether all members of the tribe of Quraysh qualify for the position of *imām*, or whether it is restricted to the descendants of the Prophet. The second, 5: 45, relates to the opinions and practices of the *Kisfiyya*, followers of Abū Manṣūr al-'Ijlī, an early Extremist group. Two other passages ibid. 4: 169, 172 may also go back to this book of Hishām, as in all likelihood the passage quoted by 'Abd al-Jabbār in his *Tathbīt*: 224 (paraphrased also at 448) on the attitudes of the early Shī'ites to the question of the Imāmate.[61] This work might also have been used by earlier heresiographers such as Zurqān, especially for quotations from Hishām on his own opinions (e.g. Abū 'l-Ḥasan al-Ash'arī 1: 109, 126–7).[62]

In Ibn al-Nadīm's list (whence also in Najāshī and *Fihrist*), this title is followed by a *Kitāb al-maydān*, but this may have been a corruption of *Kitāb al-mīzān* in Ibn al-Nadīm's source.

18. *Kitāb ikhtilāf al-nās fī 'l-imāma*

This is in all likelihood the long text quoted in *Kamāl*: 362–8 as the record of Hishām's last debate with the heads of other theological schools of his time in the house of the vizier, Yaḥyā b. Khālid al-Barmakī. The text begins with a description of the weekly sessions of theological debate in

61. On this matter, see further *Mīzān* 3: 421.
62. A similar title is given in Ibn al-Athīr, *Kāmil* 8: 28–9 for a work by Abū Shākir Maymūn b. Dayṣān, a Manichaean whose classes Hishām had allegedly attended in early life (Barqī: 92; Kashshī: 278).

the vizier's house on Sundays, and ends with the report of the debate and its aftermath in which the caliph Hārūn al-Rashīd was so incensed as to order the arrest of Hishām. Subsequently Hishām escaped to Kūfa and went into hiding there, dying shortly afterwards. The debate begins with the vizier asking Hishām and his Ibāḍī partner to debate *fī-mā ikhtalaftum fīh min al-imāma* (whence, most likely, the title). A shorter variant of this account is recorded in Kashshī: 258–63.

Wilferd Madelung has suggested[63] that this work of Hishām's may have served as the common source for the two redactions by Ḥasan b. Mūsā al-Nawbakhtī and Sa'd b. 'Abd Allāh al-Ash'arī al-Qummī of a book on early Muslim sects. In this respect, the *Kitāb al-mīzān* appears to be a better candidate. Judging by the references to the Imāmites as *Rāfiḍa* (Nawbakhtī: 76; Sa'd b. 'Abd Allāh: 78 [also 92, though in this case the word *Rāfiḍa* is probably a corruption of *Wāqifa*]) and the indifference shown to some anti-Shī'ite ideas such as Abū Ṭālib's death as a non-Muslim (Nawbakhtī: 60, edited out by Sa'd b. 'Abd Allāh), it may be argued that the common source of the two redactions might have been a Sunnī work.[64] Besides, none of the above-mentioned quotations from the *Kitāb al-mīzān* is attested in either of the two works.

19. Kitāb fī 'l-jabr wa 'l-qadar
20. Kitāb al-qadar
21. Kitāb al-istiṭā'a

There are a few quotations from Hishām on the topics of these works in later works, including Abū 'l-Ḥasan al-Ash'arī 1: 110; Kashshī: 267; *Tawḥīd*: 350–51. Bishr b. al-Mu'tamir, the Mu'tazilite theologian (d. 210), wrote a refutation of the last work, named by Ibn al-Nadīm: 205 as *Kitāb al-istiṭā'a 'alā Hishām b. al-Ḥakam*. The one line of poetry by Bishr against Hishām quoted in 'Abd al-Jabbār, *Ṭabaqāt*: 265 may have been from this latter work (for another example of poetry directed against Hishām, see Khayyāṭ: 119).

63. See his "Bemerkungen zur imamitischen Firaq-Literatur," in *Der Islam* 43 (1967): 37–52, now in his *Religious Schools and Sects in Medieval Islam*, XV.
64. However, given the fact that those references are in the form of quotations from others, even this theory is open to debate.

22. *Kitāb [fī] al-Ḥakamayn*

Ibn Bābawayh quotes a passage from this work in his *Faqīh* 3: 522 where he calls it *Faṣl li-Hishām b. al-Ḥakam ma' ba'ḍ al-mukhālifīn fī 'l-ḥakamayn bi-Ṣiffīn: 'Amr b. al-'Āṣ wa Abī Mūsā al-Ash'arī.* Judging by this passage, the work was a record of a debate between Hishām and an opponent on this topic.

23. *Kitāb al-radd 'alā 'l-Mu'tazila fī Ṭalḥa wa 'l-Zubayr*
24. *Kitāb ākhar 'alā 'l-Mu'tazila*

The second of these two anti-Mu'tazilite works seems to be the one repeatedly quoted by Ibn al-Rāwandī in his *Faḍīḥat al-Mu'tazila.* Passages from Hishām's work are thus preserved in Khayyāṭ: 108–9, 115, 116, 117, 119, 120. This may have also been the work cited by Jāḥiẓ as quoted in Abū 'l-Ḥasan al-Ash'arī 1: 104.

25. *Kitāb al-alfāẓ*

The title of this work has encouraged some recent Shī'ite scholars (e.g. Ḥasan al-Ṣadr, *Ta'sīs al-shī'a*: 310; Muḥammad Bāqir al-Ṣadr, *Durūs* 1: 52) to think of it as an early work on *uṣūl al-fiqh*. The title, however, appears in Ṭūsī's *Fihrist* as *Kitāb al-alṭāf*, a well known theological concept and an appropriate title for a work by someone deeply engaged in debates with the Mu'tazilites. Even as *Kitāb al-alfāẓ*, the work should have treated the ontological roots, rather than the etymological aspects, of words. After all, none of the early Shī'ite authors on *uṣūl al-fiqh* ever made the slightest reference to this work, let alone quoting anything from it, even indirectly.

26. *Kitāb al-ma'rifa*

The topic of the work is a popular theme for numerous theological works. However, the title may refer not to a theological work on this theme but to a long text quoted in *Kāfī* 1: 13–20 on the authority of Hishām consisting of advice given to him by Mūsā al-Kāẓim, beginning with a discussion about how to know God.

27. *Kitāb al-thamāniyat abwāb*

This may be the same as a long text quoted in Ibn Bābawayh, *Amālī*: 279–83 that describes paradise and its gates, though in the surviving text only six out of the eight gates are described.

28. *Kitāb al-akhbār [wa kayfa taṣiḥḥ]*

A quotation in Khayyāṭ: 157–8 from Hishām on the validity of a widely transmitted report (*mutawātir*) fits the title of this work.

29. *Kitāb Burayh al-Naṣrānī*

Mentioned in Abū Ghālib: 176 and *Fihrist*: 40, this text is quoted in full in *Tawḥīd*: 270–75 (a few passages also in *Kāfī* 1: 227). It is a text written in the form of a record of a fictitious debate between Hishām and a head of the Christian community of Mesopotamia.

30. *Kitāb fī 'l-jism wa 'l-ru'ya*

'Abd al-Jabbār, *Ṭabaqāt*: 152 names a book by the Mu'tazilite Abū 'Alī al-Jubbā'ī against Hishām's *Kitāb fī 'l-jism wa 'l-ru'ya*. This may well be a pejorative reference to Hishām's *Kitāb al-tawḥīd* or his book against the Mu'tazilites (see also Nasafī, *Tabṣira* 1: 219). A passage quoted by Jāḥiẓ from a book by Hishām (cited in Abū 'l-Ḥasan al-Ash'arī 1: 104) and a lengthy passage in *Kāfī* 1: 99–100 are both on the topic of *ru'ya*.

88: Hishām al-Ḥannāṭ

Hishām b. al-Muthannā, the wheat seller, a Kūfan transmitter from Ja'far al-Ṣādiq.

Barqī: 92 (as above); Najāshī: 435 (as *Hāshim* b. al-Muthannā); *Rijāl*: 319 (# 4755: *Hishām* al-Ḥannāṭ, # 4764: *Hāshim* b. al-Muthannā al-Ḥannāṭ). See also *Mashyakha*: 449 (*Hāshim* al-Ḥannāṭ); Mufīd, *Majālis* 1: 127 (*Hishām* b. al-Muthannā). The name is also spelt variously in the *isnād*s of his transmissions.

Kitāb

His notebook of *ḥadīth*, related by a number of transmitters including Ibn Abī 'Umayr (Najāshī: 435). The following quotations from this author are by the same transmitter:

- Aḥmad b. Muḥammad b. 'Īsā: 94 (cf. *Tahdhīb* 7: 326–7, 328)
- *Kāfī* 1: 306 (partially repeated in 4: 4)
  4: 55, 360, 426, 550
  5: 305
  6: 486
- Kashshī: 115–17

89: Al-Jawālīqī

Abū Muḥammad Hishām b. Sālim, the sack-maker, later the seller of fodder, a Kūfan client and a transmitter from Ja'far al-Ṣādiq and Mūsā al-Kāẓim. He was a well known Shī'ite *mutakallim* of his time whose opinions on various theological matters are recorded in general theological and heresiographical works.

For a summary of the biographical and heresiographical material on the life and opinions of this scholar, see now van Ess 1: 342–8.

1. Kitāb al-tafsīr

(Najāshī: 434). Many of the numerous comments on Qur'ānic passages quoted from this author in Shī'ite works of *tafsīr* and *ḥadīth*, including many tales of the prophets, may represent parts of the material of this work. Examples are as follows:

- Aḥmad b. Muḥammad b. 'Īsā: 53
- *Maḥāsin*: 42, 105 (also *'Iqāb*: 327–8); 114 (also *'Iqāb*: 318), 192, 200, 237 (also *Tawḥīd*: 385), 247, 257 (also *Kāfī* 2: 217), 264 (also *Kāfī* 2: 126), 321, 329 (also *'Ilal* 2: 257–8), 352 (also 'Ayyāshī 2: 285, 286), 576 (read *Hishām 'an Sulaymān b. Khālid*)
- Ṣaffār: 39 (also Ṭūsī, *Amālī*: 664), 194–5, 221, 311–12, 373–4 (also *Kāfī* 1: 174–5)

- 'Ayyāshī 1: 17, 29, 156 (two reports), 168, 189, 201, 210, 267, 279, 293, 296, 306–9, 339–40 (also Ṭūsī, *Amālī*: 657–8) 341, 357
  2: 110, 127, 177–8, 186–7, 188, 210, 254, 276–7, 283, 286, 328, 330, 334, 341 (also Ṭabrisī, *Majma'* 30: 237 quoting the lost second half of 'Ayyāshī's work)
- *Kāfī* 1: 146–7 (also *Tawḥīd*: 333), 175, 382–3, 398, 407–8 (repeated in 5: 279–80), 430, 448
  2: 8–10, 15, 80, 81, 269
  3: 256
  4: 216 (same as Ṭabrisī, *Majma'* 30: 237 quoting 'Ayyāshī)
  5: 128, 344 (and possibly 312 and 503 too)
  8: 204–5, 277–9, 338–41
- Kashshī: 43
- Ibn al-Juḥām: 217
- Nu'mānī: 228 (also *Kamāl*: 141–2)
- 'Alī b. Ibrāhīm 1: 27–8, 60, 74, 93, 95, 114, 132, 140, 165
  2: 50, 84, 100, 114, 118, 168, 198, 346
- Ibn Bābawayh, *Amālī*: 55 (also *Khiṣāl*: 218), 87, 111, 159–60 (also *Kamāl*: 524–5), 637, 672 (and possibly 600–601 [also *Tawḥīd*: 401])
- *'Ilal* 1: 10–11, 52
  2: 168, 234–6, 250
- *'Iqāb*: 253
- *Kamāl*: 138–9, 523
- *Khiṣāl*: 118, 142–3, 248, 260–61
- *Ma'ānī*: 9 (also *Tawḥīd*: 312), 31–2, 248
- *Tawḥīd*: 40, 289, 329
- *Thawāb*: 144, 194–5
- Khazzāz: 256–60 (a revised text)
- Mufīd, *Amālī*: 213
- *Ikhtiṣāṣ*: 10, 254–5, 333
- Abū Ṭālib: 359
- Ṭūsī, *Amālī*: 417–18, 658–9, 659–62 (nine reports)
- *Miṣbāḥ*: 106–7
- *Qiṣaṣ*: 41, 43, 50, 61–2, 63–4, 103–4, 108, 118, 132–3, 140–41 (two reports), 142, 164, 175, 180, 202, 208, 217, 241
- *Makārim al-akhlāq*: 129–30 (the first non-Qur'ānic part of the report also in *Maḥāsin*: 62)
- Ibn Ṭāwūs, *Yaqīn*: 264–5 (possibly)

2. *Kitāb al-ḥajj*

(Najāshī: 434). There are a fair number of quotations from this scholar on the topic of *ḥajj* (e.g. *Maḥāsin*: 68, 296 [also *Tawḥīd*: 350]; *Kāfī* 4: 272, 282, 307, 328, 359, 361, 375, 443, 493, 5: 72 [also Abān al-Sindī: 40–41; Ṭūsī, *Amālī*: 662]). The volume of the surviving material is, however, not large. It could be that the word *ḥajj* in the title is a corruption of *ḥujja*, on which topic, in its Imāmite sense, much more is quoted from this scholar. Referring to the works of the Imāmite theologians who supported the idea of explicit designation (*naṣṣ*) as the basis for legitimate succession to the Prophet, Abū Ṭālib, *Di'āma*: 27 mentions, among others, the works of the two theologians Hishām b. al-Ḥakam and Hishām b. Sālim where the *Ḥadīth al-Manzila* appears. This citation fits a *Kitāb al-ḥujja* perfectly.

3. *Kitāb al-mi'rāj*

(Najāshī: 434). This text, a description of the Prophet's Night Journey, is quoted in full in 'Alī b. Ibrāhīm 2: 3–12. Individual passages from this, or a variant, also appear in other works, such as 'Ayyāshī 2: 276–7; *'Ilal* 1: 8.

4. *Kitāb / Aṣl*

Hishām's notebook of *ḥadīth*, related by a number of transmitters including Ibn Abī 'Umayr, a close disciple of the author (see Kashshī: 279), and four others (Barqī: 91; *Mashyakha*: 424–5; Najāshī: 434; *Fihrist*: 174). The work was available in the mid-seventh century to Ibn Ṭāwūs who quotes from it in his *Iqbāl* 3: 171 and *Ghiyāth*: 5 (see further Kohlberg: 124; the quotation in *Iqbāl* 3: 171 appears on the authority of Hishām also in *Maḥāsin*: 25 [whence *Thawāb*: 160]; *Kāfī* 2: 71). A fragment of thirty-seven reports from this notebook is cited in a special chapter of Ṭūsī, *Amālī*: 657–65, some of them on Qur'ānic commentary, indicating that the notebook also contained the material which was later compiled as a separate volume on *tafsīr*.

The overwhelming majority of the close to seven hundred quotations from this scholar in Shī'ite works on *tafsīr* and *ḥadīth*, listed in Khu'ī 19: 301–305, 413–28 and *Fahāris* 10: 429, 430, 431–3, are cited on the authority of Ibn Abī 'Umayr and others specifically named as transmitters of this notebook.

90: Ḥudhayfa Bayyāʿ al-Sāburī

Abū Muḥammad Ḥudhayfa b. Manṣūr, seller of Shāpūrī clothing, a Kūfan client of Khuzāʿa and a transmitter from Muḥammad al-Bāqir and Jaʿfar al-Ṣādiq.

Barqī: 111; Kashshī: 336; Ibn al-Ghaḍā'irī: 50; Najāshī: 147–8; *Fihrist*: 65; *Rijāl*: 133, 192.

Barqī identifies this transmitter as an Arab of Khuzāʿa, but *Rijāl* as a client of that tribe. That he was from Khuzāʿa, whether by descent or as a client, is also confirmed by Ibn al-Ghaḍā'irī. *Rijāl*: 180, however, identifies Ḥasan, the son of Ḥudhayfa b. Manṣūr, also named in Najāshī: 148, as a client of Sabīʿ, a clan of Hamdān. Ibn al-Ghaḍā'irī: 50 also has this son as a *Hamdānī*. Either the father or the son might have been confused with a person of a similar name.

Kitāb

His notebook of *ḥadīth*, related by a number of transmitters (Najāshī: 148; *Fihrist*: 65). This was a work well known to Shīʿite scholars in the mid-fifth century (*Tahdhīb* 4: 169 [whence Ibn al-Barrāj, *Sharḥ*: 175). There are a good number of quotations from this author in Shīʿite works of *ḥadīth*, as listed in Khu'ī 4: 240–41, 244–5, 465–7 and *Fahāris* 8: 333, 334, including many in *Tahdhīb*. In a given case, the author of this last work (4: 167–9) notes that the citation from Ḥudhayfa does not appear in his notebook. Most other quotations from this transmitter in this and other works must have been attested in this notebook.

91: Ḥujr al-Ḥaḍramī

Abū ʿAbd Allāh Ḥujr b. Zā'ida al-Ḥaḍramī, a pious and respected member of the Shīʿite community of Kūfa in his time and a transmitter from Muḥammad al-Bāqir and Jaʿfar al-Ṣādiq. Described by his biographers as one of "sound religion" and as a very close disciple of the said Imāms, he was a staunch opponent of Mufaḍḍal al-Juʿfī, head of the Extremist *Mufawwiḍa* tendency in Imāmite Shīʿism. The *Mufawwiḍa* thus tried to discredit him by ascribing remarks to Jaʿfar al-Ṣādiq that condemn Ḥujr and support Mufaḍḍal.

Barqī: 111; Kashshī: 10; Najāshī: 148; *Fibrist*: 63; *Rijāl*: 192. See also *Ikhtiṣāṣ*: 8.

For his opposition to the Extremist Mufaḍḍal and his teachings, see Kashshī: 323, 326. On the counter-charges by the *Mufawwiḍa*, see ibid.: 321–2 (repeated in abridged form at 407); *Kāfī* 8: 373.

Kitāb

His notebook of *ḥadīth*, related by a number of Shī'ite transmitters including Ṣafwān b. Yaḥyā who quoted it from 'Abd Allāh b. Muskān from the author (Najāshī: 148; *Fibrist*: 63). Almost all of the following quotations from Ḥujr in Shī'ite works of *ḥadīth* are through the same *isnād*:

- Ḥusayn b. Sa'īd, *Zuhd*: 91
- Ṣaffār: 36, 74, 116, 177 (also *Kāfī* 1: 235), 178, 205 (also 206 with additions), 292, 322, 473
- 'Ayyāshī 1: 365
- *Kāfī* 8: 368 (also *Qiṣaṣ*: 104 with an addition)
- Kashshī: 176
- Ibn al-Juḥām: 167
- Ibn Bābawayh, *Amālī*: 572
- *Ma'ānī*: 202
- *Tahdhīb* 1: 135

92: Abū 'l-Maghrā

Abū 'l-Maghrā Ḥumayd b. al-Muthannā al-'Ijlī, the moneychanger, a Kūfan transmitter from Ja'far al-Ṣādiq and Mūsā al-Kāẓim.

Barqī: 70; *Mashyakha*: 466–7; Najāshī: 133; *Fibrist*: 60; *Rijāl*: 192.

Mashyakha identifies him as an Arab but Najāshī as a client. That he was a moneychanger is mentioned in the *Fibrist*. Barqī and *Rijāl*: 194 have Ḥumayd, the Moneychanger, as a different transmitter from Ja'far al-Ṣādiq.

Kitāb / Aṣl

His notebook of *ḥadīth*, related by a number of transmitters including Faḍāla b. Ayyūb al-Azdī, Ibn Abī 'Umayr and Ṣafwān b. Yaḥyā (Najāshī: 133; *Fibrist*: 60; also *Mashyakha*: 467). Many of the close to two hundred quotations from this author in later works, listed in Khu'ī 6: 294–6,

22: 53–4, 215–22 and *Fahāris* 8: 473, 10: 326–7, are on the authority of these transmitters. Ibn Ṭāwūs quotes from the work in his *Malāḥim*: 174 (see further Kohlberg: 124–5). A fragment of nine reports in Mufīd, *Majālis* 2: 122–3 may have been taken from this work too.

93: Ḥumayd al-Sabīʿī

Ḥumayd b. Shuʿayb al-Sabīʿī al-Hamdānī, a Kūfan transmitter from Jābir al-Juʿfī and other Shīʿite scholars of the first half and mid-second century.

Ibn al-Ghaḍāʾirī: 49–50; Najāshī: 133; *Fihrist*: 60; *Rijāl*: 192.

1. *Kitābuh ʿan Jābir*

Najāshī: 133 mentions this work as the book that Jaʿfar b. Muḥammad b. Shurayḥ quoted from Ḥumayd b. Shuʿayb from Jābir (al-Juʿfī). The notebook has survived and is published under the name of its next transmitter as *Aṣl Muḥammad b. al-Muthannā al-Ḥaḍramī*, in *al-Uṣūl al-sittat ʿashar*: 60–81.

2. *Kitāb*

His notebook of *ḥadīth*, related by a number of transmitters including ʿAbd Allāh b. Jabala whose version was the most common (Najāshī: 133; *Fihrist*: 60). Quotations from this author by the same transmitter, as in Ṣaffār: 75 and Ṭūsī, *Amālī*: 595, as well as a number of others as, for instance, in ʿAlī b. Ibrāhīm 1: 215; Khaṭīb, *Taʾrīkh* 5: 467 (whence Ibn ʿAsākir 54: 15), must go back to this notebook.

94: Ibn Abī ʾl-ʿAlāʾ

Abū ʿAlī Ḥusayn b. Abī ʾl-ʿAlāʾ, the one-eyed, the shoemaker, a Kūfan client and a transmitter from Jaʿfar al-Ṣādiq.

Barqī: 60, 79; Kashshī: 365–6; *Mashyakha*: 433; Najāshī: 52–3; *Fihrist*: 54; *Rijāl*: 131, 182. See also Bazanṭī, *Jāmiʿ*: 61.

There are conflicting accounts about the clientage of this transmitter. See Muḥammad Taqī al-Tustarī 3: 407–9 for details.

Kitāb

Najāshī: 53 reports that this transmitter had a number of works. His notebook of *ḥadīth* was related from him by various transmitters including Ibn Abī 'Umayr and Ṣafwān b. Yaḥyā (*Fihrist*: 54). Well over one hundred quotations from this author are recorded in later works, some through the same two transmitters (e.g. *Kāfī* 1: 178, 268; Ibn Qūlawayh: 152 [where Ṣafwān quotes this author through an intermediary]; *Tahdhīb* 2: 159, 278, 5: 68, 420; *Ghayba*: 163), but mostly through 'Alī b. al-Ḥakam who is in turn quoted by the scholar Aḥmad b. Muḥammad b. 'Īsā al-Ash'arī al-Qummī. For lists see Khu'ī 5: 185, 405–9; *Fahāris* 8: 420–21.

95: Ibn Abī Ghundar

Ḥusayn b. Abī Ghundar, a Kūfan transmitter from Ja'far al-Ṣādiq.

Najāshī: 55–6; *Fihrist*: 59.

Kitāb / Aṣl

His notebook of *ḥadīth*, related by Ṣafwān b. Yaḥyā (Najāshī: 55–6; *Fihrist*: 59). A fragment of this notebook, consisting of eighteen reports, has survived in Ṭūsī, *Amālī*: 666–70 (two of these reports are also attested in Ibn Qūlawayh: 125–6, 144). Other quotations from this author through the same transmitter include three reports in Ibn Qūlawayh: 199 and *Tahdhīb* 4: 258–9, 260.

96: Abū Junāda al-Salūlī

Abū Junāda Ḥuṣayn b. Mukhāriq al-Salūlī, a late second century Kūfan transmitter of *ḥadīth* with strong Shī'ite sympathies. He was a transmitter from Ja'far al-Ṣādiq and Mūsā al-Kāẓim, among others.

Ibn al-Ghaḍā'irī: 112–13; Najāshī: 145; *Fihrist*: 57–8; *Rijāl*: 191, 335; Ibn al-Muṭahhar, *Khulāṣa*: 342 (quoting Ibn 'Uqda). For Sunnī sources, see the list in the editor's footnote to *Lisān* 2: 591.

Ibn al-Ghaḍā'irī identifies this transmitter as a Zaydī (*Khulāṣa*: 342; Ibn Dāwūd: 447) and Ṭūsī as a Wāqifite (*Rijāl*: 335). The first account seems more apt as the Imāmites knew him through the Zaydīs.

He frequently quotes from Ja'far al-Ṣādiq. For examples of his transmissions from Mūsā al-Kāẓim, see 'Ayyāshī 1: 255; *Kāfī* 8:184; Ḥaskānī 1: 396, 2: 343–4.

1. *Kitāb al-tafsīr wa 'l-qirā'āt*

Described as a large book by Najāshī: 145, the work was received by him through the Zaydī Abū 'l-Faraj al-Iṣbahānī (d. 356) and by Ṭūsī (*Fihrist*: 57–8) through the Zaydī Ibn 'Uqda (d. 333), both as related by Aḥmad b. al-Ḥasan b. Sa'īd al-Khazzāz through his father from the author. Ibn al-Juḥām, Ḥaskānī, and others also quote this author through Ibn 'Uqda, but Ibn 'Asākir through a different authority, both from Aḥmad b. al-Ḥasan, from his father. Here is a list of quotations from the author on the topic through Aḥmad al-Khazzāz:

- Ibn al-Juḥām: 151, 157, 168, 180, 227 (also Ḥaskānī 1: 565), 230, 237, 317 (also Ḥaskānī 2: 240), 438 (also Ḥaskānī 2: 425), 439, 487 (also Ḥaskānī 2: 486)
- Ibn 'Adī: 490 (whence Bayhaqī 9: 51)
- Ḥaskānī 1: 52, 152, 266, 317, 388, 396, 497, 532, 565
  2: 31, 234 (also Khwārazmī, *Manāqib*: 325), 240, 343 (repeated at 344), 371, 425, 463, 486 (two reports)
- Ibn 'Asākir 14: 171–2, 425
  42: 287, 298, 360, 363, 447
- Ibn al-Jawzī, *'Ilal*: 150
- 'Abd Allāh b. Ḥamza, *Shāfī* 1: 67–8, 74 (seven versions of the same text)

Quotations from this author on the topic without, or through a different, *isnād* include passages in 'Ayyāshī 1: 255, 355 and *Kāfī* 8: 184.

2. *Kitāb jāmi' al-'ilm*

Named in *Fihrist*: 57, the title reminds one of the *Amālī Aḥmad b. 'Īsā*, known also as *Kitāb al-'ulūm*, and appears to be the same work which is quoted extensively in this latter, always through the same chain of transmission. Here is a list of these quotations, as well as a few others that may have belonged to the same work:

- Aḥmad b. ʿĪsā 1: 44, 46, 73, 144 (two reports), 258 (two reports)
  2: 435 (two reports)
  3: 6, 26, 34–5, 39, 44, 48, 49 (two reports), 50, 74, 76, 87, 97, 108 (two reports, with Abū Junāda's name missing in the *isnād* of the second), 138, 140, 141, 153, 161, 170, 172, 173 (two reports), 194
  4: 202 (four reports), 203, 211 (two reports), 212–13, 216, 217 (two reports), 219, 226, 227, 228
- *Kāfī* 4: 93
- Abū Ṭālib: 223, 267, 272, 324
- Abū ʿAbd Allāh al-Shajarī, *Adhān*: 72
- Ibn al-Maghāzilī: 261

97: Ḥusayn al-Qalānisī

Abū ʿAbd Allāh Ḥusayn b. al-Mukhtār, the hatter, a Kūfan client of Aḥmas of Bajīla, and a transmitter from Jaʿfar al-Ṣādiq and Mūsā al-Kāẓim. He joined the Wāqifites.

Barqī: 79; Najāshī: 54–5; *Fihrist*: 55; *Rijāl*: 183, 334; Ibn al-Muṭahhar, *Khulāṣa*: 338–9 (quoting Ibn ʿUqda).

That he was a Wāqifite is mentioned in *Rijāl*: 334.

Kitāb

His notebook of *ḥadīth*, related by various transmitters including Ḥammād b. ʿĪsā (Najāshī: 54–5; *Fihrist*: 55; also *Mashyakha*: 443). With close to two hundred quotations from this author in Shīʿite works of *ḥadīth*, listed in Khuʾī 6: 88, 351–5 and *Fahāris* 8: 427, 433–4, mainly through the same transmitter, it seems that the bulk of the material of the work may have survived.

98: Ḥusayn al-Aḥmasī

Abū ʿAlī Ḥusayn b. ʿUthmān, a Kūfan client of Aḥmas of Bajīla, and a transmitter from Jaʿfar al-Ṣādiq. He lived into the late second century.

Najāshī: 54; *Fibrist*: 56 (two entries); *Rijāl*: 195. See also Barqī: 79.

For his *kunya*, see below. That he lived into the late second century is indicated by a report in *Maḥāsin*: 624 where he quotes a statement from 'Alī al-Riḍā.

Kitāb

His notebook of *ḥadīth*, related by Ibn Abī 'Umayr (Najāshī: 54; *Fihrist*: 56), through whom alone the work is known (Najāshī: 54 quoting Ibn 'Uqda). The notebook has survived, on the authority of Ibn 'Uqda who received it from Ibn Abī 'Umayr through an intermediary, and is published in *al-Uṣūl al-sittat 'ashar*: 108–13. The manuscript on the basis of which the notebook is published identified the author as Ḥusayn b. 'Uthmān b. Sharīk al-'Āmirī. This is certainly wrong as parts of the contents of the notebook appear in early Shī'ite works of *ḥadīth* on the authority of Ḥusayn al-Aḥmasī.[65]

The printed version of the notebook contains forty-four reports (see further Kohlberg, *Uṣūl*: 155). There are other quotations by Ibn Abī 'Umayr from *Ḥusayn al-Aḥmasī*, as in the following instances, indicating that the surviving version is only a part of the original notebook:

- Ḥusayn b. Sa'īd, *Zuhd*: 29–30 (read *'an Abī 'Alī al-Aḥmasī* [as in the manuscript of the work mentioned in the editor's footnote # 80]; also *Kāfī* 2: 100 where the passage is quoted by Ibn Abī 'Umayr from Ḥusayn al-Aḥmasī), 51, 72 (read *'an Abī 'Alī al-Aḥmasī*; see also *Biḥār* 73: 127), 103
- *Kāfī* 1: 52
  2: 475
  4: 260

There are also quotations by the same transmitter from *Ḥusayn b. 'Uthmān*, without further distinction, many of them already attested in this notebook.[66] Examples of others which are not included in the surviving version of the notebook include the following:

---

65. Examples: *Kitāb Ḥusayn b. 'Uthmān*: 108–112, passage # 4 in *Kāfī* 4: 270; passage 11 in *Tahdhīb* 9: 118; passage 12 in *Kāfī* 4: 271; passage 13 in Ibn Qūlawayh: 296–7; passage 15 in Ḥusayn b. Sa'īd, *Zuhd*: 103; passage 39 in *Kāfī* 6: 240 (broken into two passages here).
66. The following passages from *Kitāb Ḥusayn b. 'Uthmān* are recorded in the works of *ḥadīth* on the authority of Ibn Abī 'Umayr quoting *Ḥusayn b. 'Uthmān* without further distinction: passage # 3 in *Kāfī* 3: 555; passage 7 ibid. 2: 351; passage 8 in *Khiṣāl*: 187 and *'Iqāb*: 323; passage 18 in *Kāfī* 7: 43 (repeated at 168; also *Tahdhīb* 6: 310); passage 20 in *Kāfī* 6: 80; passage 31 ibid. 4: 544; passage 32 ibid. 4: 306; passage 37 in *Maḥāsin*: 623 and *Kāfī* 6: 531; passage 44 in 'Ayyāshī 2: 210–11 and *Kāfī* 2: 157.

- *Maḥāsin*: 71 (also *Kāfī* 4: 281), 256, 548, 549, 624
- *Kāfī* 1: 545 (read *'an Ḥusayn b. 'Uthmān*)
  2: 257–8, 356, 371
  3: 204, 545, 550
  4: 423 (cf. *Tahdhīb* 5: 140 where the same report is quoted from *Ḥusayn b. 'Uthmān* through a different *isnād*)
  5: 238
  6: 179, 294
  8: 231
- Kashshī: 40
- Ibn Qūlawayh: 108, 110
- *Khiṣāl*: 24 (read *Ḥusayn b. 'Uthmān*)[67]
- *Tahdhīb* 4: 44

99: Ḥusayn al-ʿĀmirī

Ḥusayn b. ʿUthmān b. Sharīk al-Ru'āsī al-ʿĀmirī, a Kūfan transmitter from Ja'far al-Ṣādiq and Mūsā al-Kāẓim.

Kashshī: 372; Najāshī: 53; *Fihrist*: 57; *Rijāl*: 182. See also Muḥammad Taqī al-Tustarī 3: 483–4.

His brother, Ja'far b. ʿUthmān b. Sharīk al-Ru'āsī, was a companion of the prominent Imāmite *ḥadīth* transmitter of Kūfa, Abū Baṣīr Yaḥyā b. al-Qāsim al-Asadī (Kashshī: 372; Najāshī: 124–5; *Fihrist*: 44; *Rijāl*: 175; see further Ibn al-Juḥām: 214; Muḥammad Taqī al-Tustarī 2: 634–8) and author of a notebook of *ḥadīth*, related by, among others, Ibn Abī ʿUmayr (Najāshī: 125; *Fihrist*: 44) who seems to have received it from the author through an intermediary (*Mashyakha*: 527–8). Quotations from this author by the same transmitter are attested in Ṣaffār: 109 (also *Kāfī* 1: 147); *Kāfī* 2: 420, 5: 244; Kashshī: 297–8; Ibn Bābawayh, *Amālī*: 140 (also *Tahdhīb* 2: 29, 264–5); *Khiṣāl*: 411 (also *Ma'ānī*: 381); *Tahdhīb* 2: 337 (repeated in 3: 233).

Kitāb

His notebook of *ḥadīth*, related by a number of transmitters (Najāshī: 53; *Fihrist*: 57). Faḍāla b. Ayyūb quotes this author as *Ḥusayn b. 'Uthmān al-Ru'āsī* in Kashshī: 236 where Faḍāla is in turn quoted by Ḥusayn b. Sa'īd.

67. See Khu'ī 6: 331.

Close to fifty reports are quoted in the four main collections of Shīʿite *ḥadīth* through the same *isnād* (see the lists in Khuʾī 6: 330–33, 13: 434, 445–6). Quotations from *Ḥusayn b. ʿUthmān* by Faḍāla also appear in Muḥammad b. ʿAlī b. Maḥbūb: 98; *Maḥāsin*: 184, 325 and elsewhere. This body of material seems to represent the notebook in question.

100: Dhū ʾl-Damʿa

Abū ʿAbd Allāh Ḥusayn b. Zayd b. ʿAlī b. al-Ḥusayn, known as Dhū ʾl-Damʿa, a transmitter of *ḥadīth* known to both Sunnī and Shīʿite traditions. He was still a child when his father, Zayd b. ʿAlī, was killed in 122, and was adopted by Jaʿfar al-Ṣādiq, who brought him up and married him to his own niece, daughter of Muḥammad b. ʿAbd Allāh al-Arqaṭ. Ḥusayn joined the revolt of Muḥammad b. ʿAbd Allāh al-Nafs al-Zakiyya in 145 but escaped punishment after the revolt was crushed by the ʿAbbāsid Manṣūr. The latter married Ḥusayn's daughter to his own son, Muḥammad al-Mahdī, the future caliph (r. 158–169). He went blind toward the end of his life and died at the age of 76.

Bibliographical material about this transmitter is found in many Sunnī and Shīʿite sources. For lists of many of them, see the editors' footnotes to Mizzī 6: 375 and Dhahabī, *Taʾrīkh* 12 (years 181–190): 122, 13 (years 191–200): 149.

His *kunya* is given as *Abū ʿAbd Allāh* in most sources. *Abū ʾl-Ḥusayn* in the *isnād* of a report in Ṭūsī, *Amālī*: 203 is obviously wrong. The genealogical works at times have his epithet as *Dhū ʾl-ʿAbra* (e.g. ʿUbaydalī: 190; Fakhr al-Rāzī, *Shajara*: 127; Ibn Zuhra: 121; Ibn ʿInaba: 260) replacing a word with a synonym, with or without the more common form, *Dhū ʾl-Damʿa*, and at times switching freely from one to the other (e.g. ʿUbaydalī: 190, 205, 208; Ibn ʿInaba: 260, 261 ff). *Dhū ʾl-Damʿa*, however, seems to have been the one used within the family itself (see Ṭūsī, *Amālī*: 491). Ibn Samka: 383–4 thought that Ḥusayn's mother was the daughter of Abū Hāshim ʿAbd Allāh b. Muḥammad b. al-Ḥanafiyya (d. 99), who was the mother of Ḥusayn's half brother, Yaḥyā b. Zayd (d. 125) (Ibn al-Ṣūfī: 224). The genealogical sources, however, identify Ḥusayn as the son of a slave girl (e.g. Ibn al-Ṣūfī: 159; Ibn ʿInaba: 260). His marriage to the daughter of Muḥammad al-Arqaṭ is mentioned in Najāshī: 52; Fīrūzābādī, *Maghānim*: 294 (but cf. Ibn al-Ṣūfī: 144).

Barqī: 66 has him as four years old when he was orphaned, but Ibn ʿInaba: 262 as seven. Ibn al-Ṣūfī: 159 has him born in Shām. He kept his affiliation to the house of the Ḥusaynid Imāmate after Jaʿfar al-Ṣādiq passed away (see, for instance, *Maḥāsin*: 451 [read *Ḥusayn b. Zayd* for *Ḥusayn b. Yazīd*]; ʿAbd Allāh

b. Ja'far: 317). It is unanimously accepted that he died at the age of 76. Ibn Zuhra: 121 and Ibn 'Inaba: 260 have the obviously wrong dates of 134 (Ibn Zuhra) and 135 or 140 (Ibn 'Inaba) for his death. This error is particularly unexpected from Ibn 'Inaba who himself notes that Ḥusayn was a child (ibid.: 261) of seven (ibid.: 262) at the death of his father (in 122). Though not a very common corruption, *thalāthīn* could have been a corruption of *tis'īn* in a source used by the two genealogists.

The genealogical sources give long lists of his descendants, many of whom were men of fame in their own times. See, for instance, 'Ubaydalī: 190–209; Ibn al-Ṣūfī: 159–66; Fakhr al-Rāzī, *Shajara*: 127–38; Ibn 'Inaba: 261–85.

Kitāb

His notebook of *ḥadīth* that he quoted principally from Ja'far al-Ṣādiq, related from the author by a number of transmitters including the Zaydī 'Abbād b. Ya'qūb al-Rawājinī (Najāshī: 52; *Fihrist*: 55). Quotations from this author (including some through the same transmitter as, for instance, in Ibn Māja: 471; Aḥmad b. 'Īsā 1: 179, 186; Ibn 'Adī: 762; Ibn al-Rāzī, *Musalsalāt*: 243; Ibn Bābawayh, *Amālī*: 701–2; *Bishārat al-Muṣṭafā: 108*) abound in Sunnī, Zaydī and Imāmite works of *ḥadīth*. Examples are as follows:

- Ibn Māja: 471 (also *Kāfī* 5: 364 [with variations]; Ibn 'Adī: 762)
- *Maḥāsin*: 138 (whence Ibn Bābawayh, *Amālī*: 561–2; *'Ilal* 1: 134; *Ma'ānī*: 161 [read *b. Zayd* for *b. Yazīd*]), 420
- Ṣaffār: 2 (read *Ḥusayn b. Zayd* for *Ḥasan b. Zayd*)
- Aḥmad b. 'Īsā 1: 18 (also Abū Ya'lā 12: 153; Ṭabarānī, *Kabīr* 3: 86), 179, 180, 186
  3: 64, 65, 194
- 'Ayyāshī 1: 166–7, 230
  2: 220, 266 (also 2: 16 [# 35] that in the original, unabridged version of the book was from our author; see Ṭabrisī, *Majma'* 8: 47)
- Muḥammad b. Sulaymān 2: 104, 273–4
- Ṭabarī 7: 540–41 (whence *Maqātil*: 219–20)
- *Kāfī* 1: 164
  2: 497
  4: 140
  5: 144, 500
  6: 18
  7: 401
  8: 153–5 (partially also in 5: 151; the full text also in *Tawḥīd*: 275–7)

- Kashshī: 127, 128, 414–15
- Ibn Samka: 383–4
- Ibn al-Juḥām: 249 (repeated at 293), 315–16, 366 (also Ḥaskānī 2: 308–9)
- *Maqātil*: 46, 277–8 (two reports), 435–6
- Ṭabarānī, *Awsaṭ* 5: 120 (three reports, one [# 4848] also in *Khiṣāl*: 5)
- Idem, *Kabīr* 1: 208 (repeated in 22: 401; also Abū Ya'lā 1: 190; Ibn 'Adī: 762; Ibn Bābawayh, *Amālī*: 466–7; Ḥākim 3: 153–4)
  22: 249
- Idem, *Ṣaghīr* 1: 250–51 (four reports, including the three in idem, *Awsaṭ* 5: 120)
- Ibn 'Adī: 762 (three reports; one also in Abū Nu'aym, *Akhbār Iṣbahān* 1: 80–81)
- Ibn Bābawayh, *Amālī*: 378 (also *Faqīh* 3: 556–7; *Khiṣāl*: 520), 509–18 (also *Faqīh* 4:3–18), 506, 587, 701–2
- *Kamāl*: 228, 269–70 (also *Khiṣāl*: 475–6)
- *Khiṣāl*: 260, 430, 446
- Dāraquṭnī 2: 42–3
- Ibn al-Rāzī, *Musalsalāt*: 243 (cf. Ibn Bābawayh, *Amālī*: 409; *'Uyūn* 1: 250; Ṭūsī, *Amālī*: 451)
- Khazzāz: 237 (add *'an Ḥusayn b. Zayd 'an 'ammih 'Umar b. 'Alī* to the *isnād*, as in *Biḥār* 36: 388)
- Ḥākim 1: 359
  2: 588 (partially also in 3: 2)
  3: 179 (also Bayhaqī 9: 304)
- Mufīd, *Amālī*: 33, 150, 173
- *Irshād* 2: 151, 170
- Abū Ṭālib: 111
- Idem, *Mā nazal*: 92–3 (two versions; also Ḥaskānī 1: 301)
- Idem, *Ma'rifa* 1: 93
- 'Āṣimī 1: 339
- Ṭūsī, *Amālī*: 203, 447, 462–3, 491–2, 495, 499–501, 613, 632, 634
- *Miṣbāḥ*: 852
- *Tahdhīb* 1: 77
  6: 396
  7: 80 (read *Ḥusayn b. Zayd* for *Ḥasan b. Zayd*)
- *Firdaws*, two reports (Uzbak: 737, 2222)
- Abū Ṭāhir al-Silafī, *Baghdādiyya* (Uzbak: 726)
- Ibn 'Asākir 14: 223

- *Manāqib* 2: 24
- 'Abd Allāh b. Ḥamza, *Shāfī* 3: 110
- *Bishārat al-Muṣṭafā*: 108
- Ibn Abī 'l-Ḥadīd 2: 57
  3: 200

101: Ibn Abī 'l-Sammāl

Ibrāhīm b. Abī Bakr b. Abī 'l-Sammāl al-Asadī, an Arab Shī'ite from Asad Khuzayma and a descendant of the poet Sim'ān b. Hubayra b. Musāḥiq. He came from a family of Shī'ite notables. A transmitter from Mūsā al-Kāẓim, he and his brother, Ismā'īl, also a notable in the Shī'ite community, joined the Wāqifites after the death of the latter. The brothers were still alive in the time of the revolt of Abū 'l-Sarāyā in 199–200.

Barqī: 106; Kashshī: 471–4; Najāshī: 21, 101, 158–9; *Fihrist*: 9–10; *Rijāl*: 332; *Lisān* 1: 59 (quoting 'Alī b. Faḍḍāl in his book on the biography of Shī'ite transmitters). See also *Tahdhīb* 5: 248; Muḥmmad Taqī al-Tustarī 1: 134–9.

His *kunya* is given as *Abū Bakr* in Najāshī: 21. He is therefore the one meant by *Abū Bakr b. Abī 'l-Sammāl* in Barqī: 106 and a number of reports (*Kāfī*: 3: 23; *Faqīh* 1: 400 [also 4: 466]; *Thawāb*: 75; *Tahdhīb* 2: 92). *Sammāl* at times appears corrupted to *sammāk* (e.g. *Maḥāsin*: 205, 610 [here, *Ibrāhīm b. Sammāk*]; Ṣaffār: 317; *Kāfī* 3: 23, 8: 266; *Khiṣāl*: 134; *Tahdhīb* 2: 92, 3: 87, 4: 280, 5: 94, 370; Ḥasan b. Sulaymān: 13).

There are some inconsistencies in his genealogical line of descent as given in Najāshī: 21 (where he is Ibrāhīm b. Abī Bakr Muḥammad b. al-Rabī', Ibn Abī 'l-Sammāl Sim'ān b. Hubayra b. Musāḥiq), ibid.: 159 (where he is Ibrāhīm b. Abī Bakr Muḥammad b. 'Abd Allāh b. al-Najāshī, known as Ibn Abī al-Sammāl), and ibid.: 101 (where the author, himself a member of this family, gives his own genealogical line to Ibrāhīm b. Muḥammad b. 'Abd Allāh b. al-Najāshī b. 'Uthaym b. Abī 'l-Sammāl Sim'ān b. Hubayra al-Shā'ir, Ibn Musāḥiq). One way to reconcile these accounts is to suggest that the name al-Rabī' for the grandfather of Ibrāhīm might be an error for 'Abd Allāh (or that it was a name left out in the genealogical line) in Najāshī: 101, and that the author abridged the genealogical line of descent between Abū 'l-Sammāl and Ibrāhīm ibid.: 21, leaving out some names in between as was common in similar cases and as he has also done ibid.: 101 in the case of a name between Sim'ān b. Hubayra and Asad b. Khuzayma. Najāshī, the author, would be a great-grandson of our Ibn Abī 'l-Sammāl, or else a remote cousin.

His grandfather, Sim'ān b. Hubayra b. Musāḥiq, Abū 'l-Sammāl al-Asadī, was a *Jāhilī* poet who survived into the Islamic period.[68] He resided in Kūfa and was alive until the mid-first century (Ibn Manẓūr, *Tahdhīb* 10: 208–9). There is, however, some ambiguity about him in some sources. There was an Abū Sammāl al-Asadī in Kūfa in the time of 'Alī who once drank wine with the poet Qays b. 'Amr al-Najāshī al-Ḥārithī but managed to escape punishment, whereas Qays b. 'Amr al-Najāshī was caught and flogged (Ibn Qutayba, *Shi'r* 1: 329–30; see further *Manāqib* 2: 146). The *kunya* of Najāshī, the poet, was also Abū Sammāl (Ibn Mākūlā 4: 354). Some authors held that the one who drank wine but escaped punishment was our Abū 'l-Sammāl Sim'ān b. Hubayra (e.g. Ibn Ḥajar, *Iṣāba* 3: 265); others maintained that it was a different person (e.g. Ibn Nāṣir al-Dīn 5: 160). A similar confusion appears to have occurred two generations later. Najāshī: 213 reports that his own grandfather, Abū Bujayr 'Abd Allāh b. al-Najāshī, a grandson of that poet, was the governor of Ahwāz during the reign of the 'Abbāsid Manṣūr (r. 136–158). Abū 'l-Faraj, *Aghānī* 7: 274 quotes a story in which the well known poet al-Sayyid al-Ḥimyarī (d. 173) visited Ahwāz while Abū Bujayr b. Sammāk (sic) al-Asadī was in office and it happened that Ibn al-Najāshī was in the company of Ibn Sammāk in the evening. This assumes that Ibn al-Najāshī and Abū Bujayr are two different persons, though there is a good possibility that the text of *Aghānī* may be corrupt here.

As noted above, Ibrāhīm b. Abī 'l-Sammāl and his brother, Ismā'īl, joined the Wāqifites after the death of Mūsā al-Kāẓim. The text of a conversation between the two brothers and 'Alī al-Riḍā over his claim to the succession is preserved in its original form in Kashshī: 473–4. Another conversation between Ibrāhīm and 'Alī al-Riḍā is recorded in Ḥasan b. Sulaymān: 13.

Dāwūd b. Farqad (no. 52 above), a transmitter from Ja'far al-Ṣādiq and Mūsā al-Kāẓim, was a client of the descendants of Abū 'l-Sammāl and the author of a notebook of *ḥadīth*. This notebook was received by later scholars through Ibrāhīm who related it from the author (Najāshī: 159).

Kitāb / Kitāb nawādir

His notebook of *ḥadīth*, related by, among others, 'Alī b. Ḥasan b. Faḍḍāl (Najāshī: 21; *Fibrist*: 9). Quotations from this author in Shī'ite works of *ḥadīth*, many through the same transmitter, include the following examples:

- *Maḥāsin*: 205, 610
- Ṣaffār: 317

---

68. On him see Muṣ'ab al-Zubayrī: 9; Ya'qūbī 1: 230, 268 (in both cases, Shim'ān); Ibn Qutayba, *Shi'r* 1: 329–30; Ṭabarī 4: 273; Marzubānī, *Mu'jam*: 137; Dāraquṭnī, *Mu'talif*: 1240–41, 1325; Ibn Mākūlā 4: 353–4; Sam'ānī 7: 232; Ibn Manẓūr, *Tahdhīb* 10: 208–9 (the entry is missing from our version of Ibn 'Asākir's *Ta'rīkh*, the work that Ibn Manẓūr abridged; see the editor's note in Ibn 'Asākir 22: 403); Ibn Ḥajar, *Iṣāba* 3: 264–5; Ibn Nāṣir al-Dīn 5: 160 (see also the editor's footnote to Dāraquṭnī, *Mu'talif*: 1240).

- *Kāfī* 2: 388
  3: 23
  7: 7 (also *Tahdhīb* 9: 187 [read *Asadī* for *Azdī*])
  8: 266
- *Faqīh* 1: 400
- *Khiṣāl*: 134
- *Thawāb*: 29, 75, 235
- Ibn 'Ayyāsh: 54–5 (a revised text)
- *Tahdhīb* 2: 92
  3: 87
  4: 267, 280
  5: 94, 104, 136, 148, 370 (the last four are clearly different passages from a single lengthy report)
  8: 97
- Warrām: 17
- Ibn Ṭāwūs, *Jamāl*: 151
- Ḥasan b. Sulaymān: 13

102: Abū Ayyūb al-Kharrāz

Abū Ayyūb Ibrāhīm b. 'Īsā (or 'Uthmān), the tanner, a Kūfan Shī'ite transmitter from Ja'far al-Ṣādiq and Mūsā al-Kāẓim and a notable in the Shī'ite community of Kūfa in his time.

Barqī: 81; Kashshī: 366; Najāshī: 20; *Fibrist*: 8; *Rijāl*: 167.

The name of his profession is variously given as *kharrāz*, the tanner, or *khazzāz*, the furrier. The first is more likely to be correct (see Muḥammad Taqī al-Tustarī 1: 243).

Aṣl / Kitāb nawādir

His notebook of *ḥadīth*, related by Ibn Abī 'Umayr and Ṣafwān b. Yaḥyā (*Fibrist*: 8). Najāshī: 20 names a *Kitāb nawādir* by this author that was related from him by Ḥasan b. Maḥbūb. This may have been part of the same general notebook. The notebook was available in the mid-seventh century to Ibn Ṭāwūs who quoted from it in *Falāḥ*: 186 and *Sa'd*: 160 (see further Kohlberg: 224–5). Quotations from this author, many by the above-mentioned transmitters of this notebook, abound in Shīʿite works of *ḥadīth*. For a list of over six hundred of them, see Khuʾī 1: 256–8, 265–7, 359, 21: 27–34, 36–7, 283–99; *Fahāris* 8: 196–7.

103: Ibn Abī Burda

Ibrāhīm b. Mihzam b. Abī Burda al-Asadī, a Kūfan Shīʿite and a transmitter from Jaʿfar al-Ṣādiq and Mūsā al-Kāẓim. He lived a long life. His father was also a transmitter from Jaʿfar al-Ṣādiq.

Barqī: 65, 81; Najāshī: 22; *Fihrist*: 9; *Rijāl*: 167, 331 (also 146, 314, 343, all on his father).

Kitāb / Aṣl

His notebook of *ḥadīth*, related by a number of transmitters including Ḥasan b. Maḥbūb (Najāshī: 22; *Fihrist*: 9). There are a fair number of reports quoted from Ibrāhīm b. Mihzam in Shīʿite works of *ḥadīth*, listed in Khuʾī 1: 301–3, 463–5 and *Fahāris* 8: 35, some through the same transmitter as in the following examples:

- *Maḥāsin*: 250 (also *Kāfī* 2: 53)
- *Kāfī* 2: 457
  3: 156
  4: 42, 145
  5: 100
  6: 265 (also *ʿIlal* 2: 219; *Tahdhīb* 9: 90), 489, 524
- Ibn Bābawayh, *Amālī*: 286 (also *Tahdhīb* 3: 328)
- *Tahdhīb* 1: 432

There is also a citation from him in *ʿIlal* 2: 151 on the text of a non-Arabic epigraph, most likely quoted from this notebook.

104: Ibn Abī Yaḥyā

Ibrāhīm b. Muḥammad b. Abī Yaḥyā Simʿān al-Madanī, a client of the Banū Aslam and a prominent scholar of Medina. A prolific transmitter of *ḥadīth* with clear Shīʿite sympathies, for which, among others, he was criticized by Sunnī biographers, he also related from the Imāms Muḥammad al-Bāqir and Jaʿfar al-Ṣādiq. He was a teacher of Muḥammad b. Idrīs al-Shāfiʿī who studied with him as a young student and relied on his transmission. He died in 184.

Most Sunnī and Shīʿite biographical dictionaries of the transmitters of *ḥadīth* have entries on this transmitter. For a list of many of these, see the editor's footnote to Dhahabī, *Taʾrīkh* 12 (years 181–190): 63. The accounts in Ibn ʿAdī 1: 219–27, Mizzī 2: 184–91, and Ibn Ḥajar, *Tahdhīb* 1: 158–61 are among the most detailed.

Many of his biographers mention his Shīʿite sympathies (see, for instance, Yaḥyā b. Maʿīn 2: 13; ʿUqaylī 1: 63–4; Ibn ʿAdī 1: 221; Ibn Ḥibbān, *Majrūḥīn* 1: 104; Mizzī 2: 187). Najāshī: 4–15 and Ṭūsī (*Fihrist*: 3) mention his attachment to the two Shīʿite Imāms.

Ibn Abī Yaḥyā was a prolific transmitter of *ḥadīth* and author. He compiled a large work of *ḥadīth*, many times larger than the *Muwaṭṭaʾ* of his contemporary and rival, Mālik b. Anas (d. 179), as well as many smaller notebooks of *ḥadīth* (Ibn ʿAdī: 226). Nuʿaym b. Ḥammād (d. 228) spent fifty *dīnār*s on the purchase of his books (ibid. 1: 221). Another transmitter brought Ibn Abī Yaḥyā's books to him, carrying them in his own cloak, to receive permission to quote them (Ibn Ḥibbān, *Majrūḥīn* 1: 105).

Najāshī: 14–15 and Ṭūsī (*Fihrist*: 3) cite an unnamed Sunnī authority who alleged that the books of the well known historian, Muḥammad b. ʿUmar al-Wāqidī (d. 207) were all taken from Ibn Abī Yaḥyā's works. Ibn Abī Yaḥyā, however, does not seem to have been a historian, and though some of his reports in Shīʿite sources relate to historical facts (e.g. *Maḥāsin*: 378, 629; *Kāfī* 5: 376, 391, 7: 48; Furāt: 557; *ʿIlal* 2: 77), his transmissions are generally on legal topics, a fact that goes well with the description of him by some of his biographers as *faqīh*. Shīʿite sources are, however, very unclear about the identity of this scholar. As will be noted below, errors related to his name are common in Shīʿite works of *ḥadīth*, including the corruption of his *nisba*, *Madanī* or *Madīnī*, to *Madāʾinī* (see, for instance, *Maḥāsin*: 347, 629; *Kāfī* 1: 539). One wonders if that Sunnī authority mentioned by Najāshī and Ṭūsī, or, more likely, the Shīʿite source of the latter two who came across a reference to that effect in a Sunnī work, did not confuse this *Madanī*, occasionally misidentified as *Madāʾinī*, with the historian, ʿAlī b. Muḥammad al-Madāʾinī (d. 224 at the age of 93).

A Mu'tazilite (Ibn al-Nadīm: 113), as Ibn Abī Yaḥyā too was known to some of his contemporaries (Ibn Ḥibbān, *Majrūḥīn* 1: 105–7; see also Mizzī 2: 186–7; Ibn Ḥajar, *Tahdhīb* 1: 158–9), 'Alī b. Muḥammad al-Madā'inī was the author of a comprehensive work on the history of the Arabs and Islam (see Ibn al-Nadīm: 113–17 for details), from which other early historians are said to have gotten their information (Ibn Taghrībirdī 2: 259).

Kitāb mubawwab fī 'l-ḥalāl wa 'l-ḥarām 'an Ja'far b. Muḥammad

As noted above, Ibn Abī Yaḥyā was a prolific transmitter of *ḥadīth*. Shāfi'ī frequently cites him in his *Kitāb al-umm*, and many other reports have also survived from his vast transmission in Sunnī works. Even some of these, the bulk of which he quoted from the early non-Shī'ite authorities, demonstrate a Shī'ite sympathy (e.g. Khwārazmī, *Maqtal* 1: 159; see further, Ibn 'Adī 1: 222–6; Khaṭīb, *Mūḍiḥ* 1: 365–71).

The Shī'ites were interested in a book he compiled out of his transmissions from Ja'far al-Ṣādiq. Najāshī: 14 and *Fihrist*: 3 mention this work and note that it was on legal matters, divided into chapters, apparently following the order of the legal works of the time. There are quite a few quotations in Sunnī, as well as Zaydī and Imāmite Shī'ite, sources from Ja'far al-Ṣādiq on the authority of this author, mostly on legal matters or with legal implications. Examples include the following:

- Shāfi'ī, *Musnad*: 89–90, 119, 149 (two reports), 163 (two reports), 166 (two reports), 192, 349, 372, 425, 470, 502, 505, 557, 558, 571 (whence Bayhaqī 3: 198, 280, 411, 5: 114, 6: 37, 7: 313, 8: 26)
- 'Abd al-Razzāq 1: 82 (also Bayhaqī 1: 268)
  3: 292 (also Shāfi'ī, *Umm* 1: 209)
  7: 25
- *Maḥāsin*: 347 (read *Ibn Abī Yaḥyā al-Madīnī* [as in *Faqīh* 2: 266] for *Ibn Yaḥyā al-Madā'inī*), 378, 580 (read *Ibn Abī Yaḥyā* for *Ibn Yaḥyā*), 629 (read *Madīnī* [as in *Kāfī* 6: 542] for *Madā'inī*)
- Aḥmad b. 'Īsā 2: 291
  3: 119 (from Muḥammad al-Bāqir, possibly through his son, Ja'far), 124
  4: 218
- 'Ayyāshī 1: 93
  2: 218

- *Kāfī* 3: 118 (read *Ibn Abī Yaḥyā* for *Abī Yaḥyā*)
  4: 548 (read *Abī Yaḥyā al-Aslamī* for *Abī Ḥajar al-Aslamī* [also in *Faqīh* 2: 565; *'Ilal* 2: 145; Ibn Qūlawayh: 44] as in *Tahdhīb* 6: 4 [citing *Kāfī*])
  5: 376, 391
  6: 542
  7: 48 (also in Kashshī: 17–18)
- Furāt: 557
- Ibn Bisṭām: 64–5
- *'Ilal* 2: 77
- *Kamāl*: 297–99 (read *Ibn Abī Yaḥyā* for *Ibn Yaḥyā*), 300 (read *'an Ibn Abī Yaḥyā al-Madīnī*; cf. ibid.: 294–6; also *Kāfī* 1: 531 and Nu'mānī: 97–9 where Ibn Abī Yaḥyā quotes the same passage from masters other than Ja'far al-Ṣādiq).
- *Khiṣāl*: 36 (read *Ibn Abī Yaḥyā* for *Ibn Yaḥyā*)
- Abū 'Abd Allāh al-Shajarī, *Adhān*: 50–51
- Ibn Ṭāwūs, *Muhaj*: 170–71

105: Abū 'l-Ṣabbāḥ al-Kinānī

Abū 'l-Ṣabbāḥ Ibrāhīm b. Nu'aym al-'Abdī al-Kinānī, a distinguished member of the Shī'ite community of Kūfa in his time. He was a disciple of Ja'far al-Ṣādiq and Mūsā al-Kāẓim, and died after 170 at over 70 years of age.

Barqī: 53, 65, 97; Kashshī: 255, 350–52; Najāshī: 19–20; *Fihrist*: 185–6; *Rijāl*: 123, 156; Ibn Dāwūd: 19–20.

Kitāb / Aṣl

His notebook of *ḥadīth*, related by a number of transmitters including Ṣafwān b. Yaḥyā and Muḥammad b. al-Fuḍayl (Najāshī: 20; *Fihrist*: 185–6). In *Rijāl*: 123, however, Ṭūsī refers to Abū 'l-Ṣabbāḥ's *notebooks* (*uṣūl*) that Ṭūsī received through the above-mentioned two transmitters as well as Muḥammad b. Ismā'īl b. Bazī'. There are several hundred quotations from this author in Shī'ite works of *ḥadīth*, listed in Khu'ī 21: 395–400 and *Fahāris* 9: 122, mainly through the same transmitters.

106: Ibn Harāsa

Ibrāhīm b. Rajā' al-Shaybānī, also known as Ibn Harāsa, a Kūfan Sunnī ascetic with Shī'ite sympathies. He transmitted, among others, from a number of the 'Alīds including Ja'far al-Ṣādiq.

Bukhārī, *Kabīr* 1: 333; Nasā'ī, *Ḍu'afā'*: 41; 'Uqaylī 1: 69; Ibn Abī Ḥātim 2: 143; Ibn Ḥibbān, *Majrūḥīn* 1: 111; Ibn 'Adī: 243–4; Dāraquṭnī, *Ḍu'afā'*: 46; Najāshī: 23; *Fihrist*: 23; *Rijāl*: 58; Khaṭīb, *Mūḍiḥ* 1: 386–7; *Lisān* 1: 178–9 (and other sources listed in the editor's footnote).

Harāsa was the name of this transmitter's mother (Najāshī: 23; Khaṭīb, *Mūḍiḥ* 1: 387). Fīrūzābādī 2: 401 (see also Zabīdī 4: 272) notes the meaning and correct spelling of the name and mentions this transmitter. Najāshī: 23 calls him Ibn Abī Harāsa which is wrong since Harāsa, according to the same work, was the name of his mother. Khaṭīb, *Mūḍiḥ* 1: 387 identifies him as being the same as the Ibrāhīm b. Salama who related a *ḥadīth* quoted in that work. If correct, Salama should have been a grandfather. The use of the grandfather's name in place of the father's was a common practice in Arabic in cases where the name of a grandfather was a rare one and could thus serve as a family name for the descendants, distinguishing them from others. There is a Rajā' b. Salama who, like Ibrāhīm (as, for instance, in 'Āṣimī 1: 227; Ibn Ṭāwūs, *Yaqīn*: 222), related from 'Amr b. Shimr/Shamir al-Ju'fī (e.g. *'Ilal* 1: 117–18, 223; *Ma'ānī*: 58–62; also Ibn al-Juḥām: 194 [where Rajā' quotes that transmitter through an intermediary]; *Bishārat al-Muṣṭafā*: 12–13 [where the name appears as Rajā' b. *Abī* Salama[69]]).

Wakī', the Kūfan scholar (d. 197) encountered Ibrāhīm one Friday while the latter was dictating some of his transmissions to a large crowd, and made an unfriendly comment (Ibn 'Adī: 244). Ibn Abī Ḥātim 2: 143 describes him as *a'war* (one eyed). Suyūṭī, *Bughya* 1: 410 mentions an Ibrāhīm b. Rajā' b. Nūḥ, a grammarian and Qur'ān scholar from Balkh who died in 256. Nuwayhiḍ 1: 13 who names Suyūṭī's above-mentioned work as his source for information on that Qur'ānic scholar, gives 163 as the date of his death. This date does not appear in Suyūṭī's work. Wajīh: 132 misidentified our transmitter with this Qur'ānic scholar, calls the latter "Ibrāhīm b. Rajā' al-Shaybānī al-Marwazī, known as Ibn Harāsa, [after] his mother," and assigns the year 163 to this Ibn Harāsa as his date of death.

1. *Nuskha 'an Ja'far [b. Muḥammad]*

A register of his transmissions from Ja'far al-Ṣādiq (Najāshī: 23). A citation in Aḥmad b. 'Īsā 4: 312–13 from Ibrāhīm b. Rajā' al-Shaybānī

69. Rajā' b. Abī Salama Mihrān, Abū 'l-Miqdām, was a Baṣran transmitter who lived in Ramla in Palestine and died in 191 (Mizzī 9: 161–3 and the sources listed in the editor's footnote).

quoting a statement from Ja'far al-Ṣādiq on the meaning of the *Ḥadīth al-Ghadīr* (also Muḥammad b. Sulaymān 2: 377; *Bishārat al-Muṣṭafā*: 51) should go back to this work.

2. *Kitāb*

His general notebook of *ḥadīth* (*Fihrist*: 9), evidently linked at the time with the author's byname of Ibn Harāsa, since this is how the name of this author appears in almost all transmissions that he quoted from authorities other than Ja'far al-Ṣādiq. Examples of this author's Shī'ite transmissions in later works of *ḥadīth* include the following:

- Ibn Abī 'l-Dunyā, *Tawāḍu'*: 118
- Ṣaffār: 12
- Nu'mānī: 290–92
- Ibn Bābawayh, *Amālī*: 730
- Mufīd, *Amālī*: 116
- *Ḥilya* 1:64
- 'Āṣimī 2: 227
- *Tahdhīb* 6: 46 (also Abū 'Abd Allāh al-Shajarī, *Faḍl*: 44, 46)
- Khaṭīb, *Mūḍiḥ* 1: 387
- Ibn Ṭāwūs, *Yaqīn*: 222 (quoting the lost vol. 1 of the *Dalā'il al-imāma*)

107: Ibrāhīm al-Yamānī

Ibrāhīm b. 'Umar al-Yamānī al-Ṣan'ānī, a Yemeni Shī'ite who transmitted from Ja'far al-Ṣādiq and Mūsā al-Kāẓim.

Barqī: 53, 115; Ibn al-Ghaḍā'irī: 36; Najāshī: 20; *Fihrist*: 9; *Rijāl*: 123, 158, 331. See also Muḥammad Taqī al-Tustarī 1: 254.

Kitāb / Aṣl

His notebook of *ḥadīth*, related by Ḥammād b. 'Īsā al-Juhanī (Ibn al-Ghaḍā'irī: 36; Najāshī: 20; *Fihrist*: 9; *Rijāl*: 331). *Rijāl*: 123 refers to the *uṣūl* (*ḥadīth* notebooks) of this transmitter, all of which were related from him by the said Ḥammād b. 'Īsā.

With very few exceptions (*Kāfī* 1: 86, 112, 4: 168, 5: 143; Ṭūsī, *Amālī*: 735–6), all quotations from this author in Shī'ite works of *ḥadīth* are through Ḥammād b. 'Īsā (see Khu'ī 5: 231–2). Ibrāhīm was also one of the original transmitters of the Book of Sulaym b. Qays al-Hilālī, and this may have been the reason, or one of the reasons, that Ibn al-Ghaḍā'irī, who considers that book a forgery, describes Ibrāhīm as untrustworthy (Ibn al-Ghaḍā'irī: 36). Ḥammād received that book through Ibrāhīm as noted in the chain of transmission at the beginning of the text. Some of the quotations by Ḥammād from Ibrāhīm in later works are paragraphs from that work, but there are many others that do not belong there and are obviously cited from Ibrāhīm's own notebooks. Examples are as follows:

- Ḥusayn b. Sa'īd, *Zuhd*: 53, 75, 76 (also *Kāfī* 2: 453)
- Aḥmad b. Muḥammad b. 'Īsā: 60 (read *'an Ḥammād b. 'Īsā 'an Ibrāhīm b. 'Umar* as in *Kāfī* 7: 454)
- *Maḥāsin*: 99 (also Ibn Bābawayh, *Amālī*: 574; *Thawāb*: 77, 164; Mufīd, *Amālī*: 9), 289–90 (whence *'Ilal* 1: 235–6), 393, 490, 555 (whence *Kāfī* 6: 360)
- Ṣaffār: 123, 195–6, 445–6 (whence *Kāfī* 1: 271–2), 459, 462
- 'Ayyāshī 1: 12, 55 (also *Ma'ānī*: 297), 271
  2: 55, 120 (also 'Alī b. Ibrāhīm 1: 308–9), 162 (also *Kāfī* 3: 266; *'Ilal* 2: 52), 222, 261, 318
- *Kāfī* 1: 158, 271–2, 535
  2: 80, 170, 176, 197, 201, 205, 233, 361, 453, 551
  3: 44, 164, 266
  4: 70, 238–9 (also *Faqīh* 2: 256), 396, 411–12, 422–3, 535
  5: 145–6 (partially also in *Faqīh* 3: 275)
  6: 274, 360, 395
  7: 325, 454
  8: 165–6, 364 (also 'Alī b. Ibrāhīm 1: 308–9)
- Kashshī: 16–17, 53–5 (also 'Alī b. Ibrāhīm 2: 23; *Ikhtiṣāṣ*: 71–3)
- Ibn Hammām: 50
- Nu'mānī: 191, 199, 206–7 (also Ṭūsī, *Ghayba*: 339–40)
- Qāḍī Nu'mān, *Sharḥ* 1: 237
- *Faqīh* 2: 401
- *Kamāl*: 206–7 (also Ṭūsī, *Amālī*: 441), 650 (repeated at 652)
- *Khiṣāl*: 27
- *Tawḥīd*: 325–6, 359

- *Irshād* 2: 376 (also *Ghayba*: 448)
- *Ikhtiṣāṣ*: 29
- *Ghayba*: 436–7
- *Miṣbāḥ*: 302–4 (read *'an Ḥammād b. 'Īsā 'an Ibrāhīm b. 'Umar* as in Ibu Ṭāwūs, *Jamāl*: 173)
- *Tahdhīb* 1: 41
  3: 96–7
  5: 19, 79, 350
  6: 239

108: 'Īṣ al-Bajalī

Abū 'l-Qāsim 'Īṣ b. al-Qāsim b. Thābit al-Bajalī, a Kūfan Arab transmitter from Ja'far al-Ṣādiq and Mūsā al-Kāẓim.

Barqī: 103; Kashshī: 361–2; Najāshī: 302; *Fihrist*: 121; *Rijāl*: 263.

Kitāb

His notebook of *ḥadīth*, related by Ṣafwān b. Yaḥyā and Ibn Abī 'Umayr (Abū Ghālib: 161, 171; Najāshī: 302; *Fihrist*: 121). The overwhelming majority of quotations from this author are through Ṣafwān b. Yaḥyā, particularly in the case of some fifty of them which are recorded in the four main works of Shī'ite *ḥadīth* as listed in Khu'ī 13: 216–17, 418–21. Additional examples can be found in the following works:

- Aḥmad b. Muḥammad b. 'Īsā: 95, 102
- *Maḥāsin*: 453, 462, 494 (two reports), 621(see also ibid.: 452 [through Ibn Abī 'Umayr])
- Ṣaffār: 169 (two variants)
- Ibn Qūlawayh: 347 (cf. 348 where Ṣafwān quotes the same passage from 'Īṣ through an intermediary)
- Ibn Bābawayh, *Amālī*: 339–40, 398, 401–2
- Ibn Ṭāwūs, *Muḍāyaqa*: 342

109: ʿĪsā al-Mubārak

Abū Bakr ʿĪsā b. ʿAbd Allāh b. Muḥammad b. ʿUmar b. ʿAlī b. Abī Ṭālib, known as Mubārak, a great-grandson of ʿAlī, and a historian, genealogist, and poet, as well as a transmitter of *ḥadīth*. A great-nephew of Jaʿfar al-Ṣādiq, he mostly transmitted from him and from his own father, ʿAbd Allāh, known as Dāfin.

Bukhārī, *Kabīr* 6: 390–91; Barqī: 85; Ibn Abī Ḥātim 6: 280; Ibn Ḥibbān, *Majrūḥīn* 2: 121–2; idem, *Thiqāt* 8: 492; Ibn ʿAdī: 1883–5; Barqī: 85; Dāraquṭnī 2: 263; Najāshī: 295; *Fihrist*: 116, 117; *Rijāl*: 257, and other sources listed in the editor's footnote to *Lisān* 5: 375–6.

He was a son of Umm Ḥusayn, daughter of ʿAbd Allāh, brother of Jaʿfar al-Ṣādiq (ʿAqīqī: 102; Ṭabarī 7: 600 [whence *Maqātil*: 248]; Ibn al-Ṣūfī: 292 [and 94, but read *ʿAbd Allāh* for *ʿUbayd Allāh*]). This is why he refers to Jaʿfar al-Ṣādiq at times as "my uncle" (e.g. Abū Ṭālib: 59, 194). His paternal grandmother was the daughter of ʿAlī Zayn al-ʿĀbidīn (Ibn Saʿd, supplement: 249, 388; Muṣʿab al-Zubayrī: 80; Khalīfa b. Khayyāṭ, *Ṭabaqāt*: 647). Ibn ʿAdī: 1883 and Ḥākim, *Maʿrifa*: 102 identify him as a Kūfan. This is certainly not correct. A transmitter in Bukhārī, *Kabīr* 6: 390 reports that he heard him in Ray. That also seems unlikely. He was a Medinese both by origin and residence, the latter point being attested in the *isnād*s of some of his reports (e.g. Ḥaskānī 2: 227).

That he was both a prolific poet and an expert on poetry is mentioned by Muṣʿab al-Zubayrī (as quoted by Ibn ʿAsākir 32: 358, but the sentence is missing from the printed version of Muṣʿab's work); Marzubānī, *Muʿjam*: 259, as well as genealogical works such as Ibn al-Ṣūfī: 292. Six lines of an elegy which he composed for the killing of Ḥusayn b. ʿAlī Ṣāḥib Fakhkh (d. 169) are cited in *Maqātil*: 458–9 (partially also in Marzubānī: 259; Ibn al-Ṣūfī: 292). Marzubānī: 259 cites two other lines from a different poem by him. Much of the information on the revolt of Muḥammad b. ʿAbd Allāh al-Nafs al-Zakiyya (d. 145) and its background and aftermath in Ṭabarī's *Taʾrīkh* is from him (see ibid. 7: 422, 521, 529–31, 534–6, 538, 540, 541, 542, 546, 547, 549, 553, 555, 557, 560, 562, 572, 576, 578, 579, 583, 585, 586, 588, 590, 592, 598, 599–601, 603–605, 608, 611). The volume of the material suggests that ʿĪsā may have composed a book on the killing of al-Nafs al-Zakiyya. (For ʿĪsā as a source of historical material, see further, Azraqī 1: 173; Abū ʾl-Faraj, *Aghānī* 7: 21.) He is also cited as an authority on the biographical and genealogical material on the members of the House of the Prophet (e.g. Ibn Shabba as below; *Manāqib* 2: 192; Ibn Zuhra: 41–2).

For his descendants, see ʿUbaydalī: 293–5; Ibn al-Ṣūfī: 293–5; Ibn ʿInaba: 367–9.

1. *Kitāb / Nuskha*

His notebook of *ḥadīth*, related by a number of transmitters including Abū Sumayna Muḥammad b. 'Alī b. Ibrāhīm al-Qurashī and 'Alī b. Muḥammad b. Sulaymān al-Nawfalī[70] (Abū Ghālib: 146, 184; Najāshī: 295; *Fihrist*: 116, 117). The notebook was widely known in the mid-fourth century (Abū Ghālib: 146). Ibn Ḥibbān, *Majrūḥīn* 2: 123 calls it a *nuskha*. Ṭūsī received a version of the notebook ascribed to *'Īsā b. 'Abd Allāh al-Hāshimī* through Aḥmad b. Hilāl, a mid-third century transmitter, and mentions it separately in *Fihrist*: 117, clearly on the assumption that this 'Īsā may be a different person. Aḥmad b. Hilāl, however, makes it clear at times that his source is *'Īsā b. 'Abd Allāh min wuld 'Umar b. 'Alī* (*Tawḥīd*: 30; *Thawāb*: 15).

There are a large number of quotations from this author in Sunnī, Zaydī and Imāmite Shī'ite sources, many through the transmitters named above, as well as others who are regularly cited through uniform chains of transmission. The volume of this material suggests that the bulk of the work in question has survived in later works. Examples are as follows:

- 'Alī b. Asbāṭ: 124
- Azraqī 1: 173
- Bukhārī, *Kabīr* 6: 390–91 (also Ibn 'Asākir 32: 357)
- Ibn Shabba: 660, 665, 755 (whence Ibn Abī 'l-Dunyā, *Maqtal*: 120)
- *Maḥāsin*: 82–3 (also *Ma'ānī*: 164), 459 (also *Kāfī* 6: 308), 479, 486, 518, 526–7, 558–9, 570 (also *Kāfī* 6: 380–81 through two different *isnād*s)
- Ḥibarī, *Mā nazal*: 43 (also Ibn Bābawayh, *Amālī*: 579; Abū Nu'aym, *Mā nazal*: 253–4; Ḥaskānī 1: 88–92 [five variants])
- Ṣaffār 2–3 (two variants in three reports, one also in *Kāfī* 1: 30, a further variant in Ibn 'Adī: 1883), 163–4, 181 (also *Kāfī* 1: 305)
- Aḥmad b. 'Īsā 1: 15, 18, 32, 34, 130, 135, 146, 233, 237, 262
  2: 263, 264, 388, 412, 438
  3: 6, 7, 46, 138 (two reports)
  4: 259–60, 261, 315, 321, 335, 370–71 (five reports)

70. This transmitter lived in the middle of the third century, and should have received the notebook through an intermediary. In *Kāfī* 6: 391, he quotes our author through his *shaykh* (see *'Ilal* 1: 18–19), 'Alī b. Dāwūd al-Ya'qūbī, a transmitter whose transmission from our author is attested in numerous other cases too (e.g. *Kāfī* 6: 524; Ibn Bābawayh, *Amālī*: 363; *Khiṣāl*: 291; *Tahdhīb* 7: 473). This may have always been the link between Nawfalī and this notebook, even in cases where the latter leaves out the name of the intermediary.

- 'Ayyāshī 1: 21, 41, 110, 232, 288, 311, 350–51 (also *Qiṣaṣ*: 185)
  2: 64, 145–6
- Muḥammad b. Sulaymān 1: 142, 221 (repeated in 2: 384 and partially in 2: 391; also in Qāḍī Nu'mān, *Sharḥ* 1: 231), 310 (also Ṭūsī, *Amālī*: 354–5), 311, 512
  2: 81–2, 103, 104, 274, 287, 398–9 (partially also at 391), 419
- Ṭabarī: 7: 600–601 (whence *Maqātil*: 248)
- *Kāfī* 1: 286 (also 309 with a fuller text)
  3: 227
  4: 60, 189, 540
  5: 97 (also *Tahdhīb* 6: 211)
  6: 52 (read *Muḥammad b. 'Alī 'an 'Īsā b. 'Abd Allāh* as in *Tawḥīd*: 395 and *Thawāb*: 231), 391, 513, 524, 532
  7: 463
  8: 349–51
- Ibn al-Juḥām: 203 (also Ḥaskānī 1: 541)
- Furāt: 404 (same as Ibn Ḥibbān, *Majrūḥīn* 2: 122 quoting from the *Nuskha*; Ḥaskānī 2: 227), 570 (also *Khiṣāl*: 360–61), 619–20
- Nu'mānī: 156
- Ibn Ḥibbān, *Majrūḥīn* 2: 122 (six reports, directly citing the *Nuskha*; one identical with Furāt: 404; two also appear in Ibn 'Adī: 1884 [one of these two also in Ṭūsī, *Amālī*: 334–5; Ibn 'Asākir 42: 245; the other also in *Kāfī* 4: 60]; a fourth one is the same as Bukhārī, *Kabīr* 6: 390–91)
- Ṭabarānī, *Akhbār al-Ḥasan*: 65–6 (also idem, *Kabīr* 3: 41; whence Ibn 'Asākir 13: 227)
- Idem, *Awsaṭ* 6: 9
- Ibn 'Adī: 1883–5 (nineteen reports, two of them partially repeated, with a reference to nine more; many of these are cited in later biographical works as well as Shahrdār b. Shīrūya al-Daylamī's *Musnad al-Firdaws*, Ibn al-Jawzī's *al-'Ilal al-mutanāhiya* and Suyūṭī's *al-La'ālī al-maṣnū'a* from Ibn 'Adī; four of these are attested in other works independent of Ibn 'Adī: two in Dāraquṭnī, *Majrūḥīn* 2: 122 [one of the two also in *Kāfī* 4: 60; the other in Ṭūsī, *Amālī*: 334–5 and Ibn 'Asākir 42: 245]; a third one in Ṭūsī, *Amālī*: 355; a variant of a fourth in Ṣaffār: 2 and *Kāfī* 1: 30)
- Ibn Qūlawayh, *Kāmil*: 106 (partially also at 107–8 and *Khiṣāl*: 250)
- Idem, *Kitāb*: 144
- Ibn Bābawayh, *Amālī*: 64 (also *Tawḥīd*: 95; *Thawāb*: 156); 247, 363 (also Ḥaskānī 1: 76)

- *'Ilal* 2: 154–5
- *Kamāl*: 350, 415–16
- *Khiṣāl*: 91, 283–4, 291, 358
- *Ma'ānī*: 10, 164, 220, 354–6
- *Thawāb*: 37 (two reports), 53–4, 58, 134, 209
- Dāraquṭnī 1: 302
  2: 263
  4: 250
- Ḥākim, *Ma'rifa*: 50, 102 (read *'an 'Īsā b. 'Abd Allāh b. Muḥammad b. 'Umar* as in Ḥaskānī 1: 226; Ibn 'Asakīr 42: 356–7 [also in a condensed form in 45: 303])
- Abū Ṭālib: 59–61, 78, 107, 109, 194, 224, 335
- Quḍā'ī 2: 315 (also *Mīzān* 3: 315, 316)
- Bayhaqī, *Shu'ab* 4: 95
- Idem, *Sunan* 6: 349 (also Khaṭīb, *Talkhīṣ*: 247–8)
- Ṭūsī, *Amālī*: 167, 355, 454, 590
- *Tahdhīb* 1: 24, 377, 378
  3: 286, 309
  7: 394, 473
  10: 35, 106–7
- Khaṭīb, *Talkhīṣ*: 299
- Idem, *Ta'rīkh* 4: 339
- Ḥaskānī 2: 52
- *Firdaws* (Uzbak: 2300, # 73)
- Ibn 'Asākir 3: 144–5
  10: 459
  11: 312
  42: 245–6, 451
  45: 303
  54: 414
- *Kharā'ij*: 116–17
- *Manāqib* 3: 107
- Suyūṭī, *La'ālī* 1: 369
  2: 261–2

2. *Musnad 'Umar b. 'Alī b. Abī Ṭālib*

In his entry on our author, Najāshī: 295 reports that the mid-fourth century scholar of Baghdad, Abū Bakr Muḥammad b. 'Umar al-Tamīmī, known as Ibn al-Ji'ābī (d. 355), gathered the transmissions by our author from his forefathers into a single volume. This is obviously the book that Najāshī: 395 names in his entry on Ibn al-Ji'ābī and among his writings as *Kitāb musnad 'Umar b. 'Alī b. Abī Ṭālib.* The surviving quotations from 'Umar b. 'Alī on the authority of Ibn al-Ji'ābī found in later works in all likelihood go back to this work. Most of the materials quoted from 'Umar b. 'Alī are transmitted through 'Īsā, but a few items also through others, especially other members of the family.[71] This fact was also clearly reflected in Ibn al-Ji'ābī's work. While some of the surviving material of the work is indeed on the authority of 'Īsā b. 'Abd Allāh as, for instance, in Ṭūsī, *Amālī*: 354–5 (two reports), other passages are quoted through others as, for instance, in *Ḥilya* 1: 67; Abū 'l-Shaykh, *al-Targhīb wa 'l-tarhīb* (Uzbak: 2300, # 70); Mufīd, *Amālī*: 251 (see also *Khiṣāl*: 271–2).

110: 'Īsā al-Najjār

'Īsa b. Dāwūd, the carpenter, a Kūfan transmitter from Mūsā al-Kāẓim.

Najāshī: 294

Ibn 'Uqda (d. 333) and Ibn Hammām al-Iskāfī (d. 336) both quote from this author with one intermediary. The apparently widespread phenomenon of transmission by *wijāda* makes it difficult to judge whether this author could have lived well into the third century. The only internal autobiographical piece of information from the extant parts of his *Kitāb al-tafsīr* is that he transmitted from Mūsā al-Kāẓim, as Najāshī mentions.

Kitāb al-tafsīr

(Najāshī: 294) This work was at least partially available to Ibn al-Juḥām, the mid-fourth century author on the topic, who quotes a large portion of the book through a single line of transmission in his own *Tafsīr*: 127, 128, 129, 132, 135, 137–8, 140, 145, 146, 147, 149, 152, 153–4, 157–8, 159, 163, 164 (two passages), 165, 166, 167, 169–70, 171, 174–7, 179, 180, 182 (two passages), 186, 191–2, 340–44, 407, 411. The fragments quoted ibid.: 132, 140, 147, 177, 340–44 clearly retain the language and structure of the original work.

---

71. See further Najāshī: 358; Khaṭīb, *Ta'rīkh* 12: 443; also 'Āṣimī 2: 208; Ḥaskānī 2: 363; Ibn 'Asākir 42: 332, 389.

Judging by these fragments, this was a purely Shīʿite *tafsīr* similar to those of Jābir al-Juʿfī and Ibn Abī Ḥamza al-Baṭāʾinī, but not as esoteric. The fragments also show that the commentary was mixed together in this work with the text of the Qurʾān as was also the case with some later examples of the genre, such as the Qurʾānic commentary ascribed to ʿAlī b. Ibrāhīm al-Qummī.

111: Isḥāq al-Ṣayrafī

Abū Yaʿqūb Isḥāq b. ʿAmmār b. Ḥayyān, the moneychanger, a Kūfan client of the Banū Taghlib and member of a Shīʿite family of *ḥadīth* transmitters. He was both learned and wealthy and as such a distinguished member of the Shīʿite community of his time. A transmitter from Jaʿfar al-Ṣādiq and Mūsā al-Kāẓim, he reportedly died during the lifetime of the latter, possibly in or before 181.

Barqī: 83, 115; Kashshī: 402, 408–10; *Mashyakha*: 475; Najāshī: 71; *Fihrist*: 15; *Rijāl*: 162, 331. See also Muḥammad Taqī al-Tustarī 1: 757–70.

The approximate date of his death is based on an esoteric report in Kashshī: 409 according to which Mūsā al-Kāẓim predicted Ishāq's death in two years. Bearing in mind that this Imām died in 183 after four years in prison, for the story to sound probable, Isḥāq would have to have died before 182.

Kitāb / Aṣl / Kitāb nawādir

His notebook of *ḥadīth*, related by a number of Shīʿite transmitters including Ghiyāth b. Kallūb al-Bajalī and Ibn Abī ʿUmayr (Najāshī: 71; *Fihrist*, 15; *Rijāl*: 331). With close to one thousand quotations from this author in Shīʿite works of *ḥadīth*, listed in Khuʾī 3: 54–6, 430–60 and *Fahāris* 8: 139, 145–6, very many through the above-mentioned transmitters and others who narrate large numbers of passages, it appears that the entire text of this notebook is preserved in later works.

Muḥammad b. Makkī al-ʿĀmilī, known as al-Shahīd al-Awwal, a prominent Shīʿite scholar of the late eighth century (d. 786), quotes from this notebook (Āghā Buzurg 20: 112), suggesting that the notebook or a part of it may have survived into his time.

112: Isḥāq al-Kāhilī

Abū Ya'qūb Isḥāq b. Bishr b. Muqātil al-Kāhilī, a Kūfan Sunnī transmitter of *ḥadīth* with Shī'ite sympathies who transmitted from Ja'far al-Ṣādiq, among others. He lived in Baghdad and died in 228.[72]

'Uqaylī 1: 98–100; Ibn Ḥibbān, *Majrūḥīn* 1: 135–7; Ibn 'Adī: 335–6; Najāshī: 72; Khaṭīb, *Ta'rīkh* 6: 328–9, and other sources listed in the editor's footnote to *Lisān* 1: 542.

Some early authors of the biographical material on the transmitters of *ḥadīth* confused this transmitter with his more senior, and better known, contemporary Abū Ḥudhayfa Isḥāq b. Bishr al-Khurāsānī (d. 206), a historian and *ḥadīth* transmitter from Bukhārā and one time visitor to Baghdad. So did Ibn Ḥibbān, *Majrūḥīn* 1: 135–7; Najāshī: 72, as well as *Rijāl*: 162, naming only Abū Ḥudhayfa from among the two as a transmitter from Ja'far al-Ṣādiq. Judging on the basis of the surviving quotations, it was the Kūfan Kāhilī who had Shī'ite sympathies and quoted from Ja'far al-Ṣādiq, obviously, though without acknowledgement, through intermediaries (see, for instance, Ibn al-Juḥām: 489 [*'an Isḥāq b. Bishr al-Kāhilī*]; 'Āṣimī 1: 20 [*'an Isḥāq b. Bishr al-Kāhilī al-Kūfī*]; *Bishārat al-Muṣṭafā*: 152 [*'an Isḥāq b. Bishr al-Asadī*; Kāhil was a clan of Asad Khuzayma]; see further Khaṭīb, *Ta'rīkh* 6: 327 who reports that, with a single exception, only Khurāsānis quoted *ḥadīth* from Abū Ḥudhayfa). Transmission of Shī'ite transmitters from Isḥāq b. Bishr al-Kāhilī is also attested in material he quoted from masters other than Ja'far al-Ṣādiq as, for instance, in Ibn Bābawayh, *Amālī*: 672–3 (also *Thawāb*: 239).

1. *Kitāb*

Najāshī: 72 mentions that he received a book by this transmitter, related from him by a certain Aḥmad b. Sa'īd. There is a long text of a set of instructions given by God to the Prophet on his Night Journey, related from Isḥāq b. Bishr by an 'Abd al-Ḥamīd b. Aḥmad b. Sa'īd. This latter transmitter seems to be the same as the one named by Najāshī, the name *'Abd al-Ḥamīd* having been either left out by Najāshī or added in the *isnād* of this text through error.

The text, which has the format of an independent treatise, is published in a lithograph edition (Tehran, 1297, along with Ibn Shu'ba's *Tuḥaf al-'uqūl* and vol. 8 [*Rawḍa*] of Kulaynī's *Kāfī* in the same volume).

72. As can be observed from this transmitter's date of death, his transmission from Ja'far al-Ṣādiq must have been through intermediaries whose names he always leaves out. Misled by his style of direct quotation, the biographers name him as a transmitter from Ja'far al-Ṣādiq and this is also the reason why he is included in this section.

It is also quoted in Daylamī, *Irshād* 1: 373–82 (without *isnād*); *Biḥār* 71: 21–31 (with *isnād* at the end of the text) (see further Muḥammad Taqī al-Tustarī 1: 738–9).

2. *Nuskha*

A register of Kāhilī's transmissions from Ja'far al-Ṣādiq, Sufyān b. Sa'īd al-Thawrī (d. 161) and others. Ibn Ḥibbān, who mentions this *nuskha* in his *Majrūḥīn* 1: 136, found much of its contents too objectionable to quote. The tone and context seem to point to reports on the virtues of 'Alī of which quite a few are attested in Kāhilī's transmissions, including the following:

- Furāt: 242–3
- Ibn al-Juḥām: 147, 489–90 (read *Bishr* for *Bashīr*)
- Ibn Qūlawayh: 147
- Ibn Bābawayh, *Kitāb al-mi'rāj* (quoted in Ḥasan b. Sulaymān, *Muḥtaḍar* [*Biḥār* 25: 4]; also *Ta'wīl al-āyāt*: 773–4 [without *isnād*])
- 'Āṣimī: 20–21 (through two *isnāds*; also Tha'labī, *al-Kashf wa 'l-bayān* [quoted in Ibn Biṭrīq, *'Umda*: 351; also the editor's footnote to Abū Nu'aym, *Mā nazal*: 135–7]; Ḥaskānī 1: 464–5 [through six *isnāds*])
- Ibn 'Abd al-Barr, *Istī'āb*: 1744 (also *Bishārat al-Muṣṭafā*: 152; Ibn Ḥajar, *Iṣāba* 7: 354; partially also in *Mīzān* 1: 188])
- Ibn Ṭāwūs, *Yaqīn*: 484 (quoting a work of Abū 'l-Ḥusayn al-Nassāba)

There is also a quotation from Ja'far al-Ṣādiq on the authority of an Irāqi *isnād* from Isḥāq b. Bishr in the *Firdaws* (Uzbak: 2212, no. 33, whence Suyūṭī, *La'ālī* 2: 164). For examples of this author's pure Sunnī transmissions, see 'Uqaylī 1: 98–100; Ibn 'Adī: 335–6.

113: Isḥāq al-Mu'taman

Isḥāq b. Ja'far b. Muḥammad, son of Ja'far al-Ṣādiq and a transmitter from his father and brother, Mūsā al-Kāẓim. He was a respected scholar of religion in his time.

Bukhārī, *Kabīr* 1: 383; Barqī: 51, 115; Ibn Abī Ḥātim 2: 215; Ibn Ḥibbān, *Thiqāt* 8: 111; *Irshād* 2: 211; *Rijāl*: 161. See also *Kāfī* 1: 316–18; *'Uyūn* 1: 39; *Tahdhīb* 2: 317.

Lisān 1: 546–7, quoting Ibn ʿUqda, assigns the epithet *Ḥazīn* to this transmitter and quotes a report to explain why he was so called. The genealogical works, however, all give his epithet as *Muʾtaman* (see, for instance, ʿUbaydalī: 183; Ibn al-Ṣūfī: 98; Marwazī: 9, 26; Fakhr al-Rāzī, *Shajara*: 76; Ibn Zuhra: 92; Ibn ʿInaba: 249).

Ṣaḥīfa

No work is ascribed to this transmitter in Shīʿite sources. In the Sunnī tradition, however, there is a register of nineteen reports that he transmitted through his forefathers from the Prophet, known as *Ṣaḥifat Isḥāq b. Jaʿfar al-Ṣādiq ʿan ābāʾih*. The text appears in Uzbak: 709–10 as a facsimile. There are also other quotations by Isḥāq from his father in Sunnī and Shīʿite works of *ḥadīth* that are not attested in this *Ṣaḥīfa*, including the following examples:

- *Maḥāsin*: 460 (also *Kāfī* 6: 544)
- *Kāfī* 1: 308, 387–8, 448–9
- Khazzāz: 105–6 (a later contribution)
- Ṭūsī, *Amālī*: 54, 223 (repeated at 596), 495–6, 585, 596 (three reports, one a repetition of the passage at 223), 629–30
- Rāfiʿī, *Tadwīn* 4: 143–4

114: Isḥāq al-Jarīrī

Abū Yaʿqūb Isḥāq b. Jarīr al-Bajalī, a Kūfan Arab Shīʿite and a transmitter from Jaʿfar al-Ṣādiq. He lived into the last decades of the century and joined the Wāqifites after the death of Mūsā al-Kāẓim.

Barqī: 83; Najāshī: 71; *Fibrist*: 15; *Rijāl*: 161, 332. See also *Lisān* 1: 546.

He is a son of Jarīr b. Yazīd b. Jarīr b. ʿAbd Allāh al-Bajalī. His great-grandfather, Jarīr b. ʿAbd Allāh (d. 54) was a member of ʿAlī's camp who joined Muʿāwiya and became a fierce opponent of ʿAlī. Our transmitter's father, Jarīr b. Yazīd was a notable in the beginning of the ʿAbbāsid revolution (see Ṭabarī 7: 483 [see also 270]). Isḥāq himself worked for the ʿAbbāsid Abū 'l-ʿAbbās al-Saffāḥ in Ḥīra early in his life (Ibn Qūlawayh: 88).

That he joined the Wāqifites is mentioned in *Rijāl*: 332.

Kitāb / Aṣl

His notebook of *ḥadīth*, related by a number of transmitters including Ibn Abī 'Umayr and Ḥasan b. Maḥbūb (Najāshī: 71; *Fihrist*: 15). Quotations from this author, some through the same two transmitters, include the following examples:

- Aḥmad b. Muḥammad b.'Īsā: 114
- Muḥammad b. 'Alī b. Maḥbūb: 105–6 (also *Kāfī* 3: 91–2, and partially in *Maḥāsin*: 239; *'Iqāb*: 318)
- *Maḥāsin*: 89–90 (also *'Iqāb*: 249), 353, 357 (also *Faqīh* 2: 278), 559 (also *Kāfī* 6: 377)
- Ṣaffār: 439
- *Kāfī* 1: 472
  4: 586
  5: 356 (also *Tahdhīb* 7: 327 through a different transmitter), 536 (two variants, one repeated ibid. 6: 433)
  6: 520
  7: 204 (also *'Ilal* 2: 225)
- Nu'mānī: 216
- 'Alī b. Ibrāhīm 2: 244
- Ibn Qūlawayh: 87–8
- *Kamāl*: 21, 348–9
- *Tahdhīb* 2: 65
  4: 162–3
  8: 73

115: Ismā'īl al-Asadī

Ismā'īl b. 'Abd al-Khāliq b. 'Abd Rabbih, a Kūfan client of the Banū Asad and member of a Shī'ite family of transmitters of *ḥadīth*. A notable in the Shī'ite community of Kūfa with a good knowledge of religious law, he transmitted from Ja'far al-Ṣādiq and Mūsā al-Kāẓim.

Kashshī: 414; Najāshī: 27; *Fihrist*: 14; *Rijāl*: 159. See also *Kāfī* 5: 198, 203.

Kitāb

His notebook of *ḥadīth*, related by a number of transmitters including Muḥammad b. Khālid al-Ṭayālisī (d. 259) (Abū Ghālib: 148; Najāshī: 27; *Fibrist*: 14). A fragment of thirteen reports from this notebook as related by the above-mentioned transmitter is cited in 'Abd Allāh b. Ja'far: 125–9 (# 439–51). Five of these (# 441, 442, 446, 449, 451) are attested in *Kāfī* 4: 351; ibid. 3: 529; *Tahdhīb* 2: 328; ibid. 8: 55; *Kāfī* 8: 93, respectively, but all through 'Alī b. al-Ḥakam who was obviously another principal transmitter of the notebook. Other quotations from this author through Muḥammad b. Khālid al-Ṭayālisī appear in *Kāfī* 5: 198; Kashshī: 406 (repeated at 412), and Ibn Ṭāwūs, *Falāḥ*: 455–6. Other quotations through 'Alī b. al-Ḥakam are listed in Khu'ī 3: 470–71, 11: 590.

116: Ibn Abī Ziyād al-Sakūnī

Ismā'īl b. Abī Ziyād al-Sakūnī, a Kūfan client of Kinda (of which the Banū 'l-Sakūn were a clan) and a Sunnī transmitter of *ḥadīth*. He transmitted a very large number of reports from Ja'far al-Ṣādiq and is by far the most prolific non-Shī'ite source of Shī'ite *ḥadīth*.

Barqī: 82; Najāshī: 26; *Fibrist*: 13; *Rijāl*: 160. See also Khaṭīb, *Mūḍiḥ* 1: 408–410.

The name of our transmitter's father is mentioned as *Muslim* in *Mashyakha*: 459 and most of the works named above. He must be the same as the Ismā'īl b. Abī Ziyād who served as the judge of Mosul and wrote a commentary on the Qur'ān (see *Lisān* 1: 627–8 and the many sources listed in the editor's footnote; see further Khaṭīb, *Mūḍiḥ* 1: 408–10 quoting Ibn 'Uqda). The latter is said to have quoted his teacher, Thawr b. Yazīd, in his commentary on the Qur'ān (*Lisān* 1: 627), a point attested in the quotations on the topic from Ismā'īl b. Abī Ziyād al-Sakūnī in Shī'ite works of *ḥadīth* (e.g. *Tawḥīd*: 343–4).[73]

73. A variant of this passage, that as said above is related by Sakūnī from Thawr b. Yazīd, is quoted in 'Alī b. Ibrāhīm 2: 210–11 on the authority of Nawfalī, Sakūnī's principal transmitter in the Shī'ite tradition, from Sakūnī from Ja'far al-Ṣādiq. This may cast doubt on other transmissions by Nawfalī from Sakūnī, particularly where they do not agree with well established Shī'ite viewpoints, as Nawfalī or a transmitter from him may at times have misascribed the material. This sort of error can easily occur when one mistakes an authority or a chain of transmission mentioned at the beginning of a chapter for an attribution of all the quotations in that chapter.

1. Kitāb al-tafsīr

(Ibn al-Nadīm: 36; *Lisān* 1: 627). There are many quotations from this author on the topic in Shī'ite works. The one referred to above (*Tawḥīd*: 343–4) certainly represents the original language and structure of the work. Here is a list of some others:

- *Maḥāsin*: 291
- 'Ayyāshī 1: 8, 179, 238, 263, 289, 294, 319, 322, 385–6
  2: 53 (read *'an Ismā'īl al-Sha'īrī*), 108, 124, 159, 224, 256, 294, 320, 335
- *Kāfī* 2: 600, 619, 622
- 'Alī b. Ibrāhīm 2: 210–11, 339 (also *Ma'ānī*: 215)
- Ibn Qūlawayh: 163
- *Faqīh* 3: 166
- *Ma'ānī*: 216
- Abū Ṭālib: 168–9, 251, 348–9
- *Ta'wīl al-āyāt*: 542

2. Kitāb

Described as a large notebook in *Fihrist*: 13, Shī'ite scholars received this work through the transmitter Ḥusayn b. Yazīd al-Nawfalī (Najāshī: 26; see also *Mashyakha*: 459; *Fihrist*: 13). The several hundred quotations from Sakūnī through this transmitter in the four main works of Shī'ite *ḥadīth* (Khu'ī 6: 114–15, 23: 149) indicate that the bulk of the material of this notebook has survived.

3. Kitāb al-nawādir

(*Fihrist*: 13). Many of the well over one thousand citations from this author in Shī'ite works of *ḥadīth*, many listed in Khu'ī 3: 108, 185–6, 206, 461–4, 23: 103 and *Fahāris* 9: 45–7, fit the title of this work.

117: Ismā'īl al-Khath'amī

Ismā'īl b. Jābir al-Khath'amī, a Kūfan transmitter from Muḥammad al-Bāqir and Ja'far al-Ṣādiq.

Barqī: 82; Kashshī: 199, 376–7; Najāshī: 32–3; *Fihrist*: 15; *Rijāl*: 124, 160, 331.

There is some confusion about the tribal affiliation of this transmitter. See Muḥammad Taqī al-Tustarī 2: 33–9 for details (but cf. ʻAyyāshī 2: 147).

He accompanied Jaʻfar al-Ṣādiq in Mecca in 133 (Kashshī: 376–7; see also *Maḥāsin*: 356, 403).

Kitāb

His notebook of *ḥadīth*, related by Ṣafwān b. Yaḥyā (Najāshī: 33; *Fihrist*: 15; *Rijāl*: 124; see also *Mashyakha*: 426). There are some one hundred quotations from this author in later works, listed in Khuʼī 3: 464–7 and *Fahāris* 8: 159, some through the same transmitter as in the following examples:

- *Maḥāsin*: 454 (also *Kāfī* 6: 264)
- *Faqīh* 1: 63, 443, 508–9
  2: 39, 302
  3: 168
- *Maʻānī*: 298
- *Tahdhīb* 1: 41
  2: 258
  5: 298–9 (partially also in *Faqīh* 2: 351 where the transmitter from this author is not named; see further, Kashshī: 199).

118: Jaʻfar al-Ḥaḍramī

Jaʻfar b. Muḥammad b. Shurayḥ al-Ḥaḍramī, a Kūfan Shīʻite transmitter of *ḥadīth* in the late second century.

Najāshī: 133; *Fihrist*: 43.

Kitāb

(Najāshī: 133; *Fihrist*: 43). This notebook has survived and is published in *al-Uṣūl al-sittat ʻashar*: 60–81. It contains 123 reports, almost all of them from Jābir al-Juʻfī through the transmitter Ḥumayd b. Shuʻayb (no. 93 above; see further Kohlberg, *Uṣūl*: 150–1, 153–4). Apart from three reports at the very end, all of the forty three other reports that comprise the *Aṣl Muḥammad b. al-Muthannā al-Ḥaḍramī* (published in the same collection: 83–97) are also through our author (see further Kohlberg, *Uṣūl*: 154–5).

119: Ibn Darrāj

Jamīl b. Darrāj b. 'Abd Allāh, a Kūfan client of Nakha' and a prominent Shī'ite jurist in the latter part of the second century. His brother, Nūḥ (d. 182), also a Shī'ite, was the judge of Kūfa, and, later in life, of the eastern half of Baghdad. Like his brother, Jamīl went blind toward the end of his life and died late in the second century.

Barqī: 102; Kashshī: 134, 251–2, 375; Najāshī: 126–7; *Fihrist*: 44; *Rijāl*: 177, 333. See also *Ghayba*: 71.

Kashshī: 375 counts Jamīl as one of the six most learned Imāmite jurists of his generation. Sunnī sources offer useful information about the family in their entries on Nūḥ b. Darrāj. For a summary of that material, see Khaṭīb, *Ta'rīkh* 13: 315–18. For other sources, see the long lists in the editors' footnotes to Dhahabī, *Ta'rīkh* 12 (years 181–90): 427 and Mizzī 30: 43–8.

1. *Kitāb / Aṣl*

His main notebook of *ḥadīth*, related by numerous transmitters including Ibn Abī 'Umayr (Abū Ghālib: 172–3; Najāshī: 127; *Fihrist*: 44). With close to five hundred quotations from Jamīl by Ibn Abī 'Umayr in the four main works of Shī'ite *ḥadīth* alone, listed in Khu'ī 14: 418–20, 22: 102, 246–53 (the overwhelming majority of them passed down to following generations through an identical *isnād*), and many others in other works as listed in *Fahāris* 8: 307–8, it seems that the bulk of the material of this notebook, including Jamīl's own commentaries on passages he quotes from his masters (e.g. *Kāfī* 6: 98–9), has survived. A small fragment of the work is also cited by Ibn Idrīs in his *Mustaṭrafāt*: 44–5.

2. *Kitāb ishtaraka huwa wa Muḥammad b. Ḥumrān fīh*

A joint notebook, related by Ḥasan b. 'Alī al-Washshā' and Ibn Abī 'Umayr (Najāshī: 127; *Mashyakha*: 430). Surviving passages from this notebook include the following examples:

- Aḥmad b. Muḥammad b. 'Īsā: 65 (cf. *Kāfī* 6: 156)
- *Maḥāsin*: 355 (also *Kāfī* 5: 30), possibly also 238 (also Ibn Bābawayh, *Amālī* 503; cf. 'Alī b. Ibrāhīm 1: 25–6) and 320 (cf. *'Ilal* 2: 123–4)

- *Kāfī* 2: 424 (in two separate reports; cf. ibid. 5:30)
  3: 66
  4: 138
  5: 389
  6: 447
  7: 149, 221, 390
- *Faqīh* 4: 119 (cf. *Kāfī* 7: 300)
- *Tahdhīb* 1: 394, 401, 404
  3: 167
  9: 68
  10: 101

3. Kitāb ishtaraka huwa wa Murāzim b. Ḥakīm fīh

Another joint noteboook, related by ʿAlī b. Ḥadīd al-Madāʾinī, a nephew of Murāzim, the co-author of the notebook (Najāshī: 127). This may be the same notebook ascribed to Murāzim alone in the entry on him in Najāshī: 424, as the *isnād*s of both works are identical in the upper part. It may also be the same as the *Kitāb Jamīl b. Darrāj* that Abū Ghālib: 165 received through the same transmitter, ʿAlī b. Ḥadīd.

Well over fifty quotations from Jamīl through ʿAlī b. Ḥadīd in later works, listed in Khuʾī 11: 534–6, may represent part of the material of this notebook. Ḥasan b. Maḥbūb also quotes possibly from the same notebook in *Kāfī* 2: 170, 4: 27 (also *Thawāb*: 203; see also Ibn Qūlawayh: 60 [# 41], 61 [# 44] for another possible passage).

120: Jamīl al-Asadī

Jamīl b. Ṣāliḥ al-Asadī, a Kūfan transmitter from Jaʿfar al-Ṣādiq and Mūsā al-Kāẓim.

Barqī: 102; Najāshī: 127–8; *Fihrist*: 44; *Rijāl*: 177.

Kitāb / Aṣl

His notebook of *ḥadīth*, related by a number of transmitters (Najāshī: 127–8; *Fihrist*: 44). Najāshī refers to the Qummi and Kūfan versions of this notebook that were related by Ḥasan b. Maḥbūb and Ibn Abī 'Umayr, respectively. The overwhelming majority of the over two hundred quotations from this author found in Shī'ite works of *ḥadīth*, listed in Khu'ī 4: 457–62 and *Fahāris* 8: 308–9, are through the same two transmitters.

121: Jarrāḥ al-Madā'inī

Jarrāḥ al-Madā'inī, a transmitter from Ja'far al-Ṣādiq.

Barqī: 113; Najāshī: 130; *Rijāl*: 129, 179.

Rijāl: 178 has also a Jarrāḥ b. 'Abd Allāh al-Madanī among the transmitters from Ja'far al-Ṣādiq. Corruption of *Madā'inī* to *Madanī* (and its variant form of *Madīnī*) and vice versa, is not uncommon.[74] One may thus suggest that the reference in *Rijāl* helps reveal the name of our transmitter's father. However, in cases where the father's name is left unmentioned in other sources and only one source gives it as *'Abd Allāh*, it could be argued that it is used in its literal, lexicographical sense applicable to all humanity and not intended as the actual personal name of the specific individual.

Kitāb

A notebook of *ḥadīth*, related by a number of transmitters including Naḍr b. Suwayd (Najāshī: 130) who received it through Qāsim b. Sulaymān al-Baghdādī (*Mashyakha*: 437). All of the over fifty quotations from this author in the four main works of Shī'ite *ḥadīth*, listed in Khu'ī 4: 401–2 (as well as the one in Ibn Qūlawayh: 532, 533 and most likely those in 'Ayyāshī 1: 321, 379, 2: 352), are through the same chain of transmission.

122: Kathīr al-Qanbarī

Abū Ṭāriq Kathīr b. Ṭāriq, a client of the Banū Hāshim and a descendant of Qanbar, the client/servant and special aide of 'Alī. He transmitted from Zayd b. 'Alī.

74. Compare for instance, *Maḥāsin*: 347 with *Faqīh* 2: 266. For numerous other examples, see Khu'ī 21: 38–49.

Najāshī: 319. See also Ṭūsī, *Amālī*: 579, 705.

He was possibly a resident of Mecca. His transmitter, Muḥammad b. Zakariyyā b. Mu'āwiya, was a Meccan Qurashī, and one of his own masters is also known to have been a resident of that city (Ṭūsī, *Amālī*: 579).

Kitāb

His notebook of *ḥadīth*, related by the Meccan Muḥammad b. Zakariyyā (Najāshī: 319) who at times (e.g. Ṭūsī, *Amālī*: 579), and possibly always, quotes this author through his own father. Ṭūsī quotes eight reports from this author in his *Amālī*: 57–8, 579, 703–5, all through the same transmitter and thus most likely from this notebook.

123: Abū 'l-Rabī' al-Shāmī

Abū 'l-Rabī' Khālid b. Awfā al-'Anazī al-Shāmī, a transmitter from Muḥammad al-Bāqir and Ja'far al-Ṣādiq.

Barqī: 107; Najāshī: 153, 455; *Fihrist*: 186; *Rijāl*: 134, 325.

Kitāb

His notebook of *ḥadīth*, related by 'Abd Allāh b. Muskān and Khālid b. Jarīr al-Bajalī (Najāshī: 153, 455; *Fihrist*: 186). There are some one hundred quotations from this author in later works, listed in Khu'ī 7: 391–2, 21: 389–91 and *Fahāris* 8: 537, all, with a few exceptions, through Khālid b. Jarīr.[75] A few are through Ibn Muskān (e.g. *Ma'ānī*: 393; *Ta'wīl al-āyāt*: 813–14 [quoting 'Alī b. Ibrāhīm in his *Tafsīr*, the citation does not appear in the printed version of the Qur'ānic commentary ascribed to the latter]).

---

75. This seems also to be the case with quotations from this author in 'Ayyāshī 1: 192, 300, 342, 348, 361, 2: 264. Compare, for instance, ibid. 1: 192 and 348 with *'Ilal* 2: 138 and *Ma'ānī*: 240–41, respectively.

124: Khālid al-Bajalī

Khālid b. Jarīr al-Bajalī, brother of Isḥāq b. Jarīr (no. 114 above), a Kūfan Arab and a transmitter from Ja'far al-Ṣādiq.

Barqī: 87; Kashshī: 346, 422–3; Najāshī: 149–50; *Rijāl*: 201.

Kitāb

His notebook of *ḥadīth*, related by Ḥasan b. Maḥbūb (Najāshī: 150). All of the almost fifty surviving quotations from this author in later works, listed in Khu'ī 7: 7, 8, 17, 391–2 and *Fahāris* 8: 484, are through the same transmitter.

125: Khālid al-Qalānisī

Khālid b. Mādd, the hatter, a Kūfan client and a transmitter from Ja'far al-Ṣādiq.

Barqī: 87 (as *Khālid b. Ziyād*); Najāshī: 149; *Fihrist*: 66; *Rijāl*: 201 (as both *Khālid b. Mādd* and *Khālid b. Ziyād*).

With very few exceptions, the name of this transmitter's father always appears in *isnād*s as *Mādd*. In a few cases, however, it appears as *Ziyād*, *Ḥammād*, and, according to Ibn Dāwūd: 138–9, *Bād*. The last one seems to be a corruption, and the first two attempted corrections. This scenario is more plausible than the reverse, as corruption of a common name like *Ziyād* to a very uncommon form in almost all the various *isnād*s is less usual. It is also possible that the name of the author appeared unclearly in the original notebook and that the variations represent various suggestions as to how the name should be read.

His profession is given as *qalānisī* and *bayyā' al-qalānis* (*Faqīh* 2: 363).

Kitāb

His notebook of *ḥadīth*, related by the transmitter, Naḍr b. Shu'ayb (Najāshī: 149; *Fihrist*: 66; also *Mashyakha*: 444). Most surviving quotations from the author are on the authority of the same transmitter, including the following examples:

- Ṣaffār: 104, 160, 195, 309–10, 436

- *Kāfī* 1: 416–17
  2: 612 (read *'an al-Naḍr b. Shu'ayb* as in *Thawāb*: 125)
- *Faqīh* 1: 228 (see also *Kāfī* 4: 586 and Ibn Qūlawayh 73–4 [partially also at 78] where the passage is quoted from this author through other transmitters)
  2: 363
  4: 213 (also *Kāfī* 7: 20 where Khālid's name is missing from the *isnād*)
- Ibn Bābawayh, *Amālī*: 341, 370
- *Tahdhīb* 3: 329 (read *'an al-Naḍr b. Shu'ayb*)

A number of reports on the topic of *ḥajj*, all quoted by 'Amr b. 'Uthmān from 'Alī b. 'Abd Allāh al-Bajalī from this author, may also go back to this notebook. Examples include the following:

- *Maḥāsin*: 68, 70 (and a variant at 71)
- *Kāfī* 4: 252
- *Tahdhīb* 5: 468

126: Abū Sa'īd al-Qammāṭ

Abū Sa'īd Khālid b. Sa'īd, the maker of swaddling clothes, a Kūfan transmitter from Ja'far al-Ṣādiq and Mūsā al-Kāẓim.

Barqī: 119; Najāshī: 149.

Kitāb

His notebook of *ḥadīth*, related by Muḥammad b. Sinān al-Zāhirī (Najāshī: 149). Surviving quotations from this author by the same transmitter, include the following:

- *Kāfī* 2: 345
  4: 184–6 (also *'Ilal* 2: 114–16)
- Ibn Qūlawayh: 147–8 (partially also at 141–2), 322 (partially also at 296 where his name is missing from the *isnād*), 448–50 (two reports)
- *'Ilal* 2: 292
- *Khiṣāl*: 421–2 (also *Ma'ānī*: 154)
- *Tawḥīd*: 339
- *Thawāb*: 36

- *Tahdhīb* 2: 355
  7: 254 (two reports)

127: Abū 'l-'Alā' al-Khaffāf

Abū 'l-'Alā' Khālid b. Ṭahmān al-Salūlī, the shoemaker, a Kūfan Sunnī transmitter of *ḥadīth* who transmitted from Muḥammad al-Bāqir, among others.

Yaḥyā b. Ma'īn 2: 144; Bukhārī, *Kabīr* 3: 157; Muslim, *Kunā*: 619; 'Uthmān al-Dārimī, *Ta'rīkh*: 246; Barqī: 59; Dūlābī, *Kunā*: 798; Ibn Abī Ḥātim 3: 337; Ibn Ḥibbān, *Thiqāt* 6: 257; Ibn 'Adī: 891; Najāshī: 151–2, and other sources listed in the editor's footnote to Mizzī 8: 94–5.

Ibn Abī Ḥātim calls him a Shī'ite and Najāshī a Sunnī. He was a Sunnī transmitter with Shī'ite sympathies. For examples of his reports in the main Sunnī works of *ḥadīth*, see Tirmidhī 1: 281, 4: 226–7, 263, 5: 42–3 (and the sources listed in the editor's footnotes).

Nuskha 'an Abī Ja'far

A register of his transmissions from Muḥammad al-Bāqir (Najāshī: 151). It must have included the surviving quotations by this author from Muḥammad al-Bāqir as in the following examples:

- *Kāfī* 2: 664
  4: 340
- Kashshī: 211
- Ṭūsī, *Amālī*: 453
- *Tahdhīb* 2: 113 (read, most likely, *'an Abī Ja'far* for *'an Ja'far*; also in *Makārim al-akhlāq*: 120 where this author's citation from Muḥammad al-Bāqir in *Kāfī* 4: 340 [and *Faqīh* 2: 334–5] is misascribed to Ja'far al-Ṣādiq; the biographers do not mention that this author ever transmitted from Ja'far al-Ṣādiq)

128: Khallād al-Bazzāz

Khallād al-Sindī, the cloth seller, a Kūfan transmitter from Ja'far al-Ṣādiq.

Najāshī: 154; *Fihrist*: 66; *Rijāl*: 199.

Najāshī quotes a suggestion that this transmitter may be the same as Khallād b. Khalaf al-Muqri' whom he identifies as the uncle of the transmitter Abū Sumayna Muḥammad b. 'Alī al-Ṣayrafī, a client of Quraysh. In the entry on this latter transmitter, however, Najāshī: 332 identifies his uncle as Khallād b. 'Īsā. *Fihrist*: 66 names a Khallād b. Khālid al-Muqri' whose notebook was related by an *isnād* that shares its upper links with that of a quotation from our transmitter in *Tahdhīb* 5: 378.

Kitāb

His notebook of *ḥadīth*, related by Ibn Abī 'Umayr (Najāshī: 154; *Fihrist*: 66). The notebook has survived and is published in *al-Uṣūl al-sittat 'ashr*: 106–7 (see further Kohlberg, *Uṣūl*: 155). The surviving version, received through the same *isnād* as is mentioned in *Fihrist*: 66, contains eight reports, four of them also attested in other Shī'ite works of *ḥadīth* (# 1 in *Kāfī* 4: 233–4 [also *Faqīh* 2: 259; *'Ilal* 2: 139]; # 3 in *Kāfī* 2: 111 [also *Khiṣāl*: 23]; # 4 in *Kāfī* 5: 447; # 6 in *Kāfī* 7: 169). There is an additional quotation from this author in 'Alī b. Bābawayh, *Ikhwān*: 8 that is not attested in the surviving notebook.

129: Al-Khaybarī al-Ṭaḥḥān

Abū Sa'īd Khaybarī b. 'Alī, the miller, a Kūfan Extremist Shī'ite and a follower of Mufaḍḍal al-Ju'fī.

Ibn al-Ghaḍā'irī: 56; Najāshī: 154–5 (see also 55).

The *kunya* of *Abū Sa'īd* for this transmitter is mentioned in *Kāfī* 1: 52 and Ibn Qūlawayh: 166. For examples of his Extremist ideas, see Ṣaffār: 68, 438–9; *Kāfī* 1: 474.

Kitāb

His notebook of *ḥadīth*, related by Muḥammad b. Ismā'īl b. Bazī' (Ibn al-Ghaḍā'irī: 56; Najāshī: 155; *Fihrist*: 193) whose transmission from this author is attested in the following examples:

- *Kāfī* 3: 342
  4: 583 (read *'an al-Khaybarī* as in Ibn Qūlawayh: 263, 288; *Thawāb*: 111; *Tahdhīb* 6: 81)
  5: 308

- Ibn Qūlawayh: 244, 263 (repeated at 288), 280 (partially also at 278–9, 498–9; *Thawāb*: 110), 304–6 (also *Thawāb*: 118–19), 465 (repeated at 467)
- *Tahdhīb*: 6: 9

130: Kulayb al-Ṣaydāwī

Abū Muḥammad Kulayb b. Mu'āwiya b. Jabala al-Ṣaydawī al-Asadī, a Kūfan Arab from Ṣaydā, a clan of the Banū Asad, and a transmitter from Ja'far al-Ṣādiq and Mūsā al-Kāẓim.

Barqī: 59, 66; Kashshī: 339–40 (see also *Kāfī* 1: 391); Najāshī: 318; *Fihrist*: 128; *Rijāl*: 144, 274, 436.

Kitāb

Kulayb's notebook of *ḥadīth*, related by a number of transmitters (Najāshī: 318; *Fihrist*: 128; also *Mashyakha*: 456, 510). There are a fair number of quotations from this author in later works, listed in Khu'ī 14: 123–4, 372 and *Fahāris* 10:13–14, mainly through those specifically named in the above-mentioned sources as transmitters of this notebook.

131: Layth al-Murādī

Abū Baṣīr Layth b. al-Bakhtarī al-Murādī, a Kūfan transmitter from Ja'far al-Ṣādiq.

Barqī: 56, 65; Kashshī: 169–74; Ibn al-Ghaḍā'irī: 111; Najāshī: 321; *Fihrist*: 130; *Rijāl*: 144, 275, 342. See also Muḥammad Taqī al-Tustarī 8: 622–32.

Kitāb

His notebook of *ḥadīth*, related by a number of transmitters including Abū Jamīla Mufaḍḍal b. Ṣāliḥ al-Asadī (Ibn al-Nadīm: 275; Najāshī: 321; *Fihrist*: 130). There are more than sixty quotations from this author in later works, listed in Khu'ī 14: 139, 151, 372–3 and *Fahāris* 10: 23–4, many through the same transmitter.

132: Abū Mikhnaf

Abū Mikhnaf Lūṭ b. Yaḥyā al-Azdī al-Ghāmidī, a Kūfan historian whose works represent much of the records preserved by the Kūfan Shī'ites of their own early history. He transmitted from Ja'far al-Ṣādiq, among others, and died in 157.

For an analysis of the material and a list of the main biographical sources on Abū Mikhnaf, see Sezgin 1: 308–9; also Ursula Sezgin, *Abū Mikhnaf: ein Beitrag zur Historiographie der umaiyadischen Zeit* (Leiden, 1971).

Ibn al-Nadīm: 105–6 and Najāshī: 321 offer long lists of Abū Mikhnaf's works. *Fihrist*: 129–30 adds an additional item, a long sermon by 'Alī, recorded in Ibn 'Abd Rabbih 4: 76–80. Abū Mikhnaf's works were widely quoted by later historians such as Ibn Shabba, Balādhurī and Ṭabarī. Ursula Sezgin provides lists of most of these quotations. Recently, Kāmil Salmān al-Jubūrī has tried to reconstruct Abū Mikhnaf's works by compiling these excerpts, organized according to the titles of his works as given in the bibliographical sources, in a two volume work as *Nuṣūṣ min Ta'rīkh Abī Mikhnaf* (Beirut, 1999).

133: Ibn 'Aṭiyya al-Aḥmasī

Abū 'l-Ḥusayn Mālik b. 'Aṭiyya al-Aḥmasī al-Bajalī, a Kūfan Arab Shī'ite and a transmitter from Ja'far al-Ṣādiq.[76]

Barqī: 113; Kashshī: 367–8; Najāshī: 422–3; *Fihrist*: 170; *Rijāl*: 302. See also *Kāfī* 8: 268.

76. There was also a Muḥammad b. 'Aṭiyya, the wheat seller, among the transmitters from Ja'far al-Ṣādiq who was a Kūfan client (Barqī: 70; Najāshī: 356; *Rijāl*: 290) and author of a notebook of *ḥadīth* related by Ibn Abī 'Umayr (Najāshī: 356). There are a number of quotations from this author in later works, listed in Khu'ī 16: 283 and *Fahāris* 10: 221, but only one is through the same transmitter (*Kāfī* 4: 161–2). However, some other citations from this author are in the style of quotations from a book as, for instance, those in *Kāfī* 8: 94–5; *Tahdhīb* 1: 312–13 (# 907, cf. # 909).

Kitāb

His notebook of *ḥadīth*, related by a number of transmitters including Ḥasan b. Maḥbūb (Najāshī: 423; *Fihrist*: 170). There are well over one hundred quotations from this author in Shī'ite works of *ḥadīth*, listed in Khu'ī 14: 374–8 and *Fahāris* 10: 30–31, the overwhelming majority of them through the same transmitter.

134: Al-Ḍabbī al-Khazzāz

Ma'mar (or Mu'ammar) b. Yaḥyā b. Sām (or Sālim, or Bassām) al-Ḍabbī, the furrier, a Kūfan transmitter from Muḥammad al-Bāqir and Ja'far al-Ṣādiq, known to both Sunnī and Shī'ite circles of *ḥadīth* transmission of his time.

Bukhārī, *Kabīr* 7: 377; Fasawī 3: 233; Barqī: 52, 66; Ibn Abī Ḥātim 8: 258; Ibn Ḥibbān, *Thiqāt* 7: 485; Najāshī: 425; *Rijāl*: 145, 307; Ibn Mākūlā 7: 270, and other sources listed in the editor's footnote to Mizzī 28: 323.

Kitāb

His notebook of *ḥadīth*, related by the transmitter Tha'laba b. Maymūn (Najāshī: 425). A fair number of quotations from this author survive in Shī'ite and Sunnī works of *ḥadīth*, many through the same transmitter. For Shī'ite works, see the lists in Khu'ī 18: 473–4 and *Fahāris* 10: 331. For examples of quotations from him in Sunnī works, see Bukhārī, *Ṣaḥīḥ* 1: 75; Ṭabarī, *Tafsīr* 5: 261 (see the editor's footnote 1 to the Cairo, 1950 edition of this source, 9: 168), both from Muḥammad al-Bāqir.

135: Ibn Ḥāzim al-Bajalī

Abū Ayyūb Manṣūr b. Ḥāzim, a Kūfan client of Bajīla and a learned member of the Shī'ite community of Kūfa in his time. He was a transmitter from Ja'far al-Ṣādiq.

Barqī: 100; Kashshī: 420–21; Najāshī: 413; *Fihrist*: 164; *Rijāl*: 306. See also *Kāfī* 1: 86, 5: 422.

1. *Uṣūl al-sharā'i'*

A small book that the *mutakallim* Yūnus b. 'Abd al-Raḥmān al-Qummī related from this author (Najāshī: 413). A fragment in *Kāfī* 1: 188–9 (partially also at 168–9; the full text also in Kashshī: 420–21) may originally have been part of this work.

2. *Kitāb al-ḥajj*

(Najāshī: 413). Quotations from this author on the topic of the pilgrimage to Mecca, all possibly from this work, include the following examples:

- 'Ayyāshī 1: 92
- *Kāfī* 4: 233, 236, 295–6 (two reports), 333, 381, 382, 390, 416, 421, 445, 481, 495, 516–17
- *Faqīh* 2: 256, 354, 487, 504
- *'Ilal* 2: 130, 138
- *Thawāb*: 73
- *Tahdhīb* 5: 84, 110, 129–30, 141, 190, 203–4, 248, 249, 298, 299, 344, 346, 374, 375, 376, 379–80, 389, 402
- Ibn Ṭāwūs, *Iqbāl* 1: 341

3. *Kitāb*

His notebook of *ḥadīth*, related by Ibn Abī 'Umayr, Ṣafwān b. Yaḥyā and Sayf b. 'Amīra al-Nakha'ī (*Fihrist*: 164; also *Mashyakha*: 434). Ibn Abī 'Umayr seems to have received the notebook through an intermediary (see, for instance, *Kāfī* 4: 295, 381, 495, 509; *Tahdhīb* 5: 36, 39, 42, 219) though at times he leaves out his name (e.g. *Kāfī* 1: 39, 397, 2: 105, 6: 179, 7: 440; *Tahdhīb* 5: 249, 374). Most of the close to five hundred quotations from this author in later works, listed in Khu'ī 18: 338, 342–4, 484–95 and *Fahāris* 10: 354, are, however, on the authority of the other two above-mentioned transmitters of this notebook.

136: Manṣūr al-Sarrāj

Abū Yaḥyā Manṣūr b. Yūnus Buzurj, the saddler, a Kūfan client of Quraysh and a transmitter from Ja'far al-Ṣādiq and Mūsā al-Kāẓim. He joined the Wāqifites after the death of the latter Imām.

Barqī: 100; Kashshī: 468–9; Najāshī: 413; *Fibrist*: 164; *Rijāl*: 306, 343. See also *Kamāl*: 516, 517–18.

Kitāb

His notebook of *ḥadīth*, related by Ibn Abī 'Umayr, 'Alī b. Ḥadīd and Muḥammad b. Ismā'īl b. Bazī' (Najāshī: 413; *Fibrist*: 164; *Rijāl*: 343; also *Mashyakha*: 485). The overwhelming majority of the over one hundred and fifty quotations from this author in later works, listed in Khu'ī 18: 338, 340, 341–2, 353–6, 498–502 and *Fahāris* 8: 213, 10: 354, 357, are through the same transmitters.

137: Ibn Muslim

Marwān b. Muslim, a Kūfan transmitter from Ja'far al-Ṣādiq and his disciples.

Najāshī: 419; *Fibrist*: 169–70

Kitāb

His notebook of *ḥadīth*, related by a number of transmitters including 'Alī b. Ya'qūb al-Hāshimī and Ḥasan b. 'Alī b. Faḍḍāl (Najāshī: 419; *Fibrist*: 169–70; also *Mashyakha*: 477). The overwhelming majority of the close to one hundred quotations from this author in later works, listed in Khu'ī 18: 122–4, 409–11 and *Fahāris* 10: 297, are through the same two transmitters.

138: Mas'ada al-Raba'ī

Abū Muḥammad Mas'ada b. Ṣadaqa al-Raba'ī was a Baṣran transmitter from Ja'far al-Ṣādiq.

Barqī: 98; Kashshī: 390; Najāshī: 415; *Fibrist*: 167; *Rijāl*: 146, 306; *Mīzān* 4: 98; *Lisān* 6: 690.

The *kunya* of this transmitter is variously given as *Abū Muḥammad* (Najāshī: 415; *Rijāl*: 306), *Abū Bishr* (Najāshī: 415 quoting an unspecified source, but this is mentioned in *Kāfī* 2: 652 as the *kunya* of Mas'ada b. al-Yasa') and *Abū 'l-Yasa'* (Rāfi'ī 2: 477, in the *isnād* of a variant of the text in *Kāfī* 2: 652). His *nisba* is also variously given as *Raba'ī* (normally in the *isnāds* as also in *Mashyakha*: 440), *'Abdī* (normally in biographical sources, but also in the *isnāds* as in Aḥmad b. 'Īsā 4: 297; Ṭūsī, *Amālī*: 572 [also Khaṭīb, *Ta'rīkh* 14: 23]), *'Absī* (*Rijāl*: 306), and *'Aysī* (Furāt: 364). As already encountered above in several instances, *'Abdī* refers to the Banū 'Abd al-Qays, a clan of Rabī'a. Thus, there is no conflict between the two *nisbas* of *Raba'ī* and *'Abdī*. Descendants of 'Abd al-Qays can also be called *'Abqasī*, of which the words *'Absī* and *'Aysī*, as above, seem to be corrupt forms.

Kashshī and *Rijāl*: 146 identify this transmitter as a non-Shī'ite (see also *Tahdhīb* 6: 168). His quotations from Ja'far al-Ṣādiq also point to a non-Shī'ite provenance, always in style (both in using the Imām's first name instead of following the common Imāmite practice of referring to him by his *kunya*, as well as in using him as an intermediary to the Prophet only as against the overwhelming Imāmite practice of stopping with the Imām as the ultimate authority of a *ḥadīth*), and occasionally in content (see, for instance, *Tahdhīb* 9: 162). Nevertheless a number of his reports have strong Shī'ite overtones (e.g. 'Abd Allāh b. Ja'far: 9; 'Ayyāshī 2: 141 [which is from Mas'ada as attested by Ḥaskānī 1: 356]; Ibn Qūlawayh: 306–7), stronger than a Sunnī can comfortably accommodate. (There are, of course, later contributions and accretions which are anachronistically voiced through Mas'ada as, for instance, in Khazzāz: 260–62; *Dalā'il al-imāma*: 530–34.) In 'Alī b. Ibrāhīm 1: 176, he virtually asks Ja'far al-Ṣādiq whether a Shī'ite can work for the government, a somewhat unusual question if the enquirer is not a Shī'ite himself.

Some of the biographical details of this transmitter are strikingly similar to those of a contemporary of his, Mas'ada b. Ziyād al-Raba'ī, and, to a lesser extent, to those of another contemporary of both, Mas'ada b. al-Yasa' al-Bāhilī (see further, Muḥammad Taqī al-Tustarī 10: 54–6). Similar texts are at times attributed to one in one source and to another in another.[77] However, it is clearly understood from 'Abd Allāh b. Ja'far al-Ḥimyarī's *Qurb al-isnād* that there were different notebooks ascribed to the first two names in the middle of the third century, as he always quotes the two in separate bulks properly distinguished from each other.

---

77. For Mas'ada b. Ziyād, compare, for instance, *Kāfī* 5: 65, 298, 439, 6: 439 (all from Mas'ada b. Ṣadaqa) with 'Abd Allāh b. Ja'far: 79 (# 258), 84 (# 276), *Tahdhīb* 7: 314 (# 1303), and *Thawāb*: 291 (all from Mas'ada b. Ziyād), respectively; compare also *Khiṣāl*: 55 with 'Abd Allāh b. Ja'far: 46 (# 150). As for Mas'ada b. al-Yasa', compare *Kāfī* 2: 652 (from Mas'ada b. al-Yasa') with a variant in Rāfi'ī 2: 477 (from Abū 'l-Yasa' Mas'ada b. Ṣadaqa), and *Maḥāsin*: 476 (from Mas'ada b. al-Yasa') with *Kāfī* 6; 323 (from Mas'ada b. Ṣadaqa b. al-Yasa' [most likely to be read *'an Mas'ada b. Ṣadaqa Abī 'l-Yasa'*]). There were clearly some early uncertainties about the *isnāds* where a *Mas'ada* quoted from Ja'far al-Ṣādiq.

1. *Kitāb khuṭab Amīr al-Mu'minīn*

(Najāshī: 415). Numerous quotations in later Shī'ite works of sermons and other statements ascribed to 'Alī on the authority of this author may represent parts of the contents of this work. Examples include the following:

- 'Abd Allāh b. Ja'far: 1, 10, 11, 12 (two quotes), 13, 45, 50, 55, 63, 70, 72, 73, 76
- *Maḥāsin*: 585
- 'Ayyāshī 1: 7–8, 13, 102–3, 163, 242, 384
  2: 9, 17–18, 203, 223
- *Kāfī* 1: 54–5, 57–8, 60–61
  2: 219, 300, 670
  3: 118–19
  4: 4–6, 31, 43, 220, 323, 352, 534–5
  6: 221–2
  7: 460 (also 'Alī b. Ibrāhīm 2: 60–61)
  8: 63–66, 239–40 (also *'Ilal* 2: 148)
- Furāt: 55–6
- Khaṣībī: 362 (also *Kamāl*: 302)
- Ibn Bābawayh, *Amālī*: 170–71
- *Faqīh* 2: 71–2
- *'Ilal* 2: 209
- *Tawḥīd*: 48–56 (also 'Āṣimī 1: 168–72; *Nahj al-balāgha*: 124–36 [sermon 91], both with variations)
- *Irshād* 1: 290–91, 291–4
- Abū Ṭālib: 182–4, 193–5, 339
- Ṭūsī, *Amālī*: 572 (also Khaṭīb, *Ta'rīkh* 14: 23)
- *Tahdhīb* 4: 281, 299
  6: 147–8
  9: 162, 173
  10: 81
  (see also 1: 331 [repeated in 3: 332])
- Ibn 'Asākir 36: 390 (also *Mīzān* 4: 98)
- *Iḥtijāj* 1: 626–31
- *Manāqib* 2: 97 (see also 2: 264 where *Mas'ada b. al-Yasa'* may be a corruption of *Mas'ada Abī 'l-Yasa'*; a similar suggestion can be offered about Ibn Qūlawayh: 530; see also Fakhār b. Ma'add: 25)

Most of the above quotations from this author are on the authority of Hārūn b. Muslim b. Sa'dān al-Kātib (alive in 240), who is identified as the transmitter of the work in Najāshī: 415, but a few are on the authority of another mid-third century transmitter, Ja'far b. 'Abd Allāh al-Muḥammadī, who quotes the author through Abū Rawḥ Faraj b. Farwa (*Kāfī* 5: 4–6, 8: 63–6; Furāt: 55–6 [see also 364, 425]; *Tawḥīd*: 48–56 [also 'Āṣimī 1: 168–72]; Abū Ṭālib: 193–5) al-Sulamī ('Āṣimī 1: 168). A late eighth century author, Ḥasan b. Sulaymān al-Ḥillī, describes a collection of the sermons of 'Alī, a copy of which he had seen with a note by Raḍī al-Dīn 'Alī b. Ṭāwūs (d. 664) on it. Part of the book was quoted through Abū Rawḥ Faraj b. Farwa from Mas'ada b. Ṣadaqa (Ḥasan b. Sulaymān: 195).

2. *Kitāb*

His notebook of *ḥadīth*, related by the late third-century scholar, 'Abd Allāh b. Ja'far al-Ḥimyarī, from the above-mentioned Hārūn b. Muslim al-Kātib, from the author (*Fihrist*: 167). 'Abd Allāh b. Ja'far quotes several small and large fragments of this notebook in his *Qurb al-isnād*: 1–13 (# 1–39), 45–50 (# 147–63 with the exception of # 159), 54–6 (# 178–81), 62–79 (# 198–255), some 117 reports in total. Almost all of the many other quotations by Mas'ada from Ja'far al-Ṣādiq, listed in Khu'ī 18: 135–9, 414–16 and *Fahāris* 10: 301–2, are through the same transmitter. Sunnī and Zaydī sources, however, quote Mas'ada at times through Faraj b. Farwa (as noted above), Sa'īd b. 'Amr al-'Anazī (e.g. Aḥmad b. 'Īsā 1: 70, 4: 297, 299; Ibn 'Asākir 36: 390), or others.

139: Mas'ada al-Bāhilī

Mas'ada b. al-Yasa' b. Qays al-Bāhilī, a Baṣran Sunnī transmitter of *ḥadīth* who occasionally lived in Mecca. He transmitted principally from Ja'far al-Ṣādiq.

Aḥmad, *'Ilal* 3: 267; Bukhārī, *Awsaṭ* 2: 125; idem, *Kabīr* 8: 26; Barqī: 98; 'Uqaylī 4: 245; Ibn Abī Ḥātim 8: 370–71; Ibn Ḥibbān, *Majrūḥīn* 3: 35; Ibn 'Adī: 2386–7; Dāraquṭnī, *Ḍu'afā'*: 159; Najāshī: 415; *Fihrist*: 167; *Rijāl*: 306, and other sources listed in the editor's footnote to *Lisān* 6: 691.

Kitāb

His notebook of *ḥadīth* (Najāshī: 415; *Fihrist*: 167). As noted, this author transmitted principally from Ja'far al-Ṣādiq, thereby attracting the attention of the Shī'ites. There are examples of his transmission from other early authorities (e.g. Abū Ya'lā 4: 132; 'Uqaylī 4: 245; Ṭabarānī, *Ṣaghīr* 1: 84; Ibn 'Adī: 2386 [three reports]; Dāraquṭnī 4: 99; *Lisān* 6: 691), but most of his surviving quotations are indeed from Ja'far al-Ṣādiq, as in the following examples:

- *Maḥāsin*: 459, 476, 491, 570, 576 (all from him through the same *isnād*)
- 'Abd Allāh b. Ja'far: 159
- Aḥmad b. 'Īsā 1: 250
- Ṭabarī, *Tafsīr* 13: 124
- *Kāfī* 2: 652 (cf. Rāfi'ī 2: 477)
  6: 524
- Ibn Ḥibbān, *Majrūḥīn* 3: 35 (also *Lisān* 6: 692, quoting Ibn Abī Khaythama [d. 279] in his *al-Ta'rīkh al-kabīr*)
- Ibn 'Adī: 2386–7 (three reports)
- Dāraquṭnī 1: 70
- *Irshād* 1: 124–8
- Bayhaqī, *Shu'ab* 5: 92, 106 (from Ibn 'Adī: 2387; a fuller text in *Mīzān* 4: 98)
- *Firdaws* (Uzbak: 2214)
- *Manāqib* 2: 264

140: Ibn Ziyād al-Raba'ī

Mas'ada b. Ziyād al-Raba'ī, a Kūfan transmitter from Ja'far al-Ṣādiq.

Barqī: 98; Najāshī: 415; *Fihrist*: 167; *Rijāl*: 146, 306.

1. *Kitāb fī 'l-ḥalāl wa 'l-ḥarām*

A book on legal matters, organized in chapters, related from the author by 'Abd Allāh b. Ja'far al-Ḥimyarī through Hārūn b. Muslim b. Sa'dān al-Kātib (Najāshī: 415). A few quotations from the author on legal matters qualify for inclusion in this work, as in the following examples:

- 'Abd Allāh b. Ja'far: 81–5
- *Kāfī* 6: 437
- *Faqīh* 3: 292, 451 (also *Khiṣāl*: 438; *Tahdhīb* 8: 198)
- *'Iqāb*: 290, 291–2
- *Tahdhīb* 7: 184, 474

The overwhelming majority of quotations from this transmitter are, however, on non-legal matters.

2. *Kitāb*

A notebook of *ḥadīth*, related by 'Abd Allāh b. Ja'far al-Ḥimyarī through the aforementioned Hārūn b. Muslim (Abū Ghālib: 183; *Fihrist*: 167). The two sections of twenty-nine reports in total that 'Abd Allāh b. Ja'far quotes in his *Qurb al-isnād*: 28–9 (# 92–5) and 79–86 (# 256–81) through Hārūn b. Muslim from this author are clearly taken from this notebook and not from the author's organized work on legal matters. A copy of the notebook was still available in the mid-seventh century to Ibn Ṭāwūs who quotes from it in his *Muḥāsaba*: 34–5 and *Falāḥ*: 376–7 (see further Kohlberg: 125).

Apart from the above, there are a fair number of other quotations from this author in other Shī'ite works of *ḥadīth*, all, with a single exception, through Hārūn b. Muslim, including the following examples:

- *Maḥāsin*: 509, 539 (also *Kāfī* 6: 352), 545
- Ṣaffār: 8
- 'Ayyāshī 1: 283
- *Kāfī* 1: 531–2
  3: 18 (also *'Ilal* 1: 271; *Tahdhīb* 1: 44)
  5: 352
  6: 437
- Ibn Qūlawayh: 530
- Ibn Bābawayh, *Amālī*: 167 (also *Khiṣāl*: 114; *Ma'ānī*: 232), 363 (also *Thawāb*: 221)
- *Faqīh* 3: 292, 386, 451 (also *Khiṣāl*: 438; *Tahdhīb* 8: 198)
- *'Ilal* 1: 11
- *'Iqāb*: 290, 291–2, 303–4 (two reports)
- *Khiṣāl*: 55 (cf. 'Abd Allāh b. Ja'far: 46 where the same report is ascribed to Mas'ada b. Ṣadaqa), 85, 113, 296 (also *'Iqāb*: 302)
- *Ma'ānī*: 399

- Mufīd, *Amālī*: 227–8 (repeated at 292)
- Ṭūsī, *Amālī*: 203 (read *Mas'ada* for *Sa'īd*), 543
- *Tahdhīb* 7: 184, 474, 475
  10: 206

141: Misma' Kurdīn

Abū Sayyār Misma' b. 'Abd al-Malik, known as Kurdīn, a Baṣran Arab Shī'ite from the prominent family of the *Masāmi'a* and head of the tribe of Bakr b. Wā'il, a clan of Rabī'a, in Baṣra. He was a transmitter from Ja'far al-Ṣādiq.

Barqī: 111; Kashshī: 310; *Mashyakha*: 451; Najāshī: 420; Ibn Ḥazm, *Jamhara*: 301; *Fibrist*: 128–9; *Rijāl*: 145, 312; Ibn Mākūlā 7: 181. See also Ibn Qūlawayh: 203; *Ikhtiṣāṣ*: 290.

For the *Masāmi'a*, see the entry on them in the *Encyclopaedia of Islam*, 2nd edn., 6: 640 (P. Crone; also Yaqūt, *Mu'jam* 5: 122). Ibn Ḥazm, *Jamhara*: 301 reports that our transmitter, with a number of his family members, joined the revolt of Ibrāhīm b. 'Abd Allāh b. al-Ḥasan, brother of al-Nafs al-Zakiyya, in Baṣra against the 'Abbāsid Manṣūr in 145.

Misma' was a source for the littérateur and historian of Baṣra, Abū 'Ubayda Ma'mar b. al-Muthannā (d. 209), who quotes a statement from Muḥammad al-Bāqir through him in Jāḥiẓ, *Bayān* 3: 290, and a poem by Farazdaq (d. 110) in praise of the Bakr b. Wā'il in Ṭabarī 5: 245.

Kitāb

His notebook of *ḥadīth*, related by 'Abd al-Raḥmān b. 'Abd Allāh al-Aṣamm (*Fihrist*: 129). Most of some two hundred and fifty quotations from this transmitter in Shī'ite works of *ḥadīth*, listed in Khu'ī 18: 154–61, 416–21 and *Fahāris* 10: 10, 310, are through the same transmitter. The work was still available in the mid-seventh century to Ibn Ṭāwūs, who quotes from it in his *Falāḥ*: 333 (read *Misma' Kurdīn* for *Kurdīn b. Misma'*) (see further Kohlberg: 226).

142: Ibn Khunays

Abū ʿAbd Allāh Muʿallā b. Khunays, the cloth seller, a Kūfan client who resided in Medina and acted as an aide to Jaʿfar al-Ṣādiq. He was killed by order of the ʿAbbāsid Dāwūd b. ʿAlī, the governor of Medina, in 133.

Barqī: 78; Kashshī: 376–82 (see also 247, 248); *Mashyakha*: 468–9; Ibn al-Ghaḍāʾirī: 87; Najāshī: 417; *Rijāl*: 304. See also Ibn Saʿd 5: 249–50; *Kāfī* 2: 513, 557; Mizzī 20: 396.

Dāwūd b. ʿAlī was appointed by Abū 'l-ʿAbbās al-Saffāḥ as governor of Medina very late in 132, held that post for three months, and died in Rabīʿ I, 133 (Ṭabarī 7: 459). A report in Ṣaffār: 218; *Kāfī* 2: 513, and Kashshī: 377–8 suggests that Dāwūd died shortly after the execution of Muʿallā b. Khunays.

Kitāb

A notebook of *ḥadīth*, related by Ṣafwān b. Yaḥyā from Abū ʿUthmān al-Aḥwal from Muʿallā b. Khunays (Najāshī: 417; *Fihrist* [Calcutta, 1853]: 334–5). This must be the same as the *Kitāb* of Abū ʿUthmān al-Aḥwal named in Najāshī: 458; *Fihrist*: 188 (see Muḥammad Taqī al-Tustarī 10: 163). There are numerous quotations from Muʿallā by Abū ʿUthmān al-Aḥwal, almost always related by Ṣafwān, as in the following examples:

- Aḥmad b. Muḥammad b. ʿĪsā: 84 (whence *Tahdhīb* 7: 261)
- *Maḥāsin*: 235 (also *Kamāl*: 231), 365 (three reports, one also in *Kāfī*: 3: 23), 458 (also *Kāfī* 6: 272), 561 (also *Kāfī* 3: 23), 575 (also *Kāfī* 6: 383)
- Ṣaffār: 39 (also 41 with variations), 158, 162, 474 (also *Kāfī* 1: 277)
- *Kāfī* 3: 336
  5: 257 (also *Tahdhīb* 6: 380 with variations)
- Ibn al-Juḥām: 200–201, 203
- *Kamāl*: 650 (repeated at 652)
- *Tahdhīb* 2: 262
  3: 48
  7: 233
  8: 324[78]

78. In two of the cases listed above (*Kāfī* 3: 336; *Tahdhīb* 8: 324), Abū ʿUthmān al-Aḥwal is quoted by a transmitter other than Ṣafwān. In Aḥmad b. Muḥammad b. ʿĪsā: 84 and *Kamāl* 650, 652, on the other hand, Ṣafwān quotes Muʿallā through a transmitter other than Abū ʿUthmān al-Aḥwal.

143: Al-Duhnī

Abū 'l-Qāsim Mu'āwiya b. 'Ammār al-Duhnī, a Kūfan transmitter from Ja'far al-Ṣādiq and Mūsā al-Kāẓim. His father, 'Ammār b. Khabbāb (d. 133), was also a transmitter from Muḥammad al-Bāqir, among others, and well known in Sunnī circles. A seller of Shāpūrī clothing by profession, Mu'āwiya was a distinguished member of the Shī'ite community of Kūfa. He died in 175.

Yaḥyā b. Ma'īn 2: 573; Ibn al-Junayd: 161; Bukhārī, *Kabīr* 7: 335–6; Barqī: 90; Ibn Abī Ḥātim 8: 385; Kashshī: 308–9; Ibn Ḥibbān, *Thiqāt* 9: 167; Najāshī: 411; *Fibrist*: 166; *Rijāl*: 303, and other sources listed in the editor's footnote to Mizzī 28: 202.

For 'Ammār al-Duhnī, father of our transmitter, see Mizzī 21: 208–9 and the many sources listed in the editor's footnote. Ziriklī 7: 262 seems to have confused our transmitter with his father.

His profession is mentioned by Kashshī (see also *Tahdhīb* 2: 362). For his relations with the Sunnī community of Kūfa, see, for instance, *Kāfī* 7: 19. For examples of his transmissions in the Sunnī tradition, see Bukhārī, *Khalq af'āl al-'ibād*: 9 (a variant also at 21; also 'Uthmān al-Dārimī, *Jahmiyya*: 88); Muslim: 99; Ibn 'Asākir 42: 374.

1. *Kitāb al-ḥajj*

This was the most widely transmitted work of this author, related from him by a large number of transmitters (Najāshī: 411; *Fihrist*: 166). With over three hundred passages from this author on the topic, some as long as several pages (e.g. *Kāfī* 4: 245–8), quoted overwhelmingly by those specified by Najāshī and Ṭūsī as transmitters of the book, the whole contents of this work seem to have survived. Here is a list of those citations:[79]

- Aḥmad b. Muḥammad b. 'Īsā: 137–9
- *Maḥāsin*: 63, 65, 72, 335–6 (two reports), 337–8 (two reports), 340
- 'Ayyāshī 1: 91, 92, 94, 95, 97, 99, 190 (partially also in *Tawḥīd*: 344 [see the editor's footnote]), 343
- *Kāfī* 4: 184, 194 (two reports), 202, 210 (two reports), 226, 227 (two reports), 228, 229, 231, 232 (two reports), 240, 245–8, 250–51 (two

79. Two passages from this author's notebook (# 8 below): 22–3 also deal with the topic of this work.

reports), 253, 257 (repeated in 263), 258, 261–2, 265, 272, 274–6 (three reports), 282 (two reports), 284–5, 289, 290, 291–2 (three reports), 295, 296, 297, 298–9 (two reports), 304, 305, 306, 307, 311, 315, 317, 318, 319–20, 323, 326, 331–2 (two reports), 334, 335–6, 338, 339, 340–41 (two reports), 348–9 (two reports), 353, 355, 357 (two reports), 360, 361, 362, 363, 364, 366, 369–70 (two reports), 372, 373–4, 375, 377, 378, 379, 381, 382–3 (two reports), 391, 393 (two reports), 394, 395, 396, 398, 399, 400–401 (three reports), 402–3, 404, 405, 406–7, 409, 410–11 (two reports), 417, 419, 422 (two reports), 423, 425, 429, 430, 431–2, 434–5, 436, 437 (three reports), 438–9 (three reports), 440–41 (two reports), 448, 452, 454, 458, 460, 461–4 (four reports), 467, 468–9 (two reports), 471, 472, 476, 477, 478–9, 480–81, 483–5 (five reports), 487, 488–9, 490–91 (two reports), 493–4, 497, 498 (see the editor's footnote 2), 499, 500, 502–3, 505, 508, 509, 510–12, 513, 514, 517, 518, 519 (two reports), 520, 521, 524, 526, 527, 528, 529, 530–31 (two reports), 533, 535, 536, 537, 539 (two reports), 540, 550–51, 553–4, 557, 558, 560, 563, 565–6 (two reports)
6: 91
7: 19

- 'Alī b. Ibrāhīm 2: 66
- Ibn Qūlawayh: 60
- Ibn Bābawayh, *Amālī*: 254–5 (partially also in *'Ilal* 2: 84)
- *Faqīh* 2: 239–40, 251–2, 253, 254, 262, 264, 265, 295, 301, 304, 306, 307–8 (two reports), 310, 318–19, 323–4 (two reports), 333–4 (two reports), 336, 340–41 (three reports), 342, 347, 349, 351, 352, 354–5, 357, 359, 360, 364, 375, 377, 380 (two reports), 386, 389, 398–400 (two reports), 404 (three reports), 406, 407, 411, 412, 416, 417 (two reports), 420, 422, 428 (two reports), 430, 432, 434, 438, 442, 447, 450, 451, 453–4, 460 (two reports), 463–5 (three reports), 466–7, 468, 471–2, 474–5 (two reports), 476, 478, 479, 481, 483–4, 488, 499, 501, 502–4 (two reports), 506, 507, 510, 511, 514, 515, 517–18, 524, 560[80]
- *'Ilal* 2: 86, 94, 99, 113–14, 117 (two reports), 118, 120, 121 (four reports), 122, 129, 147–8
- *Khiṣāl*: 278, 455, 502
- *Ma'ānī*: 338, 339
- *Thawāb*: 72 (three reports)

---

80. Many of these citations as well as those in the *Tahdhīb* are the same as, or variants of, those in the *Kāfī*.

- *Tahdhīb* 5: passages 13, 17, 19, 27, 38, 42, 52, 53, 56, 58, 59, 60, 72, 74, 81, 82, 94, 104, 115, 117, 122, 126, 129, 131, 139, 154, 161, 166, 173, 175, 183, 193, 227, 232, 233, 235, 236, 237, 238, 253, 256, 258, 272, 293, 299, 300, 309, 319, 327, 329, 334, 337, 338, 339, 349, 357, 404, 409, 413, 422, 445, 448, 450, 475, 476, 479, 481, 487, 492, 495, 503, 509, 512, 513, 519, 521, 524, 528, 533, 537, 539, 557, 593, 595, 596, 600, 608, 611, 619, 623, 626, 633, 635, 637, 650, 661, 671, 679, 680, 697, 713, 725, 726, 728, 733, 751, 770, 771, 788, 790, 815, 821, 826, 834, 838, 844, 853, 857 (repeated at 865), 866, 867, 868, 876, 878, 888, 898, 899, 903, 904, 907, 911, 922, 926, 930, 934, 939, 941, 945, 951, 952, 953, 957, 964, 967, 970, 973, 974, 978, 983, 998, 999, 1003, 1006, 1013, 1023, 1028, 1030, 1038, 1039, 1041, 1055, 1076, 1083, 1085, 1095, 1097, 1098, 1099, 1100, 1104, 1109, 1117, 1152, 1157, 1161, 1165, 1166, 1167, 1170, 1179, 1187, 1194, 1206, 1207, 1219, 1264, 1269, 1271, 1273, 1276, 1277, 1280, 1288, 1290, 1295, 1296, 1301, 1307, 1309, 1318, 1321, 1350, 1358, 1362, 1376, 1379, 1386, 1387, 1396, 1408, 1409, 1412, 1417, 1423, 1428, 1432, 1437, 1456 (repeated at 1614), 1465, 1467, 1472, 1475, 1490, 1501, 1509, 1519, 1523, 1531, 1550, 1557, 1574, 1575, 1588, 1589, 1596, 1614, 1621, 1636, 1637, 1651, 1653, 1656, 1659, 1668, 1677, 1695, 1709, 1726, 1743, 1746, 1747, 1763[81]
- *Qiṣaṣ*: 47–8

The section quoted in Aḥmad b. Muḥammad b. ʿĪsā: 137–9 may represent the original style of the work.

2. *Kitāb al-duʿā'*

(Najāshī: 411). Examples of relevant passages:

- Muʿāwiya b. ʿAmmār: 21
- Aḥmad b. Muḥammad b. ʿĪsā: 137
- Muḥammad b. ʿAlī b. Maḥbūb: 97–8
- *Maḥāsin*: 35, 65
- Ṣaffār: 218 (a shorter text in *Kāfī* 2: 513)
- *Kāfī* 2: 477–8, 484–5 (two variants), 493, 504–5, 520, 529, 542, 549, 550–51, 568, 582–3, 584
  3: 416

81. See also ibid. 2:43, 9: 228.

4: 284–5, 311, 401, 402–3, 406–7, 411, 430, 431–2, 434–5, 452, 460, 461–2 (two reports), 463–4, 467, 468–9 (two reports), 471, 478–9, 480–81, 498 (see the editor's footnote 2), 511–12, 528, 530, 530–31, 550–51, 553–4, 557, 558, 560, 563
8: 142

- Ibn Bisṭām: 74
- Ibn Bābawayh, *Amālī*: 483 (partially also in *'Ilal* 1: 239)
- *Faqīh* 1: 471
  2: 542–3
- *'Ilal* 2: 148
- *Khiṣāl*: 101 (see the editor's footnote)
- *Thawāb*: 184 (also Ṭūsī, *Amālī*: 677 with variations)
- *Miṣbāḥ*: 63–6, 75–9, 111–14, 217–20 (see also Ibn Ṭāwūs, *Falāḥ*: 319–22 [read *Sulaymān b. Khālid 'an Mu'āwiya b. 'Ammār*], 362–4, 408, 424–7, 444–7)
- *Tahdhīb* 2: 104
  5: 50–51, 77, 91–2, 100, 101–2, 104–5, 107–8, 136, 143, 144, 145–6, 148, 177, 178, 179, 182–3, 187–8, 188–9, 191, 192, 198, 251–2, 276, 278, 280–81, 288[82]
- Ibn Ṭāwūs, *Falāḥ*: 492
- Idem, *Fatḥ*: 236
- Idem, *Iqbāl* 1: 459

Most of these citations relate to various ceremonies of *ḥajj*, but many of them and others (e.g. *Kāfī* 2: 529, 530, 550–51, 8: 142; *Faqīh* 1: 471, 2: 542–3; *Miṣbāḥ*: 63–6, 75–9, 111–14, 217–20) may originally have belonged to an independent work on *du'ā'*.

3. *Kitāb yawm wa layla*

(Najāshī: 411; *Fibrist*: 166). Examples of possible surviving passages:

- *Faqīh* 1: 219
- *'Ilal* 2: 53
- *Tahdhīb* 2: 40, 65, 69, 75, 77, 87, 122, 127 (and a variant at 128), 129, 130, 174, 243
- *Miṣbāḥ*: 63–6, 75–9, 111–14, 217–20

---

82. Many of these citations are the same as, or variants of, those in the *Kāfī*, as above.

4. *Kitāb al-ṣalāt*

(Najāshī: 411). Examples of relevant passages (other than those listed under the previous work):

- Muḥammad b. ʿAlī b. Maḥbūb: 98–9
- *Kāfī* 3: 310 (two reports), 312–13, 319, 329, 340, 357, 382, 389–90, 426, 427, 451, 460
  8: 79
- Ibn Bābawayh, *Amālī*: 254–5
- *Faqīh* 1: 271, 276
- *ʿIlal* 2: 23, 51
- *Thawāb*: 63 (two reports)
- *Tahdhīb* 2: 15, 16, 48, 83, 92, 146, 161, 162–3, 167, 172, 197, 233, 238, 247, 294–5, 303, 333, 343, 362, 375, 382–3
  3: 7, 16, 141, 156, 168, 210, 229, 285, 295–6
  5: 279
- *Miṣbāḥ*: 733–4
- Muḥaqqiq, *Muʿtabar* 2: 193 (also Ibn al-Muṭahhar, *Muntahā* 5: 115)
- Shahīd I, *Dhikrā* 3: 330

5. *Kitāb al-zakāt*

(*Fihrist*: 166). Examples of relevant passages:

- Muʿāwiya b. ʿAmmār: 21–2
- *Kāfī* 4: 40
- *Tahdhīb* 2: 238
  4: 44, 63, 72

6. *Kitāb al-ṭalāq*

(Najāshī: 411). A few relevant passages:

- *Kāfī* 6: 91, 105, 115
- *Tahdhīb* 8: 64

7. *Kitāb mazār Amīr al-Muʾminīn*

(Najāshī: 411). No part of this work appears to have survived. There are, however, a number of quotations from this author in *Kāfī* 4: 550–51,

558–60, 563 and Ibn Qūlawayh: 48–51, 60, 64–5, 66, 68–9 on the excellences and rites of visiting the tomb and mosque of the Prophet in Medina. One is tempted to suggest that Najāshī, or his source, had the tomb of the Prophet in mind but mentioned the tomb of 'Alī instead, possibly an unconscious slip or a mere slip of the pen.

8. Kitāb

(Ibn al-Nadīm: 275). Mu'āwiya b. 'Ammār was a prolific transmitter of *ḥadīth.* There are close to one thousand quotations from him in Shī'ite works of *ḥadīth,* listed in Khu'ī 18: 429–46 and *Fahāris* 10: 319, 321–2. Several hundred of these reports were organized by him in his thematic works, but most of these and others must originally have been recorded in a notebook, possibly the one mentioned by Ibn al-Nadīm: 275 as *Kitāb.* A small fragment from the *Kitāb Mu'āwiya b. 'Ammār* has survived in Ibn Idrīs, *Mustaṭrafāt*: 21–3.

144: Mu'āwiya al-Bajalī

Mu'āwiya b. Wahb al-Bajalī, a Kūfan Arab transmitter from Ja'far al-Ṣādiq.

Barqī: 90; Najāshī: 412; *Fihrist*: 166; *Rijāl*: 303. See also Zayd al-Narsī: 44–5; *Khiṣāl*: 10.

1. Kitāb faḍā'il al-ḥajj

(Najāshī: 412). The following quotations from this author on the excellences of the *ḥajj* and related matters fit the title of this work:

- *Kāfī* 4: 279, 359
- *Faqīh* 2: 308 (a variant also in *Tahdhīb* 5: 64)
- *Tahdhīb* 5: 22, 84, 112, 428, 441, 474

2. Kitāb

His notebook of *ḥadīth*, related by a number of transmitters (Abū Ghālib: 164, 165; *Fihrist*: 166; also *Mashyakha*: 440). Close to three hundred quotations from this author in Imāmite Shī'ite works of *ḥadīth*,[83] overwhelmingly through those specified in the above-mentioned sources as transmitters of this work, may represent the better part of the notebook. See the lists in Khu'ī 18: 219–23, 447–53; *Fahāris* 10: 322–3.

145: Abū Jamīla

Abū Jamīla Mufaḍḍal b. Ṣāliḥ, the slave merchant, a Kūfan client of the Banū Asad and a transmitter known to both the Sunnī and the Shī'ite communities of Kūfa. He transmitted from Ja'far al-Ṣādiq, among others, and is generally considered unreliable by the scholars of *ḥadīth*. He died late in the second century.

Bukhārī, *Kabīr* 7: 405; Barqī: 90; 'Uqaylī 4: 241–2; Ibn Abī Ḥātim 8: 316–17; Ibn Ḥibbān, *Majrūḥīn* 3: 22; Ibn 'Adī: 2405–6; Ibn al-Ghaḍā'irī: 88; *Fihrist*: 170; *Rijāl*: 307, and other sources listed in the editor's footnote to Mizzī 28: 409.

For examples of his transmissions in Sunnī works, see Aḥmad, *Faḍā'il*: 764; Tirmidhī 4: 341–2; Ṭabarī, *Tahdhīb, Ibn 'Abbās*: 85; 'Uqaylī 2: 312, 4: 242; Ibn 'Adī 6: 2405; Khaṭīb, *Ta'rīkh* 5: 467; Ibn 'Asākir 13: 221.

Kitāb

His notebook of *ḥadīth*, related by Ḥasan b. 'Alī b. Faḍḍāl (*Fihrist*: 170). There are close to five hundred quotations from this author in Shī'ite works of *ḥadīth*, many through the same transmitter. For lists see Khu'ī 18: 284–9, 476–80, 21: 96–101, 360–68; *Fahāris* 8: 309–10, 10: 336.

146: Mufaḍḍal al-Ju'fī

Abū 'Abd Allāh Mufaḍḍal b. 'Umar, the moneychanger, a Kūfan client of Ju'fī and leader of the *Mufawwiḍa* school of Shī'ite Extremism. He transmitted from Ja'far al-Ṣādiq and Mūsā al-Kāẓim, and died during the lifetime of the latter before 179.

83. There are also a number of quotations from this author in other works as, for instance, Qāḍī Nu'mān, *Sharḥ* 1: 241; Abū Ṭālib: 119.

Barqī: 90; Kashshī: 321–9; Ibn al-Ghaḍā'irī: 87–8; Najāshī: 416; *Fihrist*: 169; *Rijāl*: 307. See also *Kāfī* 2: 24, 8: 231, 374.

A number of works are attributed to Mufaḍḍal, especially in the Nuṣayrī Extremist tradition. Most of these ascriptions, however, seem to be post mortem. A few of these works are mentioned by Najāshī who also notes that they are spurious.

1. *Waṣiyyat al-Mufaḍḍal*

(Najāshī: 416; *Fihrist*: 169). The text of an alleged testament of Mufaḍḍal to the Shī'ite community, quoted in full in Ibn Shu'ba: 513–15. A long, carefully drafted paragraph towards the end explains the *raison d'être* of the text as a vindication of Mufaḍḍal, revealing at the same time some valuable information about the degree of resentment against him among the Kūfan Shī'ite community of his time.

2. *Kitāb fakkir / Kitāb fī bad' al-khalq wa 'l-ḥathth 'alā 'l-i'tibār*

Related by Muḥammad b. Sinān al-Zāhirī (Najāshī: 416), this is obviously the text known as *Tawḥīd al-Mufaḍḍal*, written in the style of a collection of lessons by Ja'far al-Ṣādiq to Mufaḍḍal in which the Imām argues for the existence of God. Najāshī calls it the book of "*Fakkir*" (Think!), clearly because many paragraphs throughout the work begin with this expression. The text has survived on the alleged authority of the same transmitter and is published, separately (Najaf, 1375, and other editions) as well as in *Biḥār* 3: 57–151.

3. *Al-Ihlīlaja*

(*Ma'ālim*: 124). The text of an alleged letter of Ja'far al-Ṣādiq in answer to a question from Mufaḍḍal on the existence and unity of God. It is in the form of a conversation between Ja'far al-Ṣādiq and an Indian physician. One of the propositions of the text is that astrology and medicine as known at the time were based on God's revelation (see further *Biḥār* 3: 56, footnote). The full text of the treatise has survived (*Biḥār* 3: 152–96; see further, Kohlberg: 187).

4. *Kitāb al-haft wa 'l-aẓilla*

A Nuṣayrī Extremist text ascribed to Mufaḍḍal as another collection of lessons he received from Ja'far al-Ṣādiq. It offers an esoteric explanation of the world and its history as well as some tenets of religion. It is a text revered by the Nuṣayrīs and is available in a number of Beirut editions (ed. 'Ārif Tāmir, 1960, 1969; ed. Muṣṭafā Ghālib, 1964). A similar text of this genre attributed to Mufaḍḍal, *Kitāb atṣirāṭ*, has recently been published by Leonardo Capezzone in the *Revista degli Studi Orientali* 69 (1995): 295–414.

5. *Mā yakūn 'ind ẓuhūr al-Mahdī*

A long, esoteric and apocalyptic text attributed to Mufaḍḍal in Khaṣībī: 392–437 where the full text is quoted (read *'an Muḥammad b. al-Mufaḍḍal 'an al-Mufaḍḍal b. 'Umar* as in the following two sources), with variants in Ḥasan b. Sulaymān: 178–92 and *Biḥār* 53: 1–35, on the situation of the world when the *Mahdī* rises up against the unjust and on what he will do. The text also takes up sectarian issues such as the *mut'a* marriage and *raj'a*, as well as the purely Extremist ideas of cycles and aeons. The last few pages of the text that contains these matters of Extremist cosmology are trimmed out in the latter two works.

6. *Kitāb 'ilal al-sharā'i'*

(Najāshī: 415). The following quotations from Mufaḍḍal are relevant to the topic of this work:

- *Kāfī* 1: 272–6 (partially also in *'Ilal* 2: 7–8)
  3: 147, 159 (partially also in *'Ilal* 1: 176)
  6: 242–3
- *'Ilal* 1: 155–6
  2: 48–9 (two reports), 210, 219, 272.

7. *Kitāb mā iftaraḍ Allāh 'alā 'l-jawāriḥ min al-īmān / Kitāb al-īmān wa 'l- islām*

(Najāshī: 416). This is clearly the long text quoted in full in Ṣaffār: 526–36 (partially also in *'Ilal* 1: 238–9) as a letter written by Ja'far al-Ṣādiq in reply to Mufaḍḍal. The text is related by Qāsim b. al-Rabī (al-Ṣaḥḥāf), from Muḥammad b. Sinān, from a certain Ṣabbāḥ al-Madā'inī, from Mufaḍḍal.

It must be the same as *Risālat Mayyāḥ* mentioned by Najāshī; 424–5, a work he received through the same chain of transmission.

8. *Du'ā' Samāt*[84] / *Du'ā' Shabbūr*

The text of a *du'ā'* that Muḥammad b. 'Uthmān al-'Amrī, the second Agent of the Twelfth Imām, released to the Shī'ite community as a text related from Ja'far al-Ṣādiq by Mufaḍḍal. The introductory note to the text explains that many Muslims at the time used to recite the *Shabbūr* of the Jews as a curse against the thieves and robbers. The matter was brought to the attention of the Agent who endorsed the practice but said that the text used by the Jews[85] was incomplete and that he was in possession of the full text[86] as related to him by his father, the first Agent, who quoted it through two intermediaries from Mufaḍḍal (*Biḥār* 90: 96–101). The text of the *du'ā'* is also quoted in *Miṣbāḥ*: 416–19; Ibn Ṭāwūs, *Jamāl*: 321–4.

9. *Kitāb yawm wa layla*

(Najāshī: 416).

---

84. Such has always been the popular pronounciation of that name among the Shī'a (see Balāghī, *Farhang*: 105), though later scholars, who try to accommodate the word within the rules of Arabic inflexion, suggest *Simāt* as a plural for *sima*, a sign (*Biḥār* 90: 102 quoting the early tenth century Shī'ite scholar, Ibrāhīm b. 'Alī al-Kaf'amī, in his monograph on this prayer).

85. See *Talmud*, *Mo'ed Katan*: 17a–17b where the paragraph talks about the concept of *shammetha*, of which clearly *samāt* is the Arabicized form. The word in Hebrew is reportedly derived from *sham-mithah* "death is there" (equivalent to Arabic *thamma 'l-mawt*). On the effect of the *shammetha*, it is said that it "adheres to one like grease to the oven ... Cast a *shammetha* on the dog's tail and it will do its work. For there was a dog that used to eat the Rabbis' shoes and they did not know what it was [that did it], so they pronounced a *shammetha* on the culprit, and the dog's tail caught fire and got burnt."

86. This "full" text seems to only add the mention of the Prophet Muḥammad and his family to the original text in a number of instances towards the end. No other significant modification appears to have been introduced. Even the name of Ishmael that naturally did not exist in the original Hebrew text, while Abraham, Isaac and Jacob are repeatedly mentioned, is still missing from the text. The early ninth century Shī'ite scholar, Ibn Fahd (d. 841) noted the absence and suggested an appendix to the text in which the reader is reminded of "the names missing from the text" (*Biḥār* 90: 99). Both in that appendix and in another suggested by an earlier scholar (ibid. 90: 100 citing Ibn Bāqī's *Ikhtiyār al-Miṣbāḥ*), it is also noted that no one in the entire Shī'ite community had the slightest idea what all of those references to concepts and events in the history of the Jewish community that formed the entire text of that *du'ā'* were about.

10. Kitāb

His notebook of *ḥadīth*, related by the transmitter, Abū Shu'ayb al-Maḥāmilī (*Fibrist*: 169).

147: Muḥammad al-Ḥalabī

Abū Ja'far Muḥammad b. 'Alī b. Abī Shu'ba al-Ḥalabī, a distinguished member of the Shī'ite community of Kūfa in his time and a transmitter from Muḥammad al-Bāqir and Ja'far al-Ṣādiq. He died during the lifetime of the latter, thus in or before 148.

Barqī: 69; Kashshī: 488; Najāshī: 325 (see also 98); *Fibrist*: 130; *Rijāl*: 145, 290.

Barqī: 69, 73 and Najāshī: 230 note that the Kūfan family of the Āl Abī Shu'ba to which this transmitter belonged was known as *Ḥalabī* because its members used to travel frequently to Aleppo on business.

1. Kitāb al-tafsīr

(Najāshī: 325). The following quotations from this author on the topic most likely belonged to this work:

- Ṣaffār: 60 (also 'Ayyāshī 2: 224)
- 'Ayyāshī 1: 22, 24, 108, 132, 134–5, 175, 178–9, 236–7, 380, 383
  2: 25, 48, 66, 224, 231, 253, 309
- Ibn al-Juḥām: 195, 304, 319, 392
- 'Alī b. Ibrāhīm 2: 388
- Ibn Qūlawayh: 182 (also *Qiṣaṣ*: 221)
- *Tawḥīd*: 154–5

There is a peculiar *isnād* that 'Ayyāshī 2: 224 and others (e.g. *Maḥāsin*: 121–2 [also *'Iqāb*: 289]; *Kāfī* 1: 443, 6: 402, 404 [read *'an Zurāra* in the two latter cases]; Ibn al-Juḥām: 195) have repeatedly quoted in their citations from this author. The *isnād* depicts our author quoting on the combined authority of several prominent mid-second century Shī'ite scholars of Kūfa, all of whom simultaneously and uniformly quote the relevant material from Muḥammad al-Bāqir, or from both him and Ja'far al-Ṣādiq. This may indicate that all the other passages cited on that collective authority in the *Tafsīr* of ʿAyyāshī, where the names of the second transmitters are normally omitted in the surviving abridged version, have been quoted from our author, more specifically from the work in question. Here is a list of these passages:

- ʿAyyāshī 1: 112, 119, 125, 127, 138, 160, 201, 224, 249, 272, 280, 304, 356, 374, 378, 384–5, 386
  2: 12, 53–4, 61–2, 70, 75, 89, 92, 104, 106, 110, 111, 127, 154, 200, 204–5, 225, 252, 274, 279, 284, 297, 309, 316, 318, 325, 326, 329–30, 338, 353

There is a long citation from *Muḥammad al-Ḥalabī* in *Taʾwīl al-āyāt*: 585–9 (citing Ibn al-Juḥām, but missing in the reconstructed version of his work). The passage has the style and flavor of a work of this period. The *isnād* of the citation (Ibn Abī ʿUmayr, fram Ḥammād, from Ḥalabī), however, points to ʿUbayd Allāh b. ʿAlī al-Ḥalabī, the brother of our author, whose work is related through this latter chain (see below, no. 204). The name *Muḥammad* before the *nisba* of *Ḥalabī* in *Taʾwīl al-āyāt* may therefore be an error.

2. *Kitāb mubawwab fī ʾl-ḥalāl wa ʾl-ḥarām*

A collection of statements of the Imāms on legal matters, organized in chapters (Najāshī: 325), and related from the author by ʿAbd Allāh b. Muskān and Abū Jamīla Mufaḍḍal b. Ṣāliḥ (Abū Ghālib: 161; Najāshī: 325; *Fihrist*: 130; see also *Mashyakha*: 427). As noted before, ʿAbd Allāh b. Muskān's book of the lawful and unlawful was in fact a copy of Ḥalabī's work to which Ibn Muskān added some extra material (Najāshī: 214).

Most of the several hundred quotations from this author on matters of law recorded in Shīʿite works of *ḥadīth*, listed in Khūʾī 17: 353–4, 18: 73, 404–6, 23: 333–41 and *Fahāris* 8: 450–52, 10: 126, 194, are through the same two transmitters.

148: Ṣāḥib al-Ṭāq

Abū Jaʿfar Muḥammad b. ʿAlī b. al-Nuʿmān b. Abī Ṭurayfa al-Aḥwal, the moneychanger, known to the Shīʿites as Muʾmin al-Ṭāq but among the

Sunnīs as Shayṭān al-Ṭāq, a Kūfan client of Bajīla and a prominent Shī'ite *mutakallim* of the mid-second century. He was also a jurist and a poet.

Barqī: 64, 121; Marzubānī, *Akhbār*: 87–95; Kashshī: 185–91; Abū 'l-Faraj, *Aghānī* 7: 245; Ibn al-Nadīm: 224; Najāshī: 325–6; *Fihrist*: 131–2; *Rijāl*: 296, 343; Khaṭīb, *Talkhīṣ*: 249; Ṣafadī 4: 104–5; *Lisān* 6: 378–9 and many other sources. There is also a monograph on him by Muḥammad Ḥusayn al-Muẓaffar as *Mu'min al-Ṭāq* (Najaf, 1965). For an account of the main biographical material about this scholar and his theological views, see now van Ess 1: 336–42.

In Shī'ite *ḥadīth*, he is normally referred to as *Ṣāḥib al-Ṭāq* (*Kāfī* 1: 101, 351, 2: 125, 7: 314; Kashshī: 185, 186, 190, 282; Ibn Bābawayh, *Amālī*: 381–2 [also *Khiṣāl*: 153; *Ma'ānī*: 196]); *Thawāb*: 162; Najāshī: 325; *Manāqib* 1: 259, 274, 4: 290) or *Ṭāqī* (*Kāfī* 1: 172; *Manāqib* 1: 269, 270, 4: 246, 277). According to Ibn al-Nadīm: 224 (see footnote 4; whence *Fihrist*: 191 and *Rijāl*: 296), he was also known as *Shāh Ṭāq*. That seems to have been the origin of the other epithets, with *Ṣāḥib al-Ṭāq* being the Arabicized, and *Shayṭān al-Ṭāq* the Sunnī pejorative, phonetically linked forms. *Mu'min al-Ṭāq* was clearly the Shī'ite rebuttal to the latter, and *Ṭāqī* the neutral, abbreviated form.

For examples of his poetry, see Marzubānī, *Akhbār*: 89–90; Ṣafadī 4: 104. Marzubānī mentions a trip by this scholar to Baṣra. This is also attested in *Kāfī* 8: 93.

Ibn al-Nadīm: 224; Najāshī: 325–6, and *Fihrist*: 132 offer partially different lists of this scholar's writings. Shahrastānī, *Milal* 1: 219, who adds an additional title, quotes the general structure of a work by this scholar called *Ifal lā tafal*, described by Najāshī as a fine and extensive work. Abū Ṭālib, *Di'āma*: 27 reports that the *Ḥadīth al-Manzila*, a text used by Shī'ite theologians in their sectarian debates with the Sunnīs, is attested in the works of this scholar. Ibn Ḥazm, who erroneously identifies him as *Muḥammad b. Ja'far b. al-Nu'mān* (*Fiṣal* 2: 269, 4: 158, 5: 39) refers to an argument by him in his book on the Imāmate (ibid. 5: 39). A paragraph quoted in 'Abd al-Jalīl al-Qazwīnī: 285 from a book by Muḥmmad b. Nu'mān al-Aḥwal on the Imām's knowledge of the unseen may have belonged to that work too. The text of a long debate between him and the Khārijite Ibn Abī Khudra[87] quoted in *Iḥtijāj* 2: 308–13 may well be the same as the *Kitāb al-iḥtijāj fī imāmat Amīr al-Mu'minīn* named in Najāshī's list; and another of a debate between him and a Khārijite recorded in Marzubānī, *Akhbār*: 90–95 may be the same as the *Kitāb kalāmih 'alā 'l-Khawārij* in the same list.

---

87. Ibn Mākūlā 3: 128–9 mentions a Khārijite Ḥabīb b. Khudra from this period.

149: Abū 'Amr al-Zubayrī

Abū 'Amr Muḥammad b. 'Amr b. 'Abd Allāh b. 'Umar b. Muṣ'ab b. Zubayr b. al-'Awwām, a Shī'ite theologian and a transmitter from Ja'far al-Ṣādiq.

Najāshī: 220, 339.

For his genealogical line, see Zubayr b. Bakkār, *Jambara* 1: 333.

Kitāb al-ṣūra

A book on the Imāmate that Najāshī: 339 describes as a fine work. The long quotations from this author on theological topics in *Kāfī* 2: 33–7, 40–42, 389–91 (in an abridged form also in 'Ayyāshī 1: 48–9; 'Alī b. Ibrāhīm 1: 32–3 [read *Abī 'Amr al-Zubayrī* for *Abī 'Umar al-Zubaydī*]), 5: 13–19 (with ending formula, clearly taken from a book or chapter), and many of the shorter citations in 'Ayyāshī 1: 51, 60–61, 63–4 (two passages), 67, 135–6, 153, 157, 169–70, 195 (two passages), 198, 228, 282, 322–3, 361, 2: 72, 105, 231, 293, 323–4 may be remnants from this work.

150: Ibn Furāt

Muḥammad b. Furāt, a Kūfan transmitter from Ja'far al-Ṣādiq.

Kashshī: 221–2; Najāshī: 363. See also *Kāfī* 7: 436.

Najāshī identifies this transmitter as a Ju'fī. A comparison between the narratives, transmitters and teachers of our transmitter with Abū 'Alī Muḥammad b. Furāt al-Tamīmī al-Kūfī, named in Sunnī sources, makes it clear that the two are one and the same. The following sources that have entries on the latter should, therefore, be added to the few works named above for biographical materials about our transmitter:

Yaḥyā b. Ma'īn 2: 533; Bukhārī, *Awsaṭ* 2: 139; idem, *Kabīr* 1: 208; 'Uqaylī 4: 123–4; Ibn Abī Ḥātim 8: 59; Ibn Ḥibbān, *Majrūḥīn* 2: 281–2; Ibn 'Adī: 2148–50; Khaṭīb, *Ta'rīkh* 3: 163–4, and other sources listed in the editor's footnote to Mizzī 26: 269.

Sunnī sources mention a *nisba* of *Jarmī* for this transmitter. *Jarm* was a clan of Quḍā'a, not of Tamīm. The two *nisbas of Tamīmī* and *Jarmī* would not therefore go well together, unless the second was an attribution to a place.[88] *Rijāl*: 292 names a Muḥammad b. al-Furāt al-Jarāmī among the transmitters from Ja'far al-Ṣādiq. Muḥammad Taqī al-Tustarī 9: 508 suggests that this latter is the same as our transmitter and that the correct form of the *nisba* may be *Ḥarāmī*, in attribution to Ḥarām b. Ka'b b. Sa'd, the ancestor of a clan of Tamīm. *Ju'fī* too may have been a corruption of *Jarmī, Jarāmī, or Ḥarāmī*.

According to a report in Mizzī 26: 272, this transmitter lived for 120 years. Someone may have understood quotations by and from this transmitter to always signify actual hearing, and, thus, come up with this figure by calculating the time between the date of death of the supposed master and birth date of the supposed student of this transmitter.

Kitāb

His notebook of *ḥadīth*, related by the mid-third century 'Abbād b. Ya'qūb al-Rawājinī (Najāshī: 363), possibly by *wijāda* or through an intermediary whose name he leaves out in his transmissions from this author as in Aḥmad b. 'Īsā 1: 179; Ibn 'Adī: 2150 (two reports); Ḥaskānī 2: 299.[89] There are a fair number of quotations from this author in Sunnī, Zaydī, and Imāmite Shī'ite works of *ḥadīth*. For examples of those in Sunnī works, see Ibn Māja: 794 [also Abū Ya'lā 10: 39 with a longer text]; 'Uqaylī 4: 123–4 [two reports]; Ibn 'Adī: 2149–50 [nine reports]; *Firdaws* [Uzbak: 714]). For those in Zaydī works, see, for instance, Aḥmad b. 'Īsā 1: 179, 3: 8, 9, 4: 262. For those in Imāmite Shī'ite works, see the lists in Khu'ī 17: 127–8, 130 and *Fahāris* 10: 221.

151: Ibn Ḥakīm al-Khath'amī

Abū Ja'far Muḥammad b. Ḥakīm, a Kūfan client of Khath'am, a Shī'ite *mutakallim* and transmitter from Ja'far al-Ṣādiq and Mūsā al-Kāẓim.

Barqī: 67, 116; Kashshī: 448–9; Najāshī: 357; *Fihrist*: 149; *Rijāl*: 280, 342.

---

88. According to Najāshī: 340, the Shī'ite transmitter Muḥammad b. Khālid al-Ṭayālisī (d. 259) *kān yaskun bi 'l-Kūfa fī Ṣaḥrā' Jarm*. The place is not mentioned by Yāqūt and a desert was not normally counted as part of a town. *Ṣaḥrā'* is most likely a corruption, possibly of *ḍāḥiya*, the district of the city where members of the tribe of Jarm lived. Najāshī: 198 also reports that the transmitter Ṣafwān b. Mihrān al-Jammāl *kān yaskun Banī Ḥarām bi 'l-Kūfa*.
89. The last citation appears also in Ibn al-Juḥām: 356 but through a different transmitter.

That he was a *mutakallim* is well documented in *Kāfī* 2: 513–14; Kashshī: 448–9 (see also 166–7; *Maḥāsin*: 212 [also Ṣaffār: 302; *Kāfī*: 1: 56]). His opinion on the theological concept of *istiṭāʿa* is quoted in Abū 'l-Ḥasan al-Ashʿarī 1: 112 (see also ʿAyyāshī 2: 351–2). For his theological reports, see *Kāfī* 1: 102, 105, 106 (the latter two also in *Tawḥīd*: 97, 99), 116 (also *Maʿānī*: 12), 154, 163 (also *Tawḥīd*: 410), 2: 284–5, 387.

Kitāb

His notebook of *ḥadīth*, related by a number of transmitters including Ḥasan b. Maḥbūb (Najāshī: 357; *Fihrist*: 149). It was received by Ibn Abī ʿUmayr through Ibn Maḥbūb (Najāshī: 357, though Ibn Abī ʿUmayr at times quotes our author directly, as in *Mashyakha*: 489 and numerous other cases, or through intermediaries other than Ibn Maḥbūb, as in *Kāfī* 1: 116 [also *Maʿānī*: 12]), and by Ḥammād b. ʿĪsā through Ḥarīz b. ʿAbd Allāh al-Sijistānī (*Mashyakha*: 489). Many, if not most, of the close to one hundred quotations from our author in later works, listed in Khuʾī 16: 30, 33–5 and *Fahāris* 10: 126, are through the above-mentioned transmitters.

152: Al-Nahdī al-Bazzāz

Abū Jaʿfar Muḥammad b. Ḥumrān, the cloth seller, a Kūfan client of the Banū Nahd of Quḍāʿa, who lived in Jarjarāyā, a village in Nahrawān, between Wāsiṭ and Baghdad. He was a transmitter from Jaʿfar al-Ṣādiq.

Barqī: 68; Najāshī: 359; *Rijāl*: 281.

1. Kitāb

His notebook of *ḥadīth*, related by many transmitters including ʿAlī b. Asbāṭ (Najāshī: 359, but cf. Ṭūsī, *Amālī*: 418), Ibn Abī ʿUmayr, ʿAbd al-Raḥmān b. Abī Najrān (*Mashyakha*: 489–90; *Fihrist*: 148[90]), and Ḥasan b. ʿAlī al-Washshāʾ (Abān al-Sindī: 41). The overwhelming majority of the close to one hundred and fifty quotations from this author in later works, listed in Khuʾī 16: 39–40, 350–54 and *Fahāris* 10: 127, are through the same transmitters.

90. This source, however, identified the author as *Muḥammad b. Ḥumrān b. Aʿyan, client of the Banū Shaybān*. This was a different person. Both *Mashyakha* and Najāshī clearly knew this notebook as belonging to Muḥammad b. Ḥumrān al-Nahdī (see Khuʾī 16: 42).

2. *Kitāb ishtaraka Jamīl wa Muḥammad b. Ḥumrān fīh*

A notebook that this transmitter had in common with Jamīl b. Darrāj (no. 119 above), related from them by Ḥasan b. ʻAlī al-Washshā' (Najāshī: 127) and Ibn Abī ʻUmayr (*Mashyakha*: 430–31). As already noted, the following passages are clearly remnants from this shared notebook:

- Aḥmad b. Muḥammad b. ʻĪsā: 65 (cf. *Kāfī* 6: 156)
- *Maḥāsin*: 355 (also *Kāfī* 5: 30); possibly also 238 (also Ibn Bābawayh, *Amālī*: 503; cf. ʻAlī b. Ibrāhīm 1: 25–6) and 320 (cf. *'Ilal* 2: 123–4).
- *Kāfī* 2: 424 (in two separate reports; cf. ibid. 5: 30)
  3: 66 (also *Faqīh* 1: 109 with a variation)
  4: 138
  5: 389
  6: 447
  7: 149, 221, 390
- *Faqīh* 4: 119 (cf. *Kāfī* 7: 300)
- *Tahdhīb* 1: 394, 401, 404
  3: 167
  9: 68
  10: 101

153: Al-Za'farānī al-Maflūj

Abū al-Naḍr Muḥammad b. Maymūn al-Tamīmī al-Za'farānī, the cripple, a Kūfan Sunnī transmitter who used to live in the vicinity of Masjid Simāk, close to the district of the ironsmith shops of Kūfa (see above, no. 42). He transmitted from Ja'far al-Ṣādiq, among others.

Yaḥyā b. Ma'īn 2: 541; Bukhārī, *Kabīr* 1: 234; ʻUqaylī 4: 137; Ibn Abī Ḥātim 8: 80–81; Ibn Ḥibbān, *Majrūḥīn* 2: 281; Ibn ʻAdī: 2268; Najāshī: 355; *Rijāl*: 295, and other sources listed in the editor's footnote to Mizzī 26: 541.

Nuskha 'an Abī 'Abd Allāh

A register of his transmissions from Ja'far al-Ṣādiq, related from the author by Muḥammad b. ʻUbayd al-Muḥāribī (Najāshī: 355). The following quotations by this author from Ja'far al-Ṣādiq, recorded mainly on the authority of the same transmitter, clearly go back to this register:

- Abū Dāwūd 3: 345
- Aḥmad b. 'Īsā 1: 139
  3: 22, 33, 72, 89, 99, 121, 149
  4: 296
- 'Uqaylī 4: 137
- Ibn 'Adī: 2268
- Abū Ṭālib: 57

154: Al-Thaqafī al-Ṭaḥḥān

Abū Ja'far Muḥammad b. Muslim b. Rabāḥ, the miller, a Kūfan client of Thaqīf, a distinguished jurist, and one of the most prominent Shī'ite transmitters of *ḥadīth* in the second century. He died in 150, aged nearly 70.

Barqī: 50, 64; Kashshī: 161–9 (see also 9–10, 136–7, 170, 185, 201, 238–9); Najāshī: 323–4; *Rijāl*: 144, 294, 342. See also *Kāfī* 5: 149.

He is certainly different from Abū 'Abd Allāh Muḥammad b. Muslim al-Ṭā'ifī al-Makkī who lived and died in Mecca in 177 (on him see the many sources listed in the editors' footnotes to Mizzī 26: 412 and Dhahabī, *Ta'rīkh* 11 [years 171–80]: 351). Muḥammad Taqī al-Tustarī 9: 579 does not note the difference and quotes, in his entry on our transmitter, a passage from *Mīzān* 4: 41 that relates to that Meccan Sunnī transmitter.

1. *Kitāb*

Muḥammad b. Muslim reportedly resided in Medina for four years to study with Muḥammad al-Bāqir and then frequented the house of his successor, Ja'far al-Ṣādiq. He is quoted as saying that he received thirty thousand *ḥadīths* from the first and sixteen thousand from the latter (Kashshī: 167). With close to two thousand reports quoted on his authority in the four main collections of Shī'ite *ḥadīth* and many more in others, he is one of the most prolific transmitters of Shī'ite *ḥadīth*. He must have had notebooks of his transmissions. In a conversation between him and Ibn Abī Laylā, the judge of Kūfa for 33 years (d. 148), the judge asks him if he has a written record of a *ḥadīth* he said he heard from Muḥammad al-Bāqir, "in a book." Muḥammad b. Muslim answers in the affirmative but says he will not show the book to the judge unless he promises not to look at any other part of it (*Kāfī* 7: 34–5 [also *Faqīh* 4: 246; *Ma'ānī*: 219–20]). The transmitter Ṣafwān b. Yaḥyā quotes a passage he found in a *Kitāb* by Muḥammad b. Muslim (*Tahdhīb* 9: 340).

His notebook(s), however, did not survive into the following centuries as none of his biographers mention any. Two recently published works attempt to collect all surviving reports quoted on the authority of this transmitter:

- *Musnad Muḥammad b. Muslim al-Thaqafī al-Ṭā'ifī* (sic), by Bashīr al-Muḥammadī al-Māzandarānī (Qum, 1416)
- *Mā rawāh al-ḥawāriyyūn*, by Kāẓim Ja'far al-Miṣbāḥ, vols. 1–3 (Qum, 1410's). This work contains some 2582 quotations from our transmitter.

2. *Kitāb al-arba'imi'at mas'ala fī abwāb al-ḥalāl wa 'l-ḥarām*

(Najāshī: 324). Khaṭīb, who received the text through the Shī'ite transmitter Ḥarīz b. 'Abd Allāh al-Sijistānī, describes it as "four hundred pieces of advice that help one in matters both spiritual and material." He reports that in length, it is a full pamphlet (Khaṭīb, *Talkhīs*: 494). The text is quoted in full in *Khiṣāl*: 610–37 (also Ibn Shu'ba: 100–125, with variations and without *isnād*).

155: Ibn Qays al-Bajalī

Abū 'Abd Allāh Muḥammad b. Qays al-Bajalī, a Kūfan transmitter from Muḥammad al-Bāqir and Ja'far al-Ṣādiq. He died in 151.

Najāshī: 323; *Fihrist*: 131; *Rijāl*: 293.

This transmitter is certainly different from the Kūfan Sunnī transmitter of the same period, Muḥammad b. Qays al-Asadī al-Wālibī (on him see Mizzī 26: 318–21 and the many sources listed in the editor's footnote) who too reportedly transmitted from Muḥammad al-Bāqir, among others (Najāshī: 324; for an example of his alleged transmission from Muḥammad al-Bāqir, see 'Abd al-Razzāq 10: 35). The Shī'ites do not seem ever to have related from Muḥammad b. Qays al-Wālibī.[91] His occasional transmission of mostly Sunnī material from 'Alī through intermediaries (e.g. Ibn Abī Shayba 6: 420, 12: 333; Aḥmad, *Faḍā'il*: 531–2; Ibn Shabba: 1269; Fākihī 5: 166–7; Ibn 'Adī: 2255) has, however, encouraged Najāshī: 324, or his source, who did not even have an accurate picture of the real identity of this latter transmitter,[92] to attribute a *Kitāb fī qaḍāyā Amīr al-Mu'minīn* to him. It may be that the confusion originally began with a Sunnī transmitter who, persuaded by these reports, misattributed the work on the topic by the Shī'ite Muḥammad b. Qays al-Bajalī (mentioned below) to the Sunnī Wālibī. Najāshī noted that the alleged work of Wālibī "equalled" the one by our transmitter, apparently in content.

1. *Kitāb qaḍāyā Amīr al-Mu'minīn*

A well known book (Najāshī: 323), related from the author by a number of transmitters including 'Āṣim b. Ḥumayd al-Ḥannāṭ (*Mashyakha*: 526–7; Najāshī: 323; *Fihrist*: 131), and the author's son, 'Ubayd b. Muḥammad b. Qays al-Bajalī, who is in turn quoted by the transmitter 'Abbād b. Ya'qūb al-Rawājinī (*Fihrist*: 108; for examples of Rawājinī's citations from 'Ubayd b. Muḥammad b. Qays al-Bajalī from his father, see Aḥmad b. 'Īsā 4: 299; *Kāfī* 6: 336). The beginning sentence of the work quoted in *Fihrist*: 108 is the same as that of the similar book by 'Ubayd Allāh b. Abī Rāfi' (see above) as given in Najāshī: 6, indicating that Muḥammad b. Qays took a copy of that earlier work, which was endorsed by Muḥammad al-Bāqir as in *Fihrist*: 108, and incorporated into it other material he had heard from the latter from or about 'Alī. There are many quotations from this author of material that relates to the topic of this work, quoted predominantly by 'Āṣim b. Ḥumayd al-Ḥannāṭ. A recent book by Bashīr al-Muḥammadī al-Māzandarānī, *Musnad Muḥammad b. Qays al-Bajalī* (Qum, 1409), has collected most of these quotations.

91. The Shī'ite *ḥadīth* transmitters of Kūfa at the time clearly knew only of one Muḥammad b. Qays and so did not feel the need to further define his name. Most confusions in cases like this came about in the following periods, especially when larger collections of *ḥadīth* mingled reports from various localities together and thus ended up with many similar names without proper distinctions.

92. Najāshī thus identifies Muḥammad b. Qays al-Asadī as a close associate of the Umayyad 'Umar b. 'Abd al-'Azīz and then of Yazīd b. 'Abd al-Malik, one of whom sent him as his emissary to Byzantium to ransom Muslim prisoners of war. These details should belong to Muḥammad b. Qays al-Madanī, a client of the family of Abū Sufyān and 'Umar b. 'Abd al-'Azīz's personal story teller (*qāṣṣ*) (on him see Mizzī 26: 323–6 and the many sources listed in the editor's footnote) who too appears in Sunnī sources, possibly inaccurately, as an occasional transmitter of material quoted from 'Alī (e.g. Aḥmad, *Faḍā'il*: 725).

2. *Al-Masā'il*

A register of a series of questions that this transmitter asked from Muḥammad al-Bāqir, together with their answers, related by 'Āṣim b. Ḥumayd (*Rijāl*: 293). Numerous passages from this register, either with (as, for instance, in Aḥmad b. Muḥammad b. 'Īsā: 47, 112; *Kāfī* 5: 113, 443, 482 [also *Tahdhīb* 8: 203–4], 6: 63, 150, 7: 261 [also *'Ilal* 2: 268], 400) or without the initial formula "I asked him," appear in the works of *ḥadīth*. Most of the surviving passages are collected in the above-mentioned *Musnad Muḥammad b. Qays al-Bajalī*.

3. *Aṣl*

His notebook of *ḥadīth*, related by Ibn Abī 'Umayr (*Fihrist*: 131). There are quotations from our author by this transmitter, through (as in *Kāfī* 6: 214) or without (as ibid. 6: 284) an intermediary. The surviving passages of this genre are also collected in the above-mentioned work.

156: Al-Nahshalī

Muḥammad b. Tamīm al-Nahshalī al-Tamīmī, allegedly a Baṣran transmitter from Mūsā al-Kāẓim.

Ibn Abī Ḥātim 7: 215; Ibn 'Adī: 753; Najāshī: 365; *Lisān* 5: 753.

This name is known principally through Abū Sa'īd Ḥasan b. 'Alī al-'Adawī (d. 318), a transmitter with a reputation for forgery (see Khaṭīb, *Ta'rīkh* 7: 381–4; *Lisān* 2: 425–8 [and the many other sources listed in the editor's footnote to the latter work 2: 425]; see also Ibn al-Ghaḍā'irī: 53, 54–5). *Lisān* 5: 753 reports that 'Abd Allāh b. Aḥmad b. Ḥanbal (d. 290) also quoted from him, presumably in his surviving *Musnad Ahl al-Bayt* (Ziriklī 4: 65). Should a transmitter such as Muḥammad b. Tamīm al-Nahshalī al-Tamīmī have ever existed, he would have lived into the third decade of the third century when 'Adawī (born 210) and 'Abd Allāh b. Aḥmad (born 213) could have heard *ḥadīth* from him. Alternatively, the transmissions by these two could have been through a written record.

Kitāb

Allegedly a notebook of Nahshalī's transmissions from Mūsā al-Kāẓim, related from the author by Ḥasan b. 'Alī al-'Adawī (Najāshī: 365). Three examples of quotations from Mūsā al-Kāẓim by Muḥammad b. Tamīm al-Nahshalī appear in Ibn ʿAdī: 753–4, all related from Nahshalī by ʿAdawī (in the edition of Ibn ʿAdī's *Kāmil* used for this study, the second report is quoted on the authority of Muḥammad b. Ṣadaqa, but Ibn al-Jawzī, *Mawḍūʿāt* 3: 67 and Suyūṭī, *Laʾālī* 2: 275 both quote Ibn ʿAdī citing that passage also from Nahshalī).

157: Ibn Abī Ḥamza

Muḥammad b. Thābit b. Dīnār al-Thumālī, a Kūfan client of the Banū ʿAwf b. Aslam of Azd and a transmitter from Jaʿfar al-Ṣādiq and Mūsā al-Kāẓim. He was a son of the prominent Shīʿite scholar of the first half of the second century, Abū Ḥamza al-Thumālī (no. 201 below).

Barqī: 68; Kashshī: 203 (repeated at 406); Najāshī: 358; *Fihrist*: 148; *Rijāl*: 145, 313.

Kitāb

His notebook of *ḥadīth*, related by Ibn Abī ʿUmayr (Najāshī: 358; *Fihrist*: 148). There are over two hundred and fifty quotations from this author in Shīʿite works of *ḥadīth*, listed in Khuʾī 14: 238–42, 403–12 and *Fahāris* 10: 128, many through the same transmitter.

158: Muḥammad Ibn Abī Rāfiʿ

Muḥammad b. ʿUbayd Allāh b. Abī Rāfiʿ al-Madanī, the grandson of Abū Rāfiʿ, the Prophet's servant, and son of ʿUbayd Allāh, the official scribe of ʿAlī. He related the works of his father and quoted *ḥadīth* from Muḥammad al-Bāqir, among others. He died in 157.

Yaḥyā b. Maʿīn 2: 529; Bukhārī, *Kabīr* 1: 271; ʿUqaylī 4: 104; Ibn Abī Ḥātim 8: 2; Ibn Ḥibbān, *Majrūḥīn* 2: 249–50; idem, *Thiqāt* 7: 400; Dāraquṭnī, *Ḍuʿafāʾ*: 147; Ibn ʿAdī: 2125–6; Najāshī: 6, 353; *Rijāl*: 287; Mizzī 26: 36–8 (and other sources listed in the editor's footnote).

Ibn ʿAdī: 2126 identifies this transmitter as a Kūfan quoted by the Kūfans and as one of the Shīʿites of that city. This does not seem correct. Like his father and other members of the family, Muḥammad too must have lived and died in Medina. Abū Ḥātim describes his son, Muʿammar, as "a Medinese *shaykh* who was in Baghdad" (Mizzī 28: 330).

His transmission from Muḥammad al-Bāqir is attested in a number of reports (e.g. *Firdaws* [Uzbak: 731, # 206]). He also quoted from Zayd b. ʿAlī (e.g. Ibn Abī 'l-Ḥadīd 4: 107) and other members of the House of the Prophet (e.g. Aḥmad 1: 78 [cf. Baḥshal: 195]; *Ḥilya* 1: 74, 388).

Nuskha

A register of *ḥadīth*, related from this transmitter by his son, Muʿammar (whom Abū Ḥātim met in Baghdad in 213, and on him see Mizzī 28: 329–31 and the sources listed in the editor's footnote), as noted by Ibn Ḥibbān, *Majrūḥīn* 3: 38. Najāshī: 353 also has him as an author of a book, though the sentence that should specify the work intended is missing from the existing version of this source. The *isnād* given by Najāshī for this unspecified work is, however, identical in the upper part with that given by him for the book of Ibn Abī Rāfiʿ that this transmitter quoted from the author, his father (Najāshī: 6).

Many quotations from this author,[93] some through his son Muʿammar,[94] appear in Sunnī and Shīʿite works of *ḥadīth*. Ṭabarānī, *Kabīr* 1: 318–22 (# 939–55 and 958) has eighteen of them in one section and another, ibid. 4: 184. Muḥammad b. Sulaymān quotes in his *Manāqib* some twenty others, all on the virtues of ʿAlī, as follows:

> 1: 236, 262 (a longer version at 285; also Ṭabarānī, *Kabīr* 1: 320, # 952; Ḥākim 3: 183), 277, 280, 283 (repeated at 286; also Ibn al-Juḥām: 282 [read *'an Ibn Abī Rāfiʿ* as in the editor's footnote 3]), 284, 310, 334, 364 (also Abū Ṭālib: 75; Ṭabrisī, *Iʿlām*: 191–2), 385–6 (read *'an Muḥammad b. 'Ubayd Allāh b. Abī Rāfiʿ 'an abīh*), 392 (also Ibn al-Juḥām: 391), 395 (also Ibn ʿAdī: 2126), 397, 428 (repeated in 2: 405; also Ṭabarānī, *Kabīr* 1: 319; Qāḍī Nuʿmān, *Sharḥ* 1: 232; Zubayr b. Bakkār, *Muwaffaqiyyāt*: 313), 474, 485–6, 489, 491 (a longer version at 495, partially also in 2: 536; also *Irshād* 1: 87), 507–8
>
> 2: 283 (repeated at 471)

---

93. At times, however, he is misidentified as Muḥammad b. ʿUbayd Allāh b. ʿAlī b. Abī Rāfiʿ (see above, section I, no. 4, the entry on ʿUbayd Allāh b. Abī Rāfiʿ).

94. They include five quotations in Ibn ʿAdī: 2443 (two also in Rūyānī 1: 473–4, another also in Ibn Māja: 153, another also in Ibn Saʿd 1: 376 through a transmitter other than Muʿammar), a sixth in Ṭabarī, *Tahdhīb, Ibn 'Abbās*: 511, and a seventh in Haythamī, *Majmaʿ al-baḥrayn* 6: 159–60.

Other quotations from this author, many through the transmitter named by Najāshī, include the following:

- Ibn Sa‘d 3: 15–16
- Aḥmad 1: 78 (read *‘an Muḥammad b. ‘Ubayd Allāh b. Abī Rāfi‘* as in the Beirut, 1995 edition, as well as in Baḥshal: 195), 121
- Ibn Māja: 242, 395 (same as Ṭabarānī, *Kabīr* 1: 318, # 940), 411–12 (same as Ṭabarānī, *Kabīr* 1: 318, # 943)
- Ṣaffār: 85
- Rūyānī 1: 455, 461 (two reports, both also in Ṭabarānī, *Kabīr* 1: 320–21 [# 954, 955, the latter also in Abū Nu‘aym, *Mā nazal*: 62–3; Ibn al-Juḥām: 98–99)
- Ibn al-Juḥām: 203 (read *‘an Muḥammad b. ‘Ubayd Allāh b. Abī Rāfi‘* as in *Biḥār* 37: 271)
- Ibn Qūlawayh: 113 (read *‘an Ibn Abī Rāfi‘*)
- *Irshād* 1: 73–4
- *Ḥilya* 1: 74, 388
- *Firdaws* (Uzbak: 731, # 206)
- Ṭabrisī, *I‘lām*: 187
- Ibn ‘Asākir 14: 128–9, 130 (see also Ṭabarānī, *Kabīr* 4: 155–6), 162 42: 141–2, 270
- Ibn Abī ’l-Ḥadīd 4: 107
- Ibn al-Qayyim, *Ṭuruq*: 67–8

The long text in Ṭusī, *Amālī*: 463–72 from ‘Ubayd Allāh b. Abī Rāfi‘ and others may have also belonged to the work in question as some passages of it are attested elsewhere on the authority of our author.

159: Ibn ‘Udhāfir al-Ṣayrafī

Muḥammad b. ‘Udhāfir al-Madā’inī, the moneychanger, a Kūfan client of Khuzā‘a and a transmitter from Ja‘far al-Ṣādiq and Mūsā al-Kāẓim. He died late in the second century at the age of 93.

Barqī: 69, 119; Najāshī: 359–60; *Fibrist*: 148; *Rijāl*: 291, 343; Ibn Mākūlā 5: 170.

Kitāb

His notebook of *ḥadīth*, related by a number of transmitters including Muḥammad b. Ismā'īl b. Bazī' and 'Amr b. 'Uthmān (Najāshī: 360; *Fihrist*: 148; *Rijāl*: 343), possibly also Muḥammad b. 'Umar b. Yazīd who is the intermediary between this author and Mūsā b. al-Qāsim al-Bajalī, author of a book on the *ḥajj* in which he repeatedly quoted from our author. The overwhelming majority of the quotations from Muḥammad b. 'Udhāfir in Sunnī (e.g. Khaṭīb, *Talkhīṣ*: 41) and Shī'ite works of *ḥadīth*, over one hundred of them listed in Khu'ī 16: 279–80, 435–7 and *Fahāris* 10: 181, are through the same transmitters.

160: Muḥammad al-Khath'amī

Muḥammad b. Yaḥyā al-Khath'amī, a Kūfan transmitter from Ja'far al-Ṣādiq.

Najāshī: 359; *Fihrist*: 162; *Rijāl*: 297.

This transmitter is most likely the same as the Muḥammad b. Yaḥyā al-Khazzāz named also in Najāshī: 359. See especially Ibn Qūlawayh: 156, # 17 and 18 (compare also *Kāfī* 6: 200 with *Tahdhīb* 6: 398 and other similar cases mentioned in Muḥammad Taqī al-Tustarī 9: 650 and Khu'ī 18: 391–3).

Kitāb

His notebook of *ḥadīth*, related by a number of transmitters including Ibn Abī 'Umayr (Najāshī: 359; *Fihrist*: 162). There are a good number of quotations from this author in later works, some through the same transmitter. For lists see Khu'ī 18: 26–9, 33–6, 386–92 and *Fahāris* 10: 274–6. The notebook was still available in the mid-seventh century to Ibn Ṭāwūs who calls it *Aṣl* and quotes a passage from it in his *Faraj*: 86 (see further Kohlberg: 125–6).

161: Munakhkhal al-Raqqī

Munakhkhal b. Jamīl al-Asadī al-Raqqī, seller of slave girls, a Kūfan esoteric Shī'ite who principally transmitted from Jābir al-Ju'fī.

Kashshī: 368; Ibn al-Ghaḍā'irī: 89, 110; Najāshī: 421; *Fibrist*: 169; *Rijāl*: 312.

Najāshī reports that Munakhkhal transmitted from Ja'far al-Ṣādiq, too. This is attested in a report in *Kāfī* 1: 417.

1. *Kitāb al-tafsīr*

Related from the author by Muḥammad b. Sinān al-Zāhirī (Najāshī: 421), this was clearly a collection of mostly esoteric reports on the Qur'ān, almost all quoted from the author's principal teacher, Jābir al-Ju'fī. There are numerous quotations on the topic from this author in later works, all, with a single exception, from Jābir, and all quoted from Munakhkhal by the same Muḥammad b. Sinān, through 'Ammār b. Marwān al-Yashkurī al-Khazzāz. Examples include the following:

- Ṣaffār: 193 (also *Kāfī* 1: 228), 294 (whence *Ikhtiṣāṣ*: 278), 399 (whence *Ikhtiṣāṣ*: 278), 399 (whence *Ikhtiṣāṣ*: 332), 500
- *Kāfī* 1: 417 (three reports), 418
- Furāt: 54
- Ibn al-Juḥām: 145
- 'Alī b. Ibrāhīm 2: 104, 111, 255
- Ibn Bisṭām: 23, 69
- *Ma'ānī*: 167
- Abū 'Abd Allāh al-Shajarī, *Adhān*: 21 (possibly; repeated at 82)
- Ḥasan b. Sulaymān: 17–18, 26 (two reports)

2. *Kitāb*

Related by Muḥammad b. al-Ḥusayn b. Abī 'l-Khaṭṭāb through Muḥammad b. Sinān al-Zāhirī (*Fibrist*: 169) who, as noted above, quotes this author through 'Ammār b. Marwān. A good number of non-Qur'ānic quotations from this author, almost all through this chain of transmission, may have belonged to this work. Examples are as follows:

- Ṣaffār: 20–21, 28 (read *'an Munakhkhal 'an Jābir*), 104, 144, 187–8, 317, 447 (also *Kāfī* 1: 272)
- Kashshī: 14–15 (through a different *isnād*)
- Nu'mānī: 200–201
- *Ikhtiṣāṣ*: 117
- *Ghayba*: 187
- *Tahdhīb* 2: 109 (repeated at 321)

162: Murāzim al-Madā'inī

Abū Muḥammad Murāzim b. Ḥakīm al-Madā'inī, a client of Azd and a transmitter from Ja'far al-Ṣādiq and Mūsā al-Kāẓim. He died after 183.

Barqī: 117; Najāshī: 424; *Fibrist*: 170; *Rijāl*: 311, 342. See also *Kāfī* 2: 344–5, 4: 506.

Murāzim was a member of an originally Kūfan Shī'ite family of transmitters of *ḥadīth* who lived in the Sabāṭ district of Ctesiphon. His brother, Ḥadīd, was a *mutakallim* and a transmitter from Ja'far al-Ṣādiq (Najāshī: 148; Khaṭīb, *Ta'rīkh* 8: 280). Najāshī and *Fibrist*: 63–4 name a notebook of *ḥadīth* by Ḥadīd, not attested through the transmitters specified in those two sources, nor quoted by his son, 'Alī, himself a widely quoted transmitter. Murāzim's other brother, Muḥammad (Najāshī: 424; *Rijāl*: 280),[95] and son, Muḥammad (Najāshī: 365; *Fibrist*: 155), are also named in the sources.[96]

1. *Kitāb*

His notebook of *ḥadīth*, related by his nephew 'Alī b. Ḥadīd (Najāshī: 424; *Fibrist*: 170), and possibly by Ibn Abī 'Umayr (*Mashyakha*: 463). There are close to one hundred quotations from this author in later works, listed in Khu'ī 18: 110–13, 407–9 and *Fahāris* 10: 293, predominently through the same transmitters.

2. *Kitāb ishtaraka Jamīl b. Darrāj wa Murāzim b. Ḥakīm fīh*

A notebook he had jointly with Jamīl b. Darrāj (no. 119 above), related by 'Alī b. Ḥadīd (Najāshī: 127). *Jamīl 'an Murāzim* in *Kāfī* 2: 170, 4: 27 (also *Thawāb*: 203) may refer to this joint notebook. Alternatively, it might have originally read *Jamīl wa Murāzim* if a joint notebook implied a register of reports filled out in part by one transmitter and in part by the other.

---

95. *Maḥāsin*: 479 has a quotation from Ja'far b. Muḥammad b. Ḥakīm, from his father, from Ḥadīd. *Kāfī* 6: 324 has Ja'far b. Muḥammad b. Ḥakīm, from Murāzim. These may be family *isnāds*, and this Ja'far possibly a nephew of Murāzim and not the Khath'amī named in Najāshī: 357.

96. *Ḥafṣ akhī Murāzim* in *Kāfī* 1: 102, however, seems to be a corruption of *Ḥadīd akhī Murāzim*, as is *Jarīr b. Ḥakīm akhū Murāzim* in *Rijāl*: 179.

163: Mūsā al-Wāsiṭī

Mūsā b. Bakr al-Wāsiṭī, a Kūfan Shī'ite who was originally from Wāsiṭ. He was a transmitter from Ja'far al-Ṣādiq and Mūsā al-Kāẓim, and joined the Wāqifites after the death of the latter.

Barqī: 85, 117, 118; Kashshī: 328, 438; Najāshī: 407; *Fihrist*: 162; *Rijāl*: 301, 343.

He was a personal aide to Mūsā al-Kāẓim as noted in a report quoted by Kashshī (also 'Abd Allāh b. Ja'far: 333; see also *Kāfī* 5: 94, 6: 332, 489). That he joined the Wāqifites is noted in *Rijāl*: 343.

Kitāb

His notebook of *ḥadīth*, related by 'Alī b. al-Ḥakam (Najāshī: 407), Ibn Abī 'Umayr and Ṣafwān b. Yaḥyā (*Fihrist*: 162). The notebook is also mentioned in the *Kāfī* where a number of passages are quoted from it through Ḥasan b. Muḥammad b. Samā'a (*Kāfī* 7: 97, continued at 104). A fragment of the work is included in Ibn Idrīs, *Mustaṭrafāt*: 17–19.

There are close to three hundred quotations from this author in later works, listed in Khu'ī 19: 22–31, 340–47 and *Fahāris* 10: 365–6, mainly through the same transmitters.

164: Mūsā al-Marwazī

Mūsā b. Ibrāhīm al-Marwazī, a Sunnī resident of Baghdad who was formerly associated with the police force of the city but later joined the circles of transmitters of *ḥadīth*. He heard *ḥadīth* from Mūsā al-Kāẓim when the latter was in the city as a prisoner. He was reportedly still alive in 229.

'Uqaylī 4: 166; Najāshī: 407–8; *Fihrist*: 163; *Rijāl*: 343; Khaṭīb, *Ta'rīkh* 13: 38–9; *Lisān* 7: 94–5 (and other sources listed in the editor's footnote).

Kitāb / Musnad al-Imām Mūsā b. Ja'far

A notebook of the *ḥadīth*s that he heard from Mūsā al-Kāẓim, related from the author by Muḥammad b. Khalaf al-Marwazī (Najāshī: 407–8).

The work has survived in an old manuscript in the Ẓāhiriyya Library of Damascus and is published (ed. Muḥammad Ḥusayn al-Ḥusaynī al-Jalālī, Tehran, 1352sh/1973–4) as *Musnad al-Imām Mūsā b. Ja'far.* It contains fifty-nine reports, with an appendix by the editor where a number of quotations by the author from Mūsā al-Kāẓim, not attested in this text, are gathered from other works.

165: Mūsā al-Numayrī

Mūsā b. Ukayl al-Numayrī, a Kūfan transmitter from Ja'far al-Ṣādiq.

Barqī: 85; Najāshī: 408–9; *Fihrist*: 162; *Rijāl*: 314.

Kitāb

His notebook of *ḥadīth*, related by a number of transmitters (Najāshī: 409; *Fihrist*: 162). The overwhelming majority of the close to fifty quotations from this author in later works are through uniform *isnād*s to the transmitters 'Alī b. 'Uqba and Dhubyān b. Ḥakīm al-Awdī who at times quote this author together (e.g. *Tahdhīb* 1: 459, 6: 242; Ibn Ṭāwūs, *Jamāl*: 278), but mostly separately. They most likely quoted from this notebook. For the list of their quotations, see Khu'ī 19: 19–21, 338–9 (see also ibid. 7: 421, 12: 313–14).

166: Abū Hārūn al-Makfūf

Mūsā b. 'Umayr al-Qurashī al-Ja'dī, the blind, a Kūfan client of the family of Ja'da b. Hubayra al-Makhzūmī, 'Alī's nephew and governor of Khurāsān, and a transmitter known to both Sunnī and Shī'ite circles of *ḥadīth* transmission in his time. He lived in Baghdad and transmitted from Ja'far al-Ṣādiq, among others.

Abū Zur'a al-Rāzī: 532; Fasawī 3: 121; Barqī: 58, 108; Nasā'ī, *Ḍu'afā'*: 224; ' Uqaylī 4: 159–60; Ibn Abī Ḥātim 8: 155; Ibn 'Adī: 2340–41; Kashshī: 222–3; Najāshī: 409 (as Mūsā b. 'Umayr *al-Hudhalī*, possibly a corruption of *Ja'dī*); *Fihrist*: 183; *Rijāl*:

150, 301; Khaṭīb, *Ta'rīkh* 13: 20–21; Mizzī 29: 128–9 (and other sources named in the editor's footnote). See also *Kāfī* 5: 480; *Tahdhīb* 10: 224–5.

For examples of this transmitter's Sunnī reports, see Ibn 'Adī: 2340–41 where seven instances are quoted.

Kitāb

His notebook of *ḥadīth*, related by 'Abbād b. Ya'qūb al-Rawājinī (Najāshī: 409) and 'Ubays b. Hishām (*Fihrist*: 183). The following quotations from this author are on the authority of 'Abbād:

- Aḥmad, *Faḍā'il*: 619 (repeated at 668)
- Aḥmad b. 'Īsā 4: 267
- Ibn 'Adī: 2341 (three reports, one also in Abū Ṭālib: 317)
- Abū Ṭālib: 400, 424

Other "Shī'ite" quotations from him include the following examples:

- *Kāfī* 3: 306, 314–15, 343
  6: 39
  8: 102, 266
- Ibn Qūlawayh: 208 (repeated at 210–11)
- *Ḥilya* 3: 186
- Ibn 'Asākir 26: 323 (read *Ḥasan b. Maḥbūb al-Sarrād 'an Mūsā b. 'Umayr al-Kūfī*)

167: Mushma'ill al-Nāshirī

Mushma'ill b. Sa'd al-Asadī al-Nāshirī, a Kūfan Shī'ite and a transmitter from Ja'far al-Ṣādiq.

Barqī: 112; Najāshī: 420; *Fihrist*: 171; *Rijāl*: 311. See also Ibn Bābawayh, *Amālī*: 581–2.

Kitāb al-diyāt

A joint book by this author and his brother, Ḥakam, related from them by 'Ubays b. Hishām al-Nāshirī (Najāshī: 420, also 136–7). There are a number of quotations from this author in later works, some through the same transmitter, but all legal transmissions of this author concern matters of inheritance (e.g. *Kāfī* 7: 91, 110, 126 [also *Faqīh* 4: 262; *Tahdhīb* 9: 294–5, read *'an Mushma'ill* for *'an Ismā'īl*]; *Tahdhīb* 9: 283). One may therefore suggest that the word *diyāt* in Najāshī's source may have been a corruption of *mīrāth*. Alternatively, the work may have been entitled *Kitāb al-farā'iḍ*, a term that would normally refer to shares of inheritance but could also mean at the time the monetary compensation for the loss of life or injuries inflicted upon a fellow human being. Najāshī or his source may have reworded the title to fit what they thought the book's content was about.

168: Muthannā al-Ḥannāṭ

Muthannā b. al-Walīd, the wheat seller, a Kūfan client and a transmitter from Ja'far al-Ṣādiq.

Barqī: 104; Kashshī: 338; Najāshī: 414; *Fihrist*: 167.

Kitāb / Aṣl

His notebook of *ḥadīth*, related by a number of transmitters including Ḥasan b. 'Alī b. Yūsuf b. Baqqāḥ (Najāshī: 414) and Ḥasan b. 'Alī al-Washshā' (Abū Ghālib: 172; Najāshī: 414; *Fihrist*: 167). The notebook has survived, and is published in *al-Uṣūl al-sittat 'ashar*: 102–5. It contains twenty-three reports (see further Kohlberg, *Uṣūl*: 155). There are, however, many other quotations from this author in later works, listed in Khu'ī 14: 178–80, 183–7, 379–86 and *Fahāris* 10: 36–7, many through the same transmitters. This may indicate that the surviving text is a shorter version of the original and much longer notebook of Muthannā al-Ḥannāṭ, or a fragment of it.

169: Ibn Abī Zuhayr

Abū Muḥammad Muṭṭalib b. Ziyād b. Abī Zuhayr, a Kūfan client and a Sunnī transmitter of *ḥadīth* with Shī'ite sympathies. He transmitted from Ja'far al-Ṣādiq, among others, and died in 185.

Ibn Sa'd 6: 360; Yaḥyā b. Ma'īn 2: 570; 'Ijlī: 431; Bukhārī, *Kabīr* 8: 8; Fasawī 3: 180; Barqī: 110; Ibn Abī Ḥātim 8: 360; Ibn 'Adī: 2455; Najāshī: 423; *Fihrist*: 168; *Rijāl*: 311, and other sources listed in the editors' footnotes to Mizzī 28: 78 and Dhahabī, *Ta'rīkh* 12 (years 181–190): 400.

He is commonly identified as *al-Thaqafī al-Zuhrī al-Qurashī*. Ibn Sa'd explains that he was called *Thaqafī* because he lived among the Thaqīf, presumably in their district in Kūfa, and was called *Qurashī* and *Zuhrī* because he was a client of Jābir b. Samura b. Junāda al-Suwā'ī (d. 74), a companion of the Prophet and nephew of Sa'd b. Abī Waqqāṣ (d. 55), whose father was a confederate (*ḥalīf*) of the Banū Zuhra b. Kilāb, a clan of Quraysh (see further, Mizzī 4: 438–9).

He also transmits from Zayd b. 'Alī (Mizzī 28: 78) and, through intermediaries, from Muḥammad al-Bāqir (e.g. Aḥmad b. 'Īsā 4: 340). For his Shī'ite sympathies see Ibn Abī Shayba 12: 59 (also Muḥammad b. Sulaymān 2: 389, 406, 409; Dhahabī, *Siyar* 8: 296–7); Aḥmad 1: 126 (also Ṭabarānī, *Awsaṭ* 1: 94, 5: 153–4, 7: 379; idem, *Ṣaghīr* 1: 261–2); Ibn Abī 'Āṣim: 895–6 (also Nasā'ī, *Khaṣā'iṣ*: 122–3; idem, *Sunan* 7: 429; Khaṭīb, *Ta'rīkh* 8: 53; Ibn 'Asākir 42: 163–4); Ibn Bābawayh, *Amālī*: 64; Mufīd, *Kāfi'a*: 38–9; Ibn Abī 'l-Ḥadīd 13: 221–2.

Nuskha 'an Ja'far b. Muḥammad

A register of his transmissions from Ja'far al-Ṣādiq, related by Aḥmad b. Muḥammad b. Khālid al-Barqī through his father (Najāshī: 423; also *Fihrist*: 168 [as a *kitāb*]). There is in fact a passage in *Maḥāsin*: 498 (whence *Kāfī* 6: 335) that Barqī quotes from his father, from this author, from Ja'far al-Ṣādiq. Other quotations by this author from Ja'far al-Ṣādiq are normally through intermediaries as in *Kāfī* 5: 517, 6: 515; Ibn Bisṭām: 84.

170: Qāsim al-'Ijlī

Qāsim b. Burayd b. Mu'āwiya al-'Ijlī, a Kūfan transmitter from Ja'far al-Ṣādiq and his disciples. He was the son of Burayd b. Mu'āwiya (no. 51 above), a distinguished member of the Shī'ite community of Kūfa in the mid-second century who died in 150.

Najāshī: 313–14; *Rijāl*: 273, 342.

Kitāb

His notebook of *ḥadīth*, related by Faḍāla b. Ayyūb (Najāshī: 313–14). Most of the over fifty surviving quotations from this author in later works, listed in Khu'ī 14: 13, 346, 347–8 and *Fahāris* 9: 554, are on the authority of the same transmitter.

171: Qāsim al-Baghdādī

Qāsim b. Sulaymān, a Kūfan who resided in Baghdad and a transmitter from Ja'far al-Ṣādiq and his disciples.

Najāshī: 314; *Fihrist*: 127–8; *Rijāl*: 273.

Kitāb

His notebook of *ḥadīth*, related by Ḥusayn b. Sa'īd through Naḍr b. Suwayd from the author (Najāshī: 314; *Fihrist*: 127–8; also *Mashyakha*: 479). Close to one hundred quotations from this author have survived in later works through this *isnād*. For lists see Khu'ī 14: 22, 348–56; *Fahāris* 9: 558.

172: Ibn 'Urwa

Abū Muḥammad Qāsim b. 'Urwa, a resident of Baghdad and an aide to Abū Ayyūb al-Khūzī, the vizier of the 'Abbāsid Manṣūr.[97] He transmitted from the disciples of Ja'far al-Ṣādiq.

Kashshī: 372; Najāshī: 314–15; *Fihrist*: 127; *Rijāl*: 273, 436.

---

97. Abū Ayyūb Sulaymān b. Makhlad (or Dāwūd) al-Khūzī al-Mūriyānī (d. 154) who served as the vizier of Manṣūr until 153. On him see especially Jahshiyārī: 65–87 (also Ṭabarī 8: 42, 44 [and numerous pages in vol. 7]; Mas'ūdī 4: 133; Ibn Khallikān 2: 410–14).

Kitāb

His notebook of *ḥadīth*, related by 'Abbās b. Ma'rūf, Ḥusayn b. Sa'īd and Muḥammad b. Khālid al-Barqī, among others (Najāshī: 314–15; *Fibrist*: 127; *Rijāl*: 273). Quotations by the same transmitters from this author abound in later works. See the lists in Khū'ī 5: 472–3, 9: 487, 498, 16: 361–2; *Fahāris* 9: 559.

173: Rabī' al-Aṣamm

Rabī' b. Muḥammad b. 'Umar b. Ḥassān al-Muslī al-Madhḥijī, a Kūfan transmitter from Ja'far al-Ṣādiq.

Najāshī: 164; *Fibrist*: 70; *Rijāl*: 203.

Kitāb / Aṣl

His notebook of *ḥadīth*, related by Ḥasan b. Maḥbūb and 'Abbās b. 'Āmir al-Qaṣabānī, among others (Najāshī: 164; *Fibrist*: 70). The transmitter 'Alī b. al-Ḥakam also seems to have been a principal transmitter of this notebook. Almost all of some fifty quotations from this author in later works, listed in Khu'ī 7: 166, 174–5, 177, 430–31 and *Fahāris* 8: 536, are on the authority of the said transmitters. The notebook was still available in the mid-seventh century to Ibn Ṭāwūs, who quoted from it in his *Falāḥ*: 382–3, 387–8 and *Muḥāsaba*: 54–5 (see further Kohlberg: 126).

174: Rifā'a al-Nakhkhās

Rifā'a b. Mūsā al-Asadī, the slave merchant, a Kūfan transmitter from Ja'far al-Ṣādiq and Mūsā al-Kāẓim. He reportedly joined the Wāqifites after the death of the latter, but later left that group and returned to mainstream Imāmism.

Barqī: 109; Najāshī: 166; *Fibrist*: 71; *Rijāl*: 205; *Ghayba*: 71. See also *Kāfī* 6: 78; Najafī 32: 130.

Kitāb mubawwab fī 'l-farā'iḍ

A work on matters of religious law, organized in chapters (Najāshī: 166), related by a number of transmitters including Ibn Abī 'Umayr and Ṣafwān b. Yaḥyā (Abū Ghālib: 177; *Fihrist*: 71; see also *Mashyakha*: 452). Quotations from this author by these and other prominent transmitters in matters of religious law abound in Shī'ite works of *ḥadīth*. For lists see Khu'ī 7: 198–200, 431–7; *Fahāris* 8: 542–3.

175: Ibn Abī Sabra

Abū Nu'aym Rib'ī b. 'Abd Allāh b. al-Jārūd b. Abī Sabra al-Hudhalī, a Baṣran transmitter of *ḥadīth* known to both Sunnī and Shī'ite traditions. His grandfather, Jārūd (d. 120) was also a *ḥadīth* transmitter and was quoted by Rib'ī. Rib'ī was a disciple of the Baṣran Shī'ite scholar Fuḍayl b. Yasār, from whom he transmitted much *ḥadīth*. He also transmitted from Muḥammad al-Bāqir and Ja'far al-Ṣādiq, among others.

Bukhārī, *Kabīr* 3: 327–8; Barqī: 101; Ibn Abī Ḥātim 3: 509; Kashshī: 362; Ibn Ḥibbān, *Thiqāt* 6: 308; Najāshī: 167; *Fihrist*: 70; *Rijāl*: 205.

For an example of Rib'ī's transmission in the Sunnī tradition, see Abū Dāwūd 2: 9. He quoted that report from his grandfather, Jārūd, as also in Ṣaffār: 58. A later transmitter of this latter report, 'Abbās b. Ma'rūf, misidentified this Jārūd (ibid.: 56). The name is wrongly amended to *Abī 'l- Jārūd* in *Kāfī* 1: 221.[98]

Kitāb / Aṣl

His notebook of *ḥadīth*, related by a number of Shī'ite transmitters including Ḥammād b. 'Īsā and Ibn Abī 'Umayr (Najāshī: 167; *Fihrist*: 70; also *Mashyakha*: 468). With a few exceptions, all of the over one hundred quotations from Rib'ī in Shī'ite works of *ḥadīth*, listed in Khu'ī 7: 160–61,

98. The editor obviously misidentified this Jārūd with the much better known Abū 'l- Jārūd Ziyād b. al-Mundhir (see above, section II, no. 13). The misidentification is not unprecedented. Abū 'l-Mundhir Jārūd b. al-Mundhir al-Kindī, the coppersmith, a Kūfan transmitter from Ja'far al-Ṣādiq and author of a notebook of *ḥadīth* (Barqī: 60, 105; Najāshī: 130; *Fihrist*: 45; *Rijāl*: 129, 179; with a few quotations on his authority in *Kāfī* 2: 144, 3: 135, 6: 5, 6, 405; Kashshī: 127; *Tahdhīb* 2: 259) has repeatedly been misidentified with Abū 'l- Jārūd. Compare, for instance, *Khiṣāl*: 132 and *Ma'ānī*: 193 with *Kāfī* 2: 144, and *Kāfī* 6: 405 with *Tahdhīb* 9: 109.

164–5, 424–30 and *Fahāris* 8: 53–4, are through Ḥammād, with the remainder through Ibn Abī ʿUmayr and others.

At the end of Ribʿī's entry in Najāshī, there is a reference to the *Kitāb al-rāhib wa 'l-rāhiba* of Ḥasan b. Rāshid (see no. 83 above). The reference is in all likelihood misplaced. That text, a sectarian polemic written in the form of a conversation between Mūsā al-Kāẓim and a monk and a nun from Yemen, is quoted in full on the authority of Ḥasan b. Rāshid in *Kāfī* 1: 481–4 and is not related to Ribʿī.

176: Rawḥ b. ʿAbd al-Raḥīm

Rawḥ b. ʿAbd al-Raḥīm b. Rawḥ, a Kūfan transmitter from Jaʿfar al-Ṣādiq. He was a nephew of Muʿallā b. Khunays (no. 142 above).

Najāshī: 168; *Rijāl*: 204. See also *Kāfī* 2: 147.

Kitāb

His notebook of *ḥadīth*, related by the transmitter Ghālib b. ʿUthmān (Najāshī: 168; also *Mashyakha*: 521). There are a number of quotations from this author in the four main works of Shīʿite *ḥadīth*, as listed in Khu'ī 7: 204–5, 206, 437 (and an additional one in *Maḥāsin*: 577), all, with a single exception, through the same transmitter.

177: Al-Khulqānī

Abū 'l-ʿAbbās Ruzayq b. al-Zubayr b. Abī 'l-Zarqā' al-Khulqānī, a Kūfan transmitter from Jaʿfar al-Ṣādiq.

Najāshī: 168; *Fibrist*: 74; *Rijāl*: 205.

That he was a Kūfan is not mentioned by his biographers but appears from a report in Ṭūsī, *Amālī*: 698.

Kitāb

(Ibn al-Nadīm: 275). This was Ruzayq's notebook of *ḥadīth*, related by Muḥammad b. Hammām al-Iskāfī (d. 336) from ʿAbd Allāh b. Jaʿfar al-Ḥimyarī from Muḥammad b. Khālid al-Ṭayālisī from the author (Najāshī: 168), and by Abū 'l-Mufaḍḍal al-Shaybānī (d. 387) from Ḥumayd b. Ziyād (d. 310) from Qāsim b. Ismā'īl al-Qurashī (possibly from Ja'far b. Bashīr as may be indicated by an *isnād* in *Kāfī* 8: 217) from the author (*Fihrist*: 74).

The notebook has partially survived in Ṭūsī, *Amālī*: 694–700 (a section of twenty reports, half of which [ibid.: 694–7, # 1478–87] are quoted from a copy handed down through the latter *isnād*,[99] and the other half [ibid.: 697–700, # 1488–97] from a copy received through the first *isnād*; two of these reports are also attested in *Kāfī* 8: 217–18 with a different *isnād*). There are other quotations from Ruzayq in works of *ḥadīth* that are not included in the surviving section. Examples are as follows:

- *Kāfī* 6: 507
- Ibn al-Rāzī, *'Arūs*: 157
- *Manāqib* 3: 223

178: Al-Fazārī al-Ḥadhdhā'

Ṣabbāḥ b. Ṣabīḥ (or Ṣubayḥ), the shoemaker, a Kūfan client of Fazāra and the *imām* of the Mosque of Dār al-Lu'lu' in Kūfa. He was a transmitter from Ja'far al-Ṣādiq and Mūsā al-Kāẓim.

Barqī: 97; Najāshī: 201–2; *Fihrist*: 85; *Rijāl*: 226.

Kitāb

His notebook of *ḥadīth*, related by a number of transmitters including 'Ubays b. Hishām (Najāshī: 202; *Fihrist*: 85). There are a fair number of quotations from this author, listed in Khu'ī 9: 93–94, 97, 385–7 and *Fahāris* 9: 121, by various transmitters including 'Ubays b. Hishām.[100] In the Sunnī tradition, a quotation from him related by his son Muḥammad, appears in Khaṭīb, *Talkhīṣ*: 394–5.

99. As attested in *Biḥār* 63: 406. The *isnād* that should appear in the beginning of this section, and to which the sentence "*wa bi-hādhā 'l-isnād*" at the beginning of all subsequent reports refers, is missing from the edition of Ṭūsī's *Amālī* used in the present work.
100. See, for instance, *Kāfī* 2: 348 (read *Ṣabbāḥ al-Ḥadhdhā'* for *Ṣāliḥ al-Ḥadhdhā'* [the confusion of the two names is not unusual; cf. *Kāfī* 3: 69 with *'Ilal* 1: 262]).

179: Ṣabbāḥ al-Muzanī

Abū Muḥammad Ṣabbāḥ b. Yaḥyā al-Muzanī, a Kūfan transmitter of *ḥadīth*. Clearly a Shī'ite, though possibly not an Imāmite, he was also known to Zaydī and Sunnī circles of *ḥadīth* transmission of his time. He transmitted from the disciples of Muḥammad al-Bāqir and Ja'far al-Ṣādiq, among others.

Bukhārī, *Kābīr* 4: 314–15; Barqī: 97; 'Uqaylī 2: 212; Ibn Abī Ḥātim 4: 442; Kashshī: 44; Ibn Ḥibbān, *Majrūḥīn* 1: 377; Ibn 'Adī: 1402; Ibn al-Ghaḍā'irī: 70; Najāshī: 201; *Fihrist*: 85; *Rijāl*: 226; *Lisān* 3: 559 (and other sources listed in the editor's footnote). See also Furāt: 440.

Kitāb

His notebook of *ḥadīth*, related by a number of transmitters (Najāshī: 201; *Fihrist*: 85). There are a fair number of quotations from this author in Shī'ite works of *ḥadīth*, listed in Khu'ī 9: 98–9 and *Fahāris* 9: 122. His transmissions also appear in Sunnī and Zaydī works, as in the following examples:

- Bukhārī, *Kabīr* 4: 314–15 (two reports)
- Muḥammad b. Sulaymān 1: 215, 312–13 (repeated at 430–31), 352, 360–61
- Ṭabarī, *Tafsīr* 10: 5
  22: 8
- 'Uqaylī 2: 86, 202
- Ṭabarānī, *Kabīr* 12: 79 (read *Muzanī* for *Madīnī*)
- *Ḥilya* 3: 187–8
- Abū 'Abd Allāh al-Shajarī, *Adhān*: 50, 87
- Ibn 'Asākir 1: 297
  42: 296
- 'Abd Allāh b. Ḥamza, *Shāfī* 1: 73, 92, 105–6

180: Sa'd al-Zāmm

Sa'd b. Abī Khalaf, known as al-Zāmm, a Kūfan client of the Banū Zuhra b. Kilāb of Quraysh, and a transmitter from Ja'far al-Ṣādiq and Mūsā al-Kāẓim.

Barqī: 98; Najāshī: 178–9; *Fihrist*: 76; *Rijāl*: 212, 338.

Kitāb

His notebook of *ḥadīth*, related by a number of transmitters, including Ibn Abī 'Umayr (Najāshī: 178–9) and Ḥasan b. Maḥbūb (*Fihrist*: 76). Almost all the quotations from this author in later works, listed in Khu'ī 8: 49, 394–6 and *Fahāris* 9: 22, are through the same transmitters.

181: Ṣafwān al-Jammāl

Abū Muḥammad Ṣafwān b. Mihrān b. al-Mughīra, the cameleer, a Kūfan client of the Banū Kāhil of Asad Khuzayma and a transmitter from Ja'far al-Ṣādiq and Mūsā al-Kāẓim.

Barqī: 110; Kashshī: 440–41; Najāshī: 198; *Fihrist*: 84; *Rijāl*: 227. See also 'Ayyāshī 1: 381.

Kitāb

His notebook of *ḥadīth*, related by a number of transmitters (Najāshī: 198; *Fihrist*: 84; also *Mashyakha*: 436). Quotations from this author, some through the transmitters specifically named in these sources, abound in later works. For lists see Khu'ī 9: 122–3, 137–8, 428, 463–5; *Fahāris* 9: 132, 133–4, 135.

182: Sa'īd al-A'raj

Abū 'Abd Allāh Sa'īd b. 'Abd Allāh al-Taymī, the lame, possibly the oil seller, a Kūfan client and a transmitter from Ja'far al-Ṣādiq and Mūsā al-Kāẓim.

Barqī: 97; Kashshī: 427–8; Najāshī: 181; *Fihrist*: 77; *Rijāl*: 213. See also Muḥammad Taqī al-Tustarī 5: 100–103, 105–106 (cf. Khu'ī 8: 122).

Kitāb / Aṣl

His notebook of *ḥadīth*, related by a number of transmitters including 'Alī b. al-Nu'mān, Ṣafwān b. Yaḥyā (Najāshī: 181; *Fihrist*: 77; *Rijāl*: 213) and 'Abd al-Karīm b. 'Amr al-Khath'amī (*Mashyakha*: 472). The overwhelming majority of the quotations from this author in later works, listed in Khu'ī 8: 107–8, 123–4, 431–4 and *Fahāris* 9: 31, 35, are on the authority of the same transmitters.

183: Ibn Ghazwān

Sa'īd b. Ghazwān, a Kūfan client of the Banū Asad and a notable in the Shī'ite community of Kūfa in his time. He transmitted from Ja'far al-Ṣādiq.

Barqī: 97; Najāshī: 181–2; *Fihrist*: 77; *Rijāl*: 214. See also Kashshī: 279.

Kitāb / Aṣl

His notebook of *ḥadīth*, related by a number of Shī'ite transmitters including Ibn Abī 'Umayr (Najāshī: 182; *Fihrist*: 77). Almost all of the surviving quotations from this author in later works, listed in Khu'ī 8: 128 and *Fahāris* 9: 37, are through the same transmitter.

184: Al-Ḍuba'ī al-Ḥannāṭ

Sa'īd b. Yasār, the wheat seller, a Kūfan client of the Banū Ḍubay'a, a clan of the Banū 'Ijl, and a transmitter from Ja'far al-Ṣādiq and Mūsā al-Kāẓim.

Barqī: 97; *Mashyakha*: 522; Najāshī: 181; *Fihrist*: 77; *Rijāl*: 213.

Kitāb / Aṣl

His notebook of *ḥadīth*, related by a number of Shī'ite transmitters (Najāshī: 181) including Ṣafwān b. Yaḥyā and 'Alī b. al-Nu'mān (*Fihrist*: 77). Most of the quotations from this author in later works, listed in Khu'ī 8: 143–4, 435–8 and *Fahāris* 9: 40, are through the same two transmitters.

185: Ibn 'Uqba

Ṣāliḥ b. 'Uqba b. Qays b. Sim'ān b. Abī Rubayḥa, a client and a transmitter with esoteric tendencies. He lived in the latter half of the second century.

Barqī: 80; Ibn al-Ghaḍā'irī: 69; Najāshī: 200; *Fihrist*: 84–5; *Rijāl*: 227, 338.

Kitāb

His notebook of *ḥadīth*, related by Muḥammad b. Ismā'īl b. Bazī' (Najāshī: 200; *Fihrist*: 84–5). Quotations from this author in later works, listed in Khu'ī 9: 76–7, 380–85 and *Fahāris* 9: 117–18, are predominantly on the authority of the same transmitter.

186: Ṣāliḥ al-Qammāṭ

Abū Sa'īd Ṣāliḥ b. Sa'īd, the maker of swaddling clothes, a client of the Banī Asad and a transmitter from Ja'far al-Ṣādiq.

Najāshī: 199; *Fihrist*: 85; *Rijāl*: 225.

Kitāb

His notebook of *ḥadīth*, related by a number of transmitters including 'Ubays b. Hishām (Najāshī: 199) and Ibrāhīm b. Hāshim (*Fihrist*: 85). The surviving quotations from this author, listed in Khu'ī 9: 65–9, 377–8 and *Fahāris* 9: 37, 116, 577, are mainly on the authority of the same two transmitters.

187: Abū Khadīja al-Jammāl

Abū Khadīja (also known as Abū Salama) Sālim b. Mukram b. 'Abd Allāh al-Kunāsī, the cameleer, a Kūfan client of the Banū Asad and a former follower of the heresiarch Abū 'l-Khaṭṭāb (d. ca. 138); he joined the mainstream Imāmite Shī'ites after surviving the massacre of Abū 'l-Khaṭṭāb and his followers. He was a transmitter from Ja'far al-Ṣādiq.

Barqī: 89; Kashshī: 352–3; Najāshī: 188; *Fihrist*: 79–80; *Rijāl*: 217. See also Nawbakhtī: 69–70; Abū 'l-Ḥasan al-Ash'arī 1: 81.

Kitāb

His notebook of *ḥadīth*, related by a number of Shī'ite transmitters (Najāshī: 188) including his associate Aḥmad b. 'Ā'idh al-Aḥmasī and 'Abd al-Raḥmān b. Abī Hāshim al-Bazzāz (*Fihrist*: 80; also *Mashyakha*: 478). The overwhelming majority of the many quotations from this author in later works, listed in Khu'ī 8: 17, 23, 26–7, 381, 21: 143–4, 386–7 and *Fahāris* 7: 490–91, 9: 6, 8, are through the same two transmitters.

188: Sallām al-Hāshimī

Sallām b. 'Abd Allāh al-Hāshimī, a transmitter from Ja'far al-Ṣādiq.

Najāshī: 189

Kitāb

A small book, related by Abū Sumayna Muḥammad b. 'Alī al-Ṣayrafī (Najāshī: 189). This seems to be the text quoted in full in *Kāfī* 1: 343–5 on the authority of the same transmitter. Another quotation from Sallām through the same Ṣayrafī appears in Nu'mānī: 271–2.

189: Ibn Abī 'Amra

Abū 'Alī Sallām b. Abī 'Amra al-Khurāsānī, a Kūfan transmitter of *ḥadīth* known to both Sunnī and Shī'ite circles of *ḥadīth* transmission at the time. He transmitted from Muḥammad al-Bāqir and Ja'far al-Ṣādiq, among others.

Yaḥyā b. Ma'īn 2: 423; Bukhārī, *Kabīr* 4: 133; Fasawī 3: 40; Ibn Abī Ḥātim 4: 258; Ibn Ḥibbān, *Majrūḥīn* 1: 341; Ibn 'Adī: 1155; Najāshī: 189; *Fihrist*: 82 (as *Sallām b. 'Amr*, possibly a corruption); *Rijāl*: 218; Mizzī 12: 293–4 (and other sources listed in the editor's footnote). See also *Kāfī* 1: 400.

Kitāb

His notebook of *ḥadīth*, related by Ibn 'Uqda from Qāsim b. Muḥammad b. al-Ḥusayn b. Ḥāzim from 'Abd Allāh b. Jabala from the author (Najāshī: 189; *Fihrist*: 82). The notebook has survived on the same *isnād* and is published in *al-Uṣūl al-sittat 'ashar*: 117–19. The surviving text contains ten reports (see further Kohlberg, *Uṣūl*: 156) and seems to be part of a larger notebook as numerous other quotations from this author appear in the sources (see *Fahāris* 9: 49), at least one (Ibn Qūlawayh: 72) through 'Abd Allāh b. Jabala, the first transmitter of this notebook. Two of the reports of the surviving notebook are attested in other early sources: one in Tirmidhī 4: 26, the other in Ibn al-Juḥām: 217.

190: Samā'a Bayyā' al-Qazz

Samā'a b. Mihrān b. 'Abd al-Raḥmān, a producer and dealer in silk cocoons, a Kūfan client of the Ḥaḍārima in whose district in Kūfa he had a mosque, though he lived in the district of Kinda in the city. He was a prolific transmitter from Ja'far al-Ṣādiq, Mūsā al-Kāẓim and their disciples. He died in Medina.

Barqī: 109, 117; Najāshī: 193–4; *Rijāl*: 221, 337.

Kitāb

His notebook of *ḥadīth*, related by many transmitters including 'Uthmān b. 'Īsā al-'Āmirī (Najāshī: 194; also *Mashyakha*: 427). There are close to one thousand quotations from this author in Shī'ite works of *ḥadīth*, listed in Khu'ī 8: 294–302, 463–83 and *Fahāris* 9: 66–8, mainly through the same transmitter.

191: Al-Sarī al-Sulamī

Sarī b. 'Abd Allāh b. Ya'qūb al-Sulamī, a Kūfan transmitter known to both Sunnī and Shī'ite communities of the city and a transmitter from Ja'far al-Ṣādiq, among others.

Ibn 'Adī: 1297–8; Najāshī: 194; *Rijāl*: 222; *Lisān* 3: 230 (and other sources listed in the editor's footnote).

Kitāb

His notebook of *ḥadīth*, related by 'Abbād b. Ya'qūb al-Rawājinī (Najāshī: 194). There are a number of quotations from Ja'far al-Ṣādiq by this author recorded in the sources on the authority of the same transmitter. Examples are as follows:[101]

- Aḥmad b. 'Īsā 3: 88, 119, 124 (also 4: 201, 204, both through a different transmitter)
- Ṭabarī, *Tahdhīb, Ibn 'Abbās*: 348
- Ibn 'Adī: 1297–8 (two reports, with a reference to his "other transmissions from Ja'far al-Ṣādiq")

101. See also 'Ayyāshī 2: 259.

192: Sayf al-Nakha'ī

Sayf b. 'Amīra al-Nakha'ī, a Kūfan transmitter from Ja'far al-Ṣādiq and Mūsā al-Kāẓim.

Barqī: 103, 116; Ibn Ḥibbān, *Thiqāt* 8: 299–300; Najāshī: 189; *Fihrist*: 78–9; *Rijāl*: 222, 337; Mizzī 12: 327–8.

Kitāb

His notebook of *ḥadīth* (Ibn al-Nadīm: 275; Abū Ghālib: 148; Najāshī: 189; *Fihrist*: 78–9; *Rijāl*: 337), related by groups of Shī'ite transmitters (Najāshī: 189) including Muḥammad b. Khālid al-Ṭayālisī (Abū Ghālib: 148; Najāshī: 189), 'Alī b. al-Ḥakam al-Nakha'ī (*Fihrist*: 78–9) and his son 'Alī b. Sayf (*Mashyakha*: 491–2; cf. Muḥammad Taqī al-Tustarī 5: 380).

There are close to three hundred quotations from this author in Shī'ite works of *ḥadīth*, listed in Khu'ī 8: 361–3, 366–9, 538–53 and *Fahāris* 9: 85, 86–7, many, if not most, through the same transmitters. The same is true with some of the quotations from this author in Sunnī sources (e.g. Dāraquṭnī 1: 91; Khaṭīb, *Talkhīṣ*: 517; Ḥaskānī 1: 359).

193: Al-'Aqarqūfī

Shu'ayb b. Ya'qūb al-'Aqarqūfī, a nephew of the prominent Imāmite *ḥadīth* transmitter of Kūfa, Abū Baṣīr Yaḥyā b. al-Qāsim al-Asadī, and a transmitter from Ja'far al-Ṣādiq and Mūsā al-Kāẓim.

Barqī: 84; Kashshī: 442–3; Najāshī: 194; *Fihrist*: 82; *Rijāl*: 224, 338.

Kitāb / Aṣl

His notebook of *ḥadīth*, related by Ḥammād b. 'Īsā, Ibn Abī 'Umayr and others (Najāshī: 195; *Fihrist*: 82). The overwhelming majority of the close to one hundred quotations from this author in later works, listed in Khu'ī 9: 27–9, 36–8, 365–8 and *Fahāris* 9: 99, 100, are through the same two transmitters.

194: Ibn ʻUyayna

Abū Muḥammad Sufyān b. ʻUyayna, the one eyed, the furrier, a Kūfan client of the Banū Hilāl b. ʻĀmir of Hawāzin and a prominent Sunnī transmitter of *ḥadīth* who transmitted from Jaʻfar al-Ṣādiq among many others. He moved to Mecca where he lived until his death in 198 at the age of 89.

Every Sunnī biographical dictionary of the transmitters of *ḥadīth* has an entry on Sufyān b. ʻUyayna. For lists of very many of these as well as other sources, see the editors' footnotes to Mizzī 11: 177–96 and Dhahabī, *Tā'rikh* 13 (years 191–200): 189–91. See also the entries on him in Sezgin 1: 96 and the *Encyclopaedia of Islam*, 2nd edn., 9: 772 (S. Spectorsky).

That he transmitted from Jaʻfar al-Ṣādiq is noted in many Sunnī (see Mizzī 11: 179 and its sources) and Shīʻite (e.g. Barqī: 103; see also Kashshī: 390; *ʻUyūn* 2: 16; *Rijāl*: 220) sources.

Nuskha ʻan Jaʻfar b. Muḥammad

A register of Sufyān's transmissions from Jaʻfar al-Ṣādiq (Najāshī: 190). Many of the numerous quotations from Jaʻfar al-Ṣādiq on the authority of this author in Sunnī and Shīʻite works of *ḥadīth* should most probably go back to this register, including the following examples:

- Shāfiʻī, *Musnad*: 65, 180, 559 (also Ibn al-Ashʻath: 211; cf. Shāfiʻī, *Umm* 1: 247, where Sufyān quotes this passage from *Jaʻfar*, and ʻAbd al-Razzāq 3: 550; Aḥmad 1: 205; Abū Dāwūd 3: 195; Tirmidhī 2: 313; Ibn Māja: 514, where he quotes it from *Jaʻfar b. Khālid*)
- ʻAbd al-Razzāq 1: 19
  3: 474, 502, 572
- Ḥumaydī 2: 342, 343 (two reports), 344, 345 (two reports)
- Ibn Saʻd 2: 223
- Aḥmad 4: 97 (two reports)
- Ibn Māja: 972
- *Maḥāsin*: 233 (also *Kāfī* 1: 50; *Khiṣāl*: 239; *Maʻānī*: 394–5), 550 (whence *Kāfī* 6: 358)
- *Kāfī* 1: 406
  2: 16 (see also *Biḥār* 70: 59 for what seems to be another part of the same report), 72, 129, 164 (repeated with a partially different *isnād* at 298), 415–16

4: 521–2 (also 'Alī b. Ibrāhīm 1: 70; partially also in *Faqīh* 2: 480)
- Furāt: 505–6 (also Ibn al-Juḥām: 405–6; Tha'labī, *al-Kashf wa 'l-bayān* [as quoted in Ibn Ṭāwūs, *Ṭarā'if* 1: 226–7])
- Abū Ya'lā 3: 375
- Ibn 'Adī: 557
- Khazzāz: 61–2 (a report with the full list of the names of the twelve Imāms)
- *'Ilal* 2: 260
- Ṭūsī, *Amālī*: 211, 609
- *Manāqib* 2: 245
  3: 318 (cf. Ibn Biṭrīq, *'Umda*: 461–2)
- Sibṭ Ibn al-Jawzī: 178, 180 (also Kanjī: 468, 470; Irbilī 2: 332–2)

195: Sulaym al-Farrā'

Sulaym, maker of fur cloaks, a Kūfan transmitter from Ja'far al-Ṣādiq and Mūsā al-Kāẓim.

Najāshī: 193; *Rijāl*: 219. He may be the same as the Abū 'Abd Allāh al-Farrā' named in *Mashyakha*: 442 and *Fihrist*: 187.

Kitāb

His notebook of *ḥadīth*, related by a number of transmitters including Ibn Abī 'Umayr (Najāshī: 193; see also *Fihrist*: 187). There are a fair number of quotations from this author in later works, listed in Khu'ī 8: 215, 229–30, 445–6, 21: 229, mainly through the same transmitter.

196: Al-Daylamī

Sulaymān al-Daylamī, a slave merchant who traveled to Khurāsān in the course of his trade and bought slaves from the region of Daylam in northern Iran, bringing them to Kūfa. He was an Extremist. He transmitted from Ja'far al-Ṣādiq and Mūsā al-Kāẓim.

Kashshī: 375; Ibn al-Ghaḍā'irī: 67; Najāshī: 182; *Fihrist*: 78; *Rijāl*: 216.

Najāshī identifies this transmitter as the son of 'Abd Allāh but Ibn al-Ghaḍā'irī as the son of Zakariyyā. According to a report in Najāshī, he was a Kūfan from the tribe of Bajīla, but his son, Muḥammad, is identified as a Baṣran in *Rijāl*: 343, 363 (also 'Ayyāshī 1: 194; *Kāfī* 8: 50 [read *baṣrī* as in the editor's footnote]).

Kashshī, Ibn al-Ghaḍā'irī and Najāshī all know him as an Extremist. The last two also identify him as a liar, a distinction to which a number of his transmissions may well attest.

1. *Kitāb yawm wa layla*

A work related by his son Muḥammad (Najāshī: 182). Two reports quoted from this author through the same transmitter in *Kāfī* 3: 326 and *Tahdhīb* 2: 122 fit the title of this work.

2. *Kitāb*

His notebook of *ḥadīth*, related by his above-mentioned son, Muḥammad (*Fihrist*: 78). All of the close to forty quotations from this author, some of considerable length and most listed in Khu'ī 8: 446–7, 463 and *Fahāris* 9: 61, are through this son.

197: Abū 'l-Rabī' al-Aqṭa'

Abū 'l-Rabī' Sulaymān b. Khālid b. Dihqān b. Nāfila, a Kūfan jurist, transmitter of *ḥadīth*, and expert on the text of the Qur'ān who participated in Zayd b. 'Alī's revolt against the Umayyads in 122 and lost an arm in the event. He was a disciple of Muḥammad al-Bāqir and Ja'far al-Ṣādiq, and died during the lifetime of the latter, thus in or before 148.

Barqī: 56, 88; Kashshī: 356–61; *Mashyakha*: 439; Najāshī: 183; *Rijāl*: 215–16. See also *Kāfī* 5: 467, 8: 250–52.

Kitāb

His notebook of *ḥadīth*, related by 'Abd Allāh b. Muskān (Najāshī: 183) and Hishām b. Sālim (*Mashyakha*: 439). Most of the close to three hundred quotations from this author in Shī'ite works of *ḥadīth*, listed in Khu'ī 8: 252–4, 451–7 and *Fahāris* 9: 60, are through the same two transmitters.

198: Suwayd al-Qallā'

Suwayd b. Muslim al-Qallā', a Kūfan client and a transmitter from Ja'far al-Ṣādiq.

Najāshī: 191; *Fihrist*: 78; *Rijāl*: 223.

Kitāb

His notebook of *ḥadīth*, related by 'Alī b. al-Nu'mān al-Nakha'ī (Najāshī: 191; *Fihrist*: 78). All surviving quotations from this author in later works, listed in Khu'ī 8: 328–9, 488–9, are through the same transmitter.

199: Ṭalḥa al-Shāmī

Ṭalḥa b. Zayd al-Shāmī, a Sunnī transmitter of *ḥadīth* who transmitted from Ja'far al-Ṣādiq, among others. Originally from Damascus, he lived in Raqqa and/or Wāsiṭ.

Bukhārī, *Kabīr* 4: 351; Fasawī 3: 402; Barqī: 111; Nasā'ī, *Ḍu'afā'*: 143; Ibn Abī Ḥātim 4: 479–80; 'Uqaylī 2: 225–6; Ibn Ḥibbān, *Majrūḥīn* 1: 383–4; Ibn 'Adī: 1427–31; Najāshī: 207; *Fihrist*: 86; *Rijāl*: 138, 228: Ibn 'Asākir 25: 24–9; Mizzī 13: 395–8 (and the many sources named in the editor's footnote).

'Uqaylī asserts that this transmitter was in Wāsiṭ. Most others report that he lived in Raqqa (see also Khazzāz: 226). 'Abbād b. Ya'qūb quotes 'Abd Allāh b. al-Ḥasan through Ṭalḥa Bayyā' al-Sāburī in Aḥmad b. 'Īsā 1: 404 (where there is also a quotation from Ja'far al-Ṣādiq through Ṭalḥa in 4: 226). It is not clear whether this refers to Ṭalḥa b. Zayd or a different person.

Kitāb

His notebook of *ḥadīth*, related in various versions by different transmitters (Najāshī: 207), including Muḥammad b. Sinān al-Zāhirī

(*Fihrist*: 86), Muḥammad b. Yaḥyā al-Khazzāz (*Mashyakha*: 480) and possibly 'Abd Allāh b. al-Mughīra.[102] The overwhelming majority of the well over one hundred quotations from this author in Shī'ite works of *ḥadīth*, predominantly from Ja'far al-Ṣādiq, are through the first two transmitters of this notebook. For lists see Khu'ī 9: 164–7, 467–70; *Fahāris* 9: 156. For an example of a quotation from Ja'far al-Ṣādiq through our author in Sunnī sources, see Dāraquṭnī 4: 215 (whence Bayhaqī 10: 173).

200: Al-Sha'rānī

Abū Ṭālib al-Azdī al-Sha'rānī, a Baṣran transmitter from the students of Ja'far al-Ṣādiq.

Ibn al-Ghaḍā'irī: 104; Najāshī: 457, 459–60; *Fibrist*: 187.

Kitāb

A notebook of *ḥadīth*, related by Muḥammad b. Khālid al-Barqī as mentioned in all three sources named above. The following quotations must therefore go back to this notebook:

- *Maḥāsin*: 636
- Ṣaffār: 27, 104, 109, 241, 357, 430[103]
- *Kāfī* 1: 269–70, 417
  2: 578–9 (read *al-Barqī 'an Abī Ṭālib*)
  4: 279
  5: 78
  6: 295

102. This may be indicated by the many quotations from our author through this latter transmitter in, for instance, *Maḥāsin*: 198, 211, 231, 252, 291, 295, 440, 632, 634; *Kāfī* 1: 41, 2: 136, 6: 533; *'Iqāb*: 270; *Ikhtiṣāṣ*: 262 (read *wa Muḥammad b. Sinān*).

103. With the exception of the passage on p. 104, the name of the transmitter from our author is left out in all the quotations from him in this source.

201: Abū Ḥamza al-Thumālī

Abū Ḥamza Thābit b. Dīnār al-Thumālī, a Kūfan client and a prominent scholar and transmitter of *ḥadīth* in the Shī'ite community of his time. He transmitted from 'Alī Zayn al-'Ābidīn, Muḥammad al-Bāqir and Ja'far al-Ṣādiq, and died in 148–150.

Ibn Sa'd 6: 345; Yaḥyā b. Ma'īn 2: 69; Bukhārī, *Kabīr* 2: 165; Fasawī 3: 56; Barqī: 46, 49, 115; Nasā'ī, *Ḍu'afā*: 69; 'Uqaylī 1: 172; Ibn Abī Ḥātim 2: 450–51; Kashshī: 201–3; Ibn Ḥibbān, *Majrūḥīn* 1: 206; Ibn 'Adī: 520; *Mashyakha*: 444; Najāshī: 115–16; *Fihrist*: 41–2; *Rijāl*: 129, 333; Mizzī 4: 357–9 (and other sources listed in the editor's footnote). See also Tirmidhī 3: 423; *Kāfī* 2: 180, 4: 453; Qālī 3: 200; Ḥākim 2: 219.

1. *Tafsīr al-Qur'ān*

(Ibn al-Nadīm: 36; Najāshī: 115–16). A commentary on the Qur'ān on the basis of quotations from the Imāms. This was a well known work in the early centuries, used by such later commentators on the Qur'ān as 'Ayyāshī, Abū Isḥāq al-Tha'labī in *al-Kashf wa 'l-bayān*, and Ṭabrisī in his *Majma' al-bayān*, and referred to by Shahrastānī in his *Mafātīḥ* 1: 170. Ibn Shahrāshūb also quotes from it in *Manāqib* 3: 61 and elsewhere (see ibid. 1: 11). There are many quotations from Abū Ḥamza on the topic in later works, most of them presumably from this work. Recently, 'Abd al-Razzāq Ḥirz al-Dīn has attempted to reconstruct the work by compiling these quotations into a volume entitled *Tafsīr al-Qur'ān al-karīm li-Abī Ḥamza Thābit b. Dīnār al-Thumālī* (Qum, 1420).

2. *Kitāb*

(*Rijāl*: 333). His notebook of *ḥadīth*, related by Ḥasan b. Maḥbūb (*Fihrist*: 41), who must have received it through an intermediary or by *wijāda* (see Kashshī: 585; Najāshī: 82). There are hundreds of quotations from this author in Sunnī and Shī'ite sources, many through the same transmitter. For lists of those in Imāmite Shī'ite sources, see Khu'ī 3: 392–3, 21: 132–6, 371–84, 23: 66; *Fahāris* 8: 255–6, 260–62, 469–70. Examples of similar material in Sunnī and Zaydī works include the following:

- Sayf b. ʻUmar, *Jamal*: 243–4
- ʻAbd al-Razzāq 2: 236
- Ibn Abī Shayba 1: 9 (also Ibn Māja: 143; Tirmidhī 1: 93–4)
- Tirmidhī 3: 422–3
- Ibn Qutayba, *ʻUyūn* 3: 174
- Bazzār 2: 85
- Aḥmad b. ʻĪsā 1: 137
  2: 306
- Ṭabarī 5: 465
- Kharā'iṭī, *Makārim*: 106
- Ṭabarānī, *Ṣaghīr* 2: 82
- Ibn ʻAdī: 520 (three reports)
- Ḥākim 2: 519
- Abū Ṭālib, *Amālī*: 298–9, 313–14, 369–70
- Idem, *Di'āma*: 216
- *Ḥilya* 1: 79–80
  3: 135–6 (two reports), 138, 139–41, 181–2, 183–4
  7: 123
- Khaṭīb, *Bukhalā'*: 57
- Idem, *Mūḍiḥ* 2: 12–13 (two reports)
- Idem, *Talkhīṣ*: 383;
- Idem, *Ta'rīkh* 11: 97
  12: 384
- Bayhaqī, *Dalā'il* 5: 341
- Ibn ʻAsākir 26: 323
  41: 396
  42: 336, 386–7
  50: 251–5
  54: 293
  69: 203
- *Mīzān* 1: 363

3. *Kitāb al-nawādir*

Related from the author by Ḥasan b. Maḥbūb (Najāshī: 116; *Fibrist*: 41). Many of Abū Ḥamza's numerous transmissions mentioned above fit the title of this work.

4. *Kitāb al-zuhd*

(*Fihrist*: 41–2). This should be the same as the text quoted from Abū Ḥamza in *Kāfī* 8: 14–17 as *Ṣaḥīfat 'Alī b. al-Ḥusayn wa kalāmuh fī 'l-zuhd.*

5. *Risālat al-ḥuqūq*

Quoted by Abū Ḥamza from 'Alī Zayn al-'Ābidīn (Najāshī: 116), this text has survived and is published (see above, section I, no. 6, the entry on 'Alī Zayn al-'Ābidīn).

6. *Du'ā' Abī Ḥamza*

The text of a long supplication ascribed to 'Alī Zayn al-'Ābidīn, quoted in full in *Miṣbāḥ*: 582–98 and Ibn Ṭāwūs, *Iqbāl* 1: 157–75 on the authority of Abū Ḥamza.

202: Abū Ismā'īl al-Ṣā'igh

Abū Ismā'īl Thābit b. Shurayḥ al-Anbārī, the jeweler, a Kūfan client of Azd and a transmitter from the disciples of Ja'far al-Ṣādiq.

Najāshī: 116; *Fibrist*: 42; *Rijāl*: 174, 418.

Kitāb fī anwā' al-fiqh / Kitāb

A collection of his transmissions on legal matters, related from him by groups of transmitters including 'Ubays b. Hishām al-Nāshirī and Ṣāliḥ b. Khālid al-Maḥāmilī (Najāshī: 116; *Fihrist*: 42). All surviving quotations from this author on legal matters are recorded in later works on the authority of the same two transmitters who sometimes appear singly (e.g. *Kāfī* 2: 495, 7: 161; *Tahdhīb* 7: 90–91 [# 385, 386]), but mostly both together (e.g. *Kāfī* 6: 84; *Tahdhīb* 2: 247–8, 7: 90 [# 383], 114, 118, 186–7 [two reports]).

203: Abū Isḥāq al-Naḥwī

Abū Isḥāq Tha'laba b. Maymūn, a Kūfan client of the Banū Asad and a prominent scholar in the Shī'ite community of Kūfa in the latter half of the second century. He was an expert on the text of the Qur'ān as well as a jurist, grammarian, and lexicographer. As a *ḥadīth* transmitter he related from Ja'far al-Ṣādiq and his disciples. He lived in the district of Masjid Simāk in Kūfa (see no. 42 above).

Barqī: 106, 117, 118; Kashshī: 412 (see also 375); Najāshī: 117–18; *Rijāl*: 174, 333. See also *Kāfī* 1: 265; *Tahdhīb* 1: 249.

Kitāb

(Abū Ghālib: 184; Najāshī: 118; *Rijāl*: 333). His notebook of *ḥadīth*, related by groups of transmitters including 'Abd Allāh b. Muḥammad al-Asadī al-Ḥajjāl (Najāshī: 118; also *Mashyakha*: 525; Abū Ghālib: 184) and Ḥasan b. 'Alī b. Faḍḍāl (as appears from the *isnād*s of his transmissions from our author). There are close to two hundred quotations from this author in later works, listed in Khu'ī 3: 410–12, 529–40; 21: 19, 279 and *Fahāris* 8: 257–8, predominantly through the same two transmitters.

204: 'Ubayd Allāh al-Ḥalabī

'Ubayd Allāh b. 'Alī b. Abī Shu'ba al-Ḥalabī, brother of Muḥammad (no. 147 above), a distinguished member of the Shī'ite community of Kūfa in the mid-second century. He transmitted from Ja'far al-Ṣādiq.

Barqī: 73; Najāshī: 231; *Fibrist*: 106–7; *Rijāl*: 234.

1. Al-Jāmi' / Kitāb

Allegedly the first systematic legal work ever written in the Shī'ite community (Barqī: 73), it was reportedly presented to Ja'far al-Ṣādiq who praised the book and corrected it (Najāshī: 231; *Fibrist*: 106). A large work organized in chapters (Najāshī: 366), it was a well known source of reference within the Shīʿite community until the late fourth century (*Faqīh* 1: 3) and the early fifth century (Murtaḍa, *Mayyāfāriqiyyāt*: 279; idem, *Rassiyya al-ūlā*: 331). Qāḍī Nuʿmān, who refers to this work as *Jāmiʿ al-Ḥalabī* or *al-Kitāb al-maʿrūf bi 'l-Jāmiʿ*, seems to have incorporated the entire work in his own *Īḍāḥ*, as attested by the many quotations from it in the small surviving fragment of the latter work: 4b, 21b, 24a, 27a, 39a, 40b, 41b, 43b, 55b, 56b, 57a, 59a, 60b, 63b, 64b, 65b, 67b, 82b, 86a, 93b, 107b, 108b–109a, 110b, 115a, 118a, 119b, 126a, 129b.

This book was related from the author by many Shīʿite transmitters, with slight differences at the beginning of the text in the various versions (Najāshī: 231) as well as minor variations in the main body of the text (see, for example, 'Ayyāshī 1: 76). The most common version was that related by Ibn Abī 'Umayr from Ḥammād b. 'Uthmān from the author (Abū Ghālib: 162; Najāshī: 231; *Fihrist*: 106), to which Ibn Abī 'Umayr occasionally added some additional material (*Maʿānī*: 149–50). This version of the book appears to have been preserved in its entirety in later works, as shown by almost a thousand quotations from this author through the same chain of transmission in the four main works of Shīʿite *ḥadīth*, as listed in Khu'ī 6: 189, 217, 390–400, 419–21.

The book was still available in the mid-seventh century to Ibn Ṭāwūs who cites from it in his *Muḍāyaqa*: 340–41 (two paragraphs) and *Iqbāl* 1: 48–9 (see further Kohlberg: 126).

2. *Kitāb al-masā'il*

A collection of questions on legal matters posed to Jaʿfar al-Ṣādiq together with his answers. This seems to have been part of the larger version of Ḥalabī's *Kitāb* referred to in *Rijāl*: 431, but (as attested by paragraphs cited from it in Qāḍī Nuʿmān's *Īḍāḥ*) different in style from the former book as the material of the book in question related to specific questions of detail and the paragraphs were in the original question and answer format (compare, for instance, the paragraph in *Īḍāḥ*: 64a from *Kitāb al-masā'il* with ibid.: 4b from *Jāmiʿ*).

Many of the responses by Jaʿfar al-Ṣādiq to various questions, quoted by Ḥalabī in his many transmissions listed in Khu'ī 11: 419–21, 23: 333–41 and *Fahāris* 8: 450–52, 9: 308, 310, may have originally belonged to this work. Qāḍī Nuʿmān frequently cited from this work in his *Īḍāḥ*, including the following cases found in the surviving fragment of that work:

15a, 17b, 23a, 24a, 26b, 31a, 32b, 33a, 35b, 39a, 41b, 43a, 49a, 52b, 53b, 62b, 64a, 67a, 85b, 86a, 91a, 91b, 94a, 96b, 97b–98a, 102a, 103a, 105a, 107a, 115a, 119b, 121a–121b, 122b, 125b, 126a, 129a

In 39a, he quotes a passage from both works (*fī kitāb al-Ḥalabī al-ma'rūf bi-Kitāb al-masā'īl wa fī kitābih al-ma'rūf bi 'l-Jāmi'*).

205: Al-Waṣṣāfī

'Ubayd Allāh b. al-Walīd b. 'Abd al-Raḥmān al-Waṣṣāfī al-'Ijlī, a Kūfan transmitter of *ḥadīth* known to both Sunnī and Shī'ite circles of *ḥadīth* transmission of Kūfa and a transmitter from Muḥammad al-Bāqir and Ja'far al-Ṣādiq, among others.

Khalīfa b. Khayyāṭ, *Ṭabaqāt*: 391; Yaḥyā b. Ma'īn 2: 384; Bukhārī, *Kabīr* 5: 402; Fasawī 1: 718; Barqī: 51; 'Uthmān al-Dārimī, *Ta'rīkh*: 158; Nasā'ī, *Ḍu'afā'*: 155; 'Uqaylī 3: 128–9; Ibn Abī Ḥātim 5: 336; Ibn Ḥibbān, *Majrūḥīn* 2: 63; Ibn Adī: 1630–31; Dāraquṭnī, *Ḍu'afā'*: 116; Najāshī: 231; *Rijāl*: 234; Mizzī 19: 173–5 (and other sources listed in the editor's footnotes).

His *kunya* is given as *Abū Ismā'īl* by Ibn 'Adī: 1630, but as *Abū Sa'īd* by Najāshī. That he had a son named *Sa'īd* is attested in Mizzī 19: 174. His transmissions appear in Bukhārī's *Adab*, Ibn Māja and Tirmidhī (as well as Ibn 'Adī: 1630–31), among others.

Kitāb

His notebook of *ḥadīth*, related by a number of transmitters including 'Abd Allāh b. Muskān (Abū Ghālib: 174; Najāshī: 231). The following quotations from this author in Shī'ite works of *ḥadīth*, some through the same transmitter, may go back to this notebook:

- Ḥusayn b. Sa'īd, *Zuhd*: 31 (also *Kāfī* 4: 8, 28, 29–30 [read *'Ubayd Allāh* for *'Abd Allāh* in both, as in Ibn Bābawayh, *Amālī*: 326–7 and Ṭūsī, *Amālī*: 603]), 38 (read as above)
- *Maḥāsin*: 30 (read *Isḥāq 'an 'Ubayd Allāh b. al-Walīd* as in *Kāfī* 2: 517; *Thawāb*: 16), 98, 193, 284 (by Ibn Muskān; also in 'Ayyāshī 2: 29; *Kāfī* 2: 188–9, 4: 15 and *Thawāb*: 205 provide other parts of this report; a different version of the report appears in *Kāfī* 8: 42–9 on a different authority), 294, 388, 391 (also *Kāfī* 2: 202), 392 (three variants of the same text)

- Aḥmad b. ʿĪsā 2: 307
  4: 340, 361
- *Kāfī* 2: 95 (also Ṭūsī, *Amālī*: 204), 110, 156, 165, 188–9 (by Ibn Muskān), 668 (see also 2: 156)
  4: 15
- *Thawāb*: 205–6
- Ṭūsī, *Amālī*: 264

Examples of his Shīʿite transmissions in Sunnī sources include the following:

- Ibn Saʿd, *Ḥusayn*: 34–5
- Ibn Abī Shayba 8: 550 (also Bukhārī, *Adab*: 419–20)
- Ibn Abī 'l-Dunyā, *Iṣlāḥ*: 328 (also idem, *Tawāḍuʿ*: 173–4)
- Ibn Ḥibbān, *Majrūḥīn* 2: 64 (also *Ḥilya* 5: 10; Khaṭīb, *Ta'rīkh* 6: 301; Abū Ṭālib: 445)
- Ibn ʿAdī: 1631 (also *Ḥilya* 5: 10–11)
- *Ḥilya* 3: 187
- ʿĀṣimī 1: 16–17
- Ibn ʿAsākir 13: 247
  54: 293
- Ibn Kathīr 1: 514

206: ʿUbayd b. Zurāra

ʿUbayd b. Zurāra b. Aʿyan, a Kūfan client of the Banū Shaybān of Bakr b. Wā'il and member of the prominent Shīʿite family of the Āl Aʿyan (see below, no. 234). He was a Shīʿite *mutakallim* as well as a *ḥadīth* transmitter, mainly from Jaʿfar al-Ṣādiq.

Barqī: 74; Ibn al-Nadīm: 276; *Mashyakha*: 441; Abū Ghālib: 114; Najāshī: 233–4; *Fihrist*: 107–8; *Rijāl*: 243. See also Nawbakhtī: 79; Saʿd b. ʿAbd Allāh: 88; Kashshī; 154; *Ma'ānī*: 266–7 (also *ʿUyūn* 1: 310–11).

For an example of his theological views, see Abū 'l-Ḥasan al-Ashʿarī 1: 112.

Kitāb

His notebook of *ḥadīth*, related by a number of transmitters including Ḥammād b. ʿUthmān (Najāshī: 233–4) and Qāsim b. Ismāʿīl al-Qurashī

(*Fibrist*: 107–8). Many of the over two hundred citations from this author in the four main works of Shī'ite *ḥadīth,* listed in Khu'ī 11: 44–5, 49–52, 412–19, are through Ḥammād b. 'Uthmān, as well as 'Abd Allāh b. Bukayr who seems to have been another principal transmitter of this notebook.

207: Udaym

Abū 'l-Ḥurr Udaym b. al-Ḥurr was a Kūfan client and a transmitter from Ja'far al-Ṣādiq.

Kashshī: 347; Najāshī: 106; *Rijāl:* 156; *Lisān* 1: 512.

There are some doubts about the tribal affiliation and profession of this transmitter. While Najāshī identifies him as *Ju'fī*, Ṭūsī (*Rijāl:* 156) calls him a *Khath'amī.* Yet in the chain of transmission of a report he quoted from Ja'far al-Ṣādiq, he is referred to as *Khuzā'ī* (*Tahdhīb* 5: 329). These names look similar in the Arabic script and the disagreement may have been caused by misreadings. However, his brother, Ayyūb, who like Udaym has been identified by Barqī: 84 and Najāshī: 103 as Ju'fī, is described in *Rijāl*: 331 as the client of Ṭarīf, probably referring to a member of the tribe of Ju'fī who was so named and not to Ṭarīf, the clan of Khazraj. As for profession, both Udaym ('Āṣim b. Ḥumayd: 40; *Kāfī* 5: 426) and his brother, Ayyūb (*Maḥāsin*: 276; also *Kāfī* 5: 78 where the adjective may refer to either Udaym or Ayyūb) are described as *Bayyā' al-Harawī,* that is, seller of the clothing made in Herat (see above, no. 50). However, Kashshī: 347 says that Udaym was a shoemaker. The two also had a third brother named Yaḥyā, also a transmitter of *ḥadīth* (see *Kāfī* 1: 373), possibly the same as the one mentioned by Barqī: 86 and *Rijāl*: 322 as Yaḥyā, brother of Ādam.[104] *Ādam* was in all likelihood the real name of our transmitter and *Udaym* its diminutive form, as in the case of the early third century Imāmite author, 'Ubays b. Hishām al-Nāshirī whose real name was 'Abbās.[105]

Aṣl

(Najāshī: 106). Kashshī: 347 reports that Udaym transmitted over forty *ḥadīths* from Ja'far al-Ṣādiq. The few surviving quotations from Udaym in the early collections of Shī'ite *ḥadīth* may represent this notebook, including the following examples:

104. *Dārim* in the case of "Yaḥyā, the brother of Dārim" in *Kāfī* 2: 106 does not seem to be a corruption as the man appears as Yaḥyā b. Zakariyyā in *Maḥāsin*: 182.
105. See Najāshī: 280.

- ʿĀṣim b. Ḥumayd: 40
- Aḥmad b. Muḥammad b. ʿĪsā: 108–9 (also *Kāfī* 5: 426)
- *Maḥāsin*: 460–61
- Ṣaffār: 177, 291, 386 (whence *Ikhtiṣāṣ*: 330–31), 427
- *Kāfī* 3: 75
- *Tahdhīb* 1: 16
  2: 167–8, 260
  5: 329
  7: 305

208: Abū Ḥafṣ al-Kalbī

Abū Ḥafṣ ʿUmar b. Abān, a Kūfan client of the Banū Kalb b. Wabara of Quḍāʿa and a transmitter from Muḥammad al-Bāqir and Jaʿfar al-Ṣādiq.

Barqī: 93; Najāshī: 285 (see also 28); *Fihrist*: 114; *Rijāl*: 253.

Kitāb

His notebook of *ḥadīth*, related by a number of transmitters including ʿAbbās b. ʿĀmir al-Qaṣabānī (Najāshī: 285; *Fihrist*: 114). There are a good number of quotations from this author in later works, listed in Khuʾī 13: 10–11, 361–3 and *Fahāris* 9: 454, some (e.g. *Kamāl*: 349) through the same transmitter but mostly through Faḍāla b. Ayyūb who seems to have been another principal transmitter of this notebook.

209: ʿUmar al-Thaqafī

ʿUmar b. ʿAbd Allāh b. Yaʿlā b. Murra al-Thaqafī, a Kūfan Sunnī transmitter of *ḥadīth* who was accused by his colleagues of irreligiousity on account of his wine drinking. He occasionally transmitted from Muḥammad al-Bāqir, among others.

Yaḥyā b. Maʿīn 2: 431; Bukhārī, *Kabīr* 2: 113, 6: 170; Fasawī 3: 111; Nasāʾī, *Ḍuʿafāʾ*: 191; ʿUqaylī 3: 176–7; Ibn Abī Ḥātim 3: 118–19; Ibn Ḥibbān, *Majrūḥīn* 2: 91; Ibn

'Adī: 1692–3; Najāshī: 286; Mizzī 21: 417–20 (and other sources listed in the editor's footnote).

Ibn Māja and Abū Dāwūd quote him in their works (see also Ibn 'Adī: 1692–3 for six other reports; also Bukhārī, *Kabīr* 6: 170). For an example of his transmission from Muḥammad al-Bāqir, see *Kāfī* 8: 122–3 (also 'Alī b. Ibrāhīm 1: 98–9).

Nuskha

A register of reports that this transmitter quoted from his father 'Abd Allāh, who quoted from his own father Ya'lā b. Murra (a Companion, on whom see Mizzī 32: 398–9) from 'Alī (Najāshī: 286). There are quotations from 'Alī in later works that this author relates through the same family *isnād* and thus clearly belong to this register (e.g. Naṣr b. Muzāḥim: 135–6; Muḥammad b. Sulaymān 2: 481 [also Ibn 'Adī: 1654; whence Ibn 'Asākir 42: 270]; Mufīd, *Amālī*: 113). The register was not, however, entirely from 'Alī as attested by a number of reports that this author quotes through the same *isnād* from the Prophet without 'Alī as the intermediary or even as the subject.[106] Five of these are cited in Ṭabarānī, *Kabīr* 22: 261–2 (the first also in idem, *Ṭiwāl*: 137–8 [see also Aḥmad 4: 170, 173 where the same report is quoted from Ya'lā b. Murra through a different *isnād*]; the third and the fourth also in 'Uqaylī 3: 177), a sixth one in Aḥmad 4: 171 (see also Ṭabarānī, *Kabīr* 22: 266 where this report is quoted from 'Umar's father, 'Abd Allāh b. Ya'lā, by a different transmitter), possibly a seventh in Aḥmad 4: 174–5 (read, most likely, *'Umar b. 'Abd Allāh* b. Ya'lā b. Murra for *'Amr b. 'Uthmān* b. Ya'lā b. Murra; no son of Ya'lā b. Murra is named elsewhere as 'Uthmān, nor a grandson as 'Amr b. 'Uthmān), and an eighth in Bayhaqī 4: 145 (from *'Umar b. Ya'lā b. Murra*; cf. Aḥmad 4: 177 [quoting the same report from 'Amr b. Ya'lā b. Murra]; Ṭabarānī, *Kabīr* 22: 264 [from 'Imrān al-Thaqafī from Ya'lā b. Murra]; ibid. 22: 263 [from the son of Ya'lā b. Murra]). In Aḥmad 4: 173, our author quotes his grandfather, Ya'lā, through another family member.

106. There is of course the less likely possibility that the *Nuskha* in question did not include everything that this transmitter quoted through that family *isnād*.

210: Ibn Udhayna

'Umar b. Udhayna, from the Banū 'Abd al-Qays of Asad Rabī'a, by descent or as a client, a prominent Shī'ite transmitter from Ja'far al-Ṣādiq and Mūsā al-Kāẓim.

Barqī: 69, 115; Kashshī: 334; Najāshī: 283–4; *Fihrist*: 113; *Rijāl*: 254, 313, 339.

There are considerable discrepancies between the different accounts regarding some significant biographical details of this transmitter (see Muḥammad Taqī al-Tustarī 8: 160–62). It is not unlikely that some of the details may relate to a different person with a similar name.

1. *Kitāb al-farā'iḍ*

On the laws of inheritance, related by Ibn Abī 'Umayr (Najāshī: 283–4; also mentioned in *Fihrist*: 113). The bulk of the material of this work seems to have survived in *Kāfī* 7: 35, 80, 82, 85, 87, 91–2, 93, 94–5, 96, 98, 100–103, 109, 128 (also *Faqīh* 4: 263–4, 265, 268, 277–9, 280, 284, 349; 'Alī b, Ibrāhīm 1: 160) on the authority of the same transmitter. The passage ibid. 7: 91 may have been the opening paragraph of the book.

2. *Kitāb*

His notebook of *ḥadīth*, related by Ibn Abī 'Umayr and Ṣafwān b. Yaḥyā (Abū Ghālib: 163; *Fihrist*: 113; *Rijāl*: 339). There were in fact two versions of this notebook which differed in length (*Fihrist*: 113). Abū Ghālib: 163 received the whole of one version and the third part of the other, both as related by Ibn Abī 'Umayr. The overwhelming majority of the over five hundred quotations from this author in later works, listed in Khu'ī 13: 20–21, 363–74, 22: 354–62, are through the same transmitter. Ibn Ṭāwūs quotes from the book of 'Umar b. Udhayna in *Falāḥ*: 185–6 (see further Kohlberg: 229) a passage that appears in the surviving abridged version of 'Ayyāshī 1: 127 without *isnād*. A passage in *Tahdhīb* 8: 28 may also belong to a book by our author.

211: 'Umar Bayyā' al-Sāburī

Abū 'l-Aswad 'Umar b. Yazīd, seller of Shāpūrī clothing, a Kūfan client of Thaqīf and a transmitter from Ja'far al-Ṣādiq and Mūsā al-Kāẓim.

Barqī: 93, 115; Kashshī: 331; Najāshī: 283; *Fihrist*: 113; *Rijāl*: 252, 339. See also Nawbakhtī: 78; Sa'd b. 'Abd Allāh: 88; Muḥammad Taqī al-Tustarī 8: 225–7, 234–6.

Kitāb fī manāsik al-ḥajj wa farā'iḍih

A book on the rituals of the *ḥajj* with all of its material quoted from Ja'far al-Ṣādiq (Najāshī: 283). It was related from the author by Muḥammad b. 'Udhāfir and others (ibid.; see also *Fihrist*: 113; *Rijāl*: 339). The author himself regularly attended the annual pilgrimage to Mecca (Najāshī: 283).

The following citations from this author on the topic, predominantly through the same transmitter, are probably from the work in question:

- 'Ayyāshī 1: 86
- *Kāfī* 4: 245, 251, 260, 308, 309, 327, 419, 452–3 (also *Tahdhīb* 5: 445–6 with variations), 471, 543
- Ibn Qūlawayh: 449–50
- *Thawāb*: 71
- *Tahdhīb* 5: 22, 34, 44, 56, 70, 71, 85, 92, 95–6 (two reports), 139, 143, 157, 169, 172, 173, 240, 245, 250, 264, 300, 313, 334, 338, 394, 435–6 (two reports)

212: 'Uqba al-Asadī

'Uqba b. Khālid, a Kūfan client of the Banū Asad and a transmitter from Ja'far al-Ṣādiq.

Barqī: 109; Kashshī: 344; Najāshī: 299; *Fihrist*: 118, *Rijāl*: 261. See also *Kāfī* 4: 34.

Kitāb

His notebook of *ḥadīth*, related by his son ʻAlī (no. 37 above) and Muḥammad b. ʻAbd Allāh b. Hilāl (Najāshī: 299; *Fihrist*: 118). Most of the over fifty quotations from this author in later works, listed in Khu'ī 11: 447–9 and *Fahāris* 9: 335, 336, are through the same two transmitters.

213: Ibn Abī Maymūna

Wahb b. ʻAbd Rabbih b. Abī Maymūna b. Yasār, a Kūfan client of the Banū Asad and member of a distinguished Shīʻite family of Kūfa at the time. He was a transmitter from Jaʻfar al-Ṣādiq.

Barqī: 103; Kashshī: 413–14; Najāshī: 430 (see also 27); *Fihrist*: 172; *Rijāl*: 317.

Kitāb

His notebook of *ḥadīth*, related by Ḥasan b. Maḥbūb (Najāshī: 430; *Fihrist*: 172). There are a fair number of quotations from this author in later works, listed in Khu'ī 19: 395–6 and *Fahāris* 10: 458, mainly through the same transmitter.

214: Abū 'l-Bakhtarī

Abū 'l-Bakhtarī Wahb b. Wahb b. Kathīr b. ʻAbd Allāh b. Zamaʻa al-Qurashī al-Madanī, a Sunnī transmitter of *ḥadīth* notorious for unreliability and forgery. Born and raised in Medina, he later moved to Baghdad where he was appointed by Hārūn al-Rashīd as a judge. In 192, he moved back to Medina as the judge of the town for a while, was dismissed in 194 and returned to Iraq where he again served as judge for a while from 195 on, and died in Baghdad in 199 or 200. He was reportedly a stepson of Jaʻfar al-Ṣādiq and ascribed much of his own transmission to him.

Ibn Sa'd 7: 239–40; Yaḥyā b. Ma'īn 2: 637; Muṣ'ab al-Zubayrī: 222; Khalīfa b. Khayyāṭ, *Ṭabaqāt*: 853; Bukhārī, *Kabīr* 8: 170; Barqī: 67; Wakī' 1: 243–54; 'Uqaylī 4: 324–5; Ibn Abī Ḥātim 9: 25–6; Kashshī: 309–10; Ibn Ḥibbān, *Majrūḥīn* 3: 74–5; Ibn 'Adī: 2526–9; Ibn al-Nadīm: 113; Ibn al-Ghaḍā'irī: 100; Najāshī: 430; *Fihrist*: 105,173; *Rijāl*: 317; Khaṭīb, *Ta'rīkh* 13: 451–7; *Lisān* 7: 344–9 (and the many other sources listed in the editor's footnote).

For the dates of his service as a judge in different towns, see especially Wakī' 1: 243–54; Khalīfa b. Khayyāṭ, *Ta'rīkh*: 753, 759.

1. *Kitāb*

Abū 'l-Bakhtarī wrote a number of books, some of which are named in the sources (Ibn al-Nadīm: 113 [whence Sezgin 1: 267]; Najāshī: 430; *Fihrist*: 173). The one of interest to the Shī'ites was his notebook of transmissions from Ja'far al-Ṣādiq.[107] This notebook was related from him by a number of Shī'ite transmitters including Sindī b. Muḥammad al-Bazzāz, as well as Aḥmad b. Muḥammad b. Khālid al-Barqī who quoted it from the author through his own father (Najāshī: 430; *Fihrist*: 105–6, 173). Almost all of the over one hundred and fifty quotations from Ja'far al-Ṣādiq by this author in Shī'ite works of *ḥadīth*, many listed in Khu'ī 19: 201–3, 210–13, 394–5, 396 and *Fahāris* 10: 459, are recorded on the authority of the same two transmitters. 'Abd Allāh b. Ja'far al-Ḥimyarī quotes a large section of this notebook comprising 136 reports as related by Sindī al-Bazzāz in his own *Qurb al-isnād*: 51–4, 130–39, 160, 176 (# 165–77 [except for 167–9], 454–579, 583–4, 645). Other quotations from Ja'far al-Ṣādiq by Abū 'l-Bakhtarī can be found in Sunnī and Zaydī sources as in the following examples:

- Yaḥyā b. Ma'īn 2: 175 (also Ibn 'Adī: 2526 and others)
- Ibn Qutayba, *Gharīb al-ḥadīth* 1: 523
- Wakī' 1: 253
- 'Āṣimī 1: 150–51
- Abū 'Abd Allāh al-Shajarī, *Adhān*: 52
- *Firdaws* (three reports [Uzbak: 652, 720, 733])
- Suyūṭī, *La'ālī* 1: 103–4

---

107. Ironically, Abū 'l-Bakhtarī was notorious for ascribing his own forgeries to Ja'far al-Ṣādiq (see especially Wakī' 1: 248, 252–3 [whence Khaṭīb, *Ta'rīkh* 13: 452–3, 455]). Shī'ite scholars were well aware of this fact (Kashshī: 309; Najāshī: 430; Ibn al-Ghaḍā'irī: 100) but nevertheless quoted some of his transmissions that were not transparent forgeries, in the hope that some may be genuine.

2. *Tafsīr [sūrat] Qul huwa 'llāhu aḥad*

A commentary on chapter 112 of the Qur'ān, either as an independent tract or part of a larger work on *tafsīr* by Abū 'l-Bakhtarī. The text is quoted in full by Ibn Bābawayh in his *Tawḥīd*: 88–93 (partially also in *Ma'ānī*: 7–8). This is a valuable text as it offers a good insight into the original style of the author and, very likely, of some other works of this genre from the latter part of the second century.

215: Ibn Ṣubayḥ

Walīd b. Ṣubayḥ, a Kūfan client of the Banū Asad and a transmitter from Ja'far al-Ṣādiq.

Barqī: 104; Kashshī: 319; Najāshī: 431; *Rijāl*: 316. See also *Kāfī* 2: 510, 3: 562, 4: 118.

Kitāb

His notebook of *ḥadīth*, related by his son 'Abbās (Najāshī: 431). There are a good number of quotations from this author in later works, listed in Khu'ī 19: 193, 195–7, 393–4 and *Fahāris* 10: 452, many through the same transmitter.

216: Al-Mantūf

Abū 'Alī Wuhayb b. Ḥafṣ al-Jurayrī, the slave merchant, known as al-Mantūf, a Kūfan client of the Banū Asad and a transmitter from the prominent Imāmite *ḥadīth* transmitter of Kūfa, Abū Baṣīr Yaḥyā b. al-Qāsim al-Asadī. He joined the Wāqifites after the death of Mūsā al-Kāẓim.

Mashyakha: 465; Najāshī: 431; *Fihrist*: 173; *Rijāl*: 317.

1. *Tafsīr al-qur'ān*

A commentary on the Qur'ān, related by Ḥasan b. Muḥammad b. Samā'a (Najāshī: 431). The following quotations on the topic from this author, mostly through the same transmitter, should represent part of the material of this work:

(A) **GENERAL:**

- *Kāfī* 2: 601
- Ibn Ṭāwūs, *Iqbāl* 1: 232

(B) **ON SPECIFIC VERSES:**

- *Tahdhīb* 2: 43–4 (on Qur'ān 2: 142)
- *Ghayba*: 477–8 (on 2: 148)
- *Tahdhīb* 5: 235–6 (on 2: 196)
- Ṣaffār: 203; 'Alī b. Ibrāhīm 2: 451(on 3: 7)
- *Tahdhīb* 8: 243 (on 4: 23)
- Nu'mānī: 51–2 (on 4: 58)
- *Kāfī* 7: 119 (on 8: 75)
- Ḥasan b. Sulaymān: 21 (see also 'Ayyāshī 2: 113 where the text appears without *isnād* in the current version) (on 9: 111–12)
- *Kāfī* 2: 95 (on 20: 1–2)
- Ibid. 8: 229 (on 23: 60)
- Ibid. 3: 504 (on 23: 99)
- *Irshād* 2: 373 (on 26: 4)
- *Kāfī* 6: 139 (on 33: 28)
- Ibid. 2: 496 (on 37: 180)
- Nu'mānī: 269 (on 41: 53)
- 'Alī b. Ibrāhīm 2: 303 (on 47: 16)
- *Tahdhīb* 6: 153 (on 76: 8)

2. *Kitāb fī 'l-sharā'i'*

A book on matters of law, organized in chapters, related by Ḥasan b. Muḥammad b. Samā'a (Najāshī: 421). It should be identical with the work named in the *Fibrist*: 173 as *Kitāb*, related by Muḥammad b. Ḥusayn b. Abī 'l-Khaṭṭāb.

With very few exceptions, all of the over fifty quotations from this author on legal matters, listed in Khu'ī 19: 204–7, 214–17, 396–8, are on the authority of the same two transmitters.

217: Wuhayb al-Karābīsī

Abū Bakr Wuhayb b. Khālid b. 'Ajlān, a seller of canvas, a Baṣran client of Bāhila of Qays 'Aylān, and a Sunnī transmitter of *ḥadīth* who transmitted from Ja'far al-Ṣādiq, among others. He died in 165 or 169 at the age of 58.

Ibn Sa'd 7: 211; Yaḥyā b. Ma'īn 2: 637; Khalīfa b. Khayyāṭ, *Ta'rīkh*: 478; Bukhārī, *Kabīr* 8: 177; 'Ijlī: 467; Fasawī 2: 129–32; Ibn Abī Ḥātim 9: 34–5; Ibn Ḥibbān, *Mashāhīr*: 252; idem, *Thiqāt* 7: 560, and other sources listed in the editors' footnotes to Mizzī 31: 164–8 and Dhahabī, *Ta'rīkh* 10 (years 161–170): 503–4.

Nuskha 'an Abī 'Abd Allāh

A register of *ḥadīth*s that Wuhayb related from Ja'far al-Ṣādiq (Najāshī: 431). There are a number of quotations from Ja'far al-Ṣādiq through this transmitter in later works (e.g. Ṭayālisī 3: 245–6, 246–9 [the lengthy report on the Prophet's pilgrimage to Mecca; also in Abū Ya'lā 4: 23–6; Ibn Ḥibbān 9: 250–52]; Aḥmad 3: 365; Bukhārī, *Adab*: 322) that may go back to this register.

218: Yaḥyā al-Rāzī

Yaḥyā b. al-'Alā' al-Bajalī al-Rāzī, a Kūfan Sunnī transmitter who moved to Ray as the town's judge. He transmitted *ḥadīth* from Ja'far al-Ṣādiq, among others.

Yaḥyā b. Ma'īn 2: 651; Bukhārī, *Kabīr* 8: 297; Abū Zur'a al-Rāzī: 527, 669; Fasawī 3: 141; Barqī: 86 (see also 53); Nasā'ī, *Ḍu'afā'*: 249; 'Uqaylī 4: 437; Ibn Abī Ḥātim 9: 179–80; Ibn Ḥibbān, *Majrūḥīn* 3: 115–16; Ibn 'Adī: 2655–8; Dāraquṭnī, *Ḍu'afā'*: 177; Najāshī: 126, 444; *Rijāl*: 149, 321; Mizzī 31: 484–8 (and other sources listed in the editor's footnote).

Rijāl: 321 has him as Yaḥyā b. al-'Alā' b. Khālid but *Fihrist*: 178 as Yaḥyā b. Abī 'l-'Alā' al-Rāzī. Ibn 'Adī: 2655 identifies him as a Medinese by origin but most others as a Kūfan. He lived in a district or suburb of Ray called Fawarzād (Mizzī 31: 484; perhaps the same as the *Farrazād* of Yāqūt 4: 249, which could be the present day Faraḥzād of Tehran; there is also a *Furārd* named in Yāqūt 4: 279 as a village of Ray). That he was the judge of Ray is attested in *Ḥilya* 3: 201 and Najāshī: 126. That he transmitted from Ja'far al-Ṣādiq is mentioned by Najāshī: 126; Mizzī 23: 484, and others.

Kitāb

His notebook of *ḥadīth*, related by a number of transmitters including his son, Abū Muḥammad Ja'far (Najāshī: 126, 444; see also *Fihrist*: 178). The Shī'ites were interested in this notebook because of the author's transmissions from Ja'far al-Ṣādiq. A fair number of these are quoted in Shī'ite works of *ḥadīth*, as listed in Khu'ī 20: 23–5, 251 and *Fahāris* 10: 473, some through the *isnād* specified in *Fihrist*: 178 (e.g. *'Ilal* 2: 87–8) but most through Abān b. 'Uthmān al-Aḥmar who seems to have been a principal transmitter of this notebook. There are other quotations from Ja'far al-Ṣādiq through this author in Sunnī and Zaydī works. Examples include the following:

- 'Abd al-Razzāq 5: 486–9 (whence Ṭabarānī, *Kabīr* 22: 410–12; 'Āṣimī 1: 142–4)
- Aḥmad b. 'Īsā 4: 203
- *Ḥilya* 3: 201
- Ṭabarānī, *Akhbār al-Ḥasan*: 69 (also idem, *Kabīr* 3: 44; Ibn 'Adī: 2657)
- Ibn al-Maghāzilī: 111–12 (also Khuzā'ī: 161–2)

Other "Shī'ite" transmissions of his appear in Muḥammad b. Sulaymān 1: 297, 439; Khaṭīb, *Mūḍiḥ* 1: 190.

219: Yaḥyā al-Ḥalabī

Yaḥyā b. 'Imrān b. 'Alī b. Abī Shu'ba al-Ḥalabī, a Kūfan client and a member of the prominent Shī'ite family of the Āl Abī Shu'ba (see above nos. 147 and 204). He was a transmitter from Ja'far al-Ṣādiq and his disciples.

Najāshī: 444; *Fihrist*: 177; *Rijāl*: 323, 346.

Kitāb

His notebook of *ḥadīth*, related by a large number of Shī'ite transmitters including Ibn Abī 'Umayr[108] and Naḍr b. Suwayd al-Ṣayrafī (Najāshī: 444; *Fihrist*: 177; *Rijāl*: 346). The overwhelming majority of the close to two hundred quotations from this author in Shī'ite works of *ḥadīth*, listed in Khu'ī 20: 70–73, 98–9, 251–3, 254–8 and *Fahāris* 10: 467, 474, are through Naḍr b. Suwayd.

220: Abū Baṣīr

Abū Muḥammad Yaḥyā b. al-Qāsim, the blind (as also implied by his alternative *kunya* of *Abū Baṣīr*), a Kūfan client of the Banū Asad and arguably the most prolific Shī'ite transmitter of *ḥadīth* in the second century. He transmitted from Muḥammad al-Bāqir and Ja'far al-Ṣādiq, and died in 149–50.

Barqī: 53, 64; Kashshī: 173; Najāshī: 441; *Fihrist*: 178; *Rijāl*: 149, 321, 346.

With close to three thousand transmissions in Shī'ite works of *ḥadīth*, as listed in Khu'ī 21: 45–63, 300–343 and *Fahāris* 8: 222–8, Abū Baṣīr is indeed a major transmitter of Imāmite Shī'ite *ḥadīth*. Najāshī: 441 ascribes a *Kitāb yawm wa layla* to him, and *Fihrist*: 178 another book on the rituals of *ḥajj*. Both works were related from him by his guide and associate, 'Alī b. Abī Ḥamza al-Baṭā'inī, and seem to have been compiled by this latter from the transmissions dictated to him on the two topics by Abū Baṣīr. For the material quoted by this transmitter from Abū Baṣīr on the two topics, see the lists in Khu'ī 11: 493–8, 22: 229–30.

---

108. This transmitter at times quotes Yaḥyā al-Ḥalabī through an intermediary, as in Aḥmad b. Muḥammad b. 'Īsā: 133. This may have always been the case even in the instances where he appears as if he quotes directly from our author, as in *Kāfī* 3: 465–6.

221: Yaḥyā al-Qaṭṭan

Yaḥyā b. Sa'īd b. Farrukh, the cotton seller, a Baṣran client of Tamīm and a prominent Sunnī scholar of *ḥadīth*; he was a major source of biographical data on the transmitters of *ḥadīth* in the second century. He transmitted from many authorities of the time including Ja'far al-Ṣādiq, and died in 198 at the age of 78.

Ibn Sa'd 7: 215; Yaḥyā b. Ma'īn 2: 645; Bukhārī, *Kabīr* 8: 276; 'Ijlī: 472; Ibn Abī Ḥātim 1: 232–51, 9: 150–51; Khaṭīb, *Ta'rīkh* 31: 329–43, and the many other sources listed in the editors' footnotes to Mizzī 31: 330 and Dhahabī, *Ta'rīkh* 13 (years 191–200): 463–71.

He was a source of biographical data for Ibn Sa'd, Aḥmad (in his *'Ilal*), Fasawī, Wakī' al-Ḍabbī, Abū Zur'a al-Dimashqī and Ibn Abī Ḥātim. That he transmitted *ḥadīth* from Ja'far al-Ṣādiq is noted in *Rijāl*: 321; Mizzī: 330, and other sources (see also Ibn 'Adī: 556).

Nuskha 'an Abī 'Abd Allāh

A register of *ḥadīth*s that this author transmitted from Ja'far al-Ṣādiq (Najāshī: 443). Quotations from Ja'far al-Ṣādiq through this transmitter in later works, many probably from this register, include the following examples:

- 'Abd al-Razzāq 3: 572
- Ibn Abī Shayba 3: 240 (repeated in 14: 558)
- Aḥmad 3: 319 (two reports), 320–21 (a lengthy report on the Prophet's pilgrimage to Mecca that Ja'far al-Ṣādiq dictated to this transmitter [Ibn 'Adī: 556]; also Abū Dāwūd 2: 187; Nasā'ī [where individual paragraphs from this text are scattered throughout the relevant chapter; see the editor's footnote to 4: 49 for a list of some 40 cases of this]; Abū Ya'lā 4: 23–6 and other works)
  6: 292 (also Nasā'ī 1: 147)
- Ibn Shabba: 161–2
- 'Ayyāshī 2: 123[109]

---

109. The passage in this source is quoted from *Yaḥyā b. Sa'īd* without further identification. The transmitter may have therefore been Yaḥyā b. Sa'īd b. Qays al-Anṣārī al-Madanī (d. 148), a *shaykh* of Yaḥyā b. Sa'īd al-Qaṭṭān, who also quotes Ja'far al-Ṣādiq (e.g. Muslim: 869; 'Alī b. Muḥammad al-Ḥimyarī: 55; Ibn 'Adī: 557), Muḥammad al-Bāqir (e.g. Ṭabarānī, *Awsaṭ* 1: 150–51 [also *Khiṣāl*: 500; Ṭūsī, *Amālī*: 516]; Abū Ṭālib: 302), and 'Alī Zayn al-'Ābidīn (e.g. *Ḥilya* 3: 136).

- 'Alī b. Ibrāhīm 2: 284, 344
- Abū Ya'lā 4: 208–9
- Ibn 'Adī: 557 (two reports)
- *Khiṣāl*: 65
- *Qiṣaṣ*: 196–7

222: Ya'qūb al-Aḥmar

Ya'qūb b. Sālim al-Aḥmar, the cloth seller, a Kūfan client of Kinda and a transmitter from Ja'far al-Ṣādiq.

Barqī: 83, 119; Najāshī: 449; *Rijāl*: 323, 324, 346. See also Ibn 'Adī: 580.

Kitāb mubawwab fī 'l-ḥalāl wa 'l-ḥarām

A work on matters of law organized in chapters, related from the author by his much better known nephew 'Alī b. Asbāṭ (Najāshī: 449). Quotations from this author on legal matters by the same nephew abound in later works. For lists see Khu'ī 20: 127–8, 135–7, 264–6; *Fahāris* 10: 488, 490.

223: Ya'qūb al-Sarrāj

Ya'qūb, the saddler, a Kūfan transmitter from Ja'far al-Ṣādiq.

Barqī: 83; Ibn al-Ghaḍā'irī: 102; Najāshī: 451; *Fihrist*: 180; *Rijāl*: 324.

Kitāb

His notebook of *ḥadīth*, related by Ḥasan b. Maḥbūb (Najāshī: 451; *Fihrist*: 180). With the exception of two or three reports of a dubious nature, all quotations from this author, listed in Khu'ī 20: 286 and *Fahāris* 10: 490, are through the same transmitter.

224: Ya'qūb al-Maythamī

Abū Muḥammad Yaqūb b. Shu'ayb b. Maytham b. Yaḥyā al-Tammār, a client of the Banū Asad and a grandson of Maytham al-Tammār, the devout partisan of 'Alī. He was a transmitter from Ja'far al-Ṣādiq.

Barqī: 83; Najāshī: 450; *Fibrist*: 180; *Rijāl*: 149, 323, 345.

Kitāb / Aṣl

His notebook of *ḥadīth*, related by a number of Shī'ite transmitters including Ṣafwān b. Yaḥyā, Ibn Abī 'Umayr,[110] and Ḥammād b. 'Uthmān (Abū Ghālib: 161, 177; Najāshī: 450; *Fibrist*: 180; *Rijāl*: 345; also *Mashyakha*: 477). Most of the well over one hundred quotations from this author in later works, listed in Khu'ī 20: 266–70 and *Fahāris* 10: 490–91, 492, are through Ṣafwān, and many of the rest through the other transmitters of the notebook as named above. The notebook was well known in the time of Mufīd (d. 413), who did not find a certain passage ascribed to this author in his *Kitāb* "in which he recorded all that he transmitted from Ja'far al-Ṣādiq" (Mufīd, *'Adadiyya*: 24). The assertion of Ibn Dāwūd: 389 that Ya'qūb transmitted five thousand *ḥadīth*s, a point not mentioned by earlier biographers, may refer to the number of reports in this notebook and indicate that either Ibn Dāwūd or his source had access to a copy.

225: Yāsīn al-Ḍarīr

Yāsīn, the blind, the oil seller, a Baṣran transmitter of *ḥadīth* in the latter half of the second century.

Najāshī: 453; *Fibrist*: 183.

---

110. According to Abū Ghālib: 177, Ibn Abī 'Umayr received this notebook through 'Abd Allāh b. al-Mughīra and Muḥammad b. Abī Ḥamza al-Thumālī. He occasionally cites this author through others as well (as, for instance, in *'Ilal* 1: 63).

Kitāb

His notebook of *ḥadīth*, related by Muḥammad b. ʿĪsā b. ʿUbayd al-Yaqṭīnī (Najāshī: 453; *Fihrist*: 183; also *Mashyakha*: 516), who may have received it through an intermediary or by *wijāda*. Quotations from this author in later works, listed in Khuʾī 20: 10–11, 13–14, 249–50 and *Fahāris* 10: 462, are mainly through the same transmitter.

226: Abū Khālid al-Qammāṭ

Abū Khālid Yazīd, the maker of swaddling clothes, a Kūfan client of the Banū ʿIjl and a transmitter from Jaʿfar al-Ṣādiq.

Barqī: 87; Kashshī: 411–12; Najāshī: 452; *Rijāl*: 325.

Kitāb

His notebook of *ḥadīth*, related by a number of transmitters including Ṣafwān b. Yaḥyā (Najāshī: 452; see also *Fihrist*: 184). There are a good number of quotations from this author in later works, listed in Khuʾī 21: 384–6 and *Fahāris* 9: 576–7, some through the same transmitter.

227: Yūnus al-Duhnī

Abū ʿAlī Yūnus b. Yaʿqūb b. Qays al-Bajalī al-Duhnī, a nephew of Muʿāwiya b. ʿAmmār (no. 143 above), a Kūfan Faṭḥite who transmitted from Jaʿfar al-Ṣādiq and Mūsā al-Kāẓim. He died in Medina late in the second century.

Barqī: 84; Kashshī: 385–8 (also 345); Najāshī: 446; *Fihrist*: 182; *Rijāl*: 323, 345, 368. See also *Kāfī* 4: 257; *Mashyakha*: 523.

1. *Kitāb al-ḥajj*

A work on the pilgrimage to Mecca, related by Ḥasan b. ʿAlī b. Faḍḍāl (Najāshī: 446). The following quotations on the topic from this author recorded in later sources on the authority of the same transmitter should represent part of the material of this work:

- *Kāfī* 4: 235 (also ʿAbd Allāh b. Jaʿfar: 314; *Tahdhīb* 5: 349, each through a different transmitter from Yūnus), 245, 257, 296, 299, 303–4, 320, 368, 383, 399, 429, 444, 447, 455, 466, 472 (also *Faqīh* 2: 469–70), 488, 505, 530, 534 (also *Tahdhīb* 5: 435), 556, 563 (also Ibn Qūlawayh: 69)
- *Tahdhīb* 5: 208 (also *Faqīh* 2: 491 and *Khiṣāl*: 356 through a different transmitter from Yūnus), 279, 368–9, 474

Other quotations from this author on the topic include the following:

- ʿAbd Allāh b. Jaʿfar: 161–2, 301 (two reports, the second also in *Faqīh* 2: 563)
- Ibn Qūlawayh: 318 (see also 299)
- *Faqīh* 2: 393, 455 (also *Tahdhīb* 5: 95)
- *ʿIlal* 2: 130
- *Thawāb*: 74
- *Tahdhīb* 5: 56, 126, 186, 306, 335, 350, 363, 482

2. *Kitāb*

His notebook of *ḥadīth*, related by Ḥakam b. Miskīn al-Thaqafī and Ibn Abī ʿUmayr (*Mashyakha*: 452; *Fihrist*: 182). This must have been different from the book on *ḥajj* by this author as most quotations from him by these two transmitters are on other topics. Lists of several hundred citations from this author in later works, including some by these two transmitters, are given in Khuʾī 20: 334–45 (see also 287, 290–91, 292); *Fahāris* 10: 508–9.

228: Zakariyyā al-Muʾmin

Abū ʿAbd Allāh Zakariyyā b. Muḥammad al-Azdī al-Muʾmin, a Wāqifite who transmitted *ḥadīth* from the disciples of Jaʿfar al-Ṣādiq and Mūsā al-Kāẓim.

Barqī: 105; Najāshī: 172; *Fibrist*: 73; *Rijāl*: 358.

Kitāb / Aṣl

His notebook of *ḥadīth*, related by Muḥammad b. ʿĪsā b. ʿUbayd al-Yaqṭīnī (Ibn al-Nadīm: 275; Najāshī: 172; *Fihrist*: 73; *Rijāl*: 409). Most of the quotations from this author in later works, listed in Khu'ī 7: 292, 481–3, 21: 416–17 and *Fahāris* 8: 559, 10: 377, are through the same transmitter. Ibn Ṭāwūs quotes from this notebook in his *Falāḥ*: 472 (see further Kohlberg: 126).

229: Zayd al-Narsī

Zayd al-Narsī, allegedly a transmitter from Jaʿfar al-Ṣādiq and Mūsā al-Kāẓim.

Ibn al-Ghaḍā'irī: 61–2; Najāshī: 174; *Fihrist*: 71; *Rijāl*: 206.

Kitāb / Aṣl

A notebook of *ḥadīth*, related by Ibn Abī ʿUmayr (Ibn al-Ghaḍā'irī: 62; Najāshī: 174; *Fihrist*: 71). Muḥammad b. al-Ḥasan b. Aḥmad b. al-Walīd al-Qummī (d. 343), the prominent fourth century Shīʿite scholar of *ḥadīth*, and, following him, his student Ibn Bābawayh, maintained that this notebook as well as another ascribed to a Zayd al-Zarrād (no. 231 below) were forged by a later transmitter (Ibn al-Ghaḍā'irī: 62; *Fihrist*: 71 quoting Ibn Bābawayh's *Fihrist* [possibly referring to his *Maṣābīḥ* named by Najāshī: 390–91]). The notebook, consisting of forty-nine reports, has survived on the authority of Ibn Abī ʿUmayr, and is published in *al-Uṣūl al-sittat ʿashar*: 43–58. For an evaluation of the material of this notebook, see Muḥammad Taqī al-Tustarī 4: 549–51 (see further Kohlberg, *Uṣūl*: 152–4).

230: Zayd al-Shaḥḥām

Abū Usāma Zayd b. Yūnus al-Shaḥḥām, a Kūfan client of Azd and a transmitter from Muḥammad al-Bāqir and Jaʿfar al-Ṣādiq.

Barqī: 65; Kashshī: 337 (see also 210); Najāshī: 175; *Fihrist*: 71; *Rijāl*: 135, 206.

Kitāb

His notebook of *ḥadīth*, related by a number of transmitters including Ṣafwān b. Yaḥyā and Abū Jamīla Mufaḍḍal b. Ṣāliḥ al-Asadī (Najāshī: 175; *Fihrist*: 71). Quotations from this author in later works, mostly through Abū Jamīla but some through Ṣafwān as well as others, abound in later works. For lists of over two hundred of them see Khu'ī 7: 366–8, 489–5, 21: 12–13, 277–8; *Fahāris* 8: 137–8, 570–71, 574.

231: Zayd al-Zarrād

Zayd, the maker of chain mail, allegedly a Kūfan transmitter from Ja'far al-Ṣādiq.

Ibn al-Ghaḍā'irī: 61–2; Najāshī: 174; *Fihrist*: 71; *Rijāl*: 206.

Kitāb / Aṣl

A notebook of *ḥadīth*, related by Ibn Abī 'Umayr (Ibn al-Ghaḍā'irī: 62; Najāshī: 174). As noted in no. 229 above, this notebook and the one ascribed to a Zayd al-Narsī were considered by some fourth century Shī'ite scholars of *ḥadīth* to have been later forgeries. The notebook, consisting of thirty-four reports, has survived on the authority of Ibn Abī 'Umayr, and is published in *al-Uṣūl al-sittat 'ashar*: 2–13 (see further Kohlberg, *Uṣūl*: 150–51, 153–4).

232: Ziyād al-Qandī

Abū 'l-Faḍl Ziyād b. Marwān al-Anbārī, the confectioner, a client of the Banū Hāshim who lived in Baghdad. He worked in the state treasury as an assistant to Jarrāḥ b. Malīḥ al-Ru'āsī (d. 176–186), who was the state treasurer during the reign of Hārūn al-Rashīd. Ziyād was later imprisoned for a while for the embezzlement of public funds. He was also a financial agent for Mūsā al-Kāẓim in Baghdad, and was a founding father of the Wāqifite tendency after the death of the latter.

Barqī: 119; Kashshī: 466–7, 493; Najāshī: 171; *Fihrist*: 72; *Rijāl*: 208, 337.

For his position in the state treasury and subsequent imprisonment, see *Kāfī* 3: 328 (see also ibid. 5: 326); Khaṭīb, *Ta'rīkh* 1: 89. For his major role in Wāqifism, see Kashshī: 466–7; *Ghayba*: 63–5, 352.

Kitāb

His notebook of *ḥadīth*, related by a number of transmitters including Ya'qūb b. Yazīd al-Anbārī and Muḥammad b. 'Īsā b. 'Ubayd al-Yaqṭīnī (Najāshī: 171; *Fibrist*: 72; *Rijāl*: 337; also *Mashyakha*: 466). Most of the quotations from this author in later works, listed in Khu'ī 7: 319–20, 328–9, 484–7 and *Fahāris* 8: 564–5 (see also Abū Ṭālib: 378 for a further example), are through the same two transmitters. Ibn Bābawayh quotes directly from this work in *Faqīh* 1: 405.

233: Zur'a al-Ḥaḍramī

Abū Muḥammad Zur'a b. Muḥammad al-Ḥaḍramī, a Kūfan Shī'ite transmitter of *ḥadīth* in the latter half of the second century who accompanied Samā'a b. Mihrān, the prominent Shī'ite scholar of Kūfa at the time, and succeeded him as the *imām* of the mosque of the Ḥaḍārima in that city. He joined the Wāqifites after the death of Mūsā al-Kāẓim and died during the lifetime of 'Alī al-Riḍā, apparently before the end of the century.

Barqī: 118; Kashshī: 476–7; Najāshī: 176 (see also 193); *Fibrist*: 75; *Rijāl*: 211, 337, 427. See also 'Ayyāshī 1: 372.

Kitāb / Aṣl

His notebook of *ḥadīth*, related by a number of transmitters including Ḥasan b. Sa'īd al-Ahwāzī and Ḥasan b. Muḥammad al-Ḥaḍramī (Najāshī: 176; *Fibrist*: 75; see also *Mashyakha*: 427). Most of the over two hundred quotations from this author in later works, listed in Khu'ī 7: 258–60, 263–4, 474–80 and *Fahāris* 8: 557, are through the same two transmitters.

234: Zurāra b. A'yan

Abū 'l-Ḥasan Zurāra b. A'yan b. Sunsun, a Kūfan client of the Banū Shaybān, the most distinguished member of the originally Byzantine family of the Āl A'yan, and the most prominent Shī'ite scholar of his generation. An expert on the text of the Qur'ān, jurist, *mutakallim*, and poet, he was a transmitter from Muḥammad al-Bāqir and Ja'far al-Ṣādiq. He died in Kūfa in 148–149.

Barqī: 57, 63, 115; 'Uqaylī 2: 96–7; Ibn Abī Ḥātim 3: 604; Ibn 'Adī: 1095; Kashshī: 133–61, 170, 185, 210, 238–40; Ibn al-Nadīm: 276; Abū Ghālib: 133–6; Najāshī: 175; *Fihrist*: 74–5; *Rijāl*: 136, 210–11, 337; *Lisān* 3: 128–9. See also Fasawī 2: 671–2; *Kamāl*: 74–6; Ibn Ḥazm, *Jamhara*: 53; Nashwān: 164.

On the Āl A'yan, the prominent Kūfan Shī'ite family of the second century, there is a monograph by Abū Ghālib al-Zurārī, a later member of the family, that has survived. According to him, the family came from Byzantium. Zurāra's father, the son of a Christian monk, fell into the hands of slave merchants and was sold in the land of Islam as a slave (Abū Ghālib: 128–9; also Ghaḍā'irī: 193, though in a different version of the story ibid.: 191, it is said that Zurāra's father was a Persian by origin).

His status as the most prominent Shī'ite jurist of the time is noted by Kashshī: 238 and others. Some of his legal opinions and arguments, apart from what he transmitted from the Imāms, are quoted in the sources (e.g. 'Ayyāshī 1: 287; *Kāfī* 5: 451, 7: 83, 100–101, 104). For his theological opinions, quoted mostly in the heresiographical sources, see now van Ess 1: 321–30. A poem of seven lines attributed to him as the head of *Shmṭiyya* or, as in some manuscripts, *Taymiyya* (the latter also in Kashshī: 152; for the significance of both of these names in this context, see Muḥammad Taqī al-Tustarī 4: 435–6) appears in Jāḥiẓ, *Ḥayawān* 7: 122–3. Fakhr al-Rāzī, *Muḥaṣṣal*: 365 quotes four additional lines of the same poem.

A report in Kashshī: 143 suggests that Zurāra kept a written record of what he had heard from Ja'far al-Ṣādiq. Sunnī sources refer to a notebook he had of his transmissions from Muḥammad al-Bāqir ('Uqaylī 2: 96, whence *Lisān* 3: 129). Some of the quotations from him in later works are in the style of passages from books and not of oral transmission (see, for instance, *Kāfī* 7: 83, 100–101). *Fihrist*: 74–5 mentions that he had a number of books, though the author knew only of a *Kitāb al-istiṭā'a wa 'l-jabr* from among them. Najāshī: 175 did not receive this work but found it mentioned by Ibn Bābawayh. With close to two thousand quotations from him in Shī'ite works of *ḥadīth*, Zurāra was, however, one of the most prolific Shī'ite transmitters of *ḥadīth*. Two recent works attempt to compile all of these quotations, classified in order of their subject matter:

- *Musnad Zurāra b. A'yan*, by Bashīr al-Muḥammadī al-Māzandarānī, Qum, 1413 (1920 passages in total)
- *Mā rawāh al-ḥawāriyyūn*, by Kāẓim Ja'far al-Miṣbāḥ, vols. 4–6 (Qum, 1418–21) (2323 passages in total).

Bibliography

Where a reference to an author of multiple works is given in the text without a specific title following the author's name, the particular work referred to is marked with an asterisk in the list that follows.

ABĀN AL-SINDĪ = Abān b. Muḥammad al-Bajalī, Sindī al-Bazzāz (mid-3rd century):
Kitāb Abān, a fragment of it in Ibn Idrīs, *Mustaṭrafāt* (Qum, 1987): 39–44 (erroneously attributed to Abān b. Taghlib, but is probably by Abān al-Sindī)

'ABBĀD B. YA'QŪB al-Rawājinī al-Kūfī (d. 250):
Aṣl Abī Sa'īd 'Abbād al-'Uṣfurī, Tehran, 1371 (in the collection of *al-Uṣūl al-sittat 'ashar*: 14–19)

'ABD B. ḤAMĪD (d. 249):
Al-Muntakhab min Musnad 'Abd b. Ḥamīd, ed. M. 'A. Shalbāya, Kuwait, 1985

'ABD ALLĀH B. AḤMAD b. Ḥanbal al-Shaybānī al-Baghdādī (d. 290):
Kitāb al-Sunna, ed. M. S. al-Qaḥṭānī, Dammām, 1986

'ABD ALLĀH B. ḤAMZA b. Sulaymān, al-Manṣūr bi-'llāh (d. 614):
– *Al-'Iqd al-thamīn*, ed. 'A. 'A. al-Wajīh, Amman, 2001
– *Al-Shāfī*, Beirut, 1406

'ABD ALLĀH B. JA'FAR al-Ḥimyarī al-Qummī (late 3rd century):
Qurb al-isnād, Qum, 1413

'ABD AL-'AZĪZ AL-ṬABĀṬABĀ'Ī (d. 1416):
Ahl al-Bayt fī 'l-maktaba al-'Arabiyya, Qum, 1417

'ABD AL-JABBĀR AL-RIFĀ'Ī:
Mu'jam mā kutib 'an al-Rasūl wa 'l-A'imma, Tehran, 1371sh/ 1992

'ABD AL-JABBĀR b. Aḥmad al-Asadābādī al-Hamadhānī (d. 415):
– *Tathbīt dalā'il al-nubuwwa*, ed. 'A. 'Uthmān, Beirut, 1966
– *Al-Mughnī fī abwāb al-tawḥīd wa 'l-adl*, vol. 20, ed. 'A. Maḥmūd and S. Dunyā, Cairo, 1966

– *Ṭabaqāt al-Mu'tazila*, ed. F. Sayyid, Tunis, 1974 (in the collection of *Faḍl al-i'tizāl wa ṭabaqāt al-Mu'tazila*: 135–350)
'ABD AL-JALĪL AL-QAZWĪNĪ (alive in 556):
Kitāb al-naqḍ, ed. J. M. Urmawī, Tehran, 1358sh/ 1980
'ABD AL-KARĪM AL-ṬABARĪ (d. 478):
Al-Talkhīṣ fī 'l-qirā'āt al-thamān, ed. M. Ḥ. Mūsā, Jiddah, 1992
'ABD AL-KARĪM B. ṬĀWŪS al-Ḥillī (d. 692):
Farḥat al-gharī, Najaf, 1368
'ABD AL-QĀDIR AL-JĪLĀNĪ (d. 561):
Al-Ghunya li-ṭālibī ṭarīq al-ḥaqq, Cairo, 1322
'ABD AL-QĀHIR AL-BAGHDĀDĪ (d. 429):
– *Al-Farq bayn al-firaq*, ed. M. M. 'Abd al-Ḥamīd, Cairo, n. d.
– *Uṣūl al-dīn*, Beirut, 1981
'ABD AL-RAZZĀQ b. Hammām al-Ṣan'ānī (d. 211):
– *Muṣannaf*, ed. Ḥ. R. al-A'ẓamī, Beirut, 1970
– *Tafsīr al-Qur'ān*, ed. M. M. 'Abduh, Beirut, 1999
ABŪ 'L-'ABBĀS AL-ḤASANĪ (d. 352):
Akhbār al-Ḥusayn b. 'Alī al-Fakhkhī min kitāb al-Maṣābīḥ, ed. M. Jarrār, Beirut, 1995 (together with Aḥmad b. Sahl al-Rāzī's *Akhbār Fakhkh*: 275–328)
ABŪ 'ABD ALLĀH AL-SHAJARĪ (d. 445):
– *Al-adhān bi-ḥayyi 'alā khayr al-'amal*, ed. Y. A. al-Fuḍayl, n. p., 1399
– *Faḍl ziyārat al-Ḥusayn*, ed. A. al-Ḥusaynī, Qum, 1403
ABŪ 'L-'ALĀ' AL-HAMADHĀNĪ (d. 569):
Ghāyat al-ikhtiṣār, ed. A. M. F. Ṭal'at, Jiddah, 1994
ABŪ 'L-'ALĀ' AL-MA'ARRĪ (d. 449):
Risālat al-ghufrān, ed. Bint al-Shāṭi', Cairo, 1950
ABŪ 'L-'ARAB = Muḥammad b. Aḥmad al-Tamīmī (d. 333):
Kitāb al-miḥan, ed. Y. al-Jubūrī, Beirut, 1983
ABŪ 'AWĀNA = Ya'qūb b. Isḥāq al-Isfarā'īnī (d. 316):
Musnad, Hyderabad, 1362
ABŪ DĀWŪD = Sulaymān b. al-Ash'ath al-Sijistānī (d. 275):
Sunan, ed. M. M. 'Abd al-Ḥamīd, Cairo, 1935
ABŪ 'L-FARAJ = 'Alī b. al-Ḥusayn al-Iṣbahānī (d. 356):
– *Al-Aghānī*, Cairo, 1927
– *Maqātil al-Ṭālibiyyīn*, ed. S. A. Ṣaqr, Cairo, 1949
ABŪ GHĀLIB = Aḥmad b. Muḥammad al-Zurārī (d. 368):
Risālat Abī Ghālib al-Zurārī, ed. M. R. al-Ḥusaynī, Qum, 1411
ABŪ 'L-ḤASAN AL-ASH'ARĪ (d. 324):
Maqālāt al-Islāmiyyīn, ed. M. M. 'Abd al-Ḥamīd, Cairo, 1969
ABŪ 'L-ḤASAN AL-SHA'RĀNĪ (d. 1393):
His marginal notes on Muḥammad Ṣāliḥ al-Māzandarānī, *Sharḥ al-Kāfī*, Tehran, 1382
ABŪ ḤAYYĀN al-Tawḥīdī (d. 414):
Al-Baṣā'ir wa 'l-dhakhā'ir, ed. W. al-Qāḍī, Beirut, 1988
ABŪ HILĀL AL-'ASKARĪ (alive in 395):
– *Kitāb al-awā'il*, ed. W. Qaṣṣāb and M. al-Miṣrī, Riyadh, 1981
– *Dīwān al-ma'ānī*, ed. A. Ḥ. Basj, Beirut, 1994

ABŪ MANṢŪR AL-ṬABRISĪ (early 6th century):
Al-Iḥtijāj, ed. I. al-Bahādurī and M. H. Bih, Qum, 1413
ABŪ NU'AYM = Aḥmad b. 'Abd Allāh al-Iṣbahānī (d. 430):
– *Dhikr akhbār Iṣbahān*, ed. S. Dedering, Leiden, 1931
– *Faḍā'il al-Khulafā' al-Arba'a*, ed. Ṣ. M. al-'Uqayl, Medina, 1997
– *Faḍīlat al-'ādilīn min al-wulāt*, ed. M. Ḥ. Āl Salmān, Riyadh, 1997
– *Ḥilyat al-awliyā'*, Cairo, 1932
– *Mā nazal min al-Qur'ān fī 'Alī*, ed. M. B. al-Maḥmūdī, Tehran, 1406 (as *al-Nūr al-mushta'il)*
– *Ma'rifat al-Ṣaḥāba*, ed. 'A. Y. al-'Azāzī, Riyadh, 1998
– *Shu'arā' = al-Muntakhab min Kitāb al-shu'arā'*, ed. I. Ṣāliḥ, Damascus, 1994
– *Ṣifat al-janna*, ed. 'A. R. 'Abd Allāh, Damascus, 1986
ABŪ ṬĀHIR AL-SILAFĪ (d. 576):
Mu'jam al-safar, ed. 'A. 'U. al-Bārūdī, Beirut, 1993
ABŪ ṬĀLIB = Yaḥyā b. al-Ḥusayn al-Hārūnī (d. 424):
– *Al-Di'āma fī tathbīt al-imāma*, ed. Nājī Ḥasan, Beirut, 1981 (as *Nuṣrat madhāhib al-Zaydiyya* by Ṣāḥib b. 'Abbād*)*
– *Al-Ifāda fī ta'rīkh al-a'imma al-sāda*, ed. M. Y. S. 'Azzān, Ṣan'ā', 1996
*– *Taysīr al-maṭālib min Amālī al-imām Abī Ṭālib*, re-organized by Ja'far b. Aḥmad b. 'Abd al-Salām al-Buhlūlī (d. 573), ed. Y. 'A. al-Fuḍayl, Beirut, 1975
ABŪ 'UBAYD = Qāsim b. Sallām al-Harawī (d. 224):
– *Kitāb al-amwāl*, ed. M. Ḥ. al-Faqī, Cairo, 1353
– *l-Nāsikh wa 'l-mansūkh fī 'l-Qur'ān*, ed. M. S. al-Mudayfir, Riyadh, 1990
ABŪ YA'LĀ = Aḥmad b. 'Alī b. al-Muthannā al-Mawṣilī (d. 307):
Musnad, ed. Ḥ. S. Asad, Damascus and Beirut, 1984
ABŪ YŪSUF = Ya'qūb b. Ibrāhīm al-Anṣārī (d. 182):
Kitāb al-kharāj, Cairo, 1352
ABŪ ZUR'A AL-DIMASHQĪ (d. 281):
Ta'rīkh, ed. Sh. N. al-Qūjānī, Damascus, n. d.
ABŪ ZUR'A AL-RĀZĪ (d. 264):
Kitāb al-ḍu'afā', ed. S. al-Hāshimī, Medina, 1989 (as *Abū Zur'a al- Rāzī wa juhūduh fī 'l-sunna al-Nabawiyya)*
ĀGHĀ BUZURG al-Ṭihrānī (d. 1389):
Al-Dharī'a ilā taṣānīf al-Shī'a, Najaf and Tehran, 1353
AḤMAD = Abū 'Abd Allāh Aḥmad b. Muḥammad b. Ḥanbal al-Shaybānī al-Marwazī (d. 241):
– *Faḍā'il al-Ṣaḥāba*, ed. W. M. 'Abbās, Beirut, 1983
– *Al-'Ilal wa ma'rifat al-rijāl*, ed. W. M. 'Abbās, Beirut and Riyadh, 1988
– *Musnad*, Būlāq, 1313
– *Zuhd*, Beirut, n. d.
AḤMAD AL-DĪNAWARĪ (d. 333):
Al-Mujālasa wa jawāhir al-'ilm, ed. M. Ḥ. Āl Salmān, Beirut, 1998
AḤMAD B. 'ĪSĀ = *Kitāb al-'ulūm al-shahīr bi-Amālī Aḥmad b. 'Īsā*, by Muḥammad b. Manṣūr al-Murādī al-Kūfī (alive in 290), n. p., n. d.
AḤMAD B. MUḤAMMAD B. 'ĪSĀ al-Ash'arī al-Qummī (mid-3rd century):
Kitāb al-nawādir, Qum, 1408

AḤMAD B. SAHL AL-RĀZĪ (early 4th century):
Akhbār Fakhkh, ed. M. Jarrār, Beirut, 1995
AḤMAD B. YAḤYĀ AL-NĀṢIR (d. 315):
Kitāb al-najāt, ed. W. Madelung, Wiesbaden, 1985
ĀJURRĪ = Abū 'Ubayd Muḥammad b. 'Alī b. 'Uthmān (alive in 300):
Su'ālāt, ed. 'A. 'A. al-Bastawī, Mecca and Beirut, 1997
'ALĀ' B. RAZĪN al-Qallā' (mid-2nd century):
Mukhtaṣar Aṣl 'Alā' b. Razīn, Tehran, 1371 (in *al-Uṣul al-sittat 'ashar.* 149–57)
'ALĪ B. BĀBAWAYH al-Qummī (d. 329):
– *Al-Imāma wa 'l-tabṣira min al-ḥayra*, ed. M. R. al-Ḥusaynī, Beirut, 1987
– *Muṣādaqat al-ikhwān*, ed. M. Mishkāt, Tehran, 1366
'ALĪ B. IBRĀHĪM b. Hāshim al-Qummī (alive in 307) (attrib.):
Tafsīr al-Qummī, ed. Ṭ. M. al-Jazā'irī, Najaf, 1386
'ALĪ B. JA'FAR AL-'URAYḌĪ (early 3rd century):
Masā'il, Mashhad, 1409
'ALĪ B. MUḤAMMAD AL-ḤIMYARĪ (d. 323):
Juz', ed. 'A. S. al-Bu'aymī, Riyadh, 1998
'ALĪ B. AL-MUṬAHHAR = 'Alī b. Yūsuf b. al-Muṭahhar al-Ḥillī (late 7th century):
'Al-'Udad al-qawiyya, ed. M. al-Rajā'ī, Qum, 1408
ALĪ NAQĪ MUNZAWĪ:
Fihrist-i . . . Kitābkhāna-yi Dānishgāh-i Tehran, vol. 2, Tehran, 1332sh/ 1953
'AQĪQĪ = Yaḥyā b. al-Ḥasan b. Ja'far al-Madanī (d. 277):
Kitāb al-mu'aqqibīn min wuld Amīr al-Mu'minīn, ed. M. al-Kāẓim, Qum, 2001
'ĀṢIM B. ḤUMAYD al-Ḥannāṭ (late 2nd century):
Aṣl, Tehran, 1371 (in *al-Uṣūl al-sittat 'ashar.* 20–41)
'ĀṢIMĪ = Aḥmad b. Muḥammad b. 'Āṣim al-Karrāmī (early 5th century):
Zayn al-fatā, ed. M. B. al-Maḥmūdī, Qum, 1418
ASĪRĪ = Shams al-Dīn Muḥammad b. Yaḥyā Lāhījī (d. 912):
Dīwān-i ash'ār wa rasā'il, ed. B. Zanjānī, Tehran, 1978
'AYYĀSHĪ = Abū 'l-Naḍr Muḥammad b. Mas'ūd al-Sulamī al-Samarqandī (early 4th century):
Kitāb al-tafsīr, ed. H. al-Rasūlī, Qum, 1380
A'ẒAMĪ, Muḥammad Muṣṭafā:
– *Dirāsāt fī 'l-ḥadīth al-Nabawī*, Riyadh, 1396
– *Ḥadīth, Methodology and Literature*, Indianapolis, 1977
AZHARĪ = Abū Manṣūr Muḥammad b. Aḥmad al-Shāfi'ī (d. 370):
Ma'ānī al-qirā'āt, ed. 'I. M. Darwīsh and 'I. Ḥ. al-Qawzī, Riyadh, 1991
AZRAQĪ = Abū 'l-Walīd Muḥammad b. 'Abd Allāh (d. ca. 250):
Akhbār Makka, ed. R. Ṣ. Malḥas, Madrid, n. d.
BAḤSHAL = Abū 'l-Ḥasan Aslam b. Sahl al-Wāsiṭī (d. 292):
Ta'rīkh Wāsiṭ, ed. K. 'Awwād, Baghdad, 1967
BAHĀ' AL-DĪN AL-'ĀMILĪ (d. 1030):
Al-Kashkūl, ed. M. Ṣ. al-Naṣīrī, Qum, 1378
BĀKHARZĪ = Abū 'l-Mafākhir Yaḥyā b. Aḥmad (d. 736):
Awrād al-aḥbāb, ed. I. Afshār, Tehran, 1966

BALĀDHURĪ = Aḥmad b. Muḥammad. Yaḥyā b. Jābir (d. 279):
*– *Ansāb al-ashrāf*, ed. M. F. al-ʿAẓm, Damascus, 1996
– *Futūḥ al-buldān*, ed. Ṣ. al-Munajjid, Cairo, 1956
BALĀGHĪ, ʿAbd al-Ḥujjat:
Farhang-i Samāt, Tehran, 1371
BĀQILLĀNĪ = Muḥammad b. al-Ṭayyib al-Baṣrī (d. 403):
Nukat al-Intiṣār, ed. M. Z. Salāma, Alexandria, 1971
BAR-ASHER, Meir M.:
Scripture and Exegesis in Early Imami Shiism, Leiden, 1999
BARQĪ = Aḥmad b. Muḥammad b. Khālid al-Qummī (d. 274–280):
– *Al-Maḥāsin*, ed. J. M. Urmawī, Tehran, 1370
*– *Rijāl* (attrib.), ed. J. Q. al-Iṣfahānī, Qum and Tehran, 1419
BAYĀḌĪ = Zayn al-Dīn ʿAlī b. Yūnus al-ʿĀmilī al-Nabāṭī (d. 877):
Al-Ṣirāṭ al-mustaqīm, ed. M. B. al-Bihbūdī, Tehran, 1384
BAYHAQĪ = Abū Bakr Aḥmad b. Ḥusayn al-Naysābūrī (d. 458):
– *Dalāʾil al-nubuwwa*, ed. ʿA. Qalʿajī, Beirut, 1985
– *Faḍāʾil al-awqāt*, ed. ʿA. ʿA. M. al-Qaysī, Jiddah, 1997
– *Shuʿab al-īmān*, ed. M. B. Zaghlūl, Beirut, 1990
*– *Al-Sunan al-kubrā*, Hyderabad, 1344
BAZANṬĪ = Aḥmad b. Muḥammad b. Abī Naṣr (d. 221):
– *Jāmiʿ = al-Aḥādīth al-muntazaʿa min Jāmiʿ al-Bazanṭī*, a fragment in Ibn Idrīs, *Mustaṭrafāt* (Qum, 1987): 53–64
– *Nawādir = al-Aḥādīth al-muntazaʿa min Nawādir al-Bazanṭī*, a fragment in Ibn Idrīs, *Mustaṭrafāt* (Qum, 1987): 25–37
BAZZĀR = Abū Bakr Aḥmad b. ʿAmr (d. 292):
Al-Baḥr al-zakhkhār al-maʿrūf bi-Musnad al-Bazzār, ed. M. Zayn Allāh, Medina and Beirut, 1988
BIḤĀR = *Biḥār al-anwār*, by Muḥammad Bāqir b. Muḥammad Taqī al-Majlisī (d. 1110), Tehran, 1376
BISHĀRAT AL-MUṢṬAFĀ, by Muḥammad b. Abī ʾl-Qāsim al-Ṭabarī (6th century), Najaf, 1963
BUKHĀRĪ = Muḥammad b. Ismāʿīl al-Juʿfī (d. 256):
– *Al-Adab al-mufrad*, ed. K. Y. al-Ḥūt, Beirut, 1984
– *Khalq afʿāl al-ʿibād*, Beirut, 1984
– *Khayr al-kalām fī ʾl-qirāʾa khalf al-imām*, ed. ʿĀ. ʿA. Mazīd, Cairo, 2001
– *Rafʿ al-yadayn fī ʾl-ṣalāt*, ed. B. al-Rāshidī, Beirut, 1996
*– *Ṣaḥīḥ*, ed. L. Krehl, Leiden, 1862
– *Al-Taʾrīkh al-awsaṭ*, ed. M. I. al-Luḥaydān, Riyadh, 1998
– *Al-Taʾrīkh al-kabīr*, Beirut, n. d. (reprint of Hyderabad, 1360)
BULQAYNĪ = ʿUmar b. Raslān al-Kinānī al-ʿAsqalānī (d. 805):
Maḥāsin al-iṣṭilāḥ, ed. ʿĀ. ʿA. Bint al-Shāṭiʾ, Cairo, 1974 (together with *Muqaddamat Ibn al-Ṣalāḥ*)
BURSĪ = Rajab b. Muḥammad al-Ḥillī (alive in 813):
Mashāriq anwār al-yaqīn, Beirut, 1379
CHESTER BEATTY = *The Chester Beatty Library, A Handbook of the Arabic Manuscripts*, by Arthur J. Arberry, Dublin, 1955

COOK, Michael:
Early Muslim Dogma, Cambridge, 1981
DA'Ā'IM = *Da'ā'im al-Islām*, by Qāḍī Nu'mān (d. 363), ed. Ā. 'A. A. Fayḍī, Cairo, 1951
DALĀ'IL AL-IMĀMA, attributed to Abū Ja'far Muḥammad b. Jarīr b. Rustam al-Ṭabarī (5th century), Qum, 1413
DAMĪRĪ = Kamāl al-Dīn Muḥammad b. Mūsā (d. 808):
Ḥayāt al-ḥayawān, Cairo, 1970
DĀNĪ = Abū 'Amr 'Uthmān b. Sa'īd al-Andalusī (d. 444):
Al-Muktafā fī 'l-waqf wa 'l-ibtidā', ed. Y. 'A. al-Mar'ashlī, Beirut, 1984
DĀNISHPAZHŪH, Muḥammad Taqī:
*Fihrist-i *... Kitābkhāna-yi Dānishgāh-i Tehran*, vol. 5, Tehran, 1956
DĀRAQUṬNĪ = 'Alī b. 'Umar b. Aḥmad al-Baghdādī (d. 385):
– *Kitāb al-ḍu'afā' wa 'l-matrūkīn*, ed. Ṣ. B. al-Sāmarrā'ī, Beirut, 1984
– *Al-Mu'talif wa 'l-mukhtalif*, ed. M. 'A. 'Abd al-Qādir, Beirut, 1986
*– *Sunan*, Medina, 1966
DĀRIMĪ = 'Abd Allāh b. 'Abd al-Raḥmān al-Tamīmī al-Samarqandī (d. 255):
Sunan, Damascus, 1349
DAYLAMĪ = Ḥasan b. Abī 'l-Ḥasan Muḥammad (8th century):
– *A'lam al-dīn*, Beirut, 1988
– *Irshād al-qulūb*, ed. H. al-Mīlānī, Tehran and Qum, 1417
DHAHABĪ = Muḥammad b. Aḥmad b. 'Uthmān al-Dimashqī (d. 748):
– *Al-'Ibar fī khabar man ghabar*, ed. Ṣ. al-Munajjid, Kuwait, 1966
– *Al-Kāshif*, ed. M. 'Awwāma and A. M. N. al-Khaṭīb, Jiddah, 1992
– *Ma'rifat al-qurrā' al-kibār*, ed. B. 'A. Ma'rūf et al., Beirut, 1984
– *Al-Mughnī fī 'l-ḍu'afā'*, ed. N. 'Itr, Aleppo, 1971
– *Siyar a'lām al-nubalā'*, ed. Sh. al-Arna'ūṭ et al., Beirut, 1981
– *Tadhkirat al-ḥuffāẓ*, Hyderabad, 1955
– *Ta'rīkh al-Islām*, ed. 'U. 'A. Tadmurī, Beirut, 1987
– *Al-'Uluww li 'l-'Alī al-Ghaffār*, Medina, 1968
DŪLĀBĪ = Abū Bishr Muḥammad b. Aḥmad b. Ḥammād (d. 310):
Al-Kunā wa 'l-asmā', ed. N. M. al-Fāryābī, Beirut, 2000
DURUST b. Abī Manṣūr al-Wāsiṭī (late 2nd century):
Mā wujid min Kitāb Durust b. Abī Manṣūr, Tehran, 1371 (in *al-Uṣul al-sittat 'ashar*: 158–69)
ESS, Josef van:
Theologie und Gesellschaft im 2. und 3. Jahrhundert Hidschra, Berlin and New York, 1991
FAHĀRIS = *Fahāris Biḥār al-anwār*, ed. M. al-Khātamī, Beirut, 1992
FAKHĀR B. MA'ADD al-Mūsawī (d. 630):
Al-Ḥujja 'alā 'l-dhāhib ilā takfīr Abī Ṭālib, Najaf, 1351
FAKHR AL-RĀZĪ = Fakhr al-Dīn Muḥammad b. 'Umar al-Tamīmī (d. 606):
Al-Shajara al-mubāraka, ed. M. al-Rajā'ī, Qum, 1409
FĀKIHĪ = Muḥammad b. Isḥāq b. al-'Abbās al-Makkī (alive in 272):
Akhbār Makka, ed. 'A. 'A. Duhaysh, Beirut, 1994
FAQĪH = *Man lā yaḥḍuruh al-faqīh*, by Ibn Bābawayh (d. 381), ed. 'A. A. al-Ghaffārī, Tehran, 1392

FASAWĪ = Ya'qūb b. Sufyān (d. 277):

*– *Al-Ma'rifa wa 'l-ta'rīkh*, ed. A. Ḍ. al-'Umarī, Baghdad, 1974

– *Al-Sunna*, Baghdad, 1976 (together with vol. 3 of the author's *al- Ma'rifa wa 'l-ta'rīkh*: 384–403)

FAYḌ = Muḥammad Muḥsin b. Murtaḍā al-Kāshānī (d. 1091):

Kalimāt maknūna, ed. 'A. 'Uṭāridī, Tehran, 1383

FAZĀRĪ = Abū Isḥāq Ibrāhīm b. Muḥammad b. al-Ḥārith (d. 188):

Kitāb al-siyar, ed. F. Ḥamāda, Beirut, 1987

FIHRIST = *Kitāb al-fihrist*, by Ṭūsī (d. 460), ed. M. Ṣ. Āl Baḥr al-'Ulūm, Najaf, 1356

FIRDAWS = *Musnad al-Firdaws*, by Abū Manṣūr Shahrdār b. Shīrūya al-Daylamī al-Hamadhānī (d. 558), the excerpts printed in facsimile in Uzbek, *Musnad 'Alī b. Abī Ṭālib*, Damascus and Beirut, 1995

FĪRŪZĀBĀDĪ = Majd al-Dīn Muḥammad b. Ya'qūb al-Shīrazī (d. 817):

– *Al-Maghānim al-muṭāba fī ma'ālim Ṭāba*, ed. Ḥ. al-Jāsir, Riyadh, [1969]

*– *Al-Qāmūs al-muḥīṭ*, Beirut, 1995

FURĀT b. Ibrāhīm al-Kūfī (early 4th century):

Tafsīr, ed. M. al-Kāẓim, Tehran, 1990

GHAḌĀ'IRĪ = Ḥusayn b. 'Ubayd Allāh al-Wāsiṭī al-Baghdādī (d. 411):

Takmilat Risālat Abī Ghālib, ed. M. R. al-Ḥusaynī, Qum, 1411 (together with Abū Ghālib al-Zurārī, *Risāla*: 185–94)

GHAYBA = *Kitāb al-ghayba*, by Ṭūsī (d. 460), Qum, 1411

ḤĀFIẒ ḤUSAYN Karbalā'ī Tabrīzī (d. 997):

Rawḍāt al-jinān, ed. J. Sulṭān al-Qurrā'ī, Tehran, 1970

ḤĀJĪ KHALĪFA = Muṣṭafā b. 'Abd Allāh Kātib Chelebī (d. 1067):

Kashf al-ẓunūn, Istanbul, 1941

ḤĀKIM = Abū 'Abd Allāh Muḥammad b. 'Abd Allāh al-Naysābūrī (d. 405):

– *Ma'rifat 'ulūm al-ḥadīth*, ed. S. M. Ḥusayn, Hyderabad, 1935

*–*Al-Mustadrak 'alā 'l-Ṣaḥīḥayn*, Hyderabad, 1340

ḤAMMĀD B. ISḤĀQ b. Ismā'īl al-Baghdādī (d. 267):

Tarakat al-Nabī wa 'l-subul allatī wajjahahā fīhā, ed. A. Ḍ. al-'Umarī, n. p., 1984

ḤAMMŪ'Ī = Ibrāhīm b. Muḥammad b. Ḥammūya al-Juwaynī (d. 722):

Farā'id al-simṭayn, ed. M. B. al-Maḥmūdī, Beirut, 1978

ḤASAN B. MAḤBŪB al-Sarrād (d. 224):

Al-Mashyakha, a fragment of it in Ibn Idrīs, *Mustaṭrafāt* (Qum, 1987): 77–91

ḤASAN B. MUḤAMMAD AL-QUMMĪ (alive in 379):

Ta'rīkh Qum, translated into Persian by Ḥasan b. 'Alī b. 'Abd al-Malik al-Qummī in 805–6, ed. J. Ṭihrānī, Tehran, 1313sh/ 1934–5

ḤASAN AL-ṢADR = Ḥasan b. Hādī al-'Āmilī al-Kāẓimī (d. 1354):

Ta'sīs al-Shī'a li-funūn al-Islām, Baghdad, n. d.

ḤASAN B. SULAYMĀN al-Ḥillī (early 9th century):

Mukhtaṣar Baṣā'ir al-darajāt, Najaf, 1950

ḤASANZĀDA Āmulī, Ḥasan:

Minhāj al-barā'a fī sharḥ Nahj al-balāgha, by Ḥabīb Allāh b. Muḥammad al-Hāshimī al-Khu'ī (d. 1324), supplement (vols. 15–19), Tehran, 1383–7

HĀSHIM AL-BAḤRĀNĪ = Hāshim b. Sulaymān b. Ismā'īl al-Ḥusaynī (d. 1107):

– *Madīnat al-ma'ājiz*, ed. 'I. M. al-Hamadānī, Qum 1413

– *Al-Maḥajja fī-mā nazal fī 'l-Qā'im al-Ḥujja*, ed. M. M. al-Mīlānī, Beirut, 1990
ḤASKĀNĪ = 'Ubayd Allāh b. 'Abd Allāh b. Aḥmad al-Naysābūrī, al-Ḥākim (5th century):
Shawāhid al-tanzīl, ed. M. B. al-Maḥmūdī, Tehran, 1990
ḤAYDAR AL-ĀMULĪ = Rukn al-Dīn Ḥaydar b. 'Alī al-Ḥusaynī (late 8th century):
– *Jāmi' al-asrār*, ed. H. Corbin and U. Yahya, Tehran, 1969
– *Al-Muḥīṭ al-a'ẓam*, ed. M. M. al-Tabrīzī, Tehran, 1414
– *Al-Muqaddamāt min kitāb Naṣṣ al-nuṣūṣ*, ed. H. Corbin and O. Yahya, Tehran, 1974
ḤAYDARKHĀNĪ, Ḥusayn:
– 1989 = his introduction to the Persian translation of Najm al-Dīn Kubrā (d. 618), *Fawā'iḥ al-jamāl*, translated by M. B. Sā'idī, Tehran, 1368sh/ 1989
– 1992 = his introduction to the edition of 'Alā' al-Dawla Simnānī (d. 736), *Manāẓir al-maḥāḍir*, Tehran, 1371sh/ 1992
HAYTHAMĪ = Nūr al-Dīn 'Alī b. Abī Bakr (d. 807):
– *Majma' al-baḥrayn*, ed. 'A. M. Nadhīr, Riyadh, 1992
– *Majma' al-zawā'id*, Cairo, 1352
ḤIBARĪ = Ḥusayn b. al-Ḥakam (d. 286):
Mā nazal min al-Qur'ān fī Ahl al-Bayt, ed. A. al-Ḥusaynī, Qum, 1975
ḤILYA = *Ḥilyat al-awliyā*, by Abū Nu'aym (d. 430), Cairo, 1932
ḤIMMAṢĪ = Sadīd al-Dīn Maḥmūd b. 'Alī al-Rāzī (alive in 583):
Al-Munqidh min al-taqlīd, Qum, 1412
ḤIRZ AL-DĪN, Muḥammad:
Marāqid al-ma'ārif, Najaf, 1969
ḤUMAYDĪ = Abū Bakr 'Abd Allāh b. al-Zubayr al-Qurashī (d. 219):
Musnad, ed. Ḥ. S. A. al-Dārānī, Damascus, 1996
ḤURR AL-'ĀMILĪ = Muḥammad b. al-Ḥasan al-Mashgharī (d. 1104):
– *Ithbāt al-hudāt*, ed. H. al-Rasūlī, Qum, 1378
– *Wasā'il al-Shī'a*, ed. 'A. R. al-Shīrāzī and M. al-Rāzī, Tehran, 1376
ḤUSAYN B. 'ABD AL-WAHHĀB (alive in 448):
'Uyūn al-mu'jizāt, Najaf, 1369
ḤUSAYN b. SA'ĪD al-Ahwāzī (first half of 3rd century):
– *Kitāb al-mu'min*, Qum, 1401
– *Kitāb al-zuhd*, ed. Gh. 'Irfāniyān, Qum, 1402
ḤUSAYN B. 'UTHMĀN al-Aḥmasī (late 2nd century):
Kitāb, Tehran, 1371 (in *al-Uṣūl al-sittat 'ashar*: 108–13 erroneously attributed to Ḥusayn b. 'Uthmān b. Sharīk al-'Āmirī)
IBN 'ABD AL-BARR = Abū 'Umar Yūsuf b. 'Abd Allāh al-Qurṭubī (d. 463):
– *Al-Istī'āb*, ed. 'A. M. al-Bajāwī, Cairo, 1960
– *Jāmi' bayān al-'ilm wa faḍlih*, ed. A. A. al-Zuhayrī, Dammām, etc., 1994
– *Tamhīd*, ed. 'A. al-Ṣiddīq, Rabat, 1967
IBN 'ABD RABBIH = Aḥmad b. Muḥammad al-Qurṭubī (d. 328):
Al-'Iqd al-farīd, ed. A. Amīn et al., Cairo, 1940
IBN ABĪ 'ĀṢIM = Abū Bakr Aḥmad b. 'Amr b. 'Āṣim (d. 287):
Al-Sunna, ed. B. F. al-Jawābira, Riyadh, 1998
IBN ABĪ DĀWŪD = Abū Bakr 'Abd Allāh b. Sulaymān al-Sijīstānī (d. 316):
Kitāb al-maṣāḥif, ed. A. Jeffery, Leiden, 1937 (with the editor's *Materials for the History of the Text of the Qur'ān*)

IBN ABĪ 'L-DUNYĀ = 'Abd Allāh b. Muḥammad b. 'Ubayd al-Qurashī al-Baghdādī (d. 281):
– *Al-Ahwāl*, ed. M. F. al-Sayyid, Cairo, 1993
– *Faḍā'il Ramaḍān*, ed. 'A. Ḥ. Al-Manṣūr, Riyadh, 1995
– *Al-Hamm wa 'l-ḥuzn*, ed. M. F. al-Sayyid, Cairo, 1991
– *Al-Ikhwān*, ed. M. 'A. 'Aṭā, Beirut, 1988
– *Iṣlāḥ al-māl*, ed. M. Mufliḥ al-Quḍāt, al-Manṣūra, 1990
– *Al-'Iyāl*, ed. N. 'A. Khalaf, Dammām, 1990
– *Maqtal Amīr al-Mu'minīn*, ed. M. B. al-Maḥmūdī, Tehran, 1990
– *Al-Mawt*, ed. L. Kinberg, Haifa, 1983
– *Al-Ṣamt wa ḥifẓ al-lisān*, ed. M. 'A. Khalaf, Beirut, 1986
– *Ṣifat al-janna*, ed. N. 'A. Khalaf, Beirut and Amman, 1997
– *Ṣifat al-nār*, ed. M. 'A. M. al-Sa'dānī, Riyadh, 2000
– *Al-Shukr*, ed. M. S. B. Zaghlūl, Beirut, 1993
– *Al-Tahajjud wa qiyām al-layl*, ed. M. J. F. al-Ḥārithī, Riyadh, 1998
– *Al-Tawāḍu' wa 'l-khamūl*, ed. L. M. al-Ṣaghīr and N. 'A. Khalaf, Cairo, n. d.

IBN ABĪ 'L-FAWĀRIS = Muḥammad b. Muslim al-Rāzī (alive in 586):
Arba'ūna ḥadīthan fī faḍā'il Amīr al-Mu'minīn, ed. R. Qubādlū, Qum, 1379sh/ 2000 (in *Mīrath-i ḥadīth-i Shī'a* 5: 63–163)

IBN ABĪ 'L-ḤADĪD = 'Izz al-Dīn 'Abd al-Ḥamīd b. Hibat Allāh al-Madā'inī (d. 655):
Sharḥ Nahj al-balāgha, ed. M. A. Ibrāhīm, Cairo, 1959

IBN ABĪ ḤĀTIM = 'Abd al-Raḥmān b. 'Umar al-Ḥanẓalī al-Rāzī (d. 327):
– *'Ilal al-ḥadīth*, Cairo, 1343
*– *Al-Jarḥ wa 'l-ta'dīl*, Beirut, n. d. (reprint of Hyderabad, 1952)
– *Al-Marāsīl*, ed. Sh. N. al-Qūjānī, Beirut, 1977
– *Tafsīr al-Qur'ān al-'aẓīm*, ed. A. M. al-Ṭayyib, Mecca and Riyadh, 1999

IBN ABĪ RĀFI' = 'Ubayd Allāh b. Abī Rāfi' al-Madanī (mid-1st century):
Tasmiyat man shahida ma'a 'Alī ḥurūbah, Qum, 1409 (in Qāḍī Nu'mān, *Sharḥ al-akhbār* 2: 16–36)

IBN ABĪ SHAYBA = Abū Bakr 'Abd Allāh b. Muḥammad b. Abī Shayba al-'Absī (d. 235):
Muṣannaf, ed. 'A. Kh. al-Afghānī et al., Hyderabad, 1966 [vols. 1–5], Bombay, 1400 [vols. 6–15], Riyadh, 1988 [*al-juz' al-mafqūd*]

IBN ABĪ 'L-THALJ = Abū Bakr Muḥammad b. Aḥmad al-Kātib al-Baghdādī (d. 325):
Ta'rīkh al-A'imma, ed. M. R. al-Ḥusaynī, Qum, 1410 (as *Ta'rīkh Ahl al-Bayt naqlan 'an al-A'imma)*

IBN 'ADĪ = Abū Aḥmad 'Abd Allāh b. 'Adī al-Jurjānī (d. 365):
Al-Kāmil fī ḍu'afā' al-rijāl, Beirut, 1984

IBN AL-'ADĪM = Kamāl al-Dīn 'Umar b. Aḥmad b. Hibat Allāh al-'Aqīlī (d. 660):
Bughyat al-ṭalab fī ta'rīkh Ḥalab, ed. S. Zakkār, Damascus, 1989

IBN 'ARABĪ = Muḥyī al-Dīn Muḥammad b. 'Alī al-Ṭā'ī al-Andalusī (d. 638):
Fuṣūṣ al-ḥikam, ed. A. 'Afīfī, Cairo, 1946

IBN 'ASĀKIR = 'Alī b. Ḥasan b. Hibat Allāh (d. 573):
– *Al-Arba'ūn al-buldāniyya*, ed. M. M. al-Ḥāfiẓ, Damascus, 1992
*– *Ta'rīkh madīnat Dimashq*, ed. 'A. Shīrī, Damascus, 1995

IBN AL-ASH'ATH = Muḥammad b. Muḥammad b. al-Ash'ath al-Kūfī (mid-4th century):
Al-Ash'athiyyāt, Tehran, n. d. (together with 'Abd Allāh b. Ja'far al-Ḥimyarī's *Qurb al-isnād*)
IBN A'THAM = Aḥmad b. Muḥammad b. A'tham al-Kūfī (d. ca. 314):
Kitāb al-futūḥ, Hyderabad, 1968, and its Persian translation by Muḥammad b. Aḥmad Mustawfī Harawī (6th century), ed. Gh. Ṭ. Majd, Tehran, 1993
IBN AL-ATHĪR = 'Izz al-Dīn 'Alī b. Muḥammad al-Jazarī (d. 630):
*– *Al-Kāmil fī 'l-ta'rīkh*, Beirut, 1965
– *Usd al-ghāba*, Cairo, 1285
IBN 'AYYĀSH = Aḥmad b. Muḥammad b. 'Ubayd Allāh al-Jawharī al-Baghdādī (d. 401):
Muqtaḍab al-athar, ed. H. al-Rasūlī, Qum, 1379
IBN BĀBAWAYH = Abū Ja'far Muḥammad b. 'Alī b. Bābawayh al-Qummī, al-Ṣadūq (d. 381):
– *Al-Amālī*, Qum, 1417
– *Faḍā'il al-ashhur al-thalātha*, ed. Gh. 'Irfāniyān, Najaf, 1396
– *Faḍā'il al-Shī'a*, ed. M. al-Badrī, Qum, 1421 (together with the author's *Mawā'iẓ*: 269–335)
IBN AL-BĀDHISH = Abū Ja'far Aḥmad b. 'Alī b. Khalaf al-Gharnāṭī (d. 540):
Al-Iqnā' fī 'l-qirā'āt al-sab', ed. 'A. Qaṭāmish, Damascus, 1402
IBN AL-BARRĀJ = Qāḍī 'Abd al-'Azīz b. Niḥrīr al-Shāmī (d. 481):
Sharḥ Jumal al-'ilm wa 'l-'amal, ed. K. M. Shānachī, Mashhad, 1974
IBN BISṬĀM = 'Abd Allāh and Ḥusayn, sons of Bisṭām b. Sābūr al-Zayyāt (early 4th century):
Ṭibb al-A'imma, Najaf, 1965
IBN BIṬRĪQ = Yaḥyā b. al-Ḥasan al-Asadī al-Ḥillī (d. 600):
– *Khaṣā'iṣ al-waḥy al-mubīn*, ed. M. B. al-Maḥmūdī, Tehran, 1406
– *'Umdat 'uyūn ṣiḥāḥ al-akhbār*, ed. M. al-Maḥmūdī and I. al-Bahādurī, Tehran, 1412
IBN DA'B = 'Abū 'l-Walīd 'Īsā b. Yazīd al-Laythī al-Madanī (d. 171):
Kitāb fī faḍl Amīr al-Mu'minīn, ed. 'A. A. al-Ghaffārī, Tehran, 1379 (in *Ikhtiṣāṣ*: 144–60)
IBN DĀWŪD = Taqī al-Dīn Ḥasan b. 'Alī b. Dāwūd al-Ḥillī (alive in 707):
Kitāb al-rijāl, ed. J. M. Urmawī, Tehran, 1342sh/ 1963–4
IBN AL-DUBAYTHĪ = Muḥammad b. Sa'īd b. Yaḥyā al-Wāsiṭī (d. 637):
Dhayl Ta'rīkh Madīnat al-Salām Baghdād, ed. B. 'A. Ma'rūf, Baghdad, 1974
IBN DURAYD = Muḥammad b. al-Ḥasan b. Durayd al-Azdī (d. 321):
Al-Ishtiqāq, ed. F. Wüstenfeld, Göttingen, 1854
IBN FAHD = Aḥmad b. Muḥammad b. Fahd al-Asadī al-Ḥillī (d. 841):
'Uddat al-dā'ī, ed. A. M. al-Qummī, Beirut, 1987
IBN FUNDUQ = Abū 'l-Ḥasan 'Alī b. Zayd al-Bayhaqī (d. 565):
Ta'rīkh-i Bayhaq, ed. A. Bahmanyār, Tehran, 1317sh/ 1938–9
IBN GHALBŪN = Abū 'l-Ḥasan Ṭāhir b. 'Abd al-Mun'im al-Ḥalabī (d. 399):
Al-Tadhkira fī 'l-qirā'āt, ed. 'A. B. Ibrāhīm, Cairo, 1990
IBN ḤAJAR = Shihāb al-Dīn Aḥmad b. 'Alī al-'Asqalānī (d. 852):
– *Fatḥ al-bārī*, Būlāq, 1300

– *Al-Iṣāba*, ed. 'A. M. al-Bajāwī, Cairo, 1970
– *Tabṣīr al-muntabih*, ed. 'A. M. al-Bajāwī and M. 'A. al-Najjār, Cairo, 1964
– *Tahdhīb al-Tahdhīb*, Hyderabad, 1325
– *Taqrīb al-Tahdhīb*, ed. M. 'A. 'Aṭā, Beirut, 1993
IBN ḤAMDŪN = Bahā' al-Dīn Muḥammad b. al-Ḥasan al-Baghdādī (d. 562):
Al-Tadhkira al-Ḥamdūniyya, ed. I. and B. 'Abbās, Beirut, 1996
IBN HAMMĀM = Abū 'Alī Muḥammad b. Hammām b. Suhayl al-Iskāfī al-Kātib (d. 336):
– *Muntakhab al-Anwār fī ta'rīkh al-A'imma al-aṭhār*, ed. M. Mihrīzī and 'A. Ṣ. Khu'ī, Qum, 1379sh/ 2000 (in *Mīrāth-i ḥadīth-i Shī'a* 5: 13–62)
*– *Al-Tamḥīṣ*, Qum, 1404 (together with Ḥusayn b. Sa'īd's *Kitāb al- mu'min*)
IBN HĀNI' = Isḥāq b. Ibrāhīm b. Hāni' al-Naysābūrī (d. 275):
Masā'il al-imām Aḥmad b. Ḥanbal, ed. Z. al-Shāwīsh, Beirut, 1400
IBN AL-HAYTHAM = Abū 'Abd Allāh Ja'far b. Aḥmad b. Muḥammad b. al-Aswad (4th century):
Kitāb al-munāẓarāt, ed. W. Madelung and P. Walker, London, 2001
IBN ḤAZM = Abū Muḥammad 'Alī b. Aḥmad b. Sa'īd al-Qurṭubī (d. 456):
– *Al-Fiṣal*, ed. M. I. Naṣr and 'A. 'Umayra, Riyadh, 1982
– *Jamharat ansāb al-'Arab*, ed. E. Lévi-Provençal, Cairo, 1948
*– *Al-Muḥallā*, ed. A. M. Shākir, Cairo, 1347
IBN ḤIBBĀN = Abū Ḥātim Muḥammad b. Ḥibbān al-Bustī (d. 354):
– *Al-Majrūḥīn*, ed. M. I. Zāyid, Aleppo, 1975
– *Mashāhīr 'ulamā' al-amṣār*, ed. M. 'A. Ibrāhīm, al-Manṣūra, 1991
– *Ṣaḥīḥ = al-Iḥsān fī taqrīb Ṣaḥīḥ Ibn Ḥibbān*, by 'Alā' al-Dīn 'Alī b. Balbān al-Fārsī (d. 739), ed. Sh. al-Arna'ūṭ and Ḥ. al-Asad, Beirut, 1984
– *Al-Sīra al-Nabawiyya*, ed. 'A. M. 'U. 'Allūsh, Beirut etc., 2000
– *Al-Thiqāt*, Hyderabad, 1973
IBN HISHĀM = Abū Muḥammad 'Abd al-Malik b. Hishām al-Ḥimyarī (d. 218):
*– *Al-Sīra al-Nabawiyya*, ed. M. al-Saqqā et al., Cairo, 1936
– *Al-Tījān fī mulūk Ḥimyar*, Hyderabad, 1347
IBN IDRĪS = Muḥammad b. Idrīs al-'Ijlī al-Ḥillī (d. 598):
Mustaṭrafāt, Qum, 1987
IBN AL-'IMĀD = 'Abd al-Ḥayy b. 'Imād al-'Akrī al-Ḥanbalī (d. 1089):
Shadharāt al-dhahab, ed. 'A. and M. al-Arna'ūṭ, Damascus and Beirut, 1986
IBN 'INABA = Jamāl al-Dīn Aḥmad b. 'Alī al-Dāwūdī al-Ḥasanī (d. 828):
'Umdat al-ṭālib, ed. M. Ḥ. Āl al-Ṭāliqānī, Najaf, 1961
IBN AL-JA'D = Abū 'l-Ḥasan 'Alī b. al-Ja'd b. 'Ubayd al-Jawharī (d. 230):
Musnad, ed. 'A. 'A. 'Abd al-Hādī, Kuwait, 1985
IBN AL-JAWZĪ = Abū 'l-Faraj 'Abd al-Raḥmān b. 'Alī al-Qurashī al-Baghdādī (d. 597):
– *Al-'Ilal al-mutanāhiya*, ed. Kh. al-Mays, Beirut, 1983
– *Al-Mawḍū'āt*, ed. 'A. M. 'Uthmān, Medina, 1966
– *Ṣifat al-ṣafwa*, Hyderabad, 1355
IBN AL-JAZARĪ = Shams al-Dīn Muḥammad b. Muḥammad b. 'Alī al-Dimashqī (d. 833):
– *Asnā al-maṭālib*, ed. M. B. al-Maḥmūdī, Beirut, 1983

– *Ghāyat al-nihāya*, ed. G. Bergsträsser, Cairo, 1932
IBN JINNĪ = Abū 'l-Fatḥ 'Uthmān b. Jinnī al-Mawṣilī (d. 392):
Al-Muḥtasib, ed. 'A. N. Nāṣif et al., Cairo, 1966
IBN AL-JUḤĀM = Muḥammad b. al-'Abbās b. Māhyār al-Bazzāz (alive in 328):
Ta'wīl mā nazal min al-Qur'ān al-karīm fī 'l-Nabī wa ālih, ed. F. T. al-Ḥassūn, Qum, 1420
IBN AL-JUNAYD = Ibrāhīm b. 'Abd Allāh b. al-Junayd (mid-3rd century):
Su'ālāt Ibn al-Junayd li-Yaḥyā b. Ma'īn, ed. S. A. al-Nūrī and M. M. Khalīl, Beirut, 1990
IBN JUZAYY = Muḥammad b. Aḥmad al-Kalbī al-Gharnāṭī (d. 741):
Al-Tashīl, Cairo, 1355
IBN AL-KALBT = Abū 'l-Mundhir Hishām b. Muḥammad b. al-Sā'ib (d. 204):
– *Jamharat al-nasab*, ed. N. Ḥasan, Beirut, 1986
– *Nasab Ma'add wa 'l-Yaman al-Kabīr*, ed. Nājī Ḥasan, Beirut, 1988
IBN KATHĪR = Abū 'l-Fidā' Ismā'īl b. 'Umar al-Qurashī al-Dimashqī (d. 774):
– *Al-Bidāya wa 'l-nihāya*, Cairo, 1351
– *Jāmi' al-masānīd*, ed. 'A. A. Qal'ajī, Beirut, 1994
*– *Tafsīr*, Beirut, 1966
IBN KHĀLAWAYH = Ḥusayn b. Aḥmad al-Hamadhānī al-Naḥwī (d. 370):
– *Al-Badī' = Mukhtaṣar fī shawādhdh al-qirā'āt min kitāb al- Badī'*, ed. G. Bergsträsser, Cairo, 1934
– *I'rāb al-qirā'āt al-sab'*, ed. 'A. S. al-'Uthaymīn, Cairo, 1992
IBN KHALLIKĀN = Abū 'l-'Abbās Aḥmad b. Muḥammad al-Barmakī al-Irbilī (d. 681):
Wafayāt al-a'yān, ed. I. 'Abbās, Beirut, 1968
IBN AL-MAGHĀZILĪ = Abū 'l-Ḥasan 'Alī b. Muḥammad al-Wāsiṭī al-Jullābī (d. 483):
Manāqib 'Alī b. 'Abī Ṭālib, ed. M. B. al-Bihbūdī, Tehran, 1402
IBN MĀJA = Muḥammad b. Yazīd al-Qazwīnī (d. 273):
Sunan, ed. M. F. 'Abd al-Bāqī, Cairo, 1954
IBN MĀKŪLĀ = Abū Naṣr 'Alī b. Hibat Allāh al-'Ijlī al-'Ukbarī (d. 475):
Al-Ikmāl, Hyderabad, 1962
IBN MANẒŪR = Abū 'l-Faḍl Muḥammad b. Mukarram al-Anṣārī (d. 711):
*– *Lisān al-'Arab*, Beirut, n. d.
– *Mukhtaṣar Ta'rīkh Dimashq*, ed. R. 'A. Murād, Damascus, 1984
IBN MARDAWAYH = Abū Bakr Aḥmad b. Mūsā al-Iṣbahānī (d. 410):
Juz' fīh mā intaqā ... Ibn Mardawayh 'alā ... al-Ṭabarānī min ḥadīthih li-ahl al-Baṣra, ed. B. al-Badr, Riyadh, 2000
IBN AL-MASHHADĪ = Muḥammad b. Ja'far al-Ḥā'irī (6th century):
Al-Mazār al-kabīr, ed. J. al-Qayyūmī, Qum, 1999
IBN MAYTHAM = Kamāl al-Dīn Maytham b. 'Alī b. Maytham al-Baḥrānī (d. 679):
Sharḥ Nahj al-balāgha, Tehran, 1378
IBN MIHRĀN = Abū Bakr Aḥmad b. al-Ḥusayn b. Mihrān al-Iṣbahānī (d. 381):
– *Al-Ghāya fī 'l-qirā'āt al-'ashr*, ed. M. Gh. al-Janbāz, Riyadh, 1985
– *Al-Mabsūṭ fī 'l-qirā'āt al-'ashr*, ed. S. Ḥ. Hākimī, Damascus, 1980
IBN AL-MUQRI' = Muḥammad b. Ibrāhīm b. Zādhān al-Iṣbahānī al-Khāzin (d. 381):
Al-Mu'jam, ed. 'Ā. Sa'd, Riyadh, 1998

IBN AL-MUṬAHHAR = Jamāl al-Dīn Ḥasan b. Yūsuf b. al-Muṭahhar al-Ḥillī, al-'Allāma (d. 726):
– *Ajwibat al-masā'il al-Muhannā'iyya,* Qum, 1401
– *Al-Dalā'il al-burhāniyya*, ed. J. M. Urmawī, Tehran, 1358sh/ 1979 (in the editor's endnotes to Thaqafī, *Kitāb al-ghārāt*: 837–80)
– *Khulāṣat al-aqwāl*, ed. J. Q. al-Iṣfahānī, Qum, 1417
– *Mukhtalaf al-Shī'a*, Qum, 1413

IBN AL-NADĪM = Abū 'l-Faraj Muḥammad b. Isḥāq al-Baghdādī al-Warrāq (late 4th century):
Al-Fihrist, ed. R. Tajaddud, Tehran, n. d.

IBN AL-NAJJĀR = Muḥibb al-Dīn Muḥammad b. Maḥmūd al-Baghdādī (d. 643):
Al-Mustafād min Dhayl Ta'rīkh Baghdad, by Aḥmad b. Aybak al-Ḥusāmī al-Dimyāṭī (d. 749), ed. M. M. Khalaf, Beirut, 1986

IBN NĀṢIR AL-DĪN = Muḥammad b. 'Abd Allāh al-Qaysī al-Dimashqī (d. 842):
Tawḍīḥ al-Mushtabih, ed. M. N. al-'Irqsūsī, Beirut, 1993

IBN AL-QAYSARĀNĪ = Abū 'l-Faḍl Muḥammad b. Ṭāhir al-Shaybānī al-Maqdisī (d. 507):
– *Al-Mu'talif wa 'l-mukhtalif*, ed. K. Y. al-Ḥūt, Beirut, 1991
– *Ṣafwat al-taṣawwuf*, ed. Gh. M. 'Adra, Beirut, 1995

IBN AL-QAYYIM = Muḥammad b. Abī Bakr b. Ayyūb al-Barda'ī al-Dimashqī (d. 751)
– *Aḥkām ahl al-dhimma*, ed. Ṣ. al-Ṣāliḥ, Damascus, 1961
– *Al-Ṭuruq al-ḥukmiyya*, ed. M. J. Ghāzī, Cairo, 1977

IBN QIBA = Abū Ja'far Muḥammad b. 'Abd al-Raḥmān b. Qiba al-Rāzī (late 3rd century):
Naqḍ Kitāb al-ishhād, ed. H. Modarressi, Princeton, 1993 (in the editor's *Crisis and Consolidation in the Formative Period of Shī'ite Islam*: 171–201)

IBN QUDĀMA = Muwaffaq al-Dīn 'Abd Allāh b. Aḥmad (d. 620):
Al-Mughnī, ed. 'A. 'A. al-Turkī and 'A. M. al-Ḥulw, Cairo 1986

IBN QŪLAWAYH = Abū 'l-Qāsim Ja'far b. Muḥammad b. Qūlawayh al-Qummī (d. 369):
*– *Kāmil al-ziyārāt*, Beirut, 1997
– *Kitāb* (a fragment of it in Ibn Idrīs, *Mustaṭrafāt*, Qum, 1987: 141–7)

IBN QUTAYBA = Abū Muḥammad 'Abd Allāh b. Muslim al-Dīnawarī (d. 276):
– *Gharīb al-ḥadīth*, ed. 'A. al-Jubūrī, Baghdad, 1977
– *Al-Ma'ārif*, ed. Th. 'Ukāsha, Cairo, 1960
– *Al-Shi'r wa 'l-shu'arā'*, ed. M. M. Shākir, Cairo, 1966
– *'Uyūn al-akhbār*, Cairo, 1925

IBN RAJAB = Abū 'l-Faraj 'Abd al-Raḥmān b. Aḥmad al-Baghdādī (d. 795):
Sharḥ 'Ilal al-Tirmidhī, ed. Ṣ. J. al-Ḥumayd, Baghdad, 1396

IBN AL-RĀZĪ = Abū Muḥammad Ja'far b. Aḥmad b. 'Alī al-Qummī (late 4th century):
– *Al-'Arūs*, ed. M. Ḥ. al-Nayshābūrī, Mashhad, 1413 (together with the author's *Jāmi' al-aḥādīth*: 143–68)
– *Al-Ghāyāt*, ed. M. Ḥ. al-Nayshābūrī, Mashhad, 1413 (together with the author's *Jāmi' al-aḥādīth*: 169–235)
– *Al-Musalsalāt*, ed. M. Ḥ. al-Nayshābūrī, Mashhad, 1413 (together with the author's *Jāmi' al-aḥādīth*: 237–68)

IBN RUSTA = Abū ʿAlī Aḥmad b. ʿUmar al-Iṣbahānī (alive in 290):
Al-Aʿlāq al-nafīsa, ed. M. J. De Goeje, Leiden, 1892 (together with Yaʿqūbī's *Kitāb al-buldān)*
IBN AL-ṢABBĀGH = ʿAlī b. Muḥammad b. Aḥmad al-Makkī (d. 855):
Al-Fuṣūl al-muhimma, Najaf, 1950
IBN SAʿD = Muḥammad b. Saʿd Kātib al-Wāqidī (d. 230):
*– *Kitāb al-ṭabaqāt al-kabīr*, ed. M. ʿA. ʿAṭā, Beirut, 1990
– *Ḥasan* = *Tarjamat al-Imām al-Ḥasan min al-qism ghayr al-maṭbūʿ min Kitāb al-ṭabaqāt*, ed. ʿA. al-Ṭabāṭabāʾī, Qum, 1416
– *Ḥusayn* = *Tarjamat al-Imām al-Ḥusayn wa maqtaluh*, ed. ʿA. al-Ṭabāṭabāʾī, Beirut, 1995
– Supplement = *al-Qism al-mutammim li-tābiʿī ahl al-Madīna wa man baʿdihim*, ed. Z. M. Manṣūr, Medina, 1987
IBN SAMKA = Abū ʿAlī Aḥmad b. Ismāʿīl b. Samka al-Bajalī al-Qummī (early 4th century):
Al-ʿAbbāsī, ed. ʿA. al-Dūrī and ʿA. al-Muṭṭalibī, Beirut, 1971(as *Akhbār al-dawla al-ʿAbbāsiyya*)[1]
IBN SAYYID AL-NĀS = Abū ʾl-Fatḥ Muḥammad b. Muḥammad al-Yaʿmurī (d. 734):
ʿUyūn al-athar, Beirut, 1977
IBN SHABBA = Abū Zayd ʿUmar b. Shabba al-Numayrī al-Baṣrī (d. 262):
Taʾrīkh al-Madīna al-munawwara, ed. F. M. Shaltūt, Beirut, 1990
IBN SHĀDHĀN = Abū ʾl-Ḥasan Muḥammad b. Aḥmad b. ʿAlī al-Qummī (early 5th century):
Miʾat manqaba, Qum, 1407

1. Moshe Sharon was apparently the first to suggest in an article published in 1973 (as quoted in his *Black Banners from the East*: 233–6) that this printed volume is a part of the *Kitāb al-ʿAbbāsī* quoted in Ḥasan b. Muḥammad al-Qummī, *Taʾrīkh Qum*: 145–6, 200, 236, 237 (see Modarressi, *Kitābshināsī*: 19) as the last two quotations are attested in this printed volume: 184–5, 165 (respectively). There is a further quotation from the author, Abū ʿAlī Aḥmad b. Samka al-Naḥwī, in *Taʾrīkh Qum*: 217–18, almost certainly from this work though not so specified. There is also a quotation in *Manāqib* 3: 191 from *Taʾrīkh al-Qummī* which may refer to the work in question, or, assuming a possible corruption in the name, to the *Taʾrīkh* of Aḥmad b. Ibrāhīm al-ʿAmmī, a student of the historian ʿAbd al-Azīz b. Yaḥyā al-Jalūdī (d. 332) (Najāshī: 96; *Fihrist*: 30; *Rijāl*: 411, 416). Sharon, however, did not know the author of the work, and the editors failed to take note of the author's transmission from ʿAlī b. Ibrāhīm al-Qummī (alive in 307) in p. 32 of their edited volume, from Sulaym b. Qays al-Hilālī in pp. 45–7, and from other Shīʿite sources in numerous other instances. The author was a teacher of the Būyid vizier Abū ʾl-Faḍl b. al-ʿAmīd (d. 360) for whom he wrote a treatise in 200 folios. The text of one of his communications with Ibn al-ʿAmīd is preserved in an old manuscript copied in 754 in the private collection of Aṣghar Mahdawī in Tehran (*cat.*: 142–3) (now also available in a facsimile edition as *Jung-i Mahdawī* [Tehran, 1380sh/2001]; the relevant text is on pages 192–3 of this edition). He was a student of Aḥmad b. Muḥammad b. Khālid al-Barqī (d. 274–280), a littérateur and author of numerous works (Najāshī: 97; *Fihrist*: 31; *Rijāl*: 417). In the story in *Taʾrīkh Qum*: 217–18, he is in the company of Abū Muslim Muḥammad b. Baḥr al-Iṣbahānī in his visits to the prominent ʿAlīds of Qum when the latter came to the town as governor in the year 309 (ibid.: 106, 142).

IBN SHĀHĪN = 'Umar b. Aḥmad al-Baghdādī (d. 385):
– *Al-Nāsikh wa 'l-mansūkh fī 'l-Qur'ān*, ed. M. I. al-Ḥifnāwī, al-Manṣūra, 1995
– *Sunna* = *Sharḥ madhāhib ahl al-sunna*, ed. 'Ā. Muḥammad, n. p., 1995
– *Al-Targhīb fī faḍā'il al-a'māl*, ed. Ṣ. A. M. al-Wu'ayl, Dammām, 1995
– *Thiqāt* = *Ta'rīkh asmā' al-thiqāt mimman nuqil 'anhum al-'ilm*, ed. 'A. A. Qal'ajī, Beirut, 1986
IBN SHU'BA = Abū Muḥammad Ḥasan b. 'Alī al-Ḥarrānī (mid-4th century):
Tuḥaf al-'uqūl, ed. 'A. A. al-Ghaffārī, Tehran, 1376
IBN AL-ṢŪFĪ = 'Alī b. Abī 'l-Ghanā'im Muḥammad al-'Umarī al-Shajarī (mid-5th century):
Al-Majdī fī ansāb al-Ṭālibiyyīn, ed. A. M. al-Dāmghānī, Qum, 1409
IBN AL-SUNNĪ = Aḥmad b. Muḥammad b. Asbāṭ al-Dīnawarī (d. 364):
'Amal al-yawm wa 'l-layla, Hyderabad, 1315
IBN TAGHRĪBIRDĪ = Yūsuf b. Taghrībirdī b. 'Abd Allāh al-Atābakī (d. 874):
Al-Nujūm al-zāhira, Cairo, 1963
IBN ṬĀWŪS = Raḍī al-Dīn 'Alī b. Mūsā b. Ṭāwūs al-Ḥasanī al-Ḥillī (d. 664):
– *Falāḥ al-sā'il*, ed. Gh. al-Majīdī, Qum, 1419
– *Faraj al-mahmūm*, Najaf, 1368
– *Fatḥ al-abwāb*, ed. Ḥ. al-Khaffāf, Qum, 1409
– *Ghiyāth sulṭān al-warā*, Qum, 1408 (excerpts, together with Ḥusayn b. Muḥammad b. Naṣr al-Ḥulwānī, *Nuzhat al-nāẓir*)
– *Al-Ijāzāt li-kashf ṭuruq al-mafāzāt*, its introduction quoted in *Biḥār* 107: 37–44
– *Al-Iqbāl*, ed. J. Q. al-Iṣfahānī, Qum, 1993
– *Jamāl al-usbū'*, ed. J. al-Qayyūmī, Tehran, 1371sh/ 1992–3
– *Kashf al-maḥajja*, Najaf, 1370
– *Al-Luhūf*, Tehran, 1321
– *Muḍāyaqa* = *Risālat 'adam muḍāyaqat al-fawā'it*, ed. M. 'A. Ṭ. al- Marāghī, Qum, 1407 (in *Turāthunā*, 7–8 [1407]: 331–59)
– *Muḥāsabat al-nafs*, ed. J. Q. al-Iṣfahānī, Qum, 1419
– *Muhaj al-da'awāt*, Tehran, 1416
– *Sa'd al-su'ūd*, ed. F. T. al-Ḥassūn, Qum, 1421
– *Al-Taḥṣīn*, Beirut, 1989 (together with the author's *al-Yaqīn*)
– *Al-Ṭarā'if*, ed. 'A. 'Āshūr, Beirut, 1999
– *Al-Yaqīn*, ed. Anṣārī, Beirut, 1989
IBN ṬAYFŪR = Aḥmad b. Muḥammad. Abī Ṭāhir Ṭayfūr al-Khurāsānī (d. 280):
Balāghāt al-nisā', Beirut, 1972
IBN WAḌḌĀḤ = Muḥammad b. Waḍḍāḥ al-Qurṭubī (d. 287):
Kitāb fīh mā jā'a fī 'l-bida', ed. B. 'A. al-Badr, Riyadh, 1996
IBN YŪSUF Shīrāzī, Ḍiyā' al-Dīn (d. 1408):
Fihrist-i Kitābkhāna-yi Madrasa-yi 'Ālī-yi Sipahsālār, Tehran, 1315sh/ 1936–7
IBN ZANJAWAYH = Ḥamīd b. Makhlad b. Qutayba al-Azdī al-Nasā'ī (d. 251):
Amwāl, ed. S. D. Fayyāḍ, Riyadh, 1986
IBN ZUHRA = Tāj al-Dīn b. Muḥammad b. Ḥamza al-Ḥalabī (alive in 753):
Ghāyat al-ikhtiṣār, ed. M. Ṣ. Baḥr al-'Ulūm, Najaf, 1962
IBRĀHĪM AL-BAYHAQĪ (late 3rd century):
Al-Maḥāsin wa 'l-masāwī, ed. M. A. Ibrāhīm, Cairo, n. d.

IḤTIJĀJ = *Al-Iḥtijāj 'alā ahl al-lijāj*, by Abū Manṣūr Aḥmad b. 'Alī b. Abī Ṭālib al-Ṭabrisī (early 6th century), ed. I. al-Bahādurī and M. H. Bih, Qum, 1413

'IJLĪ = Abū 'l-Ḥasan Aḥmad b. 'Abd Allāh b. Ṣāliḥ al-Kūfī (d. 261):
Ta'rīkh al-thiqāt, ed. 'A. Qal'ajī, Beirut, 1984

IKHTIṢĀṢ = *Kitāb al-Ikhtiṣāṣ*, attributed to Mufīd (d. 413), ed. 'A. A. al-Ghaffārī, Tehran, 1379

'ILAL = *'Ilal al-sharā'i'*, by Ibn Bābawayh (d. 381), ed. F. Ṭ. al-Yazdī, Qum, 1377

'ĪNĀTHĪ = Muḥammad b. al-Ḥusayn b. al-Qāsim al-'Āmilī (alive in 1068):
Al-Ithnā'ashariyya, Qum, 1406 (in 'Alī al-Mishkīnī al-Ardabīlī's abridgement as *al-Mawā'iẓ al-'adadiyya*)

'IQĀB = *'Iqāb al-a'māl*, by Ibn Bābawayh (d. 381), ed. 'A. A. al-Ghaffārī, Tehran, 1391 (together with the author's *Thawāb al-a'māl*: 241–347)

IRSHĀD = *al-Irshād ilā ma'rifat ḥujaj Allāh 'alā 'l-'ibād*, by Mufīd (d. 413), Beirut, 1995

ISKĀFĪ = Abū Ja'far Muḥammad b. 'Abd Allāh (d. 240):
Naqḍ al-'Uthmāniyya, ed. 'A. M. Hārūn, Cairo, 1955 (together with Jāḥiẓ, *'Uthmāniyya*: 281–343)

ISMĀ'ĪL AL-TAMĪMĪ = Abū 'l-Qāsim Ismā'īl b. Muḥammad b. al-Faḍl al-Iṣbahānī (d. 535):
Al-Ḥujja fī bayān al-maḥajja, ed. M. M. Abū Raḥīm, Riyadh, 1990

IṢṬAKHRĪ = Abū Isḥāq Ibrāhīm b. Muḥammad (early 4th century):
Al-Masālik wa 'l-mamālik, ed. M. J. 'A. al-Ḥīnī, Cairo, 1958

ISTIBṢĀR = *al-Istibṣār fī mā ikhtalaf min al-akhbār*, by Ṭūsī (d. 460), ed. Ḥ. M. al-Kharsān, Najaf, 1375

JA'FAR AL-ḤAḌRAMĪ = Ja'far b. Muḥammad b. Shurayḥ (late 2nd century):
Kitāb, Tehran, 1371 (in *al-Uṣūl al-sittat 'ashar*: 60–81)

JA'FAR B. MUḤAMMAD B. SINĀN al-Dihqān (mid-3rd century):
Kitāb, a small fragment of it in Ibn Idrīs, *Mustaṭrafāt* (Qum, 1987): 127

JĀḤIẒ = Abū 'Uthmān 'Amr b. Baḥr al-Baṣrī (d. 255):
– *Al-Bayān wa 'l-tabyīn*, ed. 'A. M. Hārūn, Cairo, 1948
– *Al-Ḥayawān*, ed. 'A. M. Hārūn, Cairo, 1938

JAHSHIYĀRĪ = Muḥammad b. 'Abdūs al-Kūfī (d. 331):
Al-Wuzarā' wa 'l-kuttāb, ed. 'A. al-Ṣāwī, Baghdad, 1938

JALĀLĪ = Muḥammad Riḍā al-Ḥusaynī al-Jalālī:
– *Tadwīn al-sunna al-sharīfa*, Qum, 1413
– "*Al-Tasmiyāt, ṭalī'at al-mu'allafāt fī 'l-ḥaḍāra al-Islāmiyya*," in *Turāthunā* 15 (1409): 11–75

JĀMI' AL-AKHBĀR, by Muḥammad b. Muḥammad al-Sabzawārī (alive in 679), ed. 'A. Āl Ja'far, Qum, 1414

JEFFERY, Arthur:
Materials for the History of the Text of the Qur'ān, Leiden, 1937

JISHUMĪ = Abū Sa'd Muḥassan b. Muḥammad b. Kirāma al-Bayhaqī (d. 494):
– *Jalā' al-abṣār*, ed. W. Madelung, Beirut, 1987 (in the editor's *Akhbār a'imma al-Zaydiyya*: 119–33)
– *Risālat Iblīs ilā ikhwānih al-manāḥīs*, ed. H. Modarressi, Beirut, 1995

JUBĀ'Ī = Shams al-Dīn Muḥammad b. 'Alī b. al-Ḥasan al-Jubā'ī al-'Āmilī (d. 886):
Majmū'a (MS 604, Malik Library, Tehran; see its catalogue 5: 105–12; also Āghā

Buzurg 20: 112), the excerpts quoted in *Biḥār* 107: 1–214 (see especially pp. 1–25, 27–31, 34–6, 47–50, 143–6, 181–2, 203–14 and many other cases not so acknowledged as in pp. 179–8 [cf. ibid. 60: 222–3])

JUMAḤĪ = Muḥammad b. Sallām b. 'Ubayd Allāh al-Baṣrī (d. 232):
Ṭabaqāt fuḥūl al-shu'arā', ed. A. M. Shākir, Cairo, 1988

JUNG-I MAHDAWĪ (an anthology compiled in 753–4), facsimile edition: Tehran, 1380sh [2001]

JUWAYNĪ = Bahā' al-Dīn Muḥammad b. 'Alā' al-Dīn Muḥammad, 'Aṭā Malik (d. 681):
Tārīkh-i jahangushā, ed. M. Qazwīnī, Leiden, 1912

KAF'AMĪ = Taqī al-Dīn Ibrāhīm b. 'Alī (d. 905):
Al-Miṣbāḥ, ed. Ḥ. al-A'lamī, Beirut, 1994

KĀFĪ, by Abū Ja'far Muḥammad b. Ya'qūb al-Kulaynī (d. 329), ed. 'A. A. al-Ghaffārī, Tehran, 1377

KAḤḤĀLA, 'Umar Riḍā (d. 1408):
Mu'jam qabā'il al-'Arab, Beirut, 1968

KALĀBĀDHĪ = Abū Bakr Muḥammad b. Ibrāhīm b. Ya'qūb al-Bukhārī (d. 384):
Baḥr al-fawā'id, ed. M. H. Ismā'īl and A. F. al-Mazīdī, Beirut, 1999

KAMĀL = *Kamāl al-dīn*, by Ibn Bābawayh (d. 381), ed. 'A. A. al-Ghaffārī, Tehran, 1390

KANJĪ = Muḥammad b. Yūsuf b. Ṭalḥa (d. 658):
Kifāyat al-ṭālib, ed. M. H. al-Amīnī, Najaf, 1970

KARĀJIKĪ = Abū 'l-Fatḥ Muḥammad b. 'Uthmān (d. 449):
Kanz al-fawā'id, Tabrīz, 1322

KASHSHĪ = Abū 'Amr Muḥammad b. 'Umar b. 'Abd al-'Azīz (early 4th century):
Rijāl = *Kitāb ma'rifat al-nāqilīn*, abridged by Ṭūsī (d. 460) as *Ikhtiyār ma'rifat al-rijāl*, ed. Ḥ. al-Muṣṭafawī, Mashhad, 1348sh/ 1970

KĀWUSHĪ DAR NAHJ AL-BALĀGHA, Tehran, 1985

KHAFĀJĪ = Shihāb al-Dīn Aḥmad b. Muḥammad b. 'Umar al-Miṣrī (d. 1069):
Nasīm al-riyāḍ fī sharḥ Shifā al-Qāḍī 'Iyāḍ, Cairo, 1325

KHALĪFA B. KHAYYĀṬ al-'Uṣfurī al-Baṣrī (d. 240):
– *Ṭabaqāt*, ed. S. Zakkār, Damascus, 1966
– *Ta'rīkh*, ed. A. Ḍ. al-'Umarī, Baghdad, 1967

KHARĀ'IJ = *al-Kharā'ij wa 'l-jarā'iḥ*, by Quṭb al-Dīn Sa'īd b. Hibat Allāh al-Rāwandī (d. 573), Qum, 1409

KHARĀ'IṬĪ = Abū Bakr Muḥammad b. Ja'far b. Sahl al-Sāmurrī (d. 327):
Makārim al-akhlāq, ed. S. S. al-Khandaqāwī, Cairo, 1990

KHAZZĀZ = Abū 'l-Qāsim 'Alī b. Muḥammad b. 'Alī al-Qummī al-Rāzī (late 4th century):
Kifāyat al-athar, ed. 'A. Ḥ. Kūhkamarī, Qum, 1401

KHAṢĪBĪ[2] = Abū 'Abd Allāh Ḥusayn b. Ḥamdān b. al-Khaṣīb[3] al-Junbulā'ī (d. 346 or 358):
Al-Hidāya al-kubrā, Beirut, 1986

2. This is how the name is pronounced by this person's followers, the Nuṣayriyya, in our time. *Khuṣaybī* in Modarressi, *Crisis*: passim must thus be corrected.
3. See Khaṣībī: 54.

KHAṬĪB = Abū Bakr Aḥmad b. Muḥammad. 'Alī b. Thābit al-Baghdādī (d. 463):
– *Al-Bukhalā'*, ed. A. Maṭlūb et al., Baghdad, 1964
– *Al-Faqīh wa 'l-mutafaqqih*, n. p., 1975
– *Al-Jāmi' li-akhlāq al-rāwī wa ādāb al-sāmi'*, ed. M. al-Ṭaḥḥān, Riyadh, 1983
– *Al-Kifāya fī 'ilm al-riwāya*, ed. 'A. M. 'Abd al-Ḥalīm and 'A. Maḥmūd, Cairo, 1972
– *Mūḍiḥ awhām al-jam' wa 'l-tafrīq*, Hyderabad, 1960
– *Al-Muttafiq wa 'l-muftariq*, ed. M. Ṣ. Ā. al-Ḥāmidī, Damascus and Beirut, 1977
– *Al-Sābiq wa 'l-lāḥiq*, ed. M. M. al-Zahrānī, Riyadh, 1982
– *Talkhīṣ al-mutashābih*, ed. M. Ḥ. Āl Salmān and A. al-Shuqayrāt, Riyadh, 1997
– *Taqyīd al-'ilm*, ed. Y. al-'Ishsh, Damascus, 1949
– *Ta'rīkh Baghdad*, Cairo, 1931
KHAṬṬĀBĪ = Ḥamd b. Muḥammad b. Sulaymān al-Bustī (d. 388):
Gharīb al-ḥadīth, ed.'A. I. al-Gharbāwī, Damascus, 1982
KHAYYĀṬ = Abū 'l-Ḥusayn 'Abd al-Raḥīm b. Muḥammad b. 'Uthmān al-Baghdādī (late 3rd century):
Al-Intiṣār, ed. H. S. Nyberg, Cairo, 1925
KHAZZĀZ = Abū 'l-Qāsim 'Alī b. Muḥammad b. 'Alī al-Qummī al-Rāzī (late 4th century):
Kifāyat al-athar, ed. 'A. Ḥ. Kūhkamarī, Qum, 1401
KHIṢĀL, by Ibn Bābawayh (d. 381), ed. 'A. A. al-Ghaffārī, Tehran, 1389
KHU'Ī = Abū 'l-Qāsim b. 'Alī Akbar al-Mūsawī (d. 1413):
Mu'jam rijāl al-ḥadīth, Beirut, 1983
KHUZĀ'Ī = 'Abd al-Raḥmān b. Aḥmad b. al-Ḥusayn al-Naysābūrī, al-Mufīd (5th century):
Al-Arba'īn 'an al-arba'īn fī faḍā'il 'Alī Amīr al-Mu'minīn, ed. M. B. al-Maḥmūdī, Tehran, 1416
KHWĀNSĀRĪ = Muḥammad Bāqir b. Zayn al-'Ābidīn al-Mūsawī al-Iṣfahānī (d. 1313):
Rawḍāt al-jannāt, ed. M. T. al-Kashfī and A. Ismā'īliyān, Tehran and Qum, 1390
KHWĀRAZMĪ = Abū 'l-Mu'ayyad Muwaffaq b. Aḥmad b. Muḥammad al-Makkī (d. 568):
– *Al-Manāqib*, ed. M. al-Maḥmūdī, Qum, 1411
– *Maqtal al-Ḥusayn*, ed. M. al-Samāwī, Qum, 1418
KITĀB AL-HAFT, attributed to Mufaḍḍal b. 'Umar al-Ju'fī (d. 179), ed. M. Ghālib, Beirut, 1964
KITĀB SULAYM b. Qays al-Hilālī, Najaf, n. d. (2nd edn.)
KOHLBERG, Etan:
*– *A Medieval Muslim Scholar at Work*, Leiden, etc., 1992
– *"Al-uṣūl al-arba'umi'a,"* in *Jerusalem Studies in Arabic and Islam* 10 (1987): 128–66 (now in his collection of articles, *Belief and Law in Imāmī Shī'ism*, VII)
LĀLIKĀ'Ī = Abū 'l-Qāsim Hibat Allāh b. al-Ḥasan b. Manṣūr (d. 418):
Sharḥ uṣūl i'tiqād ahl al-sunna wa 'l-jamā'a, ed. A. A. Ḥ. al-Ghāmidī, Riyadh, 1994
LISĀN = *Lisān al-Mīzān*, by Ibn Ḥajar (d. 852), ed. M. 'A. al-Mar'ashlī, Beirut, 1995
LUWAYN = Abū Ja'far Muḥammad b. Sulaymān b. Ḥabīb al-Maṣīṣī (d. 245):
Juz' fīh min ḥadīth Luwayn, ed. Gh. 'A. Ghunaym, Riyadh, 1998

MA'ĀLIM = *Ma'ālim al-'ulamā'*, by Ibn Shahrāshūb (d. 588), ed. M. Ṣ. Āl Baḥr al-'Ulūm, Najaf, 1961

MA'ĀNĪ = *Ma'ānī al-akhbār*, by Ibn Bābawayh (d. 381), ed. 'A. A. al-Ghaffārī, Tehran, 1379

MABĀNĪ = *Al-Mabānī fī naẓm al-ma'ānī*, anonymous, ed. A. Jeffrey, Cairo, 1954 (in *Muqaddamatān fī 'ulūm al-Qur'ān*)

MADELUNG, Wilferd:

Der Iman al-Qāsim ibn Ibrāhīm und die Glaubenslehre der Zaiditen, Berlin, 1965

MAḤĀMILĪ = Abū 'Abd Allāh Ḥusayn b. Ismā'īl al-Ḍabbī (d. 330):

Amālī, ed. I. I. al-Qaysī, Dammām and Amman, 1991

MAḤĀSIN, by Abū Ja'far Aḥmad b. Muḥammad b. Khālid al-Barqī al-Qummī (d. 274–280), ed. J. M. Urmawī, Tehran, 1370

MAḤMŪD BI-'AMRIH b. al-Ḥusayn al-Nuṣayrī (mid-5th century):

Risāla, ed. R. Strothmann, Berlin, 1908 (as *Esoterische Sonderthemen bei den Nusairi*)

MAJD AL-DĪN IBN AL-ATHĪR = Mubārak b. Muḥammad al-Shaybānī al-Jazarī (d. 606):

Al-Nihāya fī gharīb al-ḥadīth wa 'l-athar, ed. Ṭ. A. al-Zāwī and M. M. al-Tanāḥī, Cairo, 1963

MAKĀRIM AL-AKHLĀQ, by Raḍī al-Dīn Abū Naṣr Ḥasan b. al-Faḍl al-Ṭabrisī (mid-6th century), Tehran, 1376

MANĀQIB = *Manāqib Āl Abī Ṭālib*, by Ibn Shahrāshūb (d. 588), Qum, 1378

MAQĀTIL = *Maqātil al-Ṭālibiyyīn*, by Abū 'l-Faraj al-Iṣbahānī (d. 356), ed. S. A. Ṣaqr, Cairo, 1949

MAQDIST = Muṭahhar b. Ṭāhir (alive in 355):

Al-Bad' wa 'l-ta'rīkh, ed. C. Huart, Paris, 1899

MARWAZĪ = 'Izz al-Dīn Ismā'īl b. al-Ḥusayn al-Ḥusaynī (alive in 614):

Al-Fakhrī fī ansāb al-Ṭalibiyyīn, ed. M. al-Rajā'ī, Qum, *1409*

MARZUBĀNĪ = Abū 'Abd Allāh Muḥammad b. 'Imrān al-Khurāsānī (d. 384):

– *Akhbār shu'arā' al-Shī'a*, ed. M. H. al-Amīnī, Beirut, 1993

– *Mu'jam al-shu'arā'*, Cairo, 1354

MASHYAKHA = *Mashyakhat Man lā yaḥḍuruh al-faqīh*, by Ibn Bābawayh (d. 381), ed. 'A. A. al-Ghaffārī, Tehran, 1392 (at the end of the author's *Faqīh* 4: 421–588)

MAS'ŪDĪ = Abū 'l-Ḥasan 'Alī b. al-Ḥusayn al-Hudhalī al-Baghdādī (d. 346):

*– *Murūj al-dhahab*, ed. Ch. Pellat, Beirut, 1965

– *Al-Tanbīh wa 'l-ishrāf*, ed. 'A. I. al-Ṣāwī, Baghdad, 1938

MAWĀ'IẒ, by Ibn Bābawayh (d. 381), ed. M. al-Badrī, Qum, 1421

MAYMŪN AL-ṬABARĀNĪ = Abū Sa'īd Maymūn b. al-Qāsim al-Nuṣayrī (early 5th century):

Majmū' al-a'yād = *Sabīl rāḥat al-arwāḥ*, ed. R. Strothmann, Berlin, 1946 (as vol. 27 of *Der Islam*)

MIṢBĀḤ = *Miṣbāḥ al-mutahajjid*, by Ṭūsī (d. 460), Beirut, 1991

MISHKĀT AL-ANWĀR, by 'Alī b. Ḥasan al-Ṭabrisī (7th century), Najaf, 1965

MIYĀNAJĪ, 'Alī al-Aḥmadī (d. 1420):

Makātīb al-Rasūl, Qum, 1998

MĪZĀN = *Mīzān al-i'tidāl*, by Dhahabī (d. 748), ed. 'A. M. al-Bajāwī, Cairo, 1963

MIZZĪ = Jamāl al-Dīn Yūsuf b. ʻAbd al-Raḥmān (d. 742):
Tahdhīb al-Kamāl, ed. B. ʻA. Maʻrūf, Beirut, 1985
MODARRESSI, Hossein:
– *Crisis and Consolidation in the Formative Period of Shīʻite Islam*, Princeton, 1993
– "Early Debates on the Integrity of the Qur'an", *Studia Islamica* 77 (1993): 5–39
– *Kitābshināsī-yi āthār-i marbūṭ bi-Qum*, Qum, 1353sh/ 1974
MUʻĀWIYA B. ʻAMMĀR al-Duhnī (d. 175):
Kitāb, a fragment of it in Ibn Idrīs, *Mustaṭrafāt* (Qum, 1987): 21–3
MU'AYYAD = al-Mu'ayyad bi-'llāh Aḥmad b. al-Ḥusayn al-Hārūnī (d. 411):
Al-Amālī al-ṣughrā, ed. ʻA. ʻA. al-Wajīh, Ṣaʻda, 1993
MUBARRAD = Abū 'l-ʻAbbās Muḥammad b. Yazīd al-Azdī al-Baṣrī (d. 286):
*– *Al-Kāmil*, ed. A. M. Shākir, Cairo, 1937
– *Al-Taʻāzī wa 'l-marāthī*, ed. M. al-Dībājī, Damascus, 1976
MUFĪD = Abū ʻAbd Allāh Muḥammad b. Muḥammad b. al-Nuʻmān al-ʻUkbarī al-Baghdādī, Ibn al-Muʻallim (d. 413):
– *ʻAdadiyya = Jawābāt masā'il ahl al-Mawṣil fī 'l-ʻadad wa 'l-ru'ya*, ed. M. M. Najaf, Qum, 1413
– *Al-Amālī*, ed. ʻA. A. al-Ghaffārī and Ḥ. Ustād-Walī, Qum, 1403
– *Al-Jamal*, ed. ʻA. Mīr-Sharīfī, Qum, 1412
– *Al-Kāfiʻa li-ibṭāl tawbat al-khāṭi'a*, ed. ʻA. A. Zamānī-Nizhād, Qum, 1413
– *Khulāṣat al-Ījāz fī 'l-mutʻa*, ed. ʻA. A. Zamānī-Nizhād, Qum, 1413
– *Majālis = al-Fuṣūl al-mukhtāra min al-ʻUyūn wa 'l-maḥāsin*, Najaf, n. d.
– *Al-Masā'il al-Ṣāghāniyya*, ed. M. al-Qāḍī, Qum, 1413
– *Masārr al-Shīʻa*, ed. M. M. Najaf, Qum, 1413
– *Al-Mazār*, Qum, 1409
– *Al-Mutʻa* (extracted from *Biḥār*), Qum, 1413
– *Taṣḥīḥ al-Iʻtiqād*, ed. Ḥ. Dargāhī, Qum, 1413
MUḤAMMAD B. ʻALĪ B. MAḤBŪB al-Ashʻarī al-Qummī (mid-3rd century):
Nawādir (a fragment of it in Ibn Idrīs, *Mustaṭrafāt*, Qum, 1987: 93–110)
MUḤAMMAD BĀQIR AL-ṢADR (d. 1401):
Durūs fī ʻilm al-uṣūl, Beirut, 1978
MUḤAMMAD B. DĀWŪD al-Iṣbahānī al-Ẓāhirī (d. 297):
Kitāb al-zahra, ed. I. al-Sāmarrā'ī, Amman, 1985
MUḤAMMAD ṢĀLIḤ AL-MĀZANDARĀNĪ (d. 1086):
Sharḥ al-Kāfī = Al-Kāfī, al-uṣūl wa 'l-rawḍa, wa sharḥ jāmiʻ li 'l-mawlā Muḥammad Ṣāliḥ al-Māzandarānī, ed. Abū 'l-Ḥasan al-Shaʻrānī, Tehran, 1382
MUḤAMMAD B. SULAYMĀN al-Kūfī (later 3rd century):
Manāqib al-Imām Amīr al-Mu'minīn, ed. M. B. al-Maḥmūdī, Qum, 1412
MUḤAMMAD TAQĪ AL-TUSTARĪ (d. 1415):
Qāmūs al-rijāl, Qum, 1410
MUḤAQQIQ = Abū 'l-Qāsim Jaʻfar b. al-Ḥasan al-Ḥillī (d. 676):
– *Al-Masā'il al-ʻIzziyya*, ed. R. al-Ustādī, Qum, 1413 (in *al-Rasā'il al- tisʻ*: 49–178)
– *Al-Muʻtabar*, Qum, 1364sh/ 1985
MUʻJAM AL-QIRĀ'ĀT AL-QUR'ĀNIYYA, by A. M. ʻUmar and ʻA. S. Mukram, Kuwait, 1988
MUNZAWĪ, Aḥmad:
Fihrist-i nuskhahāy-i khaṭṭī-yi fārsī, Tehran, 1969

MURĀD, ʻAbbās al-Ḥāj Kāẓim:
Al-Mazārāt al-maʻrūfa fī madīnat al-Kūfa, Najaf, 1971
MURTAḌĀ = Abū 'l-Qāsim ʻAlī b. al-Ḥusayn al-Mūsawī, ʻAlam al-Hudā, al-Sharīf al-Murtaḍā (d. 436):
– *Inqādh al-bashar min al-jabr wa 'l-qadar*, Qum, 1405 (in A. al-Ḥusaynī [ed.], *Rasā'il al-Sharīf al-Murtaḍā* 2: 175–247)
– *Jawābāt al-masā'il al-Rassiyya al-ūlā*, Qum, 1405 (in A. al-Ḥusaynī [ed.], *Rasā'il al-Sharīf al-Murtaḍā* 2: 313–79)
– *Al-Masā'il al-Nāṣiriyyāt*, Tehran, 1997
– *Al-Shāfī fī 'l-imāma*, ed. ʻA. Ḥ. al-Khaṭīb, Tehran, 1987
MUṢʻAB AL-ZUBAYRĪ (d. 236):
Nasab Quraysh, ed. E. Levi-Provençal, Cairo, 1953
MUSLIM = Abū 'l-Ḥusayn Muslim b. al-Ḥajjāj al-Qushayrī al-Naysābūrī (d. 261):
– *Al-Kunā wa 'l-asmā'*, ed. ʻA. M. al-Qashqarī, Medina, 1984
*– *Ṣaḥīḥ*, ed. M. F. ʻAbd al-Bāqī, Cairo, 1955
AL-MUSNAD AL-JĀMIʻ, by B. ʻA. Maʻrūf et al., Beirut and Kuwait, 1993
MUṢṬAFĀ QAṢĪR AL-ʻĀMILĪ:
Kitāb ʻAlī, Beirut, 1995
MUTTAQĪ = ʻAlā al-Dīn ʻAlī b. Ḥusām al-Dīn al-Burhānpūrī (d. 975):
Kanz al-ʻummāl, ed. B. Ḥayyānī and Ṣ. al-Saqqā', Aleppo, 1969
NAḤḤĀS = Abū Jaʻfar Aḥmad b. Muḥammad b. Ismāʻīl al-Murādī al-Miṣrī (d. 338):
Iʻrāb al-Qur'ān, ed. Z. Gh. Zāhid, Beirut, 1985
NAHJ AL-BALĀGHA, by the Sharīf al-Raḍī (d. 406), ed. Ṣ. al-Ṣāliḥ, Beirut, 1387
NAHRAWĀNĪ = Muʻāfī b. Zakariyyā al-Jarīrī (d. 390):
Al-Jalīs al-ṣāliḥ al-kāfī, Beirut, n. d.
NAJAFĪ = Muḥammad Ḥasan b. Muḥammad Bāqir (d. 1266):
Jawāhir al-kalām, ed. ʻA. al-Qūchānī, Najaf, 1377
NAJĀSHĪ = Abū 'l-ʻAbbās Aḥmad b. ʻAlī al-Asadī al-Kūfī (d. 450):
Rijāl = Fihrist asmā' muṣannifī al-Shīʻa, ed. M. Sh. al-Zanjānī, Qum, 1407
NASAFĪ = Abū 'l-Muʻīn Maymūn b. Muḥammad (d. 508):
Tabṣirat al-adilla, ed. C. Salamé, Damascus, 1990
NASĀ'Ī = Abū ʻAbd al-Raḥmān Aḥmad b. ʻAlī b. Shuʻayb (d. 303):
– *ʻAmal yawm wa layla*, ed. F. Ḥamāda, Rabat, n. d.
– *Al-Ḍuʻafā' wa 'l-matrūkīn*, ed. B. al-Ḍanāwī and K. Y. al-Ḥūt, Beirut, 1985
– *Khaṣā'iṣ al-Imām Amīr al-Mu'minīn ʻAlī b. Abī Ṭālib*, ed. M. B. al-Maḥmūdī, Beirut, 1983
*– *Sunan*, ed. Sh. al-Arna'ūṭ and Ḥ. ʻA. Shalbī, Beirut, 2001
NASHWĀN b. Saʻīd al-Ḥimyarī (d. 573):
Sharḥ risālat al-Ḥūr al-ʻīn, ed. K. Muṣṭafā, Cairo, 1948
NAṢR B. MUZĀḤIM al-Minqarī (d. 212):
Waqʻat Ṣiffīn, ed. ʻA. M. Hārūn, Cairo, 1382
NAWBAKHTĪ = Abū Muḥammad Ḥasan b. Mūsā (late 3rd century):
Firaq al-Shīʻa, ed. M. Ṣ. Baḥr al-ʻUlūm, Najaf, 1969
NUʻAYM B. ḤAMMĀD al-Marwazī (d. 228):
Kitāb al-fitan, ed. S. Zakkār, Mecca, 1991

NU'MĀNĪ = Abū 'Abd Allāh Muḥammad b. Ibrāhīm al-Kātib, Ibn Abī Zaynab (mid-4th century):
*– *Kitāb al-Ghayba*, ed. 'A. A. al-Ghaffārī, Tehran, 1397
– *Tafsīr*, Tehran, 1387 (in *Biḥār* 93: 3–97)
NUWAYHIḌ, 'Ādil:
Mu'jam al-mufassirīn, n. p., 1983
PSEUDO-NĀSHI = *Masā'il al-imāma*, attributed to 'Abd Allāh b. Muḥammad al-Anbārī, al-Nāshi' al-Akbar (d. 293), ed. J. van Ess, Beirut, 1971 (as *Frühe Mu'tazilitsche Häresiographic*)
QAḌĀYĀ AMĪR AL-MU'MINĪN, attributed to Ibrāhīm b. Hāshim al-Qummī (mid-3rd century), Damascus, 1947 (in Muḥsin al-Amīn al-'Āmilī, *'Ajā'ib aḥkām Amīr al-Mu'minīn*)
QĀḌĪ 'IYĀḌ b. Mūsā al-Sabtī (d. 544):
Al-Shifā bi-ta'rīf ḥuqūq al-Muṣṭafā, ed. 'A. M. al-Bajāwī, Cairo, 1977
QĀḌĪ NU'MĀN = Abū Ḥanīfa Nu'mān b. Muḥammad al-Tamīmī al-Maghribī (d. 363):
– *Al-Īḍāḥ*, MS, University of Tübingen
– *Iftitāḥ al-da'wa*, ed. W. al-Qāḍī, Beirut, 1970
– *Sharḥ al-akhbār*, ed. M. Ḥ. al-Jalālī, Qum, 1409
QĀLĪ = Abū 'Alī Ismā'īl b. al-Qāsim al-Baghdādī (d. 356):
Al-Amālī, Cairo, 1926
QĀRĪ = 'Alī b. Sulṭān Muḥammad al-Harawī (d. 1014):
Sharḥ al-Shifā, Cairo, 1325 (together with Khafājī's *Nasīm al-riyāḍ*)
QAYSĪ = Abū Muḥammad Makkī b. Abī Ṭālib (d. 437):
Al-Tabṣira fī 'l-qirā'āt, ed. M. Ramaḍān, Kuwait, 1985
QIṢAṢ = *Qiṣaṣ al-anbiyā'*, by Quṭb al-Dīn Sa'īd b. Hibat Allāh al-Rāwandī (d. 573), ed. Gh. 'I. al-Yazdī, Mashhad, 1409
QUḌĀ'Ī = Abū 'Abd Allāh Muḥammad b. Salāma (d. 454):
– *Dustūr ma'ālim al-ḥikam*, Beirut, 1981
– *Musnad al-Shihāb*, ed. M. 'A. al-Salafī, Beirut, 1985
AL-QUMMĪ AL-MASHHADĪ = Muḥammad b. Muḥammad Riḍā b. Ismā'īl (alive in 1107):
Kāshif al-Ghumma fī ta'rīkh al-A'imma, Mashhad, 1419
RĀFI'Ī = Abū 'l-Qāsim 'Abd al-Karīm b. Muḥammad al-Qazwīnī (d. 623):
Al-Tadwīn fī dhikr akhbār Qazwīn, ed. 'A. 'Uṭāridī, Beirut, 1987
RĀGHIB = Abū 'l-Qāsim Ḥusayn b. Muḥammad al-Iṣbahānī (d. 402):
– *Al-Mufradāt*, ed. M. S. al-Kīlānī, Cairo, 1961
– *Muhāḍarāt al-udabā'*, Beirut, 1961
RĀMHURMUZĪ = Abū Muḥammad Ḥasan b. 'Abd al-Raḥmān b. Khallād (d. 360):
Al-Muḥaddith al-fāṣil bayn al-rāwī wa 'l-wā'ī, Beirut, n. d.
RIJĀL = *Kitāb al-rijāl*, by Ṭūsī (d. 460), ed. J. Q. al-Iṣfahānī, Qum, 1415
RŪDĀNĪ = Muḥammad b. Sulaymān al-Sūsī al-Makkī (d. 1094):
Ṣilat al-khalaf, ed. M. Ḥajjī, Beirut, 1988
RŪYĀNĪ = Abū Bakr Muḥammad b. Hārūn al-Ṭabarī (d. 307):
Musnad, ed. 'A. A. Abū Yamānī, Cairo, 1995
ṢĀBRĪ = Muḥammad b. Hīlāl al-Ṣābrī (d. 480):
Al-Hafawāt al-nādira, ed. S. al-Ashtar, Damascus, 1967

ṢABRĪ IBRĀHĪM AL-SAYYID:
Nahj al-balāgha, nuskha jadīda muḥaqqaqa wa muwaththaqa, Qatar, 1986
SA'D B. 'ABD ALLĀH al-Ash'arī al-Qummī (d. 299–301):
Kitāb al-maqālāt wa 'l-firaq, ed. M. J. Mashkūr, Tehran, 1963
ṢAFADĪ = Ṣalāḥ al-Dīn Khalīl b. Aybak (d. 764):
Al-Wāfī bi-'l-wafayāt, ed. H. Ritter et al., Istanbul and Wiesbaden, 1931
ṢAFFĀR = Abū Ja'far Muḥammad b. al-Ḥasan b. Farrukh al-Qummī (d. 290):
Baṣā'ir al-darajāt, ed. M. Kūchabāghī, Tabrīz, 1381
SAHMĪ = Abū 'l-Qāsim Ḥamza b. Yūsuf al-Jurjānī (d. 427):
Ta'rīkh Jurjān, Hyderabad, 1950
SAḤNŪN = Abū Sa'īd 'Abd al-Salām b. Sa'īd al-Tanūkhī (d. 240):
Al-Mudawwana al-kubrā, Cairo, 1323
SA'ĪD B. JANĀḤ al-Kūfī al-Baghdādī (early 3rd century):
Ṣifat al-janna wa 'l-nār, Tehran, 1379 (in *Ikhtiṣāṣ*: 345–65)
SA'ĪD B. MANṢŪR (d. 227):
Sunan, ed. S. 'A. Āl Ḥumayyad, Riyadh, 1993
ṢĀLIḤ B. AḤMAD b. Ḥanbal (d. 266):
Masā'il al-imām Aḥmad b. Ḥanbal, ed. F. Dīn Muḥammad, Delhi, 1988
SAM'ĀNĪ = Abū Sa'd 'Abd al-Karīm b. Muḥammad b. Manṣūr al-Tamīmī al-Marwazī (d. 562):
– *Adab al-imlā' wa 'l-istimlā'*, ed. Sh. M. Zay'ūr, Beirut, 1984
*– *Al-Ansāb*, Hyderabad, 1962
ṢAN'Ā', Grand Mosque, Western Library:
Cat. = *Fihrist makhṭūṭāt al-Maktaba al-Gharbiyya bi-'l-Jāmi' al-Kabīr bi-Ṣan'ā'*, by A. M. 'Īsawī and M. S. al-Malīḥ, Ṣan'ā', 1978
ṢARĪFĪNĪ = Ibrāhīm b. Muḥammad b. al-Azhar (d. 641):
Ta'rīkh Naysābūr al-muntakhab min al-Siyāq, ed. M. K. al-Maḥmūdī, Qum, 1403
SAYF B. 'UMAR al-Tamīmī (late 2nd century):
– *Kitāb al-Jamal wa masīr 'Ā'isha wa 'Alī*, ed. Q. al-Sāmarrā'ī, Leiden, 1995 (together with the author's *Kitāb al-Ridda wa 'l-futūḥ*: 231–363
– *Kitāb al-Ridda wa'l-futūḥ*, ed. Q. al-Sāmarrā'ī, Leiden, 1995
SAYYĀRĪ = Aḥmad b. Muḥammad b. Sayyār al-Baṣrī al-Kātib (mid-3rd century):
Al-Qirā'āt, MS 1455, Mar'ashī Library, Qum
SEZGIN, Fuat:
Geschichte des arabischen Schrifttum, Leiden, 1967
SHABISTARĪ, 'Abd al-Ḥusayn:
Al-Fā'iq fī ruwāt wa aṣḥāb al-Imām al-Ṣādiq, Qum, 1418
SHĀDHĀN B. JIBRĪL al-Qummī (alive in 651):
Al-Faḍā'il, Najaf, 1962
SHĀFI'Ī = Abū 'Abd Allāh Muḥammad b. Idrīs al-Muṭṭalibī (d. 204):
– *Musnad al-Imām al-Shāfi'ī*, re-organized by Abū 'Amr Muḥammad b. Ja'far b. Maṭar al-Naysābūrī (d. 360), ed. S. M. al-Laḥḥām, Beirut, 1996
*– *Al-Umm*, Cairo, 1321
SHAHĪD I = Shams al-Dīn Muḥammad b. Makkī al-'Āmilī (d. 786):
– *Al-Arba'īn*, Qum, 1407
– *Dhikrā al-Shī'a*, Qum, 1419

– *Al-Mazār*, ed. M. al-Badrī, Qum, 1416
SHAHĪD II = Zayn al-Dīn b. ʻAlī b. Aḥmad al-Jubaʻī al-ʻĀmilī (d. 966):
– *Musakkin al-fu'ād*, Qum, 1407
SHAHRASTĀNĪ = Abū 'l-Fatḥ Muḥammad b. ʻAbd al-Karīm (d. 548):
– *Mafātīḥ al-asrār*, ed. M. ʻA. Ādharshab, Tehran, 1997
*– *Al-Milal wa 'l-niḥal*, ed. ʻA. ʻA. Muhannā and ʻA. Ḥ. Fāʻūr, Beirut, 1990
– *Nihāyat al-iqdām*, ed. A. Guillame, London, 1934
SHĀNACHĪ, Kāẓim Mudīr:
His introduction to the edition of *al-Ṣaḥīfa al-Sajjādiyya*, Mashhad, 1413
SHARĪF AL-RAḌĪ = Abū 'l-Ḥasan Muḥammad b. al-Ḥusayn al-Mūsawī (d. 406):
– *Ḥaqā'iq al-ta'wīl*, ed. M. R. Āl Kāshif al-Ghiṭā', Najaf, 1355
– *Khaṣā'iṣ al-A'imma*, ed. M. H. al-Amīnī, Mashhad, 1406
– *Al-Majāzāt al-Nabawiyya*, ed. Ṭ. M. al-Zaynī, Cairo, 1967
SHARON, Moshe:
Black Banners from the East, Jerusalem and Leiden, 1983
SIBṬ IBN AL-JAWZĪ = Yūsuf b. Qizughlī al-Baghdādī (d. 654):
Tadhkirat al-khawāṣṣ, Najaf, 1383
ṢIFĀT = *Ṣifāt al-Shīʻa*, by Ibn Bābawayh (d. 381), ed. M. al-Badrī, Qum, 1421 (together with the author's *al-Mawāʻiẓ*: 187–266)
ṢIFFĪN = NAṢR B. MUZĀḤIM
SIMNĀNĪ = Aḥmad b. Muḥammad al-Biyābānakī, ʻAlā' al-Dawla (d. 736):
– *Manāẓir al-maḥāḍir*, ed. Ḥ. Ḥaydarkhānī, Tehran, 1371sh/ 1992
– *Tadhkirat al-mashāyikh*, Tehran, 1971 (in M. T. Dānishpazhūh and H. Landolt [eds.], *Majmūʻa-yi sukhanrānīhā wa maqālahā dar bāra-yi falsafa wa ʻirfān-i Islāmī*: 152–60)
SUBḤĀNĪ, Jaʻfar:
Mawsūʻat ṭabaqāt al-fuqahā', Qum, 1418
ṢUBḤĪ AL-ṢĀLIḤ (d. 1407):
Mabāḥith fī ʻulūm al-Qur'ān, Beirut, 1977
SUBKĪ = Taqī al-Dīn ʻAlī b. ʻAbd al-Kāfī (d. 756):
Fatāwā al-Subkī, Cairo, 1355
SULAMĪ = Abū ʻAbd al-Raḥmān Muḥammad b. al-Ḥusayn al-Naysābūrī (d. 412):
– *Ādāb al-ṣuḥba*, ed. M. J. Kister, Jerusalem, 1954
– *Ṭabaqāt al-Ṣūfiyya*, ed. N. Sharība, Cairo, 1969
ṢŪLĪ = Abū Bakr Muḥammad b. Yaḥyā (d. 335):
Akhbār al-Rāḍī bi 'llāh wa 'l-Muttaqī bi 'llāh min kitāb al-Awrāq, ed. J. H. Dunne, Cario, 1935
ṢŪRĪ = Sadīd al-Dīn Ḥasan b. Ṭāhir b. al-Ḥusayn (6th century):
Qaḍā' ḥuqūq al-mu'minīn, ed. Ḥ. al-Khaffāf, Qum, 1408
SUYŪṬĪ = Jalāl al-Dīn ʻAbd al-Raḥmān b. Abī Bakr (d. 911):
– *Bughyat al-wuʻāt*, ed. M. A. Ibrāhīm, Cairo, 1964
– *Al-Durr al-manthūr*, Cairo, 1314
– *Al-Itqān fī ʻulūm al-Qur'ān*, ed. M. A. Ibrāhīm, Cairo, 1967
– *Al-La'ālī al-maṣnūʻa*, Cairo, n. d.
ṬABARĀNĪ = Abū 'l-Qāsim Sulaymān b. Aḥmad b. Ayyūb (d. 360):
– *Al-Aḥādīth al-ṭiwāl*, ed. M. ʻA. ʻAṭā, Beirut, 1992
– *Akhbār al-Ḥasan b. ʻAlī b. Abī Ṭālib*, ed. M. Sh. Ḍayf Allāh, Kuwait, 1992

– *Kitāb al-Du'ā'*, ed. M. S. al-Bukhārī, Beirut, 1987
– *Al-Mu'jam al-awsaṭ*, Cairo, 1995
– *Al-Mu'jam al-kabīr*, ed. Ḥ. 'A. al-Salafī, Beirut, 1983
– *Al-Mu'jam al-ṣaghīr*, ed. 'A. M. 'Uthmān, Medina, 1968
ṬABARĪ = Abū Ja'far Muḥammad b. Jarīr (d. 310):
– *Dhayl* = *al-Muntakhab min kitāb Dhayl al-Mudhayyal*, ed. M. A. Ibrāhīm, Cairo, 1974 (together with the author's *Ta'rīkh* 11: 491–687)
– *Tafsīr* = *Jāmi' al-bayān*, Cairo, 1954
– *Tahdhīb al-āthār*, ed. M. M. Shākir, Cairo, 1982
*– *Ta'rīkh*, ed. M. A. Ibrāhīm, Cairo, 1960
ṬABRISĪ = Abū 'Alī Faḍl b. al-Ḥasan, Amīn al-Islām (d. 548):
– *I'lām al-warā*, ed. 'A. A. al-Ghaffārī, Tehran, 1379
– *Majma' al-bayān*, Beirut, 1961
ṬAḤĀWĪ = Abū Ja'far Aḥmad b. Muḥammad al-Azdī (d. 321):
Sharḥ ma'ānī al-āthār, Cairo, 1969
TAHDHĪB = *Tahdhīb al-aḥkām*, by Ṭūsī (d. 360), ed. Ḥ. M. al-Kharsān, Najaf, 1958
TĀJ AL-DĪN AL-ḤUSAYNĪ al-'Āmilī (alive in 1018):
Al-Tatimma fī tawārīkh al-A'imma, Qum, 1412
TĀJ AL-DĪN AL-SUBKĪ = 'Abd al-Wahhāb b. 'Alī b. 'Abd al-Kāfī (d. 771):
Ṭabaqāt al-Shāfi'iyya, ed. 'A. M. al-Ḥulw and M. M. al-Tanāḥī, Cario, 1964
TAWḤĪD, by Ibn Bābawayh (d. 381), ed. H. Ḥ. al-Ṭihrānī, Tehran, 1387
TA'WĪL AL-ĀYĀT al-ẓāhira, by Sharaf al-Dīn 'Alī al-Ḥusaynī al-Astarābādī (10th century), Qum, 1407
ṬAYĀLISĪ = Abū Dāwūd Sulaymān b. Dāwūd b. al-Jārūd (d. 204):
Musnad, ed. M. 'A. al-Turkī, Cairo, 1999
TEHRAN, the private collection of Dr. Aṣghar Mahdawī:
Cat. = *Fihrist-i nuskhahāy-i khaṭṭī-yi kitābkhāna-yi khuṣūṣī-yi Dr. Aṣghar Mahdawī*, by M. T. Dānishpazhūh, in *Nashriyya-yi Kitābkhāna-yi Markazī-yi Dānishgāh-i Tehran dar bāra-yi nuskhahāy-i khaṭṭī* (Tehran, 1962) 2: 59–181
THAQAFĪ = Ibrāhīm b. Muḥammad al-Kūfī (d. 283):
Kitāb al-ghārāt, ed. J. M. Urmawī, Tehran, 1395
THAWĀB = *Thawāb al-a'māl*, by Ibn Bābawayh (d. 381), ed. 'A. A. al-Ghaffārī, Tehran, 1391
TIRMIDHĪ = Abū 'Īsā Muḥammad b. 'Īsā al-Sulamī (d. 279):
– *Al-Shamā'il al-Nabawiyya*, ed. F. A. Zamarlī, Beirut, 1996
*– *Sunan* = *al-Jāmi' al-kabīr*, ed. B. 'A. Ma'rūf, Beirut, 1996
ṬURAYḤĪ = Fakhr al-Dīn b. Muḥammad 'Alī (d. 1085):
Majma' al-baḥrayn, ed. A. al-Ḥusaynī, Najaf, 1961
ṬURṬŪSHĪ = Abū Bakr Muḥammad b. al-Walīd al-Qurashī, Ibn Abī Randaqa (d. 520):
Sirāj al-mulūk, Cairo, 1935
ṬŪSĪ = Abū Ja'far Muḥammad b. al-Ḥasan, Shaykh al-Ṭā'ifa (d. 460):
– *Al-Amālī*, Qum, 1993
– *'Amal Yawm wa layla*, ed. R. al-Ustādī, Qum, 1403 (in *al-Rasā'il al-'ashr li 'l- Shaykh al-Ṭūsī*: 139–52)
– *Talkhīṣ al-Shāfī*, ed. Ḥ. Āl Baḥr al-'Ulūm, Majaf, 1963

'UBAYDALĪ = Abū 'l-Ḥasan Muḥammad b. Muḥammad al-Ḥusaynī al-Baghdādī, Shaykh al-Sharaf (d. 437):
Tahdhīb al-ansāb, ed. M. K. al-Maḥmūdī, Qum, 1413
'UQAYLĪ = Abū Ja'far Muḥammad b. 'Amr b. Mūsā b. Ḥammād al-Makkī (d. 322):
Al-Ḍu'afā', ed. 'A. A. Qal'ajī, Beirut, 1984
'UṬĀRIDĪ, 'Azīz Allāh:
Musnad al-Imām al-Sajjād, Tehran, 1379sh/ 2000
'UTHMĀN AL-DĀRIMĪ = Abū Sa'īd 'Uthmān b. Sa'īd b. Khālid al-Sijistānī (d. 280):
– *Al-Radd 'alā Bishr al-Marīsī*, ed. M. Ḥ. al-Faqī, Cairo, 1939
– *Al-Radd 'alā 'l-Jahmiyya*, ed. G. Vitestam, Leiden, 1960
– *Ta'rīkh 'Uthmān b. Sa'īd al-Dārimī 'an Yaḥyā b. Ma'īn*, ed. A. M. Nūr Sayf, Damascus and Beirut, 1400
'UYŪN = *'Uyūn akhbār al-Riḍā*, by Ibn Bābawayh (d. 381), ed. M. Ḥ. al-Lājawardī, Qum, 1377
UZBAK, Yūsuf:
Musnad 'Alī b. Abī Ṭālib, ed. 'A. R. 'Alī Riḍā, Damascus and Beirut, 1995
WĀḤIDĪ = Abū 'l-Ḥasan 'Alī b. Aḥmad b. Mattawayh al-Naysābūrī (d. 468):
Asbāb al-nuzūl, ed. S. A. Ṣaqr, Cairo, 1969
WAKĪ' = Muḥammad b. Khalaf b. Ḥayyān al-Ḍabbī (d. 306):
Akhbār al-quḍāt, ed. 'A. M. al-Marāghī, Cairo, 1947
WARRĀM = Abū 'l-Ḥusayn Warrām b. Abī Firās al-Ḥamdānī al-Ḥillī (d. 606):
Tanbīh al-khawāṭir = *Majmū'at Warrām*, Tehran, 1376
YAḤYĀ B. ĀDAM al-Qurashī al-Kūfī al-Aḥwal (d. 203):
Kitāb al-kharāj, ed. A. M. Shākir, Cairo, 1347
YAḤYĀ B. MA'ĪN al-Sarakhsī al-Anbārī (d. 233):
Al-Ta'rīkh, related from the author by Abbās b. Muḥammad al-Dūrī al-Baghdādī (d. 271), ed. A. M. Nūr Sayf, Mecca, 1979 (as *Yaḥyā b. Ma'īn wa kitābuh al-Ta'rīkh)*
YAḤYĀ B. SA'ĪD al-Hudhalī al-Ḥillī (d. 689):
Al-Jāmi' li 'l-sharā'i', Qum, 1405
YA'QŪBĪ = Aḥmad b. Muḥammad b. Isḥāq b. Ja'far b. Wahb al-Baghdādī, Ibn Wāḍiḥ (alive in 292):
– *Mushākalat al-nās li-zamānihim*, ed. W. Millward, Beirut, 1962
*– *Ta'rīkh*, Beirut, 1960
YĀQŪT = Abū 'Abd Allāh Yāqūt b. 'Abd Allāh al-Ḥamawī (d. 626):
– *Irshād al-arīb*, ed. I. 'Abbās, Beirut, 1993
– *Mu'jam al-buldān*, Beirut, 1957
YŪSUF B. ḤĀTIM al-Shāmī (late 7th century):
Al-Durr al-naẓīm, Qum, 1420
ZABĪDĪ = Muḥammad Murtaḍā b. Muḥammad al-Ḥusaynī (d. 1205):
Tāj al-'arūs, Cairo, 1306
ZAMAKHSHARĪ = Abū 'l-Qāsim Maḥmūd b. 'Umar, Jār Allāh (d. 538):
Rabī' al-abrār, ed. S. al-Nu'aymī, Baghdad, 1976
ZAYD B. 'ALĪ b. al-Ḥusayn (d. 122):
Musnad, compiled by Abū 'l-Qāsim 'Abd al-'Azīz b. Isḥāq al-Baghdādī, Ibn al-Baqqāl (d. 363), Beirut, 1966

ZAYD AL-NARSĪ (late 2nd century?):
Aṣl, Tehran, 1371 (in *al-Uṣūl al-sittat 'ashar*: 42–58)
ZAYD AL-ZARRĀD (mid-2nd century?):
Aṣl, Tehran, 1371 (in *al-Uṣūl al-sittat 'ashar*: 1–13)
ZIRIKLĪ, Khayr al-Dīn (d. 1396):
Al-A'lām, Beirut, 1989
ZUBAYR B. BAKKĀR al-Qurashī al-Makkī (d. 256):
– *Al-Akhbār al-Muwaffaqiyyāt*, ed. S. M. al-'Ānī, Baghdad, 1972
– *Jamharat nasab Quraysh*, ed. M. M. Shākir, Cairo, 1381

Index

Aaron 6
Abān b. Abī ʻAyyāsh 85, 86, 110
Abān b. Taghlib 107–16
Abān b. ʻUmar al-Asadī 43
Abān b. ʻUthmān b. ʻAffān 130
Abān b. ʻUthmān al-Aḥmar 1, 29–31, 394
Abān b. Yazīd b. Aḥmad al-Baṣrī al-ʻAṭṭār 111
ʻAbbād b. Kathīr 131
ʻAbbād b. Ṣuhayb al-Kalbī 131–3
ʻAbbād b. Yaʻqūb al-Rawājinī 164, 206, 281, 341, 356, 370
ʻAbbās b. ʻAbd al-Muṭṭalib 23
ʻAbbās b. ʻĀmir al-Qaṣabānī 179, 214, 360, 385
ʻAbbās b. Maʻrūf 360, 361
ʻAbbās b. Muḥammad b. ʻAlī b. ʻAbd Allāh b. al-ʻAbbās 171
ʻAbbās b. al-Walīd b. Ṣubayḥ al-Asadī 391
ʻAbd al-Aʻlā b. ʻĀmir al-Taghlibī al-Kūfī 46, 58
ʻAbd al-ʻAẓīm b. ʻAbd Allāh al-Ḥasanī 13
ʻAbd al-ʻAzīz b. ʻAbd Allāh Al-ʻAbdī 133–4
ʻAbd al-ʻAzīz b. Isḥāq al-Kūfī, Ibn al-Baqqāl 24
ʻAbd al-ʻAzīz b. Marwān 119
ʻAbd al-ʻAzīz b. Muḥammad b. al-Ṣiddīq al-Ḥusaynī al-Ghumārī 45
ʻAbd al-ʻAzīz b. Yaḥyā al-Jalūdī 14, 16
ʻAbd al-Ghaffār b. Ḥabīb al-Ṭāʼī al-Jāzī 134–5
ʻAbd al-Ghaffār b. al-Qāsim al-Anṣārī, Abū Maryam 135–7, 167
ʻAbd al-Ḥamīd b. Aḥmad b. Saʻīd 300
ʻAbd al-Karīm b. ʻAmr al-Khathʻamī Karrām 146–7, 366
ʻAbd Allāh b. ʻAbbās 26, 149
ʻAbd Allāh b. ʻAbd al-Raḥmān al-Aṣamm 156
ʻAbd Allāh b. Abī Yaʻfūr 103–5
ʻAbd Allāh b. Aḥmad b. Ḥanbal 347
ʻAbd Allāh b. Ayyūb b. Abī ʻIlāj, Abū Bakr 139
ʻAbd Allāh b. Ayyūb al-Ashʻarī 139
ʻAbd Allāh b. Ayyūb al-Qummī, Abū Muḥammad 139
ʻAbd Allāh b. Ayyūb b. Rāshid al-Zuhrī 138–48
ʻAbd Allāh b. Bukayr al-Shaybānī 140–41, 384
ʻAbd Allāh b. Dāhir al-Rāzī 200
ʻAbd Allāh b. Ghālib al-Asadī 141–2
ʻAbd Allāh b. Ḥabīb *see* Abū ʻAbd al-Raḥmān al-Sulamī
ʻAbd Allāh b. al-Ḥakam al-Armanī 142–3
ʻAbd Allāh b. al-Ḥārith 58, 91
ʻAbd Allāh b. al-Ḥasan 131, 230
ʻAbd Allāh b. al-Ḥusayn al-Azdī 224
ʻAbd Allāh b. Ibrāhīm al-Jaʻfarī 143–5
ʻAbd Allāh b. Jabala 217, 274, 369
ʻAbd Allāh b. Jaʻfar al-Afṭaḥ 104, 199
ʻAbd Allāh b. Jaʻfar al-Ḥimyarī 241, 323, 324, 362–3
ʻAbd Allāh b. Maymūn al-Qaddāḥ 145–50
ʻAbd Allāh b. Muʻāwiya al-Ṭālibī 87
ʻAbd Allāh b. al-Mughīra 217, 376, 398
ʻAbd Allāh b. Muḥammad b. ʻAbd al-ʻAzīz al-Manīʻī al-Baghawī 21
ʻAbd Allāh b. Muḥammad al-Asadī al-Ḥajjāl 193, 380
ʻAbd Allāh b. Muḥammad al-Bāqir 294
ʻAbd Allāh b. Muḥammad b. al-Ḥanafiyya, Abū Hāshim 280
ʻAbd Allāh b. Muḥammad b. Ibrāhīm 144
ʻAbd Allāh b. Murra 58
ʻAbd Allāh b. Muskān 150–55, 273, 310, 338, 374, 382

'Abd Allāh b. al-Najāshī 284
'Abd Allāh b. al-Qāsim al-Ḥaḍramī, al-Baṭal 155–7
'Abd Allāh b. al-Qāsim al-Ḥārithī 155
'Abd Allāh b. Saba' 7
'Abd Allāh b. al-Ṣalt al-Qummī 148
'Abd Allāh b. Sharīk 164
'Abd Allāh b. Sinān 151, 157–61
'Abd Allāh b. Ṭalḥa al-Nahdī 161
'Abd Allāh b. 'Umar 75, 149
'Abd Allāh b. Waḍḍāḥ 162
'Abd Allāh b. Waḍḍāḥ al-Kūfī al-Lu'lu'ī 162
'Abd Allāh b. Ya'lā b. Murra al-Thaqafī 385
'Abd Allāh b. Yaḥyā al-Kāhilī 162–3
'Abd Allāh b. Yazīd al-Anṣārī 45
'Abd Allāh b. Yazīd al-Ibāḍī 260
'Abd Allāh b. al-Zubayr b. al-'Awwām 145
'Abd Allāh b. al-Zubayr al-Rassān 163–5
'Abd al-Malik b. Abī Sulaymān Maysara al-Fazārī al-'Arzamī 175
'Abd al-Malik b. Ḥakīm al-Khath'amī 165
'Abd al-Malik b. Marwān 119
'Abd al-Malik b. 'Utba al-Hāshimī 165–6
'Abd al-Malik b. 'Utba al-Nakha'ī 165–7
'Abd al-Mu'min b. al-Qāsim al-Anṣārī 167–8
'Abd al-Muṭṭalib b. Hāhim b. 'Abd Manāf 83
'Abd al-Qays 103
'Abd al-Raḥmān b. 'Abd Allāh al-Aṣamm 325
'Abd al-Raḥmān b. Abī 'Abd Allāh al-Baṣrī 225, 226
'Abd al-Raḥmān b. Abī Hāshim al-Bazzāz 368
'Abd al-Raḥmān b. Abī Najrān 215, 342
'Abd al-Raḥmān b. al-Ḥajjāj 168–71
'Abd al-Raḥmān b. Kathīr al-Hāshimī 171–4, 188
'Abd al-Raḥmān b. Muḥammad b. Abī Hāshim 208
'Abd al-Raḥmān b. Muḥammad al-'Arzamī 174–5
'Abd al-Raḥmān b. Muḥammad b. al-Ash'ath 74, 75
'Abd al-Raḥmān b. Muḥammad al-Azdī al-Kūfī 113
'Abd al-Raḥmān b. 'Uthmān al-Tamīmī al-Dimashqī 15
'Abd al-Razzāq Ḥirz al-Dīn 377
'Abd al-Salām b. Ṣāliḥ, Abū 'l-Ṣalt 181
'Abd al-Ṣamad b. Bashīr al-'Urāmī 76–7
'Abd al-Ṣamad b. Muḥammad 241
'Abd al-Wāḥid b. 'Umar al-Baghdādī al-Bazzāz, Abū Ṭāhir 3
Abraham 336
Abū 'l-'Abbās al-Saffāḥ 195, 302, 326
Abū 'Abd al-Raḥmān al-Sulamī, 'Abd Allāh b. Ḥabīb 3
Abū Aḥmad al-Zubayrī, Muḥammad b. 'Abd Allāh 163, 164
Abū 'Alī al-Jubbā'ī 267
Abū Arāka al-Bajalī 191, 192
Abū Ayyūb al-Kharrāz *see* Ibrāhīm b. 'Īsā
Abū Ayyūb al-Khūzī 359
Abū 'l-Bakhtarī *see* Wahb b. Wahb
Abū Bakr b. 'Ayyāsh 3
Abū Baṣīr *see* Yaḥyā b. al-Qāsim al-Asadī
Abū Bujayr b. Sammāk 284
Abū Bujayr b. Sammāk al-Asadī 284
Abū Ḍamra *see* Anas b. 'Iyāḍ al-Laythī
Abū Dharr al-Ghifārī 1, 81
Abū Fākhita 248
Abū 'l-Faraj al-Iṣbahānī 276
Abū Hāshim *see* 'Abd Allāh b. Muḥammad b. al-Ḥanafiyya
Abū Ḥamza al-Thumālī, Thābit b. Dīnār 35, 38, 184, 231, 348, 377–9
Abū Ḥanīfa 244
Abū Hārūn al-'Abdī 8
Abū Ḥudhayfa *see* Isḥāq b. Bishr al-Khurāsānī
Abū Isḥāq al-Sabī'ī, 'Amr b. 'Abd Allāh al-Hamdānī 46, 56, 59, 62
Abū Ismā'īl al-Baṣrī 226
Abū Jamīla *see* Mufaḍḍal b. Ṣāliḥ al-Asadī
Abū 'l-Jārūd, Ziyād b. al-Mundhir al-Hamdānī 37, 38, 61, 121–5, 361
Abū Kahmas 104
Abū Khadīja *see* Sālim b. Mukram
Abū Khālid al-Wāsiṭī *see* 'Amr b. Khālid
Abū 'l-Khaṭṭāb, Muḥammad b. Abī Zaynab al-Asadī 128, 213, 368
Abū Lahab 166
Abū Mālik Ḍaḥḥāk al-Ḥaḍramī 216
Abū Manṣūr al-'Ijlī 265
Abū Manṣūr al-Juhanī 82
Abū Maryam *see* 'Abd al-Ghaffār b. al-Qāsim al-Anṣārī
Abū Mikhnaf *see* Lūṭ b. Yaḥyā al-Azdī
Abū 'l-Mufaḍḍal al-Shaybānī 363
Abū Muslim 195
Abū Rāfi' 22–4, 348
Abū Rawḥ *see* Faraj b. Farwa
Abū 'l-Ṣabbāḥ al-Kinānī *see* Ibrāhīm b. Nu'aym
Abū Salama al-Khallāl 195
Abū 'l-Sammāl al-Asadī 214, 284
Abū 'l-Sarāyā, Sarī b. Manṣūr al-Shaybānī 91, 122
Abū 'l-Sarī, Ma'dān al-Shumayṭī 78
Abū Shākir Maymūn b. Dayṣān 265
Abū Shu'ayb al-Maḥāmilī 337
Abū Sufyān 346
Abū Sumayna *see* Muḥammad b. 'Alī al-Ṣayrafī
Abū Ṭālib b. 'Abd al-Muṭṭalib 44, 248, 266
Abū Ṭālib al-Sha'rānī 374
Abū Ṭālib, Yaḥyā b. al-Ḥusayn al-Hārūnī 241
Abū 'Ubayd, Qāsim b. Sallām 129, 181
Abū 'Ubayda al-Ḥadhdhā' 116–18
Abū 'Ubayda, Ma'mar b. al-Muthannā 129, 325
Abū 'Uthmān al-Aḥwal 326
Abū Yūsuf Ya'qūb b. Ibrāhīm al-Kūfī 104
Abū Zur'a al-Dimashqī 396

'Adawī 172
Ad'iyat al-Imām Zayn al-'Ābidīn 35
'Adnān 105, 192
Aḥmad b. 'Abd Allāh b. Jullīn al-Dūrī al-Warrāq, Abū Bakr 61
Aḥmad b. 'Abd al-Malik b. 'Alī al-Naysābūrī 21
Aḥmad b. 'Ā'idh al-Aḥmasī 177, 368
Aḥmad b. 'Alī b. Abī Ṭālib al-Ṭabrisī, Abū Manṣūr 22
Aḥmad b. 'Alī al-'Aqīqī 117
Aḥmad b. 'Alī b. Shu'ayb al-Nasā'ī 15
Aḥmad b. al-Ḥasan b. Ismā'īl al-Maythamī 43
Aḥmad b. al-Ḥasan b. Sa'īd al-Khazzāz 276
Aḥmad b. Ḥanbal 92, 163, 205, 396
Aḥmad b. Hilāl 197
Aḥmad b. Maytham 251, 252, 254
Aḥmad b. Muḥammad b. 'Abd Rabbih 14
Aḥmad b. Muḥammad b. Abī Naṣr al-Bazanṭī 131, 138, 163, 215, 216
Aḥmad b. Muḥammad b. 'Īsā al-Ash'arī al-Qummī 151
Aḥmad b. Muḥammad b. Ja'far al-Ṣūlī al-Baṣrī 21
Aḥmad b. Muḥammad b. Khālid al-Barqī 212, 385, 390
Aḥmad b. Muḥammad b. Sa'īd al-Kūfī *see* Ibn 'Uqda
Aḥmad b. Muḥammad b. 'Ubayd Allāh al-Jawharī, Ibn 'Ayyāsh 87
Aḥmad b. Rizq al-Ghumshānī 178–9
Aḥmad b. Sa'īd 300
Aḥmad b. 'Umar al-Ḥallāl 177
Aḥmas 177, 277
Ahwāz 284
'Ā'idh b. Ḥabīb al-Bajalī al-Aḥmasī 177
'Ā'idh b. Nubāta 177
'Ā'isha 106
Ajlaḥ b. 'Abd Allāh al-Kindī 230
Akhbār 'Alī b. al-Ḥusayn 36
Akhbār Fāṭima 21
Akhbār Jābir al-Ju'fī 87
Akhbār al-Zahrā' 21
Akhṭal 202
Akhū Udaym *see* Ayyūb b. al-Ḥurr
Āl Abī Shu'ba 337, 394
Āl A'yan 140, 226, 231, 239, 383, 404
'Alā' b. Fuḍayl al-Nahdī 179–80, 225
'Alā' b. Razīn al-Qallā' 180
Aleppo 337
'Alī b. 'Abd Allāh al-Bajalī 312
'Alī b. 'Abd al-'Azīz 181–3
'Alī b. 'Abd al-'Azīz al-Fazārī *see* 'Alī b. Ghurāb
'Alī b. 'Abd al-'Azīz b. Marzubān b. Sābūr al-Baghawī, Abū 'l-Ḥasan 181
'Alī b. Abī Ḥamza al-Baṭā'inī 183–7, 299, 395
'Alī b. Abī Rāfi' 23, 28, 29
'Alī b. Abī Ṭālib 2–17
'Alī b. Aḥmad al-Fanjkirdī al-Naysābūrī 16
'Alī b. Aḥmad b. 'Umar al-Dāraquṭnī 21
'Alī b. Asbāṭ 237, 342, 397
'Alī b. 'Aṭiyya al-Ḥannāṭ 187–8
'Alī b. Dāwūd al-Ya'qūbī 295
'Alī b. Ghurāb 181, 182
'Alī b. Ghurāb al-Muḥāribī 183
'Alī b. Ḥadīd al-Madā'inī 308, 319, 353
'Alī b. al-Ḥakam al-Nakha'ī 243, 360, 371
'Alī b. al-Ḥasan b. Faḍḍāl 284
'Alī b. al-Ḥasan al-Jarmī al-Ṭāṭarī *see* 'Alī b. al-Ḥasan al-Ṭāṭarī
'Alī b. al-Ḥasan al-Ṭāṭarī 162, 218, 219
'Alī b. Ḥassān b. Kathīr al-Hāshimī 173, 188–9
'Alī b. Ismā'īl b. Ṣāliḥ al-Maythamī 43
'Alī b. Ismā'īl b. Shu'ayb al-Maythamī 43, 161
'Alī b. Ma'bad 220
'Alī b. Manṣūr 263
'Alī b. Muḥammad al-Maythamī 43
'Alī b. Muḥammad al-Madā'inī 13, 267, 288
'Alī b. [Muḥammad b.] al-Qāsim al-Kindī 28
'Alī b. al-Nu'mān al-Nakha'ī 250, 366, 367, 371
'Alī b. Muḥammad b. Sulaymān al-Nawfalī 295
'Alī b. Ri'āb al-Taḥḥān 118, 189
'Alī b. Sayf b. 'Amīra al-Nakha'ī 371
'Alī b. Shajara al-Nabbāl 191–2
'Alī b. 'Uqba b. Bashīr 193
'Alī b. 'Uqba b. Khālid al-Asadī 193–4, 213, 355, 389
'Alī b. Ya'qūb al-Hāshimī 319
'Alī b. Yaqṭīn 163, 169, 194–8
'Alī Zayn al-'Ābidīn 33–6
Amālī Aḥmad b. 'Īsā 276
A'mash *see* Sulaymān b. Mihrān
'Ammār b. Khabbāb al-Duhnī 322
'Ammār b. Marwān al-Kalbī 198
'Ammār b. Marwān al-Thawbānī 198–9
'Ammār b. Marwān al-Yashkurī al-Khazzāz 198, 352
'Ammār al-Maythamī 43
'Ammār b. Mūsā al-Sābāṭī 199–200
'Ammār b. Yāsir 81
'Ammāriyya 199
'Amr b. Abī 'l-Miqdām *see* 'Amr b. Thābit Abī 'l-Miqdām
'Amr b. al-Ḥamiq 40
'Amr b. Ḥazm 10
'Amr b. Ḥurayth al-Makhzūmī 235
'Amr b. Jumay' al-Ḥulwānī 200
'Amr b. Khālid al-Wāsiṭī, Abū Khālid 38, 202–4
'Amr b. Maymūn 103
'Amr b. Sa'īd b. al-'Āṣ 26
'Amr b. Shimr/Shamir al-Ju'fī 93, 100, 103, 204
'Amr b. Thābit Abī 'l-Miqdām 59, 93, 205–7
'Amr b. 'Uthmān 312, 351
Anas b. 'Iyāḍ al-Laythī, Abū Ḍamra 207–8
Anas b. Mālik 149
'Anbasa b. Bijād al-'Ābid 208–9
'Anbasa al-Khath'amī 208
'Anbasa b. Makhlad 208
Anwār al-'uqūl fī ash'ār Waṣī al-Rasūl 16

'Aqīl b. Abī Ṭālib 202
Al-Arba'īn fī faḍā'il al-Zahrā' 21
Armenia 221
Asad Khuzayma 163, 211, 257, 283, 300, 365
Asad Rabī'a 103, 133, 159, 176, 180
Asbadīs 227, 228
Aṣbagh b. Nubāta 17, 59–73, 119, 120
Asbāṭ b. Sālim Bayyā' al-Zuṭṭī 209–10
Ash'arids 139
Ash'ath b. Qays 26
'Āṣim b. Abī 'l-Ḍamra 56
'Āṣim b. Abī 'l-Najūd al-Kūfī 3, 109
'Āṣim b. Ḥumayd al-Ḥannāṭ 210–11, 346, 347
'Āṣim b. Sulaymān al-Kūzī 211–12
Aṣl Muḥammad b. al-Muthannā al-Ḥaḍramī 274, 306
'Āṣma'ī 108
'Aṭā' b. Abī Rabāḥ 4
'Aṭiyya b. al-Ḥārith al-Hamdānī 113
'Awsaja b. Shaddād 26
Ayyūb b. al-Ḥurr 212–13, 384
Ayyūb b. Rāshid 138
Azd 240, 348, 353, 379, 401
Azerbaijan 26, 221
'Azīz Allāh al-'Uṭāridī 22, 36

Bāhila 146, 393
Bajīla 105, 129, 168, 177, 235, 243, 277, 318, 339, 374
Bakr b. Ṣāliḥ al-Rāzī 144, 145
Bakr b. Wā'il 107, 117, 192, 205, 210, 325, 383
Balkh 290
Banū 'Abd al-Qays 103, 133, 176, 320
Banū 'Anaza 150
Banū Asad 42, 139, 141, 163, 193, 198, 208, 303, 305, 331, 366, 367, 380, 388, 389, 391, 395, 398
Banū Aslam 164, 286
Banū 'Awf 244, 348
Banū Ḍabba 211
Banū Ḍubay'a 366
Banū Hāshim 1, 158, 202, 248, 309, 402
Banū Ḥanīfa 210
Banū Ḥanẓala 118
Banū al-Ḥasan 19
Banū Hilāl b. 'Āmir 372
Banū 'Ijl 105, 117, 205, 366, 399
Banū Jurayr 107
Banū Kāhil 163, 257, 300, 365
Banū Kalb b. Wabara 385
Banū Kūz 211
Banū Layth b. Bakr b. 'Abd Manāt 207
Banū Makhzūm 145, 146, 235
Banū Minqar 226
Banū Muḥārib 183
Banū Murād 224
Banū Naṣr b. Qu'ayn 202
Banū Nahd 179, 225, 342
Banū Sa'd b. Bakr 190
Banū Sā'ida 116, 205
Banū 'l-Sakūn 304
Banū Shaybān 192, 239, 342, 383, 404
Banū Taghlib 299
Banū Tamīm 59, 118, 163, 187, 226, 227, 228, 340
Banū Wābish 192
Banū Zuhra b. Kilāb 158, 358, 365
Bashīr al-Muḥammadī al-Māzandarānī 345, 346, 405
Bashīr al-Nabbāl 191, 192
bawwāb 89
bayyā' al-Harawī 177, 212, 384
bayyā' al-ḥarīr 167
bayyā' al-jawārī 351
bayyā' al-karābīs 260
bayyā' al-qalānis 311
bayyā' al-qazz 369
bayyā' al-Sāburī 169, 238, 272, 327, 371, 388
bayyā' al-Zuṭṭī 138, 209
Beast of the Earth 91
Bishr b. al-Mu'tamir 266
Bukhārā 300
Burayd b. Mu'āwiya al-'Ijlī 213–14, 358
Butrī Zaydism 105, 256
Byzantium 140, 346, 404

Catholic 196
Christians 26, 255, 267, 362, 404
Copt 22
Ctesiphon 199, 200, 353

Ḍaḥḥāk *see* Abū Mālik al-Ḥaḍramī
Dāfin *see* 'Abd Allāh b. Muḥammad b. 'Umar b. 'Alī b. Abī Ṭālib
Damascus 135
Dārim 227, 228
Dār al-Lu'lu' 363
Dāwūd b. 'Alī 326
Dāwūd b. Farqad 214
Dāwūd b. al-Ḥuṣayn 214–15, 220
Dāwūd b. Kathīr al-Raqqī 89
Dāwūd b. Sirḥān 215–16
Daylam 373
Dharīḥ b. Muḥammad al-Muḥāribī 217
Dhubyān b. Ḥakīm al-Awdī 355
Dhū al-Dam'a *see* Ḥusayn b. Zayd b. 'Alī
al-Di'āma fī tathbīt al-imāma 241
Dīwān 'Alī 16
Dīwān Zayn al-'Ābidīn 36
Diyāt Ẓarīf b. Nāṣiḥ 13
doorkeeper 89
Du'ā' Abī Ḥamza 379
Du'ā' Kumayl 79
du'ā' al-ṣaḥīfa 34
Du'ā' Samāt 336
Du'ā' Shabbūr 336
du'āt 6
Durust b. Abī Manṣūr al-Wāsiṭī 218–20

Faḍā'il Fāṭima 21
Faḍā'il al-Zahrā' 22
Faḍāla b. Ayyūb al-Azdī 273, 279, 280, 359, 385
Faḍl b. 'Abd al-Malik al-Baqbāq 220–21
Faḍl b. Abī Qurra al-Armanī 221
Faḍl b. Dukayn al-Taymī 251
Faḍl b. Shādhān al-Naysābūrī 140
Faḍl b. Yūnus al-Kātib 222–3
Fakhkh 144
Faraḥzād 394
farā'iḍ 10, 357
Faraj b. Farwa 322
Farazdaq 325
Farrazād 393
Fārs 82
Faṣl li-Hishām b. al-Ḥakam ma' ba'ḍ al-mukhālifīn fī 'l-ḥakamayn bi-Ṣiffīn 267
Faṭḥites 104, 128, 199, 399
Fāṭima al-Zahrā' 17–21
Fawarzād 393
Fazāra 183, 363
Fourteen Infallibles 17
Fuḍayl b 'Abd Allāh al-Rassān 164
Fuḍayl b. 'Iyāḍ 223–4
Fuḍayl Sukkara 104
Fuḍayl b. 'Uthmān al-A'war 224
Fuḍayl b. Yasār al-Nahdī 179, 225–6
Fūrārd 394
Fuṣūṣ al-ḥikam 80

Gabriel 17, 18
Ghālib b. 'Uthmān al-Hamdānī al-Mish'arī 226
Ghālib b. 'Uthmān al-Minqarī 226–7, 362
Ghālib b. al-Hudhayl al-Asadī, Abū 'l-Hudhayl 141
Ghanī b. Ya'ṣur 236
Ghiyāth b. Ibrāhīm al-Nakha'ī al-Kūfī 228
Ghiyāth b. Ibrāhīm al-Tamīmī 227–9
Ghiyāth b. Kallūb al-Bajalī 299
Grand Mosque, Ṣan'ā' 34

Ḥaḍārima 369
Hādī, the 'Abbāsid 158, 194
Ḥadīd b. Ḥakīm al-Madā'inī 353
al-Ḥadīqa al-anīqa 16
Ḥadīth al-Faḍl b. Yūnus al-Kātib 222
Ḥadīth al-Ghadīr 291
Ḥadīth Kumayl 77
Ḥadīth "Ma 'l-ḥaqīqa?" 79
Ḥadīth al-Manzila 6, 339
Ḥafṣ b. al-Bakhtarī 230–31
Ḥafṣ b. Ghiyāth al-Qāḍī 231–5
Ḥafṣ b. Sālim Abū Wallād al-Ḥannāṭ 235
Ḥafṣ b. Sulaymān al-Kūfī 3
Ḥafṣ b. Sūqa al-'Amrī 235–6
Ḥajjāj b. Yūsuf al-Thaqafī 22, 60, 74, 75, 82
Ḥakam b. Abī 'l-'Āṣ 83
Ḥakam b. Miskīn al-Thaqafī al-A'mā 236–8, 400
Ḥakam b. Sa'd al-Asadī al-Nāshirī 356
ḥallāl 177
ḥalīf 358
Hamdān 45
Ḥammād b. Abī Ṭalḥa 238
Ḥammād b. 'Īsā al-Juhanī 225, 245, 246, 277, 291, 292, 342, 361, 362, 371
Ḥammād b. 'Uthmān al-Nāb 239, 381, 383, 384, 398
Ḥamza b. 'Abd al-Muṭṭalib 83
Ḥamza b. Ḥumrān al-Shaybānī 239–40
Ḥamza b. Maytham al-Tammār 42
Hamadān 62
Ḥanān b. Sadīr al-Ṣayrafī 240–42
Ḥarām b. Sa'd b. Ka'b 341
Harāsa 290
Hārith b. 'Abd Allāh b. Abī Rabī'a al-Makhzūmī 145
Ḥārith al-A'war 17, 26, 45–59, 61, 62
Ḥārith b. al-Mughīra al-Naṣrī 242–3
Ḥārith b. Muḥammad al-Aḥwal 243
Ḥarīz b. 'Abd Allāh al-Sijistānī 225, 244–7, 342, 345
Hārūn b. Ḥamza al-Ghanawī 247–8
Hārūn b. al-Jahm 248–9
Hārūn b. Khārija 249–50
Hārūn b. Muslim al-Anbārī al-Kātib 207, 322, 323, 324
Hārūn al-Rashīd 127, 142, 143, 158, 171, 223, 231, 254, 255, 266, 389, 402
Ḥasan b. al-'Abbās b. al-Ḥarīsh al-Rāzī 172
Ḥasan b. 'Abd Allāh al-Rassān 164
Ḥasan b. 'Alī al-'Adawī 347–8
Ḥasan b. 'Alī b. Abī Ḥamza 183–5
Ḥasan b. 'Alī b. Faḍḍāl 140, 148, 149, 179, 192, 193, 227, 239, 319, 333, 380, 399
Ḥasan b. 'Alī al-Washshā' 131, 178, 239, 307, 342, 343, 357
Ḥasan b. 'Alī b. Yūsuf b. Baqqāḥ 357
Ḥasan b. 'Aṭiyya al-Daghshī al-Muḥāribī, Abū Nāb 187
Ḥasan b. Ḥudhayfa b. Manṣūr 272
Ḥasan b. al-Ḥusayn al-'Uranī 254–5
Ḥasan b. Ismā'īl b. Shu'ayb al-Maythamī 43
Ḥasan b. Maḥbūb 131, 133, 142, 184, 190, 191, 223, 235, 236, 241, 243, 256, 285, 286, 309, 311, 317, 342, 360, 365, 377, 378, 389, 397
Ḥasan b. Muḥammad al-Ḥaḍramī 403
Ḥasan b. Muḥammad b. Samā'a 192, 354, 391, 392
Ḥasan b. Muḥammad b. 'Ubayd Allāh al-'Arzamī 175
Ḥasan b. Mūsā al-Nawbakhtī 266
Ḥasan al-Qapānchī 16
Ḥasan b. Rāshid 255–6, 362
Ḥasan b. Sa'īd al-Ahwāzī 403
Ḥasan b. Ṣāliḥ b. Ḥayy 256–7, 265
Ḥasan b. Shajara al-Bajalī 191
Hāshimite Shī'ism 84

Ḥassān al-Jammāl 257–8
Ḥassān b. Mihrān al-Nakha'ī 257
Ḥassān b. Ṣāliḥ al-Maythamī 43
Ḥātim b. Ismā'īl al-Madanī 258–9
Hawāzin 190, 242, 372
Ḥawthī 45
Hebrew 336
Herat 177, 212, 384
Hibat Allāh b. 'Alī, Ibn al-Shajarī 16
Ḥijāz 39
Ḥimṣ 39, 74
Ḥīra 302
Hishām b. 'Abd al-Malik 37, 83, 88, 163
Hishām b. al-Ḥakam 196, 216, 259–68
Hishām b. al-Muḥammad al-Sā'ib al-Kalbī 23
Hishām b. al-Muthannā 268–9
Hishām b. Sālim al-Jawālīqī 269–71, 374
Hīt 74, 75
holy war 234
Ḥudhayfa b. Manṣūr 272
Ḥujr b. 'Adī 40, 202
Ḥujr b. Zā'ida al-Ḥaḍramī 272–3
Ḥulwān 200
Ḥumayd b. al-Muthannā al-'Ijlī 273–4
Ḥumayd b. Shu'ayb al-Sabī'ī 93, 274, 306
Ḥumayd b. Ziyād al-Dihqān 245, 251, 363
Ḥumrān b. A'yan al-Shaybānī 239
Ḥusayn b. Abī 'l-'Alā' 274
Ḥusayn b. Abī Ghundar 275
Ḥusayn al-Aḥmasī 277–9
Ḥusayn b. 'Alī b. al-Ḥasan, Ṣāḥib Fakhkh 127, 195, 294
Ḥusayn b. 'Alwān al-Kalbī 203
Ḥusayn al-Ju'fī 204
Ḥuṣayn b. Mukhāriq al-Salūlī 275–7
Ḥusayn b. al-Mukhtār al-Qalānisī 277
Ḥusayn b. Sa'īd al-Ahwāzī 359, 360
Ḥusayn Shaykh al-Islamī al-Tūysirkānī 22
Ḥusayn b. Thuwayr b. Abī Fākhita 249
Ḥusayn b. 'Uthmān al-Aḥmasī 277–9
Ḥusayn b. 'Uthmān b. Sharīk al-'Āmirī 278, 279–80
Ḥusayn b. Yazīd al-Nawfalī 304, 305
Ḥusayn b. Zayd b. 'Alī, Dhū al-Dam'a 280–83

Ibāḍī 260, 266
Ibn 'Abbās *see* 'Abd Allāh b. 'Abbās
Ibn 'Abda *see* Muḥammad b. 'Abd al-Raḥmān al-'Abdī
Ibn Abī Ḥamza *see* 'Alī b. Abī Ḥamza al-Baṭā'inī
Ibn Abī Harāsa 290
Ibn Abī Ḥātim 396
Ibn Abī 'l-Khaṭṭāb *see* Muḥammad b. al-Ḥusayn b. Abī 'l-Khaṭṭāb
Ibn Abī Khudra 339
Ibn Abī Laylā 109
Ibn Abī 'l-Miqdām *see* 'Amr b. Thābit
Ibn Abī Rāfi' *see* 'Ubayd Allāh b. Abī Rāfi'
Ibn Abī Sabra *see* Rib'ī b. 'Abd Allāh b. al-Jārūd
Ibn Abī 'l-Sammāl 283
Ibn Abī 'Umayr, Abū Aḥmad Muḥammad b. Ziyād al-Azdī 131, 170, 187, 188, 209, 217, 218, 220, 223, 224, 226, 231, 236, 239, 241, 242, 260, 269, 271, 273, 275, 278, 279, 293, 299, 303, 307, 309, 314, 316, 318, 319, 326, 342, 343, 347, 348, 351, 354, 361, 362, 365, 366, 371, 373, 381, 387, 395, 398, 400, 401, 402
Ibn Abī 'l-Thalj *see* Muḥammad b. Aḥmad al-Kātib al-Baghdādī
Ibn Abī Ya'fūr *see* 'Abd Allāh b. Abī Ya'fūr
Ibn Abī Yaḥyā *see* Ibrāhīm b. Muḥammad b. Abī Yaḥyā
Ibn 'Arabī *see* Muḥyī 'l-Dīn b. 'Arabī
Ibn al-Ash'ath *see* 'Abd al-Raḥmān b. Muḥammad b. al-Ash'ath
Ibn 'Ayyāsh *see* Aḥmad b. Muḥammad b. 'Ubayd Allāh al-Jawharī
Ibn Fahd *see* Aḥmad b. Muḥammad b. Fahd al-Ḥillī 336
Ibn al-Ḥajjāj *see* 'Abd al-Raḥmān b. al-Ḥajjāj
Ibn Hammām *see* Muḥammad b. Hammām al-Iskāfī
Ibn al-Ḥanafiyya *see* Muḥammad Ibn al-Ḥanafiyya
Ibn Harāsa *see* Ibrāhīm b. Rajā' al-Shaybānī
Ibn al-Ḥarīsh *see* Ḥasan b. al-'Abbās b. al-Ḥarīsh al-Rāzī
Ibn al-Ji'ābī *see* Muḥammad b. 'Umar al-Tamīmī
Ibn Muskān *see* 'Abd Allāh b. Muskān
Ibn al-Najāshī 284
Ibn al-Qaddāḥ *see* 'Abd Allāh b. Maymūn al-Qaddāḥ
Ibn Rustam al-Ṭabarī 21
Ibn Shihāb al-Zuhrī, Muḥammad b. Muslim 36
Ibn Sa'd 396
Ibn Taymiyya 14
Ibn 'Uqda, Aḥmad b. Muḥammad b. Sa'īd al-Kūfī 61, 141, 230, 276, 278, 298, 369
Ibrāhīm b. 'Abd Allāh b. al-Ḥasan 127, 325
Ibrāhīm b. Abī Bakr b. Abī 'l-Sammāl al-Asadī 283–5
Ibrāhīm b. Abī Ḥafṣa al-Bajalī 105
Ibrāhīm b. Harāsa *see* Ibrāhīm b. Rajā' al-Shaybānī
Ibrāhīm b. Hāshim al-Qummī 67, 148, 241, 367
Ibrāhīm b. 'Īsā, Abū Ayyūb al-Kharrāz 285
Ibrāhīm b. Mihzam b. Abī Burayda 286
Ibrāhīm b. al-Muhājir al-Bajalī al-Kūfī 105
Ibrāhīm b. Muḥammad b. Abī Yaḥyā al-Madanī 286–8
Ibrāhīm b. Muḥammad al-Thaqafī 14
Ibrāhīm b. al-Naḍr 43
Ibrāhīm b. Nu'aym, Abū 'l-Ṣabbāḥ al-Kinānī 289
Ibrāhīm b. Rajā' al-Shaybānī, Ibn Harāsa 290–91
Ibrāhīm b. Shu'ayb al-Maythamī 43
Ibrāhīm b. 'Umar al-Yamānī 226, 291–3

Ibrāhīm b. al-Walīd 135
Ibrāhīm b. al-Zibriqān 203
If'al lā taf'al 339
Ifādat al-baṣīr 150
Al-Ihlīlaja 334
Ilyās b. Muḍar 164
'Imrān b. Maytham al-Tammār 42
'Imrān al-Thaqafī 386
'Īṣ b. al-Qāsim al-Bajalī 293
'Īsā b. 'Abd Allāh b. Muḥammad b. 'Umar b. 'Alī 131, 294–8
'Īsā b. Dāwūd al-Najjār 298–9
Isaac 336
Iṣfahān 26
Isḥāq b. 'Ammār al-Ṣayrafī 299
Isḥāq b. Bashīr al-Khurāsānī, Abū Ḥudhayfa 300
Isḥāq b. Bashīr al-Nabbāl 191
Isḥāq b. Bishr al-Kāhilī 300–301
Isḥāq b. Ghālib 141
Isḥāq b. Ja'far al-Ṣādiq 301–2
Isḥāq b. Jarīr al-Bajalī 302–3, 311
Isḥāq b. Shu'ayb al-Maythamī 43
Isḥāq b. 'Ubayd Allāh al-Fazārī al-'Arzamī 175
Ishmael 336
Ismā'īl b. Abān b. Isḥāq al-Azdī al-Warrāq 228, 229
Ismā'īl b. 'Abd al-'Azīz b. 'Abd Allāh al-'Abdī 133
Ismā'īl b. 'Abd al-Khāliq al-Asadī 303–4
Ismā'īl b. Abī Bakr b. Abī 'l-Sammāl al-Asadī 283, 284
Ismā'īl b. Abī Ziyād al-Sakūnī 304–5
Ismā'īl b. Ḥasan b. Ismā'īl al-Maythamī 43
Ismā'īl b. Isḥāq al-Jahḍamī al-Azdī 15
Ismā'īl b. Jābir al-Khath'amī 305–6
Ismā'īl b. Maytham al-Tammār 42
Ismā'īl b. Mihrān al-Sakūnī 13, 81, 250
Ismā'īl b. Shu'ayb al-Maythamī 43
Ismā'īl b. 'Ubayd Allāh b. al-Walīd al-Waṣṣāfī 382
istiṭā'a 140, 213, 217, 342

Jābir b. 'Abd Allāh al-Anṣārī 89, 149, 167
Jābir al-Ju'fī 86–103, 184, 204, 205, 274, 299, 306, 352
Jābir b. Samura b. Junāda al-Suwā'ī 358
Jacob 336
Ja'da b. Hubayra al-Makhzūmī 355
Ja'far b. 'Abd Allāh al-Muḥammadī 322
Ja'far b. Abī Ṭālib 83
Ja'far b. Bashīr al-Bajalī 217, 363
Ja'far b. Muḥammad b. Ḥakīm 165
Ja'far b. Muḥammad al-Khashshāb 230
Ja'far b. Muḥammad b. Shurayḥ al-Ḥaḍramī 306
Ja'far b. Muḥammad b. 'Ubayd Allāh al-Ash'arī 147, 148
Ja'far b. Yaḥyā b. al-'Alā' al-Bajalī al-Rāzī 394
Jafr 5, 18
Jalaba b. 'Iyāḍ 207
Jalāl al-Dīn al-Suyūṭī, 'Abd al-Raḥmān b. Abī Bakr 16, 22
Jāmi' 228, 380, 381
Jāmi' al-Ḥalabī 381
Jāmi'a 4, 18, 228
Jamīl b. Darrāj al-Nakha'ī 307–8, 343, 353
Jamīl b. Ṣāliḥ al-Asadī 308–9
Jarīr b. 'Abd Allāh al-Bajalī 235, 302
Jarīr b. Yazīd b. Jarīr b. 'Abd Allāh al-Bajalī 302
Jarjarāyā 342
Jarm 190, 340
Jarrāḥ b. 'Abd Allāh al-Madanī 309
Jarrāḥ al-Madā'inī 309
Jarrāḥ b. Malīḥ al-Ru'āsī 158, 402
Jārūd b. Abī Sabra al-Hudhalī 361
Jārūdī Zaydism 105, 121
Jawād al-Qayyūmī al-Iṣfahānī 35
Jawālīqī *see* Hishām b. Sālim
Jāziya 134
Jews 6, 59, 151, 206, 336
Jhāts 138, 209
Ju'fī 212
Juz' fī faḍā'il Fāṭima 21

Ka'ba 173
Kāhil *see* Banū Kāhil
Kahlān 105, 192
Kāmil Salmān al-Jubūrī 316
Karīm 58
Karrām *see* 'Abd al-Karīm b. 'Amr al-Khath'amī
Kathīr b. 'Ayyāsh al-Qaṭṭān 122
Kathīr b. Ṭāriq al-Qanbarī 309–10
Al-Kawthar 22
Kaydarī *see* Muḥammad b. al-Ḥusayn
Kaysānī Shī'ism 91, 110, 115
Kāẓim Ja'far al-Miṣbāḥ 345, 405
Khabar wafāt Salmān al-Fārsī 61
Khālid b. Awfā, Abū 'l-Rabī' al-Shāmī 310
Khālid b. Jarīr al-Bajalī 310, 311
Khālid b. Mādd al-Qalānisī 311–12
Khālid b. Sa'īd al-Qammāṭ 312–13
Khālid b. Ṭahmān al-Salūlī 313
Khallād b. 'Īsā 314
Khallād b. Khalaf al-Muqri' 314
Khallād b. Khālid al-Muqri' 314
Khallād al-Sindī al-Bazzāz 313–14
Khārif 45
Khārijites 190, 216, 244, 266, 339
Khath'am 137, 341
Khaybarī b. 'Alī al-Ṭaḥḥān 249, 314–15
Khazraj 212
Khilās b. 'Amr al-Hajarī al-Baṣrī 8, 46, 58
khirqa 76
Khurāsān 223, 300, 355, 373
Khuṭbat al-Wasīla 103
Khuzā'a 158, 272, 350
Khuzayma b. Yaqṭīn 195
Kinda 108, 192, 209, 304, 369
Kirmān 200

Kisā'ī, 'Alī b. Ḥamza al-Asadī al-Kūfī 109
Kisfiyya 265
Kitāb Abī Rāfi' 23
Kitāb ākhar 'alā 'l-Mu'tazila 267
Kitāb akhbār Abī Rāfi' 26
Kitāb al-akhbār [*wa kayfa taṣiḥḥ*] 268
Kitāb al-alfāẓ 267
Kitāb 'Alī 4–12
Kitāb al-alṭāf 267
Kitāb 'amal yawm wa layla 159
Kitāb al-arba'imi'at mas'ala fī abwāb al-ḥalāl wa 'l-ḥarām 345
Kitāb Aṣbagh 61
Kitāb al-aẓilla 173
Kitāb Burayh al-Naṣrānī 268
Kitāb al-dalā'il 251
Kitāb al-dilāla 'alā ḥadath al-ajsām 263
Kitāb al-dilālāt 251
Kitāb al-diyāt 12, 139, 191, 357
Kitāb al-du'ā' 329
Kitāb al-faḍā'il 97, 112, 113
Kitāb faḍā'il Amīr al-Mu'minīn 253
Kitāb faḍā'il al-ḥajj 332
Kitāb faḍā'il al-Qur'ān 250
Kitāb faḍl sūrat Innā anzalnāh 172
Kitāb Fadak 172
Kitāb fakkir 334
Kitāb al-farā'iḍ 13, 254, 387
Kitāb fī bad' al-khalq wa 'l-ḥathth 'alā 'l-i'tibār 334
Kitāb [*fī*] *al-Ḥakamayn* 267
Kitāb fī 'l-imāma 151–2
Kitāb fī 'l-jabr wa 'l-qadar 266
Kitāb fī 'l-jism wa 'l-ru'ya 267
Kitāb fī manāsik al-ḥajj wa farā'iḍih 388
Kitāb fī ṣifat al-janna wa 'l-nār 241
Kitāb al-fitan 252
Kitāb fī 'l-tawḥid 217
Kitāb al-gharīb fī 'l-Qur'ān 112
Kitāb [*fī*] *al-Ḥakamayn* 267
Kitāb al-ghayba 253
Kitāb ḥadīth al-Shūrā 103, 204
Kitāb al-haft wa 'l-aẓilla 173, 335
Kitāb al-ḥajj 271, 318, 327, 399
Kitāb al-Ḥalabī 382
Kitāb Ḥarīz 245
Kitāb Ibn Abī Rāfi' 26
Kitāb al-iḥtijāj fī imāmat Amīr al-Mu'minīn 339
Kitāb ikhtilāf al-nās fī 'l-imāma 265
Kitāb 'ilal al-sharā'i' 335
Kitāb 'ilal al-taḥrīm wa 'l-farā'iḍ 262
Kitāb al-imāma 262
Kitāb al-īmān wa 'l-islām 335
Kitāb al-istiṭā'a 266
Kitāb al-istiṭā'a 'alā Hishām b. al-Ḥakam 266
Kitāb al-istiṭā'a wa 'l-jabr 404
Kitāb Jābir al-Ju'fī 103
Kitāb Ja'far b. Muḥammad b. Shurayḥ al-Ḥaḍramī 93
Kitāb al-Jamal 99
Kitāb jāmi' al-'ilm 276
Kitāb kalāmih 'alā 'l-Khawārij 339
Kitāb khurūj Ṣāḥib Fakhkh wa maqtalih 144
Kitāb khurūj Muḥammad b. 'Abd Allāh wa maqtalih 144
Kitāb khuṭab Amīr al-Mu'minīn 81, 321
Kitāb mab'ath al-Nabī wa akhbārih 147
Kitāb mā iftaraḍ Allāh 'alā 'l-jawāriḥ min al-īmān 335
Kitāb al-majālis fī 'l-imāma 263
Kitāb al-majālis fī 'l-tawḥīd 263
Kitāb al-malāḥim 252
Kitābal-manāsik 38, 202
Kitāb maqtal Amīr al-Mu'minīn 101, 230
Kitāb maqtal al-Ḥusayn 102
Kitāb al-ma'rifa 267
Kitāb al-masā'il 347, 381, 382
Kitāb masā'il Abī 'l-Ḥasan Mūsā b. Ja'far 197
Kitāb al-masā'il allatī akhbara bihā Amīr al-Mu'minīn al-Yahūdī 59, 206
Kitāb mā su'ila 'anhu 'l-Ṣādiq min umūr al-malāḥim 196
Kitāb al-maydān 265
Kitāb maytham 43
Kitāb mazār Amīr al-Mu'minīn 331
Kitāb min al-uṣūl fī 'l-riwāya 'alā madhāhib al-Shī'a 116
Kitāb al-mi'rāj 271
Kitāb al-mīzān 265, 266
Kitāb al-mubtada' wa 'l-mab'ath wa 'l-maghāzī wa 'l-wafāt wa 'l-Saqīfa wa 'l-ridda 130
Kitāb munāẓaratihi [ma'] al-shākk bi-ḥaḍrat Ja'far 196
Kitāb musnad 'Umar b. 'Alī b. Abī Ṭālib 298
Kitāb al-mut'a 254
Kitāb al-Nahrawān 101
Kitāb al-qadar 266
Kitāb qaḍāyā Amīr al-Mu'minīn 27, 346
Kitāb al-Qā'im 252
Kitāb al-qirā'a 111
Kitāb al-radd 'alā Arasṭālīs fī 'l-tawḥīd 264
Kitāb al-radd 'alā aṣḥāb al-ithnayn 264
Kitāb al-radd 'alā aṣḥāb al-ṭabā'i' 264
Kitāb al-radd 'alā Hishām al-Jawālīqī 264
Kitāb al-radd 'alā 'l-Mu'tazila fī Ṭalḥa wa 'l-Zubayr 267
Kitāb [*al-radd*] *'alā Shayṭān al-Ṭāq* 265
Kitāb al-radd 'alā 'l-Zanādiqa 263
Kitāb al-rāhib wa 'l-rāhiba 255, 362
Kitāb al-raj'a 253
Kitāb al-ṣalāt 162, 186, 245, 253, 331
Kitāb al-ṣalāt al-kabīr 159
Kitāb al-ṣawm 247
Kitāb al-shaykh wa 'l-ghulām 264
Kitāb ṣifat al-janna wa 'l-nār 93, 147, 241
Kitāb Ṣiffīn 100, 115
Kitāb al-ṣirāṭ 335
Kitāb Sulaym b. Qays al-Hilālī 83–6, 292
Kitāb ṣulḥ al-Ḥasan 172

Kitāb al-sunan wa 'l-aḥkām wa 'l-qaḍāyā 24, 26
Kitāb al-ṣūra 340
Kitāb al-tadbīr 263
Kitāb al-tafsīr 94, 162, 184–6, 269, 298, 305, 337
Kitāb al-tafsīr wa 'l-qirā'āt 276
Kitāb al-ṭalāq 238, 331
Kitāb al-tawḥīd 264, 268
Kitāb al-thamāniyat abwāb 268
Kitāb thawāb Innā anzalnāh 172
Kitāb al-'ulūm 276
Kitāb al-umm 288
Kitāb al-waṣāyā 238
Kitāb waṣiyyat Mūsā b. Ja'far 144
Kitāb al-waṣiyya wa 'l-imāma 190
Kitāb al-waṣiyya wa 'l-radd 'alā man ankarahā 262
Kitāb yawm wa layla 330, 336, 374, 395
Kitāb al-zakāt 186, 246, 331
Kitāb al-ẓihār 238
Kitāb al-zuhd 379
Kitābuh ilā Muḥammad b. Muslim al-Zuhrī 35
Kuhayl al-Fazārī 76
Kulayb b. Mu'āwiya al-Ṣaydāwī 315
Kulthum bint Yūsuf b. 'Imrān al-Maythamī 43
Kumayl b. Ziyād al-Nakha'ī 74–80, 109
Kumayliyya 78
kunya 143, 171

lawḥ 20
Layth b. al-Bakhtarī al-Murādī 315–16
Lūṭ b. Yaḥyā al-Azdī, Abū Mikhnaf 316

Ma'dān al-Shumayṭī, Abū 'l-Sarī 78
Mahdī 19, 83, 88
Mahdī, the 'Abbāsid 157, 158, 194, 280
Majmū' 202
Mālik b. Anas 286
Mālik al-Ashtar 7, 39, 60, 202
Mālik b. 'Aṭiyya al-Aḥmasī 316–17
Mālik b. A'yan al-Juhanī 82
Ma'mar b. Yaḥyā b. Sām 317
Ma'mar b. al-Muthannā *see* Abū 'Ubayda
Ma'mūn, the 'Abbāsid 128
Manāqib Fāṭima 22
Al-Manāsik 38, 202
Manicheans 19, 20
Manṣūr 88
Manṣūr, the 'Abbāsid 19, 91, 127, 157, 158, 171, 195, 255, 280, 359
Manṣūr b. Ḥāzim al-Bajalī 317–18
Manṣūr b. Yūnus Buzurj 318–19
Maqtal Amīr al-Mu'minīn 230
Mā rawāh al-ḥawāriyyūn 345, 405
Marw 183
Marwān 83
Marwān b. Muslim 319
Mas'ada b. Ṣadaqa 13, 200, 319–20
Mas'ada b. al-Yasa' al-Bāhilī 320, 322–3
Mas'ada b. Ziyād al-Raba'ī 320, 323–5
Al-Masā'il 347, 381, 382
Masāmi'a 325
Maṣdaq b. Ṣadaqa 199
Mashhad 34
Masjid Dār al-Lu'lu' 363
Masjid al-Ḥaḍārima 369, 403
Masjid al-Ḥawāfir 202
Masjid Ju'fī 204
Masjid Simāk 202, 343, 380
Mawlid Fāṭima 21
Mā yakūn 'ind ẓuhūr al-Mahdī 335
Maymūn al-Qaddāḥ 145
Maymūn b. Sanjār 191
Maytham al-Tammār 42–4, 398
Mesopotamia 134, 171, 268
Mikhnaf b. Sulaym 26
Miqdād b. al-Aswad al-Kindī 1, 89
Misma' b. 'Abd al-Malik Kurdīn 320
Moses 6
Mosul 304
Mu'allā b. Khunays 326, 362
Mu'ammar b. Muḥammad b. 'Ubayd Allāh b. Abī Rāfi' 349
Mu'āwiya b. 'Ammār al-Duhnī 155, 326–32, 399
Mu'āwiya b. Wahb al-Bajalī 332
Mufaḍḍal b. Ṣāliḥ al-Asadī, Abū Jamīla 315, 333, 402
Mufaḍḍal b. 'Umar al-Ju'fī 173, 272, 273, 314, 333–7
Mufawwiḍa 272
Mughīra b. Sa'īd al-Bajalī 87
Mughīriyya 87
Muḥammad b. al-'Abd al-Ḥamīd 241
Muḥammad b. 'Abd Allāh al-Arqaṭ 280
Muḥammad b. 'Abd Allāh al-Haḍramī al-Kūfī, Muṭayyan 15
Muḥammad b. 'Abd Allāh b. al-Ḥasan, al-Nafs al-Zakiyya 19, 87, 127, 144, 163, 230, 280, 294, 325
Muḥammad b. 'Abd Allāh b. Hilāl 389
Muḥammad b. 'Abd Allāh al-Naysābūrī, al-Ḥākim 21
Muḥammad b. 'Abd Allāh al-Zubayrī *see* Abū Aḥmad al-Zubayrī
Muḥammad b. 'Abd al-Raḥmān 113
Muḥammad b. 'Abd al-Raḥmān al-'Abdī, Ibn 'Abda 163, 180
Muḥammad b. 'Abd al-Raḥmān b. Muḥammad b. 'Ubayd Allāh al-Fazārī 175
Muḥammad b. Abī Bakr 26
Muḥammad b. Abī Ḥamza al-Thumālī 215, 398
Muḥammad b. Abī Zaynab al-Asadī *see* Abū 'l-Khaṭṭāb
Muḥammad b. Aḥmad al-Kātib al-Baghdādī, Ibn Abī 'l-Thalj 21
Muḥammad b. 'Alī b. 'Abd Allāh b. al-'Abbās 171
Muḥammad b. 'Alī b. Abī Shu'ba al-Ḥalabī 153–5, 337–8, 380
Muḥammad b. 'Alī b. al-Nu'mān, Ṣāḥib al-Ṭāq 243, 338–9

Muḥammad b. 'Alī b. Ibrāhīm al-Qurashī, Abū Sumayna 290
Muḥammad b. 'Alī al-Ṣayrafī 368
Muḥammad al-Amīn, the 'Abbāsid 195
Muḥammad b. 'Amr al-Zubayrī 340
Muḥammad al-Arqaṭ *see* Muḥammad b. 'Abd Allāh al-Arqaṭ
Muḥammad b. 'Aṭiyya 316
Muḥammad b. Bakr al-Arḥabī al-Kūfī 123
Muḥammad b. Bakr b. Janāḥ 241
Muḥammad al-Bāqir 37–8
Muḥammad al-Bāqir al-Maḥmūdī 15
Muḥammad al-Bāqir al-Mūsawī 22
Muḥammad al-Bāqir al-Muwaḥḥid al-Abṭaḥī 35
Muḥammad b. al-Fuḍayl 289
Muḥammad b. Furāt 340–41
Muḥammad b. al-Furāt al-Jarāmī 341
Muḥammad b. Furāt al-Tamīmī al-Kūfī 340
Muḥammad b. al-Ḥadīd al-Madā'inī 353
Muḥammad b. Ḥakīm al-Khath'amī 341–2
Muḥammad b. Hammām al-Iskāfī 151, 298, 362
Muḥammad Ibn al-Ḥanafiyya 6, 40, 60
Muḥammad b. al-Ḥasan b. Aḥmad b. al-Walīd al-Qummī 401
Muḥammad b. al-Ḥasan al-Shaybānī 243
Muḥammad b. al-Ḥasan b. Ziyād al-Maythamī 43
Muḥammad b. Ḥumrān b. A'yan 343
Muḥammad b. Ḥumrān al-Nahdī 307, 342–3
Muḥammad b. al-Ḥusayn b. Abī 'l-Khaṭṭāb 156, 236–7, 352, 392
Muḥammad b. al-Ḥusayn al-Kaydarī al-Bayhaqī, Quṭb al-Dīn 16
Muḥammad Ḥusayn al-Muẓaffar 339
Muḥammad b. Idrīs al-Shāfi'ī 286
Muḥammad b. 'Īsā 149
Muḥammad b. 'Īsā b. 'Ubayd al-Yaqṭīnī 195, 219, 241, 399, 401, 403
Muḥammad b. Ismā'īl b. Bazī' 241, 289, 314, 319, 351, 367
Muḥammad b. Ja'far b. al-Nu'mān 339
Muḥammad b. Khalaf al-Marwazī 354
Muḥammad b. Khālid al-Barqī 156, 197, 249, 360, 376
Muḥammad b. Khālid al-Ṭayālisī 304, 341, 363, 371
Muḥammad al-Mahdī, the 'Abbāsid caliph 280
Muḥammad b. Makkī al-'Āmilī 299
Muḥammad b. Maymūn al-Za'farānī 343
Muḥammad b. Maytham al-Tammār 42
Muḥammad b. Mufaḍḍal 335
Muḥammad b. Murāzim al-Madā'inī 353
Muḥammad b. Muslim al-Ṭā'ifī al-Makkī 344
Muḥammad b. Muslim al-Thaqafī 104, 180, 181, 247, 344–5
Muḥammad b. Muslim al-Zuhrī *see* Ibn Shihāb
Muḥammad b. Muthannā al-Ḥaḍramī 217
Muḥammad b. Nu'mān al-Aḥwal 339
Muḥammad b. al-Qāsim b. Fuḍayl al-Nahdī 179
Muḥammad b. Qays al-Asadī al-Wālibī 345–6
Muḥammad b. Qays al-Bajalī 345–6
Muḥammad b. Qays al-Madanī 346
Muḥammad b. Rāshid 228
Muḥammad b. Ṣadaqa 348
Muḥammad b. al-Sā'ib al-Kalbī 113
Muḥammad b. Sallām al-Jumaḥī 129
Muḥammad b. Sinān al-Zāhirī 93, 123, 151, 158, 173, 179, 198, 238, 312, 335, 352, 375
Muḥammad b. Sulaymān al-Daylamī 374
Muḥammad b. Sūqa al-Kūfī al-'Ābid 236
Muḥammad b. Sūqa al-Marḍī al-Khazzāz 235, 236
Muḥammad b. Tamīm al-Nahshalī 347–8
Muḥammad b. Thābit b. Dīnār al-Thumālī 348
Muḥammad b. 'Ubayd Allāh b. Abī Rāfi' 29, 348–50
Muḥammad b. 'Ubayd Allāh al-'Arzamī 174
Muḥammad b. 'Ubayd al-Muḥāribī 343
Muḥammad b. 'Udhāfir al- Madā'inī 350–51, 388
Muḥammad b. 'Umar b. 'Alī b. Abī Ṭālib 119
Muḥammad b. 'Umar al-Māzinī al-Baṣrī 131
Muḥammad b. 'Umar al-Tamīmī, Ibn al-Ji'ābī 297–8
Muḥammad b. 'Umar b. 'Ubayd Allāh 29
Muḥammad b. 'Umar al-Wāqidī 13, 287
Muḥammad b. 'Umar b. Yazīd 351
Muḥammad b. 'Uthmān al-'Amrī 336
Muḥammad b. al-Walīd al-Khazzāz 228, 239, 351, 376
Muḥammad b. Yaḥyā al-Khath'amī 229, 351
Muḥammad b. Ya'qūb b. Shu'ayb al-Maythamī 43
Muḥammad b. Zakariyyā b. Dīnār al-Jawharī al-Ghallābī al-Baṣrī 21
Muḥammad b. Zakariyyā b. Mu'āwiya 310
Muḥsin al-Maythamī 43
Muḥassin b. Aḥmad al-Qaysī 131
Muḥyī 'l-Dīn b. 'Arabī 79
Mukhtār al-Thaqafī 6
Mu'min al-Ṭāq *see* Muḥammad b. 'Alī b. al-Nu'mān
Munakhkhal b. Jamīl al-Raqqī 351–2
Murāzim b. Ḥakīm al-Madā'inī 308, 353
Mūsā b. Bakr al-Wāsiṭī 354
Mūsā b. Ibrāhīm al-Marwazī 354–5
Mūsā b. al-Qāsim al-Bajalī 351
Mūsā b. Ranjawayh al-Armanī 143
Mūsā b. Sa'dān al-Ḥannāṭ 156
Mūsā b. Ukayl al-Numayrī 355
Mūsā b. 'Umayr Abū Hārūn al-Makfūf 355
Muṣḥaf Fāṭima 5, 6, 17
Mushma'ill b. Sa'd al-Nāshirī 356
Musnad 'Abd Allāh b. Bukayr b. A'yan 141
Musnad 'Alī 15

Musnad Ahl al-Bayt 347
Musnad Fāṭima 21, 21
Musnad al-Imām Mūsā b. Ja'far 354
Musnad al-Imām al-Sajjād 36
Musnad al-imām Zayd 203
Musnad Muḥammad b. Muslim al-Thaqafī al-Ṭā'ifī 345
Musnad Muḥammad b. Qays al-Bajalī 346
Musnad 'Umar b. 'Alī b. Abī Ṭālib 297
Musnad Zurāra b. A'yan 405
mut'a 108, 254
Mu'taman *see* Isḥāq b. Ja'far al-Ṣādiq
mutawātir 268
Mu'tazilites 131, 260, 266, 267, 268, 288
Muthannā b. al-Walīd al-Ḥannāṭ 357
Muṭṭalib b. Ziyād b. Abī Zuhayr 357–8
Muwaṭṭa' 286

nabīdh 136
Naḍr b. Shu'ayb 134, 311
Naḍr b. Suwayd al-Ṣayrafī 309, 359, 392
al-Nafs al-Zakiyya *see* Muḥammad b. 'Abd Allāh b. al-Ḥasan
Nahj al-balāgha 13–14
Nahrawān 59, 342
Najm al-Dīn Kubrā 76
Najrān 26, 255
Nakha' 307
Naṣr b. Mu'āwiya 242
Naṣr b. Muzāḥim 182, 203
Naṣṣ 262, 271
Nawbandagān 82
Nāwūsiyya 130
Night Journey 5, 271, 300
Nu'aym b. Ḥammād 287
Nūḥ b. Darrāj 307
Nuṣayriyya 139, 334, 335
Nuṣrat madhāhib al-Zaydiyya 241
Nuṣūs min tā'rīkh Abī Mikhnaf 316

Qaḍāyā Amīr al-Mu'minīn 27, 67
Qā'im 88, 250, 252, 253
Qanbar 309
Qāsim b. Aṣbagh b. Nubāta 61
Qāsim b. Burayd b. Mu'āwiya al-'Ijlī 358–9
Qāsim b. Fuḍayl b. Yasār al-Nahdī 179, 225
Qāsim b. Ismā'īl al-Qurashī 363
Qāsim b. Muḥammad b. al-Ḥusayn b. Ḥāzim 369
Qāsim b. al-Rabī' al-Ṣaḥḥāf 330
Qāsim b. Sallām *see* Abū 'Ubayd
Qāsim b. Sulaymān al-Baghdādī 309, 359
Qāsim b. 'Urwa 359–60
qāṣṣ 118
Qaṭī'at al-Rabī' 158
Qays b. 'Amr al-Najāshī al-Ḥārithī 284
Qays 'Aylān 192, 236, 393
Qays b. Sa'd b. 'Ubāda 26
Quḍā'a 190, 340, 342, 385
Quraysh 1, 41, 145, 157, 158, 248, 310, 318, 358, 365
'Qurrā' 74

Rabī' b. Muḥammad al-Muslī al-Aṣamm 360
Rabī' b. Yūnus, Ibn Abī Farwa 158
Rabī'a 105, 157, 320, 325
Rabī'a b. Sumay' 33
Raḍawī Library 34
Rāfiḍa 266
raj'a 91
Rajā' b. Abī Salama Mihrān, Abū 'l-Miqdām 290
Rajā' b. Salama 290
Ramla 290
Raqqa 202, 321
Rashīd al-Hajarī 40
Rasūl Ja'fariyān 130
Rawḥ b. 'Abd al-Raḥīm 362
Ray 200, 393, 394
ra'y 140
Riḍā Ustādī 14
Rib'ī b. 'Abd Allāh al-Hudhalī 225, 361–2
Rifā'a b. Mūsā al-Nakhkhās 360–61
Risālat Abī Ja'far ilayh 119
Risālat al-ḥuqūq 35, 379
Risāla ilā ba'ḍ aṣḥābih 35
Risālat Mayyāḥ 336
Rushayd al-Hajarī 40
Ruzayq b. Zubayr al-Khulqānī 362–3

Saba'iyya 91, 110
Sābāṭ 199, 353
Ṣabbāḥ al-Madā'inī 335
Ṣabbāḥ b. Ṣabīḥ al-Fazārī 363
Ṣabbāḥ b. Yaḥyā al-Muzanī 364
Sabī' 272
Sābirī 169
Sāburī 169
Sa'd b. 'Abd Allāh al-Ash'arī al-Qummī 266
Sa'd b. 'Abd al-Malik 119
Sa'd b. Abī Khalaf al-Zāmm 365
Sa'd b. Abī Waqqāṣ 358
Sa'd al-Khayr 119
Sa'd b. Ṭarīf al-Iskāf 118–21
Saffāḥ *see* Abū 'l-'Abbās al-Saffāḥ
Ṣafwān b. Mihrān al-Jammāl 341, 365
Ṣafwān b. Yaḥyā al-Bajalī 141, 170, 187, 208, 224, 240, 242, 273, 275, 285, 289, 293, 303, 306, 318, 326, 345, 354, 361, 366, 367, 387, 398, 399, 402
Sahand 221
Ṣāḥib b. 'Abbād 241
Ṣāḥib Fakhkh *see* Ḥusayn b. 'Alī b. al-Ḥusayn
Ṣaḥīfat 'Alī b. Abī Ṭālib 'an Rasūl Allāh 6
Ṣaḥīfat 'Alī b. al-Ḥusayn fī 'l-zuhd 35
Ṣaḥīfa al-farā'iḍ 10
Ṣaḥīfa al-Ḥārith al-A'war 46
Ṣaḥīfat Isḥāq b. Ja'far al-Ṣādiq 'an ābā'ih 302
al-Ṣaḥīfa al-kāmila 34

al-Ṣaḥīfa al-Sajjādiyya 34
al-Ṣaḥīfa al-Sajjādiyya al-jāmi'a 35
Sa'īd b. 'Abd Allāh al-A'raj 365
Sa'īd b. 'Amr al-'Anazī 322
Sa'īd b. al-'Āṣ 23
Sa'īd b. Ghazwān al-Asadī 366
Sa'īd b. Janāḥ al-Kūfī 93, 241
Sa'īd b. Yasār al-Ḍuba'ī 366–7
Ṣāliḥ b. Abī Ḥammād al-Rāzī 13
Ṣāliḥ b. Khālid al-Maḥāmilī 379
Ṣāliḥ b. Maytham al-Tammār 42, 43
Ṣāliḥ b. Sa'īd al-Qammāṭ 367
Ṣāliḥ b. 'Uqba 367
Sālim b. Abī Ḥafṣa 105–7
Sālim b. Dīnār 105
Sālim b. Mukram, Abū Khadīja al-Jammāl 177, 368
Sālim b. 'Ubayd 105
Sallām b. 'Abd Allāh al-Hāshimī 368
Sallām b. Abī 'Amra 369
Salmān al-Fārsī 1, 61, 89
Salwat al-Shī'a 16
samā' 86
Samā'a b. Mihrān al-Ḥaḍramī 369–70, 403
Ṣan'ā' 34
Saqīfa *see* Saqīfat Banī Sā'ida 116, 130, 205
Sarī b. 'Abd Allāh al-Sulamī 370
Sarī b. Manṣūr al-Shaybānī, Abū 'l-Sarāyā
Ṣaydā 315
Sayf b. Amīra al-Nakha'ī 318, 371
al-Sayyid al-Ḥimyarī 89, 284
Shabbūr 336
Shāfi'ī *see* Muḥammad b. Idrīs
al-Shahīd al-Awwal *see* Muḥammad b. Makkī al-'Āmilī
Shāh Ṭāq *see* Muḥammad b. 'Alī b. al-Nu'mān
Shajara b. Maymūn al-Bajalī 191
Shammetha 336
Shāpūrī 169, 170, 238, 272, 327, 388
Sharīf al-Raḍī, Muḥammad b. al-Ḥusayn al-Mūsawī 14
Sharīf b. Sābiq al-Tiflīsī 221
Sharīk b. 'Abd Allāh al-Nakha'ī 92, 104
Shaybān *see* Banū Shaybān
Shayṭān al-Ṭāq *see* Muḥammad b. 'Alī b. al-Nu'mān
Shiqshiqiyya 116
Shmṭiyya 404
Shu'ayb al-'Aqarqūfī 371
Shu'ayb b. Maytham al-Tammār 42, 43
Shu'ba b. al-Ḥajjāj 135
Sijistān 244
Simāk b. Makhrama b. Ḥumayn al-Asadī 202
Sim'ān b. Hubayra b. Musāḥiq 283
Sinān b. Ṭarīf al-Hāshimī 158
Sindī b. Muḥammad al-Bazzāz 390
Sufyān b. Ibrāhīm b. Mazyad al-Azdī 167
Sufyān b. Sa'īd al-Thawrī 301
Sufyān b. 'Uyayna 108, 109, 372–3
Sulaym al-Farrā' 375
Sulaym b. Qays al-Hilālī 82–6
Sulaymān b. 'Abd al-Malik 130
Sulaymān b. Dāwūd al-Minqarī 223, 232
Sulaymān al-Daylamī 373–4
Sulaymān b. Khālid al-Aqṭa' 374–5
Sulaymān b. Mihrān al-A'mash 109, 158, 232
Sulaymān b. Samā'a 211
Suwayd b. Muslim al-Qallā' 375

Tafsīr Ahl al-Bayt 94
Tafsīr al-Bāqir 37, 38, 122
Tafsīr al-bāṭin 188
Tafsīr gharīb al-Qur'ān 112, 202
Tafsīr al-Qur'ān 37, 122, 250, 377
Tafsīr [sūrat] Qul huwa 'llāhu aḥad 391
Ṭāhir b. Muḥammad b. 'Abd Allāh al-Zubayrī 164
Ṭalḥa Bayyā' al-Sāburī 375
Ṭalḥa b. 'Ubayd Allāh 106, 267
Ṭalḥa b. Zayd al-Shāmī 375
Ṭālibids 158
Tamīm *see* Banū Tamīm
Ṭarīf 212, 384
Tasmiyat man qutila ma'a 'l-Ḥusayn min wuldih wa ikhwatih wa shī'atih 164
Tasmiyat man shahida ma' 'Alī min aṣḥāb Rasūl Allāh 32
Taymī 172
Taymiyya 404
Ṭazayyud 146
Thābit b. Dīnār *see* Abū Ḥamza al-Thumālī
Thābit b. Hurmuz, Abū 'l-Miqdām 205
Thābit b. Shurayḥ al-Azdī al-Anbārī 379
Tha'laba b. Maymūn al-Naḥwī 317, 380
Thaqīf 180, 236, 344, 358, 388
Thawbān b. Sālim al-Yashkurī 198
Thawr b. Yazīd 304
Al-Thughūr al-bāsima 22
Thuwayr b. Abī Fākhita 248
Tirmidhī *see* Muḥammad b. 'Īsā al-Sulamī 162
Ṭūs 91

'Ubayd b. Muḥammad b. Qays al-Bajalī 346
'Ubayd b. Yaqṭīn 195
'Ubayd b. Zurāra b. A'yan 383–4
'Ubayd Allāh b. 'Abd Allāh al-Wāsiṭī al-Dihqān 218–19
'Ubayd Allāh b. Abī Rāfi' 17, 23, 24, 26–32, 346, 348, 350
'Ubayd Allāh b. Aḥmad b. Ya'qūb al-Anbārī 21
'Ubayd Allāh b. 'Alī b. Abī Rāfi' 28
'Ubayd Allāh b. 'Alī al-Ḥalabī 338, 380–82
'Ubayd Allāh b. al-Walīd al-Waṣṣāfī 382–3
'Ubays b. Hishām al-Nāshirī 138, 176, 356, 363, 367, 379, 384
Udaym b. al-Ḥurr 212, 384–5
'Umar b. Abān al-Kalbī 385
'Umar b. 'Abd al-'Azīz 346

'Umar b. 'Abd Allāh b. Ya'lā al-Thaqafī 385–6
'Umar b. Aḥmad b. Shāhīn al-Marrūdhī al-Baghdādī 21
'Umar b. 'Alī b. Abī Ṭālib 297, 298
'Umar b. Ḥafṣ b. Ghiyāth 232
'Umar b. Udhayna 214, 387
'Umar b. Yazīd al-Thaqafī 388
Umm Hāni', daughter of Abū Ṭālib 248
Umm Ḥusayn, daughter of 'Abd Allāh b. Muḥammad al-Bāqir 294
Uqayshir 202
'Uqba b. Khālid al-Asadī 388
Usayyidīs 227–8
Uṣūl al-sharā'i' 318
'Uthmān b. Ḥunayf 10, 26
'Uthmān b. 'Īsā al-Ru'āsī 250, 370
'Uthmāniyya 57, 80, 88, 202

Wahb b. 'Abd Rabbih 389
Wahb b. Wahb, Abū 'l-Bakhtarī 389–91
Wakī' al-Ḍabbī 396
Wakī' b. al-Jarrāḥ 58, 202, 290
Walīd b. Ṣubayḥ al-Asadī 391
Wāqifa 111, 128, 137, 138, 155, 156, 162, 169, 183, 184, 214, 218, 223, 227, 240, 276, 277, 283, 302, 318, 354, 360, 391, 400, 402, 403
Wāsiṭ 202, 203, 259, 342, 354, 375
waṣiyya 262
Waṣiyyat Amīr al-Mu'minīn 78
Waṣiyyat al-Mufaḍḍal 334
wijāda 86, 106, 298, 341
Wuhayb b. Ḥafṣ al-Mantūf 391
Wuhayb b. Khālid al-Karābīsī 393

Ya'fūriyya 104
Yaḥyā b. 'Abd Allāh b. al-Ḥasan 144, 254
Yaḥyā b. al-'Alā' al-Rāzī 393
Yaḥyā b. al-Ḥurr 384
Yaḥyā b. 'Imrān al-Ḥalabī 250, 394–5
Yaḥyā b. Khālid al-Barmakī 216, 265
Yaḥyā b. Muḥammad b. Ṣā'id al-Baghdādī 15
Yaḥyā b. al-Qāsim al-Asadī, Abū Baṣīr 162, 184, 278, 371, 391, 395
Yaḥyā b. Sa'īd al-Qaṭṭān 92, 396
Yaḥyā b. Sa'īd b. Qays al-Anṣārī al-Madanī 396
Yaḥyā b. Zakariyyā 384
Yaḥyā b. Zayd 280
Ya'lā b. Murra al-Thaqafī 385
Yamān b. Ri'āb 190
Yaqṭīn b. Mūsā 195
Ya'qūb b. Iṣḥāq al-Fasawī 162, 396
Ya'qūb b. Maytham al-Tammār 42, 43
Ya'qūb b. Sālim al-Aḥmar 397
Ya'qūb al-Sarrāj 397
Ya'qūb b. Shayba al-Baṣrī 15
Ya'qūb b. Shu'ayb al-Maythamī 43, 398
Ya'qūb b. Yaqṭīn 195
Ya'qūb b. Yazīd al-Anbārī 403
Yashkur 180
Yāsin al-Ḍarīr 398–9
Yazīd I 26, 83
Yazīd b. 'Abd al-Malik 346
Yazīd Abū Khālid al-Qammāṭ 399
Yazīd b. Isḥāq al-Ghanawī, Sha'ar 247
Yūnus b. 'Abd al-Raḥmān al-Qummī 89, 196, 200, 242, 244, 318
Yūnus b. 'Imrān al-Maythamī 43
Yūnus b. Ya'qūb al-Duhnī 242, 399–400
Yūnus b. Ẓabyān 89
Yūsuf b. al-Ḥārith al-Kumandānī 175
Yūsuf b. 'Imrān al-Maythamī 43
Yūsuf Uzbak 16

Ẓāhiriyya Library 355
Zakariyyā b. Muḥammad al-Mu'min 400–401
Zam'a b. Subay' 33
Zayd b. 'Abd Allāh b. Dārim 228
Zayd b. 'Alī 35, 38, 119, 121, 163, 195, 202, 203, 230, 280, 374
Zayd al-Narsī 401, 402
Zayd b. 'Umar 230
Zayd b. Wahb 13, 80–82
Zayd b. Yūnus al-Shaḥḥām 401–2
Zayd al-Zarrād 401, 402
Zaydān b. 'Umar 230
Zindīq 263
Ziyād b. Aḥmar al-'Ijlī al-Kūfī 117
Ziyād b. Aḥram 117
Ziyād b. al-Mundhir al-Hamdānī *see* Abū 'l-Jārūd
Ziyād b. Marwān al-Qandī 402–3
Ziyād b. Sūqa 235
Zubayr b. al-'Awwām 106, 267
Zuhayr b. Mu'āwiya al-Ju'fī al-Kūfī 92
Zur'a b. Muḥammad al-Ḥaḍramī 403
Zurāra b. A'yan 177, 213, 247, 404–5
Zurqān 265

www.ingramcontent.com/pod-product-compliance
Lightning Source LLC
Chambersburg PA
CBHW071115080526
44587CB00013B/1346
* 9 7 8 1 8 5 1 6 8 3 3 1 4 *